ADVANCED MICROSOFT® VISUAL BASIC® 6.0

SECOND EDITION

The Mandelbrot Set
(International) Limited

Microsoft Press

Advanced Microsoft Visual Basic 6.0, Second Edition

Published by **Microsoft Press**
A Division of Microsoft Corporation
One Microsoft Way
Redmond, Washington 98052-6399

Library of Congress Cataloging-in-Publication Data
Advanced Microsoft Visual Basic 6.0 / The Mandelbrot Set
   (International) Limited. -- 2nd ed.
      p.   cm.
    Rev. ed. of: Advanced Microsoft Visual Basic 5, c1997.
    Includes index.
    ISBN 1-57231-893-7
    1. Microsoft Visual BASIC.   2. BASIC (Computer program language)
  I. Mandelbrot Set (International) Limited.   II. Title: Advanced
Microsoft Visual Basic 5.
  QA76.73.B3A345   1998
  005.26'8--dc21   98-42530
                                                     CIP

Printed and bound in the United States of America.

3 4 5 6 7 8 9 WCWC 3 2 1 0 9

Distributed in Canada by ITP Nelson, a division of Thomson Canada Limited.

A CIP catalogue record for this book is available from the British Library.

Microsoft Press books are available through booksellers and distributors worldwide. For further information about international editions, contact your local Microsoft Corporation office or contact Microsoft Press International directly at fax (425) 936-7329. Visit our Web site at mspress.microsoft.com.

Intel is a registered trademark of Intel Corporation. ROOS, VBA2000, and Visual DateScope 2000 are trademarks of The Mandelbrot Set (International) Limited. ActiveMovie, ActiveX, Developer Studio, DirectShow, JScript, Microsoft, Microsoft Press, Visual Basic, Visual C++, Visual FoxPro, Visual InterDev, Visual J++, Visual SourceSafe, Visual Studio, Win32, Windows, and Windows NT are either registered trademarks or trademarks of Microsoft Corporation in the United States and/or other countries. Other product and company names mentioned herein may be the trademarks of their respective owners.

Acquisitions Editor: Stephen Guty
Project Editor: Wendy Zucker
Technical Editors: Marc Young, Jean Ross

CONTENTS

CHAPTER **1**

PETER J. MORRIS

ON ERROR GOTO HELL

CHAPTER **2**

ADAM MAGEE

TAKING CARE OF BUSINESS (OBJECTS)

CHAPTER **3**

ROGER
SWIFT

IIS THIS A TEMPLATE
I SEE BEFORE ME?

CHAPTER **4**

JON
BURN

PROGRAMMING WITH VARIANTS   132

CHAPTER **7**

PETER J.
MORRIS

MINUTIAE

CHAPTER **8**

ST**EVE**
OVERALL

VISUAL BASIC PROGRAMMER'S GUIDE TO SUCCESSFUL DATING

CHAPTER 9

JON PERKINS

"WELL, AT LEAST IT COMPILED OK!"

CHAPTER **10**

PHIL
RIDLEY

STARTING WITH BASES LOADED

CHAPTER **13**

MARK HURST

PROGRAMMING ON PURPOSE

A WINDOW ON DETAILED DESIGN   **540**

CHAPTER 14

CHRIS DE BELLOT
STEVE OVERALL

CHAPTER 15

MARK SEWELL

TABLE OF CONTENTS

CHAPTER **16**

ROSS

ACCESSIBILITY IN VISUAL BASIC

CHAPTER **17**

PETER J
MORRIS

MARK
SEWELL

THREE STEPS TO EMPLOYMENT HEAVEN

APPENDIX A

PETER J. MORRIS
MARK DEAKIN

CODING CONVENTIONS 787

FOREWORD

Since its inception in 1991, Microsoft Visual Basic has revolutionized the way developers create applications for Microsoft Windows. Through features such as IntelliSense, statement completion, ActiveX Control creation, a native code compiler, and database access, Microsoft has worked hard to keep developers well-equipped with the latest innovations in rapid application development. In Visual Basic 6 Professional and Enterprise Editions, Visual Basic has been expanded to make developers even more productive in what they do most often—access data, whether in a relational database (such as Microsoft SQL Server 7 or Oracle 8) or in a nonrelational data store (such as a directory service). Recognizing a rapid upsurgence in the adoption of the Web as a true cross-platform application environment, Microsoft has added new technologies to support client (Dynamic HTML) and server (WebClasses). These new features, along with literally hundreds of other enhancements and optimizations, bring the development of enterprise-wide, line-of-business applications within the reach of millions of developers who have mastered Visual Basic. In addition, these features provide the power and performance needed to create applications that run in mission-critical scenarios.

The Mandelbrot Set (International) Limited (TMS) is one of the companies that I see pushing the limits of Visual Basic most frequently. TMS is recognized worldwide as a leader in Visual Basic consulting and development. I've worked with TMS for some time now, and I've seen in their technical papers, books, and presentations that they are able to bestow a level of technical clarity not often seen in this industry. About once or twice a month, I'll get questions or insights from Peet Morris (the technical director of TMS) that are so advanced they rival the understanding of the product normally seen only by the chief architects of the product itself.

I first met Peet Morris at VBITS in San Francisco just about a year ago. I attended Peet's session and was immediately taken with his technical skill and knew that he would be an invaluable resource in the future. We immediately hit it off both technically and personally, and since then he's done sessions for us at conferences such as Microsoft TechEd this past summer in New Orleans. Peet's sessions were consistently among the most highly rated for their technical content. I eagerly anticipate Peet's visits to Redmond, where we talk about going out for a pint of Guinness but instead end up doing something trivial, such as watching the last episode of *Seinfeld* with friends while discussing the intricacies of Visual Basic's threading model or subclassing of date functions.

Understand that this book is not your canonical, learn-to-become-a-professional-programmer-in-*x*-days text. It's also not designed to provide you with a laundry list of all the new features of Visual Basic 6. This book is intended for the working professional, thus exploring in depth many of the topics that beginning books either ignore or gloss over. Drawing on the many and varied strengths of the experts at TMS, each chapter drills down into topics that are not often considered carefully in the course of day-to-day project development. The lessons learned from this book are the gems that one might unearth at a VBITS conference or in a technical course outside the classroom and away from the podium, where developers gain insight through open dialogue.

Life on the edge takes a lot of work and talent, and TMS has often had to learn the "how" the hard way. This book is your chance to benefit from their combined experience. If you're working with Visual Basic and trying to push the envelope, you'll find a lot of useful information here.

Sean P. Alexander
Lead Technical Product Manager, Visual Basic
Developer Tools Division
Microsoft Corporation

PREFACE

When we originally approached Microsoft Press with the idea of writing an advanced Visual Basic book that was a bit different from the rest, we wondered what reaction we'd get. We were particularly keen on incorporating three features:

- The book was to be a focused collection of the writings and opinions of many individuals. Perhaps, healthily, some of these people would disagree with one another.

- By including material about advanced real-world issues, we wanted the book to be of real interest to corporate managers and developers who were trying to push the tool to its limits.

- Through content and a mix of engaging writing styles, we wanted the book to be entertaining and highly readable.

We expected each author to write about a subject he or she felt passionately about. The subject had to be relevant to real-world programming issues. It also had to be drawn from practical, real-life experience gained from developing and consulting in the trenches—you'll find no code describing how to flip a window upside down in this book!

Microsoft Press liked our ideas, and we're pleased to say that the first edition of this book, which targeted Visual Basic 5, was a runaway bestseller. We have now written a substantially updated second edition for Visual Basic 6.

At The Mandelbrot Set (International) Limited, or just plain TMS, we've been committed to Visual Basic since version 1—in fact, Peet Morris did the world's first public showing of the tool. We're also the British company behind two successful programmer toolkits for both Visual Basic 3 and 4, including Micro-Help's Code Complete. In our ISV position, we've been in on the early testing programs for Visual Basic and were the first site in Europe to have access to version 6—we've been using Visual Basic 6 for a long time!

What else do we do? We spend the bulk of our time on the road developing Visual Basic software and consulting for mostly blue-chip clients. Over the years, we've become familiar with all the issues around enterprise-level development with Visual Basic. From time to time, we also write articles for various Visual Basic–oriented publications, speak at events such as VBITS and TechEd, and run advanced Visual Basic training courses and seminars.

Because of our background and our experience, we're in a superb position to write authoritatively on Visual Basic 6, the most significant upgrade yet.

WHO SHOULD READ THIS BOOK?

This book is geared toward two broad audiences. *Technical managers* responsible for planning, designing, and supporting Visual Basic applications should read it with a view to understanding what they can and can't expect from the teams they are or will be managing and what capabilities Visual Basic 6 has. *Developers* responsible for designing, programming, and implementing Visual Basic applications within the corporate arena should study it to find out how other experts handle the common, yet often complex and frustrating, problems they are likely to encounter (or are already wrestling with).

WHAT IS COVERED IN THIS BOOK?

This book covers a wide range of Visual Basic topics. Here's a brief sample of the subjects discussed: designing server side objects, CE development, building base code, mixed language programming, designing distributed applications, debugging, migration issues, error handling, the Year 2000 problem as it relates to Visual Basic 6 and Visual Basic for Applications, software testing, reusability, successful enterprise development, recruiting great developers, developing for people with disabilities, coding conventions, and numerous other mission-critical aspects of Visual Basic development. There is really no start and end—just dip into whatever chapter takes your fancy. By the time you've finished reading this book, you'll understand how to make the most of this marvelous technology.

ACKNOWLEDGMENTS

Our sincere thanks to the following people:

The entire TMS authoring team. You sacrificed much personal time and effort to deliver high-quality work under tight deadlines. In particular, thanks to Treesje Verlinden (Project Manager) for cracking the whip!

The rest of TMS for supporting, and putting up with, the authoring team!

Jim Brown, Steve Guty, Wendy Zucker, Marc Young, Rebecca McKay, Jean Ross, Bill Teel, Michael Victor, Travis Beaven, and everyone else at Microsoft Press (you know who you are) for getting such a high-quality job done.

From the Visual Basic team, Sean Alexander and everyone else who has supported us. What a truly great product you've made—well done.

Scott Swanson, who originally suggested to Microsoft Press that these Brits were the guys to do the book.

And last, but by no means least, Helen, William, Katie, Amy, Fiona, and Daniel, for all their love and support.

AND FINALLY

We hope you enjoy this book and get as much pleasure out of it as we did in writing it. If you'd like to contact any of the individual chapter authors, send an e-mail message to the address shown at the beginning of each chapter.

Peter J. Morris and Mark Sewell
TMS Directors and Cofounders

The Mandelbrot Set
(International) Limited

Using the Companion CD

Complete sample applications and code used in this book are provided on the companion CD located at the back of the book. The files for the sample programs are contained in the CD's SAMPLES folder. They are organized according to the chapter in the book in which they are discussed. (For example, Chapter 1 samples are located in the \SAMPLES\CHAP01 folder.) You can browse these files on the CD, or you can install them on your hard drive. Installing them requires approximately 12 MB of disk space.

To install the sample files on your hard drive, place the CD in your CD-ROM drive and follow these steps:

1. Click on the CD-ROM drive in Windows Explorer.
2. Double-click SETUP.EXE in the root directory of the CD.

or

1. Select Run from the Start menu.
2. Type *d:\setup* in the Run dialog box (where *d* is the drive letter of your CD drive).

NOTE

If you try to browse the files on the CD without installing them and you're unable to read some of the files, your CD driver software probably doesn't support long filenames. If this is the case, you must run the setup program to install the sample files in order to browse them.

To uninstall the sample files, do the following:

1. Open the Control Panel, and select Add/Remove Programs.
2. On the Install/Uninstall tab, select Advanced Visual Basic 6.
3. Click Add/Remove.
4. Click Yes when prompted.

If you have trouble running any of the sample files, review the text in the appropriate chapter in the book. You can also refer to the README.TXT file in the root directory of the CD, and some of the chapter subfolders also have their own README.TXT files.

Also contained on the CD is an AVI file you can run from the CD to find out more about the authors and The Mandelbrot Set (International) Limited.

On Error GoTo Hell

A Methodical Approach to Error Handling

PETER MORRIS

Peet is the Technical Director and a cofounder of The Mandelbrot Set (International) Limited (TMS). Peet, a former Microsoft employee, is acknowledged industry-wide as a Microsoft Windows and Visual Basic expert and is a frequent speaker at events such as VBITS and TechEd. As a developer and lecturer, he has taught Windows (SDK) API, Advanced Windows API, Visual Basic (all levels), OS/2 Presentation Manager, C, C++, Advanced C and C++, Pascal, compiler theory, OWL, Smalltalk, and CommonView. For more about Peet, turn to page 274.

Since the first edition of this book was released, this chapter has been tidied up a little. I've added some new rules and sidebars about handling errors in components and controls, as well as some examples of handling errors on a server.

What is an error? The short answer is, "Something that's expensive to fix." Dealing with errors is costly in terms of both money and time. As you probably know already, your test cycle will be longer, more complex, and less effective if you don't build appropriate error handling into your code right from the start. You should do all you can to reduce and handle errors in order to reduce costs, deliver quality code, and keep to schedules.

One way to eradicate errors—a way that I'll dismiss immediately—is to write error-free code. I don't think it's possible to write such pristine code. A more realistic way to deal with errors effectively is to plan for them properly so that when they do occur:

- The application doesn't crash.
- The error's root cause (and thus cure) is relatively easy to determine.
- The error is as acceptable and as invisible to the user as is humanly possible.

So what must we do to put a good error handling scheme in place? It's a deceptively simple question with a big (subjective) set of answers. I think that acquiring and then using some fundamental knowledge is where we should start:

- Ensure that all your developers truly understand how Visual Basic raises and then dispatches and handles errors.
- Make sure that those same developers understand the consequences of writing code that is hard to debug and the true costs of any unhandled error.
- Develop a suitable error handling strategy that's based on your understanding of the preceding two points and that takes into account your budget and line of business.
- Apply your strategy; demand self-discipline and team discipline.

Handling errors properly in Visual Basic is also a good idea because of the alternative: Visual Basic's default error handling rules are rather severe. Unhandled errors are reported, and then an *End* statement is executed. Keep in mind that an *End* statement stops your application dead—no form Query-Unload or Unload events, no class Terminate events, not much of anything in fact.

To help you develop an effective strategy for dealing with errors, I'll go over some ideas that I consider vital to the process. These are presented (in no particular order) as a series of tips. "Pick 'n mix" those you think will suit you, your company, and of course your development project. Each tip is empirical, and we have employed them in the code we write at The Mandelbrot Set (International) Limited (TMS). I hope they serve you as well as they have served us!

Tip 1: Inconsistent as it is, try to mimic Visual Basic's own error handling scheme as much as possible.

When you call a Visual Basic routine that can fail, what is the standard way that the routine signals the failure to you? It probably won't be via a return value. If it were, procedures, for one, would have trouble signaling failure. Most (but not all) routines raise an error (an exception) when they want to signal failure. (This applies to procedures, functions, and methods.) For example, *CreateObject* raises an exception if it cannot create an object—for whatever reason; *Open* does the same if it cannot open a file for you. (Not all routines raise such exceptions. For example, the *Choose* function returns Null [thus, it requires a Variant to hold its return value just in case it ever fails] if you index into it incorrectly.) In other words, if a routine works correctly, this fact is signaled to the caller by the absence of any error condition.

Routines such as *Open* work like this primarily so that they can be used more flexibly. For example, by not handling the error internally, perhaps by prompting the user in some way, the caller is free to handle errors in the most suitable way. The caller can also use routines in ways perhaps not thought of by their writers. Listing 1-1 is an example using *GetAttr* to determine whether the machine has a particular drive. Because this routine raises exceptions, we can use it to determine whether or not a disk drive exists.

LISTING 1-1

Using error handling to test for a disk drive

```
Public Function bDriveExists(ByVal sDriveAndFile As String) _
    As Boolean
' ====================================================================
'
' Module: modFileUtilities. Function: bDriveExists.
'
' Object: General
'
' Author - Peter J. Morris. TMS Ltd.
' Template fitted : Date - 01/01/97    Time - 00:00
'
' Function's Purpose/Description in Brief
'
' Determines whether the drive given in sDriveAndFile
' exists. Raises an exception if no drive string is given.
'
' Revision History:
'
```

>>

LISTING 1-1
>>

```
' BY              WHY AND WHEN              AFFECTED
' Peter J. Morris. TMS Ltd. - Original Code 01/01/97, 00:00
'
' INPUTS - sDriveAndFile - holds the drive name, e.g., "C".
'          Later holds the name of the drive and the filename
'          on the drive to be created.
'
'
' OUTPUTS - Via return. Boolean. True if drive exists;
'           else False.
'
' MAY RAISE EXCEPTIONS
'
' NOTES: Uses formals as variables.
'        Uses delayed error handling.
'
' =================================================================

    ' Set up general error handler.
    On Error GoTo Error_General_bDriveExists:

    Const sProcSig = MODULE_NAME & "General_bDriveExists"

    ' ========== Body Code Starts ==========
    ' These are usually a little more public - shown local
    ' for readability only.
    Dim lErr As Long
    Dim lErl As Long
    Dim sErr As String

    ' Constants placed here instead of in typelib for
    ' readability only.
    Const nPATH_NOT_FOUND        As Integer = 76
    Const nINTERNAL_ERROR_START  As Integer = 1000
    Const nERROR_NO_DRIVE_CODE   As Integer = 1001

    ' Always default to failure.
    bDriveExists = False

    If sDriveAndFile <> "" Then

        ' "Trim" the drive name.
        sDriveAndFile = Left$(sDriveAndFile, 1)

        ' Root directory.
```

```
        sDriveAndFile = sDriveAndFile & ":\"

        ' Enter error-critical section - delay the handling
        ' of any possible resultant exception.
        On Error Resume Next

        Call VBA.FileSystem.GetAttr(sDriveAndFile)

        ' Preserve the error context. See notes later on
        ' subclassing VBA's error object and adding your own
        ' "push" and "pop" methods to do this.
        GoSub PreserveContext

        ' Exit error-critical section.
        On Error GoTo Error_General_bDriveExists:

        Select Case nErr

            Case nPATH_NOT_FOUND:
                bDriveExists = False

            ' Covers no error (error 0) and all other errors.
            ' As far as we're concerned, these aren't
            ' errors; e.g., "drive not ready" is OK.
            Case Else
                bDriveExists = True

        End Select

    Else

        ' No drive given, so flag error.
        Err.Raise nLoadErrorDescription(nERROR_NO_DRIVE_CODE)

    End If

    ' ========== Body Code Ends ==========

    Exit Function

' Error handler
Error_General_bDriveExists:

    ' Preserve the error context. See notes later on
    ' subclassing VBA's error object and adding your own "push"
```

>>

LISTING 1-1

```
' and "pop" methods to do this.
GoSub PreserveContext


' **
' In error; roll back stuff in here.
' **


' **
' Log error.
' **


' Reraise as appropriate - handle internal errors
' further only.
If (lErr < nINTERNAL_ERROR_START) Or _
   (lErr = nERROR_NO_DRIVE_CODE) Then

    VBA.Err.Raise lErr

Else

    ' Ask the user what he or she wants to do with this
    ' error.
    Select Case MsgBox("Error in " & sProcSig & " " _
                    & CStr(lErr) & " " & _
                    CStr(lErl) & " " & sErr, _
                    vbAbortRetryIgnore + vbExclamation, _
                    sMsgBoxTitle)
        Case vbAbort
            Resume Exit_General_bDriveExists:

        Case vbRetry
            Resume

        Case vbIgnore
            Resume Next

        Case Else
            VBA.Interaction.MsgBox _
                            "Unexpected error" _
                            , vbOKOnly + vbCritical _
                            , "Error"

            End

    End Select

End If
```

```
Exit_General_bDriveExists:

    Exit Function

PreserveContext:

    lErr = VBA.Err.Number
    lErl = VBA.Erl
    sErr = VBA.Err.Description

    Return

End Function
```

Here are a few comments on this routine:

- Although it's a fabricated example, I've tried to make sure that it works and is complete.

- It handles errors.

- It uses delayed error handling internally.

- It's not right for you! You'll need to rework the code and the structure to suit your particular needs and philosophy.

- The error handler might raise errors.

- It doesn't handle errors occurring in the error handler.

- It uses a local subroutine, *PreserveContext*. This subroutine is called only from within this routine, so we use a *GoSub* to create it. The result is that *PreserveContext* is truly private and fast—and it doesn't pollute the global name space. (This routine preserves the key values found in the error object. Tip 11 explains a way to do this using a replacement *Err* object.)

Within *bDriveExists*, I've chosen to flag parameter errors and send the information back to the caller by using exceptions. The actual exception is raised using the *Raise* method of the Visual Basic error object (*Err.Raise*) and the return value of a function (*nLoadErrorDescription*). This return value is used to load the correct error string (typically held in string resources and *not* a database since you want to always be able to get hold of the string quickly). This string is placed into *Err.Description* just before the *Raise* method is applied to the error object. Reraising, without reporting, errors like this allows you to build a transaction model of error handling into your code. (See Tip 14 for more on this topic.)

The *nLoadErrorDescription* function is typically passed the error number (a constant telling it what string to load), and it returns this same number to the caller upon completion. In other words, the function *could* look something like this (omitting any boilerplate code):

```
Public Function nLoadErrorDescription(ByVal nCode As Integer)

    ' Return the same error code we're passed.
    nLoadErrorDescription = nCode

    ' Load the error text for nCode from some source and assign it
    ' to Err.Description.
    Err.Description = LoadResString(nCode)

    Exit Function

End Function
```

In this example, we're using a string resource to hold the error text. In reality, the *routine* we normally use to retrieve an error string (and, indeed, to resolve the constant) is contained in what we call a ROOS—that's a Resource Only Object Server, which we'll come back to in Tip 10.

A good error handler is often complex, so we must ask ourselves another question: What will happen if we get an error in the error handler? Well, if we're in the same local scope as the original error, the error is passed back up the call chain to the next available error handler. (See Tip 5 for more information on the call chain and this mechanism.) In other words, if you're in the routine proper when this second error occurs, it will be handled "above" your routine; if that's Visual Basic, you're dead! "OK," you say, "to handle it more locally, I must have an error handler within my error handler." Sounds good—trouble is, it doesn't work as you might expect. Sure, you can have an *On Error Goto xyz* (or *On Error Resume Next* or *On Error Resume 0*) in your error handler, but the trap will not be set; your code will not jump to *xyz* if an error occurs in your error handler. The way to handle an error in your error handler is to do it in another procedure. If you call another procedure from your error handler, that routine can have an error trap set. The net effect is that you *can* have error handling in your error handler just as long as another routine handles the error. The ability to handle errors in error handlers is fundamental to applying a transaction processing model of error handling to your application, a subject I'll explain further in Tip 14.

To recap, the reason *GetAttr* doesn't handle many (if any) internal errors is that to do so would take away its very flexibility. If the routine "told" you that the drive didn't exist, by using, say, a message box, you couldn't use it the way we did in *bDriveExists*.

If you're still not convinced, I'll be saying a little more on why raising errors is better than returning True or False later. But for now, let's think BASICA!

Tip 2: Use line numbers in your source code.

Line numbers!? Yup, just like those used in "real" Basic. Bear with me here—I'll convince you!

In older versions of Basic, line numbers were mandatory and often used as "jump targets." A jump target is a line number used with a *GoTo*, such as *GoTo 2000*. The *2000* identifies the start of a block of code to execute next. After *GoTo* came *GoSub* (and *Return*). Now you had a "Basic subroutine," albeit one with a strange name: *GoSub 2000*. You can think of the (line) number almost as an address (just as in C). These days, of course, Basic *is* Visual Basic and we use symbolic names for labeling such jump targets (real subroutines, just like those in C and other programming languages). Line numbers have become a peculiarity designed to allow nothing more than some level of backward compatibility with some other version of Basic.

Or then again, maybe not. In Visual Basic, *Erl*, a Visual Basic (undocumented in Visual Basic 4, 5, and 6 but present in all versions of Visual Basic thus far) "global variable," gives you access to the line number of any erroring line of code. So by using line numbers and by using *Erl* in your error handlers, you can determine which line of code erred—wow! What happens to *Erl* if you don't use line numbers? Easy—it will always be 0.

Of course, you won't want to start typing line numbers in by hand. You need some automation. At TMS, we add line numbers to our code using an internal tool we originally developed for working with Visual Basic 2. It now works as an add-in under Visual Basic 6. There are tools on the market that can do the same for your code.

After the first edition of our book came out, we received lots of mail asking us where such a line numbering tool could be obtained. The demand was so great, and the available tools were so few, that we put an FOC line number wizard on our web site (*www.themandelbrotset.com/html/downloads.htm*). That tool is still there, so please feel free to download a copy of it.

At TMS, we don't work with line numbers in our source code, however. We add them only when we're doing a ship build—that is, when we want to ship a binary to, say, beta testers or to manufacturing for an impending release. We use our internal tool to build a new version of the code, complete with line numbers, and then we make an executable from that. We store the line numbered source code in our source control system and ship the executable. We cross-reference the EXE version number (the Auto Increment option is just great here) to the source code stored in the source control system. Every time we do a new build for shipping, we create a new subproject whose name is the version number of the build and then store the line numbered source code in it along with a copy of the binary image. If an error report comes in, we can easily refer back to the source code to find the erroring line (*very easy* if you're using Microsoft Visual SourceSafe). Typically, the error report will contain details of the module, routine, and line number of the error.

Listing 1-2 is a typical Click event, line numbers and all.

LISTING 1-2

Generic Click event with line numbers

```
Private Sub Command1_Click()
' ==============================================================
' Module Type : Form
' Module Name : Form1
' Object      : Command1
' Proc Type   : Sub
' Proc Name   : Click
' Scope       : Private
' Author      :
' Date        : 01/01/97 00:00
'
' History     : 01/01/97 00:00: Peter J. Morris : Original Code.
' ==============================================================

' Set up general error handler.
On Error GoTo Error_In_Command1_Click:

1   Dim sErrorDescription As String

2   Const sProcSig = MODULE_NAME & "Command1_Click"
```

```
        ' ========== Body Code Starts ==========

3  Debug.Print bDriveExists("")

        ' ========== Body Code Ends ==========

4  Exit Sub

' Error handler
Error_In_Command1_Click:

5  With Err
6      sErrorDescription = "Error '" & .Number & " " & _
        .Description & "' occurred in " & sProcSig & _
        IIf(Erl <> 0, " at line " & CStr(Erl) & ".", ".")
7  End With

8  Select Case MsgBox(sErrorDescription, _
                    vbAbortRetryIgnore, _
                    App.Title & " Error")

        Case vbAbort
9          Resume Exit_Command1_Click:
10         Case vbRetry
11             Resume
12         Case vbIgnore
13             Resume Next
14         Case Else
15             End

16  End Select

Exit_Command1_Click:

End Sub
```

Notice in Listing 1-2 that *sProcSig* is made up of the module name (*Form1*) and the routine name (*Command1_Click*). Notice also that the error handler examines *Erl* to "see" whether line numbers have been used. Figure 1-1 shows what's typically displayed when an error occurs using this kind of scheme.

FIGURE 1-1

Error and line number information

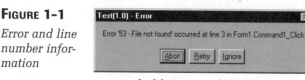

Of course, the actual code that makes up the error handler is entirely up to you. If you use this scheme, I recommend you have a module-level constant to hold your module name and use a routine-level constant to hold the routine name plus the module name:

Module Declaration Section

```
Private Const MODULE_NAME As String = "Form1."
```

Command1_Click Event

```
Const sProcSig As String = MODULE_NAME & "Command1_Click"
```

Tip 3: Raise exceptions when possible because return values *will* be ignored.

This tip supplements Tip 1: "Inconsistent as it is, try to mimic Visual Basic's own error handling scheme as much as possible." Since Visual Basic 4, a function can be called like a subroutine. (In Visual Basic 3 and earlier, it couldn't.) To demonstrate this, consider the following code fragments:

```
Sub Command1_Click ()

    Debug.Print SomeFunc()
    Call SomeFunc

End Sub


Function SomeFunc () As Integer

    SomeFunc = 42

End Function
```

The line *Call SomeFunc* is illegal in Visual Basic 3 but legal in Visual Basic 4 and later. (It's VBA!) In case you're wondering why this is so, the facility was added to VBA (Visual Basic for Applications) to allow you to write routines that were more consistent with some of Visual Basic's own routines, such as *MsgBox*, which acts sometimes like a function and sometimes like a statement (or a C type procedure if you're used to that language). (In Tip 4, you'll find out how to write your own *MsgBox* routine.)

A side effect of all this is that routines that return some indication of success or failure might now have that result ignored. As C and SDK programmers know only too well, this *will* cause problems! In Visual Basic 3, the programmer always had to use the return value. Typically, he or she would use it correctly. If a programmer can ignore a routine's returned value (say it's not a database handle but a True/False value—that is, either it worked or it failed), however, he or she usually will ignore it.

Exceptions, on the other hand, cannot easily be ignored (except by using *On Error Resume Next* or *On Error Resume 0*—both easy to test for and legislate against). Also, keep in mind that "newer" Visual Basic developers sometimes lack the necessary self-discipline to use and test return values correctly. By raising exceptions, you force them to test and then to take some appropriate action in one place: the error handler.

Another reason to use exceptions is that not using them can cause your code to become more difficult to follow—all those (un)necessary conditional tests to see that things have worked correctly. This kind of scheme, in which you try some code and determine that it didn't work by catching a thrown exception, is pretty close to "structured exception handling" as used in C++ and Microsoft Windows NT. For more on structured exception handling, see the MSDN Library Help. (Select the Contents tab, and follow this path: Visual C++ Documentation; Reference; C/C++ Language and C++ Libraries; C++ Language Reference; Statements; Exception Handling; Structured Exception Handling.)

Here's an example of a structured exception handling type of scheme:

```
Private Sub SomeWhere()

    If a() Then
        ⋮
        If b() Then
            ⋮
            If c() Then
                ⋮
            End If
        End If
    End If

End Sub
```

This example is not too hard to figure out. But I'm sure you've seen far more complex examples of nesting conditionals, and you get the idea! Here's the same code using exceptions to signal errors in *a*, *b*, or *c*:

```
Private Sub SomeWhere()

' TRY
On Error Goto ????

    a()
        ⋮
    b()
        ⋮
    c()
        ⋮

' CATCH
????

    ' Handle exception here.

End Sub
```

Can you see the flow any easier here? What's implied by the presence of the error handler is that to get to the call to *b*, *a* must function correctly. By losing the *If*, you're losing some plain readability, but you're also gaining some readability—the code is certainly less cluttered. Of course, sometimes code is clear just because you're used to it. Consider replacing *b*, for instance, with a call to *Open*. If you were to use the *If...Then* scheme to check for errors, you couldn't check for any errors in *Open* because you can't put conditional statements around a procedure. So it's easy for you to accept the fact that after *Open* is called, if an error occurs, the statement following *Open* will not run. It works the same with the *b* function. If an error occurs in the *b* function, the error routine rather than the statement that follows *b* will execute.

If you adopt this kind of error handling scheme, just make sure that you have projectwide collaboration on error codes and meanings. And by the way, if the functions *a*, *b*, and *c* already exist (as used previously with the *If* statements), we'll be using this "new" ability to ignore returned values to our advantage.

NOTE

> Once again, if a routine's returned value can be ignored, a programmer will probably ignore it!

Tip 4: Automatically log critical *MsgBox* errors.

One way to log critical *MsgBox* errors is by *not* using the standard message box provided by VBA's *Interaction.MsgBox* routine. When you refer to an object or a property in code, Visual Basic searches each object library you reference to resolve it. Object library references are set up in Visual Basic's References dialog box. (Open the References dialog box by selecting References from the Project menu.) The up arrow and down arrow buttons in the dialog box move references up and down in a list so that they can be arranged by priority. If two items in the list use the same name for an object, Visual Basic uses the definition provided by the item listed higher in the Available References list box. The three topmost references (Visual Basic For Applications, Visual Basic Runtime Objects And Procedures, and Visual Basic Objects And Procedures) cannot be demoted (or shuffled about). The caveat to all this prioritizing works in our favor—internal modules are always searched first.

Visual Basic 6 allows you to subclass its internal routines such as *MsgBox* and replace them with your own (through aggregation). Recall that in the code shown earlier (in Listing 1-1) some of the calls to *MsgBox* were prefixed with *VBA*. This explicitly scopes the call to VBA's *MsgBox* method via the Visual Basic For Applications type library reference. However, calls to plain old *MsgBox* go straight to our own internal message box routine.

A typical call to our new message box might look like this:

```
MsgBox "Error text in here", _
       vbYesNo + vbHelpButton + vbCritical, sMsgBoxTitle
```

The vbHelpButton flag is not a standard Visual Basic constant but rather an internal constant. It's used to indicate to *MsgBox* that it should add a Help button. Also, by adding vbCritical, we're saying that this message (error) is extremely serious. *MsgBox* will now log this error to a log file.

To replace *MsgBox*, all you have to do is write a function (an application method really) named *MsgBox* and give it the following signature. (The real *MsgBox* method has more arguments that you might also want to add to your replacement; use the Object Browser to explore the real method further.)

```
Public Function MsgBox _
( _
    ByVal isText As String _
    , Optional ByVal inButtons As Integer _
    , Optional ByVal isTitle As String  _
)
```

Here's an example of a trivial implementation:

```
Public Function MsgBox _
( _
    ByVal isText As String _
    , Optional ByVal inButtons As Integer _
    , Optional ByVal isTitle As String _
)

    Dim nResult As Integer

    nResult = VBA.Interaction.MsgBox(isText, inButtons, isTitle)

    If Not IsMissing(inButtons) Then
        If (inButtons And vbCritical) = vbCritical Then
            Call LogError(isText, inButtons, isTitle, nResult)
        End If
    End If

    MsgBox = nResult

End Function
```

Here we're logging (implied by the call to *LogError*) the main message text of a message box that contains the vbCritical button style. Notice that we're using the VBA implementation of *MsgBox* to produce the real message box on screen. (You could use just *VBA.MsgBox* here, but we prefer *VBA.Interaction.MsgBox* for clarity.) Within your code, you use *MsgBox* just as you always have. Notice also that in our call to *LogError* we're logging away the user's response (*nResult*) too—"I'm sure I said 'Cancel'!"

Another good idea with any message box is always to display the application's version number in its title; that is, modify the code above to look like this:

```
sTitle = App.EXEName & "(" & App.Major & "." & _
                           App.Minor & "." & _
                           App.Revision & ")"

nResult = VBA.Interaction.MsgBox(isText, inButtons, _
                           sTitle & isTitle)
```

Figure 1-2 shows the message box that results from this code.

FIGURE 1-2

Using your version number in message boxes

Of course, you don't have to use VBA's *MsgBox* method to produce the message box. You could create your own message box, using, say, a form. We create our own custom message boxes because we often want more control over the appearance and functionality of the message box. For example, we often use extra buttons (such as a Help button, which is what the vbHelpButton constant was all about) in our message boxes.

One nifty way to log error events (or any other event you might consider useful) is to use the *App* object's *LogEvent* method, which logs an event to the application's log target. On Windows NT platforms, the log target is the NT Event Log; on Windows 9x machines, the log target writes to a file specified in the *App.LogPath* property. By default, if no file is specified, events are written to a file named VBEVENTS.LOG.

This code

```
Call App.LogEvent("PeetM", vbLogEventTypeInformation)
Call App.LogEvent(Time$, vbLogEventTypeError)
```

produces this output in the log:

```
Information Application C:\WINDOWS\vbevents.log: Thread ID:
    -1902549 ,Logged: PeetM
Error Application C:\WINDOWS\vbevents.log: Thread ID:
    -1902449 ,Logged: 15:11:32
```

Interestingly, *App.LogPath* and *App.LogMode* are not available at design time and are available as read-only at run time, so how do you set them? You set them with *App.StartLogging*. A disadvantage to these routines is that *App.LogEvent* is available only in a built executable—not very useful for debugging in the Integrated Development Environment (IDE)! Now the good news: you can improve on this behavior by using the Win32 API directly from your application to log events to the NT Event Log (under Windows NT) or to a file (under Windows 9x). If you're going to log events this way I would suggest that you do so by ignoring the advice given in the Support Online article, *HOWTO: Write to the NT Event Log from Visual Basic*. (You can find this article by searching for article ID Q154576 on Microsoft's web site, *http://www.microsoft.com*.) Instead, wrap the necessary API calls (steal the code required from the *HOWTO* article) within a replacement *App* object that is contained within an ActiveX DLL (to which you have a reference in your project). This means that you'll still use *App.LogEvent* and the other routines, but instead of calling into the "real" *App* object, you're calling into the one you've provided in the DLL (which is compiled, of course). You can write this DLL so that you can easily change *App.LogFile* or any other routine (if you're running Windows 9x).

Tip 5: Have an error handler in every routine.

Because Visual Basic nests routines into local address space, all errors happen locally. An unhandled error in some routine that might be handled above that routine, in another error handler, should be considered unhandled because it will probably destabilize the application.

Let's go over that again, but more slowly. Visual Basic handles local errors. By this, I mean that whenever an error handler is called it always thinks it's acting upon an error produced locally within the routine the error handler is in. (Indeed, a bit of obscure syntax, normally unused because it's implied, *On Local Error GoTo*, gives this little secret away.) So if we write some functions named *SubA*, *SubB*, and *SubC* and arrange for *SubA* to call *SubB* and *SubB* in turn to call *SubC*, we can spot the potential problem. (See Figure 1-3.) If *SubC* generates an error, who handles it? Well, it all depends. If *we* don't handle it, Visual Basic will. Visual Basic looks up *Err.Number* in its list of error strings, produces a message box with the string, and then executes an *End* for you. If, as in Figure 1-3, *SubA* handles errors, Visual Basic will search up through the call chain until it finds *SubA* (and its error handler) and use that error handler instead of its own default error handler. Our error handler in *SubA*, however, now *thinks* that the error happened locally to it; that is, any *Resume* clause we might ultimately execute in the error handler works entirely within the local *SubA* routine.

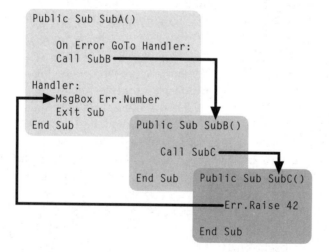

Figure 1-3   *The call chain in action*

Your code always runs in the context of some event handler; that is, any entry point into your code must ultimately be in the form of an event handler. So substituting *SubA* with, say, *Form_Load*, you could now write a catchall error handler by providing an error handler in *Form_Load*. Now, when *SubC* generates its error (I'm assuming here that these functions are only ever called from *Form_Load*), Visual Basic will find the local error handler in *Form_Load* and execute it. Ultimately, this error handler will execute a *Resume* statement. For argument's sake, let's say that it's *Resume Next*.

The *Next* here means after the call to *SubB*. OK, so what's the problem? If a problem exists, it's buried inside *SubB* and *SubC*—we don't know what they did! Imagine this scenario. Maybe *SubC* opened some files or perhaps a database or two, and somewhere within *SubC*, it was also going to close them. What happens if the erroring code happened somewhere in between these two operations—say, the files or databases got opened but were never closed? Again it depends, but loosely speaking, it means trouble.

NOTE

The situation described above could be worse, however. Maybe instead of *Resume Next* we simply used *Resume*, that is, try again. This will result in an attempt to open the same files again; and as we all know, this attempt may fail for many reasons—perhaps instead of using *FreeFile*, you used hard-coded file handle IDs, or maybe you opened the files last time with exclusive access.

Unfortunately, when Visual Basic executes an error handler, there's no easy way of telling whether the error handler was really local to the error. So there's no way to guarantee that you handled it properly. And of course, there's no way to install a global error handler that's called automatically by Visual Basic whenever an error occurs. There's no way around it: to write professional and robust applications, we must have error handlers *absolutely everywhere!*

Tip 6: Write meaningful error logs (to a central location if possible).

By way of an example, Listing 1-3 is a typical log file entry produced by our internal application template code. No explanation is provided because most of the entry is pretty obvious.

```
*****************************************************************
* Error Entry Start. TEST. Created 21 March 1998 19:01
*****************************************************************
The Application:
----------------


C:\TMS\TEMPLATE\TEST.EXE  Version 1.0.15
OS App Name C:\TMS\TEMPLATE\TEST.EXE

The Error:
----------
An error has occurred in C:\TMS\TEMPLATE\TEST.EXE - the TMS error code associated
with this error is 000053. If the problem persists, please report the error to TMS
support. The error occurred at line 100.

The error probably occurred in frmMainForm.cmd1_Click.
The standard VB error text for this error is 'File not found'.

Active Environment Variables:
-----------------------------
TMP=C:\WINDOWS\TEMP
winbootdir=C:\WINDOWS
COMSPEC=C:\COMMAND.COM
PATH=C:\WINDOWS;C:\WINDOWS\COMMAND;C:\;C:\DOS
TEMP=C:\TEMP
DIRCMD=/OGN/L
PROMPT=$e[0m[$e[1;33m$p$e[0m]$_$g
CMDLINE=WIN
windir=C:\WINDOWS

Relevant Directories:          Attr:
---------------------
Windows DIR C:\WINDOWS          - 16
System  DIR C:\WINDOWS\SYSTEM - 16
Current DIR C:\TMS\TEMPLATE     - 16
Versions:
---------
Windows    - 3.95
DOS        - 7.0
Mode       - Enhanced
CPU        - 486 or Better
COPRO      - True
Windows 95 - True (4.03.1214)B
```

LISTING 1-3   *Typical log file entry*

```
Resources:
----------
Free Mem (Rough) 15,752 MB
Free GDI  (%) 79
Free USER (%) 69
Free Handles 103


Other:
------
Threads          - 64
VMs              - 4
Registered Owner - Peter J. Morris


**********************************************************************
* Error Entry End. TEST
**********************************************************************


**********************************************************************
* Stack Dump Start. TEST. Created 21 March 1998 19:01
**********************************************************************
Stack Frame: 001 of 003 AppObject   - Run        Called @ line 70 CheckStack
Stack Frame: 002 of 003 AppObject   - CheckStack Called @ line 10 cmd1_Click
Stack Frame: 003 of 003 frmMainForm - cmd1_Click
**********************************************************************
* Stack Dump End. TEST
**********************************************************************


**********************************************************************
* DAO Errors Start. TEST. Created 21 March 1998 19:01
**********************************************************************
No Errors
**********************************************************************
* DAO Errors End. TEST
**********************************************************************
```

Also, see the note on stack frames later in this chapter for a fuller explanation of the Stack log entries.

The log files you write can be centralized; that is, all your applications can write to a single file or perhaps to many different files held in a central location. That "file" could be a Microsoft Jet database. Now if you log meaningful information of the same kind from different sources to a database, what have you got? Useful data, that's what! At TMS, we created a system like this once for a client. All the data gathered was analyzed in real time by another Visual

Basic application and displayed on a machine in the company's support department. The application had some standard queries it could throw at the data (How's application *xyz* performing today?), as well as a query editor that the company could use to build its own queries on the data. (Show me all the Automation errors that occurred for user *abc* this year, and sort them by error code.) All the results could be graphed, too—an ability that, as is usual, allows the true nature of the data statistics to become apparent.

After a little while, it wasn't just Support that accessed this database. User education used it to spot users who were experiencing errors because of a lack of training, and developers used it to check on how their beta release was running. Remember, users are generally bad at reporting errors. Most prefer to Ctrl+Alt+Delete and try again before contacting support. By logging errors automatically, you don't need the user to report the error (sometimes incorrectly or with missing information: "Let's see, it said something about…"); it's *always* done by the application, and *all* the necessary information is logged *automatically*.

Figure 1-4 shows an example of the kind of output that's easy to produce from the log:

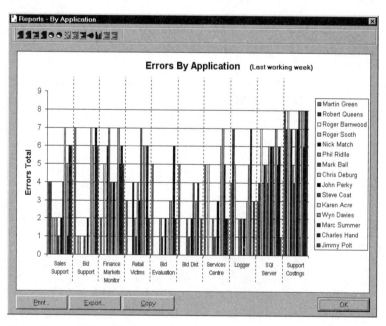

FIGURE 1-4   *Graphing error log data*

This chart shows how many users have produced trappable errors in various interesting applications.

Whenever we hit an error, we determine whether we're running in Visual Basic's IDE and then log or output different error text and do some other stuff differently depending on the result of that test. The reason we do this is that programmers are not end users, meaning that a programmer doesn't mind seeing "Input past end of file," but users almost always mind! If you know which context you're running in, you can easily switch messages.

The test we do internally at TMS to determine whether we're running in the IDE involves a routine called *InDesign*. Here's the code (the explanation follows):

```
Public Function InDesign() As Boolean

    ' *****************************************
    ' The only thing Debug.Assert is good for!
    ' *****************************************

    Static nCallCount   As Integer
    Static bRet         As Boolean   ' By default this is set to False.

    nCallCount = nCallCount + 1

    Select Case nCallCount

        Case 1: ' First time in
            Debug.Assert InDesign()

        Case 2: ' Second time in so we must have executed Debug.Assert...
            bRet = True

    End Select

    ' If Debug.Assert called, we need to return True to prevent the trap.
    InDesign = bRet

    ' Reset for future calls.
    nCallCount = 0

End Function
```

In the earlier versions of Visual Basic (previous to Visual Basic 6), *InDesign* used API calls to determine whether the Visual Basic IDE was kicking around. The version of *InDesign* (not shown here) in the first edition of our book evolved from some Visual Basic 4 code and therefore needed to cater to both the 16-bit and 32-bit worlds. We modified this code for the pure 32-bit world and replaced it with what amounts to a call to *GetModuleHandle*:

```
Private Function InDesign() As Boolean

    InDesign = 0 < GetModuleHandle("VBA5.DLL")

End Function
```

The only problem with this code was that you needed to know the name of the DLL that implements the IDE, which in this case was VBA5.DLL. Who knew that this would be VBA6.DLL for version 6 and who knows what it will be for version 7 and so on? By the way, this code works because if the application is running under the IDE in Win32, the IDE (and its DLLs and so on) must be loaded into the same process space as the application. The DLLs of other processes cannot be seen (easily, anyway); ergo, if you can see it you must have it loaded, and if you have it loaded you must be running in the IDE.

Anyway, back to the *InDesign* code shown earlier. This "new" cut of the code should work for all future versions of Visual Basic (as well as for version 6). This code essentially uses the fact that *Debug.Assert* is coded in such a way as to make it suboptimal (an explanation of this statement follows shortly). Because the *Debug* object effectively goes away when you make an EXE, it follows that methods applied to it, like *Print*, also have no effect—in fact, they don't even run. Because the *Assert* method is such a method, we can make use of this disappearing act to determine whether the code is running in design mode.

The first time we call the function, which requires only a simple *If InDesign Then* statement, *nCallCount* is zero and *bRet* is False (initialized by default). Notice that both variables are declared as static, meaning they are accessed locally but stored globally. In other words, they are shared, persistent objects that can be accessed only within the scope of the subroutine in which they're declared. We increment *nCallCount* and then execute the *Select Case* statement. Obviously *nCallCount* is now 1, so the *Case 1* code executes. At this point, if we're running in design mode, the *Debug.Assert* line causes us to reenter the routine. This time, *nCallCount = nCallCount + 1* increments the static *nCallCount* to 2, and the *Case 2* code sets *bRet* to True. Note that True is returned to the call made to *Debug.Assert* from the first entry into *InDesign*. Because we've asserted something that's True, we don't execute a *Stop* here. Instead, we return to the line of code to be executed after the call to *Debug.Assert*, which is the *InDesign = bRet* code (again). Once more we return True (because *bRet* is still set to True from the previous call to *InDesign*). This final value of True is now returned to the original caller to indicate, "Yes, we are running in design mode."

Now consider what happens if we're running as an EXE. Basically this means that the line *Debug.Assert InDesign* is missing from the routine. In this case, the only call made to our routine returns the state of *bRet*—False by default. If you're worried about the clock cycles taken here (that as an EXE we increment an integer and then set it to zero again), don't be—it's fast! If you insist, however, you can wrap the routine so that it's called just once, perhaps upon application start-up.

OK, why did I say that *Debug.Assert* was suboptimal? Normally assertions are used to implement what is known in the trade as a "soft if." Consider this code:

```
nFile = FreeFile
```

If *FreeFile* fails, what does *nFile* equal? Actually, like *Open*, *FreeFile* raises an exception to indicate failure (maybe it knows that return values can, and will, be ignored), but for the sake of argument let's say *FreeFile* returns 0. To detect this, as you should if you're building really critical applications that must cope with and recover from every possibility, expand the code to this:

```
nFile = FreeFile

If nFile <> 0 Then
    ⋮
End If
```

Adding the conditional test and the indentation complicates the code. The execution time increases due to the branch, the evaluation of both the expressions on either side of the angle brackets, and of course the comparison itself. For all we know, we may never need this code—after all, what is the probability that *FreeFile* will fail in real life? To test this, sanitize the code, and make it more efficient, we would use a "soft if" conditional instead of a "hard if" conditional:

```
nFile = FreeFile

Assert nFile <> 0

⋮
```

Here we're asserting our belief that *FreeFile* will never return 0. (Note that we've lost the indentation.) Now we build the application and send it out to test. If the assertion fails, the probability that we've run out of file handles surely approaches 1, whereas if it doesn't fail, the probability approaches 0. In this case, we can decide that the likelihood of failure is so remote that we can effectively ignore it. If the assertion never fails, we use conditional compilation to remove it and build the final EXE. In fact, we'd normally remove all assertions either by turning them into "hard ifs" or by removing them alto-gether. Never ship with assertions in your code. By the way, all of the previous was C-speak (for example, I'd do it this way in C or C++), and therein lies the rub. In Visual Basic you can't do otherwise because *Debug.Assert* is removed for you whenever you build an EXE. "Great," you say. "So now I must never ship with assertions in my code?" (I just said this practice was a good one, but only when you ship the final EXE.) "How do I determine if an assertion failed during a test if it's not even there?" Aha—the plot thickens. Assertions in Vi-sual Basic seem to be there solely for the developer and not the tester, mean-ing they work only in the IDE environment. In other words, suboptimal. That is, of course, unless you ship the source and IDE when you go out to beta!

Back to the story. By using *InDesign* we can, as mentioned earlier, do things a little differently at run time depending upon whether we're running in the IDE. We at TMS usually store the result of a single call to *InDesign* in a property of the *App* object called *InDesign*. (We replace the real *App* object with our own—also called *App*—and set this property at application start-up.)

Another use of *App.InDesign* is to turn off your own error handling altogether. Now I know that Visual Basic allows you to Break On All Errors, but that's rarely useful, especially if you implement delayed error handling. Instead, use *App.InDesign* to conditionally turn error handling on or off:

```
If Not App.InDesign Then On Error GoTo ...
```

The reason for this is that one of the last things you want within the IDE is active error handlers. Imagine you're hitting F8 and tracing through your code. I'm sure you know what happens next—you suddenly find yourself in an error handler. What you really want is for Visual Basic to issue a *Stop* for you on the erroring line (which it will do by default if you're using the IDE and hit an error and don't have an error handler active). The code above causes that to happen even when your error handling code has been added. Only if you're running as an EXE will the error trap become enabled.

Tip 7: Use assertions.

I've already briefed you on some stuff about assertions; here's the full scoop.

Assertions are routines (in Visual Basic) that use expressions to *assert* that something is or is not True. For example, you might have a line of code like this in your project:

```
nFile = FreeFile
```

So how do you know if it works? Maybe you think that it raises an exception if all your file handles are taken up. (The Help file doesn't tell you.) We wouldn't leave this to chance. What we'd do during both unit and system testing is use assertions to check our assumption that all is indeed well. We would have a line that looks like this following the line above:

```
Call Assert(nFile <> 0, "FreeFile")
```

This checks that *nFile* is not set to 0. Assertions are easy to use and extremely handy. They would be even better if Visual Basic had a "stringizing" preprocessor like the one that comes with most C compilers. Then *it* could fill in the second parameter for you with the asserted expression, like this:

```
Call Assert(nFile <> 0, "nFile <> 0")
```

Assertions should be removed at run time. They serve only for testing during development, a kind of soft error handler, if you will. (This removal could be done using the *App.InDesign* property described earlier.) If an assertion regularly fails during development, we usually place a real test around it; that is, we test for it specifically in code. For the preceding example, we would replace

```
Call Assert(nFile <> 0, "FreeFile")
```

with

```
If nFile = 0 Then
    Err.Raise ????
End If
```

If an assertion doesn't fail regularly (or at all) during development, we remove the assertion. See Chapter XX for more on writing and using assertions and on the *Debug* object's *Assert* method (which I haven't used here).

If you're asking yourself, "Why isn't he using *Debug.Assert*?" you need to go back and read all of Tip 6 on page XXX.

Tip 8: Don't retrofit blind error handlers.

The best error handlers are written when the routine they protect is being written. Tools that insert error handlers for you help but are not the answer. These tools can be used to retrofit semi-intelligent error handlers into your code once you're through writing—but is this a good idea? Your application will be error handler–enabled, that's for sure; but how *dynamic* will it be in its handling of any errors? Not very!

We rarely use any kind of tool for this purpose because in fitting a blind error handler there is little chance of adding any code that could recover from a given error situation. In other words, by fitting an error handler after the fact, you might just as well put this line of pseudocode in each routine:

```
On Error Condition Report Error
```

You're handling errors but in a blind, automated fashion. No recovery is possible here. In a nutshell, a blind error handler is potentially of little real use, although it is of course better than having no error handling at all. Think "exception" as you write the code and use automation tools only to provide a template from which to work.

Tip 9: Trace the stack.

As you saw in the log file in Listing 1-3 on page 22, we dump the VBA call stack when we hit an unexpected error because it can be useful for working out later what went wrong and why. We build an internal representation of VBA's stack (because VBA's stack is not actually available—shame), using two fundamental routines: *TrTraceIn* and *TrTraceOut*. Here they are in a typical routine:

```
Public Sub Testing()

' Set up general error handler.
On Error GoTo Error_General_Testing:
    Const sProcSig = MODULE & " General.Testing"
    Call TrTraceIn(sProcSig)

    ' ========== Body Code Starts ==========
    ⋮
    ' ========== Body Code Ends ==========

    Call TrTraceOut(sProcSig)
    Exit Sub

' Error handler.
Error_General_Testing:
    ⋮
End Sub
```

These routines are inserted by hand or by using the same internal tool I mentioned earlier in Tip 2 that adds line numbers to code. Notice that *sProcSig* is being passed into these routines so that the stack can be built containing the name of the module and the routine.

The stack frame object we use internally (not shown here) uses a Visual Basic collection with a class wrapper for its implementation. The class name we use is *CStackFrame*. As a prefix, *C* means class, and its single instance is named *oStackFrame*. We drop the *o* prefix if we're replacing a standard class such as *Err* or *App*.

Tip 10: Use a ROOS (Resource Only Object Server).

A basic ROOS (pronounced "ruse") is a little like a string table resource except that it runs in-process or out-of-process as an Automation server. A ROOS provides a structured interface to a set of objects and properties that enables us to build more flexible error handling routines.

For example, the ROOS holds a project's error constants (or rather the values mapped to the symbols used in the code that are resolved from the object's type library). The ROOS also holds a set of string resources that hold the actual error text for a given error and the methods used to load and process errors at run time. To change the language used in error reports or perhaps the vocabulary being used (for example, user vs. programmer), simply use a different ROOS. (No more DLLs with weird names!)

Tip 11: Replace useful intrinsic objects with your own.

Our main ROOS contains a set of alternative standard object classes, *TMSErr* and *TMSApp*, for example. These are instantiated as *Err* and *App* at application start-up as part of our application template initialization. (All our Visual Basic applications are built on this template.) By creating objects like this, we can add methods, properties, and so on to what looks like one of Visual Basic's own objects.

For example, our error object has extra methods named *Push* and *Pop*. These, mostly for historical reasons, are *really* useful methods because it's not clear in Visual Basic when *Err.Clear* is actually applied to the *Err* object—that is, when the outstanding error, which you've been called to handle, is automatically cleared. This can easily result in the reporting of error 0. Watch out for this because you'll see it a lot!

Usually, an error is mistakenly cleared in this way when someone is handling an error and from within the error handler he or she calls some other routine that causes Visual Basic to execute an *Err.Clear*. All sorts of things can make Visual Basic execute an *Err.Clear*. The result in this case is that the error is lost! These kinds of mistakes are really hard to find. They're also really easy to put in—lines of code that cause this to happen, that is!

The Help file under Err Object used to include this Caution about losing the error context.

If you set up an error handler using On Error GoTo and that handler calls another procedure, the properties of the Err object *may be* reset to zero and zero-length strings. To retain values for later use, assign the values of Err properties to variables before calling another procedure, or before executing Resume, On Error, Exit Sub, Exit Function, or Exit Property statements.

Of course, if you do reset *Err.Number* (perhaps by using *On Error GoTo* in the called routine), when you return to the calling routine the error will be lost. The answer, of course, is to preserve, or push, the error context onto some kind of error stack. We do this with *Err.Push*. It's the first line of code in the error handler—*always*. (By the way, Visual Basic won't do an *Err.Clear* on the call to *Err.Push* but only on its return—guaranteed.) Here's an example of how this push and pop method of error handling looks in practice:

```
Private Sub Command1_Click()

    On Error GoTo error_handler:

    VBA.Err.Raise 42

    Exit Sub

error_handler:

    Err.Push
    Call SomeFunc
    Err.Pop
    MsgBox Err.Description
    Resume Next

End Sub
```

Here we're raising an error (42, as it happens) and handling it in our error handler just below. The message box reports the error correctly as being an

Application Defined Error. If we were to comment out the *Err.Push* and *Err.Pop* routines and rerun the code, the error information would be lost and the message box would be empty (as *Err.Number* and *Err.Description* have been reset to some suitable "nothing"), assuming the call to *SomeFunc* completes successfully. In other words, when we come to show the message box, there's no outstanding error to report! (The call to *Err.Push* is the first statement in the error handler. This is easy to check for during a code review.)

NOTE

> If we assume that Visual Basic itself raises exceptions by calling *Err.Raise* and that *Err.Raise* simply sets other properties of *Err*, such as *Err.Number*, our own *Err.Number* obviously won't be called to set *VBA.Err* properties (as it would if we simply had a line of code that read, say, *Err.Number = 42*). This is a pity because if it did call our *Err.Number*, we could detect (what with our *Err.Number* being called first before any other routines) that an error was being raised and automatically look after preserving the error context; that is, we could do an *Err.Push* automatically without having it appear in each error handler.

All sound good to you? Here's a sample implementation of a new *Err* object that contains *Pop* and *Push* methods:

In a class called ErrObject

```
Private e() As ErrObjectState

Private Type ErrObjectState

    Description As String
    HelpContext As Long
    HelpFile    As String
    Number      As Long

End Type

Public Property Get Description() As String

    Description = VBA.Err.Description

End Property
```

>>

```
Public Property Let Description(ByVal s As String)

    VBA.Err.Description = s

End Property

Public Property Get HelpContext() As Long

    HelpContext = VBA.Err.HelpContext

End Property

Public Property Let HelpContext(ByVal l As Long)

    VBA.Err.HelpContext = l

End Property

Public Property Get HelpFile() As String

    HelpFile = VBA.Err.HelpFile

End Property

Public Property Let HelpFile(ByVal s As String)

    VBA.Err.HelpFile = s

End Property

Public Property Get Number() As Long

    Number = VBA.Err.Number

End Property

Public Property Let Number(ByVal l As Long)

    VBA.Err.Number = l

End Property

Public Property Get Source() As String

    Source = VBA.Err.Source

End Property
```

```vba
Public Property Let Source(ByVal s As String)

    VBA.Err.Source = s

End Property

Public Sub Clear()

    VBA.Err.Clear

    Description = VBA.Err.Description
    HelpContext = VBA.Err.HelpContext
    HelpFile = VBA.Err.HelpFile
    Number = VBA.Err.Number

End Sub

Public Sub Push()

    ReDim Preserve e(UBound(e) + 1) As ErrObjectState

    With e(UBound(e))

        .Description = Description
        .HelpContext = HelpContext
        .HelpFile = HelpFile
        .Number = Number

    End With

End Sub

Public Sub Pop()

    With e(UBound(e))

        Description = .Description
        HelpContext = .HelpContext
        HelpFile = .HelpFile
        Number = .Number

    End With
```

```
    If UBound(e) Then
        ReDim e(UBound(e) - 1) As ErrObjectState
    Else
        VBA.Err.Raise Number:=28 ' Out of stack space - underflow
    End If

End Sub

Private Sub Class_Initialize()

    ReDim e(0) As ErrObjectState

End Sub

Private Sub Class_Terminate()

    Erase e()

End Sub
```

In Sub Main

```
Set Err = New ErrObject
```

In Global Module

```
Public Err As ErrObject
```

As you can see, our new *Err* object maintains a stack of a user-defined type (UDT) called *ErrObjectState*. An instance of this type basically holds information from the last error. In Sub Main we create our only *ErrObject*—note that it's called *Err*. This means that calls to methods like *Err.Number* will be directed to our object. In other words, *Err* refers to our instance of *ErrObject* and not the global instance *VBA.Err*. This means, of course, that we have to provide stubs for all the methods that are normally part of the global *Err* object: *Number*, *Description*, *Source*, and so on.

Note that we've left *LastDLLError* off the list. This is because when we pop the stack we'd need to write a value back into *VBA.Err.LastDLLError* and, unfortunately, this is a read-only property!

Another object we replace is the *Debug* object. We do this because we sometimes want to see what debug messages might be emitting from a built executable.

As you know, "normal" *Debug.Print* calls are thrown away by Visual Basic when your application is running as an executable; "special" *Debug.Print* calls, however, can be captured even when the application is running as an executable.

Replacing this object is a little trickier than replacing the *Err* object because the *Debug* object name cannot be overloaded; that is, you have to call your new object something like *Debugger*. This new object can be designed to write to Visual Basic's Immediate window so that it becomes a complete replacement for the *Debug* object. Chapter 6 shows how you can write your own *Assert* method so that you can also replace the *Debug* object's *Assert* method.

Tip 12: Check DLL version errors.

Debugging and defensive programming techniques can be used even in post-implementation. We always protect our applications against bad dynamic links (with DLLs and with ActiveX components such as OCXs) by using another internal tool. For a great example of why you should do this, see Chapter 8, Steve Overall's chapter about the Year 2000.

One of the really great things about Windows is that the dynamic linking mechanism, which links one module into another at run time, is not defined as part of some vendor's object file format but is instead part of the operating system itself. This means, for example, that it's really easy to do mixed language programming (whereas with static linking it's really hard because you're at the mercy of some vendor's linker—you just have to hope that it will understand). Unfortunately, this same mechanism can also get you into trouble because it's not until run time that you can resolve a link. Who knows what you'll end up linking to in the end—perhaps to an old and buggy version of some OCX. Oops!

By the way, don't use a GUID (explained below) to determine the version of any component. The GUID will almost always stay the same unless the object's interface has changed; it doesn't change for a bug fix or an upgrade. On the other hand, the object's version number should change whenever the binary image changes; that is, it should change whenever you build something (such as a bug fix or an interface change) that differs in any way from some previous version. The version number, not the GUID, tells you whether you're using the latest incarnation of an object or application.

Because it affects your application externally, this kind of versioning problem can be extremely hard to diagnose from afar (or for that matter, from anear).

So how do you check DLL version numbers? There are two ways of doing this since the underlying VERSIONINFO resource (which contains the version information) usually contains the information twice. A VERSIONINFO resource contains the version number both as a string and as a binary value. The latter is the most accurate, although the former is the one shown to you by applications like Microsoft Windows Explorer.

Here's an example. On my machine, OLEAUT32.DLL has a version number reported by Windows Explorer of 2.30.4261, whereas Microsoft System Information (MSINFO32.EXE version 2.51) shows the same file having a version number of 2.30.4261.1. Is Windows Explorer missing a *.1* for some reason? Let's experiment further to find out. Here's another one—OPENGL32.DLL. (You can follow along if you have the file on your hard disk.) Windows Explorer reports this DLL as being version 4.00, yet Microsoft System Information says it's version 4.0.1379.1. Which is right? They both are, sort of. One version number is the string (4.00); the other is the binary (4.0.1379.1). As I mentioned earlier, the binary version number is more accurate, which is why it's used by the Windows' versioning API, Microsoft System Information, and of course all good installation program generators like InstallShield.

GLOBALLY UNIQUE IDENTIFIERS (GUIDs)

A GUID (Globally Unique Identifier) is a 128-bit integer that can be used by COM (Component Object Model) to identify ActiveX components. Each GUID is guaranteed to be unique in the world. GUIDs are actually UUIDs (Universally Unique Identifiers) as defined by the Open Software Foundation's Distributed Computing Environment. GUIDs are used in Visual Basic mainly to identify the components you use in your projects (referenced under the References and Components items of the Project menu) and to help ensure that COM components do not accidentally connect to the "wrong" component, interface, or method even in networks with millions of component objects. The GUID is the actual name of a component, not the string you and I use to name it, or its filename. For example, a component we've probably all used before is F9043C88-F6F2-101A-A3C9-08002B2F49FB. You and I most likely refer to this component as the "Microsoft Common Dialog Control," or more simply, COMDLG32.OCX. (I have two of these on my machine, both with the same GUID. Their versions are different, however. One is 5.00.3112, and the other is 6.00.8169. Which do you link with?)

To determine a component's GUID, look in your project's VBP file. You'll see something like this if you use the Common Dialog control:

```
Object={F9043C88-F6F2-101A-A3C9-08002B2F49FB}#1.2#0;
COMDLG32.OCX
```

Visual Basic creates GUIDs for you automatically (for every ActiveX control you build). If you want to create them externally to Visual Basic, you can use either GUIDGEN.EXE or UUIDGEN.EXE, Microsoft utilities that come with the Visual C++ compiler, the ActiveX SDK, and on the Visual Basic 6 CD. You'll also find a Visual Basic program to generate GUIDs (in Chapter 7, my chapter on type libraries).

To see some sample code that determines a file's real version number, refer to the VB98\WIZARDS\PDWIZARD\SETUP1 source code. Everything you need is in there and ready for you to borrow!

By the way, when you compile your project, Visual Basic sets the string and binary version numbers to the number you enter on the Make tab of the Project Properties dialog box. For example, if you set your version number to, say, 1.2.3 in the Project Properties dialog box and build the EXE (or whatever) and then examine its version number using Windows Explorer and Microsoft System Information, you'll find that Windows Explorer reports the version number as 1.02.0003 while Microsoft System Information reports it as 1.2.0.3.

Backward Compatibility

Once you've got your version-checking code in place should you assume backward compatibility?

I'd say you should normally assume that 1.2.3 is simply a "better" 1.2.2 and so forth, although again I urge you to see Chapter 8 to find out what Steve has to say about OLEAUT32.DLL and to see a DLL that changed its functionality, not just its version number.

Normally a version number increment shows that the disk image has been altered, maybe with a bug fix. Bottom line: whenever the binary image changes, the version number should change also. An interface GUID change means that some interface has changed. Bottom line: whenever the interface changes, the GUID (and of course the version number) must change. If you don't have an interface, you're probably working with a DLL; in addition to being a binary file, this DLL has both entry points and behavior. Bottom line: if the behavior of a DLL changes or an entry point in it is modified, you must also change the filename.

To make the version numbers of your software even more accessible to your consumers, you might want to build an interface into your components, maybe called VERSIONINFO, that returns the version number of the EXE or DLL. All it would take is one Property Get:

```
Public Property Get VersionNumber() As String
    VersionNumber = App.Major & "." & App.Minor & "." & App.Revision
End Property
```

Tip 13: Use Microsoft System Information (MSINFO32.EXE) when you can.

When you're trying to help a user with some problem (especially if you're in support), you often need to know a lot of technical stuff about the user's machine, such as what is loaded into memory or how the operating system is configured. Getting this information out of the user, even figuring out where to find it all in the first place, can be time-consuming and difficult. (Asking the user to continually hit Ctrl+Alt+Delete in an attempt to bring up the Task List and "see" what's running can be a dangerous practice: *User:* "Oh, my machine's rebooting." *Support:* "What did you do?" *User:* "What you told me to do—hit Ctrl+Alt+Delete again!") Microsoft thought so too, so they provided their users with an application to gather this information automatically: Microsoft System Information (MSINFO32.EXE). The good news is that you can use this application to help your customers.

Microsoft System Information comes with applications such as Microsoft Word and Microsoft Excel. If you have one of those applications installed, you're almost certain to have Microsoft System Information installed too. It also ships with Visual Basic 6. If you haven't seen this applet before, choose About Microsoft Visual Basic from the Help menu and click the System Info button. You'll see a window similar to Figure 1-5.

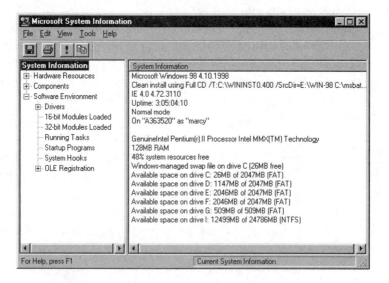

Figure 1-5   *Running MSINFO32.EXE opens the Microsoft System Information application*

The bottom line is that if your user is a Microsoft Office user or has an application such as Microsoft Excel installed, Microsoft System Information will be available. All you need to do then to provide the same information on the user's system is to run the same application!

To determine whether you've got this application to work with, look in the following location in the Registry:

```
HKEY_LOCAL_MACHINE\SOFTWARE\Microsoft\Shared Tools\MSInfo\Path
```

In the following example, we use the registration API in ADVAPI32.DLL to retrieve the value of the Registry key. We can then check to see whether the application really exists. If it does, *Shell* it!

Declaration Section

```
Option Explicit

Private Const REG_SZ                   As Long = 1
Private Const ERROR_SUCCESS            As Long = 0
Private Const HKEY_LOCAL_MACHINE       As Long = &H80000002
Private Const STANDARD_RIGHTS_ALL      As Long = &H1F0000
Private Const KEY_QUERY_VALUE          As Long = &H1
Private Const KEY_ENUMERATE_SUB_KEYS   As Long = &H8
Private Const KEY_NOTIFY               As Long = &H10
Private Const SYNCHRONIZE              As Long = &H100000
Private Const READ_CONTROL             As Long = &H20000
Private Const STANDARD_RIGHTS_READ     As Long = (READ_CONTROL)
Private Const KEY_READ                 As Long = _
                              ((STANDARD_RIGHTS_READ _
                              Or KEY_QUERY_VALUE _
                              Or KEY_ENUMERATE_SUB_KEYS _
                              Or KEY_NOTIFY) _
                              And (Not SYNCHRONIZE))


Private Declare Function WinRegOpenKeyEx Lib "advapi32.dll" _
Alias "RegOpenKeyExA" (ByVal hKey As Long, _
                   ByVal lpSubKey As String, _
                   ByVal ulOptions As Long, _
                   ByVal samDesired As Long, _
                   phkResult As Long) As Long
```

>>

```
Private Declare Function WinRegQueryValueEx Lib _
"advapi32.dll" Alias "RegQueryValueExA" _
                    (ByVal hKey As Long, _
                     ByVal lpValueName As String, _
                     ByVal lpReserved As Long, _
                     lpType As Long, lpData As Any, _
                     lpcbData As Long) As Long

Private Declare Function WinRegCloseKey Lib "advapi32" _
Alias "RegCloseKey" (ByVal hKey As Long) As Long
```

Form Load Event

```
Private Sub Form_Load()

    Dim hKey    As Long
    Dim lType   As Long
    Dim Buffer As String

    ' Need some space to write string into - DLL routine
    ' expects us to allocate this space before the call.
    Buffer = Space(255)

    ' Always expect failure!
    cmdSystemInfo.Visible = False

    ' This will work if Microsoft System Information is installed.
    If WinRegOpenKeyEx( _
                HKEY_LOCAL_MACHINE _
                , "SOFTWARE\Microsoft\Shared Tools\MSInfo" _
                , 0 _
                , KEY_READ _
                , hKey _
                ) = ERROR_SUCCESS Then

        ' Read the Path value - happens to include the filename
        ' too, e.g.,
        ' "C:\Program Files\Common Files\Microsoft Shared\
        ' MSinfo\msinfo32.exe".
        If WinRegQueryValueEx( _
                        hKey _
                        , "Path" _
                        , 0 _
                        , lType _
                        , ByVal Buffer _
```

```
                    , Len(Buffer) _
                    ) = ERROR_SUCCESS Then
    ' Make sure we read a string back. If we did...
    If lType = REG_SZ Then
        ' Make sure the Registry and reality are in
        ' alignment!
        ' Note: Using FileAttr() means you're
        ' suffering from paranoia<g>.
        If Dir$(Buffer) <> "" Then
            ' Put the path into the button's Tag
            ' property and make the button visible.
            cmdSystemInfo.Tag = Buffer
            cmdSystemInfo.Visible = True
        End If
    End If

End If

' We open - we close.
Call WinRegCloseKey(hKey)

End If

End Sub
```

Button Click Event

```
Private Sub cmdSystemInfo_Click()

    ' If we got clicked, we must be visible and therefore
    ' must have our Tag property set to the name of the
    ' Microsoft System Information application - Shell it!
    Call Shell(cmdSystemInfo.Tag, vbNormalFocus)

End Sub
```

In the code above, as the form loads (maybe this is an About box?) it detects whether or not Microsoft System Information exists. If it does, the form makes a command button visible and sets its *Tag* property to point to the program. When the form becomes visible, the button either will or won't be visible. If it is visible, you have Microsoft System Information on your machine. When you click the button, it simply calls *Shell* with the value in its *Tag* property. For more information on the APIs used in this example, see the appropriate Win32 documentation.

One of the neat little extras that came first with Visual Basic 5 was the little wizard dialog "thang" that allowed you to add standard dialog boxes to your application. One of these standard dialog boxes is an About dialog box. You'll notice that the About dialog box comes complete with a System Info button. The dialog box displays the Microsoft System Information utility using code similar to that shown on the previous page. (I think ours is cooler so I've left it here in the second edition.) This raises an interesting question, however. Is Microsoft implicitly giving you and me permission to ship MSINFO32.EXE (and anything that it needs) with an EXE? I'm afraid I don't know the answer to this one—sorry!

Tip 14: Treat error handling like transaction processing.

When you hit an error, always attempt to bring the application back to a known and stable condition; that is, roll back from the error. To do this, you'll need to handle errors locally (to roll back within the scope of the erroring procedure) and more globally by propagating the error back up through each entry in the call chain.

Here's how you proceed. When your most local (immediate) error trap gets hit, make sure you clean up as required locally first. For example, make sure you close any files that you opened in this routine. Once that's done, and if this routine is not an event handler, reraise the error (in reality, you might raise some other error here) and repeat this process for each previous stack frame (a stack frame refers to an entry in the call chain); that is, continue this process for each preceding call until you get back up to an event handler. If you've cleaned up locally all the way through the call chain and if you had an error handler for each stack frame (so that you didn't jump over some routines), you should now have effectively rolled back from the error. It will seem as though the error never really happened. Note that by *not* reporting errors from anywhere other than an event handler, you will not have shown your user a stream of message boxes.

Localized error handling might need error handling itself. Look at the following code fragment:

```
On Error GoTo Error_Handler:

    Dim nFile As Integer

    nFile = FreeFile
    Open "c:\time.txt" For Output Access Write As nFile
```

```
    Print #nFile, Time$
    Close nFile

    Exit Sub

Error_Handler:

    ' Roll back!
    Close nFile

    Exit Sub
```

Imagine you have opened a file and are attempting to roll back in your error handler. How do you know whether or not you opened the file? In other words, did the error occur before or after the line of code that opens the file? If you attempt to close the file and it's not open, you'll cause an error—but if it's open, you don't want to leave it open as you're trying to roll back! I guess you could use *Erl* to determine where your code erred, but this implies that you're editing line numbered source code—yuck. (You'll recall from Tip 2 that we added line numbers only to the code for the final EXE, not to the code we're still editing.) Probably the best way to determine what did or did not get done is to limit the possibilities; that is, keep your routines small (so that you have only a small problem domain). Of course, that's not going to help us here. What we need to do is apply a little investigation!

Given this type of problem, you're probably going to have to test the file handle to see whether it points to an open file. In the code above, we would probably use *FileAttr(nFile, 1)* to determine whether or not the file *nFile* is open for writing. If the file is not open, *FileAttr* raises an exception (of course). And obviously, you can't handle this locally because you can't set an error trap from within an error trap unless your error handling is in another routine! (Refer to Tip 5 on page 20 for details.)

Tip 15: Don't test your own software or write your own test plans.

Do you have dedicated testers where you work? Possibly not—not many companies do. Many companies say they "can't afford such a luxury." Well, in my opinion, they're a luxury that's really worth it (as many of the leading software development companies in the world already know).

Independent testers should (and often do) exhibit the following characteristics:

- Are impartial
- Are less informed about the usage and the type of input your code expects
- Are usually more knowledgeable about the usage and the type of input your code doesn't expect
- Are more likely than you to spend time trying to break code
- Are typically more leery of your interfaces and more critical of your coupling
- Are into doing you damage and breaking your code
- Are more informed than you about system limits
- Unlike you, actually want to find bugs in your software.

From time to time, Microsoft talks about its ratio of developers to testers: around 1:1. You do the math; for every programmer there's a tester. In fact, rumor has it that some developers occasionally get shifted to being testers. This could happen if a developer consistently develops very buggy software. Nothing like a shift to testing to improve one's knowledge and appreciation of what good solid code involves.

Tip 16: Stress test your applications.

Years ago, the Windows SDK (Software Development Kit) shipped with an applet named SHAKER.EXE. This applet simply ran around allocating and releasing memory blocks. When and what it actually allocated or released was random!

What was it for, then? Well, before the days of protect mode and virtual memory addressing, you could access any arbitrary memory location through a simple pointer (using C as a programming language, of course). Often, and erroneously, these pointers would be stored in nonrefreshed static variables as an application yielded control to the operating system. This access—or similar access—would cause the problems for which SHAKER.EXE was used to try to uncover.

In between handling one event and a subsequent one, Windows could move (as it can now) both your code and data around. If you'd used a static pointer to, say, point to some data, you'd quickly discover that it was no longer pointing to what you intended. (Modern virtual addressing methods make this problem go away.) So what was the point of SHAKER.EXE? It turned out that, back then, even though your application was being naughty and had stored a static pointer, you didn't know it most of the time; the Windows memory manager hadn't moved your data around between your handling of two events. The bottom line was that you didn't really know you had a problem until memory moved, and on your machine, that rarely, if ever, happened. Customers, however, did see the problem because they were running both your application and others and had loaded their systems to a point that the memory manager was starting to move memory blocks around to accommodate everyone. The whole thing was like attempting to hold a party in a small closet. Initially, everyone had plenty of room. As more people arrived and the closet filled up, however, some of the guests were bound to get their feet stepped on sooner or later. SHAKER.EXE shook the operating system on the developer's machine until something fell off!

OK, so why the history lesson? Basically, the lesson is a good one and one we can still use. In fact, an associated application, named STRESS.EXE, still ships in Visual C++. (See Figure 1-6.)

Like SHAKER.EXE, STRESS.EXE is used to make the operating system appear more loaded or busy than it actually is. For example, by using STRESS.EXE you can allocate all of your machine's free memory, making it look really loaded—or, reading from Tip 6 on, you can find out what happens when you run out of file handles.

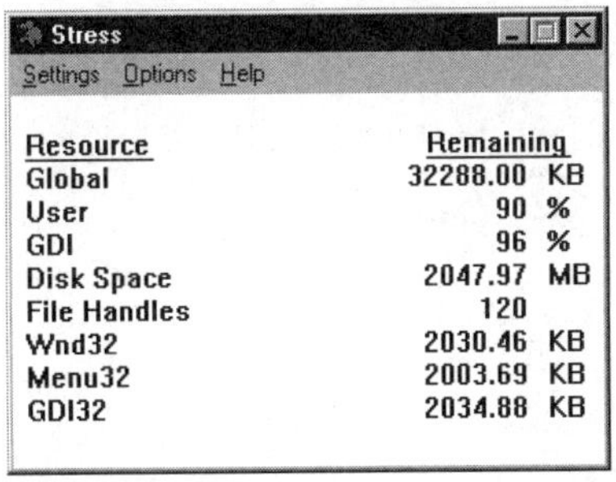

FIGURE 1-6

Stress me (STRESS.EXE)

Stress		
Settings	Options	Help

Resource	Remaining	
Global	32288.00	KB
User	90	%
GDI	96	%
Disk Space	2047.97	MB
File Handles	120	
Wnd32	2030.46	KB
Menu32	2003.69	KB
GDI32	2034.88	KB

Tools such as STRESS.EXE can present your code with a more realistic, perhaps even hostile, environment in which to work. Such conditions can cause many hidden problems to rise to the surface—problems you can fix at that point instead of later in response to a client's frustrated phone call. I'd certainly recommend using them.

Tip 17: Use automated testing tools.

See Chapter 9, "Well, At Least It Compiled OK!" for coverage of this broad and very important subject.

Tip 18: Consider error values.

Let's suppose you still want to return an indication of success from a function (instead of using exceptions). What values would you use to indicate whether or not something worked?

Normally, 0 (or False) is returned for failure, and -1 (True) for success. What are the alternatives? Some programmers like to return 0 for success and some other value for failure—the reason for failure is encoded in the value being returned. Other programmers prefer to return a negative value for failure that again encodes the reason.

By using the first alternative, we can quickly come up with some pretty weird-looking code:

```
If CreateThing() <> True Then ' It worked!
```

or

```
If Not CreateThing() Then ' It worked!
```

or

```
If CreateThing() = False Then ' It worked!
```

or

```
If CreateThing() = SUCCESS Then ' It worked!
```

SUCCESS, of course, is defined as 0.

To capture failure, you can't just do the same, though:

```
If Not CreateThing() Then ' It worked!
Else
    ' Failed!
    ' What do we do?
End If
```

Here the reason for failure is lost. We need to hold it in some variable:

```
nResult = CreateThing()

If nResult <> SUCCESS Then
    ' Failed!
    ' What do we do?
End If
```

All very messy, especially where the language lacks the ability to do an assignment in a conditional expression (as is the case in Visual Basic and is *not* the case in C).

Consider someone writing the test using implicit expression evaluation:

```
If CreateThing() Then
```

If *CreateThing* works, it returns 0, which causes the conditional *not* to execute any code in the body of the compound statement. Yikes! Imagine what code fails to execute all because someone forgot to test against *SUCCESS*.

Because any nonzero value is evaluated as True (in an *If*), using a value other than 0 (say, a negative value) to indicate failure can be equally dangerous. Given that in any conditional expression you don't have to test against an explicit value and that nonzero means execute the compound statement, the language conspires against you here not to use 0 as a code indicating success.

I'd advise sticking to True meaning success and False meaning failure. In the case of failure, I'd implement a mechanism such as the one used in C (*errno*) or perhaps Win32's *GetLastError*. The latter returns the value of the last error (easily implemented in a project—you could even add a history feature or automatic logging of errors).

Tip 19: Tighten up Visual Basic's type checking.

Visual Basic itself doesn't always help you detect errors or error conditions. For example, consider the following code fragment:

```
Private Sub Fu(ByVal d As Date)
    ⋮
End Sub

Call Fu("01 01 98")
```

Is this code legal? If you ask around, quite often you'll find that developers say no, but it is perfectly legal. No type mismatch occurs (something that worries those who suspect this is illegal).

The reason the code is legal lies in Visual Basic itself. Visual Basic knows that the *Fu* procedure requires a *Date* type argument, so it automatically tries to convert the string constant "01 01 98" into a *Date* value to satisfy the call. If it can convert the string constant, it will. In other words, it does this kind of thing:

```
' The call :
'
' Call Fu("01 01 98")
'
' Equates to …
'
Const d As String = "01 01 98"
```

>>

```
If IsDate(d) Then

    Dim Local_d As Date

    Local_d = CDate(d)

    Call Fu(Local_d)

Else

    Err.Raise Number:=13

End If
```

Now you see that Visual Basic can make the call by performing the cast (type coercion) for you. Note that you can even pass the argument by reference simply by qualifying the argument with the *ByRef* keyword, as in *Call Fu(ByRef "01 01 98")*. All you're passing by reference, in fact, is an anonymous variable that Visual Basic creates solely for this procedure call. By the way, all *ByVal* arguments in Visual Basic are passed by reference in this same fashion. That is, when it encounters a *ByVal* argument, Visual Basic creates an anonymous variable, copies the argument into the variable, and then passes a reference to the variable to the procedure. Interestingly, a variable passed by reference must be of the correct type before the call can succeed. (This makes perfect sense given that Visual Basic can trust itself to create those anonymous variables with the correct type; it can't trust user-written code to do the right thing, so Visual Basic has to enforce by-reference type checking strictly.)

So what's wrong with this automatic type coercion anyway? I hope you can see that the problem in the case above is that the cast is not helpful. We're passing an ambiguous date expression but receiving an actual, unambiguous date. This is because all date variables are merely offsets from December 30, 1899, and therefore unambiguous (for example, 1.5 is noon on December 31, 1899). There's no way "inside" of *Fu* to detect this fact and to refuse to work on the data passed. (Maybe that's how it should be? Maybe we should rely on our consumers to pass us the correct data type? No, I don't think so.)

One way to fix this [part of the] problem is to use *Variants*, which are some of the few things I normally encourage people to use. Have a look at this:

```
Call Fu("01 01 98")

Private Sub Fu(ByVal v As Variant)
```

```
Dim d As Date

If vbString = VarType(v) Then

    If True = IsDate(CStr(v)) Then

        If 0 = InStr(1, CStr(v), CStr(Year(CDate(v))), 1) Then
            Err.Raise Number:=13
        Else
            d = CDate(v)
        End If

    End If

End If

' Use d here…

End Sub
```

The good thing about a *Variant* (and the bad?) is that it can hold any kind of data type. You can even ask the *Variant* what it's referencing by using *VarType*, which is very useful. Because we type the formal argument as *Variant* we'll receive in it a type equal to the type of the expression we passed. In the code above, *VarType(v)* will return *vbString*, not *vbDate*.

Knowing this, we can check the argument types using *VarType*. In the code above, we're checking to see if we're being passed a string expression. If the answer is yes, we're then checking to see that the string represents a valid date (even an ambiguous one). If again the answer is yes, we convert the input string into a date and then use *InStr* to see if the year in the converted date appears in the original input string. If it doesn't, we must have been passed an ambiguous date.

Here's that last paragraph rephrased and broken down a bit. Remember that a *Date* always holds an exact year because it actually holds an offset from December 30, 1899. Therefore, *Year(a_Date_variable)* will always give us back a full four-digit year (assuming that *a_Date_variable* represents a date after the year 999). On the other hand, the string that "seeds" the *Date* variable can hold only an offset—98 in the example. Obviously then, if we convert 98 to a *Date* (see Chapter 8 for more on this topic), we'll get something like 1998 or 2098 in the resulting *Date* variable. When converted to a string, those years are either "1998" or "2098"—neither of which appears in "01 01 98." We can say with some conviction, therefore, that the input string contains an ambiguous date expression, or even that its data type ("ambiguous date") is in error and will throw a type mismatch error.

All this date validation can be put inside a *Validate* routine, of course:

```
Private Sub Fu(ByVal v As Variant)

    Dim d As Date

    Call Validate(v, d)

    ' Use d here - we don't get here if there's a problem with 'v'...

End Sub
```

In this *Validate* routine *d* is set to cast(*v*) if *v* is not ambiguous. If it is ambiguous, an exception is thrown. An exciting addition to this rule is that the same technique can also be applied to Visual Basic's built-in routines via Interface Subclassing.

How often have you wanted an *Option NoImplicitTypes*? I have, constantly. Here's how you can almost get to this situation:

```
Private Sub SomeSub()

    MsgBox DateAdd("yyyy", 100, "01 01 98")

End Sub


Public Function DateAdd( _
                    ByVal Interval As String _
                  , ByVal Number As Integer _
                  , ByVal v As Variant _
                    )

    Call Vali_Date(v)

    DateAdd = VBA.DateTime.DateAdd(Interval, Number, CDate(v))

End Function


Private Sub Vali_Date(ByVal v As Variant)
```

```
' If 'v' is a string containing a valid date expression ...
If vbString = VarType(v) And IsDate(CStr(v)) Then

    ' If we've got a four digit year then we're OK,
    ' else we throw an err.
    If 0 = InStr(1, CStr(v), _
                Format$(Year(CDate(v)), "0000"), 1) Then
        Err.Raise Number:=13
    End If

End If

End Sub
```

In this code, the line *MsgBox DateAdd(...)* in *SomeSub* will result in a runtime exception being thrown because the date expression being passed is ambiguous ("01 01 98"). If the string were made "Y2K Safe"—that is, 01 01 1998—the call will complete correctly. We have altered the implementation of *DateAdd*; you could almost say we inherited it and beefed up its type checking.

Obviously this same technique can be applied liberally so that all the VBA type checking (and your own type checking) is tightened up across procedure calls like this. The really nice thing about doing this with Visual Basic's routines is that instead of finding, say, each call to *DateAdd* to check that its last argument is type safe, you can build the test into the replacement *DateAdd* procedure. One single replacement tests all calls. In fact, you can do this using a kind of *Option NoImplicitTypes*.

Use this somewhere, perhaps in your main module:

```
#Const NoImplicitTypes = True
```

Then wrap your validation routines appropriately:

```
Private Sub Vali_Date(ByVal v As Variant)

    #If NoImplicitTypes = True Then

    ' If 'v' is…
    If …
    End If

    #End If

End Sub
```

You now almost have an *Option NoImplicitTypes.* I say almost because we can't get rid of all implicit type conversions very easily (that's why I used "[part of the]" earlier). Take the following code, for example:

```
Dim d As Date

d = txtEnteredDate.Text
```

Your validation routines won't prevent *d* from being assigned an ambiguous date when *txtEnteredDate.Text* is "01 01 98", but at least you're closer to *Option NoImplicitTypes* than you would be without the routines.

Actually, at TMS we use a DateBox control, and even that control cannot stop this sort of use. (See Chapter 8 for more discussion about this, and see the companion CD for a demonstration.) A DateBox returns a *Date* type, not a *Text* type, and it's meant to be used like this:

```
Dim d As Date

d = dteEnteredDate.Date
```

Of course, it can still be used like this:

```
Dim s As String

s = dteEnteredDate.Date
```

Hmm, a date in a string! But at least *s* will contain a non–Y2K-Challenged date.

Might Microsoft add such an *Option NoImplicitTypes* in the future? Send them e-mail asking for it if you think it's worthwhile *(mswish@microsoft.com).*

A Not-Too-Small Aside into Smart Types, or "Smarties"

Another way to protect yourself against this kind of coercion is to use a smart type (we call these things Smarties, which is the name of a candy-coated confection) as an lvalue (the thing on the left-hand side of the assignment operator). A smart type is a type with vitamins added, one that can do something instead of doing nothing. The difference between smart types and "dumb" types is a little like the difference between public properties that are implemented using variables versus public properties implemented using property procedures. Here's some test code that we can feed back into the code above that was compromised:

```
Dim d As New iDate

d = txtEnteredDate.Text
```

>>

Note that we're using a slightly modified version of the code here, in which *d* is defined as an instance (*New*) of *iDate* instead of just *Date*. (Of course, *iDate* means Intelligent Date.) Here's the code behind the class *iDate*:

In a class called iDate

```
Private d As Date
Public Property Get Value() As Variant

    Value = CVar(d)

End Property
Public Property Let Value(ByVal v As Variant)

    If vbDate = VarType(v) Then
        d = CDate(v)
    Else
        Err.Raise 13
    End If

End Property
```

OK then, back to the code under the spotlight. First you'll notice that I'm not using *d.Value = txtEnteredDate.Text*. This is because I've nominated the *Value* property as the default property. (Highlight *Value* in the Code window, select Procedure Attributes from the Tools menu, click Advanced >> in the Procedure Attributes dialog box, and then set Procedure ID to *(Default).*) This is the key to smart types, or at least it's the thing that makes them easier to use. The default property is the one that's used when you don't specify a property name. This means that you can do stuff like *Print Left$(s, 1)* instead of having to do *Print Left$(s.Value, 1)*. Cool, huh? Here's that test code again:

```
Dim d As New iDate

d = txtEnteredDate.Text
```

If you bear in mind this implementation of an *iDate*, you see that this code raises a Type Mismatch exception because the *Value* Property Let procedure, to which the expression *txtEnteredDate.Text* is passed as *v*, now validates that *v* contains a real date. To get the code to work we need to do something a little more rigid:

```
Dim d As New iDate

d = CDate(txtEnteredDate.Text)
```

Just what the doctor ordered. Or, in the case of a date, does this perhaps make the situation worse? One reason why you might not want to explicitly convert the text to a date is that an ambiguous date expression in *txtEnteredDate.Text* is now converted in a way that's hidden from the validation code in the *d.Value* Property Let procedure. Perhaps we could alter the code a little, like this:

```
Public Property Let Value(ByVal v As Variant)

    If vbString = VarType(v) And IsDate(CStr(v)) Then

        ' If we've got a four digit year then we're OK,
        ' else we throw an err.
        If 0 = InStr(1, CStr(v), _
                    Format$(Year(CDate(v)), "0000"), 1) Then
            Err.Raise Number:=13
        End If

    End If

    d = CDate(v)

End Property
```

Here I've basically borrowed the code I showed earlier in this chapter which checks whether a date string is ambiguous. Now the following code works only if *txtEnteredDate.Text* contains a date like "01 01 1900":

```
Dim d As New iDate

d = txtEnteredDate.Text
```

Another cool thing about Smarties is that you can use them within an existing project fairly easily, in these different ways:

1. Add the class file(s) that implement your smart types.
2. Use search and replace to turn dumb types into Smarties.
3. Run your code and thoroughly exercise (exorcise) it to find your coercion woes.
4. Use search and replace again to swap back to dumb types (if you want).

Actually, I'll come clean here—it's not always this easy to use Smarties. Let's look at some pitfalls. Consider what happens when we search for *As String* and replace with *As New iString*. For one thing we'll end up with a few procedure calls like *SomeSub(s As New iString)*, which obviously is illegal. We'll also get some other not-so-obvious—dare I say subtle?—problems.

Say you've got *SomeSub(ByVal s As iString)*; you might get another problem here because now you're passing an object reference *by value*. *ByVal* protects the variable that you're passing so that it cannot be altered in a called procedure (a copy is passed and possibly altered in its place). The theory is that if I have *s = Time$* in the called procedure, the original *s* (or whatever it was called in the calling procedure) still retains its old value. And it does; however, remember that the value we're protecting is the *value of the variable*. In our case that's the object reference, not the object itself. In C-speak, we can't change the object pointer, but because we have a copy of the pointer, we can access and change any of the object's properties. Here's an example that I hope shows this very subtle problem.

These two work the same:

```
Private Sub cmdTest_Click()

    Dim s As New iString

    s = Time$

    Call SomeSub(s)

    MsgBox s

End Sub

Sub SomeSub(ByRef s As iString)

    s = s & " " & Date$

    MsgBox s

End Sub
```

```
Private Sub cmdTest_Click()

    Dim s As String

    s = Time$

    Call SomeSub(s)

    MsgBox s

End Sub

Sub SomeSub(ByRef s As String)

    s = s & " " & Date$

    MsgBox s

End Sub
```

The assignment to *s* in both versions of *SomeSub* affects each instance of *s* declared in *cmdTest_Click*.

These two don't work the same:

```
Private Sub cmdTest_Click()

    Dim s As New iString

    s = Time$

    Call SomeSub(s)

    MsgBox s

End Sub

Sub SomeSub(ByVal s As iString)

    s = s & " " & Date$

    MsgBox s

End Sub
```

```
Private Sub cmdTest_Click()

    Dim s As String

    s = Time$

    Call SomeSub(s)

    MsgBox s

End Sub

Sub SomeSub(ByVal s As String)

    s = s & " " & Date$

    MsgBox s

End Sub
```

The assignment to *s* in the *SomeSub* on the left *still* affects the instance of *s* declared in the *cmdTest_Click* on the left.

Let me again run through why this is. This happens because we're not passing the string within the object when we pass an *iString*; we're passing a copy of the object reference. Or, if you like, we're passing a pointer to the string. So it doesn't matter whether we pass the object by reference or by value—the called procedure has complete access to the object's properties.

You also cannot change *iString* to *String* in the procedure signature (if you did, you would defeat the purpose of all this, for one thing) and still pass *ByRef* because you're effectively trying to pass off an *iString* as a *String*, and you'll get a type mismatch.

Another area where you'll have problems is in casting (coercion). Consider this:

```
Private Function SomeFunc(s As iString) As iString

    SomeFunc = s

End Function
```

Look OK to you? But it doesn't work! It can't work because = *s*, remember, means = *s.Value*—a *String*—and that's not an *iString* as implied by the assignment to *SomeFunc*. There's *no way* Visual Basic can coerce a *String* into an *iString* reference. (Maybe this is good because it's pretty strongly emphasized.) Could we coerce a *String* into an *iString* reference if we wrote a conversion operator (*CiStr*, for example)? Yes, but that would be overkill because we've already got a real *iString* in the preceding code. What we need to do is change the code to *Set SomeFunc = s*. *Set* is the way you assign an object pointer to an object variable. Anyway, it's simply a semantics change and so should be rejected out of hand. What we need is some way to describe to the language how to construct an *iString* from a *String* and then assign this new *iString*— not using *Set*—to the function name. (This is all getting us too close to C++, so I'll leave this well alone, although you might want to consider where you'd like Visual Basic to head as a language).

Anyway, you can see that this is getting messy, right? The bottom line is that you can do a good job of replacing dumb types with Smarties, but it's usually something that's best done right from the start of a project. For now, let's look at something that's easier to do on existing projects: another slant on type enforcement.

Type Checking Smarties   How do you determine whether you're dealing with an *As Object* object or with a Smartie? Easy—use *VarType*. Consider this code; does it beep?

```
Dim o As New iInteger

If vbObjectiInteger = VarType(o) Then Beep
```

Normally all object types return the same *VarType* value (*vbObject* or 9), so how does *VarType* know about Smarties (assuming that *vbObjectiInteger* hasn't also been defined as 9)? Simple; see Tip 4. We subclass *VarType* and then add the necessary intelligence we need for it to be able to differentiate between ordinary objects and Smarties. For example, *VarType* might be defined like this

```
Public Function VarType(ByVal exp As Variant) _
    As Integer ' vbVarType++

    Select Case VBA.VarType(exp)

        Case vbObject:
```

```
            Select Case TypeName(exp)

                Case "iInteger"
                    VarType = vbObjectiInteger

                Case "iSingle"
                    VarType = vbObjectiSingle

                Case Else
                    VarType = VBA.VarType(exp)

            End Select

        Case Else

            VarType = VBA.VarType(exp)

    End Select

End Function
```

The constants *vbObjectiInteger*, *vbObjectiSingle*, etc. are defined publicly and initialized on program start-up like this:

```
Public Sub main()

    vbObjectiInteger = WinGlobalAddAtom(CreateGUID)
    vbObjectiSingle  = WinGlobalAddAtom(CreateGUID)
    ' Etc…

    DoStartup

End Sub
```

WinGlobalAddAtom is an alias for the API *GlobalAddAtom*. This Windows API creates a unique value (in the range &HC000 through &HFFFF) for every unique string you pass it, and hopefully there will be no future clashes with whatever *VarType* will return. (So we have a variable constant: *variable* in that we don't know what *GlobalAddAtom* will return when we call it for the first time, but *constant* in that on subsequent calls *GlobalAddAtom* will return the same value it returned on the first call). It's basically a hash-table "thang." I want a unique value for each Smartie type I use, so I must pass a unique string to *Global-AddAtom*. I create one of these by calling the *CreateGUID* routine documented in my Chapter 7, "Minutiae: Some Stuff About Visual Basic." This routine always returns a unique GUID string (something like C54D0E6D-E8DE-11D1-A614-0060806A9738), although in a pinch you could use the class name. The bottom line is that each Smartie will have a unique value which *VarType* will recognize and return!

Why not just use any old constant value? Basically I want to try to be less predictable (clashable with) and more unique, although one downside is this: because I cannot initialize a constant in this way, those *vbObjectiInteger* and others are variables and could be reassigned some erroneous values later in our code. Actually, that's a lie because they cannot be reassigned a new value. Why not? Because they're Smarties, too. To be precise, they're another kind of Smartie—*Long*s that can have one-time initialization only. (See Chapter 7 for the code that implements them.)

You might also want to consider whether to enforce at least strict type checking on procedure call arguments and set up some kind of convention within your coding standards whereby parameters are received as *Variant*s (as outlined earlier), tested, and then coerced into a "correct" local variable of the desired type. Another advantage of this scheme is that it mandates a "fast pass by value" handling of arguments and thus can be used indirectly to reduce coupling. It's fast because it's actually a pass by reference!

In the following code, note that despite passing *n* to *Fu* by reference (which is the default passing mechanism, of course) we cannot alter it in *Fu* (if we're disciplined). This is because we work only in that routine on the local variable, *d*.

In a form (say):

```
Private Sub cmdTest_Click()

    Dim n As Integer

    n = 100

    Call Fu(n)

End Sub

Public Sub Fu(vD As Variant)

    Dim d As Single
```

```
        d = IntegerToReal(vD)

        ' Use d safely ...

End Sub
```

In a testing module:

```
Public Function IntegerToReal(ByVal vI As Variant) As Double

    #If True = NoImplicitTypes Then

        Select Case VarType(vI)

            Case vbInteger, vbLong:
                IntegerToReal = CDbl(vI)

            Case Else
                Err.Raise VBErrTypeMismatch

        End Select

    #Else

        IntegerToReal = CDbl(vI)

    #End If

End Function
```

Here we're implying that our coding standards mandate *some* type checking. We're allowing integers (both *Long* and *Short*) to be *implicitly coerced* into either *Single*s or *Double*s. Therefore, if we call *Fu* as *Call Fu(100)*, we're OK. But if we call it as, say, *Call Fu("100")*, this will fail (if *NoImplicitTypes* is set to –1 in code using *#Const*, or in the IDE using the Project Properties dialog box). Note that *d* in *Fu* is defined as a *Single* but that *IntegerToReal* is returning a *Double*. This is always OK because an integer will always fit in to a *Single*; that is, we won't overflow here at all. To speed up the code, perhaps during the final build, you can simply define *NoImplicitTypes* as 0, in which case the routine forgoes type checking.

Of course, depending on your level of concern (or is that paranoia?), you can turn this up as much as you like. For instance, you could refuse to convert, say, a *Long* integer to a *Single/Double*. You're limited only to whatever *VarType* is limited to, meaning that you can detect any type as long as *VarType* does.

Tip 20: Define constants using a TypeLib or an Enum.

When you create error values try not to use the so-called Magic Numbers. Thirteen is such a number, as in *Err.Raise Number:=13*. What does 13 mean? Basically it's a pain to resolve, so attempt always to use more meaningful names.

Visual Basic doesn't come with a set of symbolic constants defined for its own errors so I thought I'd put one together for you. Here's a snippet:

```
Public Enum vbErrorCodes
    VBErrReturnWithoutGoSub                     = 3
    VBErrInvalidProcedureCall                   = 5
    VBErrOverflow                               = 6
    VBErrOutOfMemory                            = 7
    VBErrSubscriptOutOfRange                    = 9
    VBErrThisArrayIsFixedOrTemporarilyLocked    = 10
    VBErrDivisionByZero                         = 11
    VBErrTypeMismatch                           = 13
    VBErrOutOfStringSpace                       = 14
    VBErrExpressionTooComplex                   = 16
    VBErrCantPerformRequestedOperation          = 17
    VBErrUserInterruptOccurred                  = 18
    VBErrResumeWithoutError                     = 20
    VBErrOutOfStackSpace                        = 28
    VBErrSubFunctionOrPropertyNotDefined        = 35
    ⋮
End Enum
```

Once you've added it to your project, this snippet is browsable via Visual Basic's Object Browser. You'll find the code on the companion CD. To see how you might define constants using a type library, see Chapter 7.

Tip 21: Keep error text in a resource file.

Resource files (RES files) are good things in which to keep your error text and messages, and most C developers use them all the time, especially if they're shipping products internationally. That said, Visual Basic itself uses resource files—recognize some of these sample strings taken from Visual Basic's own resources?

```
STRINGTABLE FIXED IMPURE
BEGIN
    3                       "Return without GoSub"
    5                       "Invalid procedure call or argument"
```

>>

>>

```
6                        "Overflow"
7                        "Out of memory"
  ⋮
13029                    "Sa&ve Project Group"
13030                    "Sav&e Project Group As..."
13031                    "Ma&ke %s..."
  ⋮
23284                    "Compile Error in File '|1', Line |2 : |3"
  ⋮
END
```

In fact, Visual Basic 6 uses a total of 2,934 resource files.

The *%s* in string 13031 is used to indicate (to a standard C library function) where a substring should be inserted—the binary name (?.EXE, ?.DLL, ?.OCX) in this case. The |*1*, |*2*, and |*3* in string 23284 shows where replacement strings should be inserted, this time using a different technique. In fact, this latter technique (which you can use even on the *%s* strings) can be seen operating if you look at *ResolveResString* in the Visual Basic source code for SETUP1.VBP. It looks more or less like this (this is slightly tidied up):

```
'-------------------------------------------------------------
' FUNCTION: ResolveResString
' Reads string resource and replaces given macros with given
' values
'
' Example, given a resource number of, say, 14:
'    "Could not read '|1' in drive |2"
' The call
'    ResolveResString(14, "|1", "TXTFILE.TXT", "|2", "A:")
' would return the string
'    "Could not read 'TXTFILE.TXT' in drive A:"
'
' IN: [nResID]        - resource identifier
'     [vReplacements] - pairs of macro/replacement value
'-------------------------------------------------------------
'
Public Function ResolveResString( _
                            ByVal nResID As Integer _
                            , ParamArray vReplacements() As Variant _
                            ) As String

    Dim nMacro     As Integer
    Dim sResString As String

    sResString = LoadResString(nResID)

    ' For each macro/value pair passed in ...
```

```
For nMacro = LBound(vReplacements) To UBound(vReplacements) Step 2

    Dim sMacro As String
    Dim sValue As String

    sMacro = CStr(vReplacements(nMacro))
    sValue = vbNullString

    If nMacro < UBound(vReplacements) Then
        sValue = vReplacements(nMacro + 1)
    End If

    ' Replace all occurrences of sMacro with sValue.
    Dim nPos As Integer

    Do
        nPos = InStr(sResString, sMacro)

        If 0 <> nPos Then
            sResString = Left$(sResString, nPos - 1) & _
                         sValue & _
                         Mid$(sResString, nPos + Len(sMacro))
        End If

    Loop Until nPos = 0

Next nMacro

ResolveResString = sResString

End Function
```

To see all this code work, compile the strings and add them to your project. (Save the strings as an RC file, and then run the resource compiler on the RC file like so: *C:\rc -r ?.rc.* Add the resulting RES file to your application by selecting Add File from the Project menu.) Then add this code to Form1's Load event:

```
MsgBox ResolveResString( _
                    23284 _
                    , "|1" _
                    , "Fubar.bas" _
                    , "|2" _
                    , "42" _
                    , "|3" _
                    , ResolveResString(7) _
                    )
```

This will produce the following message box:

Test Resource File

Compile Error in File 'Fubar.bas', Line 42 : Out of memory

OK

Keeping message text in a resource file keeps strings (which could include SQL strings) neatly together in one place, and also flags them as discardable data, stuff that Windows can throw away if it must. Don't worry about this—Windows can reload strings from your binary image if it needs them. Your code is treated in exactly the same way and you've never worried about that being discarded, have you? Keeping read-only data together like this allows Visual Basic and Windows to better optimize how they use memory. Resource files also provide something akin to reuse as they usually allow you to be "cleverer" in your building of SQL and error text—they might even provide a way for you to share data like this across several applications and components. (See the notes on using a ROOS earlier in this chapter.)

Tip 22: Always handle errors in controls and components (that you build).

Errors in controls

When a control raises an unhandled error (by the control), the error is reported and the control becomes disabled—it actually appears hatched—or the application terminates. (See Figure 1-7 and Figure 1-8.)

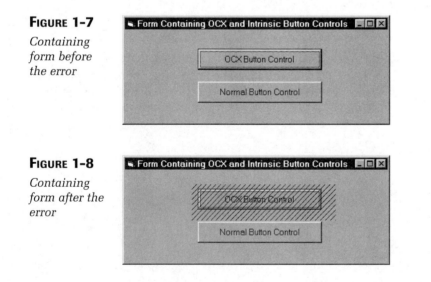

FIGURE 1-7

Containing form before the error

FIGURE 1-8

Containing form after the error

It's important to know that errors in a UserControl can be propagated to two different levels. If the errors are caused wholly by the control, they will be handled by the control only. If the errors are instigated via a call to an external interface on the control, from the containing application, they will be handled by the container. Another way to state this is to say that whatever is at the top of the call stack will handle unhandled errors. If you call into a control, say from a menu selection in the container, the first entry in your call stack will be the container's code. That's where the *mnuWhatever_Click* occurred. If the control raises an error now, the call stack is searched for a handler, all the way to the top. In this case, any unhandled control error has to be handled in the container, and if you don't handle it there, you're dead when the container stops and, ergo, so does the control. However, if the control has its own UI or maybe a button, your top-level event could be a *Whatever_Click* generated on the control itself. The top of your call stack is now your control code and any unhandled errors cause only the control to die. The container survives, albeit with a weird-looking control on it. (See Figure 1-8.)

This means that you must fragment your error handling across containers and controls, not an optimal option. Or you need some way of raising the error on the container even if the container's code isn't on the stack at the moment the error occurs. A sort of *Container.Err.Raise* thing is required.

In each of our container applications (those applications that contain User-Controls), we have a class called *ControlErrors* (usually one instance only). This class has a bundle of miscellaneous code in it that I won't cover here, and a method that looks something like this:

```
Public Sub Raise(ParamArray v() As Variant)

On Error GoTo ControlErrorHandler:

    ' Basically turns a notification into an error -
    ' one easy way to populate the Err object.
    Err.Raise v(0), v(1), v(2), v(3), v(4)

    Exit Sub

ControlErrorHandler:

    MsgBox "An error " & Err.Number & " occurred in " & Err.Source & _
           " UserControl.  The error is described as " & Err.Description

End Sub
```

In each container application we declare a new instance of *ControlErrors*, and for each of our UserControls we do what's shown on the following page.

```
If True = UserControl1.UsesControlErrors Then

    Set UserControl1.ErrObject = o

End If
```

UsesControlErrors returns True if the UserControl has been written to "know" about a *ControlErrors* object.

In each control—to complete the picture—we have something like this (*UsesControlErrors* is not shown):

```
Private ContainerControlErrors As Object

Private Sub SomeUIWidget_Click()

On Error GoTo ErrorHandler:

    Err.Raise ErrorValue

    Exit Sub

ErrorHandler:

    ' Handle top-level event error.

    ' Report error higher up?
    If Not ContainerControlErrors Is Nothing Then

        ContainerControlErrors.Raise ErrorValue

    End If

End Sub

Public Property Set ErrObject(ByVal o As Object)

    Set ContainerControlErrors = o

End Property
```

We know from this context that *SomeUIWidget_Click* is a top-level event handler (so we must handle errors here), and we can make a choice as to whether we handle the error locally or pass it on up the call chain. Of course, we can't issue a *Resume Next* from the container once we've handled the (reporting of the) error—that's normal Visual Basic. But we do at least have a mechanism whereby we can report errors to container code, perhaps signalling that we (the control) are about to perform a *Resume Next* or whatever.

Errors in OLE servers

Raising errors in a Visual Basic OLE Automation server is much the same as for a stand-alone application. However, some consideration must be given to the fact that your server may not be running in an environment in which errors will be visible to the user. For example, it may be running as a service on a remote machine. In these cases, consider these two points:

1. Don't display any error messages. If the component is running on a remote machine, or as a service with no user logged on, the user will not see the error message. This will cause the client application to lock up because the error cannot be acknowledged.

2. Trap *every* error in *every* procedure. If Visual Basic's default error handler were executed in a remote server, and assuming you could acknowledge the resulting message box, the result would be the death of your object. This would cause an Automation error to be generated in the client on the line where the object's method or property was invoked. Because the object has now died, you will have a reference in your client to a nonexistent object.

To handle errors in server components, first trap and log the error at the source. In each procedure, ensure that you have an *Err.Raise* to guarantee that the error is passed back up the call stack. When the error is raised within the top-level procedure, the error will propagate to the client. This will leave your object in a tidy state; indeed, you may continue to use the same object.

If you are raising a user-defined error within your component you should add the constant *vbObjectError* (&H80040000&). Using *vbObjectError* causes the error to be reported as an Automation error. To extract the user-defined error number, subtract *vbObjectError* from *Err.Number*. Do not use *vbObjectError* with Visual Basic–defined errors; otherwise, an "Invalid procedure call" error will be generated.

Tip 23: Use symbolic debugging information.

For extra tricky debugging, you should check out the Visual Studio debugger (which you get to by starting Visual C++). You obviously need the whole thing, in Visual Studio terms, to use this debugger in Visual Basic (or have a third-party debugger that can use the symbolic debugging information produced by Visual Basic). You'll also need some instructions on using the debugger, as it's one of the least documented features that I've ever seen.

To use the Visual Studio debugger, if you have it, do the following.

Build your Visual Basic application using the Compile To Native Code option. On the Compile tab of the Project Properties dialog box, select the Create Symbolic Debug Info and No Optimization options. Make sure that you build the EXE/DLL/OCX (I'll assume you're debugging a simple EXE from here on in) so that the binary is stored in the same folder as the source code. Start Visual C++, select Open from the File menu, and then select your built EXE file. Select Open from the File menu again (more than once if necessary) to select the source files you want to debug and trace through (FRM, BAS, CLS, etc.). Move the cursor to the line(s) where you want to start your debugging, and hit F9 to set a breakpoint. Once you've done this, hit F5. If you've set a breakpoint on, say, a *Form_Load* that runs as the program starts, you should immediately have broken to the debugger at this point. One more thing—use F10 to step through your code, not F8.

See your Visual Studio documentation (and Chapter 7) for more on how to use the debugger.

MORE ON CLIENT/SERVER ERROR HANDLING

Components should be nonintrusive about their errors. Instead of raising their own errors in message boxes, or through other UI, directly to the user, the components should pass any error that cannot be handled and corrected entirely within the component to their client's code, where the developer can decide how to handle it.

It is possible and even highly likely that a component you're using is itself a client of other components. What should you do when your component gets an error from one that it's using? Well, if you can't recover from the error, you should encapsulate it. It's bad practice merely to raise the other component's error to your client, since your client may well know nothing about this other component and is just dealing with your component. This means that you need to provide meaningful errors from your own component. Rather than passing up other component's errors or Visual Basic errors to your client, you need to define your own and use these. Public constants or Enums with good names are an excellent way of doing this, since they give a source for all errors in your component, and also should give strong clues about each error in its name.

When defining your own error numbers in components, remember that you should use *vbObjectError* and that currently Microsoft recommends keeping numbers added to it in a range between 512 and 65535.

```
Constant vbBaseErr        As long = 512
Constant ComponentBaseErr As long = vbObjectError + vbBaseErr
Constant MaxErr           As long = vbObjectError + 65535
```

Remember that there are two occasions when you can safely raise an error in Visual Basic:

>>

1. When error handling is turned off
2. When in a procedure's error handler

It is possible to raise events to pass errors to clients in some circumstances. The standard Visual Basic Data control has an error event, for instance.

Logging errors and tracing procedure stacks in components raises some special problems. It clearly makes sense to log errors, which are sent back to a client from a component. Thus, if you're creating an OCX, you would raise an error and expect that the client code would log that error in its error log. Components on remote machines may also have specific requirements about where to log.

For components there are a number of possible error log locations:

- Files (either flat files or Structured OLE storages)
- NT Event Log (but beware of using this with components deployed in Microsoft Transaction Server)
- Databases (but always have some other means to fall back on if your database connections fail)

It makes sense to add other information to a component's error log, because it's useful to know the UserID or Logon name, the machine name, the process ID, and the thread ID. We frequently use a class for this purpose, which returns the following:

- Process ID
- Thread ID
- Machine name
- Network version info
- LanGroup
- LanRoot
- Current user name
- Logon server
- Domain
- Number of users currently logged on
- Other available domains

This information is useful for sorting information in a component's error log.

Taking Care
of Business (Ojects)

Building More Effective Business Objects

ADAM MAGEE

Adam Magee is a software developer who specializes in building enterprise applications. He has worked with many large companies in the United Kingdom and in Australia, helping them to implement tiered architecture solutions. His particular focus is on the design and process of building efficient, high performance, distributable business objects. Some developers would like to see Adam in a deep gully position but he prefers it at backward square leg.

Taking care of business every day
Taking care of business every way
I've been taking care of business, it's all mine
Taking care of business and working overtime
Work out!

> "Taking Care of Business"
> by Bachmann Turner Overdrive

Business objects are big news. Everyone says the key to building distributed enterprise applications is business objects. Lots of 'em.

Business objects are cool and funky—we need business objects! You need business objects! Everyone needs business objects!

This chapter presents a design pattern for developing solid, scalable, robust business objects, designed for (and from) real-life distributed enterprise applications.

The architecture we propose at The Mandelbrot Set (International) Limited (TMS) for building distributed business object–based applications breaks down into various layers of functionality.

The data access layer (DAL) is the layer that talks to the data source. The interface of this layer should be the same regardless of the type of data source being accessed.

The business object layer is the actual layer that models the entities within your application—the real data, such as Employees, Projects, Departments, and so forth. In Unified Modeling Language (UML) parlance, these are called entity objects.

The action object layer represents the processes that occur on the business objects: these processes are determined by the application requirements. In UML, these action object layers are called control objects.

The client application layer, such as a Microsoft Visual Basic form, an ActiveX document, or an Active Server Page (ASP) on a Web server, is known as an interface object in UML.

This chapter concentrates on the middle business object layer and introduces the concepts of action objects, factory objects, and worker objects.

Data Access Layer

The most common question I get asked by Visual Basic developers is, "What type of DAL should I use? Data Access Objects (DAO), Open Database Connectivity (ODBC) API, ODBCDirect, Remote Data Objects (RDO), ActiveX Data Objects (ADO), VBSQL, vendor-specific library, smoke signals, semaphores, Morse code, underwater subsonic communications?" The answer is never easy. (Although in windier climates I would advise against smoke signals.)

What I do think is a good approach to data access is to create a simple abstract data interface for your applications. This way, you can change your data access method without affecting the other components in your application. Also, a simple data interface means that developers have a much lower learning curve and can become productive more quickly.

Remember that we are trying to create a design pattern for business object development in corporate database–centric applications. These applications typically either send or receive data or they request a particular action to be performed; as such, a simple, straightforward approach is required. I like simplicity—it leads to high-quality code.

So am I saying don't use ADO? No, not at all. Most Microsoft-based solutions are well suited to using ADO inside the DAL. But by concentrating your ADO code (or any database connection library for that matter) into one component, you achieve a more maintainable, cohesive approach. Besides, ADO is still a complex beast. If you take into account that many of ADO's features are restricted by the type of database source (such as handling text fields and locking methodologies), you'll find that the benefits of a stable, easily understood DAL far outweigh the cost of slightly reinventing the wheel.

Not only is abstracting the data access methodology important, but abstracting the input and output from this component are important as well. The DAL should return the same data construct regardless of the database source.

But enough theoretical waffling—let's look at something real.

Data Access Layer Specifics

The DAL presented here is essentially the same DAL that TMS uses in enterprise applications for its clients. I'll describe the operation of the DAL in detail here, but I'll concentrate only on *using* a DAL, not on building one. Remember that we want to concentrate on business object development, so this is the data object that our business objects will interface with.

The DAL below consists of only six methods. All other aspects of database operation (for instance, cursor types, locking models, parameter information, and type translation) are encapsulated and managed by the DAL itself.

cDAL INTERFACE

Member	Description
OpenRecordset	Returns a recordset of data
UpdateRecordset	Updates a recordset of data
ExecuteCommand	Executes a command that doesn't involve a recordset
BeginTransaction	Starts a transaction
CommitTransaction	Commits a transaction
RollbackTransaction	Rolls back a transaction

What's all this recordset malarkey? Well, this is (surprise, surprise) an abstracted custom recordset (*cRecordset*). We must investigate this recordset carefully before we look at the operation of the DAL itself.

Recordset

The method TMS uses for sending and receiving data to and from the database is a custom recordset object (*cRecordset*). In this chapter, whenever I mention recordset, I am referring to this custom *cRecordset* implementation, rather than to the various DAO/RDO/ADO incarnations.

A recordset is returned from the DAL by calling the *OpenRecordset* method. This recordset is completely disconnected from the data source. Updating a recordset will have no effect on the central data source until you call the *UpdateRecordset* method on the DAL.

We could have easily returned an array of data from our DAL, especially since ADO and RDO nicely support *GetRows*, which does exactly that, but arrays are limited in a number of ways.

Array manipulation is horrible. In Visual Basic, you can resize only the last dimension of an array, so forget about adding columns easily. Also, arrays are not self-documenting. Retrieving information from an array means relying on such hideous devices as constants for field names and the associated constant maintenance, or the low-performance method of looping through indexes looking for fields.

Enabling varying rows and columns involves using a data structure known as a ragged array—essentially an array of arrays—which can be cumbersome and counterintuitive to develop against.

The advantage of using a custom recordset object is that we can present the data in a way that is familiar to most programmers, but we also get full control of what is happening inside the recordset. We can again simplify and customize its operation to support the rest of our components.

Notice the *Serialize* method, which allows us to move these objects easily across machine boundaries. More on this powerful method later. For the moment, let's look at the typical interface of a *cRecordset*.

cRECORDSET INTERFACE

Member	Description
MoveFirst	Moves to first record
MoveNext	Moves to next record
MovePrevious	Moves to previous record
MoveLast	Moves to last record
Name	Shows the name of the recordset
Fields	Returns a *Field* object
Synchronize	Refreshes the contents of the recordset
RowStatus	Shows whether this row has been created, updated, or deleted
RowCount	Shows the number of records in the recordset
AbsolutePosition	Shows the current position in the recordset
Edit	Copies the current row to a buffer for modification
AddNew	Creates an empty row in a buffer for modification
Update	Commits the modification in the buffer to the recordset
Serialize	Converts or sets the contents of the recordset to an array

This table shows the details of the interface for the *cField* object, which is returned from the *cRecordset* object.

cFIELD INTERFACE

Member	Description
Name	Name of the field
Value	Contents of the field
Type	Visual Basic data type
Length	Length of the field

Retrieving a Recordset

So how can we utilize this *cRecordset* with our DAL? Here's an example of retrieving a recordset from the DAL and displaying information:

```
Dim oDAL     As New cDAL
Dim oRec     As New cRecordset

Set oRec = oDAL.OpenRecordset("Employees")
oRec.MoveFirst
MsgBox oRec.Fields("FirstName").Value
```

Please forgive me for being a bit naughty in using automatically instantiated object variables, but this has been done purely for code readability.

Notice that the details involved in setting up the data connection and finding the data source are all abstracted by the DAL. Internally, the DAL is determining where the Employees data lives and is retrieving the data and creating a custom recordset. In a single-system DAL, the location of the data could be assumed to be in a stored procedure on a Microsoft SQL Server; in a multidata source system, the DAL might be keying into a local database to determine the location and type of the Employees data source. The implementation is dependent upon the requirements of the particular environment.

Also, the operation in the DAL is stateless. After retrieving the recordset, the DAL can be closed down and the recordset can survive independently. This operation is critical when considering moving these components to a hosted environment, such as Microsoft Transaction Server (MTS).

Statelessness is important because it determines whether components will scale. The term *scale* means that the performance of this object will not degrade when usage of the object is increased. An example of scaling might be moving from two or three users of this object to two or three hundred. A stateless object essentially contains no module-level variables. Each method call is independent and does not rely on any previous operation, such as setting properties or other method calls. Because the object has no internal state to maintain, the same copy of the object can be reused for many clients. There is no need for each client to have a unique instance of the object, which also allows products such as Microsoft Transaction Server to provide high-performance caching of these stateless components.

Serializing a Recordset

Two of the primary reasons for employing a custom recordset are serialization and software locking. Because passing objects across machines causes a considerable performance penalty, we need a way of efficiently moving a recordset from one physical tier to another.

Serialization allows you to export the contents of your objects (such as the variables) as a primitive data type. What can you do with this primitive data type? Well, you can use it to re-create that object in another environment—maybe in another process, maybe in another machine. All you need is the class for the object you have serialized to support the repopulation of its internal variables from this primitive data type. The process of serialization has tremendous performance advantages in that we can completely transfer an object to another machine and then utilize the object natively in that environment without incurring the tremendous performance cost that is inherent in accessing objects across machine boundaries.

The *cRecordset* object stores its data and state internally in four arrays. The *Serialize* property supports exposing these arrays to and receiving them from the outside world, so transferring a recordset from one physical tier to another is simply a matter of using the *Serialize* property on the *cRecordset*. Here's an example:

```
Dim oRec      As New cRecordset
Dim oDAL      As New cDAL  ' Assume this DAL is on another machine.

oRec.Serialize = oDAL.OpenRecordset("Employees").Serialize
Set oDAL = Nothing
MsgBox oRec.RecordCount
```

Now we have a recordset that can live independently. It can even be passed to another machine and then updated by a DAL on that machine, if required.

Locking a Recordset

We need to keep track of whether the data on the central data source has changed since we made our copy. This is the job of one of the arrays inside the *cRecordset*, known affectionately as the CRUD array.

The CRUD array indicates whether this row has been Created, Updated, Deleted, or just plain old Read. Also stored is a globally unique identifier (GUID) for this particular row. This unique identifier must be automatically updated when a row is modified on the data source. These two parameters are used by the DAL in the *UpdateRecordset* method to determine whether a row needs updating and whether this row has been modified by someone since the client received the recordset. This process is a form of software locking, although it could be internally implemented just as easily using timestamps (if a given data source supports them).

Updating a Recordset

Updating a *cRecordset* object through the DAL occurs by way of the *UpdateRecordset* method. *UpdateRecordset* will scan through the internal arrays in the recordset and perform the required database operation. The unique row identifier is used to retrieve each row for modification, so if someone has updated a row while the recordset has been in operation this row will not be found and an error will be raised to alert the developer to this fact. The following is an example of updating a row in a recordset and persisting that change to the data source:

```
Dim oRec     As New cRecordset
Dim oDAL
    As New cDAL  ' Assume local DAL so don't need serialization

Set oRec = oDAL.OpenRecordset("Employees")
oRec.Edit
oRec.Fields("FirstName") = "Adam Magee"
oRec.Update
oDAL.UpdateRecordset oRec
```

Synchronizing a Recordset

After a *cRecordset* object has been used by *UpdateRecordset* to successfully update the data source, the *cRecordset* object needs to have the same changes committed to itself, which is accomplished by means of the *Synchronize* method.

Using the *Synchronize* method will remove all Deleted rows from the recordset and will set any Updated or Created rows to Read status. This gives the developer using the *cRecordset* object control over committing changes and also means the recordset state can be maintained in the event of an *UpdateRecordset* failure. Here is an example of synchronizing a recordset after a row has been updated:

```
oDAL.UpdateRecordset oRec
oRec.Synchronize
Parameters
```

Simply supplying the name of a *cRecordset* object to *OpenRecordset* is usually not enough information, except maybe when retrieving entire sets of data, so we need a way of supplying parameters to a DAL *cRecordset* operation.

This is achieved by using a *cParams* object. The *cParams* object is simply a collection of *cParam* objects, which have a name and a value. The *cParams* object, like the *cRecordset* object, can also be serialized. This is useful if the parameters need to be maintained on another machine.

cPARAMS INTERFACE

Member	Description
Add	Adds a new *cParam* object with a name and a value
Item	Returns a *cParam* object
Count	Returns the count of collected *cParam* objects
Remove	Removes a *cParam* object
Serialize	Converts or sets the content of *cParams* object into an array

cPARAM INTERFACE

Member	Description
Name	Name of the parameter
Value	Variant value of the parameter

Here is an example of retrieving a recordset with parameters:

```
Dim oDAL As New cDAL
Dim oRec As New cRecordset
Dim oPar As New cParams

oPar.AddField "EmpID", "673"
oPar.AddField "CurrentlyEmployed", "Yes"

Set oRec = oDAL.OpenRecordset("Employees", oPar)

MsgBox oRec.RecordCount
```

We can see now that only two well-defined objects are parameters to the DAL—*cRecordset* and *cParams*—and both of these objects support serialization, giving a consistent, distributed operation-aware interface.

Commands

A lot of database operations do not involve, or should not involve, *cRecordset* objects. For instance, checking and changing a password are two operations that do not require the overhead of instantiating and maintaining a *cRecordset*. This is where you use the *ExecuteCommand* method of the DAL. The *ExecuteCommand* method takes as parameters both the name of the command to perform and a *cParams* object.

Any output *cParam* objects generated by the command are automatically populated into the *cParams* object if they are not supplied by default. Here's an example of checking a password:

```
Dim oDAL As New cDAL
Dim oPar As New cParams

oPar.Add "UserID", "637"
oPar.Add "Password", "Chebs"
oPar.Add "PasswordValid", ""        ' The DAL would have added this output
                                    ' parameter if we had left it out.
oDAL.ExecuteCommand "CheckPassword", oPar

If oPar("PasswordValid").Value = "False" Then
    Msgbox "Sorry Invalid Password", vbExclamation
End If
```

Transactions

Most corporate data sources support transactions; our DAL must enable this functionality as well. This is relatively easy if you are using data libraries such as DAO or RDO, since it is a trivial task to simply map these transactions onto the underlying calls. If your data source does not support transactions, you might have to implement this functionality yourself. If so, may the force be with you. The three transaction commands are *BeginTransaction*, *CommitTransaction*, and *RollbackTransaction*.

The DAL is taking care of all the specifics for our transaction, leaving us to concentrate on the manipulation code. In the case of a transaction that must occur across business objects, we'll see later how these business objects will all support the same DAL. Here's an example of updating a field inside a transaction:

```
Dim oRec As New cRecordset
Dim oDAL As New cDAL  ' Assume local DAL so don't need serialization

With oDAL
    .BeginTransaction
    Set oRec = oDAL.OpenRecordset("Employees")
    With oRec
        .Edit
        .Fields("FirstName") = "Steve Gray"
        .Update
    End With
    .UpdateRecordset oRec
    .CommitTransaction
End With
Wrap Up
```

So that's a look at how our abstracted data interface works. I hope you can see how the combination of *cDAL*, *cRecordset*, and *cParams* presents a consistent logical interface to any particular type of data source. There is comprehensive support for distributed operation in the sense that the DAL is completely state-less and that the input and output objects (*cParams* and *cRecordset*) both support serialization.

Factory-Worker Objects

So what, really, is a business object and how is it implemented? Well, in the Visual Basic world, a business object is a public object that exposes business-specific attributes. The approach TMS takes toward business objects is to employ the action-factory-worker model. We'll come to the action objects later, but for now we'll concentrate on the factory-worker objects.

A quick note about terminology: in this design pattern there is no such thing as an atomic "business object" itself. The combination of the interaction between action, worker, and factory can be described as a logical business object.

Factory-Worker Model

The factory-worker model stipulates that for each particular type of business object an associated management class will exist. The purpose of the management class is to control the creation and population of data in the business objects. This management class is referred to as a factory class. The interface of every factory class is identical (except under exceptional circumstances).

Likewise, the worker class is the actual business object. Business objects cannot be instantiated without an associated factory class. In Visual Basic–speak we say that they are "Public Not Creatable"—the only way to gain access to a worker object is through the publicly instantiable/creatable factory class. So when we refer to a business object we are actually talking about the combination of the factory and worker objects, since each is dependent on the other.

Shared recordset implementation

Adding all this factory-worker code to your application isn't going to make it any faster. If your worker objects had 30 properties each and you wanted to create 1000 worker objects, the factory class would have to receive 1000 rows from the database and then populate each worker with the 30 fields. This would require 30,000 data operations! Needless to say, a substantial overhead.

What you need is a method of populating the worker objects in a high-performance fashion. The Shared Recordset Model solves this problem, which means that one *cRecordset* is retrieved from the DAL and each worker object is given a reference to a particular row in that recordset. This way, when a property is accessed on the worker object, the object retrieves the data from the recordset rather than from explicit internal variables, saving us the overhead of populating each worker object with its own data.

Populating each worker object involves instantiating only the object and then passing an object reference to the Shared Recordset and a row identifier, rather than setting all properties in the worker object individually. The worker object uses this object reference to the recordset to retrieve or write data from its particular row when a property of the business object is accessed. But to establish the real benefits of using the factory-worker approach, we need to discuss briefly how distributed clients interface with our business objects. This is covered in much greater detail in the sections, "Action Objects" and "Clients," later in this chapter.

To make a long story short, distributed clients send and receive recordsets only. Distributed clients have no direct interface to the business objects themselves. This is the role of action objects. Action objects act as the brokers between client applications and business objects. The recordset supports serialization, so the clients use this "serializable" recordset as a means of transferring data to and from the client tier to the business tier via the action object.

It's quite common for a client to request information that originates from a single business object. Say, for example, that the client requests all the information about an organization's employees. What the client application wants to receive is a recordset containing all the Employee Detail information from an action object. The EmployeeDetail recordset contains 1800 employees with 30 fields of data for each row.

Let's look at what's involved in transferring this information from the business objects to the client if we don't use the Shared Recordset implementation.

1. The client requests the EmployeeDetail recordset from the *Employee Maintenance* action object.

2. The *Employee Maintenance* action object creates an *Employee* factory object.

3. The *Employee* factory object obtains an Employee recordset from the DAL.

4. The *Employee* factory object creates an *Employee* worker object for each of the rows in the recordset.

5. The *Employee* factory object sets the corresponding property on the *Employee* worker object for each of the fields in that row of the recordset.

    We now have a factory-worker object containing information for our 1800 employees. But the client needs all this information in a recordset, so the client follows these steps:

6. The *Employee Maintenance* action object creates a recordset.

7. The *Employee Maintenance* action object retrieves each *Employee* worker object from the *Employee* factory object and creates a row in the recordset.

8. Each property on that *Employee* worker object is copied into a field in the recordset.

9. This recordset is returned to the client and serialized on the client side.

10. The client releases the reference to the action object.

Basically, the business object gets a recordset, tears it apart, and then the action object re-creates exactly the same recordset we had in the first place. In this case, we had 1800 × 30 data items that were set and then retrieved, for a total of 108,000 data operations performed on the recordsets!

Let's look at the difference if we use the Shared Recordset Model.

1. The client requests an EmployeeDetail recordset from the *Employee Maintenance* action object.

2. The *Employee Maintenance* action object creates an *Employee* factory object.

3. The *Employee* factory object obtains an Employee recordset from the DAL.

4. The *Employee* factory object keeps a reference to the recordset.

NOTE

Notice that at this point the factory will not create any objects; rather, it will create the objects only the first time they are requested—in essence, it will create a Just In Time (JIT) object.

5. The *Employee Maintenance* action object obtains a reference to the recordset from the *Employee* factory object via the *Recordset* property.

6. This recordset is returned to the client and serialized on the client side.

7. The client releases the reference to the action object.

Total data operations on the recordset—zero. We can now return large sets of data from a business object in a high-performance fashion. But this leads to the question of why you should bother with the business objects at all. If all the client is doing is requesting a recordset from the DAL, why the heck doesn't it just use the DAL directly?

Well, to do so would completely ignore the compelling arguments for object-oriented programming. We want contained, self-documenting abstracted objects to represent our core business, and this scenario is only receiving data, not performing any methods on these objects.

Remember that this is a particular case when a client, on a separate physical tier, requests a set of data that directly correlates to a single business object. The data will often need to be aggregated from one or more business objects. So the action object, which exists on the same physical tier as the business object, will have full access to the direct worker object properties to perform this data packaging role.

A client will often request that a complex set of business logic be performed. The action object will perform this logic by dealing directly with the worker objects and the explicit interfaces they provide. Thus, the action objects can fully exploit the power of using the objects directly.

Using the worker objects directly on the business tier means we are creating much more readable, self-documenting code. But because of the advantages of the Shared Recordset implementation, we are not creating a problem in terms of performance. If we need to shift massive amounts of data to the client, we can still do it and maintain a true business object approach at the same time— we have the best of both worlds.

Now that we have covered the general architecture of the action-factory–worker-recordset interaction, we can take a closer look at the code inside the factory and worker objects that makes all this interaction possible.

Factory Objects

The interface for the factory object is as follows:

cFactory Interface

Member	Description
Create	Initializes the business object with a DAL object
Populate	Creates worker objects according to any passed-in parameter object
Item	Returns a worker object
Count	Returns the number of worker objects contained in the factory
Add	Adds an existing worker object to the factory
AddNew	Returns a new empty worker object
Persist	Updates all changes in the worker objects to the database
Remove	Removes a worker object from the factory
Recordset	Returns the internal factory recordset
Delete	Deletes a worker object from the data source and the factory
Parameters	Returns the parameters that can be used to create worker objects

Creating a factory object

Creating the factory is simple. The code below demonstrates the use of the *Create* method to instantiate a factory object. This code exists in the action objects (which we'll cover later). This sample action object uses the *Employees* business object to perform a business process.

```
Dim ocDAL As New cDAL
Dim ocfEmployees As New cfEmployees
ocfEmployees.Create ocDAL
```

Hold it—what's the DAL doing here? Isn't the purpose of business objects to remove the dependency on the DAL? Yes, it is. But something important is happening here, and it has everything to do with transactions. The scope and lifetime of the action object determines the scope and lifetime of our transaction for the business objects as well.

Say our action object needs to access four different factory objects and change data in each of them. Somehow each business object needs to be contained in the same transaction. This is achieved by having the action object instantiate the DAL, activating the transaction and passing that DAL to all four factory objects it creates. This way, all our worker object activities inside the action object can be safely contained in a transaction, if required. More on action objects and transactions later.

So what does the Create code look like? Too easy:

```
Public Sub Create(i_ocDAL As cDAL)
    Set oPicDAL = i_ocDAL ' Set a module-level reference to the DAL.
End Sub
```

Populating a factory object

Creating a factory object isn't really that exciting—the fun part is populating this factory with worker objects, or at least looking like we're doing so!

```
Dim ocDAL           As New cDAL
Dim ofcEmployees    As New cfEmployees
Dim ocParams        As New cParams
ofcEmployees.Create oDAL
ocParams.Add "Department", "Engineering"
ofcEmployees.Populate ocParams
```

Here a recordset has been defined in the DAL as Employees, which can take the parameter *Department* to retrieve all employees for a particular department. Good old *cParams* is used to send parameters to the factory object, just like it does with the DAL. What a chipper little class it is!

So there you have it—the factory object now contains all the worker objects ready for us to use. But how does this *Populate* method work?

```
Private oPicRecordset As cRecordset
Public Sub Populate (Optional i_ocParams as cParams)
    Set oPicRecordset = oPicDAL.OpenRecordset("Employees", i_ocParams)
End Sub
```

The important point here is that the *Populate* method is only retrieving the recordset—it is not creating the worker objects. Creating the worker objects is left for when the user accesses the worker objects via either the *Item* or *Count* method.

Some readers might argue that using *cParams* instead of explicit parameters detracts from the design. The downside of using *cParams* is that the parameters cannot be determined for this class at design time and do not contribute to the self-documenting properties of components. In a way I agree, but using explicit parameters also has its limitations.

The reason I tend to use *cParams* rather than explicit parameters in the factory object *Populate* method is that the interface to the factory class is inherently stable. With *cParams* all factory objects have the same interface, so if parameters for the underlying data source change (as we all know they do in the real world) the public interface of our components will not be affected, thereby limiting the dreaded Visual Basic nightmare of incompatible components.

Also of interest in the *Populate* method is that the *cParams* object is optional. A *Populate* method that happens without a set of *cParams* is determined to be the default *Populate* method and in most cases will retrieve all appropriate objects for that factory. This functionality is implemented in the DAL.

Obtaining a worker object

After we have populated the factory object, we can retrieve worker objects via the *Item* method as shown here:

```
Dim ocDAL          As New cDAL
Dim ofcEmployees   As New cfEmployees
Dim owcEmployee    As New cwEmployee
Dim ocParams       As New cParams

ofcEmployees.Create ocDAL
ocParams.Add "Department", "Engineering"
ofcEmployees.Populate ocParams
Set owcEmployee = ofcEmployees.Item("EdmundsM")
MsgBox owcEmployee.Department
```

At this point, the *Item* method will initiate the instantiation of worker objects. (Nothing like a bit of instantiation initiation.)

```
Public Property Get Item(i_vKey As Variant) As cwEmployee
    If colPicwEmployee Is Nothing Then PiCreateWorkerObjects
    Set Item = colPicwEmployee(i_vKey).Item
End Property
```

So what does *PiCreateWorkerObjects* do?

```
Private Sub PiCreateWorkerObjects
    Dim owcEmployee As cwEmployee

    Do Until oPicRecordset.EOF
        Set owcEmployee = New cwEmployee
        owcEmployee.Create oPicRecordset, oPicDAL
        oPicRecordset.MoveNext
    Loop
End Sub
```

Here we can see the payback in performance for using the Shared Recordset Model. Initializing the worker object simply involves calling the *Create* method of the worker and passing in a reference to *oPicRecordset* and *oPicDAL*. The receiving worker object will store the current row reference and use this to retrieve its data.

But why is the DAL reference there? The DAL reference is needed so that a worker object has the ability to create a factory of its own. This is the way object model hierarchies are built up. (More on this later.)

The *Item* method is also the default method of the class, enabling us to use the coding-friendly syntax of

```
ocfEmployees("637").Name
```

Counting the worker objects

Couldn't be simpler:

```
MsgBox CStr(ofcEmployees.Count)

Private Property Get Count() As Long
    Count = colPicfEmployees.Count
End Property
```

Says it all, really.

Adding workers to factories

Often you will have a factory object to which you would like to add pre-existing worker objects. You can achieve this by using the *Add* method. Sounds simple, but there are some subtle implications when using the Shared Recordset implementation. Here it is in action:

```
Dim ocDAL           As New cDAL
Dim ocfEmployees    As New cfEmployees
Dim ocwEmployee     As New cwEmployee

ocfEmployees.Create ocDAL
Set ocwEmployee = MagicEmployeeCreationFunction()
ocfEmployees.Add ocwEmployee
```

You'll run into a few interesting quirks when adding another object. First, since the worker object we're adding to our factory has its data stored in another factory somewhere, we need to create a new row in our factory's recordset and copy the data from the worker object into the new row. Then we need to set this new object's recordset reference from its old parent factory to the new parent factory, otherwise it would be living in one factory but referencing data in another—that would be very bad. To set the new reference, we must call the worker *Create* method to "bed" it into its new home.

```
Public Sub Add(i_ocwEmployee As cwEmployee)
    oPicRecordset.AddNew
    With oPicRecordset.Fields
        .("ID") = i_ocwEmployee.ID
        .("Department") = i_ocwEmployee.Department
        .("FirstName") = i_ocwEmployee.FirstName
        .("LastName") = i_ocwEmployee.LastName
    End With
    oPicRecordset.Update
    i ocwEmployee.Create oPicRecordset
End Sub
```

And there you have it—one worker object in a new factory.

Creating new workers

You use the *AddNew* method when you want to request a new worker object from the factory. In the factory, this involves adding a row to the recordset and creating a new worker object that references this added row. One minor complication here: what if I don't have already have a recordset?

Suppose that I've created a factory object, but I haven't populated it. In this case, I don't have a recordset at all, so before I can create the new worker object I have to create the recordset. Now, when I get a recordset from the DAL, it comes back already containing the required fields. But if I don't have a recordset, I'm going to have to build one manually. This is a slightly laborious task because it means performing *AddField* operations for each property on the worker object. Another way to do this would be to retrieve an empty recordset from the DAL, either by requesting the required recordset with parameters that will definitely return an empty recordset, or by having an optional parameter on the *OpenRecordset* call. In our current implementation, however, we build empty recordsets inside the factory object itself.

But before we look at the process of creating a recordset manually, let's see the *AddNew* procedure in action:

```
Dim ocDAL            As New cDAL
Dim ocfEmployees     As New cfEmployees
Dim ocwEmployee      As New cwEmployee

ocfEmployees.Create ocDAL
Set ocfEmployee = ocfEmployees.AddNew
ocfEmployee.Name = "Adam Magee"
```

This is how it is implemented:

```
Public Function AddNew() As cwEmployee
    Dim ocwEmployee As cwEmployee

    If oPicRecordset Is Nothing Then
        Set oPicRecordset = New cRecordset
        With oPicRecordset
            .AddField "ID"
            .AddField "Department"
            .AddField "FirstName"
            .AddField "LastName"
        End With
    End If
    oPicRecordset.AddNew      ' Add an empty row for the
                              ' worker object to reference.
    oPicRecordset.Update
    Set ocwEmployee = New cwEmployee
    ocwEmployee.Create oPicRecordset, oPicDAL
    colPicwWorkers.Add ocwEmployee
    Set New = ocwEmployee
End Property
```

This introduces an unavoidable maintenance problem, though. Changes to the worker object must now involve updating this code as well—not the most elegant solution, but it's worth keeping this in mind whenever changes to the worker objects are implemented.

Persistence (Perhaps?)

So now we can retrieve worker objects from the database, we can add them to other factories, and we can create new ones—all well and good—but what about saving them back to the data source? This is the role of persistence. Basically, persistence involves sending the recordset back to the database to be updated. The DAL has a method that does exactly that—*UpdateRecordset*—and we can also supply and retrieve any parameters that might be appropriate for the update operation (although most of the time *UpdateRecordset* tends to happen without any reliance on parameters at all).

```
Dim ocDAL          As New cDAL
Dim ocfEmployees   As New cfEmployees
Dim ocwEmployee    As New cwEmployee
Dim ocParams       As New cParams

ocfEmployees.Create ocDAL
ocParams.Add "Department", "Engineering"
ocfEmployees.Populate ocParams
For Each ocwEmployee In ocfEmployees
    .Salary = "Peanuts"
Next 'ocwEmployee
ocfEmployees.Persist      ' Reduce costs
```

What is this *Persist* method doing, then?

```
Public Sub Persist(Optional i_ocParams As cParams)
    oPicDAL.UpdateRecordset oPicRecordset, i_ocParams
End Sub
```

Consider it persisted.

Removing and Deleting

What about removing worker objects from factories? Well, you have two options—sack 'em or whack 'em!

A worker object can be removed from the factory, which has no effect on the underlying data source. Maybe the factory is acting as a temporary collection for worker objects while they wait for an operation to be performed on them. For example, a collection of *Employee* objects needs to have the *IncreaseSalary* method called (yeah, I know what you're thinking—that would be a pretty small collection). For one reason or another, you need to remove an *Employee* worker object from this factory (maybe the worker object had the *SpendAllDayAtWorkSurfingTheWeb* property set to True), so you would call the *Remove* method. This method just removes the worker object from this factory with no effect on the underlying data. This is the sack 'em approach.

You use the other method when you want to permanently delete an object from the underlying data source as well as from the factory. This involves calling the *Delete* method on the factory and is known as the whack 'em approach. Calling *Delete* on the factory will completely remove the worker object and mark its row in the database for deletion the next time a *Persist* is executed.

This is an important point worth repeating—if you delete an object from a factory, it is not automatically deleted from the data source. So if you want to be sure that your worker objects data is deleted promptly and permanently, make sure that you call the *Persist* method! Some of you might ask, "Well, why not call the *Persist* directly from within the *Delete* method?" You wouldn't do this because of performance. If you wanted to delete 1000 objects, say, you wouldn't want a database update operation to be called for each one—you would want it to be called only at the end when all objects have been logically deleted.

```
Dim ocDAL            As New cDAL
Dim ocfEmployees     As New cfEmployees
Dim ocwEmployee      As New cwEmployee

ocfEmployees.Create ocDAL
ocfEmployees.Populate
For Each ocwEmployee In ocfEmployees
    With ocwEmployee
        If .Salary = "Peanuts" Then
            ocfEmployees.Remove .Index    ' Save the peasants.
        Else
            ocfEmployees.Delete .Index    ' Punish the guilty.
        End If
    End With
Next  'ocwEmployee
ocfEmployees.Persist      ' Exact revenge.
```

One important point to note here is that worker objects cannot commit suicide! Only the factory object has the power to delete or remove a worker object.

```
Public Sub Remove(i_vKey As Variant)
    colPicwWorkers.Remove i_vKey
End Sub

Public Sub Delete(i_vKey as Variant)
    If VarType(i_vKey) = vbString Then
        oPicRecordset.AbsolutePosition = _
            colPicwWorkers.Item(i_vKey).AbsolutePosition
        oPicRecordset.Delete
        colPicwWorkers.Remove oPicRecordset.AbsolutePosition
    Else
        oPicRecordset.AbsolutePosition = i_vKey
        oPicRecordset.Delete
        colPicwWorkers.Remove i_vKey
    End If
End Sub
```

Getting at the Recordset

As discussed earlier, sometimes it is more efficient to deal with the internal factory recordset directly rather than with the factory object. This is primarily true when dealing with distributed clients that do not have direct access to the worker objects themselves. In this case, the factory object exports this recordset through the *Recordset* property.

The *Recordset* property can also be used to regenerate a business object. Imagine a distributed client that has accessed an *EmployeeDetails* method on an action object and has received the corresponding recordset. The distributed client then shuts the action object down (because, as we will soon see, action objects are designed to be stateless). This recordset is then modified and sent back to the action object. The action object needs to perform some operations on the business objects that are currently represented by the recordset.

The action object can create an empty factory object and assign the recordset sent back from the client to this factory. Calling the *Populate* method will now result in a set of worker objects being regenerated from this recordset! Or, if the data has just been sent back to the database, the action object could call *Persist* without performing the *Populate* method at all, again maximizing performance when the client is modifying simple sets of data.

Take particular care when using the *Recordset* property with distributed clients, though. It's important to ensure that other clients don't modify the underlying business object after the business object has been serialized as a recordset. In such a case, you'll end up with two different recordsets—the recordset on the client and the recordset inside the business object. This situation can easily be avoided by ensuring that the action objects remain as stateless as possible. In practice, this means closing down the business object immediately after the recordset has been retrieved, thereby minimizing the chance of the business object changing while a copy of the recordset exists on the client.

```
Dim ocfEmployees       As New cfEmployees
Dim ocParams           As New cParams
Dim ocRecordset        As cRecordset

Set ocfEmployees = New cfEmployees

ocParams.Add "PostCode", "GL543HG"

ocfEmployees.Create oPicDAL
ocfEmployees.Populate ocParams

Set ocRecordset = ocfEmployees.Recordset
```

Be aware that the above code is not recommended, except when you need to return sets of data to distributed clients. Data manipulation that is performed on the same tier as the factory objects should always be done by direct manipulation of the worker objects.

Determining the Parameters of a Factory

Because we don't use explicit procedure parameters in the *Populate* method of the factory class, it can be useful to be able to determine what these parameters are. The read-only *Parameters* property returns a *cParams* object populated with the valid parameter names for this factory.

The *Parameters* property is useful when designing tools that interact with business objects—such as the business object browser that we'll look at later on—since the parameters for a factory can be determined at run time. This determination allows us to automatically instantiate factory objects.

```
Dim ocfEmployees        As New cfEmployees
Dim ocParams            As New cParams

Set ocfEmployees = New cfEmployees
Set ocParams = ocfEmployee.Parameters

' Do stuff with ocParams.
```

Worker Objects

So far, we've concentrated mainly on the factory objects; now it's time to examine in greater detail the construction of the worker objects.

Factory objects all have the same interface. Worker objects all have unique interfaces. The interface of our sample *Employee* worker object is shown below.

cWorker Employee Interface

Member	Description
ID	Unique string identifier for the worker object
Name	Employee name
Salary	Employee gross salary
Department	Department the employee works in
Create	Creates a new worker object

Creating a worker

As we saw in the discussion of the factory object, creating a worker object involves passing the worker object a reference to the shared recordset and a reference to the factory's DAL object. This is what the worker does with these parameters:

```
Private oPicRecordset     As cRecordSet
Private lPiRowIndex       As Long
Private oPicDAL           As cDAL

Friend Sub Create(i_ocRecordset As cRecordSet, i_ocDAL As cDAL)
    Set oPicRecordset = i_ocRecordset
    Set oPicDAL = i_ocDAL
    lPiRowIndex = I_ocRecordset.AbsolutePosition
End Sub
```

Why is this procedure so friendly? (That is, why is it declared as *Friend* and not as *Public*?) Well, remember that these worker objects are "Public Not Creatable" because we want them instantiated only by the factory object. Because the factory and workers always live in the same component, the *Friend* designation gives the factory object exclusive access to the *Create* method. Notice also that the worker objects store the row reference in the module-level variable *lPiRowIndex*.

Identification, please

In this design pattern, an ID is required for all worker objects. This ID, or string, is used to index the worker object into the factory collection. This ID could be manually determined by each individual factory, but I like having the ID as a property on the object—it makes automating identification of individual worker objects inside each factory a lot easier.

In most cases, the ID is the corresponding database ID, but what about when a worker object is created based on a table with a multiple field primary key? In this case, the ID would return a concatenated string of these fields, even though they would exist as explicit properties in their own right.

Show me the data!

Here is the internal worker code for the *ID* property—the property responsible for setting and returning the worker object ID. Note that this code is identical for every other Property Let/Get pair in the worker object.

```
Public Property Get ID() As Long
    PiSetAbsoluteRowPosition
    ID = oPicRecordset("ID")
End Property

Public Property Let ID(i_ID As Long)
    PiSetAbsoluteRowPosition
    PiSetPropertyValue "ID", i_ID
End Property
```

The most important point here is the *PiSetAbsoluteRowPosition* call. This call is required to point the worker object to the correct row in the shared recordset. The recordset current record at this point is undefined—it could be anywhere. The call to *PiSetAbsoluteRowPosition* is required to make sure that the worker object is retrieving the correct row from the recordset.

```
Private Sub PiSetAbsoluteRowPosition()
    oPiRecordset.AbsolutePosition = lPiRowIndex
End Sub
```

Likewise, this call to *PiSetAbsoluteRowPosition* needs to happen in the Property Let. The *PiSetPropertyValue* procedure merely edits the appropriate row in the recordset.

```
Private Sub PiSetPropertyValue(i_sFieldName As String, _
                               i_vFieldValue As Variant)
    oPiRecordset.Edit
    oPiRecordset(i_sFieldName) = i_vFieldValue
    oPiRecordset.Update
End Sub
```

Methods in the madness

At the moment, all we've concentrated on are the properties of worker objects. What about methods?

An *Employee* worker object might have methods such as *AssignNewProject*. How do you implement these methods? Well, there are no special requirements here—implement the customer business methods as you see fit. Just remember that the data is in the shared recordset and that you should call *PiSetAbsolute-RowPosition* before you reference any internal data.

Worker objects creating factories

Factory objects returning workers is all well and good, but what happens when we want to create relationships between our business objects? For example, an *Employee* object might be related to the *Roles* object, which is the current assignment this employee has. In this case, the *Employee* worker object will return a reference to the *Roles* factory object. The *Employee* object will be responsible for creating the factory object and will supply any parameters required for its instantiation. This is great because it means we need only to supply parameters to the first factory object we create. Subsequent instantiations are managed by the worker objects themselves.

```
Dim ocDAL           As New cDAL
Dim ocfEmployees    As New cfEmployees
Dim ocwEmployee     As New cwEmployee
Dim ocParams        As New cParams

ocfEmployees.Create ocDAL
ocParams.Add "ID", "637"
ocfEmployees.Populate ocParams

MsgBox ocfEmployees(1).Roles.Count
```

Here the *Roles* property on the *Employee* worker object returns the *ocfRoles* factory object.

```
Public Property Get Roles() As cfRoles
    Dim ocfRoles As New cfRoles
    Dim ocParams As New cParams

    ocParams.Add "EmpID", Me.ID
    ocfRoles.Create oPicDAL
    ocfRoles.Populate ocParams
    Set Roles = ocfRoles
End Property
```

Accessing child factory objects this way is termed navigated instantiation, and you should bear in mind this important performance consideration. If I wanted to loop through each *Employee* and display the individual *Roles* for each *Employee*, one data access would retrieve all the employees via the DAL and another data access would retrieve each set of *Roles* per employee. If I had 1800 employees, there would be 1801 data access operations—one operation for the *Employees* and 1800 operations to obtain the *Roles* for each employee. This performance would be suboptimal.

In this case, it would be better to perform direct instantiation, which means you'd create the *Roles* for all employees in one call and then manually match the *Roles* to the appropriate employee. The *Roles* object would return the *EmployeeID*, which we would then use to key into the *Employee* factory object to obtain information about the *Employee* for this particular *Roles* object. The golden rule here is that navigated instantiation works well when the number of data access operations will be minimal; if you need performance, direct instantiation is the preferred method.

```
Dim ocfRoles        As New cfRoles
Dim ocfEmployees    As New cfEmployees
Dim ocwRole         As cwRole

ocfEmployees.Create oPicDAL
ocfRoles.Create oPicDAL

ocfEmployees.Populate      ' Using default populate to retrieve all objects
ocfRoles.Populate

For Each ocwRole In ocfRoles
    MsgBox ocfEmployees(ocwRole.EmpID).Name
Next ' ocwRole
```

An interesting scenario occurs when a worker object has two different properties that return the same type of factory object. For example, a worker could have a *CurrentRoles* property and a *PreviousRoles* property. The difference is that these properties supply different parameters to the underlying factory object *Populate* procedure.

Where are my children?

It's useful to be able to query a worker object to determine what factory objects it supports as children. Therefore, a worker object contains the read-only property *Factories*, which enables the code that dynamically determines the child factory objects of a worker and can automatically instantiate them. This is useful for utilities that manipulate business objects.

The *Factories* property returns a *cParams* object containing the names of the properties that return factories and the names of those factory objects that they return. Visual Basic can then use the *CallByName* function to directly instantiate the factories of children objects, if required.

The *Factories* property is hidden on the interface of worker objects because it does not form part of the business interface; rather, it's normally used by utility programs to aid in dynamically navigating the object model.

```
Dim ocfEmployees     As New cfEmployees
Dim ocfEmployee      As New cfEmployee
Dim ocParams         As New cParams


ocfEmployees.Create oPicDAL
ocfEmployees.Populate
Set ocfEmployee = ocfEmployees(1)

Set ocParams = ocfEmployee.Factories
```

Business Object Browser

After you've created the hierarchy of business objects by having worker objects return factory objects, you can dynamically interrogate this object model and represent it visually. A business object browser is a tremendously powerful tool for programmers to view both the structure and content of the business objects, because it allows the user to drag and drop business objects in the same fashion as the Microsoft Access Relationships editor.

Business object wizard

Creating business objects can be a tedious task. If the data source you're modeling has 200 major entities (easily done for even a medium-size departmental database), that's a lot of business objects you'll have to build. Considering that the factory interface is the same for each business object and that the majority of the properties are derived directly from data fields, much of this process can be automated.

A business object wizard works by analyzing a data entity and then constructing an appropriate factory and worker class. This is not a completely automated process, however! Some code, such as worker objects returning factories, must still be coded manually. Also, any business methods on the worker object obviously have to be coded by hand, but using a business object wizard will save you a lot of time.

TMS uses a business object wizard to develop factory-worker classes based on a SQL Server database. This wizard is written as an add-in for Visual Basic and increases productivity tremendously by creating business objects based on the Shared Recordset implementation. If you need simple business objects, though, you can use the Data Object wizard in Visual Basic 6.0. The mapping of relational database fields to object properties is often referred to as the business object impedance mismatch.

Business object model design guidelines

Keep it simple—avoid circular relationships like the plague. Sometimes this is unavoidable, so make sure you keep a close eye on destroying references, and anticipate that you might have to use explicit destructors on the factory objects to achieve proper teardown. Teardown is the process of manually ensuring that business objects are set to *Nothing* rather than relying on automatic class dereferencing in Visual Basic. In practice, this means you call an explicit *Destroy* method to force the release of any internal object references.

Don't just blindly re-create the database structure as an object model; "denormalization" is OK in objects. For example, if you had an Employee table with many associated lookup tables for Department Name, Project Title, and so forth, you should denormalize these into the *Employee* object; otherwise, you'll be forever looking up *Department* factory objects to retrieve the Department Name for the employee or the current Project Title. The DAL should be responsible for resolving these foreign keys into the actual values and then transposing them again when update is required. Typically, this is done by a stored procedure in a SQL relational database.

This doesn't mean you won't need a Department factory class, which is still required for retrieving and maintaining the Department data. I'm saying that instead of your Employee class returning the DepartmentID, you should denormalize it so that it returns the Department Name.

```
MsgBox ocfEmployee.DepartmentName
```

is better than

```
MsgBox ocfDepartments(ocfEmployee.DepartmentID).Name
```

But at the end of the day, the level of denormalization required is up to you to decide. There are no hard and fast rules about denormalization—just try to achieve a manageable, usable number of business objects.

Wrap Up

So there's the basic architecture for factory-worker model business objects with a Shared Recordset implementation. I feel that this approach provides a good balance between object purity and performance. The objects also return enough information about themselves to enable some great utilities to be written that assist in the development environment when creating and using business objects.

ACTION OBJECTS

Now we turn to where the rubber meets the road—the point where the client applications interface with the business objects, which is through action objects.

Action objects represent the sequence of actions that an application performs. Action objects are responsible for manipulating business objects and are the containers for procedural business logic. Remember that the distributed clients should only send and receive *cRecordset* or *cParams* objects. This is a thin-client approach. The client should be displaying data, letting the user interact with the data, and then it should be returning this data to the action object.

Action objects live in the logical business tier (with factory and worker objects). Therefore, access to these action objects from the clients should be as stateless as possible. This means that if action objects live on a separate physical tier (as in a true three-tier system), performance is maximized by minimizing cross-machine references.

The other important task of action objects is to define transaction scope; that is, when an action object is created, all subsequent operations on that action object will be in a transaction. Physically, action objects live in a Visual Basic out-of-process component or in DLLs hosted by MTS. Worker and factory objects are contained in an in-process component that also could be hosted in MTS.

The structure of action objects comes from the requirements of the application. The requirements of the application logic should be determined from an object-based analysis, preferably a UML usage scenario. This is what I refer to as the Golden Triangle.

Here's an example: Imagine the archetypal Human Resource system in any organization. One of the most basic business requirements for an HR system is that it must be able to retrieve and update employee information and the employee's associated activities. These activities are a combination of the employee's current roles and projects and are known as the usage scenario.

The user interface needed to meet this requirement could be a Visual Basic form, but it could also be an Active Server Page–based Web page.

Action Object Interface

We can imagine that a Visual Basic form that implements this usage scenario would present two major pieces of information: *EmployeeDetails* and *Activities*. We can now determine the interface of the required action object.

- *GetEmployeeDetails*
- *UpdateEmployeeDetails*
- *GetCurrentActivities*
- *UpdateCurrentActivities*

Notice that these attributes of the action object are all stateless. That is, when you retrieve a recordset from *GetEmployeeDetails*, you then shut down the action object immediately, thereby minimizing the cross-layer communication cost. Users can then modify the resulting recordset and, when they are ready to send it back for updating, you create the action object again and call the *UpdateEmployeeDetails* method. The action object does not need to be held open while the recordset is being modified. Let's look at these calls in more detail:

```
Public Function GetEmployeeDetails(Optional i_sID As String) As cRecordset

    Dim ocfEmployees        As New cfEmployees
    Dim oParams             As New cParams

    If Not IsMissing(i_sID) Then oParams.Add "ID", i_sID

    ocfEmployees.Create oPicDAL
    ocfEmployees.Populate oParams

    Set GetEmployeeDetails = ocfEmployees.Recordset

End Function
```

Likewise, the *UpdateEmployeeDetail* call looks like this:

```
Public Sub UpdateEmployeeDetail(i_ocRecordset As cRecordset)

        Dim ocfEmployees As New cfEmployees
        Dim ocRecordset  As New cRecordset

        Set ocRecordset = New cRecordset
        ocRecordset.Serialize = i_ocRecordset.Serialize ' Create local
                            ' copy of object so that business objects do
                            ' not have to refer across network.
        ocfEmployees.Create oPicDAL
        Set ocfEmployees.Recordset = ocRecordset
        ocfEmployees.Persist

        i_ocRecordset.Serialize = ocRecordset.Serialize ' Copy updated
                            ' recordset back to client.

End Sub
```

The *GetCurrentActivities* call has a bit more work to do. It must create a new recordset because the usage scenario requires that both *Roles* and *Projects* come back as one set of data. So the *GetCurrentActivities* call would create a recordset with three fields—ActivityID, ActivityValue, and ActivityType (*Roles* or *Projects*) and then populate this recordset from the *Roles* business object and the *Projects* business object. This recordset would then be returned to the client.

The *UpdateCurrentActivities* call would have to do the reverse—unpack the recordset and then apply updates to the Roles and Projects table.

Transactions in Action

So if action objects are responsible for transactions, how do they maintain transactions? When an action object is initiated, it instantiates a *cDAL* object and begins a transaction. This *cDAL* object is passed to all business objects that the action object creates so that every business object in this action object has the same transaction.

Just before the action object is destroyed, it checks a module-level variable (*bPiTransactionOK*) in the class Terminate event to see whether the transaction should be committed. This module-level variable can be set by any of the procedures within the action object. Normally, if a transaction has to be rolled back, an exception is raised to the client and *bPiTransactionOK* is set to False so that the user can be informed that something very bad has happened. Checking this module-level variable in the Terminate event ensures that the action object is responsible for protecting the transaction, not the client.

```
Private bPiTransactionOK    As Boolean
Private oPicDAL             As cDAL

Private Sub Class_Initialize()
    Set oPicDAL = New cDAL
    oPicDAL.BeginTransaction
    bPiTransactionOK = True
End Sub

Private Sub Class_Terminate()
    If bPiTransactionOK Then
        oPicDAL.CommitTransaction
    Else
        oPicDAL.RollbackTransaction
    End If
End Sub
```

Wrap Up

So now we've covered the role and design of action objects. In summary, a good analogy is that of a relational SQL database: factory-worker objects are represented by the tables and records, and action objects are represented by the stored procedures. The lifetime of the action object controls the lifetime of the implicit transaction contained within.

Action objects should be accessed in a stateless fashion—get what you want and then get the hell out of there! Stateless fashion is enabled by the supporting of serialization by *cRecordset* and *cParams*, which ensures that your applications can achieve good distributed performance.

CLIENTS

Now for the final part of the puzzle. What is the best way for our client applications to use action objects? Basically, the client should open the appropriate action object, retrieve the required recordset, and then close down that action object immediately. When the data is ready to be returned for update, the action object will be instantiated again, the relevant *Update* method will be called, and then the action object will be closed down again. Here is an example of a client calling an action object to retrieve the list of current employees:

```
Dim ocaEmployeeMaintenance    As caEmployeeMaintenance
Dim ocRecordset               As cRecordset

Set ocRecordset = New cRecordset
Set ocaEmployeeMaintenance = _
    New caEmployeeMaintenance ' Open Employee action object

ocRecordset.Serialize = _
    caEmployeeMaintenance.GetCurrentEmployees.Serialize
Set ocaEmployeeMaintenance = Nothing

' Do stuff with local ocRecordset in user interface
' ...

Set ocaEmployeeMaintenance = New caEmployeeMaintenance
ocaEmployeeMaintenace.UpdateEmployees ocRecordset
Set ocaEmployeeMaintenance = Nothing
```

This code could be in a Visual Basic form, in an Active Server Page, or even in an ActiveX document—the important thing is that the client reference to the action object is as quick as possible. The recordset maintains the data locally until the time comes to the send the data back to the action object.

Wrap Up

So there you have it, a workable approach to implementing high-performance distributed objects. With the right amount of planning and design, an awareness of distributed application issues, and the power of Visual Basic, building powerful, scalable software solutions is well within your reach.

So get out there and code those business objects!

IIS This a Template I See Before Me?

Developing Web Applications

ROGER SWIFT

Roger's origins in programming lie in a small room in a Leicestershire school, where he spent many a happy hour punching out tape on a teletype terminal before connecting to a mainframe via an acoustic coupler modem and finding that his program didn't work. Between then and the start of his Visual Basic programming career, he spent his time in the murky world of mainframes bashing out Fortran programs for scientists. Roger first saw the VB light in early 1994 and hasn't looked back since. Roger lives in Oxfordshire with his wife Kath and their young family. When not playing or watching sports Roger fights a losing battle against the jungle growing around the house.

When I first fired up Microsoft Visual Basic 5 (yes, I did say Visual Basic *5*), I was surprised to be presented with a box asking me what type of project I wanted to develop. I was even more surprised to find that there were nine project templates to choose from—who would have thought that little old Visual Basic would grow into such a multitalented individual? Since that day I have become accustomed to the variety of development options given to us by Visual Basic, and now Visual Basic 6 offers us three new templates: Data Project, IIS Application, and DHTML Application.

I'll examine the IIS Application in this chapter, going through the process of developing a simple application for Internet Information Server (just in case you hadn't worked out the acronym).

This template and the new features embodied in it are intended to give Visual Basic developers the opportunity to develop Web applications without leaving (too often) the environment they know so well. I hope I'll be able to give you a feel for the development process, because it is different from the process of a normal Visual Basic project. I also want to get you thinking differently about how your application should be structured and how your users will interact with your application, because these design issues are probably the biggest change that you as a developer of a Web application (many such applications, I hope) are going to face.

JUST WHAT IS A WEB APPLICATION?

Before I go any further, I ought to explain just what I mean by a "Web application." A Web application is an application that runs on a Web server and is accessed at the client end using an Internet browser program or other program with Web browsing facilities. In this model, all the processing in the application is performed on the Web server and the client receives HTML-coded pages that contain the user interface and client data. Of course, real-world applications contain a mixture of server-side and client-side processing. Browsers can download Microsoft ActiveX components and Java applets to add richer functionality to the interface of the application. Web pages can contain scripting code to run at the client end to provide further flexibility in the front end and preprocessing of data and requests for the back end.

The Web application model offers the prospect of a single client front end that is capable of accessing a variety of different applications on a remote server. While this front end might not be the thinnest client in the world, it can be a fairly universal client. This client could also be updatable remotely. If it doesn't have a particular capability required by an application (such as the display of a particular format of data), the client could download a component that it can use to give it that capability. Similarly, the versions of components the client already has could be checked to ensure that they are always up to date.

A Web application in the corporate intranet obviously is attractive for a variety of reasons. By having a single client application for all server applications, rollouts are simplified and client PC maintenance costs are reduced. Standard machine setups can be used with the client gradually updating itself as it accesses different applications. In the corporate environment, where there can be tight control over the software on a user machine, applications can be produced for a specific browser, thus allowing developers to fully exploit the capabilities of that browser. Web applications also allow people to work from home or away from their normal office location without losing functionality.

Developing applications for the Internet means you have a huge audience that can access your work. Unlike the corporate intranet environment, you can no longer assume that all browsers accessing your application will have the same capabilities, but this is by no means a barrier to deploying applications over the Internet.

IIS or ASP?

Before the IIS Application template was introduced to Visual Basic, developers wanting to produce Web applications had Active Server Pages (ASP) technology available to them. The ASP model allowed developers to write pages that could be accessed from a browser and that performed some processing on the Web server before returning HTML to the browser. The server-side code could be written in a variety of languages (including client-side scripting languages, such as VBScript or Microsoft JScript), so long as the server had access to a scripting engine for that language. ASP provides a number of different objects for server scripts that allow interaction with both the client and the server.

IIS applications, while based on ASP, provide a better way for Visual Basic developers to produce Web-based applications. For example, the development environment is familiar (though there are differences for IIS application development, as you'll see). The language is the same, so you don't have to learn a new scripting language. The processing code and visual interface code can be separated out to provide a cleaner project—ASP pages have script and interface code intermingled. Visual Basic is also a much more powerful language in which to develop applications than is a scripting language (even if the scripting language can call on code components to perform any tricky processing).

At the time of this writing (on the March beta of Visual Studio 6), there is some MSDN documentation on developing IIS applications but no example code (apart from the fragments appearing in the documentation). So, while I'm not flying completely blind on this one, let's say there're some low clouds and all I have are the instruments to guide me (plus a sick bag and spare underwear!).

What Does Visual Basic 6 Need for Web Application Development?

OK, so what do you need to start developing an IIS application? Even if you don't run your application you'll still need the Microsoft Active Server Pages Object Library, ASP.DLL. This is included in the project references in the IIS Application template, and one of its objects (the *Response* object) is used in the template code. However, a Web server that supports ASP is required to run your application. The Microsoft choices for development Web servers are shown in Table 3-1.

TABLE 3-1

WEB APPLICATION DEVELOPMENT SERVERS

Operating System	Development Web Server
Windows NT Server 4	Internet Information Server
Windows NT Workstation 4	Peer Web Services
Windows 9x	Personal Web Server

You can use any of these servers during application development, but you must use IIS for deployment.

Now that we have discussed IIS applications in general, let's try developing one of our own. First we'll see what the IIS Application template gives us for free. Then we'll develop a home page for our application and add further extensions to our home page to increase its usefulness to users and to ourselves.

Foundations: The Free Stuff

Assuming you've installed and set up your Web server, the next step is to fire up Visual Basic 6. Select New Project from the File menu to display the New Project dialog box, and then select the IIS Application template to start developing your new application.

Right away you'll notice something different—the Project Explorer window contains a folder called Designers in the project tree. Designers, which act as hosts for a particular type of object, appeared in Visual Basic 5, although none of the templates supplied with Visual Basic 5 used them. Designers could (and still can) be added to a project by selecting Components from the Project menu, choosing the Designers tab of the Components dialog box, and then checking a designer in the list. Designers have features that enable the development of particular objects within the Visual Basic integrated development environment

(IDE). In Visual Basic 5, two designers came as standard components; now there are seven. IIS Applications use the WebClass designer to develop *WebClass* objects. Each IIS application contains at least one *WebClass* object.

The IIS Application template provides you with a single item in your new project; a *WebClass* object named WebClass1. Even at this early stage your project is in a state where it can be run (and can demonstrate the fact that it is running). Clicking the Start button on the toolbar (or using any of the other methods to start a project in the IDE) brings up a scaled-down version of the Project Properties dialog box with only the Debugging tab visible. This allows you to specify which *WebClass* component you want to start the application with in an IIS application. This dialog box also contains a Use Existing Browser check box, which, when selected, will launch the application in a browser that's currently running. If this option is not checked, Visual Basic will launch Internet Explorer 4 to act as the client for your application. Even if Internet Explorer 4 is not your default browser, Visual Basic will still launch Internet Explorer 4 (and then ask you if you want to make it your default browser). The options available when you start the project in the IDE are shown in Table 3-2.

Table 3-2　**Project Debugging Options**

Startup Option	Possible Use
Wait For Components To Be Created	Simulates a more normal method of operation, where the application is already running on a Web server and waits for browser requests
Start Component	Opens browser and automatically accesses the specified component
Start Program	Accesses the application using a different browser or a program with browsing capabilities
Start Browser With URL	Accesses a particular part of your application or a page with a link to your application

Once you have chosen your preferred options from this dialog box, you will be prompted to save your project and its files. In an IIS application the directory where you save your project has a bit more significance than normal since this is where the temporary files created at run/debug time will be placed. It is also the same directory where the HTML template files used in the application will be stored. When your application is deployed on a Web server, the directory structure used for development will be mirrored in the production directories, the only change being to the root directory for the application. As far as IIS is concerned, all directories stemming from a virtual root directory are part of the same Web application, unless they themselves are the virtual root directory for another application.

Once you've saved your project files, you'll be prompted for the name of a virtual directory that the Web server should use to host this application during development. When you deploy your application on your production Web server, you'll be able to specify into which directory you want to place your application files. You'll also be able to specify which virtual directory you want your Web server to associate with the physical application directory. The virtual directory name will form part of the URL that browsers use to reference your application.

Finally, after selecting a name for the virtual directory, your application will start. To see your application running, you'll have to switch to a Web browser. If you've chosen to start with a particular Web class, the focus will automatically have been transferred to a browser. If you have not yet entered any code, you'll be greeted by a Web page with the heading "WebClass1's Starting Page."

It's worth taking a moment to have a look in the project directory for the application. In addition to seeing the Web class designer files and project files, you'll also see that an ASP file has been created. During development, this is a temporary file that gets created whenever you start a debug session for your application and is destroyed when you finish the debug session. If you examine this file in Notepad, you'll see that this ASP file (WEBCLASS1.ASP for the default project) contains the following code:

```
<%
Server.ScriptTimeout=600
Response.Buffer=True
Response.Expires=0

If (VarType(Application("~WC~WebClassManager")) = 0) Then
    Application.Lock
    If (VarType(Application("~WC~WebClassManager")) = 0) Then
        Set Application("~WC~WebClassManager") = _
            Server.CreateObject("WebClassRuntime.WebClassManager")
    End If
    Application.UnLock
End If

Application("~WC~WebClassManager").ProcessNoStateWebClass _
    "Project1.WebClass1", _
    Server, _
```

```
    Application, _
    Session, _
    Request, _
    Response
%>
```

This is an ASP script (as shown by the script delimiters <% and %>) that uses the ASP *Server* and *Response* objects and creates an instance of our Web class. From this script, we can see that our IIS application is a single-page ASP application that simply runs an instance of a single object. Normally, as already mentioned, an ASP application would be made up of ASP files containing a mixture of script code to be processed by the Web server and HTML to be returned to the browser.

If we now shut down the browser and return to Visual Basic, we see that the application is still running. The temporary ASP used to access our application is still in existence, so we can start the browser and run the application again. We can even connect to our application from another computer if the Web server has been set up to allow access from that computer. You must close down your application from within Visual Basic, which causes the temporary ASP file to be deleted and thus denies access to your application.

So that's the Web application equivalent of "Hello World" done without writing even a single line of code! (As far as "Hello World" applications go, a Web application is likely to greet more of the world than a C application or a Visual Basic application.)

Building a Home of Your Own

If you want your IIS application to do anything useful, now is the time to get familiar with HTML. There is no getting away from HTML in a Web application—without it you have no user interface to your application. You can distance yourself from HTML to a certain extent by having someone else design your Web pages/client interface for you, but this will probably feel alien to the majority of Visual Basic developers who are used to dragging controls from the toolbox and designing their own forms.

Using HTML to design a user interface harkens back to the days when visual elements were created by writing code that had to be executed before the developer could see what they actually looked like on screen. However, plenty of applications allow you to design your Web pages in a visual way and then generate the underlying HTML for the Web page for you automatically. An understanding of the HTML behind the page is at least useful (if not essential) for effective Web application development, because it is the HTML in your user interface that furnishes your application with events that it can respond to.

You can include HTML in your application in two ways. The most flexible technique (and the most laborious) is to include raw HTML code in your procedures. You will already have seen this approach if you've examined the code supplied by the IIS Application template. Here is an example that uses the *Write* method of the ASP *Response* object to send text to the browser:

```
Response.Write "<HTML><BODY>Hello World!!</BODY></HTML>"
```

The other way of including HTML in your application is to add HTML files to your Web class through an HTML template. When an HTML template is added to a Web class, Visual Basic takes a copy of the underlying HTML file and stores the copy in the project directory. The HTML template is referenced in the Web class by the Web item name that you assign to it when it is added to the Web class.

When adding HTML templates to a Web class, the normal default naming convention of Visual Basic is followed, meaning that the item type name is suffixed with a number that makes the name unique. While this is fine in most cases, it would seem more sensible, when adding HTML templates, that the name of the original HTML file be used to refer to the template. The copies of the files held in the project directory maintain their original names (with the addition of a numeric suffix if a file of the same name already exists in the project directory), so why not default to these names in the IDE? So, when you add an HTML template to a Web class, change the default name to that of the HTML file it represents (remember to check the project directory to see if the name has been changed).

The HTML file is now in the Web class, but no one will get to see it unless the Web class is told when to display it. An HTML file is sent to the browser when the *WriteTemplate* method of the HTML template is called within code. This can be done from the Start event of the Web class but is better placed in the Respond event of the HTML template Web item. The Respond event is the default event of any template and is called whenever the template is referenced without a specific event procedure. To reference the HTML template in code, the *NextItem* property of the Web class is set. At the end of processing an event in a Web class, if the *NextItem* property points to a Web item, processing is transferred to that Web item. This is the statement to place in the Start event of the Web class in order to have the template displayed in the browser:

```
Private Sub WebClass1_Start()
    Set NextItem = Welcome
End Sub

Private Sub Welcome_Respond()
    Welcome.WriteTemplate
End Sub
```

In the above code, when the Web class starts, the HTML template named Welcome is sent to the browser requesting the Web class's ASP.

An HTML template is able to trigger events within a Web class when the template is processed by a browser. When an HTML template is added to a Web class, its underlying HTML file is scanned for tags that have attributes that can take a URL as a value. If an attribute can have a URL for a value, it can send HTTP requests to the Web server, which can be intercepted by the Web class. The Web class can intercept these requests only if the tag attributes are connected to events in the Web items of the Web class. The connection of attributes to events is performed in the right-hand pane of the Web class designer. Attributes can be connected either to a custom event or to a Web item by right-clicking a tag in the designer and choosing one of the options presented. If the attribute is connected to a custom event, the designer automatically creates a new event for the template containing the tag. Default event names come from the tag they are connected to (combined with the name of the attribute if the tag has multiple attributes that can be connected to events, as shown in Figure 3-1).

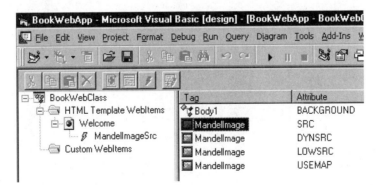

FIGURE 3-1   *Web class designer showing custom events*

If you change an event name (using the same techniques as in Windows Explorer), it is automatically updated both in the Target column of the Web class designer and the HTML Context column, but only for that tag-attribute combination. The update is not shown in other HTML Context entries belonging to the same tag until the template is refreshed in the designer. Also, if any code has been written for a custom event and the event's name is changed, the code becomes disassociated from the event and exists as a general procedure in the Web class (as happens when renaming a control in a form-based Visual Basic application). The names used for tags in the designer come from the tags themselves unless an ID or Name attribute has been set for the tag (with the ID attribute taking precedence).

Extending Your Home to Guests

Now we have a page to display when a user connects to our application. Nothing very exciting, and just maybe our visitors will want to tell us this. Being well-adjusted individuals who aren't afraid of what people might say about our work, we'll include a guestbook in our application. (See Figure 3-2.) We'll store the comments in a database and display the five most recent ones whenever anyone accesses our guestbook. We need a place for visitors to enter their comments, a mechanism for them to register their comments, and a space to display previous comments. To be helpful, we'll provide a way of clearing the comment box.

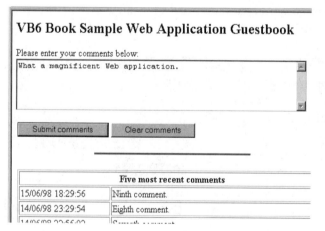

FIGURE 3-2   *Guestbook Web page*

Although the guestbook appears to be a single Web page, it has been created from two separate Web items. Everything above the horizontal rule comes from an HTML template called Guestbook that we have added to our Web class. The horizontal rule and the table below it come from a custom Web item called RecentComments. A hypertext link has been placed on our Welcome page. A connection has been made between the HREF attribute of the hyperlink and a custom event of the Welcome template, which we have called DisplayGuestbook. This custom event simply sets the *NextItem* property of the Web class to the Guestbook template and relies on the processing in the Respond event of the template to provide output to the browser. The Respond event for the Guestbook template sets the *NextItem* property to the RecentComments custom Web item before calling its own *WriteTemplate* method. At the end of the Guestbook template's Respond event, processing passes to the RecentComments custom Web item's Respond event. In this second Respond event a private procedure, *GetComments*—which is defined in the Web class, not in a Web item—is called to dynamically generate an HTML table definition containing the previous five comments. This table and a horizontal rule used to split the screen are written directly to the browser using the *Response* object of the Web server. The *GetComments* procedure uses ActiveX Data Objects (ADO) code to query our guestbook database. The query returns the comments to display in the Five Most Recent Comments table.

When the user has entered a comment, he or she clicks the button labeled Submit Comments to submit it. When this button is clicked all the responses generated by the form are gathered together and sent back to the server. Although individual input elements, like buttons or the comment text box, are not listed in the Web class designer, the form that contains them is listed in the designer. By connecting a custom event to the Form tag of the Guestbook template, we can program a response to the visitor submitting comments. Input controls in HTML are contained within sections called forms. The three attributes of forms that primarily concern us as IIS application developers in Visual Basic are: the ID attribute, which sets the name under which the form will be listed in the Web designer; the Action attribute, which we will be connecting to in order to trigger our response; and the Method attribute, which sets the mechanism by which data is sent from the browser to the server. For IIS applications written using Visual Basic, POST is the only value for the Method attribute that we can use. If we try to include an HTML template containing a Form tag with the Method attribute set to GET (or even without the Method attribute at all), the Web class designer issues a warning message (as shown in Figure 3-3) and tells us what it is going to change in our template.

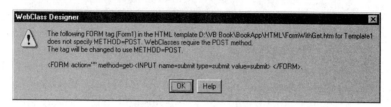

FIGURE 3-3   *Warning message issued by the Web class designer*

When the POST method is used, data is received by the server in the *Form* collection property of the *Request* object. Each element of the Form that generates data creates a member in the *Form* collection using the element's Name attribute as its key in the collection. The data returned by each element is held in the *Item* property of each collection member. Since this is the default property of the collection, we can determine if the SubmitComments button was clicked using the following piece of code:

```
If LCase$(Request.Form("submitcomments")) = "submit comments" Then
```

The value returned by this type of button (a Submit button) is always the same as the text displayed on the button. If the button had not been clicked, there would be no member of the *Form* collection with the key "submitcomments." Having received the visitor's comment about our site (in the member of the *Form* collection with the key "comments"), we then store the comment in our database. Another procedure called *AddComment* takes care of this; again, this is a private method of the Web class. The visitor remains on the Guestbook page, which has the list of recent comments updated to reflect the visitor's newly added comment.

Turning Your Home into a Business

We have a starting page for our Web application and we have a guestbook that users of our application can write comments into, but we don't as yet really have an application. How about we use our application to provide a series of technical articles, say, a whitepaper distribution application? Now, we at TMS have invested considerable resources into creating these whitepapers, so we don't want to give them away to all and sundry with no return whatsoever. So we'll provide summaries of all our whitepapers that anyone can access but will require users to provide us with some information before they can access the full text of any of the whitepapers.

To accomplish this, the first thing we'll have to do is alter our Welcome page. At a minimum, we need to describe the application so that users know what they can expect. We also want to differentiate between anonymous users who don't want to register and those users who do. Repeat users will probably want to sign in on the Welcome page and have full access to the application from then on. New users will probably want to view some of the whitepaper summaries before parting with personal information. This means that we'll have to have the facility to dynamically disable some of the features of our Web pages. We'll also want to be able to access common Web pages (such as the Registration page) from multiple locations within the application. Having obtained personal information from users, we might feel inclined to make them more at home by customizing the pages presented to them, too.

We've redesigned our Welcome page to be more descriptive of the application, added some graphical navigation buttons, and increased the number of options that a user has on this page. (See Figure 3-4.)

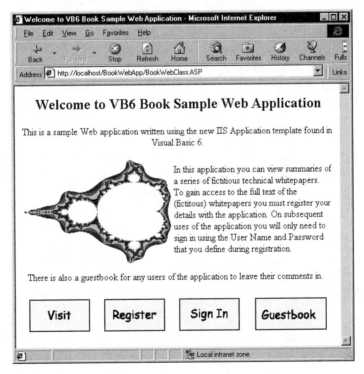

FIGURE 3-4   *New Welcome page*

Graphical navigation buttons were used partly for their visual appeal (even done as simply as this!) but they were used mostly because each graphical button can trigger an event individually. This is because the buttons actually are graphical hypertext links whose HREF attributes can be connected to custom events (or Web items) if we choose. (They are not Input tag controls wrapped inside Form tags and therefore don't have to be accessed through the *Request* object's *Form* collection.) The HREF attribute of each of the buttons references the corresponding HTML template (SignIn, Guestbook, and so forth). The Respond event in each of these templates simply calls the *WriteTemplate* method of the template to display the HTML page in the browser. So the only new feature in the Welcome template is the use of graphical buttons instead of straight text links or "proper" input buttons inside an HTML form. The guestbook itself remains the same, but there is more to comment about in the application, so it serves more of a purpose!

The Registration page is new, but the techniques behind it aren't. A single form contains all the input fields. The data entered on the page is returned in the *Request.Form* collection. To handle the registration of users in our WEBAPP.MDB database, we have added a class module to provide us with a *CUser* object. This class has properties that match the information we want to capture about our users. The CUser class also has a method, *RegisterUser*, which adds the data held in the properties of a *CUser* object to the database. This method has a return value of True if the user was successfully added to the database (the value is otherwise False). Armed with this information, we can control what happens next. If the *RegisterUser* method fails, we want to redisplay the registration form to allow the user to re-enter their details. If the user was successfully added to the database, several things should happen. First we ought to move the user to a different area of the application, away from the registration form, maybe by sending them back to the page where they jumped from to get to the registration page. Alternatively, we could send them to a fixed page of our choosing, perhaps with a "Thank you for registering" message. To make our application more welcoming, we also want to personalize the pages that we send back to users who have signed in.

Now that we have more pages in our application, we've decided that we want to use the same toolbar on several of those pages. To this end we've created a separate template called Toolbar which duplicates the functionality of the Welcome page toolbar. The next task is to edit the Welcome template to remove the section of HTML connected to the toolbar buttons and allow Visual Basic to refresh the template in the designer.

Finally we need to add code to display the Toolbar Web item at the bottom of the Welcome page. We could use the following code in the Respond event of Welcome:

```
Welcome.WriteTemplate
Toolbar.WriteTemplate
```

This does the job of putting the buttons at the bottom of the page, but it is not the code we are going to use. The *WriteTemplate* method can take the name of another template as its only argument, so it would seem that we could use this code as an alternative:

```
Welcome.WriteTemplate
Welcome.WriteTemplate Toolbar
```

If we try this code, however, we find that instead of getting buttons at the bottom of our page we get only another copy of Welcome displayed. (See Figure 3-5.)

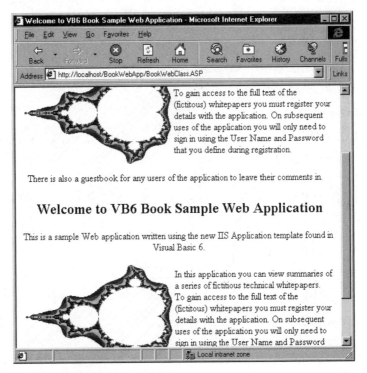

Figure 3-5   *A doubly warm Welcome!*

Toolbar.WriteTemplate Toolbar works as we would expect (perhaps "hope" would be a better word to use), which suggests that the template argument to a *WriteTemplate* call is ignored. However, we'll use this code:

```
Welcome.WriteTemplate
Set NextItem = Toolbar
```

Why use this technique? Because accessing the Toolbar via the *NextItem* property of the Web class ensures that the Respond event of Toolbar fires, which won't happen if we use the Toolbar's *WriteTemplate* method. This way, any extra processing we specify in the Respond event is applied before the template is sent to the browser.

Now that the Toolbar Web item has been added to the Welcome page, we'll add it to the Summary page, too. This page is much more interesting, both in terms of HTML construction and also in the Web class and Web item features used. The template used to construct the Summary page is called SummaryLayout. The HTML file this template is derived from uses frames to enable different sources to be used for the content of different areas of the screen within the browser. The following fragment of the original HTML file

```
<FRAMESET ROWS="25%,50%,25%">
    <FRAME SRC="" NAME="SummaryList">
    <FRAME SRC="" NAME="SummaryView">
    <FRAME SRC="" NAME="SummaryToolbar">
</FRAMESET>
```

produces the event candidates shown in Figure 3-6 when parsed by the Web class designer.

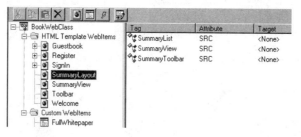

FIGURE 3-6   *Event candidates for SummaryLayout frames*

Now the question is, "Why have we designed the Summary page like this?" After all, if we wanted three different blocks of HTML code outputting to the browser, we could have strung three Web items together to produce the output.

We've structured this part of our application like this because of the features we want it to provide to our users (as will become clear later).

Since we already have our Toolbar template written and in place, we'll connect that to SummaryLayout first. We want it to be displayed at the bottom of the page, so we connect the Toolbar Web item directly to the SummaryToolbar tag that is the source for the bottom frame of the page. (See Figure 3-7.)

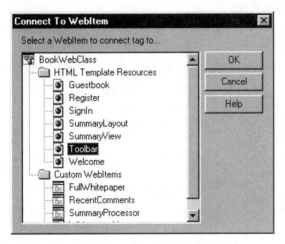

FIGURE 3-7 *The Connect To WebItem dialog box*

FATAL ERRORS IN A WEB CLASS

In a Web application, errors can occur outside of the Visual Basic code. In such cases, traditional error handling techniques (such as those discussed in Chapter 1) are not available for handling the situation gracefully. Instead, you can make use of the *FatalErrorResponse* event of the Web class. This has a single Boolean argument, *SendDefault*, which is an output argument. By setting *SendDefault* to False, the default error message is prevented from being shown in the browser. By using the *Response* object, you can send your own text to the browser to explain to the user that there has been a problem. The Web class provides an *Error* object that you can query to determine the Source, Number, and Description relating to the error. Such information can be written to the browser or logged to a file as necessary. On Windows NT 4 systems, the error is also written to the Application Log, where it can be examined in the context of other errors.

There's no problem with the article list in the top frame of the page. We'd always intended this to be generated dynamically in a custom Web item, called WhitepaperList. This Web item generates the list of available whitepapers and formats the list to make best use of the space in the top frame of the page. The names of the whitepapers are presented as hyperlinks so that clicking them sends a request to the server for the whitepaper summary. In HTML, frames can be used as targets for page requests if the frame is given a name. We've done this for the middle frame so that when the browser requests the whitepaper summary from the server, the summary is displayed in the middle frame upon receipt by the browser.

To produce a server request specific to the whitepaper that the user has selected, we use the *URLFor* method of the Web class and the UserEvent event of the SummaryView custom Web item we've created for displaying whitepaper summaries. The *URLFor* method generates, at run time, a URL either for an existing Web item event or for a run-time event. The arguments for *URLFor* are an existing Web item (which is required) and, optionally, the name of an event to fire in the Web item. If no event name is supplied, the Respond event will be fired if a request is made with this URL. If an existing event's name is used, that particular event will be fired in the Web item. The advantage of this method is the ability to specify an event that does not exist at design time—a run-time event:

```
Response.Write "<a href="""
Response.Write URLFor(SummaryProcessor, "Whitepaper 1")
Response.Write """>Whitepaper 1</a>"
```

The hyperlink defined above appears as "Whitepaper 1" in the browser and when selected will send a request to the server containing the URL for the "Whitepaper 1" event in the SummaryProcessor Web item. Since this event does not exist at design time, the *UserEvent* event procedure of the SummaryProcessor Web item is fired. A single argument is passed into the *UserEvent* event procedure that is the name of the run-time event that was triggered. This technique is well suited to presenting our whitepaper summaries, since it allows us to pass a request for the whitepaper into an event that we can use to send the summary back to the browser.

To generate the Summary page we make use of the ProcessTag event, the only standard event of a Web item that we haven't used yet. This event is fired automatically when the *WriteTemplate* method of a Web item encounters replacement tags in the template's HTML. We could generate dynamically the HTML to send back to the browser in the *UserEvent* of the SummaryProcessor

Web item. However, because the format of this page will be static, with only its content changing, we're using a template Web item with certain areas replaced as each whitepaper is requested. The template will display the whitepaper name and (obviously) the summary, so we insert placeholder tags into the template at design time, which are replaced at run time. Our template contains the following HTML code at a place where we want the whitepaper name to be displayed in the browser:

```
VB6 Book Sample Web application
<WC@WHITEPAPERNAME> Whitepaper name </WC@WHITEPAPERNAME>
Summary
```

When the *WriteTemplate* method for this Web item is called, the WC@WHITE-PAPERNAME tags in the template trigger the ProcessTag event of the template. This event is fired once for each pair of tags, which allows the text between the tags ("Whitepaper Name" in this case) to be substituted by whatever text is required. The same pair of tags is used throughout the template in areas where the whitepaper name is required. The whitepaper summary is replaced using the same technique. Tags are recognized as replacement tags because of their starting prefix; the *TagPrefix* is a property of each Web item, which is set to WC@ by default. If this prefix is changed, the new prefix should contain at least one character that is unlikely to appear elsewhere in the HTML generated by the Web item. This reduces the risk of ordinary HTML or text being processed as a replacement tag. The code used to perform the replacements is quite simple:

```
'Depending on the tag being processed, substitute either the whitepaper
'name or summary.
Select Case LCase$(TagName)
    Case "wc@whitepapername"
        TagContents = smWhitepaperName

    Case "wc@whitepapersummary"
        TagContents = smWhitepaperSummary
End Select
```

Both *TagName* and *TagContents* are passed into the event. The two variables used to replace content are set in the *SummaryProcessor_UserEvent* event procedure that is the target of all the whitepaper hyperlinks in the top frame of the Summary page.

Now we're at the point where we can display summaries of our whitepapers to users of our application, but we haven't included a mechanism for displaying the full text of our whitepapers. This can easily be done by including a hyperlink (in the form of a button, perhaps), which will request the file containing the whitepaper. As we've already stated, we want users to register (or sign in if they have previously registered) before we allow them access to the full text of our whitepapers. This being the case, we should probably display a message to that effect if the user requests a whitepaper summary without having signed in. Because we are already using text replacement tags in the SummaryView template, we'll use the same technique to place either a hyperlink button or a message in the whitepaper summary section of the page.

OK, so we know what we're going to make available as replacement text in the ProcessTag event of the SummaryView Web item, but how are we going to decide what text to supply? By adding to the functionality of our CUser class, we expose a *SignInUser* method and *SignedIn* and *FailureReason* properties. This method and these properties let us sign in a user to the application, find out the reason for failure if they were not accepted (as shown in Figure 3-8), and also check to see if they have already been signed in.

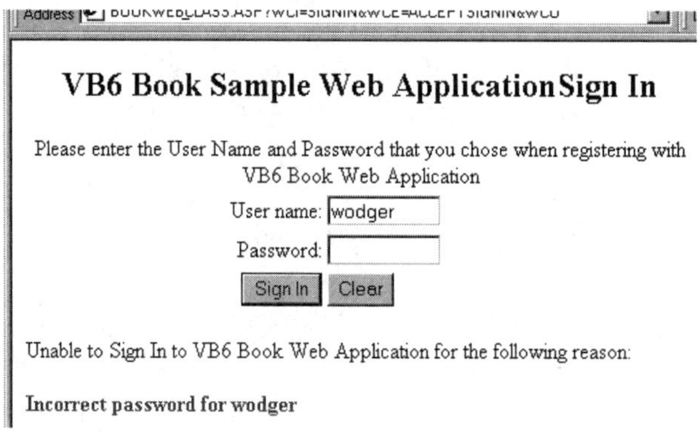

FIGURE 3-8   *Failed user sign-in*

To make the information from the *CUser* object available throughout the Web class, we define an instance of the CUser class at the Web class level. We create the *CUser* object in the Web class Initialize event (and to be tidy, destroy it in the Terminate event) and set and query its properties and methods throughout the Web class, right? If we try this approach, what happens?

Well, we can sign in to the application and be taken to the whitepaper summary page without a problem. However, when we display a whitepaper summary, we find that the information from our sign-in has disappeared and that we are asked to sign in before being able to view the full text of our whitepaper. The problem we're facing is one of application state. Unless we do something to prolong the application lifetime, each request the browser sends to the server causes an instance of the application to be created when the HTTP request is received, and causes that instance of the application to be destroyed once the HTTP request has been completed. Thus, during the sign-in process, our *CUser* object accepts the sign-in and sets its *SignedIn* property to True. When the request arrives to display a summary article, the previous instance of *CUser* is long gone and we access a new instance that has no knowledge of our previous sign-in. What can we do about this?

The easiest change we can make is to set the *StateManagement* property of the Web class to keep the Web class alive between requests. *StateManagement* can be set to *wcNoState* (the default) so that the Web class is continually created and destroyed as requests come in from the browser. The *wcRetainInstance* setting, however, keeps the Web class alive between requests. Once the *State-Management* property of the Web class is set to *wcRetainInstance*, we can sign in to the application, choose a whitepaper summary, and be presented with the opportunity to view the full whitepaper. If we look at the temporary ASP file created when we start a debugging session of our application, we can see how this property change has affected the file:

```
<%
Server.ScriptTimeout=600
Response.Buffer=True
Response.Expires=0

If (VarType(Application("~WC~WebClassManager")) = 0) Then
    Application.Lock
    If (VarType(Application("~WC~WebClassManager")) = 0) Then
        Set Application("~WC~WebClassManager") = _
            Server.CreateObject("WebClassRuntime.WebClassManager")
    End If
    Application.UnLock
End If

Application("~WC~WebClassManager").ProcessRetainInstanceWebClass _
    "BookWebApp.BookWebClass", _
    "~WC~BookWebApp.BookWebClass", _
    Server, _
    Application, _
    Session, _
    Request, _
    Response
%>
```

The difference is that the *ProcessRetainInstanceWebClass* method of the *WebClassManager* object is used instead of the *ProcessNoStateWebClass* method. The *ProcessRetainInstanceWebClass* method has an additional parameter ("~WC~BookWebApp.BookWebClass"), which is the name of the session that should be kept alive. Subsequent accesses to the application by the same user utilize the existing Web class instance by retrieving a reference to it using the same session name. Using this mechanism to maintain information between requests relies on the browser accepting cookies from the server. The server sends the name for the session as a cookie to the browser when it first accesses the application. Subsequently, whenever the browser accesses the application (until the user terminates the browser), it passes the session name cookie back to the Web server. This is how the server knows which session to associate with the request. If the user of the application has set his or her browser to refuse cookies, no session name information can be passed as a cookie. In this situation, even though we've set the *StateManagement* property of the Web class to *wcRetainInstance*, the server will generate a new session for the browser because it has no information that the browser has previously established a session on the server.

The same problem arises if we use the *Session* object directly from within our application—the browser cannot be associated with a session without accepting a cookie. If the *Session* object is available to us, we could store a user object in it to maintain our sign-in information. Alternatively, we could simply store a Boolean that gave the *SignedIn* state in the *Session* object.

We can read and write cookies directly from our application by using the *Cookies* collections of the *Response* and *Request* objects. We can control the existence of the cookies we write by setting the *Expires* property. This means that, unlike the *Session* object, we can keep information alive after the browser has been terminated so that the information can be used the next time the browser is started and our application accessed. Cookies that stay alive like this are stored permanently (until they expire, that is) on the user's hard drive, so even if the user has accepted a cookie, there is no absolute guarantee that it will still be there the next time the browser program is run.

Another mechanism that can be used to transfer data back and forth between the server and browser is to set and query the *URLData* property of the Web class. This property works by storing extra information with URLs written in pages that are sent out to the browser. If any of these URLs are activated in the browser and initiate a request on the server, the *URLData* property of the Web class is set to reflect the data that is sent back.

CONCLUSION

We've investigated many of the features available to Visual Basic developers who want to (or have to) develop Web applications. In the process, we've produced the skeleton of a functioning application—nothing to set the world on fire, but it's a start nonetheless.

This IIS Application template allows Visual Basic developers to use existing skills to create Web applications. However, to really start developing Web applications, developers should have a good knowledge of HTML, even if they don't have to write the code that is displayed in browsers. A knowledge of HTML will help Visual Basic developers get the most of the limited interaction between browser and server. Web developers also need to understand and control the lifetime of their applications and the data they rely on for operation. This definitely needs more careful consideration than for a standard Visual Basic project. Knowledge of ASP will also stand Web developers in good stead, since Web applications created with Visual Basic are based on this technology. The core objects within a Web class (*Request* and *Response*) are ASP objects, which is certainly a good reason to learn about ASP.

To produce powerful Web applications, the developers will almost certainly have to move away from a purely server-based application with the thinnest of clients and incorporate client-side scripting, DHTML, ActiveX components, and so forth, in their overall application code. This adds even more to the areas of knowledge that Visual Basic developers must enter.

No doubt that Visual Basic 6, with its IIS Application template, will kick start the development of many Web-based applications.

Programming with **V**ariants

Jon has been programming with Microsoft Windows since the mid-1980s. Originally working with C, he now uses Visual Basic for all his programming tasks. He has worked on retail software, such as the PagePlus DTP package, and a lot of other custom software in the corporate environment. Jon has also taught programming and written various articles about it. He is currently working on graphics software for business presentations.

JON BURN

Microsoft Visual Basic 6 further enhances the Variant data type from the previous version so that it can now hold user-defined types (UDTs). This creates yet another reason why you should become familiar with Variants and what they can do. In this chapter I will take an in-depth look at Variants and discuss the benefits and pitfalls of programming with them.

OVERVIEW OF VARIANTS

Variants were first introduced in version 2 of Visual Basic as a flexible data type that could hold each of the simple data types. The Variant data type was extended substantially with version 4 to include Byte, Boolean, Error, Objects, and Arrays, and a little further with version 5 to include the Decimal data type. The Decimal data type was the first data type that was not available as a "first class" data type—it is available only within a Variant—and you cannot directly declare a variable as a Decimal.

In Visual Basic 6, UDTs have been added to the list, effectively completing the set. Now a Variant can be assigned any variable or constant, whatever the type.

A variety of functions convert to these subtypes and test for these subtypes. Table 4-1 shows the development of the Variant data type through the versions of Visual Basic, along with the matching functions.

TABLE 4-1   **THE EVOLUTION OF VARIANTS**

Type	Visual Basic Name	Visual Basic Version	Convert Function	Test Function
0	Empty	2	= Empty	IsEmpty
1	Null	2	= Null	IsNull
2	Integer	2	CInt	IsNumeric*
3	Long	2	CLng	IsNumeric
4	Single	2	CSng	IsNumeric
5	Double	2	CDbl	IsNumeric
6	Currency	2	CCur	IsNumeric
7	Date	2	CVDate/CDate	IsDate
8	String	2	CStr	
9	Object	4		IsObject
10	Error	4	CVErr	IsError
11	Boolean	4	CBool	
12	Variant	4	CVar	
13	Data Object	4		
14	Decimal	5	CDec	IsNumeric
17	Byte	4	CByte	
36	UDT	6		
8192	Array	4	Array	IsArray
16384	ByRef	Never?		

* Strictly speaking, *IsNumeric* tests to see if a variable can be converted to a numeric value, and is not simply reporting on a Variant's subtype.

INTERNAL STRUCTURE

A Variant always takes up at least 16 bytes of memory and is structured as shown in Figure 4-1.

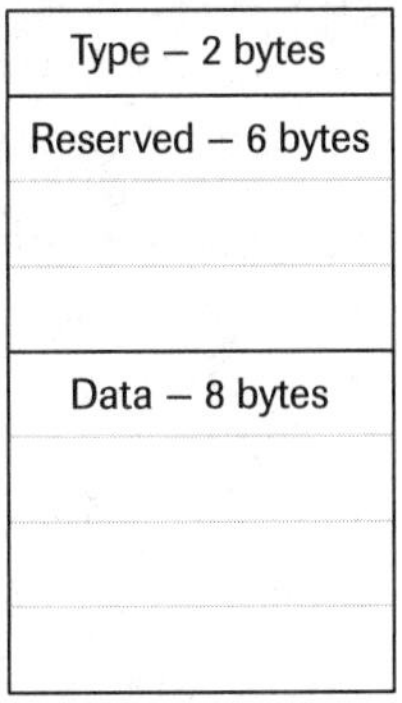

FIGURE 4-1

The structure of a Variant

| Type – 2 bytes |
| Reserved – 6 bytes |
| |
| Data – 8 bytes |
| |
| |

The first two bytes correspond to the value returned by the *VarType* function. (The *VarType* return values are defined as constants in the *VbVarType* enumeration.) For example, if the *VarType* is 2 (the value of the constant *vbInteger*), the Variant has a subtype of Integer. You cannot change this value directly, but the conversion functions (such as *CInt*) will do this for you.

The Reserved bytes have no documented function yet; their principal purpose is to pad the structure out to 16 bytes. The Data area holds the value of the variable, if the value fits into 8 bytes; otherwise, the Data area holds a pointer to the data (as with strings and so on). The type indicates how the Data portion of the Variant is to be understood or interpreted.

In this way, Variants are self-describing, meaning they contain within them all the information necessary to use them.

USING VARIANTS INSTEAD OF SIMPLE DATA TYPES

In this section I'll discuss the pros and cons of using Variants in place of simple data types such as Integer, Long, Double, and String. This is an unorthodox practice—the standard approach is to avoid the use of Variants for a number of reasons. We'll look at the counterarguments first.

Performance Doesn't Matter

Every journal article on optimizing Visual Basic includes a mention of how Variants are slower than underlying first-class data types. This should come as no surprise. For example, when iterating through a sequence with a Variant of subtype Integer, the interpreted or compiled code must decode the structure of the Variant every time the code wants to use its integer value, instead of accessing an integer value directly. There is bound to be an overhead to doing this.

Plenty of authors have made a comparison using a Variant as a counter in a *For* loop, and yes, a Variant Integer takes about 50 percent more time than an Integer when used as a loop counter. This margin decreases as the data type gets more complex, so a Variant Double is about the same as a Double, whereas, surprisingly, a Variant Currency is quicker than a Currency. If you are compiling to native code, the proportions can be much greater in certain cases.

Is this significant? Almost always it is not. The amount of time that would be saved by not using Variants would be dwarfed by the amount of time spent in loading and unloading forms and controls, painting the screen, talking to databases, and so on. Of course, this depends on the details of your own application, but in most cases it is highly unlikely that converting local variables from Variants to Integers and Strings will speed up your code *noticeably*.

When optimizing, you benefit by looking at the bigger picture. If your program is too slow, you should reassess the whole architecture of your system, concentrating in particular on the database and network aspects. Then look at user interface and algorithms. If your program is still so locally computation-intensive and time-critical that you think significant time can be saved by using Integers rather than Variants, you should be considering writing the critical portion in C++ and placing this in a DLL.

Taking a historical perspective, machines continue to grow orders of magnitude faster, which allows software to take more liberties with performance. Nowadays, it is better to concentrate on writing your code so that it works, is robust, and is extensible. If you need to sacrifice efficiency in order to do this, so be it—your code will still run fast enough anyway.

Memory Doesn't Matter

A common argument against Variants is that they take up more memory than do other data types. In place of an Integer, which normally takes just 2 bytes of memory, a Variant of 16 bytes is taking eight times more space. The ratio is less, of course, for other underlying types, but the Variant always contains some wasted space.

The question is, as with the issue of performance in the previous section, how significant is this? Again I think not very. If your program has some extremely large arrays—say, tens of thousands of integers—an argument could be made to allow Integers to be used. But they are the exception. All your normal variables in any given program are going to make no perceptible difference whether they are Variants or not.

I'm not saying that using Variants improves performance or memory. It doesn't. What I'm saying is that the effect Variants have is not a big deal—at least, not a big enough deal to outweigh the reasons for using them.

Type Safety

A more complex argument is the belief that Variants are poor programming style—that they represent an unwelcome return to the sort of dumb macro languages that encouraged sloppy, buggy programming.

The argument maintains that restricting variables to a specific type allows various logic errors to be trapped at compile time, an obviously good thing. Variants, in theory, take away this ability.

To understand this issue fully we must first look at the way non-Variant variables behave. In the following pages I have split this behavior into four key parts of the language, and have contrasted how Variants behave compared to simple data types in each of these four cases:

- Assignment
- Function Calls
- Operators and Expressions
- Visual Basic Functions

Case 1: Assignment between incompatible variables

Consider the following code fragment (Example A):

```
Dim i As Integer, s As String
s = "Hello"
i = s
```

What happens? Well, it depends on which version of Visual Basic you run. In pre-OLE versions of Visual Basic you got a *Type mismatch* error at compile time. In Visual Basic 6, there are no errors at compile time, but you get the *Type mismatch* trappable error 13 at run time when the program encounters the *i = s* line of code.

NOTE

Visual Basic 4 was rewritten using the OLE architecture; thus, versions 3 and earlier are "pre-OLE."

The difference is that the error occurs at run time instead of being trapped when you compile. Instead of you finding the error, your users do. This is a *bad* thing.

The situation is further complicated because it is not the fact that *s* is a String and *i* is an Integer that causes the problem. It is the actual *value* of *s* that determines whether the assignment can take place.

This code succeeds, with *i* set to 1234 (Example B):

```
Dim i As Integer, s As String
s = "1234"
i = s
```

This code in Example C does not succeed (you might have thought that *i* would be set to 0, but this is not the case):

```
Dim i as Integer, s As String
s = ""
i = s
```

These examples demonstrate why you get the error only at run time. At compile time the compiler cannot know what the value of *s* will be, and it is the value of *s* that decides whether an error occurs.

The behavior is exactly the same with this piece of code (Example D):

```
Dim i As Integer, s As String
s = ""
i = CInt(s)
```

As in Example C, a type mismatch error will occur. In fact, Example C is exactly the same as Example D. In Example C, a hidden call to the *CInt* function takes place. The rules that determine whether *CInt* will succeed are the same as the rules that determine whether the plain *i* = *s* will succeed. This is known as *implicit type conversion*, although some call it "evil" type coercion.

The conversion functions *CInt*, *CLng*, and so on, are called implicitly whenever there is an assignment between variables of different data types. The actual functions are implemented within the system library file OLEAUT32.DLL. If you look at the exported functions in this DLL, you'll see a mass of conversion functions. For example, you'll see *VarDecFromCy* to convert a Currency to a Decimal, or *VarBstrFromR8* to convert a string from an 8-byte Real, such as a Double. The code in this OLE DLL function determines the rules of the conversion within Visual Basic.

If the *CInt* function had worked the same way as *Val* does, the programming world would've been spared a few bugs (Example E).

```
Dim i As Integer, s As String
s = ""
i = Val(s)
```

This example succeeds because *Val* has been defined to return 0 when passed the empty string. The OLE conversion functions, being outside the mandate of Visual Basic itself, simply have different rules (Examples F and G).

```
Dim i As Integer, s As String
s = "1,234"
i = Val(s)
```

```
Dim i As Integer, s As String
s = "1,234"
i = CInt(s)
```

Examples F and G also yield different results. In Example F, *i* becomes 1, but in Example G, *i* becomes 1234. In this case the OLE conversion functions are more powerful in that they can cope with the thousands separator. Further, they also take account of the locale, or regional settings. Should your machine's regional settings be changed to German standard, Example G will yield 1 again, not 1234, because in German the comma is used as the decimal point rather than as a thousands separator. This can have both good and bad side effects.

These code fragments, on the other hand, succeed in all versions of Visual Basic (Examples H and I):

```
Dim i As Variant, s As Variant
s = "Hello"
i = s
```

```
Dim i As Variant, s As Variant
s = "1234"
i = s
```

In both the above cases, *i* is still a string, but why should that matter? By using Variants throughout our code, we eliminate the possibility of type mismatches during assignment. In this sense, using Variants can be even safer than using simple data types, because they reduce the number of run-time errors.

Let's look now at another fundamental part of the syntax and again contrast how Variants behave compared to simple data types.

LOCALE EFFECTS

Suppose you were writing a little calculator program, where the user types a number into a text box and the program displays the square of this number as the contents of the text box change.

```
Private Sub Text1_Change()
    If IsNumeric(Text1.Text) Then
        Label1.Caption = Text1.Text * Text1.Text
    Else
        Label1.Caption = ""
    End If
End Sub
```

Note that the *IsNumeric* test verifies that it is safe to multiply the contents of the two text boxes without fear of type mismatch problems. Suppose "1,000" was typed into the text box—the label underneath would show 1,000,000 or 1, depending on the regional settings.

On the one hand, it's good that you get this international behavior without performing any extra coding, but it could also be a problem if the user was not conforming to the regional setting in question. Further, to prevent this problem, if a number is to be written to a database or file, it should be written as a number *without formatting*, in case it is read at a later date on a machine where the settings are different.

Also, you should also avoid writing any code yourself that parses numeric strings. For example, if you were trying to locate the decimal point in a number using string functions, you might have a problem:

```
InStr(53.6, ".")
```

This line of code will return 3 on English/American settings, but 0 on German settings.

Note, finally, that Visual Basic itself does *not* adhere to this convention in its own source code. The number 53.6 means the same whatever the regional settings. We all take this for granted, of course.

Case 2: Function parameters and return types

Consider the following procedure:

```
Sub f(ByVal i As Integer, ByVal s As String)
End Sub
```

This procedure is called by the following code:

```
Dim i As Integer, s As String
s = "Hello"
i = 1234

Call f(s, i)
```

You'll notice I put the parameters in the wrong order.

With pre-OLE versions of Visual Basic you get a *Parameter Type Mismatch* error *at compile time*, but in Visual Basic 4, 5, and 6 the situation is the same as in the previous example—a *run-time* type mismatch, depending on the *value* in *s*, and whether the implicit *CInt* could work.

Instead, the procedure could be defined using Variants:

```
Sub f(ByVal i As Variant, ByVal s As Variant)
End Sub
```

The problem is that you might reasonably expect that after assigning 6.4 to *x* in the procedure *subByRef*, which is declared in the parameter list as a Variant, *Debug.Print* would show 6.4. But instead it shows only 6.

Now no run-time errors or compile-time type mismatch errors occur. Of course, it's not necessarily so obvious by looking at the declaration what the parameters mean, but then that's what the parameter name is for.

Returning to our survey of how Variants behave compared to simple data types, we now look at expressions involving Variants.

Case 3: Operators

I have already suggested, for the purposes of assignment and function parameters and return values, that using Variants cuts down on problematic run-time errors. Does this also apply to the use of Visual Basic's own built-in functions and operators? The answer is, "It depends on the operator or function involved."

Arithmetic operators   All the arithmetic operators (such as +, −, *, \, /, and ^) evaluate their parameters at *run time* and throw the ubiquitous type mismatch error if the parameters do not apply. With arithmetic operators, there is neither an advantage nor a disadvantage to using Variants instead of simple data types; in either case, it's the value, not the data type, that determines whether the operation can take place. In Example A, we get type mismatch errors on both lines:

```
Dim s As String, v As Variant
s = "Fred"
v = "Fred"
s = s - s
v = v - v
```

But in Example B, these lines both succeed:

```
Dim s As String, v As Variant
s = "123"
v = "123"
s = s - s
v = v - v
```

A lot of implicit type conversion is going on here. The parameters of "-" are converted at run time to Doubles before being supplied to the subtraction operator itself. *CDbl("Fred")* does not work, so both lines in Example A fail. *CDbl("123")* does work, so the subtraction succeeds in both lines of Example B.

There is one slight difference between *v* and *s* after the assignments in Example B: *s* is a string of length 1 containing the value 0, while *v* is a Variant of subtype Double containing the value 0. The subtraction operator is defined as returning a Double, so 0 is returned in both assignments. This is fine for *v - v*, which becomes a Variant of subtype Double, with value 0. On the other hand, *s* is a string, so *CStr* is called to convert the Double value to 0.

All other arithmetic operators behave in a similar way to subtraction, with the exception of +.

OPTION "STRICT TYPE CHECKING"

Some other authors have argued for the inclusion of another option along the lines of "Option Explicit" that would enforce strict type checking. Assignment between variables of different types would not be allowed and such errors would be trapped at compile time. The conversion functions such as *CInt* and *CLng* would need to be used explicitly for type conversion to take place.

This would effectively return the Visual Basic language to its pre-OLE style, and Examples A, B, and C on pages 137 and 138 would all generate compile-time errors. Example D would still return a *run-time* type mismatch, however.

Examples E, F, and G would succeed with the same results as above. In other words, code using Variants would be unaffected by the feature.

Comparison operators   We normally take the comparison operators (such as <, >, and =) for granted and don't think too much about how they behave. With Variants, comparison operators can occasionally cause problems.

The comparison operators are similar to the addition operator in that they have behavior defined for both numeric and string operands, and unfortunately this behavior is different.

A string comparison will not necessarily give the same result as numeric comparison on the same operands, as the following examples show:

```
Dim a, b, a1, b1
a = "1,000"
b = "500"
a1 = CDbl(a)
b1 = CDbl(b)
' Now a1 > b1 but a < b
```

Notice also that all four variables—*a*, *b*, *a1*, and *b1*—are *numeric* in the sense that *IsNumeric* will return True for them.

As with string and number addition, the net result is that you must always be aware of the potential bugs here and ensure that the operands are converted to a numeric or string subtype before the operator is used.

Case 4: Visual Basic's own functions

Visual Basic's own functions work well with Variants, with a few exceptions. I won't cover this exhaustively but just pick out some special points.

The Visual Basic mathematical functions works fine with Variants because they each have a single behavior that applies only to numerics, so there is no confusion. In this way, these functions are similar to the arithmetic operators. Provided the Variant passes the *IsNumeric* test, the function will perform correctly, regardless of the underlying subtype.

```
a =  Hex("1,234")
a = Log("1,234")
'etc.. No problems here
```

Type mismatch errors will be raised should the parameter not be numeric.

The string functions do not raise type mismatch errors, because all simple data types can be converted to strings (for this reason there is no *IsString* function in Visual Basic). Thus, you can apply the string functions to Variants with numeric subtypes—*Mid*, *InStr*, and so forth all function as you would expect.

However, exercise extreme caution because of the effect regional settings can have on the string version of a numeric. (This was covered earlier in the chapter.)

The function *Len* is an interesting exception, because once again it has different behavior depending on what the data type of the parameter is. For simple strings *Len* returns the length of the string. For simple nonstring data *Len* returns the number of bytes used to store the variable. However, less well known is the fact that for Variants, it returns the length of the Variant as if it were converted to a string, *regardless of the Variant's actual subtype.*

```
Dim v As Variant, i As Integer
i = 100
v = i
' The following are now true:
' Len(i) = 2
' Len(v) = 3
```

This provides one of the only ways of distinguishing a simple Integer variable from a Variant of subtype Integer at run time.

Flexibility

Some time ago, while I was working for a big software house, I heard this (presumably exaggerated) anecdote about how the company had charged a customer $1 million to upgrade the customer's software. The customer had grown in size, and account codes required five digits instead of four. That was all there was to it. Of course, the client was almost certainly being ripped off, but there are plenty of examples in which a little lack of foresight proves very costly to repair. The Year 2000 problem is a prime example. It pays to allow yourself as much flexibility and room for expansion that can be reasonably foreseen. For example, if you need to pass the number of books as a parameter to a function, why only allow less than 32,768 books (the maximum value of an Integer)? You might also need to allow for half a book too, so you wouldn't want to restrict it to Integer or Long. You'd want to allow floating-point inputs. You could at this point declare the parameter to be of type Double because this covers the range and precision of Integer and Long as well as handling floating points. But even this approach is still an unnecessary restriction. Not only might you still want the greater precision of Currency or Decimal, you might also want to pass in inputs such as *An unknown number of books.*

The solution is to declare the number of books as a Variant. The only commitment that is made is about the meaning of the parameter—that it contains a number of books—and no restriction is placed on that number. As much flexibility as possible is maintained, and the cost of those account code upgrades will diminish.

```
Function ReadBooks(ByVal numBooks As Variant)
    ' Code in here to read books
End Function
```

Suppose we want to upgrade the function so that we can pass *An unknown number of books* as a valid input. The best way of doing this is to pass a Variant of subtype Null. Null is specifically set aside for the purpose of indicating *not known*.

If the parameter had not been a Variant, you would have had some choices:

- Add another parameter to indicate that the number is unknown. A drawback of this approach is that a modification would be required everywhere this function is called. That way lies the million-dollar upgrade. If the parameter were *Optional*, you would get away with this approach, but only the first time.

- Allow a special value to indicate *unknown*—perhaps –1 or maybe –32768. We might create a constant of this value so that the code reads a little better—*Const bkNotKnown = –1*—and use that. This approach leads to bugs. Sooner or later, you or another programmer will forget that –1 is reserved and use it as an ordinary value of number of books, however unlikely that may seem at the time you choose the value of the constant.

If the parameters are Variants, you avoid these unsatisfactory choices when modifying the functions. In the same way, parameters and return types of class methods, as well as properties, should all be declared as Variants instead of first-class data types.

HUNGARIAN NOTATION

The portion of Hungarian notation that refers to data type has little relevance when programming with Variants. Indeed, as variables of different data types can be freely assigned and interchanged, the notation has little relevance in Visual Basic at all.

I still use variable prefixes, but only to assist in the categorization of variables at a semantic level. So, for example, "nCount" would be a *number* that is used as a counter of something. The *n* in this instance stands for a general numeric, not an Integer.

Defensive Coding

I have extolled the virtues of using Variants and the flexibility that they give. To be more precise, they allow the *interface* to be flexible. By declaring the number of books to be a Variant, you make it unlikely that the data type of that parameter will need to be modified again.

This flexibility of Variants has a cost to it. What happens if we call the function with an input that doesn't make sense?

```
N = ReadBooks("Ugh")
```

Inside the function, we are expecting a number—so what will it make of this? If we are performing some arithmetic operations on the number, we risk a type mismatch error when a Variant with these contents is passed. You must assert your preconditions for the function to work. If, as in this instance, the input must be numeric, be sure that this is the case:

```
Function ReadBooks(ByVal input As Variant) As Variant
    If IsNumeric(input) Then
        ' Do stuff, return no error
    Else
        ' Return error
    End If
End Function
```

In other words, you code defensively by using the set of *Is* functions to verify that a parameter is suitable for the operation you're going to perform on it.

You might think about using *Debug.Assert* in this instance, but it is no help at run time because all the calls to the *Assert* method are stripped out in compilation. So you would still need to implement your own checks anyway.

Of course, verifying that your input parameter is appropriate and satisfies the preconditions is not just about checking the type. It would also involve range checks, ensuring that we are not dividing by 0, and so on.

Is this feasible?   In practice, coding defensively like this can become a major chore, and it is easy to slip up or not bother with it. It would be prudent if you were writing an important[1] piece of component code, especially if the interface is public, to place defensive checks at your component entry points. But it is equally likely that a lot of the time you will not get around to this.

---

1. The definition of which code is *important* is naturally a personal one.

What are the consequences of *not* performing the defensive checks? While this naturally depends on what you are doing in the function, it is most likely that if there is an error it will be a type mismatch error. If the string *Ugh* in the previous example was used by an operator or built-in function that only worked with numerics, a type mismatch would occur. Interestingly, had the parameter to *ReadBooks* been declared as a Double instead of a Variant, this same error would be raised if the string *Ugh* was passed.

The only difference is that in the case of the Variant the error is raised *within* the function, not outside it. You have the choice of passing this error back to the calling client code or just swallowing the error and carrying on. The approach you take will depend on the particular circumstances and your preferences.

Using the Variant as a General Numeric Data Type

Don't get sidetracked by irrelevant machine-specific details. Almost all the time, we want to deal with numbers. For example, consider your thought process when you choose between declaring a variable to be of type Integer or type Long. You might consider what the likely values of the variable are going to be, worry a little bit about the effect on performance or memory usage, and maybe check to see how you declared a similar variable elsewhere so that you can be consistent. Save time—get into the habit of declaring all these variables as Variants.

 NOTE

All variables in my code are either Variants or references to classes. Consequently, a lot of code starts to look like this.

```
Dim Top As Variant
Dim Left As Variant
Dim Width As Variant
Dim Height As Variant
```

After a time I started to take advantage of the fact that Variants are the default, so my code typically now looks like this:

```
Dim Top, Left, Width, Height
```

I see no problem with this, but your current Visual Basic coding standards will more than likely prohibit it. You might think about changing them.

VARIANT BUGS WHEN PASSING PARAMETERS BY REFERENCE

Variants do not always work well when passed by reference, and can give rise to some hard-to-spot bugs. The problem is illustrated in the following example:

```
Private Sub Form_Load()
    Dim i As Integer
    i = 3
    subByVal i
    subByRef i
End Sub

Private Sub subByVal(ByVal x As Variant)
    x = 6.4
    Debug.Print x       'shows 6.4
End Sub

Private Sub subByRef(x As Variant)
    x = 6.4
    Debug.Print x       'shows 6
End Sub
```

Notice that the only difference between the procedures *subByVal* and *subByRef* is that the parameter is passed *ByVal* in *subByVal* and *ByRef* in *subByRef*. When *subByVal* is called, the actual parameter *i* is of type Integer. In *subByVal*, a new parameter *x* is created as a Variant of subtype Integer, and is initialized with the value 3. In other words, the subtype of the Variant *within* the procedure is defined by the type of the variable that the procedure was actually called with. When *x* is then set to a value of 6.4, it converts to a Variant of subtype Double with value 6.4. Straightforward.

When *subByRef* is called, Visual Basic has a bit more of a problem. The Integer is passed by reference, so Visual Basic cannot allow noninteger values to be placed in it. Instead of converting the Integer to a Variant, Visual Basic leaves it as an Integer. Thus, even in the procedure *subByRef* itself, where *x* is declared as a Variant, *x* is really an Integer. The assignment of *x = 6.4* will result in an implicit *CInt* call and *x* ends up with the value 6. Not so straightforward.

Procedures like *subByVal* are powerful because they can perform the same task, whatever the data type of the actual parameters. They can even perform different tasks depending on the type of the actual parameter, though this can get confusing.

Procedures like *subByRef* lead to bugs—avoid them by avoiding passing by reference.

USING VARIANTS INSTEAD OF OBJECTS

Earlier in the chapter, I extolled the use of Variants in the place of simple data types like Integer and String. Does the same argument apply for objects?

Put simply, the answer is no, because there is considerable extra value added by declaring a variable to be of a specific object type. Unlike the simple data types, we can get useful *compile-time* error messages that help prevent bugs. If the Variant (or Object) data type was used, these errors would surface only at run time—a *bad* thing.

By way of explanation, consider the following simple example. In this project there is one class, called *Cow*, which has few properties, such as *Age*, *TailLength*, and so forth. We then create a routine

```
Private Sub AgeMessage(c As Cow)
    MsgBox c.Age
End Sub
```

If you accidentally misspell *Age* and instead type

```
MsgBox c.Agg
```

provided *c* is declared as *Cow*, you will receive a *compile-time* error message so that you can correct it. If the parameter was declared as a Variant (or Object), Visual Basic cannot know whether there is a legitimate property of *c* called *Agg* until, at run time, it actually knows what the object is. Hence, all you get is a run-time error 438 instead.

Notice how this argument does *not* apply back to simple data types. Although simple data types do not have properties, they do have certain operators that may or may not be well defined for them. However, a piece of code such as this

```
Dim s As String
s = s * s
```

where the * operator is undefined for strings, will result in a *run-time* type mismatch, not a compile-time error. So the advantage of not declaring as Variant is lost.

OTHER VARIANT SUBTYPES

Flexibility is the fundamental reason to use Variants. But the built-in flexibility of Variants is not advertised enough, and consequently they tend to be underused. The use of *Empty*, *Null*, and Variant arrays—and now in version 6, UDTs—remain underused in the Visual Basic programmer community.

Empty and *Null*

Any uninitialized Variant has the *Empty* value until something is assigned to it. This is true for all variables of type Variant, whether *Public*, *Private*, *Static*, or local. This is the first feature to distinguish Variants from other data types—you cannot determine whether any other data type is uninitialized.

As well as testing for *VarType* zero, a shorthand function exists—*IsEmpty*—which does the same thing but is more readable.

In early versions of Visual Basic, once a Variant was given a value, the only way to reset it to *Empty* was to assign it to another Variant that itself was empty. In Visual Basic 5 and 6, you can also set it to the keyword *Empty*, as follows:

```
v1 = Empty
```

I like *Empty*, although I find it is one of those things that you forget about and sometimes miss opportunities to use. Coming from a C background, where there is no equivalent, isn't much help either. But it does have uses in odd places, so it's worth keeping it in the back of your mind. File under miscellaneous.

Of course, *Null* is familiar to everyone as that database "no value" value, found in all SQL databases. But as a Variant subtype it can be used to mean *no value* or *invalid value* in a more general sense—in fact, in any sense that you want to use it. Conceptually, it differs from *Empty* in that it implies you have *intentionally* set a Variant to this value for some reason, whereas *Empty* implies you just haven't gotten around to doing anything with the Variant yet.

As with *Empty*, you have an *IsNull* function and a *Null* keyword that can be used directly.

Visual Basic programmers tend to convert a variable with a Null value—read, say from a database—to something else as quickly as possible. I've seen plenty of code where Null is converted to empty strings or zeros as soon as it's pulled out of a recordset, even though this usually results in information loss and some bad assumptions. I think this stems from the fact that the tasks we want to perform with data items—such as display them in text boxes or do calculations with them—often result in the all too familiar error 94, "Invalid use of Null."

This is exacerbated by the fact that Null propagates through expressions. Any arithmetic operator (+, −, *, /, \, Mod, ^) or comparison operator (<, >, =, <>) that has a Null as one of its operands will result in a Null being the value of the overall expression, irrespective of the type or value of the other operand. This can lead to some well-known bugs, such as:

```
v = Null
If v = Null Then
    MsgBox "Hi"
End if
```

In this code, the message "Hi" will *not* be displayed because as *v* is Null, and = is just a comparison operator here, the value of the expression *v = Null* is itself Null. And Null is treated as *False* in *If...Then* clauses.

The propagation rule has some exceptions. The string concatenation operator & treats Null as an empty string "" if one of its operands is a Null. This explains, for example, the following shorthand way of removing Null when reading values from a database:

```
v = "" & v
```

This will leave *v* unchanged if it is a string, unless it is Null, in which case it will convert it to "".

Another set of exceptions is with the logical operators (And, Eqv, Imp, Not, Or, Xor). Here Null is treated as a third truth value, as in standard many-valued logic. Semantically, Null should be interpreted as *unsure* in this context, and this helps to explain the truth tables. For example:

```
v = True And Null
```

gives *v* the value Null, but

```
v = True Or Null
```

gives *v* the value True. This is because if you know A is true, but are unsure about B, then you are unsure about A and B together, but you are sure about A or B. Follow?

By the way, watch out for the Not operator. Because the truth value of Null lies halfway between True and False, Not Null must evaluate to Null in order to keep the logical model consistent. This is indeed what it does.

```
v = Not Null
If IsNull(v) Then MsgBox "Hi"   ' You guessed it...
```

That's about all on Null—I think it is the trickiest of the Variant subtypes, but once you get to grips with how it behaves, it can add a lot of value.

Arrays

Arrays are now implemented using the OLE data type named *SAFEARRAY*. This is a data type that, like Variants and classes, allows arrays to be *self-describing*. The *LBound* and number of elements for each dimension of the array are stored in this structure. Within the inner workings of OLE, all access to these arrays is through an extensive set of API calls implemented in the system library file OLEAUT32.DLL. You do not get or set the array elements directly, but you use API calls. These API calls use the *LBound* and number of elements to make sure they always write within the allocated area. This is why they are *safe* arrays—attempts to write to elements outside the allowed area are trapped within the API and gracefully dealt with.[2]

The ability to store arrays in Variants was new to Visual Basic 4, and a number of new language elements were introduced to support them such as *Array* and *IsArray*.

To set up a Variant to be an array, you can either assign it to an already existing array or use the *Array* function. The first of these methods creates a Variant whose subtype is the array value (8192) added to the value of the type of the original array. The *Array* function, on the other hand, always creates an array of Variants—*VarType 8204* (which is 8192 plus 12).

The following code shows three ways of creating a Variant array of the numbers 0, 1, 2, 3:

```
Dim v As Variant
Dim a() As Integer
Dim i As Integer

' Different ways to create Variant arrays
' 1. Use the Array function
v = Array(0, 1, 2, 3) 'of little practical use
v = Empty

' 2. Create a normal array, and assign it to a Variant.
' Iterate adding elements using a normal array...
For i = 0 To 3
    ReDim Preserve a(i) As Integer
    a(i) =  i
Next i
```

---

2. Unless this feature is disabled in the compile-time optimization.

```
' ...and copy array to a Variant
v = a
'or
v = a()
' but not v() = a()

v = Empty

' 3. Start off with Array, and then ReDim to preferred size
' avoiding use of intermediate array.
For i = 0 To 3
    ' First time we need to create array
    If IsEmpty(v) Then
        v = Array(i)
    Else
        ' From then on, ReDim Preserve will work on v
        ReDim Preserve v(i)
    End If
    v(i) = i
Next i
```

Notice that the only difference between the last two arrays is that one is a Variant holding an array of integers and the other is a Variant holding an array of Variants. It can be easy to get confused here, look at the following:

```
ReDim a(5) As Variant
```

This code is creating an array of Variants, but this is *not* a Variant array. What consequence does this have? Not much anymore. Before version 6 you could utilize array copying only with Variant arrays, but now you can do this with any variable-sized array.

So what is useful about placing an array in a Variant? As Variants can contain arrays, and they can be arrays of Variants, those contained Variants can themselves be arrays, maybe of Variants, which can also be arrays, and so on and so forth.

Just how deep can these arrays be nested? I don't know if there is a theoretical limit, but in practice I have tested at least 10 levels of nesting. This odd bit of code works fine:

```
Dim v As Variant, i As Integer

' Make v an array of two Variants, each of which is an array
' of two Variants, each of...and so on
For i = 0 To 10
    v = Array(v, v)
```

>>

```
Next i

' Set a value...
v(0)(0)(0)(0)(0)(0)(0)(0)(0)(0)(0) = 23
```

How do these compare to more standard multidimensional arrays? Well, on the positive side, they are much more flexible. The contained arrays—corresponding to the lower dimensions of a multidimensional array—do not have to have the same number of elements. Figure 4-2 explains the difference pictorially.

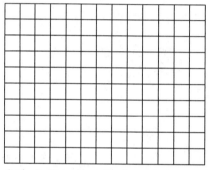

A standard two-dimensional array is a rectangle.

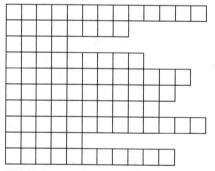

With Variant arrays, you need not waste space.

FIGURE 4-2   *The difference between a standard two-dimensional array (top) and a Variant array (bottom)*

These are sometimes known as *ragged arrays*. As you can see from the diagram, we do not have all the wasted space of a multidimensional array. However you have to contrast that with the fact that the Variant "trees" are harder to set up.

This ability of Variants to hold arrays of Variants permits some interesting new data structures in Visual Basic. One obvious example is a tree. In this piece of code, an entire directory structure is folded up and inserted in a single Variant:

```
Private Sub Form_Load()
    Dim v As Variant
    v = GetFiles("C:\") ' Places contents of C: into v
End Sub

Public Function GetFiles(ByVal vPath As Variant) As Variant
    ' NB cannot use recursion immediately as Dir
    ' does not support it, so get array of files first
    Dim vDir As Variant, vSubDir As Variant, i

    vDir = GetDir(vPath)

    ' Now loop through array, adding subdirectory information.
    If Not IsEmpty(vDir) Then
        For i = LBound(vDir) To UBound(vDir)
            ' If this is a dir, then...
            If (GetAttr(vDir(i)) And vbDirectory) = vbDirectory Then
                ' replace dir name with the dir contents.
                vDir(i) = GetFiles(vDir(i))
            End If
        Next i
    End If

    GetFiles = vDir

End Function

Private Function GetDir(ByVal vPath As Variant) As Variant
    ' This function returns a Variant that is an array
    ' of file and directory names (not including "." or "..")
    ' for a given directory path.
    Dim vRet As Variant, fname As Variant

    ' Add \ if necessary.
    If Right$(vPath, 1) <> "\" Then vPath = vPath & "\"

    ' Call the Dir function in a loop.
    fname = Dir(vPath, vbNormal & vbDirectory)
    Do While fname <> ""
        If fname <> "." And fname <> ".." Then
            vRet = AddElement(vRet, vPath & fname)
        End If
        fname = Dir()
    Loop
```

>>

>>

```
                        ' Return the array.
                        GetDir = vRet
                    End Function


                    Public Function AddElement(ByVal vArray As Variant, _
                        ByVal vElem As Variant) As Variant
                        ' This function adds an element to a Variant array
                        ' and returns an array with the element added to it.

                        Dim vRet As Variant ' To be returned

                        If IsEmpty(vArray) Then
                            ' First time through, create an array of size 1.
                            vRet = Array(vElem)
                        Else
                            vRet = vArray
                            ' From then on, ReDim Preserve will work.
                            ReDim Preserve vRet(UBound(vArray) + 1)
                            vRet(UBound(vRet)) = vElem
                        End If

                        AddElement = vRet

                    End Function
```

USING + FOR STRING CONCATENATION

This misconceived experiment with operator overloading was considered bad form even back in the days of Visual Basic 2, when the string concatenation operator & was first introduced. Yet it's still supported in Visual Basic 6. In particular, since version 4 brought in extensive implicit type conversion between numerics and strings, this issue has become even more important. It's easy to find examples of how you can get tripped up. Can you honestly be confident of what the following will print?

```
Debug.Print "56" + 48
Debug.Print "56" + "48"
Debug.Print "56" - "48"
```

What *should* happen is that adding two strings has the same effect as subtracting, multiplying, or dividing two strings—that is, the addition operator should treat the strings as numeric if it can; otherwise, it should generate a type mismatch error. Unfortunately, this is not the case. The only argument for why the operator stays in there, causing bugs, is backward compatibility.

One point to note about this code is that this is an extremely efficient way of storing a tree structure, because as *v* is a multidimensional *ragged* array, the structure contains less wasted space than its equivalent multidimensional fixed-sized array. This contrasts with the accusation usually leveled at Variants, that they waste a lot of memory space.

User-Defined Types

The rehabilitation of UDTs was the biggest surprise for me in version 6 of Visual Basic. It had looked as if UDTs were being gradually squeezed out of the language. In particular, the new language features such as classes, properties, and methods did not seem to include UDTs. Before version 6, it was not possible to

1. have a UDT as a public property of a class or form.
2. pass a UDT as a parameter *ByVal* to a sub or function.
3. have a UDT as a parameter to a public method of a class or form.
4. have a UDT as the return type of a public method of a class or form.
5. place a UDT into a Variant.

But this has suddenly changed and now it is possible in version 6 to perform most of these to a greater or lesser extent. In this chapter, I am really only concentrating on the last point, that of placing a UDT into a Variant.

Restrictions are imposed on the sorts of UDTs that can be placed in a Variant. They must be declared within a public object module. This rules out their use within Standard EXE programs, as these do not have public object modules. This is a Microsoft ActiveX–only feature. Internally, the *Data* portion of the Variant structure is always a simple pointer to an area of memory where the UDT's content is sitting. The *Type* is always 36. This prompts the question of where and how the meta-data describing the fields of the UDT is kept. Remember that all other Variant subtypes are self-describing, so UDTs must be, too. The way it works is that from the Variant you can also obtain an *IRecordInfo* interface pointer. That interface has functions that return everything you want to know about the UDT.

We are able to improve substantially on the nesting ability demonstrated earlier with Variant arrays. While it is still impossible to have a member field of a UDT be that UDT itself—a hierarchy that is commonly needed—you can use a Variant and sidestep the circular reference trap. The following code shows a simple example of an employee structure (*Emp*) in an imaginary, not-so-progressive organization (apologies for the lack of originality). The boss and an array of workers are declared as Variant—these will all in fact be *Emps* themselves. *GetEmp* is just a function that generates *Emps*.

```
' In Class1
Public Type Emp
    Name As Variant
    Boss As Variant
    Workers() As Variant
 End Type

' Anywhere Class1 is visible:
Sub main()
    Dim a As Emp
    a.Name = "Adam"
    a.Boss = GetEmp(1)
    a.Workers = Array(GetEmp(2), GetEmp(3))
End Sub

Private Function GetEmp(ByVal n) As Emp
    Dim x As Emp
    x.Name = "Fred" & n
    GetEmp = x
End Function
```

Note that this code uses the ability to return a UDT from a function. Also, the *Array* function always creates an array of Variants, so this code now works because we can convert the return value of *GetEmp* to a Variant.

INTERFACE INVIOLABILITY

If you're like me, you may well have experienced the frustration of creating ActiveX components (in-process or out-of-process, it doesn't matter) and then realizing you need to make a tiny upgrade.

You don't want to change the interface definition because then your server is no longer compatible, the CLSID has changed, and you get into all the troublesome versioning complexity. Programs and components that use your component will all have problems or be unable to automatically use your upgraded version.

There isn't a lot you can do about this. Visual Basic imposes what is a very good discipline on us with its version compatibility checking, though it is sometimes a bitter pill to swallow.

In this respect, the flexibility gained by using Variants for properties and methods' parameters can be a great headache saver.

One drawback to this is that Visual Basic does not know at compile time the actual type of *Workers*, so you might write errors that will not be found until run time, such as the following:

```
a.Workers.qwert = 74
```

Accessing an invalid property like this will not be caught at compile time. This is analagous to the behavior of using Variants to hold objects described earlier. Similarly, the *VarType* of *a.Workers* is 8204—*vbArray* + *vbVariant*. Visual Basic does not know what is in this array.

If we rewrote the above code like this:

```
' In Class1
Public Type Emp
    Name As Variant
    Boss As Variant
    Workers As Variant
End Type

' Anywhere Class1 is visible:
Sub main()
    Dim a As Emp
    ReDim a.Workers(0 To 1) As Emp

    a.Name = "Adam"
    a.Boss = GetEmp(1)

    a.Workers(0) = GetEmp(2)
    a.Workers(1) = GetEmp(3)
End Sub
```

This time the *VarType* of *a.Workers* is 8228—*vbArray* + *vbUserDefinedType*. In other words, Visual Basic knows that *Workers* is an array of *Emps*, not an array of Variants. This has similarities to the late-bound and early-bound issue with objects and classes. (See "How Binding Affects ActiveX Component Performance" in the Visual Basic Component Tools Guide.) At compile time, however, the checking of valid methods and properties is still not possible because the underlying declaration is Variant.

The alternative way of implementing this code would be to create a class called *Emp* that had other *Emps* within it—I'm sure you've often done something similar to this. What I find interesting about the examples above is the similarity they have with this sort of class/object code—*but no objects are being created here.* We should find performance much improved over a class-based approach because object creation and deletion still take a relatively long time in Visual Basic. This approach differs slightly in that an assignment from one Variant containing a UDT to another Variant results in a deep copy of the UDT. So in the above examples, if you copy an *Emp*, you get a copy of all the fields and their contents. With objects, you are just copying the reference and there is still only one underlying object in existence. Using classes rather than UDTs for this sort of situation is still preferable given the many other advantages of classes, unless you are creating hundreds or thousands of a particular object. In this case, you might find the performance improvement of UDTs compelling.

MORE ON PASSING PARAMETERS BY REFERENCE

You might be wondering, "Why should I avoid passing parameters by reference? It's often very useful." In many situations, passing parameters by reference is indicative of bad design. Just as using global variables is bad design but can be the easy or lazy way out, passing parameters by reference is a shortcut that often backfires at a later date.

Passing parameters by reference is a sign that you don't have the relationships between your functions correct. The mathematical model of a function is of the form:

```
x = f (a,b,c,..)
```

where the function acts on *a,b,c,* and so on to produce result *x*. Both sides of the equal sign are the same value. You can use either *x* or *f(a,b,c,...)* interchangeably.

Likewise in Visual Basic, functions can be used as components in expressions, as this example shows:

```
x = Sqr(Log(y))
```

This is not quite the case in a Visual Basic program, because the function *does* something in addition to returning a value. But it's still most useful to think of the return value *x* as the *result* of what that function *f does*. But if *x* contains the result, the result cannot also be in *a*, *b*, or *c*. In other words, only *x* is changed by the function. This is my simplistic conceptual model of a function, and it is at odds with the notion of passing by reference. Passing a parameter by reference often indicates one of the following:

>>

Functions are trying to do more than one task

This is going to lead to larger functions than need be, functions that are more complex than need be, and functions that are not as useful as they could be. You should break down the functions so that each one does only one task, as in the mathematical model.

A new class needs to be defined

If the function needs to return two related values, say an X and a Y value for a coordinate, create a class or UDT to hold the object that these values relate to, and return that. If the values are not sufficiently related to be able to define a class, you are almost certainly doing too much in the one function. As an example, this

```
GetCenter(f As Form, ByRef X, ByRef Y)
```

would be better written as

```
Set p = GetCenter(f As Form)
```

where *p* is an object of class Point. Alternatively

```
p = GetCenter(f as Form)
```

here *p* is a Variant UDT.

Functions are returning some data and some related meta-data

By *meta-data* I mean a description of the data returned. Functions won't need to return meta-data if you use only self-describing data types. For example, functions that return an array or a single element, depending upon some argument, should return a Variant, which can hold either, and the caller can use *IsArray* to determine what sort of data is returned.

Functions are returning some data and an indication of the function's success

It is quite common to use the return value of a function to return True, False, or perhaps an error code. The actual data value is returned as a parameter by reference. For example, consider this code fragment:

```
bRet = GetFileVersion(ByRef nVersion, filename)
```

Here the version of *filename* is returned by reference, provided the file was found correctly. If the file was not found, the function will return False and *nVersion* will not be accurate. You have a couple of alternatives.

- **Raise errors.** This has always been the Visual Basic way. (For example, Visual Basic's own *Open* works in this way.)

- **Return a Variant and use the *CVErr* function to create a Variant of subtype *vbError* holding the error condition.** The caller can then use *IsError* as follows:

```
nVersion = GetFileVersion(filename)

If IsError(nVersion) Then
    ' nVersion is unreliable, take some action...
Else
    ' nVersion is reliable, use it...
End If
```

Error raising and trapping is not to everyone's taste, so the second option might appeal to you.

Side effects when passing by reference

Bugs result when instances of parameters unexpectedly change their value. To put it at its simplest, parameters changing their value are a side effect, and side effects trip up programmers. If I call the function

```
Dim a, b
a = f(b)
```

it is immediately apparent to me that *a* is likely to change, and probably *b* will not. But I cannot guarantee that without looking at the source code for the function *f*.

It is particularly unfortunate that the default parameter-passing convention is *ByRef*, because it means that you have to do extra typing to avoid *ByRef* parameters. Because of backward compatibility, I don't think there's any chance of this being changed. However, it has been suggested by the Visual Basic team that they could fill in the *ByRef*s automatically on listback in the editor so that people can see exactly what's happening. The problem is that this would alter all old code as it is brought into the editor and cause problems with source code control.

Developing **A**pplications in **W**indows **CE**

My Two CEnts Worth

CHRIS DE BELLOT

During his career, Chris, a TMS Developer, has worked on a number of diverse applications. Chris has a great deal of experience in the three-tier client/server arena and is experienced in object design in Microsoft Visual Basic. A key member of the TMS team, Chris is highly respected for his knowledge, opinions, and experience in the design of user interface code, in particular the design of structured and reusable code, at both the code and business level. Chris is a Microsoft Certified Professional. In his spare time, Chris is a keen commercial aviation enthusiast and enjoys nothing more than landing 747s at London Heathrow's runway 27L using one of his many flight simulators.

I grabbed a beer and settled back down in front of a screen full of Visual Basic code. I'd been working on a killer app and had a few bugs left to find. Behind the project window I could see the news just starting. "Better stop," I thought, "and catch up on what's going on in the world."

My computer is connected to the television, which has a 29-inch screen. It's great for coding because I've finally got enough space for all my windows, and I have the benefit of being able to watch the TV at the same time. This, I tell myself, helps me to concentrate! Since Microsoft Windows CE took off in a big way, a whole load of new appliances have appeared on the market all incorporating Windows CE technology. My TV is just one example. Windows CE has the ability to address quite a few gigabytes of memory and the manufacturers have taken advantage of this by putting video memory in the actual television set; the 3-D video card is also built in. This means that I don't have to have these components stuffed into my PC. The processor and other components are still inside the PC case—the TV is just an I/O device that happens to have a large screen, plenty of RAM, and loads of disk space. The latter comes in handy when I use the Internet functionality built into the Windows CE operating system.

I have lots of other Windows CE devices—a stereo, an intelligent oven that can be programmed with menus on a CD-ROM. But my favorite device is my radio alarm clock. I'm really bad at getting up in the morning, and this little gadget lets me program any sequence of events, such as turning the radio on for half an hour, then chiming every 20 minutes until I get fed up and finally get out of bed. All of this was possible using conventional technology, but when Windows CE came out, the common platform was a real incentive for manufacturers to make all those devices that were perhaps too expensive to justify building before. After all, who in their right mind would take on developing a stereo with speech recognition? Oh well, it's getting a bit late now. I think I'll try out the roast lamb program in my programmable oven. It's just a shame the oven can't prepare the ingredients as well!

OK, so I don't really use my TV as a computer screen and I don't have all those gadgets—I just made it all up. But I do predict that in five years these sorts of gadgets will be commonplace. Windows CE has the potential to create a market in which affordable electronic devices can be built to cater to any need (well, almost!), so watch this space.

What Is Windows CE?

Windows CE is simply a 32-bit, non-PC operating system. You might have seen Windows CE devices, such as the handheld PC (HPC) or the palm-sized PC—these are just some of the many applications run by the Windows CE operating system. So, although this chapter devotes much time to writing applications for the HPC, it is important to realize that these devices are only a small subset of Windows CE applications. Windows CE is designed to be a component-based operating system that can be embedded into any number of devices. Being supplied as a series of configurable components allows Windows CE to meet the stringent memory and size constraints common to many electronic devices.

If you were to compare the number of Microsoft Windows NT and Microsoft Windows 9x machines with the number of 32-bit operating systems throughout the world, you might be surprised to find that Microsoft comprises only a small percentage of the market. Windows CE is Microsoft's attempt to claim a larger percentage of the 32-bit operating system market. One of Microsoft's goals is to have the Windows CE operating system embedded into devices ranging from industrial control systems to everyday consumer devices. Bill Gates recently said at a TechEd conference: "Although Windows 98 is the big thing today, I do expect that two years from now Windows NT and Windows CE volume will be as great, or greater than, Windows 98 volume."

The Windows 9x operating systems at present outsell Windows NT and Windows CE. If Bill Gates' instincts are proven correct, the picture might look drastically different in the year 2000.

Peet Morris, director of The Mandelbrot Set (International) Limited (TMS) and one of the authors of this book, also has high hopes for the future of Windows CE. Peet's view of Windows CE is summed up by the following statement:

> "I think that Windows CE is, and will become more and more, a key technology for our industry. It presents a fantastic new opportunity for developing great software and presents a new, almost unique set of challenges for developers worldwide. As the Technical Director of TMS, I'm determined that we will be a leading provider of both Windows CE–based solutions and, for the developer, the tools and technologies required to fully exploit the opportunity Windows CE presents."

The amount of interest being shown by both the electronics and developer communities is a sure sign that Windows CE is here to stay and that it will have a large impact in the marketplace. I said earlier that Windows CE is a non-PC operating system. At the time of this writing it is already possible to buy palm-sized PCs running Windows 95 with lots of memory and disk space. For programmers looking to implement applications comparable to those on the desktop, however, Windows CE is probably not the best choice of operating systems.

Target Audience

The Windows CE operating system is specifically targeted at independent hardware vendors (IHVs) and original equipment manufacturers (OEMs). Windows NT and Windows 9x are available as software packages that can be installed on a computer; however, Windows CE is designed to reside in read-only memory (ROM). It is therefore not possible for a software developer to simply buy the operating system, install it, and write software for it. The uses of Windows CE are almost unlimited in scope in the OEM and IHV markets, although some types of applications will depend on enhancements being made to the operating system even as I write.

Consider a domestic electronic device that you have at home or in your office. Chances are that the product uses custom hardware and an operating system with the code written in either assembly language or C/C++. The manufacturers might design and build their own hardware or they might buy components upon which they build. Whichever method is used to build the product, more than likely the processor has been designed specifically for the task it performs. Any change to the product's features might well involve changes to the pro-cessor unit—in short, increasing the development time and costs.

Windows CE offers the ability for a manufacturer to buy a fully customizable operating system that is based on the Microsoft Win32 API. A large base of Win32 programmers already exists; therefore, the task of programming a Windows CE device becomes that much easier. Another benefit is the amount of training and support that is available. However, the real benefits can be better understood if you consider the additional functionality available as part of the operating system.

I mentioned that Windows CE offers the ability to build a device that can be programmed using the Win32 API and standard tools like Microsoft Visual C++. However, these capabilities by themselves probably would not be enough in-centive to persuade the electronics industry to switch to Windows CE. Bear in mind that the operating system is licensed and the cost of the license fee de-pends on configuration and volume. OEMs are used to building their own hardware and maybe even writing their own operating systems. The real in-centive for using Windows CE lies in the additional components, listed below:

- Transmission Control Protocol/Internet Protocol (TCP/IP), Point-to-Point Protocol (PPP), and Telephony API (TAPI) components offer the ability to communicate using industry standard protocols. Using these communications components, the vendor can build support for the Internet and intranets in the same way that Windows programmers do. HTML support is also a feature of the operating system. Even for an OEM, the time and costs required to build these components from scratch would more than likely be prohibitive, because the develop-ment cost would price the device out of the market.

- IrDA is the infrared port communications protocol. Again, using standard programming techniques, the vendor can support infrared communication of complex data. This will be a popular form of communication for devices that are in mobile locations. For example, a telephone device installed in a vehicle will need some means of receiving updates to its software or data. A typical scenario might be a user downloading his or her PC contacts file onto a handheld device, and then transmitting the data from the handheld device to the telephone using an infrared link. The telephone also serves as an example of how much potential this technology has. For example, it is feasible that a Windows CE telephone could update new software via a telephone call from the desktop—wow! (Not "Windows On Windows."<g>)

- As most Windows CE machines don't have any disk storage available to them, the object store provides intrinsic data storage methods as part of the operating system. This is covered in more detail later in this chapter; however, the object store essentially provides database, Registry, and file system functionality. The object store is accessible via the Win32 API, so utilizing this functionality is purely a software task—the vendor does not need to build any additional hardware. I should mention at this point that the Windows CE database is not a relational database—it's an indexed sequential access method (ISAM) database, meaning it allows storage of a number of fields indexed on up to four keys. Any record might contain any data in its fields, and might contain any number of fields.

Microsoft Visual Basic, Java, and Microsoft Foundation Class run times can be incorporated into the operating system by the device manufacturer. These components are available for purchase when you buy the Windows CE license. Devices built with these components have the added advantage that the components reside, and are executed, in ROM. This is a big bonus, because, for example, the Visual Basic run time is around 600 KB in size. A Visual Basic program would not require these components to be installed again, thereby leaving more memory for the application. Corporate buyers should make note of this point, because whether these run-time components are included in the operating system is purely the manufacturer's decision. If you will be developing applications requiring any of these run times, it might pay to invest in a device with the required components built in.

COM objects are supported by Windows CE, although at present they can be created using only C++ and must be in-process DLLs. This means that for the time being it is not possible to build Distributed COM (DCOM) objects. It is important to remember that Windows CE is a fairly new technology. Although the Windows CE desktop systems are largely compatible with the Windows 9x/NT systems, the underlying code is totally new and is optimized for the Windows CE environment. This is one of the reasons why some of the tools available have limited functionality. However, Microsoft is listening carefully to its users, so you can expect these tools to become more powerful over time.

- In addition to the language support, Microsoft Internet Explorer can also be an integral part of the operating system. This is an invaluable addition for Web-enabled devices. I would imagine that a vast number of Windows CE devices will be Web-enabled—WebTV is just one example. Again, imagine having to write your own Web functionality totally from scratch! The scope of devices using World Wide Web features is limited only to the imagination.

Now that I've described all the benefits, it is probably easier to comprehend just what Windows CE has to offer. Indeed, the amount of interest being shown by the electronics industry is proof of its potential. The potential market for Windows CE devices is enormous. Based on the history of the electronics industry over the last decade, it might be safe to assume that as the Windows CE operating system is enhanced over time, more diverse applications will be developed to solve problems we experience today. Some solutions might stretch the Windows CE architecture to its limits, performing tasks that we would not have believed possible. At the moment, Microsoft envisions that Windows CE will be best suited to the three main categories of product shown in Figure 5-1.

Microsoft has divided its support for the application of Windows CE into two areas: semi-targeted products and targeted products. Essentially, for semi-targeted products, Microsoft will work with OEMs and IHVs to produce custom components for a specific purpose (for example, writing device drivers). For targeted products, Microsoft will make enhancements to the operating system itself to support features required by certain types of application. One example of a targeted product is the HPC, where the operating system has built-in support for most of the features it requires.

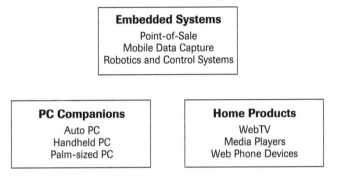

FIGURE 5-1   *The main Windows CE product categories and typical usage*

Building a Windows CE Device

Hardware vendors are generally very good at what they do, maybe because of the skills they need to produce a piece of equipment that meets the tough demands of consumer laws. When, for example, was the last time you bought a car with a bug in the electronic ignition system? OK, so you might not know if the car did have one, but compare that to the average software application! With this degree of technical ability, the average IHV or OEM will easily be able to build high-quality devices using Windows CE.

Windows CE is purchased as a set of files containing the operating system binaries—the exact content is decided by the purchaser. The Windows CE Kernel module is a mandatory requirement of the operating system; however, all other components are optional. For example, if you were building a control module for an alarm system, you might want to have a custom LCD display, in which case you would purchase Windows CE without the Graphics Device Interface (GDI) module and simply add your own. You get the Microsoft Windows CE Embedded Toolkit for Visual C++ 5 (ETK) along with the operating system. This toolkit allows you to build device drivers that interface your hardware to Windows CE and customize the operating system. (See Figure 5-2.)

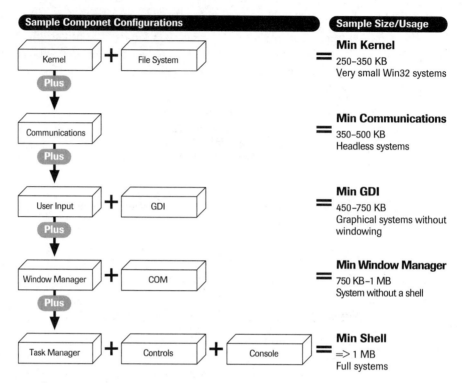

FIGURE 5-2   *Windows CE is available in various configurations to match the user's needs*

In the early days of PC software development, a major consideration was that of processor speed and disk space. As hardware has evolved, the cost of high-speed CPUs, RAM, and disk storage has plummeted, in many cases reducing the need for programmers to spend time developing code that conserves these resources—the average corporate desktop PC will usually have adequate memory and disk space to run the application. Windows makes things even easier with its virtual memory management. However, the story is very different for OEM and IHV developers. In a custom device, physical space might well be at a premium. More importantly, hardware like CPUs, ROM, RAM, and disks all consume power, which is limited in a portable device. This makes the manufacturer's task a difficult one. For example, a color display might be a nice thing to have, but you might have to cut back elsewhere so that the poor battery will last a reasonable time. (Remember the first portable phones with their enormous battery packs?) This is the reason that the Windows CE operating system is vastly reduced in size from the PC and server operating systems, and it is also why the operating system is available in component form. By including only the required functionality, the manufacturer can keep the ROM requirement small, which allows more RAM for the user.

Having purchased the Windows CE license, you now want to build and test your device. You can select a Windows CE configuration with as many or as few components as you require. For example, if you want telephony support you might choose to purchase a license that includes the TAPI module. The more components you choose, the easier it will be to build your device because much of the work will already have been done. After selecting the operating system components, the vendor must build any drivers that will interface to the device hardware. In addition, the vendor must write any vendor-specific software. For example, not all devices need to have a video display unit (VDU)/keyboard interface; a Windows CE stereo system might have a custom plasma display with a button panel. In instances like this, the vendor might need to write his or her own components—in this case a replacement GDI module and hardware drivers. The Windows CE Embedded Toolkit for Visual C++ 5 provides all the necessary support for building and testing device drivers and customizing the operating system. Once the software is written, the next step is to burn an erasable programmable read-only memory (EPROM) chip for testing. The EPROM contains the user-configured Windows CE operating system in addition to the device's software. Having the software in ROM does not prevent additional software from being loaded into RAM, but RAM software is lost should power fail. However, an advantage to having software in RAM is that it makes upgrading a much easier task. Once the device has been tested and debugged, the "real" system CPUs can be produced for the finished device. For an OEM or IHV, producing a Windows CE device should be reasonably straightforward; in many cases, it should be an easier task than at present once the OEM or IHV has mastered the intricacies of the Win32 API and Windows CE configuration.

It is easy to draw false impressions about the capabilities of the Windows CE operating system, especially if you focus too much on devices like the HPC. Consider the screen display as a prime example. When I first started to look at Windows CE seriously, I thought the operating system was bound to a miniature device that had to have a tiny screen display. In fact, nothing could be further from the truth—the Windows CE device can be of any size and can also incorporate a screen display of virtually any size.

Peripheral devices, of which I predict a weird and wonderful selection, will be designed primarily for a specific task. Windows CE allows flexibility for this specific design; for example, the operating system can support a screen resolution of 1600 x 1200 and device drivers can be built if the default does not meet a particular requirement. If I could emphasize one Windows CE concept, it is that Windows CE is a flexible and adaptable compact operating system.

Windows CE has matured somewhat over the last year or so and, as with any good product, a whole plethora of support tools and services are now available to both the OEM and software developer.

GETTING UNDER THE HOOD

Many programmers are now familiar with the Windows architecture and have some knowledge of hardware used on platforms like the Intel x86. It would be wise to understand the principles of a platform before writing an application for that platform. For this reason, this section provides a brief overview of the core components that make up Windows CE. Please bear in mind that this section is not designed to be an exhaustive reference.

Supported Architectures

Microsoft's desktop and server operating systems presently support a limited number of platforms, such as Intel x86, Alpha, MIPS, and so forth. However, to target the mass electronics market, Windows CE must provide support for a vastly larger number of processors. After all, it is unlikely that a vendor using a tried and tested processor will want to change to an unfamiliar environment that might require a whole new learning curve and changes to test-bed equipment. Microsoft's commitment to Windows CE is such that even at this relatively early stage, support is already provided for CPUs from eleven manufacturers, and the list is growing! Currently support is provided for processors from the following CPU manufacturers:

- AMD
- Digital
- Hitachi
- IBM
- Intel
- LG Semiconductors

- Motorola
- NEC
- Philips
- Toshiba
- QED

At present, the Microsoft Windows CE Toolkit for Visual C++ 5 can create programs for each of these platforms; however, the Microsoft Windows CE Toolkit for Visual Basic 5 can only create applications for HPC devices. At present, Philips and Hewlett-Packard are the two largest players in the commercial HPC market, the former using the MIPS platform and the latter using the SH3 platform from Hitachi. This supported hardware list will increase over time, I imagine, according to the demand from customers. I would also expect that the platforms available for Visual Basic will increase. This degree of flexibility is one reason why the industry is taking Windows CE very seriously.

Win32 API

Microsoft estimates that there are some 4.76 million professional developers worldwide, a large number of which currently program Win32 using languages such as Visual C++ or Visual Basic. Of this number, it is estimated that around 300,000 are embedded developers (developers who write software to control hardware devices). For this reason, basing Windows CE on the Win32 API provides a sound foundation from which to build. Don't be fooled, though; if there were not such a large user base, it is feasible that Windows CE might have been based on some other API. With a development team of around 700 on Windows CE alone, Microsoft is more than capable of achieving this!

The API set for Windows CE is very much scaled down from the desktop and server operating systems. Whereas Windows NT has around 10,000 API routines, Windows CE has a mere 1200. This isn't a bad thing, because the new versions are highly optimized and the duplicated functions that exist in the Windows NT/9x operating systems have been removed. If you will be porting from an existing application to Windows CE and you use Win32 API calls in your code, I hope you will have converted to the newer calls. For example, where a function *Foo* and *FooEx* exists you should be using the newer *FooEx* version. If you haven't then never mind, the conversion should not be too painful, although you will need to convert because the older routines do not exist in Windows CE.

The subset of API calls should be sufficient for most tasks. Remember that Windows CE has been built with a "ground-up" approach, so the immediate requirements have been dealt with first. As the operating system's development progresses, new calls will be added as required by users.

The Object Store

The object store is the collective name for the data storage elements within the Windows CE operating system. On the HPC, physical RAM is divided into application memory space and emulated disk space. The disk portion of RAM is where the object store resides. The object store is home for such items as the Registry, Windows CE databases, user files, and applications. Applications that are built into the operating system core are actually held in ROM and cannot be accessed using the object store API calls. A default Registry is also stored in ROM and therefore it, too, cannot be accessed using the API.

An important feature within the Windows CE object store is its transaction mechanism. Microsoft stipulates that if for any reason data cannot be written to the object store, the whole operation will be canceled. This mechanism works on a record level—for example, if you are writing 10 records to a database and a power loss occurs during record 8, records 1 to 7 will have been saved, but no fields in record 8 will be. This applies to the Registry and file system in the same way.

The object store comprises three elements: the database, the Registry, and the file system. These are explained in the following sections.

The Windows CE database

The Windows CE database model provides storage for non-relational data. You can create any number of databases, each with a unique ID. Each database can contain any number of records (depending on memory). A database record can have any number of fields and these fields can be of type Integer, String, Date or Byte array (also known as Binary Large Objects, or BLOBs). Each database record has its own unique ID and this ID is unique across all databases. Database records can contain up to four index keys, which can be used for searching and sorting. In addition, a field can be indexed either in ascending or descending order.

The records held in a database need not be related; for example, you can store contact information in some records and product price details in another record within the same database. A number of API functions exist to manipulate databases—these are covered in more detail later in this chapter. Microsoft has recently released a beta version of ActiveX Data Objects, (ADO) which provides full connectivity to relational databases like Microsoft SQL Server and Microsoft Access. ADO makes it possible to manipulate data in a relational database using the standard SQL to which most Windows developers are accustomed.

Even though the standard database features might sound rather limited, you should remember the kind of application for which Windows CE is designed. If you think in terms of the OEM developing a household device, you'll see that the functionality is more than adequate.

File system

The Windows CE file system has a host of functions with which to access file-based data. The file functions that exist in the normal development environment are not supported by Windows CE; instead, new functions have been provided in the API. Most Windows CE devices presently use the FAT-based file systems. However, the operating system can support installable file systems. For most current Windows CE applications, file access will be to RAM rather than to a physical hard disk, although in terms of coding the difference is transparent.

The file system can be browsed and manipulated using the Mobile Devices application that is installed as part of the Windows CE Services. This application is rather like Windows Explorer and works in the same way. You can even copy, move, or paste files between Windows Explorer and mobile devices.

Registry

Windows CE, like Windows NT/9x, uses the Registry to store system and application configuration data. However, the Windows NT Registry consists of several files, or hives, that together form the entire Registry. Windows CE does not support hives—the entire Registry is stored as a single file. The Registry file is stored in ROM and is copied to RAM when the device is booted. You should bear in mind that a Windows CE device will probably boot only after the power supply has been connected. Normally, when the device is turned off, backup batteries retain RAM memory. This design allows a feature that Microsoft calls "Instant On"—that is, the device is immediately available when switched on. It is possible to write software that saves the Registry file to a non-volatile storage device. Given the nature of the power supply for many prospective Windows CE devices, however, user data can be lost in almost any situation. Losing the Registry should not cause too many problems for an application, because more than likely any user files will be lost as well. A good design principle to employ might be for an application to back up the Registry to non-volatile storage whenever the user chooses to backup his or her files.

The RAM copy of the Registry can be accessed using the Win32 API, or Visual Basic programmers can use the built-in Registry functions. Desktop applications written in Visual Basic often need to use the API in order to access different Registry keys; for example, global application data would probably need to be saved to HKEY_LOCAL_MACHINE, whereas user specific settings would be better located under HKEY_CURRENT_USER. For Visual Basic programmers, a COM DLL is required to access keys or paths other than the default one that Visual Basic accesses: HKEY_CURRENT_USER\Software\VB and VBA Program Settings.

ActiveSync

ActiveSync is the technology introduced with Windows CE 2 that provides an easy way to keep data synchronized between a mobile device and a desktop PC. ActiveSync allows you to keep databases synchronized between your device and the desktop PC in much the same way as replication occurs between SQL Server databases. Conflict resolution is handled for you once you set up the required configuration. The synchronization operations can be performed using the Mobile Devices folder menu options, but you can also use certain API functions to control the process. The ActiveSync API calls are listed later in this chapter in the section "Visual Basic Development."

Processes and Threads

Because Windows CE is based on the Win32 API, it has full support for processes and threads. Visual C++ (and even Visual Basic 5) programmers might already be familiar with these concepts. Essentially, a process consists of one or more threads of execution, where a thread is the smallest unit of execution. Windows CE allows a maximum of 32 processes; however, the number of threads is limited only by available memory. It is possible to create threads using Visual Basic, but this is not advisable because the Visual Basic run time is not "thread safe"— that is, if two threads within the same process were to call a Visual Basic routine at the same time, some fairly nasty things might happen. However, because I know that some of you will try it, and because it is very applicable to C++ development, the section "Visual Basic Development" later in this chapter describes the thread-handling API calls. If you have trouble remembering the difference between processes and threads, you might find the diagram in Figure 5-3 helpful.

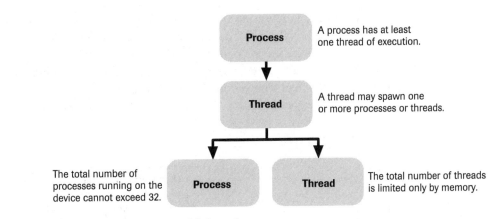

FIGURE 5-3   *Windows CE processes and threads*

The ability to assign priorities to a thread is a major requirement, especially for an operating system that will host real-time applications. Windows CE allows a thread to be assigned one of eight priority levels, as shown in Table 5-1.

TABLE 5-1   **THREAD PRIORITIES**

Priority		Typical Usage
0	THREAD_PRIORITY_TIME_CRITICAL	Used primarily for real-time threads and processing, such as device drivers. Priority 0 threads are not preempted—once started, a thread process will continue to completion. The operating system will not interrupt the thread.
1	THREAD_PRIORITY_HIGHEST	
2	THREAD_PRIORITY_ABOVE_NORMAL	Kernel threads normally run at these levels, as do normal applications.
3	THREAD_PRIORITY_NORMAL	
4	THREAD_PRIORITY_BELOW_NORMAL	
5	THREAD_PRIORITY_LOWEST	Used in instances in which it doesn't matter how long the functionality takes to complete. These will usually be background tasks, probably without their own user interface. An example might be of a thread that periodically checks to see if you have any new mail. Threads on these priority levels can expect to be interrupted often.
6	THREAD_PRIORITY_ABOVE_IDLE	
7	THREAD_PRIORITY_IDLE	

The Windows CE operating system is preemptive and as such must allocate a time slice for each thread. This is done in a "round-robin" fashion. The default time slice for a thread is 25 milliseconds, except for priority 0 threads. A priority 0 thread, once started, will retain the processor until it yields control. The scheduling mechanism uses an algorithm whereby the highest priority thread is always allocated time first. This process is better illustrated by Figure 5-4.

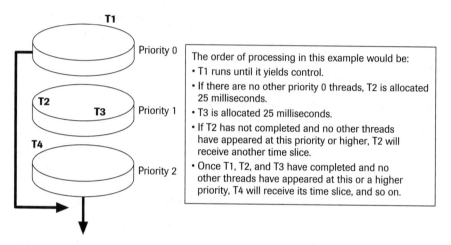

The order of processing in this example would be:
- T1 runs until it yields control.
- If there are no other priority 0 threads, T2 is allocated 25 milliseconds.
- T3 is allocated 25 milliseconds.
- If T2 has not completed and no other threads have appeared at this priority or higher, T2 will receive another time slice.
- Once T1, T2, and T3 have completed and no other threads have appeared at this or a higher priority, T4 will receive its time slice, and so on.

FIGURE 5-4   *Thread preemption in Windows CE*

Windows CE handles thread priority inheritance (a requirement of real-time systems we will discuss shortly) using a method called Priority Inversion. It is possible that a thread on a lower priority might lock a resource required by a thread on a higher priority. When this condition occurs Windows CE promotes the lower thread task to the level of the higher priority thread until the resource has been released. The Win32 API has full support for thread priority assignments. In version 2 of the Windows CE operating system the default time slice is configurable on the MIPS platform.

An additional requirement currently being developed is to increase the number of priority bands, possibly to as many as 256. This has been a frequent request from OEMs and IHVs in order to enhance real-time flexibility. Because of the way in which the preemptive multitasking works in Windows CE, it is possible to guarantee the time it will take for a thread to execute on the highest priority, an important factor in a real-time system.

Real-Time Capabilities

The ability for Windows CE to perform real-time processing is an essential element when it comes to control and monitoring systems. There is some debate as to whether the operating system currently allows "true" real-time processing. The Internet newsgroup *comp.realtime* gives this standard definition of a real-time system: "A real-time system is one in which the correctness of the computations not only depends on the logical correctness of the computation, but also on the time at which the result is produced. If the timing constraints of the system are not met, system failure is said to have occurred." In addition, this newsgroup states that a real-time operating system must also meet the following requirements:

- The operating system must be multithreaded and preemptive.
- The operating system must support thread priority.
- A system of priority inheritance must exist.
- The operating system must support predictable thread synchronization mechanisms.
- The maximum time during which an interrupt can be disabled by the operating system or device drivers must be known.
- The time it takes the interrupt to run (interrupt latency) must be within the requirements of the application.

The Windows CE operating system meets the criteria to be classed as a real-time operating system, but in its current implementation the architecture does not achieve these goals in a way that would promote the level of integrity required to host a mission critical application. To help you understand this better I should perhaps explain how the interrupt processing is performed. Interrupts are events triggered by external components to announce that an event has occurred. Because I know a little about aircraft, I shall use an aircraft warning system to draw an analogy—note that the examples are not strictly accurate but are simply designed to illustrate the point. Imagine an autopilot that is equipped with a collision avoidance system. In the event of a collision warning, the collision avoidance device should notify the autopilot, which in turn must take corrective action. This might be in the form of an audible warning and also might automatically adjust the aircraft controls to miss the obstacle. In a real-time system you would expect that once the warning (or interrupt) has occurred the autopilot will react and perform the required actions within a stipulated time. Figure 5-5 on the following page shows a simplified diagram of how such functionality might be handled by the Windows CE operating system.

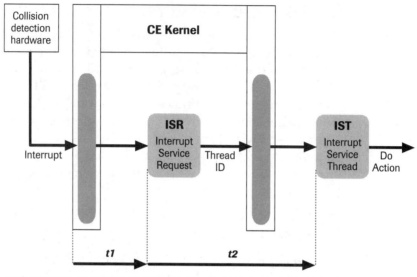

t1 and t2 represent the latency (or time taken) for each stage of the interrupt processing. Testing has shown typical times for t1 to be 1.3–7.5 microseconds. Typical times for t2 are 93–275 microseconds.

A real-time operating system must have a predictable latency (t1 + t2). Microsoft is currently working on guaranteed interrupt latencies of below 50 microseconds for Windows CE version 3.

FIGURE 5-5   *Real-time processing in Windows CE*

An external device notifies the operating system of an event by way of an interrupt, or more correctly, an interrupt request line (IRQ). Each IRQ has an associated interrupt service routine (ISR). When an interrupt occurs the Kernel calls the associated ISR, which returns the ID of the interrupt service thread (IST) for the IRQ. Once the Kernel has the thread ID it notifies the IST, which starts the required processing. There are a couple of reasons why you might not want this system in a Boeing 777 on final approach. First, interrupts cannot be nested—that is, once an interrupt has occurred no further interrupts can be processed until the IST has started for the previous interrupt. Second, imagine the scenario where there are multiple ISTs each on 0, the highest priority. Because critical threads are not preempted any further IST will not be able to run until the first IST has finished. So, in the case of our 777, whose computer also handles the fire extinguisher, we could deal with the collision warning, but we could not deal with a fire until the collision warning's IST completed. Microsoft is working hard to cater to these demanding requirements of real-time mission critical applications. Version 3 of the Windows CE operating system will be able to handle nested interrupts and will have interrupt latencies of less than 50 milliseconds.

Development Environments

One of the attractions of the Windows CE operating system is that it is possible to build software applications using industry-standard programming languages. For the OEM and IHV developers, the choice of programming language will no doubt be the ETK because of their need to write low-level device drivers. For the rest of the industry, Windows CE also provides support for C++, MFC, ActiveX Template Library (ATL), Visual Basic, and Java applications. The Visual Basic language might prove very appealing because it is so well known, but note that you cannot use the Windows CE Toolkit for Visual Basic with any version other than Visual Basic 5 at the moment—the toolkit is hard-coded to recognize only this version. Other higher-level applications, especially Web-enabled ones, can be written using Visual J++.

Whichever tool you use to write Windows CE applications, you must bear in mind that they are subsets of their respective "parents." When we discuss Visual Basic development later in this chapter, you will notice a marked reduction in the number of routines and statements available. Obviously, the scaled-down nature of the operating system means that certain functionality is not needed because Windows CE cannot support it. The other reason for some omissions is that Microsoft has included what they believe to be the most needed features for this platform—don't worry, the feature list will grow with demand. Currently four main markets exist for Windows CE (although this is growing). These are:

- Auto PC (in-vehicle computing)
- Handheld PC
- Palm-sized PC
- Embedded systems

The language you choose depends largely on which of these platforms you will be developing for. Figure 5-6 on the following page shows the various development tools available for each platform. The long-term strategy, as far as development tools is concerned, is for each toolkit to provide support for each platform. As the tools are more finely honed and expanded, the software development scene will change somewhat, presenting exciting opportunities. I personally look forward to the possibility of projects including mission-critical systems and real-time systems in the future.

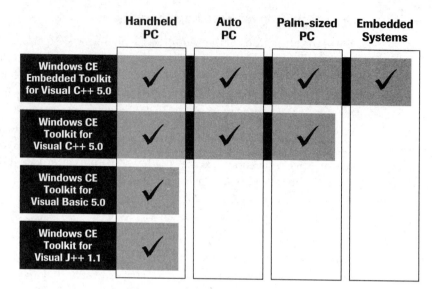

	Handheld PC	Auto PC	Palm-sized PC	Embedded Systems
Windows CE Embedded Toolkit for Visual C++ 5.0	✓	✓	✓	✓
Windows CE Toolkit for Visual C++ 5.0	✓	✓	✓	
Windows CE Toolkit for Visual Basic 5.0	✓			
Windows CE Toolkit for Visual J++ 1.1	✓			

FIGURE 5-6   *Choosing the right development tool for the job*

WINDOWS CE AND THE IT DEPARTMENT

The development of applications for Windows CE falls mainly into two camps: embedded systems for custom hardware devices and high level applications for devices such as the HPC and the palm-sized PC. I would imagine that the development of software will be split into low-level development for the OEM and IHV and high-level development for the corporate Information Technology (IT) environments. Although some companies might use custom Windows CE devices, it is probable that they will use ready-built hardware and write their own custom high-level applications.

I imagine that many corporate developers might at this moment have visions of writing sales force automation systems and so on, but they (and everybody else) must consider their hardware limitations before deciding how best the technology can be utilized in their particular environment. For example, it might not be a good idea trying to port a full-blown ordering system to an HPC because of the memory constraints. The power requirements of HPC–style devices will continue to be a hindrance that prevents mass storage capabilities, although even as I write there is a company developing a fingernail-sized hard disk capable of storing a half megabyte of data. Battery technology will improve over time, but in the past advances in this area have been nowhere near the advances in hardware technology.

For the more conventional software houses and IT departments a whole new market will open up in areas such as point-of-sale systems, bar code information retrieval, and other data capture devices. The cost benefits are numerous; for instance, businesses such as local electricity companies or traffic enforcement agencies could invest in HPC machines for their meter readers to collect data off site, and then use the ActiveSync or ADO technology to upload data to the corporate database. The cost of an HPC is probably considerably less than the cost of custom hardware devices, and, as we have discussed, writing programs for these devices is a pretty easy task.

For the time being, I do not expect to be writing any aircraft control systems. However, with the enhancements being made to the real-time capabilities of Windows CE, it is quite possible that specialist companies might open their doors to the contract market or independent software houses. Basically, the future is not set—what we are seeing in Windows CE is a way forward that opens up many new niche areas.

Visual Basic Development

To develop Windows CE applications using Visual Basic, you will need the Windows CE Toolkit for Visual Basic 5. Notice that at the moment the toolkit will not run with any other version of Visual Basic. The toolkit provides the Windows CE–specific functionality and the IDE changes needed to create and build Windows CE applications. In terms of the language, Visual Basic for Windows CE is a subset of Visual Basic, Scripting Edition. This means that much of the Visual Basic 5 language is not supported. However, enhancements have been added to the language in Visual Basic 6, but not Visual Basic 5. This chapter is aimed at developers who are already experienced in Visual Basic 5 development and, therefore, this section focuses mainly on the differences and new features of the language and environment.

The Development Environment

Creating a new Windows CE project is not much different from creating a normal Visual Basic one. A new project type, Windows CE Project, has been added, which configures the Visual Basic IDE for Windows CE development. In standard Visual Basic you can create a number of different types of project, such as Standard EXE, ActiveX EXE, and ActiveX DLL. However, a Windows CE project might only create the equivalent of a Standard EXE, or—to be more precise—a PVB file. Before you commence coding, you must configure your project's properties. The Project Properties dialog box is displayed automatically when you start a new project. Once you have dismissed the Project Properties dialog box, you will notice some changes in the IDE from that of standard Visual Basic. Figure 5-7 shows the major changes to the IDE.

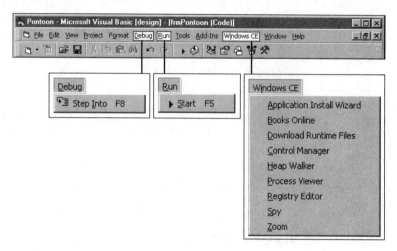

FIGURE 5-7   *Windows CE IDE changes in Visual Basic 5*

The first things you will notice are the greatly reduced number of options for the Run and Debug menus. This is because the way that Windows CE programs are run in the development environment is very different from the way a standard Visual Basic project runs. The toolkit provides an emulation environment that allows you to run and debug your applications without actually having an HPC device. I will explain the emulator in more detail later, but essentially, the emulator is part of the Windows CE Platform SDK and is supplied with the Windows CE Toolkit for Visual Basic 5.

A number of new menu options have been added to help with Windows CE development, as listed here.

- The Application Install Wizard, as the name suggests, provides the equivalent functionality as the Visual Basic Setup Wizard.

- Books Online contains reference information and is very comprehensive. Additional information can be obtained from the Microsoft Web site.

- Download Runtime Files transfers the Visual Basic run time files to the emulation and HPC device.

- Control Manager downloads ActiveX controls to either the emulation or HPC environment. Any controls you use in your application will need to reside in the environment where you choose to run or debug the application.

- Heap Walker (a scaled-down equivalent of the program supplied for other Windows versions) views the process and "heaps" information for processes running on your HPC.

- Process Viewer provides the functionality of the PVIEWxx.EXE program supplied with other versions of Visual Basic. Process Viewer lists each module loaded in memory on the HPC. You can use this application to kill processes running on your HPC and you can also view the modules being used by a particular process.

- The Registry Editor functions the same way as in the other Windows operating systems. This version, however, allows you to edit both the HPC and emulator Registries.

- The Spy utility allows you to examine details of window objects that are loaded on the HPC. Like the Windows NT/9x version, Spy allows you to view the window and class information and to view the message queue to a particular window on the HPC device.

- Zoom was originally designed to allow you to zoom in on an area of the screen to view the bit patterns. The Windows CE version has extended this functionality to allow you to also save screen shots of your HPC screen.

Windows CE Application Design Philosophy

Because of the nature of the Windows CE operating system, a new design philosophy is required in order to develop Visual Basic applications for the HPC. The foremost concern is that of memory. With such a potentially small amount of RAM you stand a good chance that your application might run out of memory or be terminated when another application requires memory resources being used by your application. Unlike Windows NT/9x, there is no virtual memory management, so if memory runs out—tough! Once the machine starts running low on memory it will look to see if there are any other applications running. If another application is found, it will be terminated; this will continue until the memory requirement has been satisfied. In effect, any program in memory is in danger of being shut down by the operating system to satisfy memory requirements. A Windows CE application must be designed with this in mind.

User transactions must be well designed so that in the event of an application being closed, user data is not left in an unpredictable state. The operating system's transaction mechanism will protect you against data integrity problems at a record level, but you can build certain scenarios into your code that increase the risk of data getting out of sync. For example, if you are writing a series of related records from various sources, it might be a good idea to collect all the data and then apply the changes in a batch, rather than as each individual item becomes available.

Another consideration is that of the power supply. The nature and size of HPC devices means that at some point the battery will run out. HPC devices usually contain backup batteries that are designed to preserve the memory while the main batteries are being changed. However, the backup batteries can be removed as well. An application must allow for the possibility of power loss. In this instance, batch operations will not be of any use. When power is lost, the entire content of the RAM is lost. The only safeguard against losing data is to back up to a PC. Do not confuse loss of power with the user switching off the device. In the latter case, RAM is not destroyed—the HPC merely enters a sleep state. When the HPC is turned on again, the device's previous state will be restored. As a Visual Basic developer, you will very likely be writing high level applications and as such, if there is a loss of power, the application will no longer be in memory. Unless the user's data has been synchronized (saved to a desktop), the data will also be lost.

In terms of visual appearance, the potentially small screen display might mean cutting back on some of the more aesthetic user interface elements—a good practice would be to make sure the elements are functional rather than cosmetic. In most cases I would advise against using unnecessary controls in your application because each control you include in your project will need to be installed on the device. This will leave less working memory. You should also give consideration to the ergonomics of the interface; for example, if you are not using default color schemes, you should make sure that the contrast is sufficient for both gray-scale and color displays.

Your First Windows CE Application

Writing a Windows CE program is much the same as writing any other Visual Basic program. However, you'll have to accustom yourself to many differences in the language and to the development environment. You'll need to carefully consider the structure of your code and the implementation of the finished application. I have written a card game named Pontoon, and I will use this application from time to time to highlight important points. Figure 5-8 shows some screen shots of the application.

Perhaps now might be a good time to explain quickly the rules of the game—it's similar to Blackjack, or 21. The player plays against the computer (dealer) with the aim of attaining a score of 21. If the score goes over 21, the game is lost. The player can choose to be dealt another card, ("twist"), and his or her score is calculated as a sum of the face values of all the player's cards. The ace has a face value of 11 and picture cards have a face value of 10. If the player decides that another card might bring his or her score over 21, he or she might decide to not take anymore cards ("stick"). After a player chooses to stick, all subsequent cards will be dealt to the dealer. If the dealer reaches a score higher than the player's and below 22, the dealer wins. But if the dealer's score exceeds 21, the dealer loses. Before the player makes the first twist he or she must select an amount to gamble. If the game is lost, the player's funds are deducted by that amount. If the player wins, his or her funds are increased by the amount gambled. That's it! The full source code for the Pontoon game is included on the CD-ROM accompanying this book.

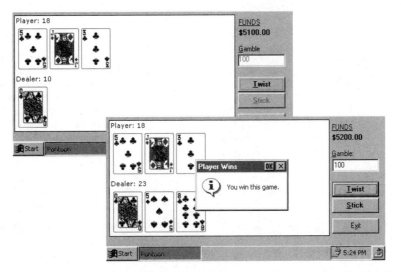

FIGURE 5-8   *The Pontoon Windows CE card game in action—I got lucky this time!*

General Design Considerations

Building a Windows CE application is essentially a compromise of various factors, more so in Visual Basic because of the small subset of available programming constructs. The common factors that you will need to consider are size, memory, maintainability, and stability. All these factors together determine the quality of the application as shown in Figure 5-9.

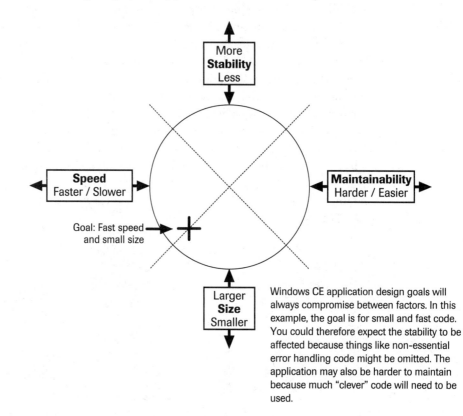

Windows CE application design goals will always compromise between factors. In this example, the goal is for small and fast code. You could therefore expect the stability to be affected because things like non-essential error handling code might be omitted. The application may also be harder to maintain because much "clever" code will need to be used.

FIGURE 5-9   *Design factors in a Windows CE application*

For my Pontoon game, the primary goals are good maintainability and small size. Various techniques are used to reduce the program size while trying to keep it reasonably understandable and maintainable; however, this may result in a loss in performance and perhaps in robustness. But the losses are not so great because stability is not a major concern. We can code to avoid obvious errors, but if an error does occur, at worst the user will get an error message. Speed is not really important here because the actual processing cycles are relatively small.

The user interface

The most obvious consideration when writing an HPC application is that of the screen display. The current HPC machines have a relatively small screen resolution, though these do vary between models. Apart from the physical dimensions, color is also an issue. Version 2 of Windows CE introduced support for 16 colors. This has improved the color contrast on monochrome displays, though devices are now available with color displays.

Windows CE supports only two window styles—fixed border or no border—and there is no Minimize or Maximize button. You can set the form's *BorderStyle* design time property to another style but any styles other than those allowed will be overridden at run time. When creating a new form, Visual Basic defaults to a size near the maximum resolution of the HPC device you are using, but you can change this default size in the Project Properties dialog box. Any size that you set here will be retained as the default for future forms you create.

A new window style has been implemented for message box windows. If you specify a button configuration of *vbOKOnly*, the message box will be displayed with the OK button in the title bar next to the Close button. Other button configurations will display message boxes in the usual format. The height of the message box has been scaled down to obscure the least amount of space on the screen. While we're on the subject of message boxes, you should be aware of a glitch in the current version of the language. The message box is not modal, but floats above its parent window. The form below the parent window can still respond to mouse events. To avoid this problem you will need to disable your form while the message box is displayed.

When designing a Windows CE form, you should evaluate the need for a border and title bar. Many of the Microsoft applications, such as Pocket Word and Pocket Excel, do not have title bars or borders. This really does increase the amount of usable screen real estate.

In terms of user interface controls, you will find that not all of the intrinsic Visual Basic controls are supported. Rather, the intrinsic user interface controls you can use are:

- Check Box
- Combo Box
- Command Button
- Frame
- Horizontal and Vertical Scroll Bars
- Label

- Line
- List Box
- Option Button
- Shape
- Text Box
- Timer

Although the remaining controls are not removed from the toolbox, a warning message will be displayed and the control will be removed if you attempt to place one of these on your form. Obviously, graphical capabilities must be retained, so two new graphical controls are available from the Components dialog box: PictureBox and ImageCtl.

These two graphical controls are replacements for the standard PictureBox and Image controls, though you should note that their class names have changed. These two controls retain the ability to display images and pictures, although there are some differences from the controls they replace. Apart from being a lightweight control, the PictureBox has undergone some changes to its methods. The methods such as *Line, Circle, Point*, and *PSet* have been removed and are now replaced by this new set of methods:

- *DrawCircle*
- *DrawLine*
- *DrawPicture*
- *DrawPoint*
- *DrawText*

Pontoon, being a card game, relies heavily on graphics. The graphical methods supported by the *Form* object in other versions of Visual Basic are not available in the Windows CE toolkit. Therefore, the PictureBox control is used for displaying the graphics.

Windows CE contains a unique set of constraints or bounds that we must work within. One such constraint is that control arrays are not permitted. You can create control arrays but you will get an error at run time if you do so. In the case of the Pontoon game, the work-around to this problem is to use a PictureBox control and draw the card graphic in the picture box. In other versions of Visual Basic, it might have been easier to simply create a control array of Image controls on the fly, and then load the required images. The Pontoon game uses the Windows CE PictureBox control as a container into which the cards can be drawn. The PictureBox control does not have the ability to be a container object, so a problem arises because you cannot place labels within the PictureBox. Because labels are lower in the z-order, you can't show labels within a picture box. To get around this problem I've used two picture boxes to display the rows of cards and I've used a Shape control to create an area around the picture boxes and labels to form a playing table.

Figure 5-10 shows the Pontoon screen at design time. The number of controls have been kept to a minimum. The screen is built up using only essential controls or elements needed to improve clarity.

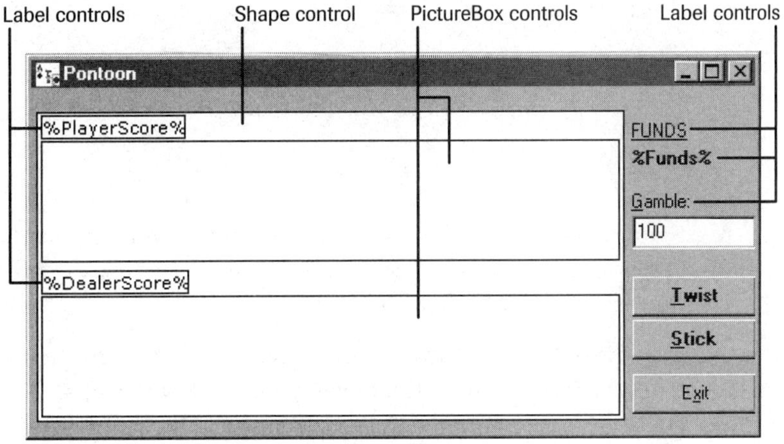

FIGURE 5-10   *The design-time layout of the Pontoon game*

You will notice that although the design-time form looks like a standard Windows NT/9x form, the form will be displayed using the Windows CE window style when the program is run—that is, with no Minimize or Maximize buttons. We have an interface where all elements are large enough to be clearly visible, resulting in little clutter on the screen.

Another important aspect of the user interface design is that of keyboard ergonomics. If I were sitting on a train playing this game, I might find it uncomfortable trying to use the stylus if the train is swaying. It might also be uncomfortable to use the accelerator keys because two hands are required. One design feature I've implemented to aid keyboard use is the *KeyPreview* property, which is used to intercept keystrokes and convert them to accelerator key presses. In an ideal world we could simply code the following in the form's KeyPress event, as shown here:

```
Private Sub Form_KeyPress(KeyAscii)
    SendKeys "%" & Chr(KeyAscii)
End Sub
```

Alas, this is not possible—the *SendKeys* statement is not supported. Instead you can achieve the coding using a method like the one I've implemented here:

```
Private Sub Form_KeyPress(KeyAscii)

    If StrComp(Chr(KeyAscii), "g", vbTextCompare) = 0 Then
        txtGambleAmount.SetFocus
    End If

    If StrComp(Chr(KeyAscii), "t", vbTextCompare) = 0 Then
        cmdTwist.Value = True
    End If

    If StrComp(Chr(KeyAscii), "s", vbTextCompare) = 0 Then
        cmdStick.Value = True
    End If

End Sub
```

Simple routines like this take no time to write but can drastically improve the ergonomics of an interface. I expect many new ideas to be developed in the future that will aid usability.

In addition to the intrinsic controls and the PictureBox and ImageCtl controls that are supplied with the development kit, you can also download a set of controls from the Microsoft Web site at *http://www.microsoft.com/windowsce/ developer*. At this site you can obtain the Microsoft Windows CE ActiveX Control Pack 1.0, which contains many more useful controls. The download is more than 5 MB but is worth downloading, because in this pack you get the following controls:

- *GridCtrl*
- *TabStrip*
- *TreeViewCtrl*
- *ListViewCtrl*
- *ImageList*
- *CommonDialog*

The addition of these controls allows you to create the same interface styles as the controls of full-blown Visual Basic applications. The list of controls will grow and I would expect a lot of new controls to emerge from third-party vendors as well.

Size and memory considerations

I said earlier that one of the goals for the Pontoon game was to be small in size. The word "size" might imply the physical file size, but an important factor is also the memory footprint of the application. You can control the program's memory footprint by enforcing restrictions on functionality and by writing more efficient code. The former method will nearly always be a business issue and, therefore, possibly might be out of the programmer's control. However, using efficient coding techniques is a trade-off against readability and maintainability. However, I'll discuss some techniques that you can use to code more efficiently.

Program variables are the obvious source of memory consumption. The Windows CE Toolkit for Visual Basic 5 allows only Variant type variables. This is a little surprising, given that Variants take more memory than a "typed" variable. Although your variables will be Variant types, you can still coerce them into a subtype using the conversion functions like *CLng*, *CCur*, and so forth, although this coercion will be performed automatically when a value is assigned to the variable. The Pontoon game makes extensive use of bit flag variables. This is an efficient way to store multiple values, providing there is no overlap in range of the bit values. By using bit values, the overall memory requirement can be reduced, but you must be careful if creating constants to represent the bits because you might end up using the same or larger amounts of memory. The following is the declaration section from the form:

```
Private m_btaDeck(12, 3)

Private m_btaPlayerCards        ' Byte Array stores cards held by player.
Private m_btaDealerCards        ' Byte Array stores cards held by dealer.
Private m_nPlayerScore          ' Player score - total value of cards held.
Private m_nDealerScore          ' Dealer score - total value of cards held.
Private m_nPlayerFunds          ' Dealer score - total value of cards held.
Private m_nGameStatusFlags      ' Long Integer of flags indicating game
                                ' status.


' Constants used with m_nGameStatusFlags.
'
Private Const m_GSF_PLAYER_HAS_21 = &H1
Private Const m_GSF_DEALER_HAS_21 = &H2
Private Const m_GSF_PLAYER_HAS_BUST = &H4
Private Const m_GSF_DEALER_HAS_BUST = &H8
Private Const m_GSF_PLAYER_HAS_HIGHER_SCORE = &H10
Private Const m_GSF_DEALER_HAS_HIGHER_SCORE = &H20
Private Const m_GSF_PLAYER_HAS_STUCK = &H40
Private Const m_GSF_IS_DEALER_TURN = &H100
```

You should note two points here. First, even though you can declare only Variant variables, it is still good practice to use scope and type prefixes. Because each variable can potentially store any value, you need to be sure that everyone knows what type of value is expected. For example, the variable *UserName* obviously contains a string, but a variable named *ItemId* could easily represent a string or numeric value. Second, you'll see that I've used hexadecimal notation to assign the bit flag constants. Bit manipulation often requires mask and other values to extrapolate the individual values within the flag variable. Using hexadecimal notation makes it much easier for others to understand the operations that are being performed, because the conversion from hexadecimal to binary is much easier than from decimal to binary.

Let's look for a moment at the variable *m_nGameStatusFlags* that I use in the Pontoon game to keep track of the game's progress. The variable is a Long Integer (32 bits) and stores nine separate values, which together provide a complete picture of the game's current status. Figure 5-11 shows how these values are stored.

The Pontoon game stores game status information as bit flags in a Long Integer variable. The chart below shows the values that are stored in each of the bit positions in the *m_nGameStatusFlags* variable.

Description	Not Used		Total cards dealt				Dealer's turn?	Player has stuck?	Dealer has higher score?	Player has higher score?	Dealer has bust?	Player has bust?	Dealer has 21 points?	Player has 21 points?
Bit number	32	...	13	12	11	10	9	8	7	6	5	4	3	2	1

You can see that this method is very efficient for conserving memory. We are storing a total of nine different values in a single Long Integer variable, and we still have space left. We could have used a Boolean variable for each of the flags; however, the Boolean variables would in fact be Variants with sub-type Boolean, which are larger than true Boolean variables.

FIGURE 5-11   *Pontoon game bit flag values*

Another technique you can use to reduce memory size is to pass all parameters by reference (*ByRef*). Doing this means that a pointer to the variable is passed and the procedure does not need to make a local copy of the variable within the procedure it is being passed to. In other versions of Visual Basic, passing by reference would not be good practice because of the potential of inadvertently changing a parameter's value, affecting code outside of a procedure. Many of the Pontoon game's functions are designed to process data that is held in module-scoped variables. However, it is still a good idea to pass the module-level variable into procedures, because this improves reuse as the procedure does not get tied to the module or form where the variable is declared.

A common problem when trying to optimize code is that complex algorithms are often created, which can be very difficult to understand. It is a good idea to encapsulate complex functionality within distinct functions so that if maintenance is required, the functionality is not shrouded by unnecessary code. An example of this encapsulation is the function below that shuffles the deck of cards in our Pontoon game.

```
Private Sub ShufflePack(btaDeck, btaHand1, btaHand2, nGameStatus)
''''''''''''''''''''''''''''''''''''''''''''''''''''''''''''''''''''''''
' Shuffle the pack. We acheive this by marking each byte in the card '
' deck array as being available (False). Obviously we cannot unmark  '
' any card that is currently held by the player or dealer.           '
''''''''''''''''''''''''''''''''''''''''''''''''''''''''''''''''''''''''
    Dim bteCard         ' Value of card being processed.
    Dim nCard           ' Counter for iterating our card values.
    Dim nSuit           ' Counter for iterating suit values.

    ' Mark each card in our array as False, meaning available.
    For nCard = LBound(btaDeck, 1) To UBound(btaDeck, 1)
        For nSuit = LBound(btaDeck, 2) To UBound(btaDeck, 2)
            btaDeck(nCard, nSuit) = False
        Next
    Next

    ' Loop through the player's cards. Each of the player's cards
    ' must be made unavailable in the deck by marking it True.
    If IsEmpty(btaHand1) = False Then
        For Each bteCard In btaHand1
            ' Calculate the array index for the card and set
            ' its element to True, indicating the card is in
            ' use. Bit 9 of the card array is the suit and bit
            ' 1-8 is the card's value.
            btaDeck(bteCard And &HF, (bteCard And &H70) \ &H10) = True
        Next
    End If
```

>>

>>

```
' Do the same for the dealer's cards.
If IsEmpty(btaHand2) = False Then
    For Each bteCard In btaHand2
        btaDeck(bteCard And &HF, (bteCard And &H70) \ &H10) = True
    Next
End If

nGameStatus = (nGameStatus And &HFF)

End Sub
```

Looking at the code above you can clearly see all the actions for shuffling the deck. Such a procedure might be called only from one location in your program, but placing the shuffling code in its own procedure will help clarify both its logic and that of the procedure that calls it. Using magic numbers instead of constants in code has always been bad practice; however, we have to consider any memory constraint criteria. In this case, maintainability has been compromised in favor of size. If you choose to make this kind of compromise, try to keep the code simple. Whenever you develop complex logic, always ensure that there are plenty of comments, because code that might be easy to understand a day after you've written it has a habit of becoming quite complex three months later.

Often your application will need to use external files and resources such as Registry entries. Do not forget to consider the size of these elements when you start designing. You will need to think carefully about what you write to storage because this eats into the overall memory of the HPC. The Pontoon game does not use any Registry entries, but it does store the card graphics in bitmap files. We have 52 cards in our deck; each one has a corresponding bitmap file of 2022 bytes. Therefore, the overall storage space required is 105,144 bytes, or 103 KB. Our program file is 24 KB and we are using the PictureBox control, which is 59 KB. We can therefore calculate that the application will require a total of 183 KB. Because the HPC device has the Visual Basic CE run-time files in ROM, we do not need to include these components in our calculation. It would be too difficult to attempt to calculate the absolute total memory requirement because of the other influences, but so long as your program is small enough to run in the available memory and you have allowed for program terminations caused by insufficient memory, you should not have any problems.

An important point to be aware of is that on the desktop operating system each card would actually take up more space than its physical size; my PC, for example, will store each card in a space 32 KB in size. This size is called an allocation unit. Essentially, when writing files to disk, the operating system always write the data in blocks of a predetermined size (32 KB in my case). If I create a file less than or equal to 32 KB, the amount of disk space allocated for the file will actually be 32 KB. If the file's size is 33 KB, it will occupy two allocation units, or 64 KB. The allocation unit size on the PC is dependent upon the size of the hard disk partition and is configurable, but it can still be quite wasteful. Windows CE does not use allocation units, so my cards will occupy only the space equivalent to the file's actual size.

Programming for Windows CE

The Windows CE Toolkit for Visual Basic 5 is based on a subset of the Visual Basic, Scripting Edition programming language, so many Visual Basic language features available in other versions are not applicable or available when writing Windows CE programs. The Windows CE toolkit uses Visual Basic's code editor and syntax checker, and for this reason you will find that many of the errors caused by using features not available to the Windows CE environment will not be reported by the syntax checker. These errors are reported only at run time. Moreover, these run-time errors do not give specific information—they simply report that an error has occurred. When you run a Windows CE application in the development environment, the Visual Basic interpreter is not used—instead a debug version of your program is created and loaded either in the emulator environment or on the HPC device. Certain errors can be detected only after your application is executed. Once your program has started it has no further interaction with Visual Basic; instead, the Windows CE debugging window interacts with your program. Figure 5-12 illustrates how Visual Basic and the Windows CE toolkit components interact when you run a program. I will explain the emulator and the debugger in more detail later in this chapter.

In a Visual Basic Windows CE program you can create as many forms as you like, but you might have only one standard module. You cannot use class modules or any other type of module, such as User Documents or Property Pages, so you will not be able to create ActiveX components. You can, however, have related documents attached to your project. You need to be careful when using the properties and methods of standard Visual Basic objects, because many of the properties and methods either are not supported or have changed. The Knowledge Base contains articles providing a full list of what has changed or the excluded functionality, so I will not repeat them all here.

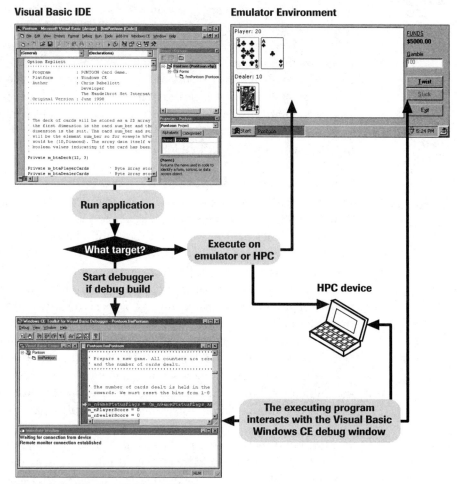

FIGURE 5-12 *The Visual Basic debugging environment for Windows CE*

What's new or changed in the language?

In addition to changes in the development environment, some new features and changes elsewhere have been added. The Books Online reference provides full documentation of the language, so I won't provide a comprehensive listing here. The following is a description of some elements that are either new or that work differently. Some elements are not new but might have missed your attention in previous versions, and they might now have a more prominent role in your designs.

One of the more common programming elements is the array. A big change here is that the lower bound of an array is always 0—this cannot be changed. A new set of functions has been included, which will make manipulation of arrays an easier task. The *Array* function was introduced in Visual Basic 5, but it might have gone unnoticed. Arrays will probably player a bigger role in your Windows CE code, so I'll describe the *Array* function.

Array function

The *Array* function takes a list of comma-separated arguments and returns an array containing the list of supplied arguments. The syntax of the *Array* function is *variable = Array(arg1 [,arg2...])*. The following code shows how you might use the *Array* function.

```
Dim ProductType
Dim Item

ProductType = Array("1 - Grocery", 1, "2 - Tobacco", 2, "3 -
    Alcohol", 3)

For Each Item In ProductType
    If IsNumeric(Item) = False Then
        List1.AddItem Item
    Else
        List1.ItemData(List1.NewIndex) = Item
    End If
Next
```

In the example above, the variable *ProductType* is initially declared as a Variant. Assigning the result from the *Array* function causes a coercion to type Variant array. The bounds of the array are 0 to 5 because Windows CE supports only 0 as the lower bound of an array. The same result could be achieved using the more conventional coding technique of declaring the variable as an array and then assigning a value to each element, but the *Array* function is more efficient for small arrays.

The arguments of the *Array* function need not be hard-coded "constant" type values, as in our example above. Because the array created is a Variant array, you can use variables or even other arrays as arguments. The example on the following page illustrates this.

```
Dim FirstArray
Dim SecondArray
Dim ThirdVariable

FirstArray = Array("A Value", "Another Value")
SecondArray = Array(FirstArray, "A Third Value")
ThirdVariable = SecondArray(0)
Print ThirdVariable(0)        ' Prints "A Value"
Print ThirdVariable(1)        ' Prints "Another Value"
Print SecondArray(1)          ' Prints "A Third Value"
```

When assigning arrays as elements of an array, remember that because the element is, in fact, an array, any variable you assign that element to will also be coerced to an array type. You can assign *SecondArray(0)* to another variable that would then, in fact, contain *FirstArray*, or you could interrogate the array *in situ*:

```
Print SecondArray(0)(0)       ' Prints "A Value"
Print SecondArray(0)(1)       ' Prints "Another Value"
```

For Each statement

The *For Each* programming construct should be familiar to nearly all programmers. With the increased support functions for array handling, you should be aware that the *For Each* construct can be used for arrays in addition to objects. (This has been available since Visual Basic 5.)

```
Dim ItemPrice
Dim Goods

Goods = Array(10, 12.54, 9.85)
For Each ItemPrice In Goods
    ItemPrice = ItemPrice + CalculateTaxOn(ItemPrice)
Next
```

In the example above, as the loop iterates, *ItemPrice* evaluates to the actual data in the array *Goods* for each element in turn.

CreateObject function

The *CreateObject* function is not new; in fact, it has been around for some time, but most Visual Basic programmers probably use the more familiar syntax *Set X = New Object*. The Windows CE Toolkit for Visual Basic 5 does not allow the declaration of API calls—the *Declare* keyword is no longer valid, nor is the *New* keyword. Therefore, it is now necessary to use the *CreateObject* function to instantiate instances of ActiveX (COM) objects.

If you have created objects in Visual Basic before, you might have noticed that the object reference held in HKEY_CLASSES_ROOT of the Registry identifies your object by ServerName.ClassName. Therefore, if you create an ActiveX component (say, CUSTOMER.DLL) with public classes of Account and History, the entry in HKEY_CLASSES_ROOT would contain the entries shown in Figure 5-13.

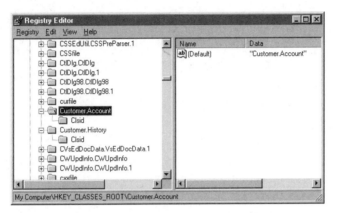

FIGURE 5-13   *Objects are identified by ServerName.ClassName*

Although you cannot build objects for Windows CE using Visual Basic, you can still use objects created in another language like Visual C++ 5 with the Windows CE Toolkit. This can be particularly useful because you have the ability to create C++ objects that wrap API functionality.

The syntax of the CreateObject function is *CreateObject(ServerName.ClassName)*. The following code shows how you would normally use this function to create a COM object instance.

```
Dim WinCeDB
WinCeDB = CreateObject("WinCeAPI.DataBaseFunctions")
WinCeDB.OpenDatabase Id, "My Database", 0, 0, vbNull
```

Some Microsoft applications like Word and Excel expose objects that you can use. I would strongly recommend using these and other Microsoft objects where possible. I would also expect a plethora of third-party objects to hit the market shortly, though you should apply your usual testing methods before using any of these.

For Next statement

A minor change has been made to the *For Next* construct. In Windows CE development you are not allowed to specify the counter variable on the Next line. The code

```
For Counter = 1 to 100
    ⋮
Next Counter
```

is invalid and will produce an error. The code would have to be written as

```
For Counter = 1 to 100
    ⋮
Next
```

in order to work.

String functions

Visual Basic string functions can no longer be used with the type suffix. Because the language supports only Variant data types, you will need to use the Variant functions instead, such as *Mid* instead of *Mid$*.

File handling

File handling is an intrinsic part of many applications. However, the file handling routines you are probably used to are not included in the language. Instead, a new ActiveX control is provided that wraps all the file functionality. The *FileSystem* component adds two controls to the toolbox: the FileSystem control and the File control. To use these you need to place them on a form.

The FileSystem control   This control provides the means to manipulate the file system, such as creating and deleting files, searching, copying, and getting or setting file attributes. The following code snippet shows how you would use a FileSystem control (*fs*) to fill a list box with file names.

```
Do
    If sFile = "" Then sFile = fs.Dir(sPath & "*.*") Else sFile = fs.Dir
    If sFile = "" Then Exit Do
    List1.AddItem sPath & sFile
Loop
```

The File control   Whereas the FileSystem control provides the functionality to manipulate the file system, the File control allows you to create, read, and write file data. This example writes data to a random access file.

```
Dim vData

Const REC_LEN = 20

Const ModeInput = 1:  Const LockShared = 1:   Const AccessRead = 1
Const ModeOutput = 2: Const LockRead = 2:     Const AccessWrite = 2
Const ModeRandom = 4: Const LockWrite = 3:    Const AccessReadWrite = 3
Const ModeAppend = 8: Const LockReadWrite = 5
Const ModeBinary = 32

vData = Array("Chris", "John", "Julie")

fl.Open "My File", ModeRandom, AccessReadWrite, LockShared, REC_LEN
fl.Put vData(0), 1    ' Write record 1
fl.Put vData(1), 2    ' Write record 2
fl.Put vData(2), 3    ' Write record 3
fl.Close
```

Language objects

The Windows CE Toolkit for Visual Basic 5 language has seven objects. These are:

- *App*
- *Clipboard*
- *Err*
- *Finance*
- *Font*
- *Form*
- *Screen*

Of these objects, the *Finance* object is new. The other objects are Windows CE implementations with reduced functionality from other Visual Basic versions. The *Finance* object, as you might expect, provides financial functions, but you must create this object yourself in order to use it, as you can see below:

```
Dim oFinance
Set oFinance = CreateObject("pVBFinFunc.pVBFinFunc")
Text1.Text = oFinance.Pmt(0.0083, 48, 12000)
```

I would recommend that you study the Books Online carefully to determine exactly the functionality of these objects.

Dealing with Errors

In terms of error handling you have two choices: don't, or use *On Error Resume Next*. You cannot use line numbers or labels in your code, so *On Error GoTo* would not work anyway. If you've been reading the various error handling articles produced by both Peet Morris and me, you are no doubt aware of the broad strategy of inserting generic catch-all error handling code throughout your application and then writing more specific handlers for anticipated errors. With the reduced error handling capabilities, a good scheme for Windows CE applications is to omit the generic handlers and just code for anticipated errors. This is because the Windows CE error handling mechanism has also been changed. If an unhandled error occurs, Visual Basic will display the default error message box; unlike other versions of Visual Basic, however, the program will not be terminated. Instead, the call stack is cleared and your application returns to an idle state (the state you were in before the last event was invoked). Beware! Your application is now in a stable state, *not* a known state. If you have written some data or manipulated some variables before the error occurred, it is possible that your application will actually be in an invalid state. The following pseudocode illustrates this:

```
Private Sub PurchaseItem_Click()
    aShoppingBasket = GetShoppingBasketList
    aCustomerAcct = GetCustomerAccount
    aShipList = GetShipList
    For Each Item In aShoppingBasket
        If aCustomerAcct(CustomerBalance) - Item(Price) > 0 Then
            AddToShipList Item(ItemCode), aCustomerAcct(CustomerNumber)
            *** ERROR ****
            DeductFromCustomer Item(ItemPrice), _
                            aCustomerAcct(CustomerNumber)
        End If
    Next
End Sub
```

In this example the unhandled error causes the procedure to exit, and code after the error will not be executed. If the *For Each* loop had already performed some iterations before the error, you would effectively have a situation where some of the orders had been placed, but not all of them. The shopping basket data would still contain both processed and unprocessed orders, which means that if the procedure were invoked again for the same customer, you would have doubled some of the orders. You can prevent errors such as this by changing the design of your program. For example, in the code above, a better idea would be to remove the item from the shopping basket immediately after an individual order has been placed, and then write a specific error handler around the transaction.

The default error message box displayed by Windows CE is shown in Figure 5-14. The error message varies depending on where the error has occurred; in this example, the error has occurred after the application's form has loaded. Errors in the *Form_Load* event procedure are a little harder to trap. This is because the *Form_Load* event procedure executes before the debugger is loaded. You cannot, therefore, set a breakpoint to trap the error. Remember that Visual Basic debugging is not integrated with the Windows CE environment, so the Break options have no effect. An error that occurs while running your application does not cause the program to break into debug mode. The only way to trap an error is to set a breakpoint in the debugger and then step through the code until the error is reached.

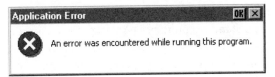

Figure 5-14   *An unhandled error message from Visual Basic for Windows CE*

The Pontoon application does not contain any error handlers. At design time and during coding, I evaluated the possibility of an error occurring. In this application there are no places where I can anticipate an error, so it would be a waste to code error handlers everywhere just in case. Remember that using *On Error Resume Next* requires lots of code to implement correctly because you need to check for an error after every line where an error could possibly occur. Another disadvantage is that because you cannot have line labels, you will effectively end up having deeply-nested conditionals. When determining your error handling requirements, it is obviously important to consider how critical the application is. If the Pontoon game has an error, the consequences are not severe. The *Err* object is available for diagnosing errors, although the *Erl* property is not present for obvious reasons.

If these limitations seem a little restrictive, I'll remind you again of the types of applications you will be creating at this stage. As Microsoft's goal to allow development for any platform in Visual Basic gets closer to reality and the hardware's capacity grows, I expect the error handling capabilities will grow to comparable levels with that of other versions of Visual Basic (or maybe even C++!).

The Windows CE Desktop Emulator

The Windows CE Desktop Emulator is a program supplied with the Windows CE Platform Software Development Kit (and also supplied with the Windows CE toolkit). The emulator is a program that runs the Windows CE operating system on your desktop. You can start the emulator by running the program manually, or it is started automatically when you run a Windows CE application from Visual Basic after having selected the target device as Emulator. You can write, test, and run your applications wholly within the emulator without having a physical HPC device at all. The Start menu of the emulator is really a dummy menu—you cannot use it to access any of the programs loaded in the emulator. To browse and copy files within the emulator's environment, you need to run the My Handheld PC program from the desktop. Even from here not all the programs will run in the emulator, though your Visual Basic programs will. The emulator's file system is stored in the object store (essentially an OBS file), meaning that you cannot copy or move files between your PC and the emulator using standard methods like drag-and-drop. To do this you need to use the program EMPFILE.EXE, which you can find in the \wce\emul\ hpc\Windows folder in the Windows CE Platform SDK folder. The location of the Windows CE Platform SDK folder obviously depends on your installation options. The following listing shows the Help information that the program displays when run from an MS-DOS window:

```
C:\Program Files\Windows CE Platform SDK\wce\emul\hpc\windows>empfile
USAGE:  EMPFILE [options]...

options:
 -c SOURCE DEST  ('put' or 'get' a file from object store)
 -d FILE         (delete a file on object store)
 -e FILE         (check to see if a file exists on object store)
 -s              (synchronize object store with wce\emul\PLATFORM\ tree)
 -r MYAPP ARGS   (run myapp.exe in the object store with arguments ARGS)

examples:
   EMPFILE -s
           (Synchronize wce\emul\PLATFORM\ tree with object store)
   EMPFILE -c c:\test.exe wce:windows\test.exe
           (Copy c:\test.exe to object store's Windows\ directory)
   EMPFILE -c wce:test.exe c:\test.exe
           (Copy test.exe from object store to c:\)
   EMPFILE -e windows\text.exe
           (verify that test.exe Exists in object store's
           Windows\ directory)
```

```
EMPFILE -d test.txt
        (Delete test.txt from object store root directory)
EMPFILE -r test.exe -10
        (Run test.exe from object store with parameter "-10")
```

You can use EMPFILE to copy files to and from the emulator and also to synchronize databases between the emulator and your PC. If you write any programs that require external files (such as bitmaps), you need to use EMPFILE to copy those files to the emulator so that these files are available when you run your program under the emulator.

Testing and Debugging Your Application

The limitations of the current version of the Windows CE toolkit mean that you will have to thoroughly test and debug your code, even more so than you do now. The debugger allows you to debug applications running either in the emulator or on the HPC. Before running your application at design time, you will first need to download the run-time files. This option is available under the Windows CE menu. This process downloads the Visual Basic run-time library files to the emulator environment and to the HPC. Once completed, you will need to be sure that you download the controls required by your application by selecting Control Manager from the Windows CE menu. Figure 5-15 shows the Control Manager screen.

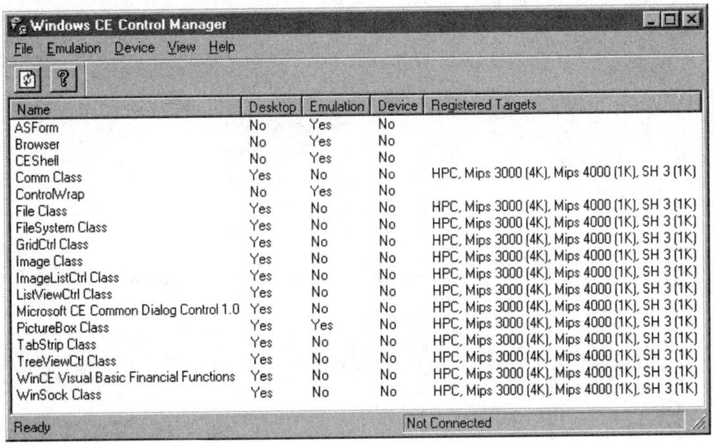

FIGURE 5-15   *Windows CE Control Manager*

You need to download only the controls you are using in your project, but they must be downloaded to either the emulator or to the HPC depending on the target you have selected. Select the controls to download and use the Emulation or Device menus to install or uninstall the controls. Once you have completed these steps you can run your program in the normal way—using F5 or the *Run* command.

Running a Windows CE application in the development environment is a little slower than normal, because the program is downloaded and run within the selected environment. The debugger application interfaces with that environment. The debug facility offers a reduced set of functionality compared to other versions of Visual Basic. Once in the debugger you can set breakpoints, but you cannot change any code. The debugger supports the same debug actions as in other versions. Figure 5-16 shows the debug window.

The biggest difference between this debug window and that which you will become accustomed to is that you cannot change code within it. To change your code you will need to stop the application, close the debugger, amend your code, and then rerun it. Unfortunately, if you keep the debug window open after stopping the application, you need to set your breakpoints again when you restart another instance of the debugger—there's no way around it!

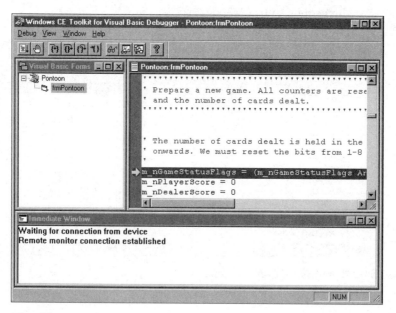

FIGURE 5-16   *The debug window*

Run-time errors in the development environment are dealt with differently than what you might be used to. Misspelled variable or function names and parameter constants are not all detected until the procedure is entered. One tip for avoiding these errors is to always type these elements in lowercase. If valid, the capitalization will be changed to that of the declaration; if not, the case will remain unchanged. This will give you a good indication that a variable name is correct.

Sometimes you might find the debug window a distraction. If this happens, you can prevent the debug window from being displayed by deselecting the Build Debug option on the Make tab of the Project Properties dialog box.

Deploying Your Application

You can get your application onto the HPC device in one of two ways, both of which are equally as easy. For one-off installation you can simply copy the application and its data files to the HPC using the Mobile Devices folder. The Mobile Devices folder works in the same way as Windows Explorer, and you can drag-and-drop files as well as create folders and shortcuts. You can also access your HPC device directly through Windows Explorer. Before copying your application you will need to compile it using the Make option, just as with a regular Visual Basic application. There are no optimization options because the compiled program is rather like a P-Code executable. The compiled application has a PVB file extension. If you are using any custom controls, you will need to install these onto the device using the Control Manager, and you will need to register ActiveX components using the REGSVRCE.EXE program (the Windows CE equivalent of REGSVR32.EXE).

For a more formal installation, you will need to use the Application Install Wizard (available from the Windows CE menu), which works in a similar way to the Setup Wizard in other versions of Visual Basic. Installation programs for Windows CE applications follow the same format. When installing from a setup program, the setup checks the status of your device and then prompts you to select the components you want to install. The application's setup files are extracted to a temporary storage area on the HPC. At this point, the PC's work is all but done and you are prompted to check your device for further messages. As soon as the PC has finished the copy process, the HPC starts installing the files. This is normally a fairly quick process; your application is then ready to run.

Extending Visual Basic Using COM DLLs

The Windows CE toolkit does not allow you to declare API functions, but you can use the *CreateObject* function to create instances of ActiveX components. Therefore, if you want to use any of the Windows CE API functions, you will need to create an ActiveX object that wraps the functionality required. Before embarking on this task, I would advise that you check the necessity for the particular API functions you want to use. Remember that the operating system itself contains only a subset of the Win32 API. Whereas the Win32 API has some 15,000 functions, the Windows CE API has only around 1200—the function you require might not even exist. I can recommend the book *Microsoft Windows CE Programmer's Guide* (Microsoft Press) as an excellent reference. This book gives complete documentation of the Windows CE API and covers topics such as communications and file and Registry access.

There are two "legitimate" areas of functionality for which you might decide to write ActiveX components. The first is the ActiveSync functionality. The Windows CE databases can be synchronized with a PC using ActiveSync. When your HPC performs its synchronization, what it is actually synchronizing are the databases on your device. The HPC is shipped with the Contacts, Calendar, Inbox, and other databases. In addition, you can create your own databases using the HPC Database application that comes with most HPC devices. The HPC Database application is normally found in the Databases icon on the desktop. You can configure ActiveSync to maintain synchronized copies of any or all these databases. Using the API you can achieve this functionality in code, which is useful if you write applications incorporating the Windows CE database functionality.

The database API functions are another area for which you might want to write wrappers. The API gives you the ability to create, open, enumerate, read, write, and delete the Windows CE database files.

To create an ActiveX wrapper you will need Visual C++ 5 and the Windows CE Toolkit for Visual C++ 5. Using this combination you can create a DLL that implements an Active Template Library (ATL) COM object, and then create instances of that object in your Visual Basic program by using the *CreateObject* function.

Staying in Control

Effective Weapons in the War Against Bugs

MARK PEARCE

Mark is a TMS Associate who has been programming professionally for the past 19 years, working mainly in the investment banking industry. In recent years, Mark has concentrated on the design and development of effective client/server systems. His interest in zero-defect software comes from a previous incarnation as a professional chess player, where one mistake can lose you your next meal. Mark's current ambitions include making more money than he spends, not ever learning any flavor of Java, and finding the perfect mountain running trail.

Program bugs are highly ecological because program code is a renewable resource. If you fix a bug, another will grow in its place. And if you cut down that bug, yet another will emerge; only this one will be a mutation with long, poisonous tentacles and revenge in its heart, and it will sit there deep in your program, cackling and making elaborate plans for the most terrible time to strike.

Every week seems to bring Visual Basic developers more powerful but also more complex language features, custom controls, APIs, tools, and operating systems. While Visual Basic 5 finally brought us a "grown-up" language with real enterprise pretensions, Visual Basic 6 arrives only a year later, along with a whole new raft of acronyms and concepts. The phrase "technological downpour," coined by a Microsoft executive, strikes a chord with both developers and their managers. In the midst of all this technological chaos, the deadlines become tougher and our tools often refuse to cooperate with one another. If whatever we build lasts at least until we've finished building it, we consider it an unexpected bonus. Yet we are expected to sculpt stable Microsoft Visual Basic code that gives our users more flexible, less costly, and easier-to-use systems.

From this chapter's point of view, the key word is "stable." It's no use being able to churn out ever larger and more capable systems with these new, improved, wash-whiter-than-white tools if all that we succeed in doing is producing more defects. Developers tend to take a casual attitude toward bugs. They know them intimately, including their origin and even their species. A typical programmer looks at bugs in the same manner as an Amazonian tribe member looks at the insect-infested jungle—as an inevitable fact of life. The typical user is more like a tourist from the big city stranded in the same jungle. Surrounded by hordes of disgustingly hairy creepy-crawlies with too many legs and a nasty habit of appearing in the most unexpected places, the user often becomes upset—which is hardly surprising. This different perspective is one that software developers need to consider if they expect to meet user expectations.

An Expensive Tale

Production bugs are expensive, often frighteningly so. They're expensive in monetary terms when it comes to locating and fixing them. They're expensive in terms of data loss and corruption. And they're expensive when it comes to the loss of user confidence in your software. Some of these factors can be difficult to measure precisely, but they exist all the same. If we examine the course of a typical production defect in hard monetary terms alone, we can get some idea of the magnitude of costs involved when developers allow bugs into their master sources.

Enter Erica, a foreign exchange dealer for a major investment bank, who notices that the software she is using to measure her open U.S. dollar position seems to be misreporting the value of certain trades. Luckily she spots the defect quickly, before any monetary loss is incurred. Being distrustful of the new software, she has been keeping track of her real position on her trade blotter, so the only real cost so far is the time she has had to devote to identifying the problem and proving that it exists. But in that time, she has lost the opportunity to make an advantageous currency trade. Defect cost so far: $5,000.

Peter, a long-time programmer in the bank's Information Systems (IS) department, is given the task of finding and fixing the defect. Although Peter is not very familiar with the software in question, the original developer's highly paid contract ended a week ago, and he's lying on a beach in Hawaii. Peter takes a day to track down the bug (a misunderstanding about when Visual Basic triggers the *LostFocus* event of a text box) and another day to fix the program, test his fix, and run some regression tests to ensure that he has not affected any other part of the program. Defect cost so far: $6,000.

Sally is asked to check Peter's work and to write up the documentation. She notices that the same problem occurs in four other programs written by the contractor and tells Peter to fix those programs too. The fixes, testing, and documentation take another three days. Defect cost so far: $9,000.

Tony in the Quality Assurance (QA) department is the next person to receive the amended programs. He spends a day running the full set of QA standard tests. Defect cost so far: $10,000.

Finally, Erica is asked to sign off the new release for production. Because of other pressing work, she performs only the minimal testing needed to convince herself that she is no longer experiencing the same problem. The bug fix now has all the signatures necessary for production release. Total defect cost: $11,000.

But wait: statistics show that some 50 percent of bug fixes lead to the introduction of at least one new bug, which brings the statistical cost of this particular bug to over $16,000! This amount doesn't include the overhead costs of production support and implementation.

This example of a typical defect found in a production environment illustrates that the financial expenses involved in finding and fixing software bugs are often large. A commonly accepted figure in the information technology (IT) industry is that this kind of problem costs an order of magnitude more at each stage of the process. In other words, if the bug in our particular example had been found by the programmer during development, it might have cost $16 to fix. Found by a tester, the cost would have been around $160. Found by a user before it had gone into production, the cost might have been $1,600. Once the problem reaches production, the potential costs are enormous.

The most expensive bug ever reported (by Gerald Weinberg in 1983), the result of a one-character change in a previously working program, cost an incredible $1.6 billion. The jury is still out on the true cost of the Year 2000 bug, but current estimates are in the region of $600 billion worldwide. (See Chapter 8 for an in-depth treatment of the Y2K problem.) Intel spent $200 million to compensate PC owners for the now notorious Pentium bug. In 1992, a fly-by-wire passenger plane crashed during an air show, killing eleven people. The crash was traced to a bug in the software controlling the plane's flight systems. A total failure caused by bugs in a new software system installed to control the dispatch of London ambulances was judged to have directly contributed to at least one patient's death. In 1996, a London brokerage house had to pay more than $1 million to its customers after new software failed to handle customer accounts properly. The list goes on and on.

Most bugs don't have such life-or-death effects; still, the need for zero-defect or low-defect software is becoming increasingly important to our civilization. We have everything from nuclear power stations to international banking systems controlled by software, making bugs both more dangerous and more expensive. This chapter is about techniques that help to reduce or eliminate bugs in production code, especially when writing Visual Basic 6 programs.

What Are We Trying to Accomplish?

The aim of this chapter is to teach you different methods of catching bugs during Visual Basic 6 program development and unit testing, before they can reach the master source files. As programmers, we are in a unique position. First, we can learn enough about bugs and their causes to eliminate large classes of them from our programs during initial development. Second, we are probably the only people who have sufficient knowledge of the internal workings of our programs to unit-test them effectively and thereby identify and remove many bugs before they ever reach our testers and users. Developers tend to be highly creative and imaginative people. The challenge is to impose a certain discipline on that talent in order to attack the bug infestation at its very source. Success in meeting this challenge will give us increased user confidence, fewer user support calls and complaints, shorter product development times, lower maintenance costs, shorter maintenance backlogs, and increased developer confidence—not to mention an ability to tamper with the reality of those developers who think that a zero-defect attitude to writing code is nonproductive.

A Guided Tour

In the first part of this chapter, we'll take a look at some of the more strategic issues involved in the high bug rate currently experienced by the IT industry. We'll also look at some of the latest ideas that leading software companies such as Microsoft and Borland use to tackle those issues. Although these ideas aren't all directly related to writing code, Visual Basic developers and their managers need to understand them and the issues behind them. As Visual Basic 6 becomes more and more the corporate tool of choice in the production of large-scale projects, we are faced with a challenge to produce complex, low-defect systems within reasonable schedules and budgets. Without a firm strategic base on which to build, the game will be lost even before we start designing and coding.

We'll also examine the role that management and developer attitudes play in helping to produce fewer bugs. One of the key ideas here is that most program bugs that reach production can be avoided by stressing the correct software development attitudes. Several studies have shown that programming teams are successful in meeting the targets they set, provided these targets are specific, nonambiguous, and appropriately weighted in importance for the project being tackled. The attitudes of developers are driven by these targets, and we'll look at ways of reinforcing the attitudes associated with low bug rates.

Then it will be time to get our hands dirty. You probably remember those medieval maps that used to mark large empty regions with the phrase "Here Be Dragons." We're going to aim for their Visual Basic 6 equivalent, boldly venturing into the regions labeled "Here Be Nasty Scaly Six-Legged Hairy Bugs" and looking at some issues directly related to Visual Basic design and coding. We'll see where some of the more notorious and ravenous bugs are sleeping and find out how we can avoid waking them—or at least how we can avoid becoming really tangled up in them. At this point, we'll sometimes have to delve into rather technical territory. This journey into technical details is unfortunately inevitable when peering at creatures worthy of some of H. R. Giger's worst creations. Once you come out on the other side unharmed, you should have a much better appreciation of when and where Visual Basic developers have to be careful.

In the final section of this chapter, we'll look at some tools that can aid the bug detection and prevention processes in several ways. Microsoft seems to have established a virtual monopoly on the term "Wizard" to describe an add-in or utility designed to help programmers with some aspect of code development. So casting around for a suitable synonym, I came up with "Sourcerer" (thanks, Don!) instead, or perhaps Sourceress. Three such tools are demonstrated and explained.

The three sourcerers

The first tool is the Assertion Sourcerer, an add-in that supplements Visual Basic 6's *Debug.Assert* statement and allows you to implement assertions even in compiled modules, ideal for testing distributed components. Next comes the Metrics Sourcerer, also an add-in. It uses a couple of fairly simple measurements to estimate the relative complexity of your Visual Basic 6 project's procedures, forms, and classes. Several studies have shown that the longer and more complex a procedure, the more likely it is to have bugs discovered in it after being released to production. The final utility is the Instrumentation Sourcerer, yet another add-in. It adds instrumentation code to your Visual Basic 6 project to track all user interactions with your application's graphical interface. This tool can be invaluable in both tracking a user's actions leading up to that elusive program bug and showing exactly how different users use your application in the real world.

"Some final thoughts" sections

Throughout this chapter, many sections end with a recommendation (entitled "Some Final Thoughts") culled from both my own experiences and those of many other people in the IT industry. Acting on these suggestions is probably less important than understanding the issues behind them, as discussed in each section. These recommendations are just opinions, candidly stated, with no reading between the lines required.

Some Strategic Issues

Before we take a closer look at Visual Basic 6, we need to examine several general factors: priorities, technological progress, and overall project organization. Without understanding and controlling these factors, the best developers in the world can't avoid producing defects. These issues are not really Visual Basic 6–specific. Their effect is more on the whole development process. To extend the bug/beastie analogy onto even shakier ground, these are the real gargoyles of the bug world. Their presence permeates a whole project, and if left unrecognized or untamed they can do severe and ongoing damage.

Priorities: The Four-Ball Juggling Act

Software development is still much more of an art than a science. Perhaps one area in which we can apply a discipline more reminiscent of normal engineering is that of understanding and weighing the different aspects of a project. In almost any project, four aspects are critical:

1. The features to be delivered to the users

2. The hardware, software, and other budgets allocated to the project

3. The time frames in which the project phases have to be completed

4. The number of known defects with which the project is allowed to go into production

Balancing these four factors against one another brings us firmly into the realm of classical engineering trade-offs. Concentrating on any one of these aspects to the exclusion of the others is almost never going to work. Instead, a continuous juggling act is required during the life of most projects. Adding a new and complicated feature might affect the number of production bugs. Refusing to relax a specific project delivery date might mean reducing the number of delivered features. Insisting on the removal of every last bug, no matter how trivial, might significantly increase the allocated budgets. So the users, managers, and developers make a series of decisions during the life of a project about what will (or won't) be done, how it will be done, and which of these four aspects takes priority at any specific time.

The major requirement here from the zero-defect point of view is that all the project members have an explicit understanding about the relative importance of each of these aspects, especially that of production bugs. This consensus gives everybody a framework on which to base their decisions. If a user asks for a big new feature at the very end of the project, he or she has no excuse for being unaware of the significant chance of production bugs associated with the new feature, or of the budget and schedule implications of preventing those bugs from reaching production. Everybody will realize that a change in any one of these four areas nearly always involves compromises in the other three.

A project I was involved with some time ago inherited a legacy Microsoft SQL Server database schema. We were not allowed to make any significant structural changes to this database, which left us with no easy way of implementing proper concurrency control. After considering our project priorities, we decided to do without proper concurrency control in order to be able to go into production on the planned date. In effect, we decided that this major design bug was acceptable given our other constraints. Knowing the original project priorities made it much easier for us to make the decision based on that framework. Without the framework, we would have spent significant time investigating potential solutions to this problem at the expense of the more important project schedules. When pointed out in black and white, our awareness of the project's priorities seems obvious. But you'd be surprised at the number of projects undertaken with vague expectations and unspecified goals. Far too often, there is confusion about exactly which features will be implemented, which bugs will be fixed, and how flexible the project deadlines and budgets really are.

Some final thoughts   Look at your project closely, and decide the priorities in order of their importance. Determine how important it is for your project to go to production with as few bugs as possible. Communicate this knowledge to all people involved in the project, including the users. Make sure that everyone has the framework in which to make project decisions based on these and other priorities.

Progress Can Be Dangerous

Avalanches have caused about four times as many deaths worldwide in the 1990s as they did in the 1950s. Today, in spite of more advanced weather forecasting, an improved understanding of how snow behaves in different climatic conditions, and the use of sophisticated locating transmitters, many more people die on the slopes. In fact, analysis shows that the technological progress made over the last four decades has actually contributed to the problem. Skiers, snowboarders, and climbers are now able to roam into increasingly remote areas and backwoods. The wider distribution of knowledge about the mountains and the availability of sophisticated instruments have also given people increased confidence in surviving an avalanche. While many more people are practicing winter sports and many more adventurers have the opportunity to push past traditional limits, the statistics show that they have paid a heavy price.

In the same way that technological progress has ironically been accompanied by a rise in the number of avalanche-related deaths, the hot new programming tools now available to developers have proved to be a major factor in the far higher bug rates that we are experiencing today compared to five or ten years ago. Back in the olden days of Microsoft Windows programming (about 1990 or so), the only tools for producing Windows programs were intricate and difficult to learn. Only developers prepared to invest the large amounts of time required to learn complex data structures and numerous application programming interface (API) calls could hope to produce something that even looked like a normal Windows program. Missing the exact esoteric incantations and laying on of hands, software developed by those outside an elite priesthood tended to collapse in a heap when its users tried to do anything out of the ordinary—or sometimes just when they tried to run it. Getting software to work properly required developers to be hardcore in their work—to understand the details of how Windows worked and what they were doing at a very low level. In short, real Windows programming was often seriously frustrating work.

With the introduction of Microsoft Visual Basic and other visual programming tools, a huge amount of the grunt work involved in producing Windows programs has been eliminated. At last, someone who hasn't had a great deal of training and experience can think about producing applications that have previously been the province of an elite group. It is no longer necessary to learn the data structures associated with a window or the API calls necessary to draw text on the screen. A simple drag-and-drop operation with a mouse now performs the work that previously took hours.

The effect has been to reduce dramatically the knowledge levels and effort needed to write Windows programs. Almost anybody who is not a technophobe can produce something that resembles, at least superficially, a normal Windows program. Although placing these tools into the hands of so many people is great news for many computer users, it has led to a startling increase in the number of bug-ridden applications and applications canceled because of runaway bug lists. Widespread use of these development tools has not been accompanied by an equally widespread understanding of how to use them properly to produce solid code.

What is necessary to prevent many types of defects is to understand the real skills required when starting your particular project. Hiring developers who understand Visual Basic alone is asking for trouble. No matter how proficient programmers are with Visual Basic, they're going to introduce bugs into their programs unless they're equipped with at least a rudimentary understanding of how the code they write is going to interact with all the other parts of the system. In a typical corporate client/server project, the skills needed cover a broad range besides technical expertise with Visual Basic. Probably the most essential element is an understanding of how to design the application architecture properly and then be able to implement the architecture as designed. In the brave new world of objects everywhere, a good understanding of Microsoft's Component Object Model (COM) and of ActiveX is also essential. In addition, any potential developer needs to understand the conventions used in normal Windows programs. He or she must understand the client/server paradigm and its advantages and disadvantages, know an appropriate SQL dialect and how to write efficient stored procedures, and be familiar with one or more of the various database communication interfaces such as Jet, ODBC, RDO, and ADO (the VB interface to OLE DB). Other areas of necessary expertise might include knowledge about the increasingly important issue of LAN and WAN bandwidth and an understanding of 16-bit and 32-bit Windows architecture together with the various flavors of Windows APIs. As third-party ActiveX controls become more widespread and more complex, it might even be necessary to hire a developer mainly for his or her expertise in the use of a specific control.

Some final thoughts   You don't hire a chainsaw expert to cut down trees—you hire a tree surgeon who is also proficient in the use of chainsaws. So to avoid the serious bugs that can result from too narrow an approach to programming, hire developers who understand client/server development and the technical requirements of your specific application, not those who only understand Visual Basic.

Dancing in Step

One of the most serious problems facing us in the battle against bugs is project size and its implications. As the size of a project team grows linearly, the number of communication channels required between the team members grows factorially (in fact, almost exponentially once the numbers reach a certain level). Traditionally, personal computer projects have been relatively small, often involving just two or three people. Now we're starting to see tools such as Visual Basic 6 being used in large-scale, mission-critical projects staffed by ten to twenty developers or more. These project teams can be spread over several locations, even over different continents, and staffed by programmers with widely varying skills and experience.

The object-oriented approach is one attempt to control this complexity. By designing discrete objects that have their internal functions hidden and that expose clearly defined interfaces for talking to other objects, we can simplify some of the problems involved in fitting together a workable application from many pieces of code produced by multiple developers.

However, programmers still have the problems associated with communicating what each one of hundreds of properties really represents and how every method and function actually works. Any assumptions a programmer makes have to be made clear to any other programmer who has to interact with the first programmer's objects. Testing has to be performed to ensure that none of the traditional implementation problems that are often found when combining components have cropped up. Where problems are found, two or more developers must often work together for a while to resolve them.

In an effort to deal with these issues, which can be a major cause of bugs, many software companies have developed the idea of working in parallel teams that join together and synchronize their work at frequent intervals, often daily. This technique enables one large team of developers to be split into several small teams, with frequent builds and periodic stabilization of their project. Small teams traditionally have several advantages over their larger counterparts. They tend to be more flexible, they communicate faster, they are less likely to have misunderstandings, and they exhibit more team spirit. An approach that divides big teams into smaller ones but still allows these smaller groups to synchronize and stabilize their work safely helps to provide small-team advantages even for large-team projects.

What is the perfect team size? To some extent, the optimum team size depends on the type of project; but studies typically show that the best number is three to four developers, with five or six as a maximum. Teams of this size communicate more effectively and are easier to control.

Having said this, I still think you need to devise an effective process that allows for the code produced by these small teams to be combined successfully into one large application. You can take several approaches to accomplish this combination. The process I recommend for enabling this "dancing in step," which is similar to the one Microsoft uses, is described here:

1. **Create a master copy of the application source.** This process depends on there being a single master copy of the application source code, from which a periodic (often daily) test build will be generated and released to users for testing.

2. **Establish a daily deadline after which the master source cannot be changed.** If nobody is permitted to change the master source code after a certain time each day, developers know when they can safely perform the synchronization steps discussed in detail in the rest of these steps.

3. **Check out.** Take a private copy of the code to be worked on from the master sources. You don't need to prevent more than one developer from checking out the same code because any conflicts will be dealt with at a later stage. (See step 8.)

4. **Make the changes.** Modify the private copy of the code to implement the new feature or bug fix.

5. **Build a private release.** Compile the private version of the code.

6. **Test the private release.** Check that the new feature or bug fix is working correctly.

7. **Perform pretesting code synchronization.** Compare the private version of the source code with the master source. The current master source could have changed since the developer checked out his or her private version of the source at the start of this process. The daily check-in deadline mentioned in step 2 ensures that the developers know when they can safely perform this synchronization.

8. **Merge the master source into the private source.** Merge the current master source into the private version of the source, thus incorporating any changes that other developers might have made. Any inconsistencies caused by other developers' changes have to be dealt with at this stage.

9. **Build a private release.** Build the new updated private version of the source.

10. **Test the private release.** Check that the new feature or bug fix still works correctly.

11. **Execute a regression test.** Test this second build to make sure that the new feature or bug fix hasn't adversely affected previous functionality.

12. **Perform pre-check-in code synchronization.** Compare the private version of the source code with the master source. Because this step is done just prior to the check-in itself (that is, before the check-in deadline), it will not be performed on the same day that the previous pretesting code synchronization (which occurs after the check-in deadline; see step 7) took place. Therefore, the master source might have changed in the intervening period.

13. **Check in.** Merge the private version of the source into the master source. You must do this before the daily check-in deadline mentioned in step 2 so that other developers can perform their private code synchronization and merges safely after the deadline.

14. **Observe later-same-day check-ins.** It is essential that you watch later check-ins that day before the deadline to check for potential indirect conflicts with the check-in described in step 13.

15. **Generate a daily build.** After the check-in deadline, build a new version of the complete application from the updated master sources. This build should be relatively stable, with appropriate punishments being allocated to project members who are responsible for any build breaks.

16. **Test the daily build.** Execute some tests, preferably automated, to ensure that basic functionality still works and that the build is reasonably stable. This build can then be released to other team members and users.

17. **Fix any problems immediately.** If the build team or the automated tests find any problems, the developer responsible for the build break or test failure should be identified and told to fix the problem immediately. It is imperative to fix the problem before it affects the next build and before that developer has the opportunity to break any more code. This should be the project's highest priority.

Although the above process looks lengthy and even somewhat painful in places, it ensures that multiple developers and teams can work simultaneously on a single application's master source code. It would be significantly more painful to experience the very frustrating and difficult bugs that traditionally arise when attempting to combine the work of several different teams of developers.

Some final thoughts   Split your larger project teams into smaller groups, and establish a process whereby these groups can merge and stabilize their code with that of the other project groups. The smaller teams will produce far fewer bugs than will the larger ones, and an effective merging process will prevent most of the bugs that would otherwise result from combining the work of the smaller teams into a coherent application.

Some Attitude Issues

One of the major themes of this chapter is that *attitude* is everything when it comes to writing zero-defect code. Developers aren't stupid, and they can write solid code when given the opportunity. Provided with a clear and unambiguous set of targets, developers are usually highly motivated and very effective at meeting those targets. If management sets a crystal-clear target of zero-defect code and then does everything sensible to encourage attitudes aimed at fulfilling that target, the probability is that the code produced by the team will have few defects. So given the goal of writing zero-defect code, let's look at some of the attitudes that are required.

Swallowing a Rhinoceros Sideways

The stark truth is that there is no such thing as zero-defect software. The joke definition passed down from generation to generation (a generation in IS being maybe 18 months or so) expresses it nicely: "Zero defects [noun]: The result of shutting down a production line." Most real-life programs contain at least a few bugs simply because writing bug-free code is so difficult. As one of my clients likes to remind me, if writing solid code were easy, everybody would be doing it. He also claims that writing flaky code is much easier—which might account for the large quantity of it generally available.

Having said this, it is really part of every professional developer's job to aim at writing bug-free code. Knowing that bugs are inevitable is no excuse for any attitude that allows them the slightest breathing space. It's all in the approach. Professional programmers know that their code is going to contain bugs, so they bench-test it, run it through the debugger, and generally hammer it every way they can to catch the problems that they know are lurking in there somewhere. If you watch the average hacker at work, you'll notice something interesting. As soon as said hacker is convinced that his program is working to his satisfaction, he stops working, leans back in his chair, shouts to his boss that he's ready to perform a production release, and then heads for the soda machine. He's happy that he has spent some considerable time trying to show that his program is correct. Now fast-forward this hacker a few years, to the point where he has become more cynical and learned much more about the art of programming. What do you see? After reaching the stage at which he used to quit, he promptly starts working again. This time, he's trying something different— rather than prove his program is correct, he's trying to prove that it's incorrect.

Perhaps one of the major differences between amateur and professional developers is that amateurs are satisfied to show that their programs appear to be bug-free, whereas professionals prefer to try showing that their programs still contain bugs. Most amateurs haven't had enough experience to realize that when they believe their program is working correctly, they are perhaps only halfway through the development process. After they've done their best to prove a negative (that their code doesn't have any bugs), they need to spend some time trying to show the opposite.

One very useful if somewhat controversial technique for estimating the number of bugs still remaining in an application is called defect seeding. Before performing extensive quality assurance or user acceptance tests, one development group deliberately seeds the application code with a set of documented defects. These defects should cover the entire functionality of the application, and range from fatal to cosmetic, just as in real life. At the point when you estimate that the testing process is near completion, given the ratio of the number of seeded defects detected to the total number of defects seeded, you can calculate the approximate number of bugs in the application by using the following formula:

$$D0 = (D1 / D2) * D3$$

D1 is the total number of seeded defects, D2 is the number of seeded defects found so far, and D3 is the number of real (i.e. non-seeded) defects found so far. The resulting figure of D0 is therefore the total number of defects in the application, and D0 minus D3 will give you the approximate number of real defects that still haven't been located.

Beware of forgetting to remove the seeded defects, or of introducing new problems when removing them. If possible, keep the seeded defect code encapsulated and thus easy to remove from the programs.

Some final thoughts   Find developers who are intelligent, knowledgeable, willing to learn, and good at delivering effective code. Find out whether they are also aware that writing bug-free code is so difficult that they must do everything possible to prevent and detect bugs. Don't hire them without this final magical factor. It's true that the first four qualities are all wonderful, but they are meaningless without this last one.

Looping the Loop

One of the most effective ways of restraining soaring bug rates is to attack the problem at its source—the programmer. Programmers have always known about the huge gap between the quality of code produced by the best and by the worst programmers. Industry surveys have verified this folklore by showing that the least effective developers in an organization produce more than twenty times the number of bugs that the most effective developers produce. It follows that an organization would benefit if its better programmers produced the majority of new code. With that in mind, some corporations have introduced the simple but revolutionary idea that programmers have to fix their own bugs—and have to fix them as soon as they are found.

This sets up what engineers call a negative feedback loop, otherwise known as evolution in action. The more bugs a programmer produces, the more time he or she is required to spend fixing those bugs. At least four benefits rapidly become apparent:

1. The more bugs a programmer produces, the less chance he or she has of working on new code and thereby introducing new bugs. Instead, the better programmers (judged by bug rate) get to write all the new code, which is therefore likely to have less bugs.

2. Programmers soon learn that writing buggy code is counterproductive. They aren't able to escape from the bugs they've introduced, so they begin to understand that writing solid code on the first pass is more effective and less wasteful of time than having to go back to old code, often several times in succession.

3. Bug-prone developers start to gain some insights into what it's like to maintain their own code. This awareness can have a salutary effect on their design and coding habits. Seeing exactly how difficult it is to test that extremely clever but error-prone algorithm teaches them to sympathize more with the maintenance programmers.

4. The software being written has very few known bugs at any time because the bugs are being fixed as soon as they're found. Runaway bug lists are stomped before they can gather any momentum. And the software is always at a point where it can be shipped almost immediately. It might not have all the features originally requested or envisioned, but those features that do exist will contain only a small number of known bugs. This ability to ship at any point in the life of a project can be very useful in today's fast-changing business world.

Some people might consider this type of feedback loop as a sort of punishment. If it does qualify as such, it's an extremely neutral punishment. What tends to happen is that the developers start to see it as a learning process. With management setting and then enforcing quality standards with this particular negative feedback loop, developers learn that producing bug-free code is very important. And like most highly motivated personalities, they soon adapt their working habits to whatever standard is set. No real crime and punishment occurs here;

the process is entirely objective. If you create a bug, you have to fix it, and you have to fix it immediately. This process should become laborious enough that it teaches developers how to prevent that type of bug in the future or how to detect that type of bug once it has been introduced.

Some final thoughts   Set a zero-defect standard and introduce processes that emphasize the importance of that standard. If management is seen to concentrate on the issue of preventing bugs, developers will respond with better practices and less defects.

Back to School

Although Visual Basic 6 is certainly not the rottweiler on speed that C++ and the Microsoft Foundation Classes (MFC) can be, there is no doubt that its increased power and size come with their own dangers. Visual Basic 6 has many powerful features, and these take a while to learn. Because the language is so big, a typical developer might use only 10 percent or even less of its features in the year he or she takes to write perhaps three or four applications. It has become increasingly hard to achieve expertise in such a large and complex language. So it is perhaps no surprise to find that many bugs stem from a misunderstanding of how Visual Basic implements a particular feature.

I'll demonstrate this premise with a fairly trivial example. An examination of the following function will reveal nothing obviously unsafe. Multiplying the two maximum possible function arguments that could be received (32767 * 32767) will never produce a result bigger than can be stored in the long variable that this function returns.

```
Private Function BonusCalc(ByVal niNumberOfWeeks As Integer, _
    ByVal niWeeklyBonus As Integer) As Long

BonusCalc = niNumberOfWeeks * niWeeklyBonus

End Function
```

Now if you happened to be diligent enough to receive a weekly bonus of $1,000 over a period of 35 weeks…well, let's just say that this particular function wouldn't deliver your expected bonus! Although the function looks safe enough, Visual Basic's intermediate calculations behind the scenes cause trouble. When multiplying the two integers together, Visual Basic attempts to store the temporary result into another *integer* before assigning it to *BonusCalc*. This, of course, causes an immediate overflow error. What you have to do instead is give the Visual Basic compiler some assistance. The following revised statement works because Visual Basic realizes that we might be dealing with longs rather than just integers:

```
BonusCalc = niNumberOfWeeks * CLng(niWeeklyBonus)
```

Dealing with these sorts of language quirks is not easy. Programmers are often pushed for time, so they sometimes tend to avoid experimenting with a feature to see how it really works in detail. For the same reasons, reading the manuals or online help is often confined to a hasty glance just to confirm syntax. These are false economies. Even given the fact that sections of some manuals appear to have been written by Urdu swineherders on some very heavy medication, those pages still contain many pearls. When you use something in Visual Basic 6 for the first time, take a few minutes to read about its subtleties in the documentation and write a short program to experiment with its implementation. Use it in several different ways within a program, and twist it into funny shapes. Find out what it can and can't handle.

Some final thoughts   Professional developers should understand the tools at their disposal at a detailed level. Learn from the manual how the tools *should* work, and then go beyond the manual and find out how they really work.

Yet More Schoolwork

Visual Basic 4 introduced the concept of object-oriented programming using the Basic language. Visual Basic 5 and 6 take this concept and elaborate on it in several ways. It is still possible to write Visual Basic 6 code that looks almost exactly like Visual Basic 3 code or that even resembles procedural COBOL code (if you are intent upon imitating a dinosaur). The modern emphasis, however, is on the use of relatively new ideas in Basic, such as abstraction and encapsulation, which aim to make applications easier to develop, understand, and maintain. Any Visual Basic developer unfamiliar with these ideas first has to learn what they are and why they are useful and then has to understand all the quirks of their implementation in Visual Basic 6. The learning curve is not trivial. For example, understanding how the *Implements* statement produces a virtual class that is Visual Basic 6's way of implementing polymorphism (and inheritance if you're a little sneaky) can require some structural remodeling of one's thought processes. This is heavy-duty object-oriented programming in the 1990s style. Trying to use it in a production environment without a clear understanding is a prime cause of new and unexpected bugs.

Developers faced with radically new concepts usually go through up to four stages of enlightenment. The first stage has to do with reading and absorbing the theory behind the concept. The second stage includes working with either code examples or actual programs written by other people that implement the new concept. The third stage involves using the new concept in their own code. Only at this point do programmers become fully aware of the subtleties involved and understand how *not* to write their code. The final stage of enlightenment arrives when the programmer learns how to implement the concept correctly, leaving no holes for the bugs to crawl through.

Some final thoughts   Developers should take all the time necessary to reach the third and fourth stages of enlightenment when learning new programming concepts or methodologies. Only then should they be allowed to implement these new ideas in production systems.

Eating Humble Pie

Most developers are continually surprised to find out how fallible they are and how difficult it is to be precise about even simple processes. The human brain is evidently not well equipped to deal with problems that require great precision to solve. It's not the actual complexity but the type of complexity that defeats us. Evolution has been successful in giving us some very sophisticated pattern-recognition algorithms and heuristics to deal with certain types of complexity. A classic example is our visual ability to recognize a human face even when seen at an angle or in lighting conditions never experienced before. Your ability to remember and compare patterns means that you can recognize your mother or father in circumstances that would completely defeat a computer program. Lacking your ability to recognize and compare patterns intelligently, the program instead has to use a brute-force approach, applying a very different type of intelligence to a potentially huge number of possibilities.

As successful as we are at handling some sorts of complexity, the complexity involved in programming computers is a different matter. The requirement is no longer to compare patterns in a holistic, or all-around, fashion but instead to be very precise about the comparison. In a section of program code, a single misplaced character, such as "+" instead of "&," can produce a nasty defect that often cannot be easily spotted because its cause is so small. So we have to watch our p's and q's very carefully, retaining our ability to look at the big picture while also ensuring that every tiny detail of the picture is correct. This endless attention to detail is not something at which the human brain is very efficient. Surrounded by a large number of potential bugs, we can sometimes struggle to maintain what often feels like a very precarious balance in our programs.

A programmer employed by my company came to me with a bug that he had found impossible to locate. When I looked at the suspect class module, the first thing I noticed was that one of the variables hadn't been declared before being used. Like every conscientious Visual Basic developer, he had set *Require Variable Declaration* in his Integrated Development Environment (IDE) to warn him about this type of problem. But in a classic case of programming oversight, he had made the perfectly reasonable assumption that setting this option meant that all undeclared variables are always recognized and stomped on. Unfortunately, it applies only to new modules developed from the point at which the flag is set. Any modules written within one developer's IDE and then imported into another programmer's IDE are never checked for undeclared variables unless that first developer also specified *Require Variable Declaration*. This is obvious when you realize how the option functions. It simply inserts *Option Explicit* at the top of each module when it is first created. What it doesn't do is act globally on all modules. This point is easy to recognize when you stop and think for a moment, but it's also very easy to miss.

Some final thoughts   Learn to be humble when programming. This stuff is seriously nontrivial (a fancy term for swallowing a rhinoceros sideways), and arrogance when you're trying to write stable code is counterproductive.

Jumping Out of The Loop

One psychological factor responsible for producing bugs and preventing their detection is an inability to jump from one mind-set to another.In our push to examine subtle details, we often overlook the obvious. The results of a study performed a decade ago showed that that 50 percent of all errors plainly visible on a screen or report were still overlooked by the programmer. The kind of mistake shown in the preceding sentence ("that" repeated) seems fairly obvious in retrospect, but did you spot it the first time through?

One reason for this tendency to overlook the obvious is that the mind-set required to find gross errors is so different from the mind-set needed to locate subtle errors that it is hard to switch between the two. We've all been in the situation in which the cause of a bug eludes us for hours, but as soon as we explain the problem to another programmer, the cause of the error immediately becomes obvious. Often in this type of confessional programming, the other developer doesn't have to say a word, just nod wisely. The mental switch from an internal monologue to an external one is sometimes all that we need to force us into a different mind-set, and we can then reevaluate our assumptions about what is happening in the code. Like one of those infuriating Magic Eye pictures, the change of focus means that what was hidden before suddenly becomes clear.

Some final thoughts   If you're stuck on a particularly nasty bug, try some lateral thinking. Use confessional programming—explain the problem to a colleague. Perhaps take a walk to get some fresh air. Work on something entirely different for a few minutes, returning later with a clearer mind for the problem. Or you can go so far as to picture yourself jumping out of that mental loop, reaching a different level of thought. All of these techniques can help you avoid endlessly traversing the same mental pathways.

GETTING OUR HANDS DIRTY

Steve Maguire, in his excellent book *Writing Solid Code* (Microsoft Press, 1995), stresses that many of the best techniques and tools developed for the eradication of bugs came from programmers asking the following two questions every time a bug is found:

- How could I have automatically detected this bug?
- How could I have prevented this bug?

In the following sections, we'll look at some of the bugs Visual Basic 6 programmers are likely to encounter, and I'll suggest, where appropriate, ways of answering both of the above questions. Applying this lesson of abstracting from the specific problem to the general solution can be especially effective when carried out in a corporate environment over a period of time. Given a suitable corporate culture, in which every developer has the opportunity to formulate general answers to specific problems, a cumulative beneficial effect can accrue. The more that reusable code is available to developers, the more it will be utilized. Likewise, the more information about the typical bugs encountered within an organization that is stored and made available in the form of a database, the more likely it is that the programmers with access to that information will search for the information and use it appropriately. In the ideal world, all this information would be contributed both in the form of reusable code and in a database of problems and solutions. Back in the real world, one or the other method may have to suffice.

Some final thoughts Document all system testing, user acceptance testing, and production bugs and their resolution. Make this information available to the developers and testers and their IS managers. Consider using an application's system testing and user acceptance bug levels to determine when that application is suitable for release to the next project phase.

In-Flight Testing: Using the *Assert* Statement

One of the most powerful debugging tools available, at least to C programmers, is the *Assert* macro. Simple in concept, it allows a programmer to write self-checking code by providing an easy method of verifying that a particular condition or assumption is true. Visual Basic programmers had no structured way of doing this until Visual Basic 5. Now we can write statements like this:

```
Debug.Assert 2 + 2 = 4

Debug.Assert bFunctionIsArrayHealthy

Select Case iUserChoice
    Case 1
        DoSomething1
    Case 2
        DoSomething2
    Case Else
        ' We should never reach here!
        Debug.Assert nUserChoice = 1 Or nUserChoice = 2
End Select
```

Debug.Assert operates in the development environment only—conditional compilation automatically drops it from the compiled EXE. It will take any expression that evaluates to either TRUE or FALSE and then drop into break mode at the point the assertion is made if that expression evaluates to FALSE. The idea is to allow you to catch bugs and other problems early by verifying that your assumptions about your program and its environment are true. You can load your program code with debug checks; in fact, you can create code that checks itself while running. Holes in your algorithms, invalid assumptions, creaky data structures, and invalid procedure arguments can all be found in flight and without any human intervention.

The power of assertions is limited only by your imagination. Suppose you were using Visual Basic 6 to control the space shuttle. (We can dream, can't we?) You might have a procedure that shuts down the shuttle's main engine in the event of an emergency, perhaps preparing to jettison the engine entirely. You would want to ensure that the shutdown had worked before the jettison took place, so the procedure for doing this would need to return some sort of status code. To check that the shutdown procedure was working correctly during debugging, you might want to perform a different version of it as well and then verify that both routines left the main engine in the same state. It is fairly common to code any mission-critical system features in this manner. The results of the two different algorithms can be checked against each other, a practice that would fail only in the relatively unlikely situation of both the algorithms having the same bug. The Visual Basic 6 code for such testing might look something like this:

```
' Normal shutdown
Set nResultOne = ShutdownTypeOne(objEngineCurrentState)

' Different shutdown
Set nResultTwo = ShutdownTypeTwo(objEngineCurrentState)

' Check that both shutdowns produced the same result.
Debug.Assert nResultOne = nResultTwo
```

When this code was released into production, you would obviously want to remove everything except the call to the normal shutdown routine and let Visual Basic 6's automatic conditional compilation drop the *Debug.Assert* statement.

You can also run periodic health checks on the major data structures in your programs, looking for uninitialized or null values, holes in arrays, and other nasty gremlins:

```
Debug.Assert bIsArrayHealthy CriticalArray
```

Assertions and *Debug.Assert* are designed for the development environment only. In the development environment, you are trading program size and speed for debug information. Once your code has reached production, the assumption is that it's been tested well and that assertions are no longer necessary. Assertions are for use during development to help prevent developers from creating bugs. On the other hand, other techniques—such as error handling or defensive programming—attempt to prevent data loss or other undesirable effects as a result of bugs that already exist.

Also, experience shows that a system loaded with assertions can run from 20 to 50 percent slower than one without the assertions, which is obviously not suitable in a production environment. But because the *Debug.Assert* statements remain in your source code, they will automatically be used again whenever your code is changed and retested in the development environment. In effect, your assertions are immortal—which is as it should be. One of the hardest trails for a maintenance programmer to follow is the one left by your own assumptions about the state of your program. Although we all try to avoid code dependencies and subtle assumptions when we're designing and writing our code, they invariably tend to creep in. Real life demands compromise, and the best-laid code design has to cope with some irregularities and subtleties. Now your assertion statements can act as beacons, showing the people who come after you what you were worried about when you wrote a particular section of code. Doesn't that give you a little frisson?

Another reason why *Debug.Assert* is an important new tool in your fight against bugs is the inexorable rise of object-oriented programming. A large part of object-oriented programming is what I call "design by contract." This is where you design and implement an object hierarchy in your Visual Basic program, and expose methods and properties of your objects for other developers (or yourself) to use. In effect, you're making a contract with these users of your program. If they invoke your methods and properties correctly, perhaps in a specific order or only under certain conditions, they will receive the services or results that they want. Now you are able to use assertions to ensure that your methods are called in the correct order, perhaps, or that the class initialization method has been invoked before any other method. Whenever you want to confirm that your class object is being used correctly and is in an internally consistent state, you can simply call a method private to that class that can then perform the series of assertions that make up the "health check."

One situation in which to be careful occurs when you're using *Debug.Assert* to invoke a procedure. You need to bear in mind that any such invocation will never be performed in the compiled version of your program. If you copy the following code into an empty project, you can see clearly what will happen:

```
Option Explicit
Dim mbIsThisDev As Boolean

Private Sub Form_Load()
mbIsThisDev = False

' If the following line executes, the MsgBox will display
' True in answer to its title "Is this development?"
' If it doesn't execute, the MsgBox will display false.

Debug.Assert SetDevFlagToTrue
MsgBox mbIsThisDev, vbOKOnly, "Is this development?"

Unload Me
End Sub
```

```
Private Function SetDevFlagToTrue() As Boolean

SetDevFlagToTrue = True
mbIsThisDev = True

End Function
```

When you run this code in the Visual Basic environment, the message box will state that it's true that your program is running within the Visual Basic IDE because the *SetDevFlagToTrue* function will be invoked. If you compile the code into an EXE, however, the message box will show FALSE. In other words, the *SetDevFlagToTrue* function is not invoked at all. Offhand, I can't think of a more roundabout method of discovering whether you're running as an EXE or in the Visual Basic 6 IDE.

When should you assert?

Once you start using assertions seriously in your code, you need to be aware of some pertinent issues. The first and most important of these is when you should assert. The golden rule is that assertions should not take the place of either defensive programming or data validation. It is important to remember, as I stated earlier, that assertions are there to help prevent developers from creating bugs—an assertion is normally used only to detect an illegal condition that should never happen if your program is working correctly. Defensive programming, on the other hand, attempts to prevent data loss or other undesirable effects as a result of bugs that already exist.

To return to the control software of our space shuttle, consider this code:

```
Function ChangeEnginePower(ByVal niPercent As Integer) As Integer
Dim lNewEnginePower As Long

Debug.Assert niPercent => -100 And niPercent =< 100
Debug.Assert mnCurrentPower => 0 And mnCurrentPower =< 100

lNewEnginePower = CLng(mnCurrentPower) + niPercent

If lNewEnginePower < 0 Or lNewEnginePower > 100
Err.Raise vbObjectError + mgInvalidEnginePower
Else
mnCurrentPower = lNewEnginePower
End If

ChangeEnginePower = mnCurrentPower

End Sub
```

Here we want to inform the developer during testing if he or she is attempting to change the engine thrust by an illegal percentage, or if the current engine thrust is illegal. This helps the developer catch bugs during development. However, we also want to program defensively so that if a bug has been created despite our assertion checks during development, it won't cause the engine to explode. The assertion is in addition to some proper argument validation that handles nasty situations such as trying to increase engine thrust beyond 100%. In other words, don't ever let assertions take the place of normal validation.

Defensive programming like the above is dangerous if you don't include the assertion statement. Although using defensive programming to write what might be called nonstop code is important for the prevention of user data loss as a result of program crashes, defensive programming can also have the unfortunate side effect of hiding bugs. Without the assertion statement, a programmer who called the *ChangeEnginePower* routine with an incorrect argument would not necessarily receive any warning of a problem. Whenever you find yourself programming defensively, think about including an assertion statement.

Explain your assertions

Perhaps the only thing more annoying than finding an assertion statement in another programmer's code and having no idea why it's there is finding a similar assertion statement in your own code. Document your assertions. A simple one- or two-line comment will normally suffice—you don't need to write a dissertation. Some assertions can be the result of quite subtle code dependencies, so in your comment try to clarify why you're asserting something, not just what you're asserting.

Beware of Boolean coercion

The final issue with *Debug.Assert* is Boolean type coercion. Later in this chapter, we'll look at Visual Basic's automatic type coercion rules and where they can lay nasty traps for you. For now, you can be content with studying the following little enigma:

```
Dim nTest As Integer
nTest = 50
Debug.Assert nTest
Debug.Assert Not nTest
```

You will find that neither of these assertions fire! Strange, but true. The reason has to do with Visual Basic coercing the integer to a Boolean. The first assertion says that *nTest = 50*, which, because nTest is nonzero, is evaluated to TRUE. The second assertion calculates *Not nTest* to be –51, which is also nonzero and again evaluated to TRUE.

However, if you compare *nTest* and *Not nTest* to the actual value of TRUE (which is –1) as in the following code, only the first assertion fires:

```
Debug.Assert nTest = True
Debug.Assert Not nTest = True
```

Some final thoughts   *Debug.Assert* is a very powerful tool for bug detection. Used properly, it can catch many bugs automatically, without any human intervention. (See the discussion of an Assertion Sourcerer beginning on page 267 for a utility that supplements *Debug.Assert*.) Also see Chapter 1 for further discussion of *Debug.Assert*.

How Sane Is Your Program?

A source-level debugger such as the one available in Visual Basic is a wonderful tool. It allows you to see into the heart of your program, watching data as it flows through your code. Instead of taking a "black box," putting input into it, and then checking the output and guessing at what actually happened between the two, you get the chance to examine the whole process in detail.

Back in the 1950s, many people were still optimistic about the possibility of creating a machine endowed with human intelligence. In 1950, English mathematician Alan Turing proposed a thought experiment to test whether a machine was intelligent. His idea was that anybody who wanted to verify a computer program's intelligence would be able to interrogate both the program in question and a human being via computer links. If after asking a series of questions, the interrogator was unable to distinguish between the human and the program, the program might legitimately be considered intelligent. This experiment had several drawbacks, the main one being that it is very difficult to devise the right type of questions. The interrogator would forever be devising new questions and wondering about the answers to the current ones.

This question-and-answer process is remarkably similar to what happens during program testing. A tester devises a number of inputs (equivalent to asking a series of questions) and then carefully examines the output (listens to the computer's answers). And like Turing's experiment, this type of black-box testing has the same drawbacks. The tester simply can't be sure whether he or she is asking the right questions or when enough questions have been asked to be reasonably sure that the program is functioning correctly.

What a debugger allows you to do is dive below the surface. No longer do you have to be satisfied with your original questions. You can observe your program's inner workings, redirect your questions in midflight to examine new issues raised by watching the effect of your original questions on the code, and be much more aware of which questions are important. Unlike a psychiatrist, who can never be sure whether a patient is sane, using a source-level debugger means that you will have a much better probability of being able to evaluate the sanity of your program.

Debugging windows

Visual Basic 6's source-level debugger has three debugging windows as part of the IDE.

- The Immediate (or Debug) window is still here, with all the familiar abilities, such as being able to execute single-line statements or subroutines.

- The Locals window is rather cool. It displays the name, value, and data type of each variable declared in the current procedure. It can also show properties. You can change the value of any variable or property merely by clicking on it and then typing the new value. This can save a lot of time during debugging.

- The Watches window also saves you some time, allowing you to watch a variable's value without having to type any statements into the Immediate window. You can easily edit the value of any *Watch* expression you've set or the *Watch* expression itself by clicking on it, just as you can in the Locals window.

Debugging hooks

One technique that many programmers have found useful when working with this type of interactive debugger is to build debugging hooks directly into their programs. These hooks, usually in the form of functions or subroutines, can be executed directly from the Immediate window when in break mode. An example might be a routine that walks any array passed to it and prints out its contents, as shown here:

```
Public Sub DemonstrateDebugHook()
Dim saTestArray(1 to 4) As Integer
saTestArray(1) = "Element one"
saTestArray(2) = "Element two"
saTestArray(3) = "Element three"
saTestArray(4) = "Element four"
```

```
Stop

End Sub

Public Sub WalkArray(ByVal vntiArray As Variant)
Dim nLoop As Integer

' Check that we really have an array.
Debug.Assert IsArray(vntiArray)

' Print the array type and number of elements.
Debug.Print "Array is of type " & TypeName(vntiArray)
nLoop = UBound(vntiArray) - LBound(vntiArray) + 1
Debug.Print "Array has " & CStr(nLoop) & " elements""

' Walk the array, and print its elements.
For nLoop = LBound(vntiArray) To UBound(vntiArray)
    Debug.Print "Element " & CStr(nLoop) & " contains:" _
        & vntiArray(nLoop)
Next nLoop

End Sub
```

When you run this code, Visual Basic will go into break mode when it hits the *Stop* statement placed in *DemonstrateDebugHook*. You can then use the Immediate window to type:

```
WalkArray saTestArray
```

This debugging hook will execute and show you all the required information about any array passed to it.

NOTE

> The array is received as a Variant so that any array type can be handled and the array can be passed by value. Whole arrays can't be passed by value in their natural state. These types of debugging hooks placed in a general debug class or module can be extremely useful, both for you and for any programmers who later have to modify or debug your code.

Exercising all the paths

Another effective way to use the debugger is to step through all new or modified code to exercise all the data paths contained within one or more procedures. You can do this quickly, often in a single test run. Every program has code that gets executed only once in a very light blue moon, usually code that handles special conditions or errors. Being able to reset the debugger to a particular source statement, change some data to force the traversal of another path, and then continue program execution from that point gives you a great deal of testing power.

```
' This code will work fine - until nDiv is zero.
If nDiv > 0 And nAnyNumber / nDiv > 1 Then
    DoSomething
Else
    DoSomethingElse
End If
```

When I first stepped through the above code while testing another programmer's work, *nDiv* had the value of 1. I stepped through to the *End If* statement—everything looked fine. Then I used the Locals window to edit the *nDiv* variable and change it to zero, set the debugger to execute the first line again, and of course the program crashed. (Visual Basic doesn't short-circuit this sort of expression evaluation. No matter what the value of *nDiv*, the second expression on the line will always be evaluated.) This ability to change data values and thereby follow all the code paths through a procedure is invaluable in detecting bugs that might otherwise take a long time to appear.

Peering Inside Stored Procedures

One of the classic bugbears of client/server programming is that it's not possible to debug stored procedures interactively. Instead, you're forced into the traditional edit-compile-test cycle, treating the stored procedure that you're developing as an impenetrable black box. Pass in some inputs, watch the outputs, and try to guess what happened in between. Visual Basic 5 and Visual Basic 6 contain something that's rather useful: a Transact-SQL (T-SQL) interactive debugger.

There are a few constraints. First of all, you must be using the Enterprise Edition of Visual Basic 6. Also, the only supported server-side configuration is Microsoft SQL Server 6.5 or later. Finally, you also need to be running SQL Server Service Pack 3 or later. When installing Visual Basic 6, select Custom from the Setup dialog box, choose Enterprise Tools, and click Select All to ensure that all the necessary client-side components are installed. Once Service Pack 3 is installed, you can install and register the T-SQL Debugger interface and Remote Automation component on the server.

The T-SQL Debugger works through a UserConnection created with Microsoft UserConnection, which is available by selecting the Add Microsoft UserConnection option of the Project menu. Once you've created a UserConnection object, just create a Query object for the T-SQL query you want to debug. This query can be either a user-defined query that you build using something like Microsoft Query, or a stored procedure.

The T-SQL Debugger interface is similar to most language debuggers, allowing you to set breakpoints, change local variables or parameters, watch global variables, and step through the code. You can also view the contents of global temporary tables that your stored procedure creates and dump the resultset of the stored procedure to the output window. If your stored procedure creates multiple resultsets, right-click the mouse button over the output window and select More Results to view the next resultset.

Some final thoughts   The combination of these two powerful interactive debuggers, including their new features, makes it even easier to step through every piece of code that you write, as soon as you write it. Such debugging usually doesn't take nearly as long as many developers assume and can be used to promote a much better understanding of the structure and stability of your programs.

NOTE

How low can you get? One of Visual Basic 6's compile options allows you to add debugging data to your native-code EXE. This gives you the ability to use a symbolic debugger, such as the one that comes with Microsoft Visual C++, to debug and analyze your programs at the machine-code level. See Chapter 7 and Chapter 1 (both by Peter Morris) for more information about doing this.

Here Be Dragons

As I told you early in this chapter, a typical medieval map of the world marked unexplored areas with the legend "Here be dragons," often with little pictures of exotic sea monsters. This section of the chapter is the modern equivalent, except that most of these creatures have been studied and this map is (I hope) much more detailed than its medieval counterpart. Now we can plunge into the murky depths of Visual Basic, where we will find a few real surprises.

Bypassing the events from hell

Visual Basic's *GotFocus* and *LostFocus* events have always been exasperating to Visual Basic programmers. They don't correspond to the normal *KillFocus* and *SetFocus* messages generated by Windows; they don't always execute in the order that you might expect; they are sometimes skipped entirely; and they can prove very troublesome when you use them for field-by-field validation.

Microsoft has left these events alone in Visual Basic 6, probably for backward compatibility reasons. However, the good news is that the technical boys and girls at Redmond do seem to have been hearing our calls for help. Visual Basic 6 gives us the *Validate* event and *CausesValidation* property, whose combined use avoids our having to use the *GotFocus* and *LostFocus* events for validation, thereby providing a mechanism to bypass all the known problems with these events. Unfortunately, the bad news is that the new mechanism for field validation is not quite complete.

Before we dive into *Validate* and *CausesValidation*, let's look at some of the problems with *GotFocus* and *LostFocus* to see why these two events should never be used for field validation. The following project contains a single window with two text box controls, an OK command button, and a Cancel command button. (See Figure 6-1.)

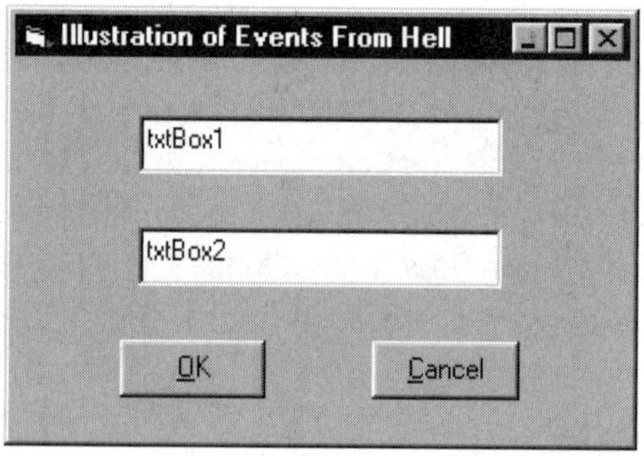

FIGURE 6-1   *Simple interface screen hides events from hell*

Both command buttons have an accelerator key. Also, the OK button's *Default* property is set to TRUE (that is, pressing the Enter key will click this button), and the Cancel button's *Cancel* property is set to TRUE (that is, pressing the Esc key will click this button). The *GotFocus* and *LostFocus* events of all four controls contain a *Debug.Print* statement that will tell you (in the Immediate window) which event has been fired. This way we can easily examine the order in which these events fire and understand some of the difficulties of using them.

When the application's window is initially displayed, focus is set to the first text box. The Immediate window shows the following:

```
Program initialization
txtBox1 GotFocus
```

Just tabbing from the first to the second text box shows the following events:

```
txtBox1 LostFocus
txtBox2 GotFocus
```

So far, everything is as expected. Now we can add some code to the *LostFocus* event of *txtBox1* to simulate a crude validation of the contents of *txtBox1*, something like this:

```
Private Sub txtBox1_LostFocus

Debug.Print "txtBox1_LostFocus"
If Len(txtBox1.Text) > 0 Then
    txtBox1.SetFocus
End If

End Sub
```

Restarting the application and putting any value into *txtBox1* followed by tabbing to *txtBox2* again shows what looks like a perfectly normal event stream:

```
txtBox1_LostFocus
txtBox2_GotFocus
txtBox2_LostFocus
txtBox1 GotFocus
```

Normally, however, we want to inform the user if a window control contains anything invalid. So in our blissful ignorance, we add a *MsgBox* statement to the *LostFocus* event of *txtBox1* to inform the user if something's wrong:

```
Private Sub txtBox1_LostFocus

Debug.Print "txtBox1_LostFocus"
If Len(txtBox1.Text) > 0 Then
    MsgBox "txtBox1 must not be empty!"
    txtBox1.SetFocus
End If

End Sub
```

Restarting the application and putting any value into *txtBox1* followed by tabbing to *txtBox2* shows the first strangeness. We can see that after the message box is displayed, *txtBox2* never receives focus—but it does lose focus!

```
txtBox1_LostFocus
txtBox2_LostFocus
txtBox1 GotFocus
```

Now we can go further to investigate what happens when both text boxes happen to have invalid values. So we add the following code to the *LostFocus* event of *txtBox2*:

```
Private Sub txtBox2_LostFocus

Debug.Print "txtBox2_LostFocus"
If Len(txtBox2.Text) = 0 Then
    MsgBox "txtBox2 must not be empty!"
    txtBox2.SetFocus
End If

End Sub
```

Restarting the application and putting any value into *txtBox1* followed by tabbing to *txtBox2* leads to a program lockup! Because both text boxes contain what are considered to be invalid values, we see no *GotFocus* events but rather a continuous cascade of *LostFocus* events as each text box tries to claim focus in order to allow the user to change its invalid contents. This problem is well known in Visual Basic, and a programmer usually gets caught by it only once before mending his or her ways.

At this point, completely removing the *MsgBox* statements only makes the situation worse. If you do try this, your program goes seriously sleepy-bye-bye. Because the *MsgBox* function no longer intervenes to give you some semblance of control over the event cascade, you're completely stuck. Whereas previously you could get access to the Task Manager to kill the hung process, you will now have to log out of Windows to regain control.

These are not the only peculiarities associated with these events. If we remove the validation code to prevent the application from hanging, we can look at the event stream when using the command buttons. Restart the application, and click the OK button. The Immediate window shows a normal event stream. Now do this again, but press Enter to trigger the OK button rather than clicking on it. The Debug window shows quite clearly that the *LostFocus* event of *txtBox1* is never triggered. Exactly the same thing happens if you use the OK button's accelerator key (Alt+O)—no *LostFocus* event is triggered. Although in the real world you might not be too worried if the Cancel button swallows a control's *LostFocus* event, it's a bit more serious when you want validation to occur when the user presses OK.

The good news with Visual Basic 6 is that you now have a much better mechanism for this type of field validation. Many controls now have a *Validate* event. The *Validate* event fires before the focus shifts to another control that has its *CausesValidation* property set to True. Because this event fires before the focus shifts and also allows you to keep focus on any control with invalid data, most of the problems discussed above go away. In addition, the *CausesValidation* property means that you have the flexibility of deciding exactly when you want to perform field validation. For instance, in the above project, you would set the OK button's *CausesValidation* property to True, but the Cancel button's *CausesValidation* property to False. Why do any validation at all if the user wants to cancel the operation? In my opinion, this is a major step forward in helping with data validation.

Note that I stated that "most" of the problems go away. Unfortunately, "most" is not quite "all." If we add Debug.Print code to the *Validate* and *Click* events in the above project, we can still see something strange. Restart the application, and with the focus on the first text box, click on the OK button to reveal a normal event stream:

```
txtBox1 Validate
txtBox1 LostFocus
cmdOK GotFocus
cmdOK Click
```

Once again restart the application, and again with the focus on the first text box, press the accelerator key of the OK button to reveal something strange:

```
txtBox1 Validate
cmdOK Click
txtBox1 LostFocus
cmdOK GotFocus
```

Hmmm. The OK button's *Click* event appears to have moved in the event stream from fourth to second. From the data validation point of view, this might not be worrisome. The *Validate* event still occurs first, and if you actually set the *Validate* event's *KeepFocus* argument to True (indicating that *txtBox1.Text* is invalid), the rest of the events are not executed—just as you would expect.

Once again, restart the application and again with the focus on the first text box, press the Enter key. Because the *Default* property of the OK button is set to True, this has the effect of clicking the OK button:

```
cmdOK Click
```

Oops! No *Validate* event, no *LostFocus* or *GotFocus* events. Pressing the Escape key to invoke the Cancel button has exactly the same effect. In essence, these two shortcut keys bypass the *Validate/CausesValidation* mechanism completely. If you don't use these shortcut keys, everything is fine. If you do use them, you need to do something such as firing each control's *Validate* event manually if your user utilizes one of these shortcuts.

Some final thoughts   Never rely on *GotFocus* and *LostFocus* events actually occurring—or occurring in the order you expect. Particularly, do not use these events for field-by-field validation—use *Validate* and *CausesValidation* instead. Note that the *Validate* event is also available for UserControls.

Evil Type Coercion

A programmer on my team had a surprise when writing Visual Basic code to extract information from a SQL Server database. Having retrieved a recordset, he wrote the following code:

```
Dim vntFirstValue As Variant, vntSecondValue As Variant
Dim nResultValue1 As Integer, nResultValue2 As Integer

vntFirstValue = Trim(rsMyRecordset!first_value)
vntSecondValue = Trim(rsMyRecordset!second_value)

nResultValue1 = vntFirstValue + vntSecondValue
nResultValue2 = vntFirstValue + vntSecondValue + 1
```

He was rather upset when he found that the "+" operator not only concatenated the two variants but also added the final numeric value. If *vntFirstValue* contained "1" and *vntSecondValue* contained "2," *nResultValue1* had the value 12 and *nResultValue2* had the value 13.

To understand exactly what's going on here, we have to look at how Visual Basic handles type coercion. Up until Visual Basic 3, type coercion was relatively rare. Although you could write Visual Basic 3 code like this:

```
txtBox.Text = 20
```

and find that it worked without giving any error, almost every other type of conversion had to be done explicitly by using statements such as *CStr* and *CInt*. Starting with Visual Basic 4, and continuing in Visual Basic 5 and 6, performance reasons dictated that automatic type coercion be introduced. Visual Basic no longer has to convert an assigned value to a Variant and then unpack it back into whatever data type is receiving the assignment. It can instead invoke a set of hard-coded coercion rules to perform direct coercion without ever involving the overhead of a Variant. Although this is often convenient and also achieves the laudable aim of good performance, it can result in some rather unexpected results. Consider the following code:

```
Sub Test()

    Dim sString As String, nInteger As Integer
    sString = "1"
    nInteger = 2
    ArgTest sString, nInteger

End Sub

Sub ArgTest(ByVal inArgument1 As Integer, _
            ByVal isArgument2 As String)
    ' Some code here
End Sub
```

In Visual Basic 3, this code would give you an immediate error at compile time because the arguments are in the wrong order. In Visual Basic 4 or later, you won't get any error because Visual Basic will attempt to coerce the string variable into the integer parameter and vice versa. This is not a pleasant change. If *inArgument1* is passed a numeric value, everything looks and performs as expected. As soon as a non-numeric value or a null string is passed, however, a run-time error occurs. This means that the detection of certain classes of bugs has been moved from compile time to run time, which is definitely not a major contribution to road safety.

The following table shows Visual Basic 6's automatic type coercion rules.

Source Type	Coerced To	Apply This Rule
Integer	Boolean	0=False, nonzero=True
Boolean	Byte	False=0, True=255
Boolean	Any numeric	False=0, True=-1 (except Byte)
String	Date	String is analyzed for MM/dd/yy and so on
Date	Numeric type	Coerce to Double and use *DateSerial(Double)*
Numeric	Date	Use number as serial date, check valid date range
Numeric	Byte	Error if negative
String	Numeric type	Treat as Double when representing a number

Some final thoughts   Any Visual Basic developer with aspirations to competence should learn the automatic type coercion rules and understand the most common situations in which type coercion's bite can be dangerous.

Arguing safely

In Visual Basic 3, passing arguments was relatively easy to understand. You passed an argument either by value (*ByVal*) or by reference (*ByRef*). Passing *ByVal* was safer because the argument consisted only of its value, not of the argument itself. Therefore, any change to that argument would have no effect outside the procedure receiving the argument. Passing *ByRef* meant that a direct reference to the argument was passed. This allowed you to change the argument if you needed to do so.

With the introduction of objects, the picture has become more complicated. The meaning of *ByVal* and *ByRef* when passing an object variable is slightly different than when passing a nonobject variable. Passing an object variable *ByVal* means that the type of object that the object variable refers to cannot change. The object that the object variable refers to is allowed to change, however, as long as it remains the same type as the original object. This rule can confuse some programmers when they first encounter it and can be a source of bugs if certain invalid assumptions are made.

Type coercion introduces another wrinkle to passing arguments. The use of *ByVal* has become more dangerous because Visual Basic will no longer trigger certain compile-time errors. In Visual Basic 3, you could never pass arguments to a procedure that expected arguments of a different type. Using *ByVal* in Visual Basic 6 means that an attempt will be made to coerce each *ByVal* argument into the argument type expected. For example, passing a string variable *ByVal* into a numeric argument type will not show any problem unless the string variable actually contains non-numeric data at run time. This means that this error check has to be delayed until run time—see the earlier section called "Evil Type Coercion" for an example and more details.

If you don't specify an argument method, the default is that arguments are passed *ByRef*. Indeed, many Visual Basic programmers use the language for a while before they realize they are using the default *ByRef* and that *ByVal* is often the better argument method. For the sake of clarity, I suggest defining the method being used every time rather than relying on the default. I'm also a firm believer in being very precise about exactly which arguments are being used for input, which for output, and which for both input and output. A good naming scheme should do something like prefix every input argument with "i" and every output argument with "o" and then perhaps use the more ugly "io" to discourage programmers from using arguments for both input and output. Input arguments should be passed *ByVal,* whereas all other arguments obviously have to be passed *ByRef.* Being precise about the nature and use of procedure arguments can make the maintenance programmer's job much easier. It can even make your job easier by forcing you to think clearly about the exact purpose of each argument.

One problem you might run into when converting from previous versions of Visual Basic to Visual Basic 6 is that you are no longer allowed to pass a control to a DLL or OCX using *ByRef.* Previously, you might have written your function declaration like this:

```
Declare Function CheckControlStatus Lib "MY.OCX" _
        (ctlMyControl As Control) As Integer
```

You are now required to specify *ByVal* rather than the default *ByRef.* Your function declaration must look like this:

```
Declare Function CheckControlStatus Lib "MY.OCX" _
        (ByVal ctlMyControl As Control) As Integer
```

This change is necessary because DLL functions now expect to receive the Windows handle of any control passed as a parameter. Omitting *ByVal* causes a pointer to the control handle to be passed rather than the control handle itself, which will result in undefined behavior and possibly a GPF.

The meaning of zero

Null, IsNull, Nothing, vbNullString, "", vbNullChar, vbNull, Empty, vbEmpty... Visual Basic 6 has enough representations of nothing and zero to confuse the most careful programmer. To prevent bugs, programmers must understand what each of these Visual Basic keywords represents and how to use each in its proper context. Let's start with the interesting stuff.

```
Private sNotInitString As String
Private sEmptyString As String
Private sNullString As String
sEmptyString = ""
sNullString = 0&
```

Looking at the three variable declarations above, a couple of questions spring to mind. What are the differences between *sNotInitString, sEmptyString,* and *sNullString?* When is it appropriate to use each declaration, and when is it dangerous? The answers to these questions are not simple, and we need to delve into the murky depths of Visual Basic's internal string representation system to understand the answers.

After some research and experimentation, the answer to the first question becomes clear but at first sight is not very illuminating. The variable *sNotInitString* is a null pointer string, held internally as a pointer that doesn't point to any memory location and that holds an internal value of 0. *sEmptyString* is a pointer to an empty string, a pointer that does point to a valid memory location. Finally, *sNullString* is neither a null string pointer nor an empty string but is just a string containing 0.

Why does *sNotInitString* contain the internal value 0? In earlier versions of Visual Basic, uninitialized variable-length strings were set internally to an empty string. Ever since the release of Visual Basic 4, however, all variables have been set to 0 internally until initialized. Developers don't normally notice the difference because, inside Visual Basic, this initial zero value of uninitialized strings always behaves as if it were an empty string. It's only when you go outside Visual Basic and start using the Windows APIs that you receive a shock. Try passing either *sNotInitString* or *sEmptyString* to any Windows API function that takes a null pointer. Passing *sNotInitString* will work fine because it really is a null pointer, whereas passing *sEmptyString* will cause the function to fail. Of such apparently trivial differences are the really nasty bugs created.

The following code snippet demonstrates what can happen if you're not careful.

```
Private Declare Function WinFindWindow Lib "user32" Alias _
    "FindWindowA" (ByVal lpClassName As Any, _
                   ByVal lpWindowName As Any) As Long

    Dim sNotInitString As String
    Dim sEmptyString As String
    Dim sNullString As String

    sEmptyString = ""
    sNullString = 0&

    Shell "Calc.exe", 1
    DoEvents
    ' This will work.
    x& = WinFindWindow(sNotInitString, "Calculator")

    ' This won't work.
    x& = WinFindWindow(sEmptyString, "Calculator")

    ' This will work.
    x& = WinFindWindow(sNullString, "Calculator")
```

Now that we've understood one nasty trap and why it occurs, the difference between the next two variable assignments becomes clearer.

```
sNullPointer = vbNullString
sEmptyString = ""
```

It's a good idea to use the former assignment rather than the latter, for two reasons. The first reason is safety. Assigning *sNullPointer* as shown here is the equivalent of *sNotInitString* in the above example. In other words, it can be passed to a DLL argument directly. However, *sEmptyString* must be assigned the value of *0&* before it can be used safely in the same way. The second reason is economy. Using "" will result in lots of empty strings being scattered throughout your program, whereas using the built-in Visual Basic constant vbNullString will mean no superfluous use of memory.

Null and *IsNull* are fairly clear. Null is a variant of type vbNull that means no valid data and typically indicates a database field with no value. The only hazard here is a temptation to compare something with Null directly, because Null will propagate through any expression that you use. Resist the temptation and use *IsNull* instead.

```
' This will always be false.
If sString = Null Then
    ' Some code here
End If
```

Continuing through Visual Basic 6's representations of nothing, vbNullChar is the next stop on our travels. This constant is relatively benign, simply CHR$(0). When you receive a string back from a Windows API function, it is normally null-terminated because that is the way the C language expects strings to look. Searching for vbNullChar is one way of determining the real length of the string. Beware of using any API string without doing this first, because null-terminated strings can cause some unexpected results in Visual Basic, especially when displayed or concatenated together.

Finally, two constants are built into Visual Basic for use with the *VarType* function. vbNull is a value returned by the *VarType* function for a variable that contains no valid data. vbEmpty is returned by *VarType* for a variable that is uninitialized. Better people than I have argued that calling these two constants vbTypeNull and vbTypeEmpty would better describe their correct purpose. The important point from the perspective of safety is that vbEmpty can be very useful for performing such tasks as ensuring that the properties of your classes have been initialized properly.

The Bug Hunt

Two very reliable methods of finding new bugs in your application are available. The first involves demonstrating the program, preferably to your boss. Almost without exception, something strange and/or unexpected will happen, often resulting in severe embarrassment. Although this phenomenon has no scientific explanation, it's been shown to happen far too often to be merely a chance occurrence.

The other guaranteed way of locating bugs is to release your application into production. Out there in a hostile world, surrounded by other unruly applications and subject to the vagaries of exotic hardware devices and unusual Registry settings, it's perhaps of little surprise that the production environment can find even the most subtle of weaknesses in your program. Then there are your users, many of whom will gleefully inform you that "your program crashed" without even attempting to explain the circumstances leading up to the crash. Trying to extract the details from them is at best infuriating, at worst impossible. So we need some simple method of trapping all possible errors and logging them in such a way as to be able to reconstruct the user's problem. Here we'll examine the minimum requirements needed to trap and report errors and thus help your user retain some control over what happens to his or her data after a program crash.

The first point to note about Visual Basic 6's error handling capabilities is that they are somewhat deficient when compared with those of most compiled languages. There is no structured exception handling, and the only way to guarantee a chance of recovery from an error is to place an error trap and an error handler into *every* procedure. To understand why, we need to look in detail at what happens when a run-time error occurs in your program.

Your program is riding happily down the information highway, and suddenly it hits a large pothole in the shape of a run-time error. Perhaps your user forgot to put a disk into drive A, or maybe the Windows Registry became corrupted. In other words, something fairly common happened. Visual Basic 6 first checks whether you have an error trap enabled in the offending procedure. If it finds one, it will branch to the enabled error handler. If not, it will search backward through the current procedure call stack looking for the first error trap it can locate. If none are found, your program will terminate abruptly with a rude error message, which is normally the last thing you want to happen. Losing a user's data in this manner is a fairly heinous crime and is not likely to endear you to either your users or the technical support people. So at the very least you need to place an error handler in the initial procedure of your program.

Unfortunately, this solution is not very satisfactory either, for two reasons. Another programmer could come along later and modify your code, inserting his or her own local error trap somewhere lower in the call stack. This means that the run-time error could be intercepted, and your "global" error trap might never get the chance to deal with it properly. Instead, your program has to be happy with some fly-by-night error handler dealing with what could be a very serious error. The other problem is that even if, through good luck, your global error trap receives the error, Visual Basic 6 provides no mechanism for retrying or bypassing an erroneous statement in a different procedure. So if the error was something as simple as being unable to locate a floppy disk, you're going to look a little silly when your program can't recover. The only way of giving your user a chance of getting around a problem is to handle it in the same procedure in which it occurred.

There is no getting away from the fact that you need to place an error trap and an error handler in every single procedure if you want to be able to respond to and recover from errors in a sensible way. The task then is to provide a minimalist method of protecting every procedure while dealing with all errors in a centralized routine. That routine must be clever enough to discriminate between the different types of errors, log each error, interrogate the user (if necessary) about which action to take, and then return control back to the procedure where the problem occurred. The other minimum requirement is to be able to raise errors correctly to your clients when you are writing ActiveX components.

Adding the following code to every procedure in your program is a good start:

```
Private Function AnyFunction() As Integer

On Error GoTo LocalError
    ' Normal procedure code goes here.

    Exit Function
LocalError:
    If Fatal("Module.AnyFunction") = vbRetry Then
        Resume
    Else
        Resume Next
    End If

End Function
```

This code can provide your program with comprehensive error handling, as long as the *Fatal* function is written correctly. *Fatal* will receive the names of the module and procedure where the error occurred, log these and other error details to a disk log file for later analysis, and then inform the program's operator about the error and ask whether it ought to retry the statement in error, ignore it, or abort the whole program. If the user chooses to abort, the *Fatal* function needs to perform a general cleanup and then shutdown the program. If the user makes any other choice, the *Fatal* function returns control back to the procedure in error, communicating what the user has chosen. The code needed for the *Fatal* function can be a little tricky. You need to think about the different types of error that can occur, including those raised by ActiveX components. You also need to think about what happens if an error ever occurs within the *Fatal* function itself. (Again, see Chapter 1 for a more detailed analysis of this type of error handling.) Here I'll examine a couple of pitfalls that can occur when handling or raising Visual Basic 6 errors that involve the use of vbObjectError.

When creating an ActiveX component, you often need to either propagate errors specific to the component back to the client application or otherwise deal with an error that occurs within the component. One accepted method for propagating errors is to use *Error.Raise*. To avoid clashes with Visual Basic 6's own range of errors, add your error number to the vbObjectError constant. Don't raise any errors within the range vbObjectError through vbObjectError + 512, as Visual Basic 6 remaps some error messages between vbObjectError and vbObject- Error + 512 to standard Automation run-time errors. User-defined errors should therefore always be in the range vbObjectError + 512 to vbObjectError + 65536. Note that if you're writing a component that in turn uses other components, it is best to remap any errors raised by these subcomponents to your own errors. Developers using your component will normally want to deal only with the methods, properties, and errors that you define, rather than being forced to deal with errors raised directly by subcomponents.

When using a universal error handler to deal with many different types of problems, always bear in mind that you might be receiving errors that have been raised using the constant vbObjectError. You can use the *And* operator (*Err.Number And vbObjectError*) to check this. If *True* is returned, you should subtract vbObjectError from the actual error number before displaying or logging the error. Because vbObjectError is mainly used internally for interclass communications, there is seldom any reason to display it in its natural state.

In any error handler that you write, make sure that the first thing it does is to save the complete error context, which is all the properties of the *Err* object. Otherwise it's all too easy to lose the error information. In the following example, if the *Terminate* event of *MyObject* has an *On Error* statement (as it must if it's to handle any error without terminating the program), the original error context will be lost and the subsequent *Err.Raise* statement will itself generate an "Illegal function call" error. Why? Because you're not allowed to raise error 0!

```
Private Sub AnySub()
On Error GoTo LocalError
' Normal code goes here

Exit Sub
LocalError:
    Set MyObject = Nothing      ' Invokes MyObject's Terminate event
    Err.Raise Err.Number, , Err.Description
End Sub
```

Another point to be careful about is raising an error in a component that might become part of a Microsoft Transaction Server (MTS) package. Any error raised by an MTS object to a client that is outside MTS causes a rollback of any work done within that process. This is the so-called "failfast" policy, designed to prevent erroneous data from being committed or distributed. Instead of raising an error, you will have to return errors using the Windows API approach, in which a function returns an error code rather than raising an error.

A final warning for you: never use the Win32 API function *GetLastError* to determine the error behind a zero returned from a call to a Win32 API function. A call to this function isn't guaranteed to be the next statement executed. Use instead the *Err.LastDLLErr* property to retrieve the error details.

Staying compatible

An innocuous set of radio buttons on the Component tab of the Project Properties dialog box allows you to control possibly one of the most important aspects of any component that you write—public interfaces. The Visual Basic documentation goes into adequate, sometimes gory, detail about how to deal with public interfaces and what happens if you do it wrong, but they can be a rather confusing area and the source of many defects.

When you compile your Visual Basic 6 component, the following Globally Unique Identifiers (GUIDs) are created:

- An ID for the type library
- A CLSID (class ID) for each creatable class in the type library
- An IID (interface ID) for the default interface of each Public class in the type library, and also one for the outgoing interface (if the class raises events)
- A MID (member ID) for each property, method, and event of each class

When a developer compiles a program that uses your component, the class IDs and interface IDs of any objects the program creates are included in the executable. The program uses the class ID to request that your component create an object, and then queries the object for the interface ID. How Visual Basic generates these GUIDs depends on the setting of the aforementioned radio buttons.

The simplest setting is No Compatibility. Each time you compile the component, new class and interface IDs are generated. There is no relation between versions of the component, and programs compiled to use one version of the component cannot use later versions. This means that any time you test your component, you will need to close and reopen your test (client) program in order for it to pick up the latest GUIDs of your component. Failing to do this will result in the infamous error message "Connection to type library or object library for remote process has been lost. Press OK for dialog to remove reference."

The next setting is Project Compatibility. In Visual Basic 5, this setting kept the type library ID constant from version to version, although all the other IDs could vary randomly. This behavior has changed in Visual Basic 6, with class IDs now also constant regardless of version. This change will help significantly with your component testing, although you might still occasionally experience the error mentioned above. If you're debugging an out-of-process component, or an in-process component in a separate instance of Visual Basic, this error typically appears if the component project is still in design mode. Running the component, and then running the test program, should eliminate the problem. If you are definitely already running the component, you might have manually switched the setting from No Compatibility to Project Compatibility. This changes the component's type library ID, so you'll need to clear the missing reference to your component from the References dialog box, then open the References dialog box again and recheck your component.

It is a good idea to create a "compatibility" file as early as possible. This is done by making a compiled version of your component and pointing the Project Compatibility dialog box at this executable. Visual Basic will then use this executable file to maintain its knowledge about the component's GUIDs from version to version, thus preventing the referencing problem mentioned above.

Binary Compatibility is the setting to use if you're developing an enhanced version of an existing component. Visual Basic will then give you dire warnings if you change your interface in such a way as to make it potentially incompatible with existing clients that use your component. Ignore these warnings at your peril! You can expect memory corruptions and other wonderful creatures if you blithely carry on. Visual Basic will not normally complain if, say, you add a new method to your interface, but adding an argument to a current method will obviously invalidate any client program that expects the method to remain unchanged.

Declaring Your Intentions

The answer to the next question might well depend on whether your primary language is Basic, Pascal, or C. What will be the data type of the variable *tmpVarB* in each of the following declarations?

```
Dim tmpVarB, tmpVarA As Integer
Dim tmpVarA As Integer, tmpVarB
```

The first declaration, if translated into C, would produce a data type of integer for *tmpVarB*. The second declaration, if translated into Pascal, would also produce a data type of integer for *tmpVarB*. Of course in Visual Basic, either declaration would produce a data type of Variant, which is the default data type if none is explicitly assigned. While this is obvious to an experienced Visual Basic developer, it can catch developers by surprise if they're accustomed to other languages.

Another declaration surprise for the unwary concerns the use of the *ReDim* statement. If you mistype the name of the array that you are attempting to redim, you will not get any warning, even if you have *Option Explicit* at the top of the relevant module or class. Instead you will get a totally new array, with the *ReDim* statement acting as a declarative statement. In addition, if another variable with the same name is created later, even in a wider scope, *ReDim* will refer to the later variable and won't necessarily cause a compilation error, even if *Option Explicit* is in effect.

Born again

When declaring a new object, you can use either of the following methods:

```
' Safer method
Dim wgtMyWidget As Widget
Set wgtMyWidget = New Widget

' Not so safe method
Dim wgtMyWidget As New Widget
```

The second method of declaring objects is less safe because it reduces your control over the object's lifetime. Because declaring the object as *New* tells Visual Basic that any time you access that variable it should create a new object if one does not exist, any reference to *wgtMyWidget* after it has been destroyed will cause it to respawn.

```
' Not so safe method
Dim wgtMyWidget As New Widget
wgtMyWidget.Name = "My widget"
Set wgtMyWidget = Nothing
If wgtMyWidget Is Nothing Then
    Debug.Print "My widget doesn't exist"
Else
    Debug.Print My widget exists"
End If
```

In the situation above, *wgtMyWidget* will always exist. Any reference to *wgtMy-Widget* will cause it to be born again if it doesn't currently exist. Even comparing the object to nothing is enough to cause a spontaneous regeneration. This means that your control over the object's lifetime is diminished, a bad situation in principle.

Safe global variables

In the restricted and hermetically sealed world of discrete components, most developers dislike global variables. The major problem is that global variables break the valuable principle of loose coupling, in which you design each of your components to be reused by itself, with no supporting infrastructure that needs to be re-rigged before reuse is a possibility. If a component you write depends upon some global variables, you are forced to rethink the context and use of these global variables every time you reuse the component. From bitter experience, most developers have found that using global variables is much riskier than using local variables, whose scope is more limited and more controllable.

You should definitely avoid making the code in your classes dependent on global data. Many instances of a class can exist simultaneously, and all of these objects share the global data in your program. Using global variables in class module code also violates the object-oriented programming concept of encapsulation, because objects created from such a class do not contain all of their data.

Another problem with global data is the increasing use of multithreading in Visual Basic to perform faster overall processing of a group of tasks that are liable to vary significantly in their individual execution time. For instance, if you write a multithreaded in-process component (such as a DLL or OCX) that provides objects, these objects are created on client threads; your component doesn't create threads of its own. All of the objects that your component supplies for a specific client thread will reside in the same "apartment" and share the same global data. However, any new client thread will have its own global data in its own apartment, completely separate from the other threads. *Sub Main* will execute once for each thread, and your component classes or controls that run on the different threads will not have access to the same global data. This includes global data such as the *App* object.

Other global data issues arise with the use of MTS with Visual Basic. MTS relies heavily on stateless components in order to improve its pooling and allocation abilities. Global and module-level data mean that an object has to be stateful (that is, keep track of its state between method invocations), so any global or module-level variables hinder an object's pooling and reuse by MTS.

However, there might be occasions when you want a single data item to be shared globally by all the components in your program, or by all the objects created from a class module. (The data created in this latter occasion is sometimes referred to as static class data.) One useful means of accomplishing this sharing is to use locking to control access to your global data. Similar to concurrency control in a multiuser database environment, a locking scheme for global data needs a way of checking out a global variable before it's used or updated, and then checking it back in after use. If any other part of the program attempts to use this global variable while it's checked out, an assertion (using *Debug.Assert*) will trap the problem and signal the potential bug.

One method of implementing this locking would be to create a standard (non-class) module that contains all of your global data. A little-known fact is that you can use properties *Get/Let/Set* even in standard modules, so you can implement all your global data as private properties of a standard module. Being a standard module, these variables will exist only once and persist for the lifetime of the program. Since the variables are actually declared as private, you can use a locking scheme to control access to them. For example, the code that controls access to a global string variable might look something like this:

```vb
'Note that this "public" variable is declared Private
'and is declared in a standard (non-class) module.
Private gsMyAppName As String
Private mbMyAppNameLocked As Boolean
Private mnMyAppNameLockId As Integer

Public Function MyAppNameCheckOut() As Integer
'Check-out the public variable when you start using it.
'Returns LockId if successful, otherwise returns zero.

    Debug.Assert mbMyAppNameLocked = False
    If mbMyAppNameLocked = False Then
        mbMyAppNameLocked = True
        mnMyAppNameLockId = mnMyAppNameLockId + 1
        MyAppNameCheckOut = mnMyAppNameLockId
    Else
        'You might want to raise an error here too,
        'to avoid the programmer overlooking the return code.
        MyAppNameCheckOut = 0
    End If

End Function

Property Get MyAppName(ByVal niLockId As Integer) As String
'Property returning the application name.
'Assert that lock id > 0, just in case nobody's calling CheckOut!
'Assert that lock ids agree, but in production will proceed anyway.
'If lock ids don't agree, you might want to raise an error.

    Debug.Assert niLockId > 0
    Debug.Assert niLockId = mnMyAppNameLockId
    MyAppName = gsMyAppName

End Property


Property Let MyAppName(ByVal niLockId As String, ByVal siNewValue As Integer)
'Property setting the application name.
'Assert that lock id > 0, just in case nobody's calling CheckOut!
```

```
'Assert that lock ids agree, but in production will proceed anyway.
'If lock ids don't agree, you might want to raise an error.

    Debug.Assert niLockId > 0
    Debug.Assert niLockId = mnMyAppNameLockId
    gsMyAppName = siNewValue

End Property


Public Function MyAppNameCheckIn() As Boolean
'Check-in the public variable when you finish using it
'Returns True if successful, otherwise returns False

    Debug.Assert mbMyAppNameLocked = True
    If mbMyAppNameLocked = True Then
        mbMyAppNameLocked = False
        MyAppNameCheckIn = True
    Else
        MyAppNameCheckIn = False
    End If

End Function
```

The simple idea behind these routines is that each item of global data has a current LockId, and you cannot use or change this piece of data without the current LockId. To use a global variable, you first need to call its *CheckOut* function to get the current LockId. This function checks that the variable is not already checked out by some other part of the program and returns a LockId of zero if it's already being used. Providing you receive a valid (non-zero) LockId, you can use it to read or change the global variable. When you've finished with the global variable, you need to call its *CheckIn* function before any other part of your program will be allowed to use it. Some code using this global string would look something like this:

```
Dim nLockId As Integer

nLockId = GlobalData.MyAppNameCheckout
If nLockId > 0 Then
    GlobalData.MyAppName(nLockId) = "New app name"
    Call GlobalData.MyAppNameCheckIn
Else
    'Oops! Somebody else is using this global variable
End If
```

This kind of locking scheme, in which public data is actually created as private data but with eternal persistence, prevents nearly all the problems mentioned above that are normally associated with global data. If you do want to use this type of scheme, you might want to think about grouping your global routines into different standard modules, depending on their type and use. If you throw all of your global data into one huge pile, you'll avoid the problems of global data, but miss out on some of the advantages of information hiding and abstract data types.

ActiveX Documents

ActiveX documents are an important part of Microsoft's component strategy. The ability to create a Visual Basic 6 application that can be run inside Microsoft Internet Explorer is theoretically very powerful, especially over an intranet where control over the browser being used is possible. Whether this potential will actually be realized is debatable, but Microsoft is certainly putting considerable effort into developing and promoting this technology.

There are some common pitfalls that you need to be aware of, especially when testing the downloading of your ActiveX document into Internet Explorer. One of the first pitfalls comes when you attempt to create a clean machine for testing purposes. If you try to delete or rename the Visual Basic 6 run-time library (MSVBVM60.DLL), you might see errors. These errors usually occur because the file is in use; you cannot delete the run time while Visual Basic is running or if the browser is viewing an ActiveX document. Try closing Visual Basic and/or your browser. Another version of this error is "An error has occurred copying Msvbvm60.dll. Ensure the location specified below is correct:". This error generally happens when there is insufficient disk space on the machine to which you are trying to download. Another pitfall pertaining to MSVB-VM60.DLL that you might encounter is receiving the prompt "Opening file *DocumentName*.VBD. What would you like to do with this file? Open it or save it to disk?" This happens if the Visual Basic run time is not installed, typically because the safety level in Internet Explorer is set to High. You should set this level to Medium or None instead, though I would not advise the latter setting.

The error "The Dynamic Link Library could not be found in the specified path" typically occurs when the ActiveX document that you have been trying to download already exists on the machine. Another error message is "Internet Explorer is opening file of unknown type: *DocumentName*.VBD from…". This error can be caused by one of several nasties. First make sure that you are using the .vbd file provided by the Package and Deployment Wizard. Then check that the CLSIDs of your .vbd and .exe files are synchronized. To preserve CLSIDs across builds in your projects, select Binary Compatibility on the Components tab of the Project Properties dialog box. Next, make sure that your actxprxy.dll file exists and is registered. Also if your ActiveX document is not signed or safe for scripting, you will need to set the browser safety level to Medium. Incidentally, if you erroneously attempt to distribute Visual Basic's core-dependent .cab files, they won't install using a browser safety level of High, since they are not signed either. Finally, do a run-time error check on your ActiveX document, as this error can be caused by errors in the document's initialization code, particularly in the *Initialize* or *InitProperties* procedures.

SOME VISUAL BASIC 6 TOOLS

We now turn to a discussion of the three Sourcerers mentioned at the beginning of the chapter. These tools—the Assertion Sourcerer, the Metrics Sourcerer, and the Instrumentation Sourcerer—will help you detect and prevent bugs in the programs you write.

Registering the Three Sourcerers

All three Sourcerers we're going to discuss are available in the CHAP06 folder on the companion CD. These Sourcerers are designed as Visual Basic 6 add-ins, running as ActiveX DLLs. To register each Sourcerer in the Microsoft Windows 95/98 or the Microsoft Windows NT system Registry, load each project in turn into the Visual Basic 6 IDE and compile it. One more step is required to use the add-ins: you must inform Visual Basic 6 itself about each add-in. This is done by creating an entry in VBAddin.INI under a section named [Add-Ins32]. This entry takes the form of the project connection class name, for example, VB6Assert.Connect=0 for the Assertion Sourcerer. To perform this automatically for all three Sourcerers, just load, compile, and run the BootStrap project available in the CHAP06 folder on the companion CD. This will add the correct entries in the VBAddin.INI file.

Assert Yourself: The Assertion Sourcerer

Although *Debug.Assert* fulfills its purpose very well, improvements to it would certainly be welcome. It would be nice if you had the ability to report assertion failures in compiled code as well as source code. Because one of the aims of the Enterprise Edition of Visual Basic 6 is to allow components to be built and then distributed across a network, it is quite likely that others in your organization will want to reference the in-process or out-of-process ActiveX servers that you have built using Visual Basic. Ensuring that assertion failures in compiled Visual Basic 6 programs were reported would be a very useful feature, enabling better testing of shared code libraries and allowing the capture of assertion failures during user acceptance testing. This kind of functionality cannot be implemented using *Debug.Assert* because these statements are dropped from your compiled program. Additionally, because you cannot drop from object code into Visual Basic's debugger on an assertion failure, you are faced with finding some alternative method of reporting the assertion failures.

Step forward the Assertion Sourcerer. This add-in supplements *Debug.Assert* with the functionality mentioned above. When you have registered the Sourcerer in the Registry and used the Add-In Manager to reference it, you can select Assertion Sourcerer from the Add-Ins menu to see the window shown in Figure 6-2.

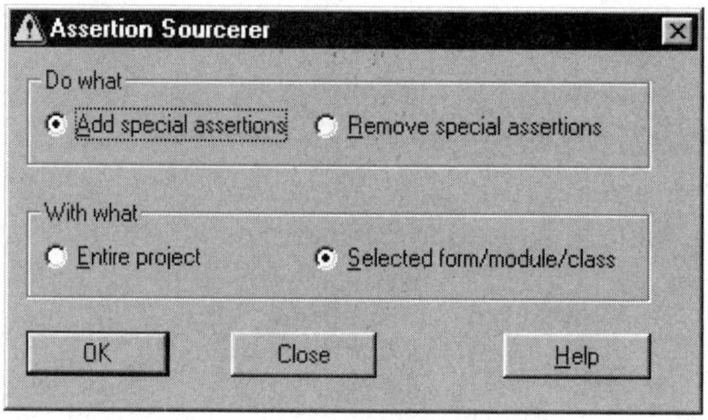

FIGURE 6-2   *The Assertion Sourcerer dialog box*

The standard assertion procedure, which supplements the *Debug.Assert* functionality, is named *BugAssert*. It is part of a small Visual Basic 6 module named DEBUG.BAS, which you should add to any project in which you want to monitor run-time assertion failures. You can then specify which of your *Debug.Assert* statements you want converted to run-time assertions; the choices are all assertions in the project or just those in the selected form, class, or module.

The Assertion Sourcerer works in a very simple manner. When you use the Assertion Sourcerer menu option on the Add-Ins menu to request that assertion calls be added to your project, the Assertion Sourcerer automatically generates and adds a line after every *Debug.Assert* statement in your selected module (or the whole project). This line is a conversion of the *Debug.Assert* statement to a version suitable for calling the *BugAssert* procedure. So

```
Debug.Assert bTest = True
```

becomes

```
Debug.Assert bTest = True
BugAssert bTest = True, "bTest = True," _
          "Project Test.VBP, module Test.CLS, line 53"
```

BugAssert's first argument is just the assertion expression itself. The second argument is a string representation of that assertion. This is required because there is no way for Visual Basic to extract and report the assertion statement being tested from just the first argument. The final argument allows the *BugAssert* procedure to report the exact location of any assertion failure for later analysis. The *BugAssert* procedure that does this reporting is relatively simple. It uses a constant to not report assertion failures, to report them to a *MsgBox*, to report them to a disk file, or to report them to both.

Before compiling your executable, you'll need to set the constant mnDebug in the DEBUG.BAS module. Now whenever your executable is invoked by any other programmer, assertion failures will be reported to the location(s) defined by this constant. Before releasing your code into production, you can tell the Assertion Sourcerer to remove all *BugAssert* statements from your program.

Complete source code for the Assertion Sourcerer is supplied on the CD accompanying this book in CHAP06\assertion so that you can modify it to suit your own purposes.

Some final thoughts   You can use the Assertion Sourcerer as a supplement to *Debug.Assert* when you want to implement assertions in compiled Visual Basic code.

Size Matters: The Metrics Sourcerer

Take any production system and log all the bugs it produces over a year or so. Then note which individual procedures are responsible for the majority of the defects. It's common for only 10 to 20 percent of a system's procedures to be responsible for 80 percent of the errors. If you examine the characteristics of these offending procedures, they will usually be more complex or longer (and sometimes both!) than their better-behaved counterparts. Keeping in mind that the earlier in the development cycle that these defects are detected the less costly it is to diagnose and fix them, any tool that helps to predict a system's problem areas before the system goes into production could prove to be very cost-effective. Step forward the Metrics Sourcerer. (See Figure 6-3.) This Visual Basic 6 add-in analyzes part or all of your project, ranking each procedure in terms of its relative complexity and length.

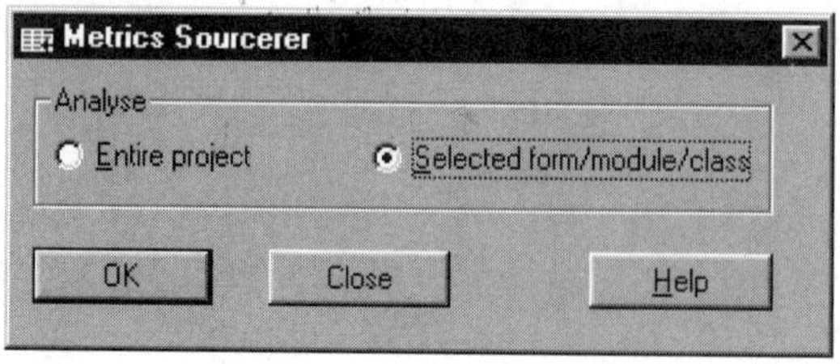

FIGURE 6-3   *The Metrics Sourcerer dialog box*

Defining complexity can be fairly controversial. Developers tend to have different ideas about what constitutes a complex procedure. Factors such as the difficulty of the algorithm or the obscurity of the Visual Basic keywords being employed can be considered useful to measure. The Metrics Sourcerer measures two rather more simple factors: the number of decision points and the number of lines of code that each procedure contains. Some evidence suggests that these are indeed useful characteristics to measure when you're looking for code routines that are likely to cause problems in the future. The number of decision points is easy to count. Certain Visual Basic 6 keywords—for example, *If...Else...End If* and *Select Case*—change the flow of a procedure, making decisions about which code to execute. The Metrics Sourcerer contains an amendable list of these keywords that it uses to count decision points. It then combines this number with the number of code lines that the procedure contains, employing a user-amendable weighting to balance the relative importance of these factors. The final analysis is then output to a text file, viewable by utilities such as WordPad and Microsoft Word. (By default, the filename is the name of your project with the extension MET.) You might also want to import the text file into Microsoft Excel for sorting purposes. There's no point in taking the output of the Metrics Sourcerer as gospel, but it would certainly be worthwhile to reexamine potentially dangerous procedures in the light of its findings.

Another factor that might be useful to measure is the number of assertion failures that each procedure in your program suffers from. This figure can be captured using the Assertion Sourcerer. Combining this figure with the numbers produced by the Metrics Sourcerer would be a very powerful pointer toward procedures that need more work before your system goes into production.

Some final thoughts   Use the Metrics Sourcerer as a guide to the procedures in your programs that need to be examined with the aim of reducing their complexity. Economical to execute in terms of time, the Metrics Sourcerer can prove to be extremely effective in reducing the number of bugs that reach production.

A Black Box:
The Instrumentation Sourcerer

When a commercial airliner experiences a serious incident or crashes, one of the most important tools available to the team that subsequently investigates the accident is the plane's black box (actually colored orange), otherwise known as the flight data recorder. This box provides vital information about the period leading up to the accident, including data about the plane's control surfaces, its instruments, and its position in the air. How easy would it be to provide this type of information in the event of user acceptance or production program bugs and crashes?

The Instrumentation Sourcerer, shown in Figure 6-4 on the following page, walks through your program code, adding a line of code at the start of every procedure. This line invokes a procedure that writes a record of each procedure that is executed to a log file on disk. (See Chapter 1 for an in-depth examination of similar techniques.) In this way, you can see a complete listing of every button that your user presses, every text box or other control that your user fills in, and every response of your program. In effect, each program can be given its own black box. The interactive nature of Windows programs allows users to pick and choose their way through the different screens available to them. Thus it has traditionally been difficult to track exactly how the user is using your program or what sequence of events leads up to a bug or a crash. The Instrumentation Sourcerer can help you to understand more about your programs and the way they are used.

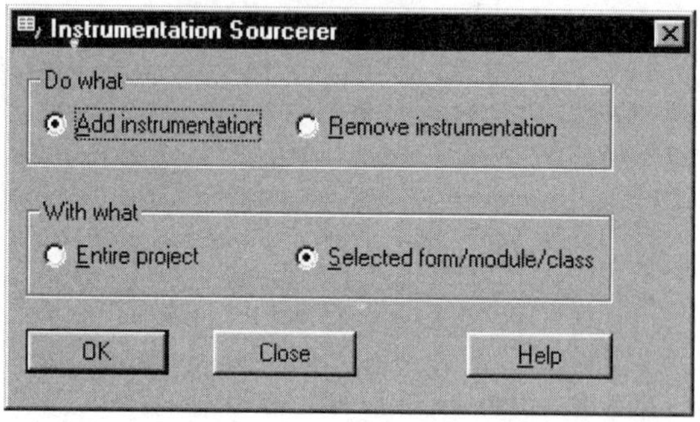

FIGURE 6-4   *The Instrumentation Sourcerer dialog box*

Configuration options allow you to selectively filter the procedures that you want to instrument. This might be useful if you want to document certain parts of a program, such as Click and KeyPress events. You can also choose how much information you want to store. Just as in an aircraft's black box, the amount of storage space for recording what can be a vast amount of information is limited. Limiting the data recorded to maybe the last 500 or 1000 procedures can help you to make the best use of the hard disk space available on your machine or on your users' machines.

Some final thoughts   The Instrumentation Sourcerer can be useful in tracking the cause of program bugs and crashes, at the same time providing an effective record of how users interact with your program in the real world.

FINAL THOUGHTS

Is it possible to write zero-defect Visual Basic 6 code? I don't believe it is—and even if it were, I doubt it would be cost-effective to implement. However, it is certainly possible to drastically reduce the number of production bugs. You just have to *want* to do it and to prepare properly using the right tools and the right attitudes. From here, you need to build your own bug lists, your own techniques, and your own antidefect tools. Although none of the ideas and techniques described in this chapter will necessarily prevent you from creating a program with a distinct resemblance to a papcastle (something drawn or modeled by a small child that you are supposed to recognize), at least your programs will have presumptions toward being zero-defect papcastles.

Final disclaimer: All the bugs in this chapter were metaphorical constructs. No actual bugs were harmed during the writing of this work.

Required Reading

The following books are highly recommended—maybe even essential—reading for any professional Visual Basic developer.

- *Hardcore Visual Basic* by Bruce McKinney (Microsoft Press, 1997)
- *Hitchhiker's Guide To Visual Basic and SQL Server, 6th Edition* by Bill Vaughan (Microsoft Press, 1998)
- *Microsoft Visual Basic 6 Programmer's Guide* by Microsoft Corporation (Microsoft Press, 1998)
- *Dan Appleman's Developing ActiveX Components With Visual Basic 5.0* by Dan Appleman (Ziff-Davis, 1997)
- *Software Project Survival Guide* by Steve McConnell (Microsoft Press, 1997)
- *Code Complete* by Steve McConnell (Microsoft Press, 1993)

Minutiae

PETER MORRIS

In addition to being a "doer," Peet also thinks and talks about writing code and is a frequent speaker at international conferences, such as VBITS and Microsoft's DevCon and TechEd. This book is Peet's second foray into the world of book writing—

his first occurred about the time he was working at Microsoft when he wrote *Windows Advanced Programming and Design* (now as rare as duck's teeth), which was a pure API, C, and Assembler SDK book. Peet's story continues on page 454.

As you can probably guess from its title, this chapter is going to cover a rather broad range of information about Visual Basic. Think of this chapter as a Visual Basic programmer's smorgasbord. You'll learn about such topics as the advantages and disadvantages of compiling to p-code and native code. You'll get some hints on how to optimize your applications beyond just writing excellent code. And you'll also receive up-to-the-minute information on such scintillating subjects as types and type libraries. So let's begin!

Stuff About the Compiler

In this section, we'll examine applications compiled to native code. We won't deal much with p-code (packed code) at all, aside from a brief introduction and some comparisons with native code.

As you probably know, Visual Basic 6 applications, just like their Visual Basic 5 counterparts, can now be "properly" compiled, unlike Visual Basic version 4 and earlier, which produced p-code executables. In other words, as well as producing p-code executables, Visual Basic 6 can produce a native code binary. Which compile option you choose is up to you. I suspect that most corporate developers will want to know more about this compiler process than they ever wanted to know about p-code.

A Little About P-Code

P-code applications are usually smaller (and slower) than native code applications. With p-code, an interpreter compresses and packages your code. Then, at run time, this same interpreter expands and, of course, runs your application. P-code applications are usually ported more easily to different processors.

The term p-code was derived from the term "pseudocode" because p-code consists of a RISC-like set of instructions for a "make-believe" processor. At run time, this processor, usually known as a stack machine (because it uses a stack for practically all its operations), is simulated by the built-in interpreter. (Just so you know, a "normal" processor uses registers and a stack primarily to pass values to and from function calls.) Because of its imaginary nature, the processor's instruction set never needs to change; instead, each instruction is mapped, via a lookup table, to a real instruction on any given processor. Logically, then, all that's required to move code from one processor to another is this mapping—code generation remains largely unaffected.

In a nutshell, p-code is an intermediate step between the high-level instructions in your Visual Basic program and the low-level native code executed by your computer's processor. At run time, Visual Basic translates each p-code statement to native code.

With p-code, typical size reduction from native code is more than 50 percent. For example, when the VisData sample that is included on the Visual Basic 5 CD is compiled to p-code, the resulting executable is less than half the size it would be if compiled to native code (396 KB vs. 792 KB). Additionally, compiling p-code is a lot faster than compiling to native code—around seven times faster. (Some of the reasons for the speed of p-code compiling will become evident later in the chapter.) You'll need to keep this compile-time difference in mind during your development and testing phases. These compile timings, and all the other timings in this chapter, were made using prerelease builds of Visual Basic 6. If you're interested in these timings, you should conduct your own tests using the actual product.

Back in the days of Visual Basic 4 and earlier, a native code compiler was, I think, one of the most requested features, so I'm not surprised to find that Microsoft put it in Visual Basic 5—and, of course, the native code compiler is basically the same feature in Visual Basic 6. Personally, however, I think that native code compilation, for many reasons (and forgetting for a second that it typically executes faster) is a backward step. I'm still convinced that p-code is ultimately a superior technology compared to native code generation, as does, apparently, Sun Microsystems, because Java is essentially doing the same thing! Ever since the first version of Visual Basic, its p-code output has been, or could have been, roughly equivalent to Java's bytecodes. If a Visual Basic program had to be instantiated using the Visual Basic "virtual machine" (that is, something like *vbrun100 <AppName>*) and if that virtual machine were to be ported to different, non-Intel architectures, Visual Basic could have perhaps led the way to what's now become "bytecode nerdvana" instead of being criticized in its p-code form for being both slow and interpreted (just like pure Java *is*, in fact) Not convinced? Here's one of Sun's own descriptions of bytecode technology.

> [On Java being a portable technology] "The Java compiler does this by generating bytecode instructions that have nothing to do with a particular computer architecture. Rather, they are designed to be both easy to interpret on any machine and easily translated into native machine code on the fly." [I'm sure the similarity between the two is obvious.]

If you want to read some more stuff about p-code that isn't specific to Visual Basic, search MSDN for "Microsoft P-Code Technology" and see Andy Padawer's excellent paper on the subject.

Generating Code

You select the code generation model you want via the somewhat hidden dialog box shown in Figure 7-1 on the next page. You get to this dialog box by choosing Properties from the Project menu.

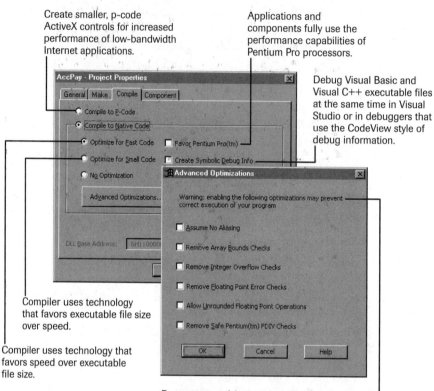

Create smaller, p-code ActiveX controls for increased performance of low-bandwidth Internet applications.

Applications and components fully use the performance capabilities of Pentium Pro processors.

Debug Visual Basic and Visual C++ executable files at the same time in Visual Studio or in debuggers that use the CodeView style of debug information.

Compiler uses technology that favors executable file size over speed.

Compiler uses technology that favors speed over executable file size.

Remove some of the automatic Visual Basic language protective features from executable files to further enhance performance, but first make sure the code doesn't need the features you're removing.

FIGURE 7-1   *Visual Basic's compiler options dialog boxes*

As you can see, some extra compilation options become available when you select Compile To Native Code. I'll discuss some of these options a little later.

When you compile to native code, the Visual Basic 6 native code generator/compiler, C2.EXE, is run once for each code component in the project. For example, if a project has a form, Form1; a standard module, Module1; and a class module, Class1; C2.EXE is run a total of three times. Each invocation's options are the same depending on which you selected in the dialog box; that is, the options you select are used to compile the entire project. In case you're interested, C2.EXE runs as a multithreaded, Win32, 32-bit console process.

Each time the native code compiler is run, a hidden process (described as 16-bit by the Windows 95 Task Manager) is started and the code generator/ compiler, also run as a hidden process, is run attached to this process. (In Windows 95, this process is run from the file WINOA386.MOD, with a process description of "Non-Windows application component for 386 enhanced mode." This file is not required if you're running under Windows NT.) As each invocation of C2.EXE terminates, the instance of WINOLDAP (the module name given to WINOA386.MOD) in which it was run is also terminated. You should now start to see why this process might be slower than selecting p-code generation (which is an internal process and doesn't use C2.EXE, although it does use LINK.EXE). Here's what the command-line arguments of a typical compilation look like (with no optimizations):

```
C2 -il C:\WINDOWS\TEMP\VB603389 -f Form1 -W3 -Gy -G5 -Gs4096
-dos -Zl -FoC:\TEMP\Form1.OBJ -QIfdiv -ML -basic
```

These flags are explained in Table 7-1.

TABLE 7-1

COMMAND-LINE FLAGS FOR THE C2 COMPILER

Flag	Explanation
-il C:\WINDOWS\TEMP\VB603389	Undocumented but also used for a C program; probably used to "name" intermediate language files
-f Form1	The input file to be compiled
-W3	Warning level 3
-Gy	Enable function-level linking
-G5	Optimize for Pentium
-Gs4096	Turn off stack probes
-dos	Undocumented but also used for a C program
-Zl	Remove default library name from OBJ file
-Fo C:\TEMP\Form1.OBJ	Name of output file
-QIfdiv	Perform Pentium FDIV erratum fix
-ML	Create a single-threaded executable file
-basic	Undocumented but appears to be a new flag for Visual Basic compilation

Some of the flags are described in more detail here as well:

-il   This flag is undocumented but "intermediate language" is a good guess for what "il" stands for. Files produced are <Signature>GL, SY, EX, IN, and DB. I have no idea what these files contain. In the command-line example in Table 7-1, the following files (long filenames shown) are generated temporarily while the application is being built:

- VB603389GL
- VB603389SY
- VB603389EX
- VB603389IN
- VB603389DB

-G5   The option optimizes the generated code to favor the Intel Pentium processor. Here's what the Microsoft Developer Network (MSDN) says about the same Visual C++ flag: "Use this option for programs meant only for the Pentium. Code created using the /G5 option does not perform as well on 80386- and 80486-based computers as code created using the /GB (Blend) option." Interestingly, by default, the -G5 switch is always used—even when you compile on a 486 machine.

-Gs[size]   If a function requires more than *size* stack space for local variables, its stack probe is activated. A stack probe is a piece of code that checks whether the space required for passed parameters and local variables is available on the stack before any attempt to allocate the space is made. -Gs0 is the same as -Ge, turn stack probes on; -Gs4096 is the default.

-ML   This option places the library name LIBC.LIB in the object file so that the linker will use LIBC.LIB to resolve external symbols. This is the compiler's default action. LIBC.LIB does not provide multithread support, by the way.

Don't bother to scan your Visual Basic 6 documentation for information about these flags because you won't find any—they are all undocumented. If you have a set of documentation for the Visual C++ compiler, however, you might be in luck. It seems that C2.EXE is taken from the Visual C++ compiler (this file is called C2.DLL in version 6 of Visual C++, although in Visual Basic 5, both Visual Basic and Visual C++ shared exactly the same file—C2.EXE). C2.EXE is, in fact, the compiler from Microsoft's Visual C++ product. Nevertheless, the above interpretation of the flag meanings is mine alone. Microsoft doesn't document how its C++ compiler works beyond describing CL.EXE (the front end to the C compiler).

Table 7-2 provides a summary of the C2 compiler incarnations at the time of this book's writing.

Table 7-2 **Comparison of Visual C++ and Visual Basic C2 Components**

Component	Product Version	Compiler Description
C2.EXE (from Visual Basic 6)	6.0.8041.0	32-Bit 80x86 Compiler Back End
C2.DLL (from Visual C++ 6)	6.0.8168.0	32-Bit 80x86 Compiler Back End
C2.EXE (from Visual Basic 5)	5.0.0.7182	32-bit Visual Basic Compiler Back End

Visual Basic itself evidently provides the compiler's first pass, unlike Visual C++ in which the first pass (the parser and some of the optimizer) of C and C++ files is provided by either C1.DLL or C1XX.DLL, respectively. In terms of compilers, VB6.EXE is seemingly analogous to CL.EXE.

The Loggers

Either the C application or the Visual Basic application listed at the end of this section (and on the CD) can be used to replace the real C2.EXE file. To replace it, follow these steps for the C version:

1. Make backup copies of C2.EXE and LINK.EXE.

2. Rename C2.EXE to C3.EXE.

3. If you want to rebuild the C application, make sure that the first real line of code in the OUTARGS.C source file reads as follows:

   ```
   strcpy(&carArgs[0], ".\\C3 ");
   ```

   The binary version on the CD already includes this line of code.

4. Copy the EXE (OUTARGS.EXE) to C2.EXE.

   ```
   copy outargs.exe c2.exe
   ```

5. Your original C2.EXE is now C3.EXE, so no damage is done.

Use Visual Basic 6 as you normally would.

The steps for using the Visual Basic version are a little different. To replace C2.EXE with the Visual Basic application, follow these steps:

1. Make backup copies of C2.EXE and LINK.EXE.

2. Compile the code to OUTARGS.EXE (make sure your project contains just the *OUTARGS.BAS* standard module—no forms or anything else).

3. Rename C2.EXE to C3.EXE. Rename LINK.EXE to L1NK.EXE. (Note that the "i" has been changed to a "1".)

4. Copy the EXE (OUTARGS.EXE) to C2.EXE and LINK.EXE. Your original C2.EXE is now C3.EXE and your LINK.EXE is now L1NK.EXE, so no damage is done.

5. Run REGEDIT.EXE, and under HKEY_CURRENT_USER\Software\VB and VBA Program Settings insert two new keys (subkeys and values as shown here):

```
HKEY_CURRENT_USER\Software\VB and VBA Program Settings\
    \C2
        \Startup
            \RealAppName      ".\C3"
    \LINK
        \Startup
            \RealAppName      ".\L1NK"
```

6. Use Visual Basic 6 as normal.

The purpose of the Visual Basic version of OUTARGS.EXE is to have the same binary self-configure from a Registry setting. This means that you only need one OUTARGS.EXE (renamed appropriately) to "spy" on any application.

The output of the Visual Basic application is a little less fully featured than that produced by the C application. After you've carried out either of these steps, the following will happen: When Visual Basic 6 runs (to compile to native code), it will run C2.EXE. C2.EXE, which is really our OUTARGS.EXE program, will log the call made to it to the file C2.OUT. (Our application logs to a file based upon its own name, <EXEname>.OUT; because our application is renamed C2.EXE, the log file will be C2.OUT.) Information logged includes the parameters that have been passed to it. C2.EXE will then shell C3.EXE (the "real" C2), passing to it, by default, all the same parameters that it was passed. The net effect is that you have logged how C2 was invoked.

The Visual Basic OUTARGS program will also be used to log the linker, if you followed the steps above. Listing 7-1 is a typical C2.OUT log (C version).

```
********** Run @ Wed Jan 1 00:00:00 1998

* EXE file...

        C2

* Command Line Arguments...

1       -il
2       C:\WINDOWS\TEMP\VB476314
3       -f
4       Form1
5       -W
6       3
7       -Gy
8       -G5
9       -Gs4096
10      -dos
11      -Z1
12      -FoC:\TEMP\Form14.OBJ
13      -QIfdiv
14      -ML
15      -basic
* 'Real' program and arguments...

        .\C3 -il C:\WINDOWS\TEMP\VB476314 -f Form1 -W 3 -Gy -G5
        -Gs4096 -dos -Z1 -FoC:\TEMP\Form14.OBJ -QIfdiv -ML -basic

********** Run End
```

LISTING 7-1   *Typical C2.OUT log file*

The Visual Basic team seems to have added a space between the -W and the 3, possibly causing C2 to interpret this as two separate switches. Since C2 doesn't error or complain, I'm assuming that it knows to treat the switch as -W3 (warning level set to 3).

By further altering the code (again, the C version is demonstrated here), you can change, add, or remove compiler switches. For example, you can add the following code to the argument processing loop to replace, say, -G5 with, say, -GB, the "blend" switch mentioned earlier in our discussion of -G5 on page 280.

```
if_(0 == strcmp(argv[nLoop], "-G5"))
{
    (void)strcat(&carArgs[0], "-GB ");

    continue;
}
```

NOTE

The C version OUTARGS.EXE doesn't like long pathnames that include spaces. Each "gap" causes the next part of the pathname to be passed to C3 as a separate command-line argument. To fix this, either alter the C code to quote delimit each pathname or copy your test Visual Basic project to, say, C:\TEMP before attempting to use it; that is, remove any long pathname. (Leave the renamed OUTARGS C2.EXE in the same folder as the real, now renamed, C3.EXE.) *Note that the Visual Basic OUTARGS.EXE doesn't have the same problem.*

To restore the "real" program, simply copy over C2.EXE with C3.EXE:

```
copy c3.exe c2.exe
```

The Linker

As I've already said, C2.EXE compiles each component to an object file. When all the components are compiled, they are linked using LINK.EXE. Table 7-3 lists the command line arguments you might find in a typical run when creating an EXE containing a single form, class module, and standard module. The only compile option switched on for this run was Create Symbolic Debug Info. This information was captured using the OUTARGS.EXE program.

Again, LINK.EXE is taken from the Visual C++ 6.0 compiler. At the time of writing, its version number was 6.00.8168.0—exactly the same version as that supplied with C2.DLL. See the Visual C++ documentation or MSDN for more information regarding these linker switches.

The linker is also used to create a p-code application, by the way. The difference in the invocation is that VBAEXE6.LIB is not linked in and that only one object file is used as input—ProjectName.OBJ.

TABLE 7-3   **COMMAND-LINE SWITCHES FOR THE LINKER**

Switch	Explanation
C:\TEMP\Form1.OBJ	Form OBJ file
C:\TEMP\Module1.OBJ	Module OBJ file
C:\TEMP\Class1.OBJ	Class OBJ file
C:\TEMP\Project1.OBJ	Project OBJ file
C:\PROGRAM FILES\VISUAL STUDIO\VB\VBAEXE6.LIB	Library of Visual Basic OBJs
/ENTRY:__vbaS	Sets the starting address for an executable file or DLL. The entry point should be a function that is defined with the *stdcall* calling convention. The parameters and the return value must be defined as documented in the Win32 API for *WinMain* (for an .EXE) or *DllEntryPoint* (for a DLL). This entry point is in your <project name>.OBJ file—here it will be in PROJECT1.OBJ. Note that *neither Sub Main* nor *Form_Load* is mentioned.
/OUT:C:\TEMP\Project1.exe	The output file—the EXE!
/BASE:0x400000	Sets a base address for the program, overriding the default location for an executable file (at 0x400000) or a DLL (at 0x10000000). The operating system first attempts to load a program at its specified or default base address. If sufficient space is not available there, the system relocates the program. To prevent relocation, use the /FIXED option. The BASE generated by Visual Basic 6 for an ActiveX DLL is 0x11000000—something that's different from the default at last.
/SUBSYSTEM:WINDOWS,4.0	Tells the operating system how to run the .EXE file. (Options include CONSOLE | WINDOWS | NATIVE | POSIX.)
/VERSION:1.0	Tells the linker to put a version number in the header of the executable file or DLL. (This option has nothing to do with a VERSIONINFO resource.) The major and minor arguments are decimal numbers in the range 0 through 65535. The default is version 0.0. Visual Basic uses the Major and Minor settings on the Make tab of the Project Properties dialog box for these values. This switch is used to document the image version as shown by DUMPBIN.EXE (another Microsoft Visual C++ tool).
/DEBUG	Creates debugging information for the executable file or DLL. The linker puts the debugging information into a program database (PDB). It updates the program database during subsequent builds of the program.

≫

TABLE 7-3

>>

Switch	Explanation
/DEBUGTYPE:{CV|COFF|BOTH}	Generates debugging information in one of three ways: Microsoft format, COFF format, or both. CV is CodeView; COFF is Common Object File Format.
/INCREMENTAL:NO	Specifies whether incremental linking is required.
/OPT:REF	Excludes unreferenced packaged functions from the executable file. Packaged functions are created using the -Gy flag at compile time (see Table 7-1 on page 279). Packaged functions have several uses (not mentioned here) and are created automatically, sometimes by the compiler. For example, C++ member functions are automatically packaged.
/MERGE:from=to	Combines the first section (from) with the second section (to), naming the resulting section "to". If the second section does not exist, LINK renames the section "from" as "to". The /MERGE option is most useful for creating VxDs and for overriding the compiler-generated section names.
/IGNORE:4078	Ignores certain warnings (defined in LINK.ERR). 4078 means that LINK found two or more sections that have the same name but different attributes.

Why these switches?

I have no idea why some of these switches are used explicitly (on the compiler also), particularly since some are set to the default anyway. Perhaps some of the reasons for using these switches will be documented later.

Using the Compiler to Optimize Your Code

The effect of the optimization options (on the Compile tab of the Project Properties dialog box and in the Advanced Optimizations dialog box) on how C2.EXE and LINK.EXE are driven is summarized in Table 7-4 (for building a standard EXE).

Obviously, -G6 means favor the Pentium Pro.

Notice that most of the switches have no effect on how C2 or LINK are started (although the EXE size changes so that we know the option is making itself known!). Since most switches have no effect, we must assume they are being acted on within VB6.EXE itself (as it seems to contain the compiler's first pass). Or perhaps the mystery files shown earlier (VB603389GL, VB603389SY, VB603389EX, VB603389IN, and VB603389DB) have some way of influencing the code generator, thus sidestepping our efforts to understand how the process is being controlled.

TABLE 7-4

THE COMPILER EFFECT

Optimization Option	C2.EXE Effect	LINK.EXE Effect
Optimize For Small Code	None	None
Optimize For Fast Code	None	None
Favor Pentium Pro	/G6 (from G5)	None
Create Symbolic Debug Info	/Zi	/DEBUG /DEBUGTYPE:CV
Assume No Aliasing	None	None
Remove Array Bounds Checks	None	None
Remove Integer Overflow Checks	None	None
Remove Floating Point Error Checks	None	None
Allow Unrounded Floating Point Operations	None	None
Remove Safe Pentium(tm) FDIV Checks	/QIfdiv Removed	None

Advanced Optimizations

Microsoft generally encourages you to play around with what they call the safe compiler options. Naturally, these are options that aren't situated beneath the Advanced Optimizations button. For those options Microsoft usually provides a disclaimer: "These might crash your program." Let's see what these Advanced Optimizations are about and why this warning is given. (See Table 7-5 on the following page.)

TABLE 7-5   **ADVANCED OPTIMIZATIONS OPTIONS**

Option	Description
Allow Unrounded Floating Point Operations	Allows the compiler to compare floating-point expressions without first rounding to the correct precision. Floating-point calculations are normally rounded off to the correct degree of precision (Single or Double) before comparisons are made. Selecting this option allows the compiler to do floating-point comparisons before rounding, when it can do so more efficiently. This improves the speed of some floating-point operations; however, this may result in calculations being maintained to a higher precision than expected, and two floating-point values not comparing equal when they might be expected to.
Assume No Aliasing	Tells the compiler that your program does not use aliasing (that your program does not refer to the same memory location by more than one name, which occurs when using *ByRef* arguments that refer to the same variable in two ways). Checking this option allows the compiler to apply optimization such as storing variables in registers and performing loop optimizations.
Remove Array Bounds Checks	Disables Visual Basic array bounds checking. By default, Visual Basic makes a check on every access to an array to determine if the index is within the range of the array. If the index is outside the bounds of the array, an error is returned. Selecting this option will turn off this error checking, which can speed up array manipulation significantly. However, if your program accesses an array with an index that is out of bounds, invalid memory locations might be accessed without warning. This can cause unexpected behavior or program crashes.
Remove Floating Point Error Checks	Disables Visual Basic floating-point error checking and turns off error checking for valid floating-point operations and numeric values assigned to floating-point variables. By default in Visual Basic, a check is made on every calculation to a variable with floating-point data types (Single and Double) to be sure that the resulting value is within the range of that data type. If the value is of the wrong magnitude, an error will occur.
	Error checking is also performed to determine if division by zero or other invalid operations are attempted. Selecting this option turns off this error checking, which can speed up floating-point calculations. If data type capacities are overflowed, however, no error will be returned and incorrect results might occur.
Remove Integer Overflow Checks	Disables Visual Basic integer overflow checking. By default in Visual Basic, a check is made on every calculation to a variable with an integer data type (Byte, Integer, Long, and Currency) to be sure that the resulting value is within range of that data type. If the value is of the wrong magnitude, an error will occur. Selecting this option will turn off this error checking, which can speed up integer calculations. If data type capacities are overflowed, however, no error will be returned and incorrect results might occur.

Option	Description
Remove Safe Pentium FDIV Checks	Disables checking for safe Pentium floating-point division and turns off the generation of special code for Pentium processors with the FDIV bug. The native code compiler automatically adds extra code for floating-point operations to make these operations safe when run on Pentium processors that have the FDIV bug. Selecting this option produces code that is smaller and faster, but which might in rare cases produce slightly incorrect results on Pentium processors with the FDIV bug.

By using the Visual C++ debugger (or any compatible debugger) with Visual Basic code that has been compiled to contain symbolic debugging information, it's possible to see more of what each option does to your code. By way of explanation, here are a few annotated examples (obviously you won't expect to see commented code like this from a debugger!):

Integer Overflow

```
Dim n As Integer

n = 100 * 200 * 300
```

Disassembly (without Integer Overflow check)

```
' Do the multiplication - ax = 300
mov         ax,offset    Form::Proc+4Ch

' Signed integer multiplication. 300 * 20000
' The 20000 is stored in Form::Proc+51h and was
' created by the compiler from the constant exp.
' 100 * 200 and held as 'immediate data'
imul        ax,ax,offset Form::Proc+51h

n = Result

mov         word ptr [n],ax
```

Disassembly (with Integer Overflow check)

```
' Do the multiplication - ax = 100
mov         ax,offset    Form::Proc+4Ch
imul        ax,ax,offset Form::Proc+51h

' Jump to error handler if the overflow flag set
jo          __vbaErrorOverflow

Else, n = Result
mov         word ptr [n],ax
```

Array Bounds

```
Dim n1        As Integer
Dim n(100)    As Integer

n1 = n(101)
```

Disassembly (without Array Bounds check)

```
' Sizeof(Integer) = 2, put in eax
push        2
pop         eax

' Integer multiplication.  2 * 101 (&H65) = result in eax.
imul        eax,eax,65h

' Get array base address in to ecx.
mov         ecx,dword ptr [ebp-20h]

n(101) (base plus offset) is in ax
mov         ax,word ptr [ecx+eax]

n1 = n(101)
mov         word ptr [n1],ax
```

Disassembly (with Array Bounds check)

```
' Address pointed to by v1 = 101, the offset we want
mov         dword ptr [unnamed_var1],65h

' Compare value thus assigned with the known size of array + 1
cmp         dword ptr [unnamed_var1],65h

' Jump above or equal to 'Call ___vbaGenerateBoundsError'
jae         Form1::Proc+6Dh

' Zero the flags and a memory location.
and         dword ptr [ebp-48h],0

' Jump to 'mov eax,dword ptr [unnamed_var1]'
jmp         Form1::Proc+75h

' Raise the VB error here
call        ___vbaGenerateBoundsError

' Store element number we want to access
mov         dword ptr [ebp-48h],eax
```

```
' Get the element we wanted to access into eax
mov          eax,dword ptr [unnamed_var1]

' Get array base address in to ecx.
mov          ecx,dword ptr [ebp-20h]

' n(101) is in ax (* 2 because sizeof(Integer) = 2
mov          ax,word ptr [ecx+eax*2]

' n1 = n(101)
mov          word ptr [n1],ax
Floating Point Error
Dim s As Single

s = s * s
```

Disassembly (without Floating Point Error check)

```
' Pushes the specified operand onto the FP stack
fld          dword ptr [s]

' Multiplies the source by the destination and returns
' the product in the destination
fmul         dword ptr [s]

' Stores the value in the floating point store (ST?)
' to the specified memory location
fstp         dword ptr [s]
```

Disassembly (with Floating Point Error check)

```
fld          dword ptr [s]
fmul         dword ptr [s]
fstp         dword ptr [s]

' Store the floating point flags in AX (no wait)
fnstsw       ax

' Test for floating point error flag set
test         al,0Dh

' Jump if zero flag not set
jne          ___vbaFPException
```

You should now have more of a feel for why these options are left partially obscured like they are, and for the warning given by Microsoft. Without a native code debugger it's really hard to see just how your code's being affected. Even with a debugger like the one that comes with Visual Studio it's not a straight-forward task to read through the assembly-language dumps and state that your code is cool and that the optimizations you've chosen are safe!

Library and object files

From Table 7-3 on page 285, you'll notice that VBAEXE6.LIB is linked in with our own OBJ file (created from our files and modules). The library contains just one component (library files contain object files), NATSUPP.OBJ. (NATSUPP might stand for "native support.") You can find this object by using *DUMPBIN /ARCHIVEMEMBERS VBAEXE6.LIB.* (DUMPBIN.EXE is the Microsoft Common Object File Format [COFF] Binary File Dumper.) NATSUPP.OBJ can be extracted for further examination using the Microsoft Library Manager, LIB.EXE:

```
lib /
extract:c:\vbadev\r6w32nd\presplit\vbarun\obj\natsupp.obj vbaexe6.lib
```

The reason for including the path to the OBJ file is that the library manager expects us to specify exactly the name of the module—including its path. (This is embedded into the library file when the object file is first put into it and is discovered using *DUMPBIN /ARCHIVEMEMBERS.*) In other words, the object file probably "lived" at this location on someone's machine in Redmond! Similarly, we can tell that the source code for this object file was named NAT-SUPP.ASM and was in the directory C:\VBADEV\RT\WIN32. It was assembled using Microsoft's Macro Assembler, Version 6.13. (6.11 is the latest version available to the public, I believe.) Interestingly, it doesn't contain any code—just data—although what looks like a jump table (a mechanism often used to facilitate calls to external routines) appears to be included. To call a routine, you look up its address in the table and then jump to it, as shown in Table 7-6.

TABLE 7-6

CONTENTS OF **NATSUPP.OBJ**

Name	Size	Content
.text	0	Readable code
.data	4	Initialized readable writable data
.debug$S	140	Initialized discardable readable data
.debug$T	4	Initialized discardable readable data

The sections are as follows:

- **.text** is where all the general-purpose code created by the compiler is output. (It's 0 bytes big, which probably means no code!)
- **.data** is where initialized data is stored.
- **.debug$S** and **.debug$T** contain, respectively, CodeView Version 4 (CV4) symbolic information (a stream of CV4 symbol records) and CV4 type information (a stream of CV4 type records), as described in the CV4 specification.

As well as statically linking with this library file, other object files reference exported functions in yet another library file, MSVBVM60.DLL This is a rather large DLL installed by the Visual Basic 6 Setup program in the WIN-DOWS\SYSTEM directory. (The file describes itself as Visual Basic Virtual Machine and at the time of writing was at version 6.0.81.76—or 6.00.8176 if you look a the version string.) Using *DUMPBIN /EXPORTS MSVBVM60.DLL* on this DLL yields some interesting symbolic information. For example, we can see that it exports a number of routines, 635 in fact! Some interesting-looking things, possibly routines for invoking methods and procedures, are in here as well: *MethCallEngine* and *ProcCallEngine*. Additionally, there are what look like stubs, prefixed with *rtc* ("run-time call," perhaps?), one for apparently all the VBA routines: *rtcIsArray*, *rtcIsDate*, *rtcIsEmpty*, … *rtcMIRR* , … *rtcMsgBox*, … *rtcQBColor*, and so on. And as with most DLLs, some cryptic, yet interesting exports, such as *Zombie_Release*, are included.

In addition to this symbolic information, the DLL contains a whole bunch of resources, which we can extract and examine using tools such as Visual C++ 6. Of all the resources the DLL contains, the one that really begs examination is the type library resource. If we disassemble this using OLEVIEW.EXE, we can see its entire type library in source form.

The type library contains all sorts of stuff as well as the interface definitions of methods and properties, such as the hidden *VarPtr*, *ObjPtr*, and *StrPtr* routines.

It turns out that this MSVBVM60.DLL is probably the run-time support DLL for any Visual Basic 6 native and p-code executable; that is, it acts like MFC42.DLL does for an MFC application. (MFC stands for Microsoft Foundation Classes, Microsoft's C++/Windows class libraries.) We can confirm this by dumping a built native code executable. Sure enough, we find that the executable imports routines from the DLL. (By the way, the Package And Deployment Wizard also lists this component as the Visual Basic Runtime.)

By dumping other separate object files, we can gather information about what is defined and where it is exported. For example, we can use *DUMPBIN /SYM-BOLS MODULE1.OBJ* to discover that a function named *Beep* will be compiled using Microsoft's C++ name decoration (name mangling) regime and thus end up being named *?Beep@Module1@@AAGXXZ*. Presumably, this function is compiled as a kind of C++ anyway; that is, in C++ it is defined as *(private: void__stdcall Module1::Beep(void))*. Or better yet, we can use *DUMPBIN /DISASM ????????.OBJ* to disassemble a module.

The same routine—*Beep*—defined in a class, Class1 for example, looks like this:

```
?Beep@Class1@@AAGXXZ (private: void __stdcall Class1::Beep(void)).
```

Maybe now we can see why, since Visual Basic 4, we've had to name modules even though they're not multiply instantiable. Each seems to become a kind of C++ class. According to the name decorations used, *Beep* is a member of the C++ Classes Class1 and Module1.

The Logger Code

As promised, Listing 7-2 shows the C source code for the spy type application we used earlier on the command line arguments of both C2.EXE and LINK.EXE. Note that a nearly equivalent Visual Basic version follows this application.

```c
/*************************************************************

Small 'C' applet used to replace Visual Basic 6 compiler
apps so as to gather their output and manipulate their
command-line switches.

See notes in main text for more details.

*************************************************************/

#include < stdio.h   >
#include < string.h  >
#include < time.h    >
#include < windows.h >

int main
(
     int    argc     // Number of command-line arguments
    ,char * argv[]    // The arguments themselves
    ,char * env []    // Environment variables
)
```

LISTING 7-2   *The OUTARGS logger application in C*

```
{
    /****************************************
    ** General declares.
    */
    #define BUFF 2048

    auto FILE *      stream;          // File to write to.

    auto struct tm * tt;             // Time stuff for time of write.
    auto time_t      t;              // ----- " " -----

    auto char        carBuff[255];   // Used for holding output
                                     // file name.

    auto char        carArgs[BUFF];  // Holds command line args
                                     // for display.
    auto int         nLoop;          // Loop counter.


    /* **************
    ** Code starts ...
    */

    // Change according to what real (renamed) application you
    // want to start.
    (void)strcpy(&carArgs[0], ".\\C3 ");

    // Get the system time and convert it to ASCII string.
    (void)time(&t);
    tt = localtime(&t);

    // Going to need to append to our exe name, so write
    // to temp buffer.
    (void)strcpy(&carBuff[0], argv[0]);

    // Now append .OUT - should contain ???.OUT after this where ???
    // could be APP.EXE or just APP, depending upon how this program
    // is run.
    (void)strcat(&carBuff[0], ".OUT");

    // Write to EXEName.OUT file (append mode)...
    if (NULL != (stream = fopen(&carBuff[0], "a")))
    {
        // Write out the time.
```

>>

LISTING 7-2

```
        (void)fprintf(stream, "********** Run @ %s\n", asctime(tt));

        // Output name of EXE file.
        (void)fprintf(stream, "* EXE file...\n\n");
        (void)fprintf(stream, "\t%s\n", argv[0]);

        /* ***************************************************
        ** Output command line args (exclude our exe name argv[0]).
        */

        (void)fprintf(stream, "\n* Command Line Arguments...\n\n");

        for (nLoop = 1; nLoop < argc; nLoop++)
        {
            (void)fprintf(stream,"%d\t%s\n", nLoop, argv[nLoop]);

            // Append to args buffer.
            (void)strcat(&carArgs[0]    , argv[nLoop]);
            (void)strcat(&carArgs[0]    , " ");
        }

        /* ****************************
        ** Output environment variables.
        */

        (void)fprintf(stream, "\n* Environment Variables...\n\n");

        for (nLoop = 0; NULL != env[nLoop]; nLoop++)
        {
          (void)fprintf(stream, "%d\t%s\n", nLoop, env[nLoop]);
        }

        /* ***************************************************
        ** Output name and args of other application to start.
        */

        (void)fprintf(stream, "\n* 'Real' program and arguments...\n\n");
        (void)fprintf(stream, "\t%s\n", &carArgs[0]);

        (void)fprintf(stream, "\n********** Run End\n\n\n");

        // All done so tidy up.
        (void)fclose(stream);

        (void)WinExec(&carArgs[0], 1);
    }

    return 0;
}
```

And the (nearly) equivalent Visual Basic application in Listing 7-3:

```vb
Sub Main()
    If 0 <> Len(Command$) Then

        Dim sRealAppName As String

        sRealAppName = GetSetting(App.EXEName, "Startup", _
                                  "RealAppName", "")

        If 0 <> Len(sRealAppName) Then

            Call Shell(sRealAppName & " " & Command$, vbHide)

            Dim nFile As Integer

            nFile = FreeFile

            Open App.EXEName & ".out" For Append Access Write As nFile

            Print #nFile, "****** Run at " & _
                          Format$(Date, "Short date") & _
                          " " & Format$(Time, "Long Time")

            Print #nFile, sRealAppName & " " & Command$

            Close nFile

        End If

    End If

End Sub
```

LISTING 7-3   *The OUTARGS logger application in Visual Basic*

STUFF ABOUT OPTIMIZATION

This section deals with how to best optimize your applications. Notice that the word "code" didn't appear in the preceding sentence. To correctly optimize the way we work and the speed with which we can ship products and solutions, we need to look beyond the code itself. In the following pages, I'll describe what I think are the most effective ways to optimize applications.

Choosing the Right Programmers

In my opinion, there's a difference between coding and programming. Professional programming is all about attitude, skill, knowledge, experience, and last but most important, the application of the correct algorithm. Selecting the right people to write your code will *always* improve the quality, reuse, and of course execution time of your application. See Chapter 17 (on recruiting great developers) for more on this subject.

Using Mixed Language Programming

Correctly written Visual Basic code can easily outperform poorly written C code. This is especially true with Visual Basic 6. (Visual Basic 6 native code is faster than p-code.) Whatever language you use, apply the correct algorithm.

At times, of course, you might have to use other languages, say, to gain some required speed advantage. One of the truly great things about Windows (all versions) is that it specifies a linkage mechanism that is defined at the operating system level. In MS-DOS, all linkages were both early and defined by the language vendor. The result was that mixed-language programming was something that only the very brave (or the very foolish) would ever have attempted. It used to be impossible, for example, to get some company's FORTRAN compiler to produce object files that could be linked with other object files generated by another company's C compiler. Neither the linker supplied with the FORTRAN compiler nor the one that came with the C compiler liked the other's object file format. The result was that mixed-language programming was almost impossible to implement. This meant, of course, that tried-and-tested code often had to be ported to another language (so that the entire program was written in one language and therefore linked).

Trouble is that these days we've largely forgotten that mixed language programming is even possible. It is! Any language compiler that can produce DLLs can almost certainly be used to do mixed-language programming. For example, it's now easy to call Microsoft COBOL routines from Visual Basic. Similarly, any language that can be used to create ActiveX components can be used to create code that can be consumed by other, language-independent, processes.

At The Mandelbrot Set (International) Limited (TMS), when we really need speed—and after we've exhausted all the algorithmic alternatives—we turn to the C compiler. We use the existing Visual Basic code as a template for writing the equivalent C code. (We have an internal rule that says we must write everything in Visual Basic first—it's easier, after all.) We then compile and test (profile) this code to see whether the application is now fast enough. If it's not, we optimize the C code. Ultimately, if it's required, we get the C compiler to generate assembly code, complete with comments (/Fc and /FA CL.EXE switches are used to do this), and discard the C code completely. Finally, we hand-tune the assembly code and build it using Microsoft's Macro Assembler 6.11.

Controlling Your Code's Speed

Don't write unnecessarily fast code. What I mean here is that you shouldn't produce fast code when you don't need to—you'll probably be wasting time. Code to the requirement. If it must be fast, take that into account as you code—not after. If it's OK to be slow(er), then again, code to the requirement. For example, you might decide to use nothing but Variants if neither size nor execution speed is important. Such a decision would simplify the code somewhat, possibly improving your delivery schedule. Keep in mind that each project has different requirements: code to them!

Putting On Your Thinking Cap

The best optimizations usually happen when people really think about the problem.[1] I remember once at TMS we had to obtain the sine of some number of degrees many times in a loop. We used Visual Basic's *Sin* routine to provide this functionality and ultimately built the application and profiled the code. We found that about 90 percent all our recalculating execution time was spent inside the *Sin* routine. We decided therefore to replace the call to Visual Basic's routine with a call to a DLL function that wrapped the C library routine of the same name. We implemented the DLL, rebuilt, and retested. The results were almost identical. We still spent most of the time inside the *Sin* routine (although now we had another external dependency to worry about—the DLL!). Next we got out the C library source code for *Sin* and had a look at how we might optimize it. The routine, coded in an assembly language, required detailed study—this was going to take time! At this point, someone said, "Why don't we just look up the required value in a previously built table?" Brilliant? Yes! Obvious? Of course!

---

1. See the famous book *Programming Pearls* by Jon Bentley for more on this approach (Addison-Wesley, 1995, ISBN 0-201-10331-1).

Staying Focused

Don't take your eyes off the ball. In the preceding example, we lost our focus. We got stuck in tune mode. We generated the lookup table and built it into the application, and then we rebuilt and retested. The problem had vanished.

"Borrowing" Code

Steal code whenever possible. Why write the code yourself if you can source it from elsewhere? Have you checked out MSDN and all the sample code it provides for an answer? The samples in particular contain some great (and some not so great) pieces of code. Unfortunately, some programmers have never discovered the VisData sample that shipped with Visual Basic 5, let alone looked through the source code. If you have Visual Basic 5, let's see if I can tempt you to browse this valuable resource. VISDATA.BAS contains the following routines. Could they be useful?

ActionQueryType	AddBrackets	AddMRU
CheckTransPending	ClearDataFields	CloseAllRecordsets
CloseCurrentDB	CompactDB	CopyData
CopyStruct	DisplayCurrentRecord	DupeTableName
Export	GetFieldType	GetFieldWidth
GetINIString	GetODBCConnectParts	GetTableList
HideDBTools	Import	ListItemNames
LoadINISettings	NewLocalISAM	MakeTableName
MsgBar	OpenLocalDB	NewMDB
ObjectExists	RefreshErrors	OpenQuery
OpenTable	SetFldProperties	RefreshTables
SaveINISettings	ShowError	SetQDFParams
ShowDBTools	StripConnect	ShutDownVisData
StripBrackets	StripOwner	StripFileName
StripNonAscii	stTrueFalse	UnloadAllForms
vFieldVal		

There's more! The BAS files in the SETUP1 project contain these routines—anything useful in here?

AbortAction	AddActionNote	AddDirSep
AddHkeyToCache	AddPerAppPath	AddQuotesToFN
AddURLDirSep	CalcDiskSpace	CalcFinalSize
CenterForm	ChangeActionKey	CheckDiskSpace

CheckDrive	CheckOverwrite-PrivateFile	CommitAction
CopyFile	CopySection	CountGroups
CountIcons	CreateIcons	CreateOSLink
CreateProgManGroup	CreateProgManItem	CreateShellLink
DecideIncrement-RefCount	DetectFile	DirExists
DisableLogging	EnableLogging	EtchedLine
ExeSelfRegister	ExitSetup	Extension
fCheckFNLength	fCreateOS-ProgramGroup	fCreateShellGroup
FileExists	fIsDepFile	fValidFilename
FValidNT-GroupName	fWithinAction	GetAppRemo-valCmdLine
GetDefMsgBoxButton	GetDepFileVerStruct	GetDiskSpaceFree
GetDrivesAllocUnit	GetDriveType	GetFileName
GetFileSize	GetFileVersion	GetFileVerStruct
GetGroup	GetLicInfoFromVBL	GetPathName
GetRemoteSupport-FileVerStruct	GetTempFilename	GetUNCShareName
GetWindowsDir	GetWindowsSysDir	GetWinPlatform
IncrementRefCount	InitDiskInfo	intGetHKEYIndex
IntGetNextFldOffset	IsDisplayNameUnique	IsNewerVer
IsSeparator	IsUNCName	IsValidDestDir
IsWin32	IsWindows95	IsWindowsNT
IsWindowsNT4-WithoutSP2	KillTempFolder	LogError
LogNote	LogSilentMsg	LogSMSMsg
LogWarning	LongPath	MakeLongPath
MakePath MoveAppRemovalFiles	MakePathAux	
MsgError	MsgFunc	MsgWarning
NewAction	NTWithShell	PackVerInfo
ParseDateTime	PerformDDE	Process-CommandLine
PromptForNextDisk	ReadIniFile	ReadProtocols
ReadSetupFileLine	ReadSetupRemoteLine	RegCloseKey
RegCreateKey	RegDeleteKey	RegEdit
RegEnumKey	RegisterApp-RemovalEXE	RegisterDAO

>>

RegisterFiles	RegisterLicense	RegisterLicenses
RegisterVBLFile	RegOpenKey	RegPathWin-CurrentVersion
RegPathWinPrograms	RegQueryNumericValue	RegQueryRefCount
RegQueryStringValue	RegSetNumericValue	RegSetStringValue
RemoteRegister	RemoveShellLink	ReplaceDouble-Quotes
ResolveDestDir	ResolveDestDirs	ResolveDir
ResolveResString	RestoreProgMan	SeparatePath-AndFileName
SetFormFont	SetMousePtr	ShowLoggingError
ShowPathDialog	SrcFileMissing	StartProcess
StrExtractFile-nameArg	strExtractFilenameItem	strGetCommon-FilesPath
StrGetDAOPath	strGetDriveFromPath	strGetHKEYString
StrGetPredefined-HKEYString	strGetProgramsFilesPath	StringFromBuffer
StripTerminator	strQuoteString	strRootDrive
StrUnQuoteString	SyncShell	TreatAsWin95
UpdateStatus	WriteAccess	WriteMIF

Calling on All Your Problem-Solving Skills

Constantly examine your approach to solving problems, and always encourage input and criticism from all quarters on the same. Think problems through. And *always* profile your code!

A truly useful code profiler would include some way to time Visual Basic's routines. For example, how fast is *Val* when compared with its near functional equivalent *CInt*? You can do some of this profiling using the subclassing technique discussed in Chapter 1 (replacing some VBA routine with one of your own—see Tip 11), but here's a small example anyway:

Declarations section

```
Option Explicit

Declare Function WinQueryPerformanceCounter Lib "kernel32" _
Alias "QueryPerformanceCounter" (lpPerformanceCount As LARGE_INTEGER) _
As Long

Declare Function WinQueryPerformanceFrequency Lib "kernel32" _
Alias "QueryPerformanceFrequency" (lpFrequency As LARGE_INTEGER) _
As Long
```

```
Type LARGE_INTEGER
     LowPart    As Long
     HighPart   As Long
End Type
```

In a module

```
Function TimeGetTime() As Single

     Static Frequency    As Long
     Dim CurrentTime     As LARGE_INTEGER

     If 0 = Frequency Then

         Call WinQueryPerformanceFrequency(CurrentTime)

         Frequency = CurrentTime.LowPart / 1000

         TimeGetTime = 0

     Else

         Call WinQueryPerformanceCounter(CurrentTime)

         TimeGetTime = CurrentTime.LowPart / Frequency

     End If

End Function
```

Replacement for *Val*

```
Public Function Val(ByVal exp As Variant) As Long

     Dim l1 As Single, l2 As Single

     l1 = TimeGetTime()

     Val = VBA.Conversion.Val(exp)

     l2 = TimeGetTime()

     Debug.Print "Val - " & l2 - l1

End Function
```

The *TimeGetTime* routine uses the high-resolution timer in the operating system to determine how many ticks it (the operating system's precision timing mechanism) is capable of per second (*WinQueryPerformanceFrequency*). *TimeGetTime* then divides this figure by 1000 to determine the number of ticks per millisecond. It stores this value in a static variable so that the value is calculated only once.

On subsequent calls, the routine simply returns a number of milliseconds; that is, it queries the system time, converts that to milliseconds, and returns this value. For the calling program to determine a quantity of time passing, it must call the routine twice and compare the results of two calls. Subtract the result of the second call from the first, and you'll get the number of milliseconds that have elapsed between the calls. This process is shown in the "Replacement for *Val*" code.

With this example, one can imagine being able to profile the whole of VBA. Unfortunately, that isn't possible. If you attempt to replace certain routines, you'll find that you can't. For example, the *CInt* routine cannot be replaced using this technique. (Your replacement *CInt* is reported as being an illegal name.) According to Microsoft, for speed, some routines were not implemented externally in the VBA ActiveX server but were kept internal—*CInt* is one of those routines.

Using Smoke and Mirrors

The best optimization is the perceived one. If you make something look or feel fast, it will generally be perceived as being fast. Give your users good feedback. For example, use a progress bar. Your code will actually run slower (it's having to recalculate and redraw the progress bar), but the user's perception of its speed, compared to not having the progress bar, will almost always be in your favor.

One of the smartest moves you can ever make is to start fast. (Compiling to native code creates "faster to start" executables.) Go to great lengths to get that first window on the screen so that your users can start using the application. Leave the logging onto the database and other such tasks until after this first window is up. Look at the best applications around: they all start, or appear to start, very quickly. If you create your applications to work the same way, the user's perception will be "Wow! This thing is usable *and* quick!" Bear in mind that lots of disk activity before your first window appears means you're slow: lots after, however, means you're busy doing smart stuff!

Because you cannot easily build multithreaded Visual Basic applications (see Chapter 13 to see some light at the end of this particular tunnel), you might say that you'll have to block sometime; that is, you're going to have to log on some-time, and you know that takes time—and the user will effectively be blocked by the action. Consider putting the logging on in a separate application imple-mented as an out-of-process ActiveX server, perhaps writing this server to provide your application with a set of data services. Use an asynchronous callback object to signal to the user interface part of your application when the database is ready to be used. When you get the signal, enable those features that have now become usable. If you take this approach, you'll find, of course, that the data services ActiveX server is blocked—waiting for the connection—but your thread of execution, in the user interface part of the application, is unaf-fected, giving your user truly smooth multitasking. The total effort is minimal; in fact, you might even get some code reuse out of the ActiveX server. The effect on the user's perception, however, can be quite dramatic.

As I've said before, compiled code is faster than p-code, so of course, one "easy" optimization everyone will expect to make is to compile to native code. Surely this will create faster-executing applications when compared to a p-code clone?

Using the *TimeGetTime* routine (discussed fully on page 304), we do indeed see some impressive improvements when we compare one against the other. For example the following loop code, on my machine (300 MHz, Pentium Pro II, 128 MB RAM), takes 13.5 milliseconds to execute as compiled p-code and just 1.15 milliseconds as native code—almost 12 times faster (optimizing for fast code and the Pentium Pro). If this kind of improvement is typical, "real" compilation is, indeed, an easy optimization.

```
Dim n As Integer
Dim d As Double

For n = 1 To 32766
    ' Do enough to confuse the optimizer.
    d = (n * 1.1) - (n * 1#)
Next
```

STUFF ABOUT OBJECTS, TYPES, AND DATA STRUCTURES

Code reuse is mostly about object orientation—the effective packaging of components to suit some plan or design. This section examines the mechanisms that exist in Visual Basic to effectively bring about code reuse. In particular, we'll look at how we can extend the type system in Visual Basic.

Visual Basic as an Object-Oriented Language

People often say that Visual Basic is not properly object oriented. I would answer that if you were comparing it with C++, you're both right and wrong. Yes, it isn't C++; it's Visual Basic!

C++ is a generic, cross-platform programming language designed around a particular programming paradigm that is, subjectively, object oriented. It is based on and influenced by other programming languages such as Simula, C, and C with Objects.[2]

Visual Basic has evolved—and has been influenced, too—according to system considerations, not primarily to different languages. It was designed to be platform specific; there's not an implementation for the VAX computer, for example. Visual Basic's object orientation, then, is not primarily language based. Its object-oriented language constructs are not there to implement object orientation directly but rather to best utilize the object-oriented features of the operating system—in Windows, of course, this means ActiveX.

ActiveX itself, however, is not a language definition but a systems-level object technology built directly into a specific range of operating systems. It is not subject to committees either, although you might consider this to be a negative point. Additionally, I think I'd call ActiveX and Visual Basic "commercial," whereas I'd probably call C++ "academic." I have nothing against C++ or any other programming language. Indeed, I'm a proponent of mixed-language programming and use C++ almost daily. What I am against, however, is a comparison of Visual Basic with C++. These two languages are as different as COBOL and FORTRAN, and both were designed to solve different problems and to cater to different markets. This all said, I'm still keen to model the world realistically in terms of objects, and I also want to encourage both high cohesion and loose coupling between and within those objects. (Here's a quick tip for the latter: Use *ByVal*—it helps!) Whether or not I achieve this cohesion and coupling with Visual Basic and ActiveX is the real question.

Cohesion and coupling

Before going any further, let me take a moment to define the terms *cohesion* and *coupling*. A component is said to be cohesive if it exhibits a high degree of functional relatedness with other related components. These related components (routines typically) should form cohesive program units (modules and

---

2. See *History of Programming Languages* for more on the evolution of C++ (Addison-Wesley, 1996, ISBN 0-201-89502-1).

classes). Every routine in a module should, for example, be essential for that module to accomplish its purpose. Generally, there are seven recognized levels of cohesion (none of which I'll cover here). Coupling is an indication of the strength of the interconnections and interactions exhibited by different program components. If components are strongly coupled, they obviously have a significant dependency on each other—neither can typically work without the other, and if you break one of the components, you'll invariably break the others that are dependent upon it. In Visual Basic, tight coupling typically comes about through the overuse and sharing of public symbols (variables, constants, properties, and routines exported by other units).

What are your intentions?

Having an object implies intention; that is, you're about to do something with the object. This intention should, in turn, define the object's behavior and its interfaces. Indeed, a strong type system implies that you know what you'll do with an object when you acquire one. After all, you know what you can do with a hammer when you pick one up! A sense of encapsulation, identity, and meaning is an obvious requirement. To add both external and procedural meaning to an object, you need to be able to add desirable qualities such as methods and properties. What does all this boil down to in Visual Basic? The class, the interface, and the object variable.

Classes are essentially Visual Basic's way of wrapping both method, which is ideally the interface, and state—that is, providing real type extensions (or as good as it gets currently). A real type is more than a description of mere data (state); it also describes the set of operations that can be applied to that state (method). Unfortunately, methods are currently nonsymbolic. One feature that C++ has that I'd love to have in Visual Basic is the ability to define symbolic methods that relate directly to a set of operators. With this ability, I could, for example, define what it means to literally add a deposit to an account using the addition operator (+). After all, the plus sign is already overloaded (defined for) in Visual Basic. For example the String type supports addition. Also, a solution will have nothing to do with ActiveX; the ability to define symbolic methods is a mere language feature.

Visual Basic "inheritance"

Visual Basic lacks an inheritance mechanism (definitely more of an ActiveX constraint) that is comparable with that of C++. To reuse another object's properties in Visual Basic, you must use something else—either composition or association (composition meaning aggregation—like in a UDT; association meaning, in Visual Basic-speak, an object reference). Historically, association is "late" composition—as a result it also invalidates strong typing. A Visual Basic object cannot, in the C++ sense, be a superclass of another type. In other words, you cannot describe a PC, say, as being either a specialization of or composed of a CPU.

NOTE

By the way, C++ type inheritance is often used badly; that is, an object that inherits from other objects exports their public interfaces. The result is that top-level objects are often bloated because they are the sum of all the public interfaces of the objects they are derived from—a sort of overprivileged and overfed upper class!

Components that are highly cohesive, yet loosely coupled, are more easily shared—if code reuse is an issue, consider rigorously promoting both of these simple philosophies.

Object polymorphism

Polymorphism is a characteristic by which an object is able to respond to stimuli in accordance with its underlying object type rather than in accordance with the type of reference used to apply the stimulus. The *Implements* statement, discussed in the next section, is Visual Basic's way of extending polymorphic types beyond that allowed by the *Object* type. Polymorphic types might be assigned (or "set") to point to and use one another, and they're useful when you know that one type has the same interface as another type (one you'd like to treat it as). The really important thing is that with polymorphism, an object responds according to its type rather than the type of reference you have to it.

Let me give you an example using two constructs that are probably familiar to you, the *Object* type and a window handle.

What is the result of this code?

```
Dim o As Object

Set o = frmMainForm

MsgBox o.Caption
```

You can see here that the *Caption* property evaluation is applied to what the pointer/object reference *o* points to rather than according to what *Object.Caption* means. That is, that object to which we bind the *Caption* access to is decided in the context of what *o* is set to when *o.Caption* is executed. (We call this behavior *late binding*, by the way.) Notice that the code doesn't error with a message that says, "The Object class doesn't support this property or method." Polymorphism says that an object responds as the type of object it is rather than according to the type of the reference we have to it. Again, notice that I didn't have to cast the reference, (using a fabricated cast operator that you might take at first glance to be an array index), like this one, for instance:

```
CForm(o).Caption
```

The object *o* knows what it is (currently) and responds accordingly. Obviously, we can alter what *o* points to:

```
Dim o As Object
If blnUseForm = True Then
    Set o = frmMainForm
Else
    Set o = cmdMainButton
End If
MsgBox o.Caption
```

Again, *o.Caption* works in either case because of polymorphism.

The second example is a window handle. This window handle is something like the object reference we used above, meaning it's basically a pointer that's bound to an object at run time. The object, of course, is a Windows' window— a data structure maintained by the operating system, an abstract type. You can treat an *hWnd* in a more consistent fashion than you can something declared *As Object*, however. Basically you can apply any method call to *hWnd* and it'll be safe. You're right in thinking that windows are sent messages, but the message value denotes some action in the underlying *hWnd*. Therefore, we can think of a call to *SendMessage* not as sending a window a message but rather as invoking some method, meaning that we can treat *SendMessage(Me.hWnd, WM_NULL, 0, 0)* as something like *hWnd.WM_NULL 0, 0*. The *WM_NULL* (a message you're not meant to respond to) is the method name, and the *0, 0* are the method's parameters. All totally polymorphic—an *hWnd* value is a particular window and it will respond accordingly.

Another similarity between the window handle and the *Object* type is that a window is truly an abstract type (meaning that you cannot create one without being specific), and so is the *Object* type. You can declare something *As Object*—though now it seems what I've just said is not true—but what you've done, in fact, is not create an *Object* instance but an instance of a pointer to any specific object (an uninitialized object reference). It's like defining a void pointer in C. The pointer has potential to point somewhere but has no implementation and therefore no sense in itself. It's only meaningful when it's actually pointing to something!

I hope you can see that polymorphism is great for extending the type system and for being able to treat objects generically while having them respond according to what they actually are. Treating objects as generically as possible is good; specialize only when you really need to.

OK, so what's the catch? Well, the problem with As-Object polymorphism is that it isn't typesafe. What would happen in my earlier example if, once I'd set *o* to point to the *cmdMainButton* command button, I tried to access the *WindowState* property instead of the *Caption* property? We'd get an error, obviously, and that's bad news all around. What we really need is a more typesafe version of *Object*, with which we can be more certain about what we might find at the other end of an object reference (but at the same time keeping the polymorphic behavior that we all want). Enter *Implements*.

Using *Implements*

The *Implements* statement provides a form of interface inheritance. A class that uses the *Implements* statement inherits the interface that follows the *Implements* keyword but not, by some magic, an implementation of that interface. A class is free to define code for the inherited interface methods, or the class can choose to leave the interface methods as blank stubs. On the other side of the *Implements* equation, we can define an interface that other classes can inherit but have nothing to do with a particular implementation.

When you inherit an interface by using the *Implements* statement, you're providing methods and properties with certain names on an object. Now, when your containing class is initialized, it should create a suitable implementation of these promised methods and properties. This can happen in one of two ways:

1. Pass method and property invocations on to the underlying implementation (by creating and maintaining a local copy of an object that actually implements the methods and properties). This mechanism is often called *forwarding*.

2. Handle the invocation entirely by itself.

How does this differ from As-Object polymorphism? Basically, when you set a typed object reference to point to an object, the object instance to which you set it must implement the interfaces specified by the type of the object reference you use in the declaration. This adds an element of type safety to the dynamic typecast, which is what you're implicitly doing, of course.

When you choose not to implement an interface other than by forwarding requests to the underlying base type (the thing you've said you implement) you can get these problems:

1. The derived class now acts like a base class—you've just provided a pass-through mechanism.

2. The base object reference is made public in the derived class (by accident), and because you cannot declare *Const* references, the reference to your implementation might be reassigned. (Actually, it's just as easy to do this via composition in Visual Basic.)

A consequence of the second problem is that you can accidentally "negate" the reference to the base object. Say, for argument's sake, that you set it to point to a Form; clearly the derived class no longer implements a base but a Form. Better hope your method names are different in a base and a Form or you're in for a surprise!

It's important to realize that *Implements* can be used with forwarding or via composition. The only difference in Visual Basic is the keyword *New*—in fact, it's even grayer than that. In class Derived, does the following code mean we're using forwarding or composition?

```
Implements Base
```

```
Private o As New Base
```

Do we contain a *Base* object or do we simply have a variable reference to a *Base* instance? Yes, it's the latter. In Visual Basic you cannot compose an object from others because you cannot really define an object—only an object reference.

Let me summarize this statement and the meaning of *Implements*. When you're given an object reference you have to consider two types: the type of the reference and the type of the object referenced (the "reference" and the "referent"). *Implements* ensures that the type of the referent must be "at least as derived as" the type of the reference. In other words, if a *Set* works, you have at least a reference type referent object attached to the reference. This leads us to the following guarantee: If the class of the reference has the indicated method or property (*Reference_Type.Reference_Method*), then the object reference—the referent—will have it, too.

Delegating objects

Delegating objects consists of two parts. Part one deals with who responds—through my interface I might get an actual implementor of the interface (the object type I have said that I implement) to respond (possibly before I respond), or I might elect to generate the whole response entirely by myself. Part two deals with who is responsible for an object; this is used in conjunction with association. Two containers might deal with a single provider object at various times. This use of association raises the question of object ownership (which container should clean up the object, reinitialize and repair it, and so forth).

Object orientation *is* modeling the requirements. Defining the requirements therefore dictates the object model and implementation method you'll employ. You can build effective sets of objects in Visual Basic, but you cannot do today all of what is possible in C++. As I said earlier, Visual Basic and C++ are two different languages, and you should learn to adapt to and utilize the strengths of each as appropriate.

Using Collections to Extend the Type System

You can also extend the type system ("type" meaning mere data at this point). At TMS, we often use a *Collection* object to represent objects that are entirely entities of state; that is, they have no methods. (You cannot append a method to a collection.) See Chapter 1 for more on building type-safe versions of Visual Basic's intrinsic types (called Smarties).

```
Dim KindaForm As New Collection

Const pHeight As String = "1"
Const pWidth  As String = "2"
Const pName   As String = "3"
' ...

With KindaForm
    .Add Key:=pHeight, Item:=Me.Height
    .Add Key:=pWidth, Item:=Me.Width
    .Add Key:=pName, Item:=Me.Name
End With

' ...

With KindaForm
    Print .Item(pHeight)
    Print .Item(pWidth)
    Print .Item(pName)
End With
```

Here we have an object named *KindaForm* that has the "properties" *pHeight*, *pWidth*, and *pName*. In other words, an existing Visual Basic type (with both properties and method) is being used to create a generic state-only object. If you're using classes to do this, you might want to consider using *Collection* objects as shown here instead.

You can add functional members to a *Collection* object with just one level of indirection by adding an object variable to the collection that is set to point to an object that has the necessary functionality defined in it. Such methods can act on the state in the other members of the collection.

So what's the difference between using a collection and creating a user-defined type (UDT)? Well, a collection is more flexible (not always an advantage) and has support for constructs such as *For Each*:

```
For Each v In KindaForm
    Print v
Next
```

The advantage of UDTs is that they have a known mapping. For example, they can be used as parameters to APIs, sent around a network and passed between mainframe and PC systems—they are just byte arrays. (See Chapter 4 for more on UDTs—they're one of Jon Burns's favorite things!) Obviously, a state-only *Collection* object doesn't mean much to a mainframe system, and passing *KindaForm* as "the thing" itself will result in your only passing an object pointer to a system that cannot interpret it. (Even if it could, the object would not be available because it's not transmitted with its address.)

Adding to *VarType*

Another "byte array" way to extend the type system is to add in new Variant types. In Visual Basic 5, the following subtypes were available via the Variant:

Visual Basic Name	VarType	Description
vbEmpty	0	Uninitialized (default)
vbNull	1	Contains no valid data
vbInteger	2	Integer
vbLong	3	Long integer
vbSingle	4	Single-precision floating-point number
vbDouble	5	Double-precision floating-point number
vbCurrency	6	Currency

Visual Basic Name	VarType	Description
vbDate	7	Date
vbString	8	String
vbObject	9	Automation object
vbError	10	Error
vbBoolean	11	Boolean
vbVariant	12	Variant (used only for arrays of Variants)
vbDataObject	13	Data access object
vbDecimal	14	Decimal
vbByte	17	Byte
vbArray	8192	Array

In Visual Basic 6, we have a new addition (and a great deal of scope for adding more—a lot of gaps!):

vbUserDefinedType	36	User-defined type

With some limitations, we can add to this list. For example, we could, with only a small amount of effort, add a new Variant subtype of 42 to represent some new entity by compiling this C code to a DLL named NEWTYPE.DLL:

```
#include "windows.h"
#include "ole2.h"
#include "oleauto.h"

#include <time.h>

typedef VARIANT * PVARIANT;

VARIANT __stdcall CVNewType(PVARIANT v)
{
    // If the passed Variant is not set yet...
    if (0 == v->vt)
    {
        // Create new type.
        v->vt = 42;

        // Set other Variant members to be meaningful
        // for this new type...

        // You do this here!
    }
```

```
    // Return the Variant, initialized/used Variants
    // unaffected by this routine.
    return *v;
}


int __stdcall EX_CInt(PVARIANT v)
{
    // Sanity check - convert only new Variant types!
    if (42 != v->vt)
    {
        return 0;
    }
    else
    {
        // Integer conversion - get our data and convert it as
        // necessary.
        // Return just a random value in this example.
        srand((unsigned)time(NULL));

        return rand();
    }
}
```

This code provides us with two routines: *CVNewType* creates, given an already created but empty Variant (it was easier), a Variant of subtype 42; *EX_CInt* converts a Variant of subtype 42 into an integer value (but doesn't convert the Variant to a new Variant type). "Converts" here means "evaluates" or "yields." Obviously, the implementation above is minimal. We're not putting any real value into this new Variant type, and when we convert one all we're doing is returning a random integer. Nevertheless, it is possible! Here's some code to test the theory:

```
Dim v As Variant

v = CVNewType(v)

Me.Print VarType(v)
Me.Print EX_CInt(v)
```

This code will output 42 and then some random number when executed against the DLL. The necessary DLL declarations are as follows:

```
Private Declare Function CVNewType Lib "NEWTYPE.DLL" _
    (ByRef v As Variant) As Variant
Private Declare Function EX_CInt   Lib "NEWTYPE.DLL" _
    (ByRef v As Variant) As Integer
```

Again, we cannot override Visual Basic's *CInt* (see page 304), and so I've had to call my routine something other than what I wanted to in this case, *EX_CInt* for "external" *CInt*. I could, of course, have overloaded *Val*:

```
Public Function Val(ByRef exp As Variant) As Variant

    Select Case VarType(exp)

        Case 42:   Val = EX_CInt(exp)
        Case Else: Val = VBA.Conversion.Val(exp)

    End Select

End Function
```

Here, if the passed Variant is of subtype 42, I know that the "real" *Val* won't be able to convert it—it doesn't know what it holds after all—so I convert it myself using *EX_CInt*. If, however, it contains an old Variant subtype, I simply pass it on to VBA to convert using the real *Val* routine.

Visual Basic has also been built, starting with version 4, to expect the sudden arrival of Variant subtypes about which nothing is known. This assertion must be true because Visual Basic 4 can be used to build ActiveX servers that have methods. In turn, these can be passed Variants as parameters. A Visual Basic 5 client (or server) can be utilized by a Visual Basic 6 client! In other words, because a Visual Basic 6 executable can pass in a Variant of subtype 14, Visual Basic must be built to expect unknown Variant types, given that the number of Variant subtypes is likely to grow at every release. You might want to consider testing for this in your Visual Basic 4 code.

Having said all this and having explained how it could work, I'm not sure of the real value currently of creating a new Variant subtype. This is especially true when, through what we must call a feature of Visual Basic, not all the conversion routines are available for subclassing. Why not use a UDT, or better still, a class to hold your new type instead of extending the Variant system?

Another limitation to creating a new Variant subtype is because of the way we cannot override operators or define them for our new types. We have to be careful that, unlike an old Variant, our new Variant is not used in certain expressions. For example, consider what might happen if we executed *Me.Print 10 + v*. Because *v* is a Variant, it needs to be converted to a numeric type to be added to the integer constant 10. When this happens, Visual Basic must logically apply *VarType* to *v* to see what internal routine it should call to convert it to a numeric value. Obviously, it's not going to like our new Variant subtype! To write expressions such as this, we'd need to do something like *Me.Print 10 + Val(v)*. This is also the reason why, in the *Val* substitute earlier, I had to pass *exp* by reference. I couldn't let Visual Basic evaluate it, even though it's received as a Variant.

Variants also *might* need destructing correctly. When they go out of scope and are destroyed, you might have to tidy up any memory they might have previously allocated. If what they represent is, say, a more complex type, we might have to allocate memory to hold the representation.

Microsoft does not encourage extending the Variant type scheme. For example, 42 might be free today, but who knows what it might represent in Visual Basic 7. We would need to bear this in mind whenever we created new Variant subtypes and make sure that we could change their *VarType* values almost arbitrarily—added complexity that is, again, less than optimal!

All in all, creating new Variant subtypes is not really a solution at the moment. If we get operator overloading and proper access to VBA's conversion routines, however, all of this is a little more attractive.

NOTE

The code to create Variant subtypes needs to be written in a language such as C. The main reason is that Visual Basic is too type safe and simply won't allow us to treat a Variant like we're doing in the DLL. In other words, accessing a Variant in Visual Basic accesses the subtype's value and storage transparently through the VARIANT structure. To access its internals, it's necessary to change the meaning of Variant access from one of value to one of representation.

Pointers

A common criticism of Visual Basic is that it doesn't have a pointer type. It cannot therefore be used for modeling elaborate data types such as linked lists. Well, of course, Visual Basic has pointers—an object variable can be treated as a pointer. Just as you can have linked lists in C, so you can have them in Visual Basic.

Creating a linked list

Let's look at an example of a circular doubly linked list where each node has a pointer to the previous and next elements in the list, as shown in Figure 7-2. Notice in the code that we have a "notional" starting point, *pHead*, which initially points to the head of the list.

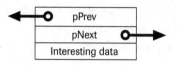

FIGURE 7-2   *A node in the list*

The Node class

```
Option Explicit

' "Pointers" to previous and next nodes
Public pNext As Node
Public pPrev As Node

' Something interesting in each node -
' the creation number (of the node)!
Public nAttribute As Integer


Private Sub Class_Initialize()

    Set pNext = Nothing
    Set pPrev = Nothing

End Sub


Private Sub Class_Terminate()

    ' When an object terminates, it will already have
    ' had to set these two members to Nothing:
    ' this code, then, is slightly redundant.
    Set pNext = Nothing
    Set pPrev = Nothing

End Sub
```

The Test form

```
Option Explicit

Private pHead    As New Node
Private pV       As Node


Public Sub CreateCircularLinkedList()
```

```
Dim p          As Node
Dim nLoop      As Integer
Static pLast   As Node      ' Points to last node created
                            ' pHead if first node.

pHead.nAttribute = 0

Set pLast = pHead

' 501 objects in list - the pHead object exists
' until killed in DeleteList.

For nLoop = 1 To 501

    Set p = New Node

    p.nAttribute = nLoop

    Set pLast.pNext = p
    Set p.pPrev = pLast

    Set pLast = p

Next

' Decrement reference count on object.
Set pLast = Nothing

' Join the two ends of the list, making a circle.
Set p.pNext = pHead
Set pHead.pPrev = p

Exit Sub

End Sub


Public Sub PrintList()

    Debug.Print "Forwards"

    Set pV = pHead

    Do
        Debug.Print pV.nAttribute

        Set pV = pV.pNext
```

>>

```
        Loop While Not pV Is pHead


        Debug.Print "Backwards"

        Set pV = pHead.pPrev

        Do
            Debug.Print pV.nAttribute

            Set pV = pV.pPrev

        Loop While Not pV Is pHead.pPrev

End Sub


Public Sub DeleteList()

    Dim p As Node

    Set pV = pHead

    Do
        Set pV = pV.pNext
        Set p = pV.pPrev

        If Not p Is Nothing Then
            Set p.pNext = Nothing
            Set p.pPrev = Nothing
        End If

        Set p = Nothing

    Loop While Not pV.pNext Is Nothing

    ' Both of these point to pHead at the end.
    Set pV = Nothing
    Set pHead = Nothing

End Sub
```

The routines *CreateCircularLinkedList*, *PrintList*, and *DeleteList* should be called in that order. I have omitted building in any protection against deleting an empty list. To keep the example as short as possible, I've also excluded some other obvious routines, such as -*InsertIntoList*.

In Visual Basic, a node will continue to exist as long as an object variable is pointing to it (because a set object variable becomes the thing that the node is set to). For example, if two object variables point to the same thing, an equality check of one against the other (using *Is*) will evaluate to True (an equivalence operator). It follows, then, that for a given object all object variables that are set to point to it have to be set to *Nothing* for it to be destroyed. Also, even though a node is deleted, if the deleted node had valid pointers to other nodes, it might continue to allow other nodes to exist. In other words, setting a node pointer, *p*, to *Nothing* has no effect on the thing pointed to by *p* if another object variable, say, *p1*, is also pointing to the thing that *p* is pointing to. This means that to delete a node we have to set the following to *Nothing*: its *pPrev* object's *pNext* pointer, its *pNext* object's *pPrev* pointer, and its own *pNext* and *pPrev* pointers (to allow other nodes to be deleted later). And don't forget the object variable we have pointing to *p* to access all the other pointers and objects. Not what you might expect!

It's obvious that an object variable can be thought of as a pointer to something and also as the thing to which it points. Remember that *Is* should be used to compare references, not =. This is why we need *Set* to have the variable point to something else; that is, trying to change the object variable using assignment semantically means changing the value of the thing to which it points, whereas *Set* means changing the object variable to point elsewhere. In fact nearly any evaluation of an object variable yields the thing to which the object variable is pointing to. An exception is when an object variable is passed to a routine as a parameter, in which case the pointer is passed, not the value (the object) that it's pointing to. (The object also has an *AddRef* applied to it.)

Linked lists that are created using objects appear to be very efficient. They are fast to create and manipulate and are as flexible as anything that can be created in C.

Visual Basic 6 (VBA) is also able to yield real pointers, or addresses. Three undocumented VBA methods—*VarPtr*, *ObjPtr*, and *StrPtr* (which are just three different VBA type library aliases pointing to the same entry point in the run-time DLL)—are used to create these pointers. You can turn an object into a pointer value using *l = ObjPtr(o)*, where *o* is the object whose address you want and *l* is a long integer in which the address of the object is put. Just resolving an object's address doesn't *AddRef* the object, however. You can pass this value around and get back to the object by memory copying *l* into a dummy object variable and then setting another object variable to this dummy (thus adding a reference to the underlying object).

```
Call CopyMemory(oDummy, 1, 4)
Set oThing = oDummy
```

CopyMemory should be defined like this:

```
Private Declare Sub CopyMemory Lib "kernel32" _
    Alias "RtlMoveMemory" (pDest As Any, pSource As Any, _
    ByVal ByteLen As Long)
```

The really neat thing here is that setting *I* doesn't add a reference to the object referenced by the argument of *ObjPtr*. Normally, when you set an object variable to point to an object, the object to which you point it (attach it, really) has its reference count incremented, meaning that the object can't be destroyed, because there are now two references to it. (This incrementing also happens if you pass the object as a parameter to a routine.) For an example of how this can hinder your cleanup of objects, see the discussion of the linked list example on page 317.

By using *VarPtr* (which yields the address of variables and UDTs), *StrPtr* (which yields the address of strings), and *ObjPtr*, you can create very real and very powerful and complex data structures.

Here's the short piece of code I used to discover that *VarPtr, ObjPtr,* and *StrPtr* are all pretty much the same thing (that is, the same function in a DLL):

```
Private Sub Form_Load()

    ' VB code to dump or match an external
    ' server method with a DLL entry point. Here it's
    ' used to dump the methods of the "_HiddenModule".

    ' Add a reference to 'TypeLib Information' (TLBINF32.DLL),
    ' which gives you TLI before running this code.

    Dim tTLInfo  As TypeLibInfo
    Dim tMemInfo As MemberInfo
    Dim sDLL     As String
    Dim sOrdinal As Integer

    Set tTLInfo = _
        TLI.TLIApplication.TypeLibInfoFromFile("MSVBVM50.DLL")

    For Each tMemInfo In _
        tTLInfo.TypeInfos.NamedItem("_HiddenModule").Members

        With tMemInfo
            tMemInfo.GetDllEntry sDLL, "", sOrdinal

            ' labDump is the label on the form where the
            ' output will be printed.
```

```
                    labDump.Caption = labDump.Caption & _
                            .Name & _
                            " is in " & _
                            sDLL & _
                            " at ordinal reference " & sOrdinal & _
                            vbCrLf
            End With

        Next

End Sub
```

The code uses TLBINF32.DLL, which can interrogate type libraries (very handy). Here I'm dumping some information on all the methods of a module (in type library parlance) named _HiddenModule. You'll see that this is the module that contains *VarPtr, ObjPtr,* and *StrPtr*, which you can discover using OLEVIEW.EXE to view MSVBVM60.DLL:

```
module _HiddenModule {
        [entry(0x60000000), vararg, helpcontext(0x000f6c9d)]
        VARIANT _stdcall Array([in] SAFEARRAY(VARIANT)* ArgList);
        [entry(0x60000001), helpcontext(0x000f735f)]
        BSTR _stdcall _B_str_InputB(
                        [in] long Number,
                        [in] short FileNumber);
        [entry(0x60000002), helpcontext(0x000f735f)]
        VARIANT _stdcall _B_var_InputB(
                        [in] long Number,
                        [in] short FileNumber);
        [entry(0x60000003), helpcontext(0x000f735f)]
        BSTR _stdcall _B_str_Input(
                        [in] long Number,
                        [in] short FileNumber);
        [entry(0x60000004), helpcontext(0x000f735f)]
        VARIANT _stdcall _B_var_Input(
                        [in] long Number,
                        [in] short FileNumber);
        [entry(0x60000005), helpcontext(0x000f65a4)]
        void _stdcall Width(
                        [in] short FileNumber,
                        [in] short Width);
        [entry(0x60000006), hidden]
        long _stdcall VarPtr([in] void* Ptr);
        [entry(0x60000007), hidden]
        long _stdcall StrPtr([in] BSTR Ptr);
        [entry(0x60000008), hidden]
        long _stdcall ObjPtr([in] IUnknown* Ptr);
    };
```

When you run the Visual Basic code beginning on page 322, you'll see this output:

```
LabelArray     is in VBA5.DLL at ordinal reference 601
_B_str_InputB is in VBA5.DLL at ordinal reference 566
_B_var_InputB is in VBA5.DLL at ordinal reference 567
_B_str_Input  is in VBA5.DLL at ordinal reference 620
_B_var_Input  is in VBA5.DLL at ordinal reference 621
Width          is in VBA5.DLL at ordinal reference 565
VarPtr         is in VBA5.DLL at ordinal reference 644
StrPtr         is in VBA5.DLL at ordinal reference 644
ObjPtr         is in VBA5.DLL at ordinal reference 644
```

This output shows the method name together with the DLL and ordinal reference (into the DLL) that implements its functionality. If you use *DUMPBIN / EXPORTS* on MSVBVM60.DLL like this:

```
dumpbin /exports msvbvm60.dll > dump
```

and then examine the dump file, you'll see that the routine at ordinal 644 is in fact *VarPtr*. In other words, *VarPtr, ObjPtr,* and *StrPtr* all do their stuff in the MSVBVM60.DLL routine *VarPtr*!

Matching the code output to the dump, we see this:

```
Method Name       DLL Routine Name
LabelArray        rtcArray
_B_str_InputB     rtcInputCount
_B_var_InputB     rtcInputCountVar
_B_str_Input      rtcInputCharCount
_B_var_Input      rtcInputCharCountVar
Width             rtcFileWidth
VarPtr            VarPtr
StrPtr            VarPtr
ObjPtr            VarPtr
```

I haven't explained what the other routines do—you can discover that for yourself.

Stuff About Type Libraries

In this section, we'll take a quick look at type libraries—not those created by Visual Basic (because they're free) but those created by hand. You'll see how to use these handmade type libraries as development tools that will help you ensure that your coding standards are correctly applied.

A type library is where Visual Basic records the description of your ActiveX server's interfaces. Put another way, a type library is a file, or perhaps part of a file, that describes the type of one or more objects. (These objects don't have to be ActiveX servers.) Type libraries do not, however, store the actual objects described—they store only information about objects. (They might also contain immediate data such as constant values.) By accessing the type library, applications can check the characteristics of an object—that is, the object's exported and named interfaces.

When ActiveX objects are exported and made public in your applications, Visual Basic creates a type library for you to describe the object's interfaces. You can also create type libraries separately using the tools found on the Visual Basic 6 CD in \TOOLS\VB\UNSUPPRT\TYPLIB.

Type libraries are usually written using a language called Object Description Language (ODL) and are compiled using MKTYPLIB.EXE. A good way to learn a little more about ODL is to study existing type libraries. You can use the OLEVIEW.EXE tool mentioned earlier to disassemble type libraries from existing DLLs, ActiveX servers, and ActiveX controls for further study.

As I just said, the information described by a type library doesn't necessarily have anything to do with ActiveX. Here are a couple of handy examples to show how you might use type libraries.

Removing *Declare* Statements

You might have noticed that throughout this book we generally prefix Windows API calls with *Win* to show that the routine being called is in Windows, that it's an API call. You've also seen how to make these calls using *Alias* within the declaration of the routine. (*Alias* allows you to rename routines.) Here *BringWindowToTop* is being renamed *WinBringWindowToTop*:

```
Declare Function WinBringWindowToTop Lib "user32" _
    Alias "BringWindowToTop" (ByVal hwnd As Long) As Long
```

However, we could use a type library to do the same thing. Here's an entire type library used to do just that:

APILIB.ODL

```
' The machine name for a type library is a GUID.
[uuid(9ca45f20-6710-11d0-9d65-00a024154cf1)]

library APILibrary
```

>>

```
{
    [dllname("user32.dll")]

    module APILibrary
    {
        [entry("BringWindowToTop")] long stdcall
            WinBringWindowToTop([in] long hWnd);
    };
};
```

MAKEFILE

```
apilib.tlb : apilib.odl makefile
    mktyplib /win32 apilib.odl
```

The MAKEFILE is used to create the TLB file given the ODL file source code. To run MAKEFILE, invoke NMAKE.EXE. If you don't have NMAKE.EXE, simply run MKTYPLIB.EXE from a command prompt like this:

```
mktyplib /win32 apilib.odl
```

The type library contains a description of an interface in APILibrary named *WinBringWindowToTop*. Once you have compiled the library, run Visual Basic and select References from the Project menu. Click the Browse button in the References dialog box to find the APILIB.TLB file, and then select it, as shown in Figure 7-3.

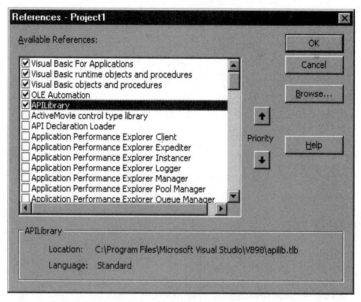

FIGURE 7-3   *Selecting APILibrary (APILIB.TLB) in the References dialog box*

Click OK and press F2 to bring up Visual Basic's Object Browser, which is shown in Figure 7-4:

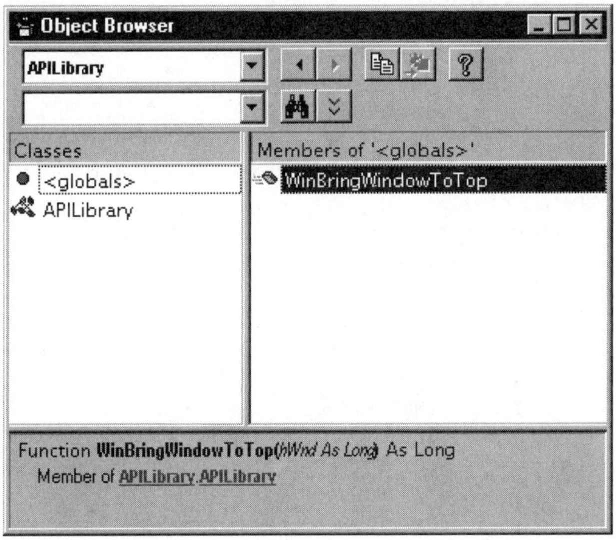

FIGURE 7-4   *APILibrary displayed in the Object Browser*

In Figure 7-4, notice that the method *WinBringWindowToTop* seems to be defined in a module and a server, both named APILibrary. Notice also that we have access to the syntax of the method. (The Quick Info help in Visual Basic will also display correctly for this method.) To use the method (which is really a function in USER32.DLL), all we have to do is enter code. No DLL declaration is now required (and so none can be entered incorrectly).

```
Call WinBringWindowToTop(frmMainForm.hWnd)
```

Another useful addition to a type library is named constants. Here's a modified APILIB.ODL:

```
[uuid(9ca45f20-6710-11d0-9d65-00a024154cf1)]

library APILibrary
{

    [dllname("user32.dll")]

    module WindowsFunctions
```

```
    {
        [entry("BringWindowToTop")] long stdcall
            WinBringWindowToTop([in] long hWnd);
        [entry("ShowWindow")] long stdcall
            WinShowWindow([in] long hwnd, [in] long nCmdShow);
    };

    typedef
    [
        uuid(010cbe00-6719-11d0-9d65-00a024154cf1),
        helpstring
        ("WinShowWindow Constants - See SDK ShowWindow for more.")
    ]
    enum
    {
        [helpstring("Hides the window, activates another")]
            SW_HIDE = 0,
        [helpstring("Maximizes the window")]
            SW_MAXIMIZE = 3,
        [helpstring("Minimizes the window activates next window")]
            SW_MINIMIZE = 6,
        [helpstring("Activates the window")]
            SW_RESTORE = 9,
        [helpstring("Activates/displays (current size and pos)" )]
            SW_SHOW = 5,
        [helpstring("Sets window state based on the SW_ flag")]
            SW_SHOWDEFAULT = 10,
        [helpstring("Activates window - displays maximized")]
            SW_SHOWMAXIMIZED = 3,
        [helpstring("Activates window - displays minimized")]
            SW_SHOWMINIMIZED = 2,
        [helpstring("Displays  window minimized")]
            SW_SHOWMINNOACTIVE = 7,
        [helpstring("Displays  window to current state.")]
            SW_SHOWNA = 8,
        [helpstring("Displays  window (current size and pos)")]
            SW_SHOWNOACTIVATE = 4,
        [helpstring("Activates and displays window")]
            SW_SHOWNORMAL = 1,
    } WinShowWindowConstants;

};
```

The library (APILibrary) now contains two sections, WindowsFunctions and WinShowWindowConstants, as shown in Figure 7-5.

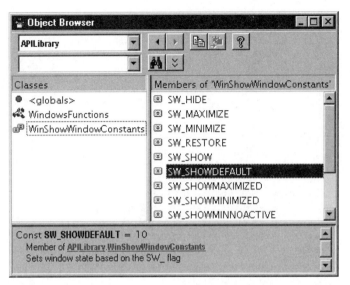

FIGURE 7-5   *APILibrary with named constants displayed in the Object Browser*

The long numbers [uuid(9ca45f20-6710-11d0-9d65-00a024154cf1)] used in the ODL file are Globally Unique IDs (GUIDs). (See Chapter 1 for more detailed information on GUIDs.) Just for your interest, here's a small Visual Basic program that'll generate GUIDs for you. No matter how many times you run this program (which outputs a GUID for each button click), it will *never* produce the same GUID twice!

Declaration section

```
Option Explicit

Private Type GUID
    D1       As Long
    D2       As Integer
    D3       As Integer
    D4(8)    As Byte
End Type

Private Declare Function WinCoCreateGuid Lib "OLE32.DLL" _
    Alias "CoCreateGuid" (g As GUID) As Long
```

CreateGUID

```
Public Function CreateGUID() As String

    Dim g          As GUID
    Dim sBuffer    As String

    Dim nLoop As Integer

    Call WinCoCreateGuid(g)

    sBuffer = PadRight0(sBuffer, Hex$(g.D1), 8, True)
    sBuffer = PadRight0(sBuffer, Hex$(g.D2), 4, True)
    sBuffer = PadRight0(sBuffer, Hex$(g.D3), 4, True)
    sBuffer = PadRight0(sBuffer, Hex$(g.D4(0)), 2)
    sBuffer = PadRight0(sBuffer, Hex$(g.D4(1)), 2, True)
    sBuffer = PadRight0(sBuffer, Hex$(g.D4(2)), 2)
    sBuffer = PadRight0(sBuffer, Hex$(g.D4(3)), 2)
    sBuffer = PadRight0(sBuffer, Hex$(g.D4(4)), 2)
    sBuffer = PadRight0(sBuffer, Hex$(g.D4(5)), 2)
    sBuffer = PadRight0(sBuffer, Hex$(g.D4(6)), 2)
    sBuffer = PadRight0(sBuffer, Hex$(g.D4(7)), 2)

    CreateGUID = sBuffer

End Function
```

PadRight0

```
Public Function PadRight0( _
                    ByVal sBuffer As String _
                    ,ByVal sBit As String _
                    ,ByVal nLenRequired As Integer _
                    ,Optional bHyp As Boolean _
                    ) As String

    PadRight0 = sBuffer & _
            sBit & _
            String$(Abs(nLenRequired - Len(sBit)), "0") & _
            IIf(bHyp = True, "-", "")

End Function
```

Command1 Click Event handler

```
Private Sub Command1_Click()

    Print CreateGUID

End Sub
```

Notice that the optional Boolean argument in *PadRight0* is set to False if it is missing in Visual Basic 6 (as it was in 5); that is, it is never actually missing. (See *IsMissing* in the Visual Basic 6 online help.) In Visual Basic 6, an optional argument typed as anything other than Variant is never missing. An Integer is set to 0, a String to "", a Boolean to False, and so on. Bear this in mind if you really need to know whether or not the argument was passed. If you do, you'll need to use *Optional Thing As Variant* and *IsMissing*. Even in Visual Basic 4 an object is never really missing; rather, it is set to be of type *vbError* (as in *VarType* will yield 10). I've no idea what the error's value is.

In Chapter 1, I mentioned using object instances as constants and referenced this chapter for the code. Well, here it is along with some explanation.

In Visual Basic you cannot initialize a constant from a variable expression. The Help file in Visual Basic 6 says, "You can't use variables, user-defined functions, or intrinsic Visual Basic functions, such as Chr, in expressions assigned to constants." In other words, the value of the constant must be derivable by the compiler at compile time. In Chapter 1, I wanted to use a constant to hold a value returned from the Windows API, like this:

```
vbObjectiSingle = WinGlobalAddAtom(CreateGUID)
```

I said that the object type of *vbObjectiSingle* was a constant Smartie type. That said, here's the code....

STUFF ABOUT SMARTIES

Here's the code for this ConstiLong class (a constant intelligent Long):

```
Private bInit    As Boolean
Private l        As Long

Public Property Let Value(ByVal v As Variant)

    If bInit Then
        Err.Raise 17
    Else
        bInit = True
    End If

    If vbLong <> VarType(v) Then
        Err.Raise 13
    Else
        l = CLng(v)
    End If

End Property
```

>>

```
Public Property Get Value() As Variant

    Value = 1

End Property
```

Class ConstiLong instances are used as constant long integers. The *Value* property is marked as the default property for the class (in common with normal Smarties). You can see that the Property Let allows one-time-only initialization of the contained value (*l*). You can also see that I'm using a Variant to type check the argument in the Let (Visual Basic then insists on my using a Variant for the Get, too). You can remove these and use a real Long if you want (and I can guarantee that you'll be set from a Long).

From Chapter 1, here's how you'd set these up (all this code is in your start-up module).

```
' Used to extend sub-classed VarType for Smartie Types
'
Public vbObjectiInteger As New ConstiLong
Public vbObjectiSingle  As New ConstiLong
Public vbObjectiString  As New ConstiLong
⋮

Sub main()

    vbObjectiInteger = WinGlobalAddAtom(CreateGUID)
    vbObjectiSingle  = WinGlobalAddAtom(CreateGUID)
    vbObjectiString  = WinGlobalAddAtom(CreateGUID)
    ⋮

End Sub
```

Obviously, I need one of these classes for each intrinsic type from which I want to make a constant—ConstiInt, ConstiString, and so on. (If you're not sure what's going on, see my aside on Smarties in Chapter 1.)

Another thing you can use Smarties for is recording assigned values. This might sound a bit weird, but it is a useful thing to do with them. What do I mean? Consider this code:

```
Dim n As New iInteger

n = SomeFunc(SomeParam)

End Sub
```

Because *iInteger* is a Smartie, it can, of course, do all sorts of stuff when its default property *Let Value* gets hit—like record the value assigned from *SomeFunc* in the Registry. Remember code where you have stuff like this?

```
' Ask the user for some info...
n = MsgBox("Show tips at startup?", vbYesNo + vbQuestion, _
            "Show Tips at Startup")


' Write away to persistent store.
Call SaveSetting(... n ...)

If vbYes = n Then ...
```

With Smarties you can have the same thing happen with just this assignment:

```
' Ask the user for some info and record it away...
n = MsgBox("Show tips at startup?", vbYesNo + vbQuestion, _
            "Show Tips at Startup")

If vbYes = n Then ...
```

Without proper construction (a parametizable constructor procedure for classes, also known as a declarative initialization), this assignment is of little real use. For example, how does *this* instance of *iInteger* know which key it should write to in the Registry? What you really need to support this kind of thing is declarative support, something like this—*Dim n As New ipInteger(kTips)*. The *ip* here means intelligent-persistent *iInteger* (a class that would implement *iInteger*); *kTips* is a value that is passed to the created *ipInteger* instance, telling it which Registry value it should be writing to. In this scenario, it would probably write to App.EXEName\Settings\kTips. Currently the only way to parameterize the construction of objects such as this is by using public variables, such as the ones shown here.

```
kTips = "Tips"

Dim n As New ipInteger: n = Nothing
```

The *n = Nothing* causes *n*'s Initialize event to trigger and read the value of the public *kTips*, which is really nasty, prone to error, and basically awful!

Of course, this code hides the fact that the value in *n* is written somewhere, so you might consider this "clever code" and discard it. It's up to you—where cleverness starts and abstraction ends is somewhat subjective. For example, what does this code look like it might do?

```
Dim n As New iInteger
```

```
n = n
```

Nothing right—the code simply assigns 0 to *n*. Well, that's what would happen if *n* were an ordinary integer, but with a Smartie we cannot be certain. As you probably know, "*Dim*-ing" an object using *New* doesn't create it—the object is created at its first use. So *n* is actually created when we read the value of *n* (because the right side of the assignment is evaluated first). This statement causes the object to be created and thus causes its Initialize event to fire. Hmm, it could be doing anything in there, like reading from the Registry and setting up its own value! Would you expect to find, if the next line read *MsgBox n*, that *n* contains, say, 42? Probably not. Of course, the code might look even more obvious:

```
n = 0
```

```
n = Nothing
```

```
Set n = Nothing
```

Notice that *n* = *Nothing* is kinda odd (in more ways than one). The statement is really "the *Value* (default) property of *n* is assigned *Nothing*," or *Call n.Value(Nothing)*, so the statement is perfectly legal and causes *Nothing* to be passed to our object as a parameter—and, of course, causes it to be created. Notice, too, that it's very different from *Set n* = *Nothing*; this statement doesn't invoke the *Value* property *Set* even though the syntax makes it appear that the default property is being accessed. To *Set* the *Value* property, of course, you need to use *Set n.Value* = *Nothing*—see the ambiguity here? (If a default were allowed for both regular assignment and *Set*, Visual Basic would have no way of knowing whether you wanted to set the default property or the object variable.) Actually, depending on whether *n* is declared *Dim n As New iInteger* or *Dim n As iInteger* (which is then set using *Set n* = *New iInteger*), even a *Set n* = *Nothing* might have no effect. A show of hands, anyone, who thinks that an object declared *Dim o As New ObjectName* can be set to *Nothing* using *Set o* = *Nothing*. That many? Think again!

You can also, of course, log more ordinary assignments using Smarties. Should you feel that some routine is periodically returning an interesting value, have the assigned-to Smartie log the assigned value to the Registry so that you can check it.

OTHER STUFF

In my humble opinion, the nicest place to eat in all of Seattle (perhaps even the world, excluding The Waterside Inn in Bray in England) is The Brooklyn Seafood, Steak & Oyster House, on the intersection of Second and University in downtown. This place is just dazzling, and I have spent many a happy, self-indulgent evening there immersed in its glow and hubbub. One of my favorite things to do there is to sit at the chef's bar and watch the show on the other side of the bar. If they're makin' flames, so much the better. The chef's bar has great old-fashioned high-back swivel chairs stationed all along it for the sole purpose of allowing you to watch, and, if you're not careful, be a part of the drama taking place there. In fact, it's a lot like sitting in a theater, except it's much more intimate and generally a lot more fun!

Understanding Software Development by Dining Out

You know, it's a privilege to watch these people work—in fact the entire restaurant staff is amazing to watch—but the chef's bar is something special. Many a time I've sat there wishing that I could get a software team to work together half as well as the chefs do, or even that I could put together applications from readily prepared components quite so easily.

You see, I reason that I should be able to do this because the two industries have some very strong similarities. Think about it. A restaurant has a development team: an architect who plans the way it's going to be (the head chef); a technical lead–cum–project manager (whoever is the main chef for the evening); and a whole bunch of developers in the guise of sous chefs. The junior developers are the general helpers and dishwashers. In the front office are customer service representatives at the reception desk and perhaps the sales reps are the waiters and waitresses—all working on commission, mostly. Of course, a management team is trying to keep up the quality, running the whole operation and trying to make a profit. (The Brooklyn has about 50 staff in all.)

Outside the organization are a whole bunch of suppliers bringing in myriad raw and cooked components ("constituents" might be a better term), all of which have well-defined interfaces and some of which must be prepared further before they can be assembled properly to form the end product. And they do it so well, too! At every lunch and dinner they take orders from customers and rapidly create meals, using what appears to be a true Rapid Application Development

(RAD) approach. They also change the menu monthly, so it wouldn't be true to say, "Well, that's fine for them because they're always producing the same thing," because they're not. So, I ask myself, why can't our industry do its thing just as easily and efficiently?

On one visit I got to chatting with Tony Cunio (head chef and co-owner). I wanted him to explain to me all the hows and whys of his trade, to explain how they consistently manage to produce the goods and yet maintain such high quality. I told him I'd like to be able to do the same. It was an interesting conversation because we each had a very strong domain vocabulary that didn't necessarily "port" too well. (For me, port is a process; for Tony, it's a drink.) It was frustrating at times—you ought to try explaining object-oriented software construction to a chef sometime!

About people, Tony says to look for people with a strong team spirit and build a strong team around you. For him, staff selection is where the quality starts. He also says that the staff have to work well under pressure and while constantly stepping on each other's feet, because they practice "full-contact cooking" at The Brooklyn. Another of Tony's passions, aside from food and cooking, is his commitment to a coaching style of management. Now coaching is a subject that I'm not going to get into deeply here, except by way of trying to define it for you.

Coaching is all about a supportive relationship between the coach and the player and a way of communication between the same. The coach doesn't pass on facts but instead helps the player discover the facts, from the inside and for himself or herself. Of course, the objective is to better the performance of the player. With coaching, perhaps, how this is achieved is what's different from the normal, more traditional style of management. You know the adage—teach me and I will listen, show me and I will learn, let me do and I will understand. Well, coaching is a bit like that, except we'd probably replace that last piece with something like, "Counsel me, guide me, and trust me, but overall, let me discover, for then I will understand and grow." At TMS, we try to coach instead of manage, but I'd say that we're still learning the techniques. So far, though, the indications are good.[3]

---

3. See *Coaching for Performance* by Sir John Whitmore for more on this highly interesting subject (Nicholas Brealey, 1996, ISBN 1-85788-170-2).

What else does Tony have to offer by way of advice to an industry that is still, relatively speaking, in its start-up phase? Well, Tony always makes sure that all his staff have the right tools for the job. After all, they can't give 100 percent without the right tools, so if they need a new filleting knife, they get one. Sounds reasonable, of course, but drawing the analogy back to the software industry, how many developers can say that they are provided with the right tools for the job? Not the majority, that's for sure. Tony says that everyone needs to be fast and technically good. Again, ask yourself how skillful and fast your average developer is—this comes straight back to your hiring practices. Tony also recommends giving people responsibility, accountability, and in making them "excuse-free," meaning there are no obstacles to being successful.

Tony is very clear about the procurement of constituents. "[The suppliers] are here for us, we're not here for them. I expect a faultless delivery, on time and to standard." And if he has a substandard component delivered to his kitchen? "It would go straight back—no question, garbage in, garbage out." (See? Some terms span whole industries!) "I'd also have words with the supplier to ensure that it didn't ever happen again." And what if it did? "Easy. We'd never use that supplier again." How many of you have worked with, or are working with, substandard components—and, I might add, regularly paying for what are little more than bug fixes just to discover new bugs in the upgrade? When I told Tony about the way the software industry procures components that are inevitably buggy, he was simply dumbstruck!

I asked Tony how he goes about the assembly of an entity from its components. Tony recommends using a methodology, a recipe, or a plan from which people learn—not so restrictive that it limits creativity and not so unencumbered that it lacks proper rigor and guidance. Could this be what we might call a coding standard? Combined with the coaching idea, this is surely a productive and enjoyable way to learn.

It seems to me that the fundamental differences between a cooking team and a software team are that

1. We don't practice "full-contact development" <g>, and
2. We take what we're given, accept it for what it is (even when we shouldn't), and nevertheless try and come up with the goods, on time and to budget! (See Chapter 17 for the hiring perspective.)

Yup, The Brooklyn has certainly taught me a thing or two about software development over the years. Talking to Tony reminded me of a saying that I first saw in Fred Brooks' Mythical Man-Month (usually called MMM), which came out in 1972. (The latest edition is ISBN 0-201-83595-9.) It's actually a quote from the menu of Antoine's Restaurant, which is at 713-717 Rue St. Louis, New Orleans, in case you're ever there.

> "Faire de la bonne cuisine demande un certain temps. Si on vous fait attendre, c'est pour mieux vous servir, et vous plaire."

which means

> "To cook well requires a certain amount of time. If you must wait it is only to serve you better and please you more."

Go visit The Brooklyn and Tony next time you're in Seattle, and see if you can figure out just how they "can" and we "can't." Maybe I'll see you there, or maybe you'll bump into Michael Jordan or some other famous regular. Perhaps you'll meet some notable Microsoft "foodies" there—who knows? Anyway, enjoy your meal!

To give you an idea of what's on on the menu and to round up this chapter, here's Tony's recipe for The Brooklyn's signature dish: Alder-Planked Salmon with Smoked Tomato and Butter Sauce. (By the way, the plank is made up of blocks of alderwood secured together using steel rods and nuts. A shallow depression is then formed in the block to hold the salmon during cooking.)

Northwest Alder-Planked Salmon with Smoked Tomato Butter Sauce

Ingredients:

- Four 8 oz. salmon fillets (skinless)
- Salt and pepper to taste
- One seasoned alder plank (see below)
- 8 oz. smoked tomato butter sauce (recipe follows)
- ¼ oz. snipped chives
- 1 oz. Brunoise Roma tomato skin

Preparation:

- Make smoked tomato butter sauce according to recipe. Set aside in warm area.
- Oven cook alder plank salmon fillets.

- Serve 2 oz. smoked tomato butter with each salmon fillet.
- Garnish sauce with snipped chives and Brunoise Roma tomato.
- Serve!

Ingredients for Smoked Tomato Butter (yield 3 cups):

- 1 oz. garlic, minced
- Two smoked tomatoes (whole)
- 1c. white wine
- 2 tbsp. lemon juice
- ¾ c. cream
- 1 lb. Butter
- ½ tsp. seasoning salt (20 parts salt to 1 part white pepper)

Preparation:

Saute garlic in oil. Deglaze pan with wine and lemon juice. Add tomatoes and reduce to almost dry (approximately two tablespoons liquid). Add cream and reduce by half. Slowly incorporate cold butter. Season and strain. Hold in warm area until ready to serve.

Plank tips

This intriguing section might inspire you to build or buy your own wood plank!

About the wood   Wood, when heated, can crack, but don't be alarmed—the steel rods and nuts are designed to prevent the plank from splitting. Make sure the nuts are screwed tightly against the wood, especially when your plank is new. The wood will slowly contract as you use it and any small cracks that develop will soon disappear.

It is especially important to season the plank when it is new. Pour one to two tablespoons of olive or vegetable oil in the hollowed oval of the plank and use a paper towel to rub the entire top of the plank, until it is lightly coated. Do not put oil on the bottom of the plank. After using your plank eight to ten times it will become well seasoned and it will be necessary to season it only on occasion.

To rekindle a stronger wood flavor after repeated use, lightly sand the plank inside the oval with fine sandpaper. Once the plank has been sanded, it should be treated like a new plank and oiled before each use until it becomes well seasoned. The bottom of the plank can also be sanded if you want to lighten the darkened wood.

Baking on wood   Cooking on wood is a unique, natural, and healthy way of cooking. The wood breathes, allowing most of the juices to stay in the food, resulting in added moisture and flavor. You will find that fewer additives, sauces, or liquids will be needed. We use the plank as a beautiful serving platter right from the oven.

Preheating your plank is important so that the wood will be warm enough to cook from the bottom as well as the top. Place the plank on the middle rack of a cold oven and set to bake at 350 degrees (do not use the preheat setting). Leaving the plank in for 10 minutes will sterilize it and prepare it for use. Enjoy using your plank to cook fish, poultry, meat, vegetables, and even bread.

Cleaning your plank   Just use warm running water and a soft-bristled brush to clean your plank. You can use a mild soap if you want. It is easiest to clean the plank within an hour or so after use. Remember, preheating the plank before use will sterilize it.

Be careful!   The plank absorbs heat and will be hot when used for cooking, so please use pot holders or oven gloves when handling it. While the plank is designed for baking, it is important to observe cooking times and the recommended temperature of 380 degrees.

Visual Basic Programmer's Guide to Successful Dating

How Does Y2K Affect Visual Basic?

Steve has played a major part over the past couple of years in The Mandelbrot Set's drive to raise awareness of the Year 2000 issue for Visual Basic developers. He has had articles published on the subject in both the Visual Basic Programmers Journal and, in Europe, the Microsoft Developer Network Journal. He lives in leafy Surrey with the mysterious "M," his record collection, and his plants. He fully intends to be in no fit state to be aware of any problems when the clocks strike midnight on December 31, 1999.

STEVE OVERALL

Hands up—how many of you have heard of the "Millennium Bug" or "Year 2000 Problem" or whatever else it has been called over the last few years? If any of you didn't raise your hands, you are either not open to suggestion or you are new to this planet. Welcome! We call it Earth.

Much has been written about this subject over the past few years. While there is a great wealth of information, most of it is aimed at the COBOL community, and what isn't tends to be very generic—limited to management guides and theoretical discussions. What I want to do in this chapter is simply look at the issue from a practical perspective, focusing on its particular relevance to Visual Basic. I will look at how Visual Basic stores and manipulates date information and, equally important, what its weaknesses are.

For me the issue is not so much what happens when the clocks strike midnight on a certain night in December 1999, but that many developers still do not fully understand how our language deals with this simple piece of data!

A LITTLE ABOUT THE DATE RULES

The Gregorian calendar, which is used throughout the western world, has a long and check-ered past. It was first introduced in 1582 by Pope Gregory XIII, after whom it is named.

Prior to the Gregorian calendar the Julian calendar was widely used. The Julian calendar had a leap year every four years. With the actual period of our orbit around the sun being 365.24219 days, there was a slow shifting of the seasons, until by the sixteenth century events such as the autumnal equinox were occur-ring up to ten days earlier than they were when the Julian calendar was intro-duced. The Gregorian calendar changed the rule for the century years so that they would not be leap years unless they were divisible by 400.

The new calendar was adopted in Catholic countries in 1582. Ten days were dropped to bring the seasons back into line. October 4 was immediately fol-lowed by October 15, with no dates in between. The United Kingdom and its colonies, which at the time included areas of North America, made the change in 1752 with the dropping of eleven days (September 2 was immediately fol-lowed by September 14).

NOTE

> Every fourth year is a leap year except those that are also divisible by 100. How-ever, those years divisible by 400 are leap years. So the year 2000 is a leap year; 1900 and 2100 are not.

SO HOW DOES VISUAL BASIC HELP MY DATING SUCCESS?

Here are some ways Visual Basic helps you get around the Year 2000 glitch.

The Date Data Type

Visual Basic has had a dedicated Date data type since version 4 and, prior to that (in versions 2 and 3), a Date Variant type with the same storage pattern. Dates can be declared and used like this:

```
Dim dteMyDate     As Date
```

```
dteMyDate = DateSerial(1998, 2, 12)
```

Or perhaps

```
dteMyDate = #2/12/98#
```

The Date data type is actually stored as an IEEE double-precision floating point value, 8 bytes long. The data stored can represent dates from January 1 100 up to December 31 9999. Days are stored as whole numbers, with zero being December 30 1899. Dates prior to this are stored as negative values, those after are positive. In the example above, February 12 1998 is stored as 35838. You can test this outcome with the following code:

```
MsgBox CDbl(DateSerial(1998, 2, 12))
```

The Date data type is also able to hold time information. Hours, minutes, and seconds are held as fractions, with noon represented as 0.5. If we take the number of seconds in a day, 86400, and divide that into 1, the answer is the fraction equal to one second: 0.000011574.... The table below shows the minimum, default, and maximum values that can be stored in a variable declared as a *Date*.

	Date	Value Stored
Minimum Value	January 1 100 00:00:00	-657434
Default Value	December 30 1899 00:00:00	0
Maximum Value	December 31 9999 23:59:59	2958465.99998843

As we can see, there is nothing wrong with the way Visual Basic stores dates. Its method is both compact and Year 2000 compliant. For example, 8 bytes would store only the date if encoded as an alphanumeric CCYYMMDD. In effect, the Date data type allows us to store the time for free.

Manipulating Dates in Visual Basic

Once all your dates are stored in Date variables, all the date manipulation functions become available. The benefits of these functions are obvious—they are Year 2000 compliant and leap year aware.

Visual Basic has a number of date manipulation functions. In this section we are going to look at them in some detail. It might seem like I am telling you something you already know, but I have seen too many supposedly good Visual Basic developers remain unaware of the range of tools that are in the box.

Date tools

Visual Basic provides a lot of properties and functions that support comparison and manipulation of dates. These properties and functions are all designed to work with the Visual Basic Date data type and should be used in preference to all other methods. The majority of these elements reside in the VBA library in a class called DateTime. You can see the details of the class in Figure 8-1.

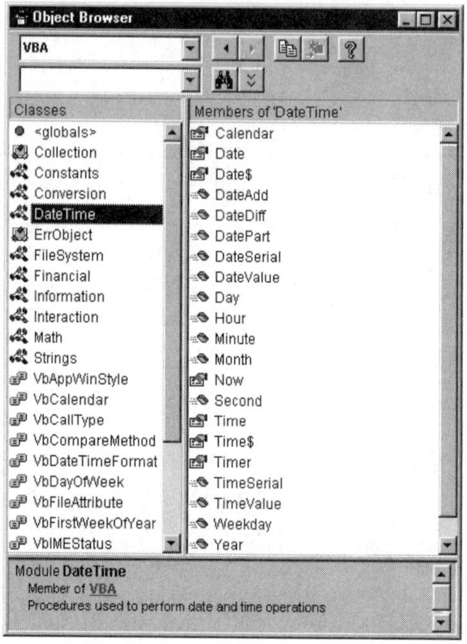

FIGURE 8-1   *The VBA.DateTime class as seen in the Visual Basic Object Browser*

TIP

With all the conversion functions, you would do well to use *IsDate* to test your expression before you perform the conversion.

The *Calendar* property   This property exposes the calendar system currently in use within your application. By default this is set to vbCalGreg, the Gregorian calendar in use throughout most of the western world. Currently the only alternative is vbCalHijri, the Hijri calendar.

The *Now, Date, Date$, Time,* and *Time$* properties   All these properties perform similar tasks. They retrieve or assign the system date or time. By far the most used is the read-only *Now* property, which returns the current system date and time as a Visual Basic Date that can be assigned directly to a Date data type variable without conversion.

The *Date* and *Time* properties can be used to assign or return just the date or time part of the current system date. When assigning, the *Date* property expects to be passed a date expression containing the date you want to set the system date to. Any time information is ignored. The date must be within the range shown in the table below. Dates outside this range will result in a run-time error (5 - Invalid Procedure Call Or Argument). The *Date$* property returns and assigns dates from Strings, with the equivalent *Date* property using Variants.

Range for VBA.DateTime.Date	Windows 9x	Windows NT
Minimum Date	January 1 1980	January 1 1980
Maximum Date	December 31 2099	December 31 2099

The *Time* and *Time$* properties perform a task similar to *Date* and *Date$*, exposing the system time.

The *Timer* property   This property returns the number of seconds that have elapsed since midnight.

The *DateDiff* function   This function performs a comparison of two dates. The value that is returned—the difference between the two dates—is reported in a time or date unit of the caller's choosing. An important point to note is that the answer will correctly reflect the fact that the year 2000 is a leap year. The following code displays the difference, in number of days (specified by the first argument), between the current system date and December 1, 2000.

```
' Display the number of days until Dec 1 2000.
MsgBox DateDiff("d", Now, #12/1/2000# _
                , vbUseSystemDayOfWeek, vbUseSystem)
```

The fourth and fifth arguments are both optional, allowing you to specify the first day of the week and the first week of the year. Both will default to the system values if omitted.

The *DateAdd* function   This function is used to modify a Visual Basic Date, with the value returned being the new Date following modification. Again this routine is fully aware of the leap year rules. The following line of code adds one month to the date January 31 2000 and returns the result February 29 2000, correctly calculating that February will have 29 days in the year 2000.

```
' Add one month to Jan 31 2000.
MsgBox DateAdd("m", 1, CDate("31 Jan 2000"))
```

The *Year, Month,* and *Day* functions The *Format$* function is often abused when a programmer needs to get only part of the information held in a date. I still come across newly written code where *Format$* has been used to do this.

```
' Getting the month of the current date, the old way
iMonth = CInt(Format$(Date, "MM"))
```

```
' And how to do it the new, more efficient way
iMonth = Month(Date)
```

Visual Basic provides the *Year*, *Month*, and *Day* functions to return these numeric values when passed a Date.

The *Hour, Minute,* and *Second* functions Not surprisingly, these functions perform a similar task to the *Year*, *Month*, and *Day* functions described above, except that they will return the numeric values representing the components of the time held in a Visual Basic Date.

The *DatePart* function This function returns the part of a passed date that you request in the unit of your choice. The above *Year*, *Month*, *Day*, *Hour*, *Minute*, and *Second* functions can perform the majority of the tasks that *DatePart* can, but the *DatePart* function does give you more flexibility, as demonstrated in the following code:

```
' Get the quarter of the current date.
MsgBox DatePart("q", Now, vbUseSystemDayOfWeek, vbUseSystem)
```

The third and fourth arguments are both optional, allowing you to specify the first day of the week and the first week of the year. Both will default to the system values if omitted.

The *Weekday* function This function will return the day of the week of the Date passed in as the first argument. The second optional argument allows you to specify the first day of the week.

```
' Get the current day of the week.
MsgBox Weekday(Now, vbUseSystemDayOfWeek)
```

The *DateValue* and *TimeValue* functions These two functions perform conversions from a String date expression to a Date data type; in this case the conversion will be of only the date for *DateValue* and the time for *TimeValue*. These functions are useful if you want to separate the two parts of a date for separate storage.

One point to note with these two functions is that you can get a Type Mismatch error if any part of the expression you are converting is not valid, even the part you are not interested in. Executing the code below will result in this error, even though the time part of the expression is valid.

```
' Try this; it causes a Type Mismatch error!
MsgBox TimeValue("29 02 1900 12:15")
```

The *DateSerial* and *TimeSerial* functions   *DateSerial* and *TimeSerial* are less flexible than *DateValue* and *TimeValue*, requiring three numeric parameters to define the date or time you want to convert. The three parameters of the *DateSerial* function are the *year*, *month*, and *day*, in that order. *TimeSerial* expects *hours*, *minutes*, and *seconds*.

```
' Assign April 12 1998 to the date.
dteMyDate = DateSerial(1998, 4, 12)

' Alternatively, assign the time 12:00:00.
dteMyDate = TimeSerial(12, 00, 00)
```

Both these functions have an interesting ability to accept values outside the normal range for each time period (excluding years). For instance, if you pass the year *1998* and the month *14* to the *DateSerial* function, it will actually return a date in the second month of 1999, having added the 14 months to 1998. The following line of code illustrates this. (Your output might look different depending on your system settings, but the date will be the same.)

```
Debug.Print "The Date is " & Format$( _
            DateSerial (1998, 2, 29), "Long Date")
The Date is 01 March 1998
```

In this instance, *DateSerial* has correctly worked out that there is no February 29 in 1998, so it has rolled the month over to March for the extra day. We can use this ability to write a function that tells us whether any year is a leap year.

```
Public Function IsLeapYear(ByVal inYear As Integer) As Boolean

    IsLeapYear = (29 = Day(DateSerial(inYear, 2, 29)))

End Function
```

Formatting and displaying dates

These functions can be found in the VBA.Strings module. All these functions are aware of the current system locale settings. Any strings returned will be in the language and style of this locale.

Locales have particular formats for such things as the date, time, and currency. For instance, a user on a PC in France would expect to read or be able to enter date information in a familiar format. Windows extends this formatting to cover common text such as the days of the week or the months of the year. Visual Basic is aware of the system locale and will use the information associated with it when interpreting and formatting dates.

The *Format* and *Format$* functions   The *Format* function and the *Format$* function are interchangeable. These functions return a string containing the passed date in the specified format. By default there are seven predefined date formats (see the table on page 352), of which "Long Date" and "Short Date" are the most useful; these two formats coincide with the formats set in the Regional Settings dialog box, shown in Figure 8-2. You can access this dialog box from the Regional Settings option in the Control Panel. The user can use the Date property page of this dialog box to modify both the Short Date and Long Date formats. These formats are directly supported by the *Format$* function.

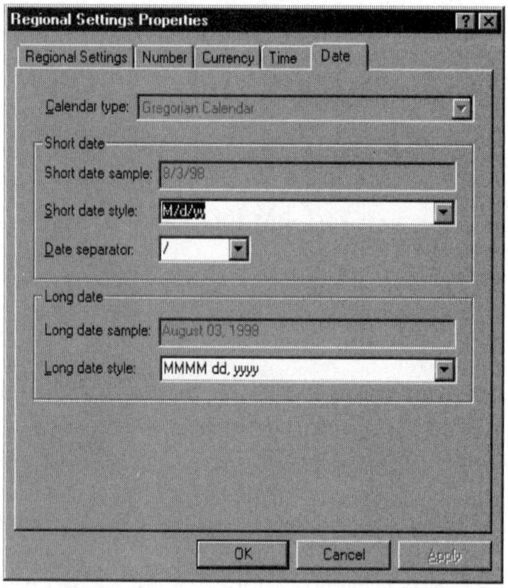

FIGURE 8-2   *The Windows Control Panel, Regional Settings Properties dialog box*

If we convert a Date to a string without applying a format, we will actually assign the date in General Date format. For the U.S. this defaults to M/d/yy;

for the U.K. and much of Europe it defaults to dd/MM/yy. The code extract below will display the date in a message box using the system General Date format. (See the table on the following page for a description of the General Date format.) You can experiment by changing the Short Date and Long Date formats and rerunning the code.

```
Dim dteMyDate As Date

dteMyDate = DateSerial(1997, 2, 12)
MsgBox CStr(dteMyDate)
```

To use any named format other than General Date, we have to explicitly specify the format with the *Format$* function. We can substitute the following line for the *MsgBox* line in the code above:

```
MsgBox Format$(dteMyDate, "Long Date" _
               , vbUseSystemDayOfWeek, vbUseSystem)
```

The third and fourth arguments are both optional, allowing you to specify the first day of the week and the first week of the year. Both will default to the system values if omitted.

The format types are very useful for displaying dates, either on line or within reports. Here the user has some control over the format via the Control Panel, and you maintain consistency with many other applications.

CAUTION

> The size of date and time formats can be changed. As this is outside your application's direct control, you should allow sufficient space for any eventuality. Even when using the default General Date format we cannot assume a fixed length string. Dates in the 20th century will be formatted with two-digit years; dates in any other century, however, will be formatted with four-digit years. This behavior is consistent, even when we move the system date into the 21st century.

Notice that the formats in the table below are purely for coercing a Date into a String; they have no effect on the date value stored. A Date displayed using the Short Date format will still hold century information (indeed, it will hold the time too); it will just be coy about it. The Short Date format is particularly open to abuse, sometimes by so-called Year 2000 experts convinced that the PC problem can be solved by changing the Short Date format to include the century.

Format Name	Description
General Date (Default)	This will use the system Short Date format. If the date to be displayed contains time information, this will also be displayed in the Long Time format.
	Dates outside 1930 to 2029 will be formatted with century information regardless of the settings for the Short Date format in the Regional Settings.
Long Date	This will use the Regional Settings system Long Date format.
Medium Date	This will use a format applicable to the current system locale.
	This cannot be set in the Regional Settings of the Control Panel.
Short Date	This will use the Regional Settings system Short Date format.
Long Time	This will use the Regional Settings system Time format.
Medium Time	This will format the time using a 12-hour format.
Short Time	This will format the time using a 24-hour format.

In addition to the predefined formats, you can apply your own formats. The weakness in using nonstandard formats for display purposes is that they are not controllable by the Regional Settings in the Control Panel. So if you are considering foreign markets for your software, you might have to modify your code for any change in regional date format (the different U.K. and U.S. formats are an obvious example). My advice is to use only the default formats wherever possible.

NOTE

Format$, *DateAdd*, and *DateDiff* are a little inconsistent with the tokens they use to represent different time periods. *Format$* uses "n" as the token for minutes and "m" or "M" for months. However, *DateAdd* and *DateDiff* expect minutes as "m," and months as "M." Because the Regional Settings dialog box also uses "M," my advice would be to always use the upper-case letter when specifying the month in any of these functions.

If you convert a Date directly to a String without using *Format*, the resulting String will follow the General Date rules except that dates outside the range 1930–1999 will be formatted with four-digit years, regardless of the settings for Short Date.

The *FormatDateTime* function   This function is new to Visual Basic in version 6. It works in a similar way to *Format$*, which we discussed on page 350. However, *FormatDateTime* uses an enumerated argument for the format instead of parsing a string. This makes it less flexible than *Format$*, but faster. If you are going to be using only the system date formats, you should use *FormatDateTime* instead of *Format$*, giving you cleaner code and a slight performance improvement.

```
' Print the current system date.
dteMyDate = FormatDateTime(Now, vbLongDate)
```

The *MonthName* function   Another addition to Visual Basic version 6, *MonthName* returns a String containing the name of the month that was passed in as an argument of type long. This function replaces one of the tricks that *Format$* had often been called upon to do in the past: getting the name of a month.

```
' Give me the full name of the current month, the old way.
MsgBox Format$(Now, "MMMM")
```

```
' Now do it the new way.
MsgBox MonthName(Month(Now), False)
```

This function has a second, optional Boolean argument that when set to True will cause the function to return the abbreviated month name. The default for this argument is False.

The *WeekdayName* function   *WeekdayName* is another addition to Visual Basic 6. It works in a similar way to *MonthName* except that it returns a String containing the name of the day of the week.

```
' Give me the name of the current day of the week,
' the old way.
MsgBox Format$(Now, "dddd", vbUseSystemDayOfWeek)
```

```
' Give me the full name of the current day of the week
' for the current system locale, the new way.
MsgBox WeekdayName(Weekday(Now, vbUseSystemDayOfWeek), _
                   False, vbUseSystemDayOfWeek)
```

Again, the remaining arguments are optional. The first, if set to True, will cause the function to return the abbreviation of the day of the week; the second tells the function what day to use as the first day of the week.

The conversion and information functions

The last set of functions we are going to look at are the conversion functions.

The *CDate* and *CVDate* functions   *CDate* and *CVDate* both convert a date expression (ambiguous or not) directly into a Date data type. The difference is that *CVDate* actually returns a Variant of type vbDate (7) and is retained for backward compatibility with earlier versions of the language. The following code demonstrates two different ways of using *CDate* to retrieve a Date.

```
Dim dteMyDate   As Date

' This assigns December 31 1999 to the date...
dteMyDate = CDate("31 Dec 1999")

' ...and so does this.
dteMyDate = CDate(36525)
```

CDate and *CVDate* perform a similar function to the *DateValue* function in the DateTime library with two exceptions. First, they can convert numeric values to a Date. The example above shows *CDate* converting the numeric serial date value of 36525 to a date of December 31 1999. Second, they will include time information in the conversion if it is present.

These functions can be found in the VBA.Conversion module, along with the other conversion functions such as *CLng* and *CInt*.

The *IsDate* function   This function performs a simple but vital task. If passed a date expression, it will return True if the expression can be converted to a Visual Basic Date successfully. This is of great use when validating dates from sources directly outside your control, such as the user (the bane of all developers' lives).

```
If True = IsDate(txtDateOfBirth.Text) Then
    ' Convert the expression entered to a date.
    dteDOB = CDate(txtDateOfBirth.Text)
Else
    ' Otherwise, inform the user of his or her mistake.
    MsgBox "Don't be silly. That is not a valid date."
End If
```

To add a final bit of complexity to everything, this function lives in a fourth module, VBA.Information.

GOING UNDER THE COVERS: DATING ASSIGNMENTS

Most of the work done with dates in Visual Basic involves processing data taken from some outside source. This can be a database, a file, an interface, the operating system, or the user. In all these instances we are subject to data that is often in a string format and that might be formatted in a way that is outside our direct control.

To make a system Year 2000 compliant, we must either enforce the rule that all dates supplied must be in a four-digit year format, or we must make the system perform a conversion to a compliant format. Often, the latter method is considered easier and more cost effective, especially where the user interface is concerned. (The latter method is referred to as "interpretation," the former as "expansion.") In each case we must quickly realize that sooner or later we will have to deal with dates that have only two-digit years.

Assigning noncompliant dates: Visual Basic's default behavior

In order to predict the resultant date from an assignment, we must find out what Visual Basic will do by default to convert to its native Date data type when presented with a noncompliant date. Invariably a noncompliant date will originate from a string, whether it is the contents of a text box or a database field.

It's time for a little detective work. We want to find out what Visual Basic does when asked to assign a date when the century is missing. As an example, try the following code:

```
Dim dteMyDate As Date

dteMyDate = CDate("12 Feb 01")

MsgBox Format$(dteMyDate, "dd MMM yyyy")
```

Under most circumstances, Visual Basic will give us the answer 12 Feb 2001. If it does not, bear with me—this is leading somewhere. Now substitute the following code for the second line:

```
dteMyDate = CDate("12 Feb 35")
```

This time the answer is likely to be 12 Feb 1935! So what is going on?

What is happening here is that Visual Basic is being smart. When the line of code *dteMyDate = CDate("12 Feb 35")* is executed, Visual Basic spots the fact that only two digits were given for the year, and applies an algorithm to expand it to four. This is something we humans do intuitively, but computers, literal beasts that they are, need to be given some rules. The algorithm used can be expressed like this:

```
If Years < 30 Then
    Century Is 21st ' 20xx
Else ' >= 29
    Century Is 20th ' 19xx
End If
```

Another, easier way to visualize this is to consider all dates with only two-digit years to be within a 100-year window, starting at 1930 and ending at 2029, as shown in Figure 8-3.

FIGURE 8-3   *The 100-year date window used by Visual Basic*

As I mentioned earlier, the results of our bit of detective work might not be consistent. This is because there is one final complication at work here. A system library file OLEAUT32.DLL specifies the date behavior for all of the 32-bit implementations of Visual Basic. This is one of the libraries at the heart of Microsoft's ActiveX and Component Object Model. Currently we know of several versions of this file. This table lists them.

OLEAUT32 File Version	Size (Bytes)	Date Window
2.1	232,720	Current Century
No version information	257,560	Current Century
2.20.4044	470,288	Current Century
2.20.4049	473,872	1930 – 2029
2.20.4054	491,792	1930 – 2029
2.20.4103	491,280	1930 – 2029
2.20.4112	490,256	1930 – 2029
2.20.4118	492,304	1930 – 2029
2.20.4122	503,808	1930 – 2029
2.30.4261 (Installed with VB6)	598,288	1930 – 2029

As you will have noticed, the earlier versions of the file have a different date window from more recent ones. Visual Basic 6 installs the latest version of this DLL as part of its setup, and will not run with some of the earlier versions. However, the important point here is that the rules have changed, and they could change again in the future. What this means, of course, is that we cannot always be entirely sure what Visual Basic is going to do with a two-digit-year date. I, for one, prefer to deal with certainties.

It is worth noting that the Setup Wizard that is shipped with Visual Basic will include the current version of OLEAUT32.DLL as part of your setup. This is an important consideration, since Visual Basic 6 executables will not work with versions of OLEAUT32 prior to the version shipped with the product. It is no longer enough to copy the EXE and its run-time DLL onto your target machine. You must provide a proper setup that includes, and registers where necessary, the additional dependencies such as OLEAUT32.DLL. The Setup Wizard is the minimum requirement for this task.

STOP THE PRESSES: MICROSOFT RELEASES WINDOWS 98

Microsoft Windows 98 puts another angle on our windowing discussion. If you select the Date tab in the Regional Settings dialog box in Windows 98, you'll see that there is a new field provided where you can change the date window in your system settings. Changing the data in this field alters the behavior of OLEAUT32.DLL, moving the default window that expands two-digit years. For this feature to work with a Visual Basic application, you must have version 2.30.xxxx or later of OLEAUT32.DLL installed on the machine, otherwise the setting is ignored. Unfortunately, Windows 98 ships with version 2.20.4122 of this file, which does not support the new window, so if you intend to make use of it you must install a newer version on the target machine. (Visual Basic 6 ships with version 2.30.4261.)

While this is definitely a real step forward, similar functionality has not been made available on either Microsoft Windows 95 or Microsoft Windows NT. For this reason, it is still of minimal use to the Visual Basic developer, unless the target operating environment can be guaranteed to be Windows 98. I have no doubt that in time this functionality will spread across all of the members of the Windows family of operating systems. Unfortunately, time is a priceless commodity in this particular field of endeavor.

The final issue with the default behavior of Visual Basic/OLEAUT32 is the range of the window itself. It is very biased toward past dates. This window is starting to get restrictive on the dates it can interpret. Certainly in some financial areas it is not uncommon to be entering dates 25 or even 30 years in the future. As an example, look at the standard mortgage, which has a term of 30 years. If I were to enter the date of the final payment for a new mortgage taken out in May 1998, it would take me through to May 2028, just one year before the end of this window. That doesn't leave a great deal of breathing space.

What we want is to implement an improved interpretation algorithm that leaves us immune to possible disruptive changes to the window used by OLEAUT32, and gives us more breathing space than the current 2029 ceiling. While there are no "silver bullets" to this issue, we can do much to improve this default behavior.

Assigning noncompliant dates: the sliding window as an alternative

By default, Visual Basic implements a "fixed window" algorithm for interpreting ambiguous dates. It uses a 100-year window that is fixed to the range 1930–2029 (barring changes to OLEAUT32). This means that any ambiguous date will be interpreted as being somewhere within that 100-year window.

A more flexible alternative is to use a custom implementation of a "sliding window" algorithm. The sliding window works by taking the noncompliant initial date and ensuring that it is converted to a date within the 100-year window, but in this case a window that moves with the current year. This is done by using a range of 100 years, bounded at the bottom by a pivot year that is calculated as an offset from the year of the current system date. This means that as the current year changes, the window changes with it. This algorithm provides a "future-proof" method of interpreting ambiguous dates because the window will always extend the same distance before and after the current year. Additionally, we are no longer using the OLEAUT32 algorithm, so changes to it will not affect us.

Figure 8-4 shows how a sliding window moves with the current system year, keeping a balanced window. Compare this to the default window in Figure 8-3, which is already very biased toward past dates. If you imagine this same situation 10 years into the future, the difference becomes even more marked.

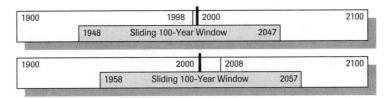

Figure 8-4   *A sliding 100-year window with a pivot year offset of –50*

Listing 8-1 below shows the function *dteCSafeDate*, which uses this sliding window algorithm to convert a date expression passed to it into a Visual Basic Date type. If you use this routine instead of assigning the date directly to a variable or use it in place of Visual Basic date conversion functions, you are able to bypass Visual Basic's default windowing behavior and apply your own more flexible date window.

Note

The CSafeDate class is included on the companion CD in the folder Chap08\ SubClass Windowed.

The *dteCSafeDate* function also allows you to select how many years in the past you would like your pivot year to be, tuning the window to the particular needs of your business. If you leave this at the default, –50, the pivot date will always be calculated as 50 years prior to the current year.

```
Private Const ERROR_TYPE_MISMATCH    As Long = 13

Public Function dteCSafeDate(ByVal ivExpression As Variant, _
                Optional ByVal inPivotOffset As Integer = -50, _
                Optional ByRef iobWindowed As Boolean = False) _
                As Date
' Convert the passed Date literal to a VB Date data type, replacing
' VB's conversion functions. It will bypass VB's date windowing
' (if necessary) by applying our own sliding window prior to the
' final conversion.
```

>>

Listing 8-1   *A date conversion function incorporating a sliding window algorithm*

LISTING 8-1
>>

```
'------------------------------------------------------------------
' If we are converting a string to a date, we delegate most of the
' work to the VBA Conversion and DateTime routines. This takes
' advantage of the fact that VB will be able to translate literals
' containing months as names. We step in ourselves only to provide
' the century where one is not present.
'------------------------------------------------------------------

    ' The literal is broken down into these parts before
    ' reassembling as a Date.
    Dim nYear      As Integer
    Dim nMonth     As Integer
    Dim nDay       As Integer
    Dim dTime      As Double

    ' This is used in our own windowing algorithm. This is the
    ' lowest year in our 100-year window used to assign century
    ' information.
    Dim nPivotYear  As Integer

    ' This is used to indicate a special case, arising from a
    ' literal that contains the year as '00'. This will be
    ' replaced temporarily with 2000 so that we can parse the date,
    ' but this flag tells our routine that the 2000 was not
    ' originally there and to treat it as 00.
    Dim bFlag00     As Boolean

    ' We temporarily assign the date to get some basic information
    ' about it.
    Dim dteTempDate As Date

    ' This indicates to the calling code whether we used our window
    ' during our conversion. Initialize it to indicate that we
    ' haven't yet; we will overwrite this later in the routine if
    ' necessary.
    iobWindowed = False

    Select Case VarType(ivExpression)

    Case vbDate
        ' The Date literal is already a Date data type. Just
        ' assign it directly.
        dteCSafeDate = ivExpression

    Case vbDouble, vbSingle
        ' If the Date literal is a Double, convert it directly to
        ' a date.
        dteCSafeDate = VBA.Conversion.CDate(ivExpression)
```

```
Case vbString
    ' If the literal is a string, we have quite a bit of
    ' work to do as the string might be in any number of
    ' different (international) formats.

    ' Check that the literal is valid to be made into a Date.
    If Not VBA.Information.IsDate(ivExpression) Then

        '-----------------------------------------------------------
        ' There is a date 02/29/00 (or equivalent) that OLEAUT32
        ' currently windows to be 02/29/2000, which is a valid
        ' date. If the used window were to change in the future,
        ' this may be reported as invalid at this point, even
        ' though our window may make it valid. Check for this
        ' date by looking for 00 in the literal and replacing it
        ' with '2000,' which will be valid regardless. We do not
        ' use the year as 2000 when applying our window, but it
        ' does allow us to continue while ignoring the assumed
        ' year.
        '-----------------------------------------------------------
        Dim nPos As Integer
        nPos = InStr(ivExpression, "00")
        If 0 = nPos Then

                ' The date did not contain the year 00, so there
                ' was some other reason why it is not valid.
                ' Raise the standard VB Type Mismatch Error.
                Err.Raise ERROR_TYPE_MISMATCH

        Else

                ' Replace the 00 with 2000, and then retest to
                ' see if it is valid.
                IvExpression = Left$(ivExpression, nPos - 1) & _
                                "2000" & _
                                Mid$(ivExpression, _
                                    nPos + 2)

                bFlag00 = True

                If Not VBA.Information.IsDate(ivExpression) Then
                    ' The date is still not valid, so accept
                    ' defeat and raise the standard VB Type
                    ' Mismatch error and exit.
                    Err.Raise ERROR_TYPE_MISMATCH
                End If
        End If
    End If
End If
```

>>

LISTING 8-1

```
'-----------------------------------------------------------
' If we have gotten here the passed date literal is one that
' VB/OLEAUT32 understands, so convert it to a temporary date
' so that we can use VB built-in routines to do the hard
' work in interpreting the passed literal. Doing this makes
' our routine compatible with any international formats
' (and languages) that would normally be supported.
'-----------------------------------------------------------
dteTempDate = VBA.Conversion.CDate(ivExpression)

' First we get the year of the Date and see if it was
' included fully in the date literal. If the century was
' specified, assign the date directly as there is no need to
' apply any windowing.
' ** If bFlag00 is set then we ourselves put
' the 2000 in there, so this test fails regardless. **
nYear = VBA.DateTime.Year(dteTempDate)
If 0 <> InStr(ivExpression, CStr(nYear)) And _
        bFlag00 = False Then

        ' We found the year in the passed date. Therefore
        ' the date already includes century information, so
        ' convert it directly into a date.
        dteCSafeDate = dteTempDate

    Else

        '---------------------------------------------------
        ' The passed date literal does not include the
        ' century. Use VB's DateTime functions to get the
        ' constituent parts of the passed date. Then
        ' overwrite the century in the year with one
        ' calculated from within our 100-year window.
        '---------------------------------------------------
        nMonth = VBA.DateTime.Month(dteTempDate)
        nDay = VBA.DateTime.Day(dteTempDate)
        dTime = VBA.DateTime.TimeValue(dteTempDate)

        ' Remove any century information that VB would have
        ' given the year.
        nYear = nYear Mod 100

        ' Get the pivot year from the current year and the
        ' offset argument.
        nPivotYear = VBA.DateTime.Year(VBA.DateTime.Now) + _
                                    inPivotOffset
```

```
                   ' Get the century for the pivot year and add that to
                   ' the year.
                   nYear = nYear + (100 * (nPivotYear \ 100))

                   ' If the year is still below the bottom of the
                   ' window (pivot year), add 100 years to bring it
                   ' within the window.
                   If nYear < nPivotYear Then
                       nYear = nYear + 100
                   End If


                   '-------------------------------------------------------
                   ' We now have all the parts of the date; it is
                   ' now time to reassemble them. We do this by
                   ' recreating the date as a string in the ISO8601
                   ' International Date format (yyyy-mm-dd) to prevent
                   ' any ambiguities caused by regional formats.
                   '
                   ' The alternative is to use the function DateSerial
                   ' but this will cause unexpected results if assigned
                   ' values outside the correct range (ie: assigning
                   ' Y1900, M2, D29 results in a date value of
                   ' Mar/01/1900 as the month is rolled over to
                   ' accommodate the extra day). It is better to cause
                   ' an error in this circumstance as that is what
                   ' CDate would do.
                   '-------------------------------------------------------
                   dteCSafeDate = CStr(nYear) & "-" & CStr(nMonth) _
                               & "-" & CStr(nDay) & " " _
                               & Format$(dTime, "hh:mm:ss")

                   ' Set the passed iobWindowed argument to True,
                   ' indicating to the calling code that we had to
                   ' apply a window to the year.
                   iobWindowed = True

            End If

        Case Else

            ' Any other variable type is not possible to convert
            Err.Raise ERROR_TYPE_MISMATCH

        End Select

    End Function
```

This is a large but generally straightforward function. We check the data type of the incoming expression. If it is numeric or already a Date, it cannot be ambiguous, so we convert the value directly to a Date and return it. The only intrinsic data type that can hold an ambiguous date is the String, so we check for this.

With strings, we do not want to have to write the code to interpret the nearly infinite number of possible combinations of format, language, and order that can make up a valid date expression, so we cheat. We still get Visual Basic to perform all of the conversion, but we make sure that there is a century present within the expression before the final conversion takes place, adding it ourselves if necessary. With this in mind, the first thing we do is look to see if the expression contains century information. If it does contain the century, it is not ambiguous, so again we can get Visual Basic to perform the conversion, as no windowing is necessary.

We do this check for century information by letting Visual Basic temporarily convert the expression to a Date; then we look for the year of the resulting date within the original expression. If it is found, the expression is safe and can be converted as is. If not, the date will need a window applied to assign it a century before the final conversion.

We must deal with one special case at this stage. Currently there is a date, Feb 29 00 (or some similar format), that the existing Visual Basic/OLEAUT32 window will interpret as Feb 29 2000, which is a valid date. Those of you who have tried entering this particular date into the older 16-bit versions of Visual Basic might have found that it is rejected as invalid. This is because it was interpreted as Feb 29 1900, which—if you have been paying attention—you know never existed. While this will not be an issue with the current window, only one in four possible interpretations of Feb 29 00 is actually a valid date. Therefore we have some code to account for this expression that might be rejected when we use Visual Basic to perform this temporary interpretation for us, but that we can interpret differently later in the routine. We do this by replacing the 00 for the year with 2000 so that it can be interpreted successfully by Visual Basic, regardless of the window applied.

If the expression does not contain the century, we will have to do some work. To avoid the default window we have to make sure that the date has a century before the final conversion. Here all we do is temporarily convert the expression to a Date, which we immediately break down into its constituent year, month, day, and time parts. The year is the only one that is of concern, so we remove any century that Visual Basic has assigned, and assign the correct century from our own window, which is calculated as 100 years starting from the current system date minus the offset to the pivot year. Once this is done we reassemble the four parts of the date, including the new year, and finally let Visual Basic perform the final conversion to the Date.

All of this probably seems quite long-winded, but the effort is well worth the flexibility that it gives you to specify your own date interpretation window.

In use, this function is a simple replacement for the date assignment functions *CDate*, *CVDate*, and *DateValue*, as shown in the code below. You can also use this same algorithm to create a function to replace the *DateSerial* function.

```
Dim dteMyDate      As Date

' Convert the ambiguous expression to "04/16/2035".
dteMyDate = dteCSafeDate("04/16/35", -50)
MsgBox FormatDateTime$(dteMyDate, vbLongDate)
```

More on assignments: implicit coercion

So the good news is that if everybody in your organization uses the *dteCSafe-Date* function to do their date conversions, the interpretation will be looked after for you in a way that is superior to the default. Oh, if only everything was that simple.

One of the strongest criticisms currently aimed at Visual Basic is that it is weakly typed. That doesn't mean I'm criticizing your keyboard skills<g>. It means that data can be coerced from one type to another very easily. Other languages such as Pascal, and to a certain extent C and C++, make you explicitly perform type conversion, also known as casting. Visual Basic is too helpful—it will do the conversion for you.

This isn't always as good an idea as it first sounds. Sure, it is one less thing for you to worry about. If you want to make an assignment, Visual Basic will be there to help you along. But try this one on for size:

```
Dim A    As Integer
Dim B    As Single

B = 3.1415926
A = B * 2

MsgBox A
```

And the answer is...6. If you assign a real number to an Integer, Visual Basic will assume you mean it, and discard the fraction. We refer to this as implicit conversion. You probably worked this one out as you typed it in, but what if the declarations were in separate parts of the application, or one of them was a public property of a component? Faults like this are among the most difficult to trace that you will come across, and Visual Basic makes them easy to create. A strongly typed language would have prevented you from assigning a Single directly to an Integer by producing an error at compile time, forcing you to convert the data explicitly.

The relevance of this type conversion to the Date issue is that you can implicitly convert other data types to Dates within Visual Basic just as easily. We have covered the explicit conversions with the *dteCSafeDate* function, but this function will sit idly on the bench if there is code making direct assignments to Dates. The following code illustrates this perfectly:

```
Dim dteDate1    As Date
Dim dteDate2    As Date

' Include the dteCSafeDate function shown above.
dteDate1 = dteCSafeDate("12/04/35", -50)
dteDate2 = "12/04/35"
MsgBox DateDiff("d", dteDate1, dteDate2)
```

Just looking at the code you would expect to see 0 displayed. When you actually see −36525 displayed you might be a little surprised, especially as this sort of thing will be an intermittent fault. If I had used the date 12/04/98, the response would be 0. This is due to the differences in the date windows used. When Visual Basic executes the line of code *dteDate2 = "12/04/35"* it does an implicit *CDate("12/04/35")* for us, whether we wanted it to or not.

One way to get around this fault is to add a new data type to the language, the CSafeDate class. This is a class module that contains a Date data type internally, but allows you to perform additional functionality when an assignment is made via the Property Procedures, in this case applying our own sliding window algorithm to expand any ambiguous dates as they are assigned. Listing 8-2 shows an implementation of the CSafeDate class (minus a private copy of the *dteCSafeDate* function). The *DateValue* property is set to be the default, allowing us to use the class in a way that is very similar to a standard Date.

```
Option Explicit

Private m_dteInternalDate        As Date
Private m_iPivotOffset           As Integer
Private m_bWindowed              As Boolean
Private Const ERROR_TYPE_MISMATCH   As Long = 13

Private Sub Class_Initialize()
    ' Initialize this class' internal properties.
    m_iPivotOffset = -50
End Sub


Public Property Get DateValue() As Variant
    DateValue = m_dteInternalDate
End Property


Public Property Let DateValue(ByVal vNewValue As Variant)
    ' Assign the passed expression to the internally
    ' held VB Date. If it cannot be assigned, dteCSafeDate
    ' will raise a Type Mismatch Error.
    m_dteInternalDate = dteCSafeDate(vNewValue, m_iPivotOffset, _
                                     m_bWindowed)
End Property


Public Property Get PivotOffset() As Integer
    PivotOffset = m_iPivotOffset
End Property


Public Property Let PivotOffset(ByVal iiOffset As Integer)
    m_iPivotOffset = iiOffset
End Property


Public Property Get IsWindowed() As Boolean
    IsWindowed = m_bWindowed
End Property
```

LISTING 8-2   *The CSafeDate class*

LISTING 8-2

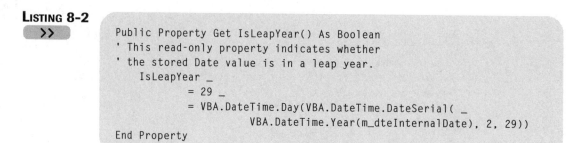

```
Public Property Get IsLeapYear() As Boolean
' This read-only property indicates whether
' the stored Date value is in a leap year.
    IsLeapYear _
            = 29 _
            = VBA.DateTime.Day(VBA.DateTime.DateSerial( _
                        VBA.DateTime.Year(m_dteInternalDate), 2, 29))
End Property
```

The CSafeDate class allows us to apply the same algorithm to dates that are implicitly assigned as to those that are explicitly assigned, using the *dteCSafe-Date* function. If you compare the following code fragment to the code on page 366, you'll see that they look very similar. This time the result of the *DateDiff* function is the expected 0. Both dates are expanded to the year 2035.

```
Dim dteDate1    As New CSafeDate
Dim dteDate2    As New CSafeDate

' Include the dteCSafeDate function
' and the CSafeDate Class.
dteDate1.DateValue = dteCSafeDate("12/04/35", -50)
dteDate2.DateValue = "12/04/35"
MsgBox DateDiff("d", dteDate1.DateValue, dteDate2.DateValue)
```

NOTE

I am issuing a call to arms. I would like to see an addition to the next version of the language, a new option. My suggestion would be "Option StrictTypes" so that professional developers like you and me can make the language switch off this easy coercion. If I am assigning a Single to an Integer, I want to know about it and I want to be made to wrap the assignment in a *CInt* before I can success-fully compile my code. If any of you agree, tell Microsoft, and we at TMS will too.

Unfortunately we are still not finished. There is one last area where implicit coercion can occur. Consider the following code segment:

```
MsgBox Year("Feb/25/25")
```

This is perfectly valid Visual Basic syntax. If you were to write the declaration for the *Year* function, it would look something like the following:

```
Public Function Year(Date As Date) As Integer
```

The danger sign here is the argument *Date As Date*; if you provide an expression that Visual Basic can convert to a date, it will do it for you. Again the language steps in and performs a quiet implicit coercion for you. So if we really want to do a thorough job in replacing Visual Basic's date windowing, we are going to have to do something about this.

A look at subclassing

A feature of Visual Basic that is often overlooked is the ability to subclass many of Visual Basic's native functions. What do we mean by subclassing? Well, I'm sure any object-orientation guru can give you a wonderful explanation full of four-, five-, and six-syllable words all ending in "tion" or "ism," but that is not the role of this chapter. In this instance subclassing means that we are taking a function that exhibits a known behavior and reimplementing and possibly modifying its behavior while keeping the external interface unchanged.

Subclassing is possible because of the way the language is structured. The built-in functions are actually methods and in some cases properties of the VBA library and its subordinates. Earlier in this chapter we looked at the various date functions built into the language and their locations. You can use the Object Browser from within the Visual Basic IDE to view these functions at their locations within the VBA modules and classes. (You can open the Object Browser by pressing the F2 function key on your keyboard.) When you make a call to one of these functions, you generally just specify its name and arguments, not its location. If you take the previous example of the *Year* function, you'll see you don't call the function as *VBA.DateTime.Year*. Because you don't specify the location in the function call, Visual Basic has to search for the function, starting with the closest scope first: the current module. If that search fails, Visual Basic will look at public methods of the other code components within the current project. If this also fails, it will finally look at the referenced objects that are listed in the References dialog box, starting at the top with the three Visual Basic libraries, which is where the built-in implementation of these Date functions resides.

From the example above you can see that if you write a function called *Year* within your application, and it is within scope when you make a call to the *Year* function, your version will be called in preference to *VBA.DateTime.Year*. In practice this means we can "improve" certain areas of the language without forcing changes to any of the code that makes use of it. Visual Basic's date logic is one such area. So guess what we are going to do!

Wouldn't it be great if we could write *CVDate*, *CDate*, and *DateValue* functions that apply our own sliding window algorithms instead of the original fixed window? This is a perfect case for subclassing, so let's give it a go. Take the above *dteCSafeDate* function and rename it *CVDate*. It works. So does renaming it *DateValue*, but if you try to rename it to *CDate* you immediately get the nasty compile error shown in Figure 8-5.

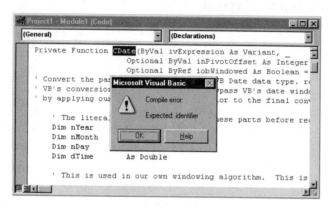

FIGURE 8-5 *Compile error when trying to subclass* CDate

You cannot currently subclass *CDate*. If you try, Visual Basic gives you a wonderfully lucid error. This is unfortunate, because subclassing works for many of the functions built into the language, and is a great way of seamlessly extending it. The ability to subclass has been in the product since Visual Basic 4, and Microsoft is not unaware of the fact that *CDate* has been overlooked; however, in Visual Basic 6 it is still not fixed.

As it turns out, there is a reason that *CDate* still can't be subclassed. It's because *CDate* is a cast operator and as such doesn't have a VBA helper function—it's *really* built in. *CDbl*, *CLng CInt*, and so forth don't work for the same reason. *CVDate* works because it's a wrapper around the "internal" routine—it's a helper! Microsoft knows this is a problem and that it's inconsistent across Visual Basic 4, Visual Basic 5, and Visual Basic 6. They haven't promised a fix, because they say that going through the helpers slows up the code (which is most likely true). Developers need to put the pressure on.

That was the bad news. The good news is that the majority of the other date functions can be subclassed. We have already shown that it is possible to subclass *CVDate* and *DateValue*. The other functions discussed in the chapter so far that you cannot subclass in this way are *Format$* and *Format*, because VBA is being rather clever in providing you with two functions with the same name. If you provide a third it gets very confused. And you cannot subclass the Date properties *Gets* and *Lets*. Because Date is a Visual Basic reserved word it will not let you use the word Date for anything other than declaring a Date variable. Although even if that was not the case, you would probably run into the same problem as with *Format* and *Format$* since you have matching *Date* and *Date$* properties.

Still, there is a great deal of scope for providing your own implementations of the remaining functions. Listing 8-3 shows a subclassed *Year* function. The key to this implementation is that our version of the *Year* function accepts a Variant as an argument, not the Date data type of the original. By using a Variant in this way we are not forcing Visual Basic to coerce the expressions into a Date when we call the function—the Variant just lets it through as is. Once the expression is in, we assign it to a local *CSafeDate* variable that will apply any expansion necessary, and we get a fully expanded date to pass to the original *VBA.DateTime.Year* function. All we are really doing is making sure any date expression is unambiguous before calling the original function.

```
Public Function Year(ByRef DateExpression As Variant) As Integer
'----------------------------------------------------------------
'   Replaces the Year function, applying a better date window.
'----------------------------------------------------------------

    Dim dteTempDate         As New CSafeDate

    ' Convert the passed expression to a SafeDate.
    ' If the expression is invalid we will get a Type
    ' Mismatch error, which we echo back to the calling code.
    dteTempDate.DateValue = DateExpression

    ' Now we have a fully expanded date; call the VB function.
    Year = VBA.DateTime.Year(dteTempDate.DateValue)

    Set dteTempDate = Nothing

End Function
```

Listing 8-3   *Subclassing the* Year *function*

This book's companion CD contains a WindowedDates project that contains two files, the CSafeDate class, and a module containing an implementation of every date function in which it is possible to subclass the original. This project is located in the Chap08\SubClass Windowed folder.

Sometimes You Have to Get Strict

The previous pages have introduced a number of elements that when used together provide a nearly complete way of applying a better windowing algorithm than that provided by default. You can take an alternative track here. Instead of trying to make the language more flexible, you can make it stricter by using a class and subclassed functions in the same way as before. This time, however, you'll reject any date expressions that do not have any century information in them.

At the center of this strategy is an algorithm that can tell whether a date expression has a century in it. Listing 8-4 shows the CStrictDate class that uses this algorithm to test any expressions as they are assigned, rejecting those that fail its test. This class can be used in place of the Date data type to enforce a strict policy of Year 2000 compliance on all dates stored. The class will reject the assignment of a date expression where the century information is not present.

At the center of this class is the *bPiIsStrictDate* function, which performs a job similar to Visual Basic's *IsDate* function. In the case of *bPiIsStrictDate*, an extra test is performed to make sure that the passed expression not only can be converted to a Date, but is also unambiguous.

```
'-----------------------------------------------------
' This is an implementation of a Strict Date data type.
' In this class, only valid and unambiguous dates are
' stored. If an assignment is attempted using an
' ambiguous date expression such as '02/02/98,' this
' is rejected as if it were an invalid value.
'-----------------------------------------------------

Option Explicit

' This is where the date is actually stored.
' As all dates this defaults to '1899-12-30'.
Private m_dteInternalDate        As Date

' This is the error that is raised if an attempt is
' made to assign an invalid date (as VB's Date does).
Private Const ERROR_TYPE_MISMATCH   As Long = 13


Private Function bPiIsStrictDate(ByVal Expression As Variant) _
                                As Boolean
'-----------------------------------------------------
' This function will return true if the passed
' date expression is a valid and unambiguous date.
' If the expression is either ambiguous or
' invalid, it will return false.
'-----------------------------------------------------


    Dim bIsDate      As Boolean

    ' OK, VB can do the hard work. Can this value
    ' be converted to a date?
    bIsDate = VBA.Information.IsDate(Expression)

    ' Additional check if the literal is a string.
    ' Is it an ambiguous date?
    If bIsDate = True And VarType(Expression) = vbString Then

        ' Search for the year within the passed string literal.
        If 0 = InStr(1, _
            VBA.Conversion.CStr(Expression), _
            VBA.DateTime.Year(VBA.Conversion.CDate(Expression)), _
            vbTextCompare) Then
```

>>

LISTING 8-4   *The CStrictDate Class*

LISTING 8-4

```
                    ' We could not find the full 4-digit year in the
                    ' passed literal; therefore the date is ambiguous
                    ' and so we mark it as invalid.
                    bIsDate = False
            End If
        End If

        ' Return whether this is a valid date or not.
        bPiIsStrictDate = bIsDate
End Function


Public Property Get DateValue() As Variant

        ' Return the date value stored internally.
        DateValue = m_dteInternalDate

End Property


Public Property Let DateValue(ByVal Expression As Variant)

        If bPiIsStrictDate(Expression) Then

                ' If the date expression does conform to our
                ' validation rules, store it.
                m_dteInternalDate = VBA.Conversion.CDate(Expression)

            Else

                ' Otherwise emulate VB and raise a standard error.
                Err.Raise ERROR_TYPE_MISMATCH
        End If
End Property

Public Property Get IsLeapYear() As Boolean
'-------------------------------------------
' This read-only property indicates
' whether the stored Date value is in
' a leap year.
'-------------------------------------------

        IsLeapYear = 29 _
                = VBA.DateTime.Day(VBA.DateTime.DateSerial( _
                VBA.DateTime.Year(m_dteInternalDate), 2, 29))

End Property
```

Being Seen with Your Dates
in Public: User Interface Issues

As I've stated earlier in this chapter, the biggest source of noncompliant dates is on the other side of the keyboard. You are most definitely not going to find a Year-2000–compliant sticker on your average user. This leaves us with some work to do. How do we both display dates and allow users to enter dates in a way that does not compromise our hard-won compliance?

Displaying Date Information

Your best course of action here is to always use the default formats when displaying dates. Within your applications this means using the *FormatDateTime* function with either vbGeneralDate or vbLongDate. Because the Short Date format generally lacks four-digit year information, avoid using vbShortDate unless space is at a premium.

By using these formats you are following standard conventions for the display of date information within the Windows environment. Users expect to see dates displayed in this way, and they expect any changes they have made through the Control Panel to be reflected across all applications. This will also make your applications friendlier to foreign markets in which the date formats might be different.

Date Entry

What is the best way of allowing users to enter dates into your applications? Sorry, there are no easy answers here. Ideally, we would like to force them to enter all dates complete with century information. In practice this isn't always a vote-winner with user groups. It might only be two extra keystrokes per date, but if you are a data entry clerk keying a thousand records a day, each record containing three date fields, that's six thousand additional keystrokes.

Simple text fields

You can enter dates in a couple of ways. The first is to use a simple TextBox control, and either write code within its events to validate a date entered, or write a new control around it. This approach has the benefit of being totally within your control (no pun intended). You can apply any rules you want because you are writing the implementation. There are a number of things to remember when taking this route.

- Never trap the input focus in the date TextBox control. If the date is invalid, don't force users to correct it before allowing them to move to another control— they might be trying to cancel an edit.

- Never force users to enter the date in a noncompliant way. Don't laugh—I have seen applications where users could only enter the date as "ddMMyy"!

- If you allow entry in a noncompliant format, always echo the date back to the input fields as soon as it has been expanded, showing the century you have applied. This allows users a chance to re-enter the date in full if they do not agree with your expansion algorithm.

NOTE

For a closer look at implementing your own date entry control see Chapter 14 by Chris De Bellott and myself. We discuss the design and implementation of a simple date entry control of just this type.

The DateTimePicker and MonthView controls

New additions to the latest version of Visual Basic are the DateTimePicker (DTPicker) and MonthView controls. Both of these can be found in the Microsoft Windows Common Controls–2 6.0 component. Either control can be used for date entry and display.

The DateTimePicker control, shown in Figure 8-6, works similarly to a drop-down combo box: users can enter information directly into the text field at the top, or if they prefer they can use the drop down to reveal a Picker from which they can select their date. The control can also be used for the display and input of time information by setting its *Format* property to dtpTime, in which case the dropdown combo box is replaced by a Spin control. You can also replace the combo box with the spinner for the date display by setting the DateTime-Picker control's *UpDown* property to True. The chosen date or time is made available to you through the control's *Value* property as a Date data type.

NOTE

When using a custom format with the DateTimePicker control, be careful to specify the month part with an upper-case *M*. If you use a lower-case *m*, the control will display minute information where you expected the month to be. This can lead to some very obscure results, such as 00/28/1998 if you set the custom format to mm/dd/yyyy.

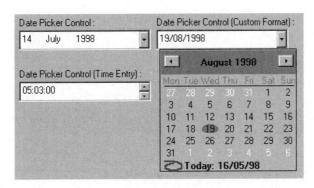

FIGURE 8-6   *Three implementations of the Microsoft DateTimePicker control*

The MonthView control, shown in Figure 8-7, is a much simpler proposition. This control gives you a view similar to the Picker of the DateTimePicker control. The user can select a date using the mouse or the cursor keys; there is no facility for typing dates in directly. Two nice features are the ability to display more than one month at a time, and the ability to select a range of dates.

FIGURE 8-7   *Two implementations of the Microsoft MonthView control*

More alternatives

Before you resort to purchasing a third-party control, there are a couple more options for you to consider. The first is a source-code control shipped with the Microsoft Visual Studio 98 Enterprise Edition (Disc 3), the Visual Studio 98 Professional Edition (Disc 2), and the Visual Basic 6 Enterprise and Professional Editions (Disc1), all at the location \Common\Tools\VB\Unsupprt\Calendar. You could use this control as the basis of your own "corporatedate" entry control with the advantage of having access to the source code so that you can be sure it is compliant. There is nothing to stop you from including the CSafe-Date class and the subclassed date functions within this control to take advantage of the improved windowing we looked at earlier in this chapter.

The other alternative is shipped with Microsoft Office 97 Professional. This is the MSCal control, which gives you a view similar to the MonthView control.

NOTE

> With all these controls, and any third-party ones you are interested in, you must perform a thorough acceptance test before clearing them for use. We're not going to recommend any particular control, purely because we feel that you have to perform these tests yourself.

THE YEAR 2000 DATEBOX CONTROL

With the added burden of Year 2000 data-entry validation, development teams might well resort to third-party controls for date display and entry. There are a number of alternative options available when it comes to date validation. However, these will undoubtedly mean having to write validation code that must be used in every part of the application that reads or displays a date. More coding effort will be required to ensure consistency than if a custom control were to be used.

If you opt for a third-party control, it is important to evaluate the control thoroughly. Do not assume that because the control is sold commercially it will be Year 2000 compliant. It might not be! Your organization might have a set of Year 2000 guidelines. If not, adopt some. The guidelines in this chapter are compliant with most industry standards including the British Standards Institute (BSI). Once you have some guidelines to follow you should test any prospective date control against those standards. I would strongly suggest rejection of controls that fail—do not rely on updates to fix problems because you might compromise the integrity of your data before an update is available.

Some developers will prefer to write a custom date control to meet specific needs. This can be a good solution if you have requirements that cannot be met by other commercial components, or if ownership of code is desired to enable future enhancements. The DateBox control described in Chapter 14 is an example of a compliant date control that provides a number of features:

- Date entry is made easy for users by allowing them to enter a date in any format, e.g. 5/2/1998 or May 2 1998.

- The control forces users to enter a 4-digit year regardless of the date format used—Long Date or Short Date.

- Incorrect dates are displayed in configurable highlighted colors so users are aware that the input contains an error.

>>

>>

- The control is configurable so that errors are not reported until the application attempts to use the date. This avoids users having to break their flow—they can fix errors when they want to.

- The control is not capable of returning an invalid date; instead, a trappable error is raised.

The DateBox control uses a Date type for the date property that prevents errors from being introduced if a date is coerced from a String type to a Date type. Obviously, in many cases an application must accept a Null value or a blank date—if a field is not mandatory, for example. These instances are allowed for by an additional property, *DateVariant*, which is a Variant type and can be data-bound. The *DateVariant* property can be set to any value; however, when the property is read-only, valid dates, a Null, or Empty can be returned—any invalid value causes a validation error.

Programmers suffer a common frustration when a third-party control offers only a percentage of the desired functionality. Achieving that other *x* percent usually requires a work-around or more commonly, a kludge! The DateBox control has some additional useful features. It allows you to disable weekdays; for example, you can stipulate that Sunday is not a valid day. You can also set a *CancelControl* property. What's that, you ask? The DateBox has an *ErrorKeep-Focus* property, which as the name suggests causes the control to regain focus if the user attempts to leave the control when it has an invalid date. Obviously, this would cause problems if the user wanted to hit the Cancel button! Therefore, setting *CancelControl* to your form's Cancel button allows DateBox to lose focus only to that control.

Chapter 14 provides a detailed overview of the DateBox design and covers some broader issues dealing with ActiveX controls in general.

WHERE TO TAKE YOUR DATES: STORAGE ISSUES

Love it or loathe it, most of the work Visual Basic is called upon to perform is to provide a front end to a database. The different database products all have different capabilities and storage patterns. Not all have a native Date or DateTime field type, and some of those that do have ones that could not be considered Y2K-friendly.

Working with Databases

Currently this field of database technology is being reshaped almost daily, as new technologies, or new versions of older technologies, emerge. Most of your database work will be done through a proprietary API, DAO, RDO, ADO, or ODBC. The latter three all depend to some extent on an additional driver layer that might be sourced from a third party. As with controls, you must perform thorough acceptance testing on any middleware that you use.

SQL issues

A major issue when working with SQL, especially if you work outside the United States, is that of date formats in your statements. The SQL standard is to use a U.S. format MM/dd/yyyy date. Certainly in other countries, such as the U.K., this format can lead to some confusion if you forget to modify the date to provide it in the U.K. format of dd/MM/yyyy. The following code shows a function for formatting any date in an SQL statement.

```
Public Function sFormatDateForSQL(ByVal idtDate As Date) As String

    ' Convert the passed Date to a string in the
    ' US format, suitable for using in an SQL Statement.
    sFormatDateForSQL = Format$(idtDate, "MM/dd/yyyy")
End Function
```

Storage patterns for legacy platforms

Wherever possible use the native date format provided by the database product. Most of the latest versions of the most popular products support dates well into the next millennium and beyond. Where a date field is not available, or is not capable of Year 2000 compliance, we will need a little cunning. Here's a look at a couple of storage patterns we can use.

Double-precision numbers   By storing your dates as double-precision numbers, you render them immediately compatible with Visual Basic's Date data type. Double-precision numbers can store time as well as date information.

***TimeSince* methods**   An alternative to the above idea is to store your dates as a Long integer containing the number of seconds, minutes, or days since a defined base date. This base will be a date such as midnight, January 1, 1980, or midnight, January 1, 2000. Conversions to and from this format can be performed using the *DateDiff* and *DateAdd* functions discussed earlier in this chapter. The following code shows an implementation of *TimeSince* methods. This implementation provides functions to convert a Date to and from a Long, using a base date of January 1, 2000.

```
Const BASE_DATE    As Date = #1/1/2000# ' Base date is 2000-01-01.
Const INTERVAL     As String = "n"      ' Interval is minutes.


Public Function lDateToTimeSince(ByVal idteDate As Date) As Long

    ' Convert the passed date and time to a Long integer
    ' containing the minutes elapsed since the base date.
    LDateToTimeSince = DateDiff(INTERVAL, BASE_DATE, idteDate)
End Function


Public Function dtDateFromTimeSince(ByVal ilMinutes As Long) As Date

    ' Convert the passed Long integer to a Date as
    ' the number of minutes since the base date.
    DtDateFromTimeSince = DateAdd(INTERVAL, ilMinutes, BASE_DATE)
End Function
```

Obviously, the choice of time interval dictates the date range available, but even if we use seconds we have a range of approximately 135 years (slightly less than 68 years before and after the base date). If storing time is not important or space is at a premium, we can use days as a time interval and store our date as a short Integer.

NOTE

This technique is actually mimicking the storage format employed by Visual Basic itself, but with a lower storage overhead. Visual Basic uses an 8-byte double-precision number to store the number of seconds before or since midnight December 30 1899. We save space by choosing a more recent base date and a more coarse time measurement.

Both the double-precision and *TimeSince* methods have the added bonus of being numeric data, which is considerably faster for a database to sort, search, and index than alphanumeric data.

WHEN IT'S TIME TO MOVE ON: MIGRATION ISSUES

A great deal of work currently being carried out in the Visual Basic world is the rewriting of applications previously written in the earlier versions of the language. This section looks at the differences between the various versions of the language and some of the date issues you can encounter. The table below summarizes the date-handling features of the different versions of Visual Basic.

Visual Basic Version	Date Data Type?	New Functions	Date Window	Other Issues
1	No	*DateValue, DateSerial, IsDate, Day, Month, Year, Weekday, Date($), Now, TimeValue, TimeSerial, Hour, Minute, Second, Time($), Timer, Format($)*	1900–1999	No native date storage. Dates either stored as Strings or Doubles.
2	Variant (Type 7)	*CVDate*	1900–1999	
3	Variant (Type 7)	*DateDiff, DateAdd, DatePart*	1900–1999	
4 (16-bit)	Date	*CDate, Weekday,* and *DatePart* updated to include optional *FirstDayOfWeek* and *FirstWeekOf-Year* argument	Current century	
4 (32-bit)	Date	*CDate, Weekday,* and *DatePart* updated to include optional *FirstDayOfWeek* and *FirstWeekOfYear* argument.	OLEAUT32	*DateSerial* does not use OLEAUT32; it uses a current century window similar to 16-bit version 4.
5	Date		OLEAUT32	
6	Date	*FormatDateTime, MonthName, WeekdayName*	OLEAUT32	

The basic split is between the 16-bit and 32-bit versions of the language. If you are migrating your code from a previous 32-bit version of the language, the date logic will work unchanged. However, if you are moving from a 16-bit version, there are some differences. The most significant difference is the complete lack of a built-in Date data type in the first version.

Note

> The 32-bit implementation of Visual Basic 4 has a strange anomaly. In this implementation the *DateSerial* function does not use the same date window as the *CDate* and *CVDate* functions, provided by OLEAUT32. *DateSerial* uses the same current century window as the 16-bit implementation of version 4. This is the only time in all the versions of Visual Basic that these functions might provide different results.

If you are migrating your code from Visual Basic 1 to Visual Basic 6, you will most likely have to deal with date storage based around Strings, with any manipulation logic having been hand-written. The quality of this logic will very much depend on the original author, but it should always be treated with suspicion. It is guilty until proven innocent, because this code would have been written in the late eighties and early nineties, when the world was only just starting to wake up to the Y2K problem. At the very least, the leap year logic will be suspect.

Migrating from code written in Visual Basic 2 and Visual Basic 3 will be more common than from Visual Basic 1. Here you might be lucky: when well written, code in these versions can be very compliant. The Variant data type did (and still does) store dates in the same format as the newer Date data type. These versions have the full complement of supporting conversion and manipulation functions. Unfortunately, there has been a real lack of awareness of the Variant type's existence for use with dates. Just as with code from Visual Basic 1, you might have to work with code that stores dates in Strings. I still come across very recent Visual Basic 3 code that is not in the least bit Year 2000 compliant (in some cases within compliance projects!).

If you have been lucky and the original author used the Variant data type, be aware of the original date window. These versions will always assume the 20th century for ambiguous dates. Any code that relies on this behavior will be in for a surprise when ported to the latest version.

Visual Basic 4 is easier to migrate from than the previous three versions. This one supports the Date data type, and from my experience most code will have been written using it. Here the only issue is the date window. The 16-bit implementation of this version uses a date window that assumes the current century for an ambiguous date. The 32-bit version uses the window provided by

OLEAUT32, although at the time of this version's release OLEAUT32 also assumed current century.

There is no real difference between Visual Basic 5 and Visual Basic 6 in terms of date usage other than the additional functions and controls available to you in version 6.

In all cases, any code you port will be as good as the original author's. We have had the tools to store and manipulate dates since version 3; however, these tools have not always been used. Even today noncompliant applications are still being produced.

What to Look Out for When Renovating Old Code

This section lists a few of the problems that can crop up when you're updating existing code.

Sorting on dates

Sorting dates will be one of the main areas where noncompliant date formats will become readily apparent to anybody. If we take, for example, the YYMMDD alphanumeric date format, it is fairly obvious that when this format starts finding dates with the year 00 these are going to be sorted before all other years. Sorting reports or displays on dates is not an uncommon feature of computer systems. This can generally be thought of as a cosmetic problem, but it can be a very visible barometer of more serious and far less visible problems lurking beneath the surface.

Dates manipulated as strings

When reviewing code written in the earlier versions of Visual Basic, we often see date manipulations carried out on Strings. Take the following piece of code:

```
Dim dteMyDate    As Date
Dim nYear        As Integer

dteMyDate = Now

nYear = Val(Right$(Format$(dteMyDate, "Long Date"), 4))

If nYear > 1999 Then
    MsgBox "Welcome to the Twenty First Century!"
End If
```

This will work, unless of course somebody has changed the format of the Long Date in the regional settings of the Control Panel. If the original programmer was more enlightened, you might see something like this:

```
nYear = Val(Format$(dteMyDate, "yyyy"))
```

Here the programmer is explicitly stating the format in which he or she would like the date to be used. If you are really lucky you might actually see the following code, which correctly avoids the conversion to a String altogether by employing Visual Basic's *Year* function:

```
nYear = Year(dteMyDate)
```

Using Visual Basic's Find dialog box can be quite revealing here. Just searching on Long Date, Short Date, Mid, Right, Left, and Format—while somewhat indiscriminate—can be very revealing. The first example above is not uncommon.

Most of the compliance problems in Visual Basic applications can eventually lead us back to the manipulation of dates as strings. This must be treated with extreme mistrust. Your first task when renovating this code must be to replace this code based around strings with the built-in date functions operating on Date data types.

Look for dates used as magic numbers

Magic number dates are date values that are used as a system indicator. Dates such as 9/9/99, 12/31/99, or 999999 are common examples. These might be used to indicate such things as records that never expire, locked or deleted records, or records that must always be displayed at the start or end of a list. They work fine until the magic date occurs, then all sorts of strange behavior can follow. Again, by using the Find dialog box, searching for these strings can be most illuminating.

Testing

Without a doubt, the Y2K problem has highlighted the importance of testing. Even if you don't convert any code, you should, at the very least, test all your Visual Basic applications to ensure that they are Year 2000 compliant.

If you have made changes, perform regression testing wherever possible, using the original test scripts for each application. If you don't have access to the original test scripts, you should attempt to test the functionality of the entire application, regardless of whether certain functionality uses date processing. This step is necessary because various changes at any level of the application could have a domino effect (for any number of reasons) on any other application functionality. Testing only the changes is not good enough.

Ensure that all test conditions and the results from all testing are well documented. The testing tasks and issues described in the following subsections might help you formulate your testing plan.

Test the user interface and third-party controls

As I have mentioned, calendar controls are at the top of the hit list for potential Y2K horror stories. There are too many commercial calendar controls for this book to cover individually, and I wouldn't be surprised if many of the existing calendars are updated to new versions fairly soon.

So if your application uses a calendar, and even if you have a new Year 2000 compliant version of that calendar, give it a good hammering. Test all conceivable scenarios. Leave no stone unturned. When testing the user interface there are a number of key dates you should test in as many different formats as possible. The table below shows a list of dates that you should use in your testing.

Valid		Invalid	Ambiguous
Dec 31 1998	Jan 1 1999	Feb 29 1900	Jan 1 00
Feb 27 1999	Feb 28 1999	Feb 29 1999	Jan 1 99
Mar 1 1999	Sep 9 1999	Feb 30 2000	Feb 29 00
Dec 31 1999	Jan 1 2000	Feb 29 2001	Jan 1 29
Feb 28 2000	Feb 29 2000	Feb 30 2004	Jan 1 30
Mar 1 2000	Dec 31 2000		
Jan 1 2001	Feb 28 2001		
Mar 1 2001	Feb 28 2004		
Feb 29 2004	Mar 1 2004		

Test Data and Conditions

Testing for the Year 2000 Problem won't be like any testing that you've done before. Here's why: in order to be 100 percent certain that your business can survive into the year 2000, you'll need to execute three completely separate system tests dealing with three sets of test data, and more than likely (depending on the size of your organization), each of these three tests will be in a different testing environment.

Regression testing of today's production environment

Having made changes to your current system, your next task is to test that all programs function as expected for the current time frame. In other words, you want to be certain that your business can continue to use its Visual Basic applications with no unexpected side effects.

In effect, this test will ensure that the systems work exactly as they did when they were originally built. This test might sound counterproductive to begin with, but it's no good announcing to the world that all your applications are Year 2000 compliant if they come crashing to their knees!

Future date testing

Having verified that your system functions correctly in the present, you'll need to create a second set of test data that will test your system's ability to cope with dates on either side of the year 2000. The particulars for this test will depend entirely on the business nature of your applications.

For example, let's suppose that your Visual Basic application maintains car insurance policies, which typically can have a life cycle of 12 months. You'll need to set your system clock to some time in 1999 and run your tests, this time looking specifically for the application's ability to process car insurance policies that will expire in the year 2000.

Your business might have a shorter future date requirement, such as a long-term car parking system that has a maximum life cycle of 6 months. In this case, you would need to ensure that the system date is set to at least August 1999 so that you can adequately test processing into the year 2000.

And the list goes on. Make sure you thoroughly understand the future date capabilities and scope of your system. Then run your system so that it is forced to process future dates that are at least in the year 2000, if not later.

Running your system in the future

The final test involves gauging the ability of your applications to function in and beyond the year 2000. Set your system date to some time beyond 2000, and run your original test scripts. Don't forget that if your system processes historical information, you should have test conditions in which you set your system clock beyond 2000, and then force your applications to look at dates before 2000.

Leap years

Include in all three of your system tests conditions that will force your application to process the last two days in February and the first two days in March. The year 2000 is a leap year, which means that February 29 2000 is a valid date. Don't be caught out by this one. I've seen much debate from mathematicians and rocket scientists on the correct way to calculate leap years, and I've naturally researched the subject myself thoroughly enough to conclude that 2000 is a leap year. In fact, I nearly had a fight with my neighbor the other day because he wouldn't accept that February has 29 days in the year 2000!

The point I'm trying to make here is that if superhumans and neighbors can disagree on the number of days in February 2000, so can programmers! It's possible that during the development of your Visual Basic applications, a programmer might have manually calculated (incorrectly) that the year 2000 is *not* a leap year, so be sure to test for it.

Recommended system dates

If you're lucky (or wise), you'll have already built automated testing procedures that don't require too much manual intervention. Otherwise, somebody is going to get very sore fingers! In a perfect world, I would suggest running your complete system test against the following system date years: 1998, 1999, 2000, 2001, 2002, 2007.

Change Your System Date

Before we get into the techniques involved in changing your system date, be warned! Some system resources and functions are date- and time-sensitive and might be switched on or off when you change the system date. Before changing your system date, make sure that you understand all of the consequences. Better still, consult an expert first.

The tests you carry out with regard to the system date serve dual purposes. Not only are you testing the ability of your applications to function correctly in the year 2000 and beyond, you are also testing how well your hardware will cope with the change. Although the hardware issue is outside the scope of this chapter, it's still an important concern, because without the hardware... say no more!

In many cases, your system date will come from one of three places: from a date value in your database, from the clock on your server, or from the clock on your PC. Retrieving the current system date from the database is a very wise move. If your Visual Basic applications do this, resetting your system date is simply a matter of changing the value in the database. That's all there is to it. But you'll still need to test the ability of your machines to function in the year 2000, and we'll look at the steps involved with that in a moment.

If your applications retrieve the system date from the PC's clock and the PC is connected to a network, chances are that your workstation retrieves its system date from the server. In this case, you should definitely consult your network administrator about changing the system date. There is one way of changing the system date without being affected by the network, and that is to disconnect the PC from the network. If you disconnect your PC, however, you will probably defeat the whole purpose of the exercise, especially with regard to testing the hardware.

If your system date is retrieved only from the PC's clock, consider the fact that on some older PCs you might not be able to set the clock beyond the year 2000. This is because the BIOS doesn't know about centuries. Whatever the case, you should run the following two tests on your PC to judge both your application's functionality and your hardware's capabilities.

System clock automatic update test

In most cases, when the clock rolls over to start the year 2000, most of us will be popping party balloons, singing, and hugging loved ones (or as Mark Mayes said in the last edition, lying at the bottom of the garden caressing an empty bottle of vodka!). I expect very few office PCs will actually be turned on over the New Year's holiday (although it has been suggested that companies should leave them on just in case), and even fewer Visual Basic applications will be running. In the spirit of completeness, however, you should test to find out whether your PC's clock will actually roll over. To do so, follow these steps:

1. Using the DOS DATE function, set the PC's date to 12/31/1999.
2. Using the DOS TIME function, set the PC's clock to 11:58:00.00.
3. Keep the power on.
4. Wait until the clock passes midnight.
5. Check the date to ensure that it is 01/01/2000.
6. Test your Visual Basic application (if appropriate).
7. Turn off the power.
8. Wait for a while.
9. Turn on the power.
10. Check the date to ensure that it is still 01/01/2000.
11. Just for good measure, test your Visual Basic application again (if appropriate).

System clock automatic update test after a power down

The more likely scenario is that all office workers will go home on the evening of Friday, December 31, 1999, having switched off their machines, and will return on Tuesday, January 4, 2000. To ensure that the PC's clock will have successfully moved on to the correct date while the power was down, perform the following test:

1. Using the DOS DATE function, set the PC's date to 12/31/1999.
2. Using the DOS TIME function, set the PC's clock to 11:58:00.00.
3. Turn off the power.
4. Wait at least three minutes.
5. Turn on the power.
6. Check the date to ensure that it is January 1 2000.
7. Test your Visual Basic application (if appropriate).

There are countless more tasks and issues concerned with testing for Year 2000 compliance. I hope the issues I've raised will set you on your path toward creating the perfect test plan. The important thing is to be sensible about testing. Consider all possible scenarios, and don't cut corners.

Consider Third-Party Tools

With the deadline now looming dangerously close, companies are finding themselves working with very tight project deadlines in their migration and renovation projects. Time spent reviewing some of the available third-party tools can pay real dividends. While none of them should be considered a one stop "silver bullet," they can seriously affect your productivity. Tools such as Visual DateScope 2000 from Class Solutions Ltd. (see Appendix D for a full description) can provide you with just the edge you need when it comes to meeting that deadline.

FIND OUT MORE ABOUT YOUR DATE'S BACKGROUND

There is one last piece in the date jigsaw. Visual Basic relies on the underlying operating system for some of its date functionality—you have already seen how it takes its date windowing from the system file OLEAUT32.DLL and how the Short Date and Long Date are based on the Regional Settings in the Control Panel. Both of these dependencies can alter the way our applications interpret and report dates.

Unfortunately, Visual Basic does not make this information freely available to you and retrieving it can be a little tricky. Listing 8-5 is a module that provides functions to get this information from the system. This module contains functions that retrieve the Long Date and Short Date formats for the current System Locale. There is also a function to retrieve the version number of OLEAUT32.DLL and another to work out which date window it provides.

This information can be used in a number of ways. You could make it available on your application's About box. Alternatively, you can check it as part of your application's startup routines. If OLEAUT32.DLL's version number is not one you expect, you can abort the startup and display a message to the user telling him or her to contact the help desk.

NOTE

You can find this application on the companion CD in the Chap08\Date Environment folder.

```
Option Explicit

' Used to hold the date format passed to
' sPiEnumDateFormatsProc so that it can be passed to
' the GetLongDateFormat and GetShortDateFormat functions
Private m_sDateFormat    As String


Private Declare Function WinGetFileVersionInfo Lib "version.dll" _
                    Alias "GetFileVersionInfoA" _
                    (ByVal lptstrFilename As String, _
                    ByVal dwHandle As Long, _
                    ByVal dwLen As Long, _
                    ByVal lpData As String) As Long

Private Declare Function WinGetFileVersionInfoSize _
                    Lib "version.dll" _
                    Alias "GetFileVersionInfoSizeA" _
                    (ByVal lptstrFilename As String, _
                    lpdwHandle As Long) As Long
```

>>

LISTING 8-5   *The Date Information module*

LISTING 8-5

```
Private Declare Function WinEnumDateFormats Lib "kernel32" _
                        Alias "EnumDateFormatsA" _
                        (ByVal lpDateFmtEnumProc As Long, _
                        ByVal Locale As Long, _
                        ByVal dwFlags As Long) As Long

Private Declare Sub WinCopyMemory Lib "kernel32" _
                        Alias "RtlMoveMemory" _
                        (ByVal lpDestination As Any, _
                        ByVal lpSource As Long, _
                        ByVal Length As Long)

Private Declare Function Winlstrlen Lib "kernel32" _
                        Alias "lstrlenA" (ByVal lpString As Long) _
                        As Long

Private Const LOCALE_SYSTEM_DEFAULT     As Long = &H400
Private Const DATE_LONGDATE             As Long = &H2
Private Const DATE_SHORTDATE            As Long = &H1

Public Function GetLongDateFormat() As String
' 32-bit VB function to retrieve the system "Long Date" format

    ' Call the API routine that will enumerate the system date
    ' format. This will call back the bPiEnumDateFormatsProc
    ' routine in this module, passing it a string containing the
    ' Long Date format.
    Call WinEnumDateFormats(AddressOf bPiEnumDateFormatsProc, _
            LOCALE_SYSTEM_DEFAULT, DATE_LONGDATE)

    ' Return the date format that will have been stored module
    ' wide by the bPiEnumDateFormatsProc.
    GetLongDateFormat = m_sDateFormat
End Function

Public Function GetShortDateFormat() As String
' 32-bit VB function to retrieve the system "Short Date" format

    ' Call the API routine that will enumerate the system date
    ' format. This will call back the bPiEnumDateFormatsProc
    ' routine in this module, passing it a string containing
    ' the system Short Date format.
    Call WinEnumDateFormats(AddressOf bPiEnumDateFormatsProc, _
            LOCALE_SYSTEM_DEFAULT, DATE_SHORTDATE)
```

```vb
        ' Return the date format that will have been stored module
        ' wide by the routine bPiEnumDateFormatsProc.
        GetShortDateFormat = m_sDateFormat
End Function

Public Function GetOLEAUT32Version() As String
' 32-bit VB function to retrieve the string version number of
' the OLEAUT32.DLL to which our process is linked. The routine
' returns the string version number.

    Dim sVerInfo    As String
    Dim sVersion    As String
    Dim n           As Integer
    Dim nPos        As Integer
    Dim sVer        As String

    Const sOLEAUT32 As String = "OLEAUT32" ' Don't need the '.DLL'.
    Const sSEARCH   As String = "FILEVERSION"

    ' Allocate space for the string version information.
    SVerInfo = String$(WinGetFileVersionInfoSize(sOLEAUT32, 0), 0)

    ' Retrieve info. If sVerInfo is "" it's OK, we don't need to
    ' test it.
    If 0 <> WinGetFileVersionInfo(sOLEAUT32, 0, Len(sVerInfo), _
                                sVerInfo) Then

            ' We might have to search for the info twice, the first
            ' time as an ANSI string, and if that doesn't work,
            ' the second time as a Unicode string.
            For n = 1 To 2

                ' Copy the version info, converting it to ANSI
                ' from Unicode if this is the second attempt to
                ' get it.
                If n = 1 Then
                        sVersion = sVerInfo
                    Else
                        sVersion = StrConv(sVerInfo, vbFromUnicode)
                End If

                ' Got version stuff - search for 'file version'.
                ' This looks like :- FileVersion ?.?.?.?
                nPos = InStr(1, sVersion, sSEARCH, 1)
```

>>

LISTING 8-5

>>

```
                        ' If we found it.
                        If 0 <> nPos Then

                            ' The version comes after the 'FileVersion'
                            ' string so chop off everything until the first
                            ' byte of the version from the front of the
                            ' string.
                            sVersion = Trim$(Mid$(sVersion, nPos + _
                                             Len(sSEARCH)))

                            ' Clear any remaining leading NULLS.
                            Do While Left$(sVersion, 1) = vbNullChar
                                sVersion = Right$(sVersion, _
                                            Len(sVersion) - 1)
                            Loop

                            ' The version is terminated by a Null (Chr$(0)).
                            NPos = InStr(sVersion, vbNullChar)

                            ' Found the end so pull off nPos bytes
                            ' to get the version.
                            If 0 <> nPos Then
                                ' String version is ...
                                sVer = Left$(sVersion, nPos - 1)
                            End If
                        End If

                        ' If we are left with some text, the
                        ' Version Info was found.
                        If sVer <> "" Then Exit For
                    Next n
            End If

        ' Set function return value to the string version in full.
        GetOLEAUT32Version = sVersion
End Function

Private Function bPiEnumDateFormatsProc(ByVal lpstrFormat As Long) _
    As Long
' The address to this function is passed to the API function
' EnumDateFormatsA that will then call it, passing a pointer
' to a string containing the requested system Date format.

    ' Store the date format module wide, so that it can be
    ' read by the originating VB function. As the value passed
```

```
        ' to this function is a pointer to a string, something that VB
        ' does not directly understand, we use another function to
        ' retrieve the string that the pointer points to.
        m_sDateFormat = sPiGetStringFromPointerANSI(lpstrFormat)


        ' Return True, indicating that
        ' EnumDateFormatsA can continue enumerating.
        BpiEnumDateFormatsProc = True
End Function


Public Function GetSystemDateWindow() As Integer
' This routine calculates the extremes of the date window
' currently provided by OLEAUT32. It does this by finding
' where the century assigned to the years 0 to 99 changes.
        Dim nYear           As Integer
        Dim nWindowedYear   As Integer
        Dim nLastYear       As Integer


        '   Setup the initial year to compare to.
        NlastYear = Year(DateSerial(0, 1, 20))


        ' Setup the return value to default to the year assigned to
        ' "00". If this routine does not detect a shift in the century
        ' applied to the values 0 - 99, the window must start at
        ' the century.
        GetSystemDateWindow = nLastYear


        ' Go through each year in a single century 0 - 99. Look for
        ' a change in the century assigned to these years. This will
        ' be the pivot date, the bottom date in the date window.
        For nYear = 0 To 99
            nWindowedYear = Year(DateSerial(nYear, 1, 20))


            ' Compare the current year to the previous one; if the
            ' century assignment has changed we have the Pivot year.
            If (nWindowedYear \ 100) <> (nLastYear \ 100) Then
                GetSystemDateWindow = nWindowedYear
            End If


            NLastYear = nWindowedYear
        Next nYear
End Function


Private Function sPiGetStringFromPointerANSI _
                (ByVal lPointer As Long) As String
```

>>

LISTING 8-5

>>

```
' This function will return the text pointed to by the passed
' pointer. VB does not support pointers, which are often
' returned by API calls. This function might be used to retrieve
' a string passed to VB by an API call as a pointer.
    Dim sBuffer       As String
    Dim lSize         As Long

    ' Get the length of the string pointed to.
    lSize = Winlstrlen(lPointer)

    ' Size the destination, so that it is large enough.
    Sbuffer = String$(lSize + 1, vbNullChar)

    ' Copy the contents of the memory pointed to
    ' by the passed Long value into the Buffer.
    WinCopyMemory sBuffer, lPointer, lSize

    ' Return the contents of the buffer, up to
    ' the first NULL (Ascii 0) which will have been
    ' used by the API to indicate the end of the string.
    sPiGetStringFromPointerANSI = _
            Left$(sBuffer, InStr(sBuffer, vbNullChar))
End Function
```

The book's companion CD contains an ActiveX EXE project named DateInfo
that uses this module to provide this information as properties of a CDateInfo
class, once you have included SystemDateInfo in your application's references.
Additionally, because the project is an EXE it can be launched manually to
provide this information visually. Figure 8-8 shows the DateInfo application.

FIGURE 8-8   *The DateInfo application when launched from the desktop*

CONCLUSION

Use the following points as your basic rules for handling dates in your Visual Basic programs:

- Always use the Date data type for holding and manipulating dates.
- If you have to assign dates that lack century information, always use a known and documented algorithm for your interpretation or expansion of them.
- Be aware of all of the leap year rules in any routines you write that manipulate dates.
- Never manipulate dates as strings.
- Wherever possible use Visual Basic's built-in date manipulation capabilities, which are many and varied.
- Assume nothing.

Many developers are rather blasé about Visual Basic's Year 2000 compliance, assuming that since the Date data type can store dates up to 9999, the language is fully compliant and they have nothing to worry about. Given that Visual Basic is without a doubt one of the world's most popular programming languages, this attitude is worrisome, to say the least. I hope this chapter has revealed that this is by no means the whole story. Not only must the language be compliant, so must the programmers. Visual Basic is like a loaded gun: it's only safe in the right hands. When used sensibly it is easy to create fully compliant applications; unfortunately, writing noncompliant ones is even easier.

"Well, at Least It Compiled OK!"

The Value of Software Testing

JON PERKINS

Jon is a TMS Associate who has been developing applications with Microsoft Visual Basic since version 1. He specializes in writing three-tier, client/server applications with Visual Basic and Microsoft SQL Server. He is also a Microsoft Certified Solution Developer and writes a regular Visual Basic column for EXE, a British software development magazine. His interests include New Age philosophy, jazz, opera, reading, cooking, and gardening. Jon and his wife, Alison, live in the Herefordshire countryside with their two cats, Solomon and Micha.

In the previous version of this book, I made the rather bold statement, "It is my belief that software development is one of the most complex tasks that human beings are called upon to perform." This assertion led to comments like, "What about people who design nuclear reactors, or the space shuttle?" Sure, there might be a lot of tasks on a list above "Write Software," but we could argue that "Write *Quality* Software" should be high up on the list too. Quality consists of many attributes, the most important being that a piece of software should perform exactly as designed. In this chapter, I will cover several ways to test Visual Basic code that illustrate this key concept: testing should be planned before code is written, and all code should be written with testing in mind.

Software development projects come in all shapes and sizes, and they also vary in their nature. In terms of business applications, a standalone telephone directory system for a medium-sized company probably exists at the "relatively simple" end of the spectrum. With an underlying Microsoft Access database and a few data-bound controls, it doesn't take much effort to put together, and because of the extensive use of pretested components it probably wouldn't be too challenging in terms of testing either. However, at the other end of the spectrum might be a major banking application that facilitates the processing of all branch-level account activity using a remote Microsoft ActiveX server set via a local SQL Server database, and then synchronizes each local set of data with the central bank's DB2 database. A system of this size is a much larger development effort that therefore requires a more thorough and comprehensive planning and design exercise, and the result is of course a greater amount of source code. The implications of a failure in the code could result in a loss of money for the bank, and this in turn leads to a loss of credibility in the business community. It is therefore imperative that the system work as expected.

Another example, perhaps closer to home for many of us, is the forthcoming Microsoft Windows NT 5. Back in the days when Windows NT existed as version 3.51, it had about 5 million lines of code. The last released version of Windows NT 4 Server was the Microsoft Enterprise Edition, which included Microsoft Internet Information Server, Microsoft Message Queue Server, and Microsoft Transaction Server (all now considered to be part of the base platform), and contained 16 million lines of code in all. At the time of this writing (April 1998), it is estimated that the final gold release of Windows NT 5 will have about 31 million lines of code. This new code also includes some fairly radical alterations to the existing technology (most notably the inclusion of Active Directory services). With so much code, the testing effort will be massive. In this particular case, the 400 or so programmers are joined by another 400 testers, providing a ratio of one tester for every developer. The overall team also has around 100 program managers and an additional 250 people who work on internationalization.

Although software development has formal guidelines that lay down techniques for drawing up logic tables, state tables, flow charts, and the like, the commercial pressures that are frequently placed on a development team often mean that a system must be ready by a certain date no matter what. Some people might choose to argue with this observation, but it happens nevertheless. One of the biggest headaches for a software developer is time—or rather, the lack of it. When your project lead sits you down and asks you to estimate the amount of time that it will take to code up an application from a design specification that he or she has given you, it is difficult to know beforehand what problems will arise during the project. You are also faced with a bit of a dilemma between giving yourself enough time to code it and not wanting to look bad because you think that the project might take longer than the project lead thinks it will. The logical part of your mind cuts in and tells you not to worry because it all looks straightforward. However, as the development cycle proceeds and the usual crop of interruptions comes and goes, you find that you are running short of time. The pressure is on for you to produce visible deliverables, so the quality aspect tends to get overlooked in the race to hit the deadline. Code is written, executed once to check that it runs correctly, and you're on to the next bit. Then, eventually, the development phase nears its end—you're a bit late, but that's because of (insert one of any number of reasons here)—and you have two weeks of testing to do before the users get it. The first week of the two-week test period is taken up with fixing a few obvious bugs and meeting with both the users and technical support over the implementation plan. At the beginning of the second week, you start to write your test plan, and you realize that there just isn't time to do it justice. The users, however, raise the alarm that there are bugs and so the implementation date is pushed back by a month while the problems are sorted out. When it finally goes live you get transferred onto another project but quietly spend the next fortnight trying to get the documentation done before anyone notices.

I dread to think how many systems have been developed under these conditions. I'm not saying that all development projects are like this, and the problems are slightly different when there is a team of developers involved rather than an individual, but it's an easy trap to fall into. The scenario I've described indicates several problems, most notably poor project management. Even more detrimental to the quality of the final deliverable, however, is the lack of co-ordinated testing. The reason I so strongly tie in testing with the project management function is that a developer who is behind schedule will often ditch the testing to get more code written. This is human nature, and discipline is required (preferably from the developer) to follow the project plan properly rather than give in to deadline urgency. It is very important to report any slippage that occurs rather than cover it up and try to fit in the extra work. The discipline I'm referring to involves writing a proper test plan beforehand and then striving to write code that can be easily tested. The project management process should ensure that the creation of the test suite is also proceeding along with the actual development. I've seen projects fall woefully behind schedule *and* be very buggy because of poor project managers working with relatively good developers. If, among a team of developers, there is one poor developer, the rest of the team will probably make up for it. However, if the project manager is poor at performing the job, the effect on the project can be disastrous, often because of resultant low morale.

Software projects often run into trouble, more so when they are team developments. The industry average for software development projects is that typically about four in every five overrun their planned time scales and budgets, and less than half actually deliver everything that they are supposed to. In the fight to deliver a bug-free system as quickly as possible, project managers often end up negotiating with the end users for a reduction in functionality so that the developers can concentrate on the key parts of the system. The remaining functionality is often promised for delivery in the next version.

In this chapter, I'll start by covering the formalities—that is, descriptions of the various phases of testing that a well-managed development project undergoes. I'll then outline a few tips that I think will help with the testing of a Visual Basic program, and I'll finish up with a discussion of test environments. I've also included a few Microsoft Word 97 Quality Tracking templates on the CD that accompanies this book. Although most companies will have their own in-house versions of these templates, I've included them as starting points for people who do not already use them. The usage of each form should be self-explanatory because of its filename. The files are called:

- BUILD LOG.DOT
- BUILD REPORT.DOT
- END USER FEEDBACK LOG.DOT
- END USER FEEDBACK REPORT.DOT
- TEST FAILURE LOG.DOT
- TEST FAILURE REPORT.DOT

Notice that I have kept these templates generic—different businesses have different requirements and audit standards, so the templates can be modified as necessary. To install them on your machine, create a new directory called TMS under the Templates subdirectory in your Microsoft Office installation, and then copy the files to this location. Now start up Microsoft Word, and select the New command from the File menu. The templates should appear under the TMS tab of the New dialog box.

It's very easy to think of the debugging process as being synonymous with the testing process. Certainly, the distinction between the two processes blurs on small systems at the unit testing stage (to be defined a bit later). Other chapters in this book cover the debugging side of the software development process, which should allow the distinction to become more apparent.

THE PURPOSE OF TESTING

Testing verifies that a software deliverable conforms precisely to the functional and design specifications that have been agreed to by the users. That's a formal definition. However, testing is also used in the detection of bugs—not to prove that there are none, but to locate any that are present. It is a sad fact that we all inadvertently code bugs into our applications. The trick is to reduce the number of bugs in a deliverable to as few as possible so that the system is completely operable. In an ideal world, we would continue to hone and refine the application ad nauseam until it was practically bug-free, but the users can't wait that long, unfortunately. As a general rule, bugs are found and eliminated exponentially— that is, it gets harder to track down bugs as time goes by, but that doesn't mean that they aren't there. When the product is released, they will pop up from time to time, but the user's perception will be—we hope—that the application is stable and robust.

THE FORMAL TEST CYCLE

Before we get our teeth too deeply into the Visual Basic way of programming, I think it's worth reviewing the different levels of testing that apply to all software development projects regardless of the programming language or target platform.

The nature of testing is so varied in its requirements that it is difficult to give generalized definitions. What is appropriate for a small (one- or two-person) application is totally unsuitable for a large (twenty-person) development, whereas the amount of formality that accompanies a large project would slow down the delivery of a small application by a wholly unreasonable amount. With this in mind, I have tried where appropriate to illustrate the relative scale that is necessary at each stage.

Unit/Component Testing

Unit testing is a test of a simple piece of code—in our case a subroutine, a function, an event, a method, or a *Property Get/Let/Set*. In formal terms, it is the smallest piece of testable code. It should be nonreliant on other units of code that have been written for this development project because they will almost certainly be only partly tested themselves. However, it is acceptable to call library routines (such as the Visual Basic built-in functions) since you can be highly confident that they are correct. The idea is to confirm that the functional specification of the unit has been correctly implemented. An example of a unit would be a single user-defined calculation.

TIP

> Sometimes it is necessary to comment out one piece of code to get another piece to work. This might be necessary during the main development cycle when, for example, the underlying code might be dependent on something that has not yet been written or that contains a known bug. If you have to comment out a piece of code, add a *Debug.Print* statement just before or after it to high-light the fact that you have done so. It's inevitable that you'll forget to remove the leading apostrophe from time to time, and adding a *Debug.Print* statement should save you from having to find out the hard way.

Component-level testing is the next level up from unit testing. A component can have fairly straightforward functionality, but it is just complex enough to warrant breaking down the actual implementation into several smaller units. For example, a logical process could be specified that calculates the monthly salary for an individual. This process might consist of the following operations:

- Extract from the database the number of hours worked in the month.
- Calculate the amount of gross pay.
- Add a bonus amount (optional).
- Make all standard deductions from this amount.

Each operation will probably have different requirements. For example, the database extraction will need error handling to allow for the usual group of possibilities (user record not found, database service not available, and so on). The calculations will need to prevent numeric type errors (divide by zero, mainly), and if they are remote components, they will have to raise fresh errors. Therefore, the entire component (for example, *CalcMonthlySalary*) will con-sist of four smaller units (*GetHoursForEmployee*, *CalcGrossPay*, *GetBonus-Amount*, and *CalcDeductions*), but *CalcMonthlySalary* will still be small enough to qualify as a unit (for testing purposes).

To test a defined unit, a series of scenarios should be devised that guarantees every line of code will be executed at some time (not necessarily in the same test). For example, if a function includes an *If..Then..Else* statement, at least two test scenarios should be devised, one to cover each path of execution. If it is a function that is being tested, defining the expected result of the test is generally easier because the return value of the function can be tested for correctness or reasonableness. However, if you are testing a subroutine, you can check only the effect(s) of calling the routine because there is no return value. I generally have a bias toward writing routines as functions where this is reasonable. For some operations, particularly GUI manipulation, it is not so necessary or beneficial because an error should generally be contained within the routine in which it occurred.

In a small system, the developer would likely perform this level of testing. In a larger system, the developer would still perform the initial test, but a separate individual would most likely conduct a more formal version of the test.

Integration Testing

This is the next level up and is concerned with confirming that no problems arise out of combining unit components into more complex processes. For example, two discrete functions might appear to test successfully in isolation, but if function B is fed the output of function A as one of its parameters, it might not perform as expected. One possible cause might be incorrect or insufficient data validation. Using the previous example of the calculation of the single net salary figure, the actual system might implement a menu or command button option to calculate the salaries for all employees and produce a report of the results. It is this entire routine that qualifies as an integration test.

As with unit testing, it is important to write test plans that will execute along all conceivable paths between the units. Integration testing, by its nature, will probably be performed by a dedicated tester—except for small projects.

System Testing

System testing is concerned with the full build of an application (or application suite). At this level, the emphasis is less on bug hunting per se, and more on checking that the various parts of the system correctly interact with each other. The level of testing that would be conducted at this phase would be more systemwide. For example, it could include correct initialization from the Registry, performance, unexpected termination of resources (for example, database connections being terminated when other parts of the system still expect them to be there), logon failures, error recovery and centralized error handling (if appropriate), correct GUI behavior, and correct help file topics, to name just a few.

A system test is conducted on a complete build of the application under construction or at least on a specified phase of it. Ideally, it should be in the state in which the end user will see it (for example, no test dialog boxes popping up and no "different ways of doing things until we code that part of the interface"). Therefore, it should be as complete as possible. In my opinion, the testing cycle should also include the system installation task and not just the execution of the application. If you are developing software for corporatewide use, it is highly unlikely that you will be performing the installations. Most large corporations have dedicated installation teams, and these people are still end users in that they will be running software that you have generated. On the other hand, if you are developing commercial software, the setup program is the first thing the "real" user will see. First impressions count. The Setup Wizard has matured into a very useful tool, but you should still test its output.[1]

User Acceptance Testing

User acceptance testing happens when a tested version of the specified deliverable is made available to a selected number of users who have already received training in the use of the system. In this scenario, the users chosen to perform the tests will be expected to give the system the kind of usage that it will receive in real life. The best way to perform this testing is to get the users to identify an appropriate set of data for the system test and to enter it into the system themselves. This data is most useful if it is real rather than hypothetical. Whatever kind of processing the system performs can then be instigated (for example, printing reports) and the results scrutinized carefully. Ideally, the development and testing team will have little or no input into this process, other than to answer questions and to confirm the existence of any bugs that crop up. Apart from this careful input of prepared data, the system should also be used "normally" for a while to determine the level of confidence that can be attributed to the system. If this confidence level is satisfactory, the system can be signed off and a system rollout can commence. If possible, a partial rollout would initially be preferable—not only for prolonged confidence tests, but also to ease the burden on the support team. These people will encounter more queries as to the use of the system during these early days than at any other time during its lifetime, so if the volume of queries can be spread out, so much the better. It also gives them an idea of the most frequently asked questions so that they can organize their knowledge base accordingly.

---

1. It's also worth having a look at SETUP1.BAS so that you can customize the way it looks and works.

Regression Testing

Regression testing is the repetition of previously run tests after changes have been made to the source code. The purpose is to verify that things in the new build still work according to specification and that no new bugs have been introduced in the intervening coding sessions. Although it is impossible to quantify precisely (some have tried), figures that I have come across from time to time suggest that for every ten bugs that are identified and cleared, perhaps another four will be introduced. This sounds like a realistic figure to me, although I would apply it more to process code rather than event handlers, which are more self-contained (which, of course, is a benefit of the object-based model that Microsoft Visual Basic employs). As you continue each test/debug iteration, the overall number of bugs in the code should decrease correspondingly until a shippable product exists.

Code Reviews

The code review (or inspection) process is a major part of the software quality cycle, and it is also one of the most important. It is an acknowledgment that the creation of test scripts or the use of automated testing packages only goes so far in assuring the quality of the code. Computers do not yet possess the levels of reasoning necessary to look at a piece of code and deduce that it is not necessarily producing the result specified by the design document. I guess when that day comes, we'll all be out of a job.

The code review is the process whereby the human mind reads, analyzes, and evaluates computer code, assessing the code in its own right instead of running it to see what the outcome is. It is, as the name suggests, a thorough examination of two elements:

- The code itself
- The flow of the code

A code review should also ascertain whether the coding style used by the developer violates whatever in-house standards might have been set (while making allowances for personal programming styles). On a fairly large project a review should probably be conducted twice. The first review should be early on in the development, for example when the first few substantial pieces of code have been written. This will allow any bad practices to be nipped in the bud before they become too widespread. A subsequent review much later in the development cycle should then be used to verify that the code meets the design criteria.

The value of this process should not be taken lightly—it's a very reliable means of eliminating defects in code. As with anything, you should start by inspecting your own code and considering what the reviewer is going to be looking for. The sorts of questions that should come up are along these lines:

- Has the design requirement been met?

- Does it conform to in-house development standards?

- Does the code check for invalid or unreasonable parameters (for example, a negative age in a customer record)?

- Is the code Year 2000 compliant?

- Are all handles to resources being closed properly?

- If a routine has an early *Exit* subroutine or function call, is everything tidied up before it leaves? For example, an RDO handle could still be open. (The current versions of Windows are much better than their predecessors were at tidying up resources, but it's still sloppy programming not to close a resource when you are done with it.)

- Are all function return codes being checked? If not, what is the point of the function being a function instead of a subroutine?[2]

- Is the code commented sufficiently?

- Are *Debug.Assert* statements used to their best advantage? We've been waiting a long time for this, so let's use it now that we have it.

- Are there any visible suggestions that infinite loops can occur? (Look for such dangerous constructs as *Do While True*.)

- Is the same variable used for different tasks within the same procedure?

- Are algorithms as efficient as possible?

TESTING VISUAL BASIC CODE

When you're writing a piece of code in any language, it is important to continually ask yourself, "How am I going to test this?" There are several general approaches that you can take.

---

2. See Peet's discussion on returning values vs. raising errors in Chapter 1.

Partner with Another Developer

One good approach to testing is to partner with another developer with the understanding that you will test each other's code. Then, as you type, you will be asking yourself, "How would I test this if I were looking at this code for the first time? Would I understand it, and would I have all the information that I needed?" Some questions are inevitable, but I have found that if you know from the outset that somebody else is going to perform a unit-level test on your code without the same assumptions or shortcuts that you have made, that is excellent news! How many times have you spent ages looking through your own code to track down a bug, only to spot it as soon as you start to walk through it with another developer? This is because we often read what we *think* we have written rather that what we actually have written. It is only in the process of single-stepping through the code for the benefit of another person that our brains finally raise those page faults and read the information from the screen rather than using the cached copy in our heads. If you're looking at somebody else's code, you don't have a cached copy in the first place, so you'll be reading what is actually there. One further benefit of this approach is that it will prompt you to comment your code more conscientiously, which is, of course, highly desirable.

Test as You Go

Testing as you go has been written about elsewhere, but it is something that I agree with so strongly that I'm repeating it here. As you produce new code, you should put yourself in a position where you can be as certain as possible of its performance before you write more code that relies on it. Most developers know from experience that the basic architecture needs to be in place and stable before they add new code. For example, when writing a remote ActiveX server that is responsible for handling the flow of data to and from SQL Server, you will need a certain amount of code to support the actual functionality of the server. The server will need some form of centralized error handler and perhaps some common code to handle database connections and disconnections. If these elements are coded, but development continues on the actual data interfaces before these common routines are tested, the first time you try to run the code, there will be many more things that can go wrong. It's common sense, I know, but I've seen this sort of thing happen time and again.

The first and most obvious way to test a new piece of code is to run it. By that, I don't mean just calling it to see whether the screen draws itself properly or whether the expected value is returned. I mean single-stepping through the code line by line. If this seems too daunting a task, you've already written more code than you should have without testing it. The benefit of this sort of approach is that you can see, while it's still fresh in your mind, whether the code is actually doing what you think it's doing. This single concept is so important that Steve Maguire devotes an entire chapter to it in his book *Writing Solid Code* (Microsoft Press, 1995).

TIP

> Sometimes you will need to code routines that perform actions that will be difficult or impossible to reverse. When such routines fail, they might leave your application in an unstable state. An example might be a complicated file moving/renaming sequence. Your ability to test such code will be limited if you know that it might fail for unavoidable reasons. If you can predict that a sequence of operations might fail and that you can't provide an undo facility, it helps the user to have a trace facility. The idea is that each action that is performed is written to a log window (for example, a text box with the multiline property set to True). If the operation fails, the user has a verbose listing of everything that has occurred up to that point and can therefore take remedial action.

Create Regular Builds

I have always been a fan of regular system builds. They force the development team to keep things tidy. If everybody knows that whatever they are doing is going to have to cooperate with other parts of the system every Friday (for example), it is less likely that horrendously buggy bits of half-completed code will be left in limbo. Code left in this state will sometimes not be returned to for several weeks, by which time the original developer will have forgotten which problems were outstanding and will have to rediscover them from scratch.

If I'm writing a set of remote ActiveX servers, I will generally try to have a new build ready each Monday morning for the other developers to use. If I'm working on a large GUI-based system, I will probably look more toward a build every other week. It's hard to be precise, however, because there are always influential factors and, of course, you need the necessary numbers of staff to do this. If you are in a team development, I suggest that this is something you should discuss among yourselves at the beginning of the coding cycle so that you can obtain a group consensus as to what is the best policy for your particular project. It is likely that you will get some slippage, and you might well decide to skip the occasional build while certain issues are resolved, but overall, creating regular builds will allow everybody to get a feel for how the project is shaping up.

If you consider yourself to be a professional developer or part of a development team, you should be using a source code control system (for example, Microsoft Visual SourceSafe). I recommend that you only check in code that will not break a build. This helps maintain the overall quality of the project by keeping an up-to-date, healthy version of the system available at all times.

Write Test Scripts at the Same Time You Code

Having stepped through your code, you need to create a more formal test program that will confirm that things do indeed work. Using a test script allows for the same test to be run again in the future, perhaps after some changes have been made. The amount of test code that you write is really a matter of judgment, but what you're trying to prove is that a path of execution works correctly and any error conditions that you would expect to be raised are raised. For critical pieces of code—the mortgage calculation algorithm for a bank, for example— it might be worthwhile to actually write the specific code a second time (preferably by someone else) and then compare results from the two. Of course, there is a 50 percent chance that if there is a discrepancy, it is in the test version of the algorithm rather than the "real" version, but this approach does provide a major confidence test. I know of a company that was so sensitive about getting the accuracy of an algorithm correct that they assigned three different developers to each code the same routine. As it happened, each piece of code produced a slightly different answer. This was beneficial because it made the analyst behind this realize that he had not nailed down the specification tight enough. This is a good example of the prototype/test scenario.

Decide Where to Put Test Code

This might seem like a strange heading, but what we need to consider is whether the nature of the development warrants a dedicated test harness program or whether a bolt-on module to the application itself would be suitable. Let's examine this further.

A major component—for example, a remote ActiveX server—has clearly defined public interfaces. We want to test that these interfaces all work correctly and that the expected results are obtained, and we also need to be sure that the appropriate error conditions are raised. Under these circumstances, it would be most suitable to write an application that links up to the remote server and systematically tests each interface. However, let's say a small, entirely self-contained GUI-based application is being created (no other components are being developed and used at the same time for the same deliverable). In this case, it might be more appropriate to write the test code as part of the application but have the test interfaces (for example, a menu item) only be visible if a specific build flag is declared.

Ensure Source Code Coverage During Testing

A series of test scripts should, of course, run every single line of code in your application. Every time you have an *If* statement, or a *Select Case* statement, the number of possible execution paths increases rapidly. This is another reason why it's so important to write test code at the same time as the "real" code—it's the only way you'll be able to keep up with every new execution path.

The Visual Basic Code Profiler (VBCP) add-in that shipped with Visual Basic 5 is able to report the number of times each line of code is executed in a run. Using VBCP while testing your code will allow you to see which lines have been executed zero times, enabling you to quickly figure out which execution paths have no coverage at all.

Understand the Test Data

This is an obvious point, but I mention it for completeness. If you are responsible for testing a system, it is vital that you understand the nature and meaning of whatever test data you are feeding to it. This is one area in which I have noticed that extra effort is required to coax the users into providing the necessary information. They are normally busy people, and once they know that their urgently needed new system is actually being developed, their priorities tend to revert to their everyday duties. Therefore, when you ask for suitable test data for the system, it should be given to you in a documented form that is a clearly defined set of data to be fed in. This pack of test data should also include an expected set of results to be achieved. This data should be enough to cover the various stages of testing (unit, integration, and system) for which the development team is responsible. You can bet that when the users start user acceptance testing, they will have a set of test data ready for themselves, so why shouldn't they have a set ready for you? Coax them, cajole them, threaten them, raise it in meetings, and get it documented, but make sure you get that data. I realize that if you are also the developer (or one of them), you might know enough about the system to be able to create your own test data on the users' behalf, but the testing process should not make allowances for any assumptions. Testing is a checking process, and it is there to verify that you have understood the finer points of the design document. If you provide your own test data, the validity of the test might be compromised.

Get the Users Involved

The intended users of a system invariably have opinions while the system is under development and, if given the opportunity to express these opinions, can provide valuable feedback. Once a logical set of requirements starts to become a real-life set of windows, dialog boxes, and charts that the user can manipulate, ideas often start to flow. This effect is the true benefit of prototyping an application because it facilitates early feedback. It is inevitable that further observations will be forthcoming that could benefit the overall usability or efficiency of the finished result. Unless you are working to very tight deadlines, this feedback should be encouraged throughout the first half of the development phase (as long as the recommendations that users make are not so fundamental that the design specification needs to be changed). A good way of providing this allowance for feedback is to make a machine available with the latest system build that is accessible to anybody. This will allow people to come along at any time and play. This is a very unstructured approach, but it can lead to a lot of useful feedback. Not only can design flaws be spotted as the system progresses, but other pairs of eyes become involved in the debugging cycle.

To make this informal approach work, it is necessary to provide a pile of blank user feedback forms that anybody can fill out and leave in some prearranged in-tray for the attention of the development team. A nominated individual should be responsible for maintaining a log of these feedback reports and should coordinate among the development team any actions that arise out of them. I've included a sample feedback form on the accompanying CD (see the list of Word templates at beginning of this chapter). Of course, a more elegant and up-to-date approach would be to use an intranet-based electronic form that captures all such feedback and bug reports.

Having extolled the virtues of allowing the users to give you continual feed-back, I must point out one disadvantage with this approach. If the currently available build is particularly buggy or slow (or both), this could quite possi-bly cause some anxiety among the users and thus could earn the system a bit of bad publicity before it gets anywhere near to going live. Again, common sense is the order of the day. Some users are familiar with the development cycle and will take early-build system instabilities in their stride, but others won't. Make the most of the users and the knowledge that they can offer, but don't give them a reason to think that the final system will be a dog!

Track Defects

I mentioned earlier the importance of good project management, and now we are going to return to this concept. Depending on the size and structure of your project, the responsibility for keeping a record of the defects will either rest with a dedicated test lead or with the project lead (who is therefore also the test lead). Developers will find bugs in their own code, and in many cases will fix them there and then. However, some bugs will be too elusive to track down quickly, or there might not be time to fix them, so they should be raised with the test lead. Faults will also be raised by the users during their own testing, and also by anybody else involved in the test program. Unfortunately, it is quite possible that faults may continue to be found after the application has been released.

A suitable defect-tracking system will allow for the severity of defects to be graded to different levels (from show-stopper to irrelevant), and for each de-fect to be allocated to a specific member of the development team. Ideally it should also tie in with the local e-mail system. It is important to maintain an efficient means of tracking all defects so that the overall health of the project can be continually monitored. Toward the end of a development of any size there is normally considerable pressure from the business for it to be released. Before this can happen, however, the project lead and the user lead will need to continually review the defect status list until a point is reached when the user lead is satisfied with the correctness of the system. This can only be prop-erly achieved by maintaining a thorough, central log of the current health of the system.

TEST PLANS

A test plan is analogous to the main design document for a system. Though focused entirely on how the system will be tested rather than on what should be in the system, the test plan should be written with the same degree of seriousness, consideration, and checking as the main design document because it determines the quality of the system. The secret of a good plan is that it should allow any team member to continue in your absence. One day in the future, you will have moved on, but the system will still be there. Companies very rarely stand still these days, and changes to their working practices—and therefore to the system—will follow. Whatever changes need to be made, the new development team will be tremendously encouraged if they have test scripts that are documented and are known to work from the start.

Test plans have other purposes than the reasons I describe above. They provide a formal basis from which to develop repeatable (that is, regression) tests. As systems evolve or as new builds are created during the debug cycle, it is essential to know that the existing stability of the system has not been broken. This can best be achieved through an ability to run the same tests over and over as each new build is produced. Also, test plans provide a basis from which the test strategy can be inspected and discussed by all interested parties.

A good test plan will start with a description of the system to be tested, followed by a brief discussion of the test's objectives. The following elements should be included in the plan:

- The objectives of the test exercise.
- A description of how the tests will be performed. This will explain the various degrees of reliance that will be made on key testing components, such as rerunnable test scripts, manual checklists, end-user involvement, and so on.
- A description of the environment in which the test will occur. For example, if your organization supports several base environment configurations, you should clearly state which of them you will be testing against.
- A listing of the test data that will need to be made available for the tests to be valid.

- A discussion of any restrictions that might be placed on the test team that could have an impact on the reliability of the test results. For example, if you are testing a system that is likely to be used by a very large number of people and that accesses a central database, it might be difficult for you to simulate this level of volume usage.

- A declaration of the relative orders of importance that you are placing on different criteria—for example, your concern for robustness compared to that of performance.

- Any features that you will not be testing, with a commentary explaining why not (to enlighten those who come after you).

- An intended test schedule showing milestones. This should tie into the overall project plan.

Then, using the same breakdown of functionality as was presented in the design specification, start to list each test scenario. Each scenario should include:

- A reference to the item to be tested

- The expected results

- Any useful comments that describe how these test results can definitely confirm that the item being tested actually works properly (success criteria)

TEST SCRIPTS

A test script can be either a set of instructions to a user or to another piece of code. Generally speaking, I am referring to code-based test scripts in this section. So a good test script should be approached in the same way as the code that it is supposed to be testing. Therefore, it should be designed, documented, commented, and tested. Tested? No, that doesn't necessarily mean writing a test script for it, but it does mean single-stepping through your test code while it runs to ensure that it is doing what you expect it to do. If the code that you are testing is a particularly important piece, the test code should be inspected and walked through as with any normal code. The following rules apply to test scripts:

- Test script functionality should be kept in sync with the application code.

- The version/revision number of the test script must be the same as the application.

- Test scripts should be version controlled, just like the application code. Use Microsoft Visual SourceSafe (or an equivalent) to keep track of any changes that you make. That way, if you need to roll back to an earlier version of the code for any reason, you will have a valid set of test scripts to go with it.

Stubs and Drivers

An application is basically a collection of software units connected by flow-control statements. The best time to test each individual unit is immediately after it has been written, if for no other reason than it is fresh in your mind (and because if you don't do it now, you'll never have the time later). Of course, having a software unit that relies on a call to another unit is only testable if you either comment out the call or substitute a dummy implementation. This dummy is known as a *stub*. Conversely, if you are testing a unit that would normally be called by a higher-level unit, you can create a temporary calling routine, called a *driver*. Let's take a closer look at these concepts.

Stubs

A stub is a temporary replacement piece of code that takes the place of a unit that has yet to be written (or made available by another developer). The implementation of the stub can be simple or somewhat complex, as conditions require. For instance, either it can be hard-coded to return a set value, or it can perform any of the following:

- Provide a validation of the input parameters.

- Provide a realistic delay so as not to convey a false impression that your new application is lightning-fast.

- Provide a quick-and-dirty implementation of the intended functionality of the unit that you are substituting. Be careful not to be too quick-and-dirty; otherwise, you'll waste valuable time debugging throwaway code.

A useful task that you can perform with a stub is to pass the input parameters into the debug window. In most cases, this will merely show you what you expect to see, but it will occasionally throw up a parameter value that you never expected. Although you would have (probably) found this out anyway, you will have immediately been given a visible sign that there is something wrong. While formalized testing is a good method of identifying bugs, so is the common sense observation process ("that can't be right…").

Drivers

These either contain or call the unit that you are testing, depending on the nature of the code. For a simple unit of code such as a calculation routine, a dedicated piece of test code in another module is sufficient to call the piece of code being tested and to check the result. The idea of using a driver is to provide a basic emulation of the calling environment to test the unit.

The advent of the ActiveX interface now means that it is possible to invoke a test container simply by creating a reference to your piece of code in a new instance of Visual Basic. This does, of course, mean that your code must be given a public declaration and so on, but this client/server-based approach truly leads to flexibility in your systems. And of course, if you are creating ActiveX documents, you can test your development only in a driver-style environment—for example, Microsoft Internet Explorer.

PLANNING A CODE COMPONENT

As I said at the beginning, the most important concept that I want this chapter to convey is the necessity of writing testable code. Less experienced Visual Basic programmers have a tendency to implement a lot of functionality directly beneath command buttons. I've certainly seen instances where there are several hundred lines of code behind a button: code that updates the screen, displays and processes the results from a File Open dialog box, reads from the registry, performs a database access, and then writes to the screen again. I've even seen code like this that exists in two places: behind a command button and again underneath a menu item. (Cut and paste can be such a useful facility.)

When you write a piece of code it needs to be as function-specific as possible. Therefore the monolithic code block that I've just described should be broken down into small routines. First of all there should be very little code behind a button—ideally, a call to another routine, but a small number of relatively safe commands is acceptable. If there is a need for a large amount of processing, there should be one procedure that controls the overall flow and control of the process, and that procedure calls function-specific routines. In the description I gave above, the database access should be a separate routine, as should the

Registry code, and so on. This is good practice, and there is no taboo in having many small private routines attached to a form, a module, a class, or whatever.[3] The testing is so much easier this way, and it also makes for much more specific error handling code. It's also tidier, of course.

It's important not to get too formal with the coding, though; we'd never get it delivered. The code that goes into making a Microsoft Windows application can be divided into two categories: process specific and interface specific. In very general terms[4] the test code that goes into the process-specific sections is what needs to be planned beforehand because it's the process that actually gets the user's work done. The interface-specific elements of the system are still important, but they demand a much greater degree of spontaneous interaction from the user.

To illustrate the planning process I have invented the following functional specification for a small DLL, and I have included an associated test plan.[5] Most real-world requirements will be more comprehensive than this but I don't feel that additional detail would add any extra weight to the point that I'm trying to get across. All software should be written from a functional specification (or design document, if you prefer). However, you'll find that if you write the test plan at the same time as (or immediately after) the functional specification, you will continually identify test scenarios that will prompt you to go back to the functional specification to add necessary error handling directives. This happened to me while I was writing the test script specification for the example DLL, even though it's only a simple demonstration.

Functional Specification

Create a prototype ActiveX DLL component (SERVERDATA.DLL) that encapsulates the StockList table of the SERVERDATA.MDB database. The table is defined as shown on the following page.

---

3. Within reason, of course. Each procedure creates an entry in the global namespace area, so don't go overboard.

4. I say in general terms because there'll always be somebody who can point out an intelligent argument to the contrary (in this case it'll probably be the GUI test product marketing executives).

5. As an aside, when the TMS book team was planning this revision we created a list of topics that we wanted to see included in this edition. One of those topics was calling ADO code from an ActiveX DLL, and this seemed a good place to include it. Therefore the code that satisfies the example specification actually exists on the CD under the \Chap09\Code directory.

Field name	Data Type	Description
ID	AutoNumber	ID number for each record
StockCode	Text (length = 8)	Stock code to identify item
Name	Text (length = 50)	Name of stock item
StockLevel	Number (Long Integer)	Number of units currently held
UnitPrice	Currency	Price of each unit

General requirements

The following characteristics should be defined for the DLL component:

1. The DLL component does not explicitly need any startup code.

2. The DLL component should have two classes defined.

   b CStockList, which provides a logical wrapper around the StockList table. Its *Instancing* property should be set to MultiUse.

   b CStockItem, which acts as a single record representation of the StockList table. Its *Instancing* property should be set to Public-NotCreatable.[6]

3. Database access should be performed via ActiveX Data Objects (ADO).

4. The database should be opened during the first call upon it, and should be closed during the Terminate event of the CStockList class. For the purposes of this prototype it can be assumed that the client application will not generate any database activity from the CStockItem class once the CStockList class has been destroyed.

CStockList

Implement the following interface:

***Add* method**   Input parameters:

StockCode As String
Name As String
StockLevel As Long
UnitPrice As Currency

---

6. In other words, a client application should be able to declare a variable of type CStockItem, but should not be able to directly create an instance of the class from the ActiveX DLL. Instead the CStockList class will pass a running instance of this class via a function call.

This method should create a new record in the StockList table and populate that record with the parameter data. It should check that the *StockCode* value has not already been used and that all numeric values are at least zero. (If there is an error, a negative value is returned.)

***Count* property (read-only)**   This property should return the number of records in the StockList table.

***Item* method function**   Input parameters:

> *StockCode As String*

This function should create, instantiate, and return an object of type CStock-Item for the record identified by the *StockCode* parameter. This function should raise an error in the event of the record not being found.

***ItemList* function**   Input parameters:

> None

This function should return a collection of all *StockCode* values that exist within the StockList table.

***StockValue* property (read-only)**   This property should return the sum of each record's StockLevel field multiplied by its UnitPrice field.

***Remove* method**   Input parameters:

> *StockCode As String*

This method should delete the record that matches the supplied *StockCode* value.

CStockItem

Implement the following interface:

***Name* property (read/write)**   *Let/Get* for the Name field.

***StockCode* property (read/write)**   *Let/Get* for the StockCode field.

***StockLevel* property (read/write)**   *Let/Get* for the StockLevel field.

***UnitPrice* property (read/write)**   *Let/Get* for the UnitPrice field.

***StockValue* property (read-only)**   *Get* property only. Calculated dynamically and is the product of the UnitPrice field and the StockLevel field.

Update **method**   This method should apply any changes that are made to any of the read/write properties.

Test Script Specification

(The idea here is that we want to methodically check each member of the public interface. Some of the test routines will automatically make use of some of the other members.)

Objective: To ensure that each member in the CStockList and CStockItem classes have been run at least once to ensure correct behavior. This is a component-level test that will be performed by the development team.

Test methodology: The two classes are implemented in an ActiveX DLL. This allows for the creation of a dedicated test harness application that will act as a normal client program. For this initial test, sample data will be hard-coded into the test harness application. (The possibility exists to extend this in the future so that test data will be read from a data file.)

Scope of this strategy: This is a generic document that outlines a method of testing without providing any test data. Reasonable test data can be created as required.

Test environment: Windows 98 (full installation), run-time files as installed by Visual Basic 6. No service packs are applied to these products at this time.

SERVERDATA.DLL test 1

Members used: *Add, Count, Item, StockValue*

Intent: Check that a record is added successfully.

1. Formulate the data for a new record that doesn't already exist in the table.

2. Create a reference to a *CStockList* object.

3. Call the *Item* method using the new *StockCode* value (from step 1) and verify that this raises a "not found" error. This is to check that the record doesn't already exist. If it does exist, this test data has already been used and so the rest of the test should be aborted.

4. Call the *Count* property. Check that this tallies with the number of records currently in the table (via Access?).

5. Call the *StockValue* property to establish the value Y of total stock currently held.

6. Calculate the value X of the new item of stock that is to be added by multiplying the StockLevel value with the UnitPrice value.

7. Call the *Add* method with the new stock data.

8. Call the *StockValue* property and verify that it is equal to the value of X + Y.

9. Call the *Item* function to obtain a reference to a *CStockItem* object. Verify that each property matches the original data. Release the reference to the *CStockItem* object.

10. Release the reference to the *CStockList* object.

SERVERDATA.DLL test 2

Members used: *Add*

Intent: Prove that a new record with a duplicate key value will be rejected.

1. Create a reference to a *CStockList* object.

2. Attempt to add a record that already exists. A predictable error should be raised (that is, client error handler should include a check for this specific error code being raised).

3. Release the reference to the *CStockList* object.

SERVERDATA.DLL test 3

Members used: *Remove*

Intent: Check that an attempt to delete a record that doesn't exist will fail gracefully.

1. Create a reference to a *CStockList* object.

2. Attempt to remove a record that doesn't exist. A predictable error should be raised.

3. Release the reference to the *CStockList* object.

SERVERDATA.DLL test 4

Members used: *Item*, *Update*

Intent: Prove that the *CStockItem.Update* method will reject an attempt to modify a record where the *StockCode* value would be the same as an existing record.

1. Create a reference to a *CStockList* object.

2. Attempt to rename a *StockCode* value to an existing value. A predictable error should be raised.

3. Release the reference to the *CStockList* object.

PERFORMANCE TESTING

Performance testing is somewhat less rigid in its documentation requirements than the other types of testing. It is concerned with the responsiveness of the system, which in turn depends on the efficiency of either the underlying code or the environment in which the system is running. For example, a database system might work fine with a single tester connected, but how does it perform when 20 users are connected? For many systems, performance is just a matter of not keeping the user waiting too long, but in other cases, it can be more crucial. For example, if you are developing a real-time data processing system that constantly has to deal with a flow of incoming data, a certain level of performance expectation should be included in the design specification.

Performance is partly up to the efficiency of the network subsystem component within Windows, but it is also up to you. For example, if you are accessing a database table, what kind of locks have you put on it? The only way to find out how it will run is through volume testing. But performance is also a matter of perception. How many times have you started a Windows operation and then spent so long looking at the hourglass that you think it has crashed, only to find two minutes later that you have control again? *The Windows Interface Guidelines for Software Design* (Microsoft Press, 1995) offers very good advice on how to show the user that things are still running fine (using progress bars, for instance).

Profiling your code is an obvious step to take when performance is an issue, particularly for processor-intensive operations. Profiling can point out where the most time is being consumed in a piece of code, which in turn will show you the most crucial piece of code to try to optimize.

PREPARING A SUITABLE TEST ENVIRONMENT

If you are testing a system for a corporate environment, it's a good idea to have a dedicated suite of test machines. As a result, machines are available for end users to try out the new system without being an inconvenience to you, and they can also focus on the task at hand by being away from their own work environment. More important, it means that you are not running the software on a machine that might contain other versions of the system (or at least some of its components) that you are developing.

The nature, size, and variety of the test environment will inevitably depend on the size of your organization. A large corporation will conceivably have dedicated test rooms containing a dozen or so test machines. This setup will not only offer the scope to test the software under different conditions but will also allow for a degree of volume testing (several different users using the same network resources at the same time, particularly if you have developed a product that accesses a shared database). If you work for a small software house or you are an independent developer, chances are you will not be able to provide yourself with many testing resources.

Most software these days has one of two target markets. The software is either intended for some form of corporate environment, or for commercial sale. Corporate environments can normally provide test environments, and if you work for a small software house or you are an independent developer, you will probably be expected to perform system testing on site anyway. (Obviously your user-acceptance tests must be on site.) If, however, there is no mention of this during your early contract negotiations or project planning, it is worth asking what sort of test facilities your employer or client will be able to provide for you. It's better to arrange this at the outset rather than muddle your way through a limited test.

Test Machine Configurations

If you are testing a system for a corporate environment, it is worthwhile having two different types of test machine configurations. A "plain-vanilla," or basic, configuration gives you a benchmark with which to work. A second configuration that contains a typical corporate build will highlight any problems you might encounter. Let's examine them in more detail.

The plain-vanilla configuration

In this configuration, a plain-vanilla machine is configured solely for the purpose of testing your new system. Preferably, the hard disk will have been formatted to remove everything relating to previous configurations. The machine should then be loaded with the following:

- The version of Windows you are testing against.

- The minimum network drivers that you need to get your configuration to work. By this, I mean that if your corporate environment runs on a TCP/IP-based protocol, check that the machine is not also running NetBEUI or IPX/SPX.

- The build (and only that build) of the system that you are testing.

This test will allow you to assess the performance in a pure environment. Whatever problems arise during this test are either straightforward bugs in your system or are fundamental problems in the way that you are trying to work with the Windows environment. By testing in such an uncontaminated environment, you can be sure that the problems are between you and Windows and that nothing else is causing any problems that arise at this stage.

I have a personal reason for being so particular about this point. A few years back, I was writing a client/server system using a non-Microsoft development tool. The product itself was buggy, and it was difficult to get any form of stable build from it at all. Eventually, everything that went wrong was blamed on the development tool. Because we concentrated on trying to get some common routines built first, my co-developer and I did not attempt to hook up to the Microsoft SQL Server service for a couple of weeks. When we did try, it wouldn't work. We both blamed the tool again. Because we had seen it done in a training course, we knew that it should work. Therefore, we reasoned, if we tried doing the same thing in different ways, we eventually would find success. We didn't. Only when we came to try something else that involved a connection to SQL Server did we find that it was the current Windows configuration that was at fault. We decided to reload Windows to get a plain-vanilla environment, and, sure enough, we got our database connection. As we reloaded each additional component one by one, we found out that the antivirus terminate-and-stay-resident (TSR) program that we were both using was interfering with the SQL Server database-library driver! When we changed to a different antivirus tool, the problem went away.

The corporate configuration

Having gained a benchmark against what works and what doesn't, you can then repeat the tests against a typical corporate environment. For example, your company might have several standard configurations. The base environment might consist of Windows 95, Office (a mixture of standard and professional editions), a couple of in-house products (an internal telephone directory application that hooks up to a SQL Server service somewhere on the network), and a third-party communication package that allows connectivity to the corporate mainframe. Typically, additional install packs are created that add department-specific software to the base environment. For example, the car fleet department will probably have an off-the-shelf car pool tracking system. Allowances need to be made in your testing platforms to take into account more diverse variations of the corporate base environment, but only if the software that you have developed is likely to run in this environment, of course.

In a perfect world, there would be no problem running your new system in these environments. However, inconsistencies do occur. Products produced by such large companies as Microsoft are tested so widely before they are commercially released for sale that issues such as machine/product incompatibility are addressed either internally or during the beta test cycle. (Indeed, the various flavors of Windows currently available do contain the occasional piece of code that detects that it is running on a specific piece of hardware or with a specific piece of software and makes allowances accordingly.) One of these inconsistencies can be attributed to executable file versions. For example, different versions of the WINSOCK.DLL file are available from different manufacturers. Only one of them can be in the Windows System or System32 directory at any time, and if it's not the one you're expecting, problems *will* occur.

Another problem that can arise in some companies—as incredible as it seems—is that key Windows components can be removed from the corporate installation to recover disk space. Many large corporations made a massive investment in PC hardware back when a 486/25 with 4 MB of RAM and a 340 MB hard disk was a good specification. These machines, now upgraded to 16 MB of RAM, might still have the original hard disks installed, so disk space will be at a premium. This is less of a problem nowadays with the relative cheapness of more powerful machines, so if your organization doesn't suffer from this situation, all is well, but it is a common problem out there. I am aware of one organization, for example, that issued a list of files that could be "safely" deleted to recover a bit of disk space. Apart from the games, help files for programs such as Terminal and the object packager (ever use that? me neither), there was also the file MMSYSTEM.DLL. This file is a key component of the multimedia system. In those days (Windows 3.1), very few of the users had any multimedia requirements, so the problem went unnoticed for a while. The fix was obviously quite straightforward, but it still would have caused problems. If your attitude is "Well, that's not my problem," you are wrong. You need to be aware of *anything* that is going to prevent your system from running properly at your company, and if a show-stopping bug is not discovered until after the rollout, you'll be the one who looks bad, no matter who you try to blame.

A good indication of the amount of effort that went into producing a build of the first version of Windows NT can be found in the book *Show-Stopper: The Break-neck Race to Create Windows NT and the Next Generation at Microsoft,* by G. Pascal Zachary (Free Press, 1994). Not only is it an interesting read, it describes well the role of the testing teams within a large development environment—larger than most of us will be exposed to during our careers, I dare say. But the book conveys very well the necessity of structure and discipline that must be maintained in large developments.

A FINAL WORD OF CAUTION

And now for the bad news: once you have completed the testing, your application or component will still probably have bugs in it. This is the nature of software development, and the true nature of testing is unfortunately to reduce the number of bugs to a small enough number that they do not detract from the usefulness and feel-good factor of the product. This includes the absence of "showstopper" bugs—there is still no excuse for shipping something that has this degree of imperfection. In running through the testing cycles, you will have reduced the number of apparent bugs to zero. At least everything should work OK. However, users are going to do things to your system that you would never have imagined, and this will give rise to problems from time to time. In all likelihood, they might trigger the occasional failure that cannot apparently be repeated. It does happen occasionally, and the cause is most typically that the pressures (commercial or otherwise) on the project management team to deliver become so strong that the team succumbs to the pressure and rushes the product out before it's ready. They then find that the users come back to them with complaints about the stability of the product. Sometimes you just can't win.

Starting with Bases Loaded

Building Base Code

Phil has been working with Microsoft Visual Basic since version 3, mainly within the finance and insurance fields. His main area of expertise is creating large, reusable business objects, using base code wherever possible. When not working seven days a week, Phil can be found watching football or playing the occasional round of golf.

PHIL RIDLEY

Do engineers reinvent the wheel every time they need to build a new piece of machinery? Of course not. So why do we, as developers, almost always do the equivalent when building new applications? C++ developers have been using MFC for years. J++ developers have AFC. So why don't we have our own equivalents? At The Mandelbrot Set (International) Limited (TMS), we've been using our own application template for a number of years for all new projects (see Appendix for more details).

In this chapter, we'll look at some of the reasons for using base code and some of the techniques that can be applied to creating your own base code. Finally we'll look at how Microsoft Visual Basic templates can be used to provide frameworks for common forms, classes, and modules.

WHY BASE CODE?

How many times have you sat down to begin a new project and wondered exactly where to start? Do you begin by creating the screens you need, writing the low-level functions, or (as often seems to happen) do you just leap in somewhere in the middle? Then maybe somewhere down the line, you suddenly realize that you need to decide how to handle and report errors. This can leave you having to retrofit an error handling strategy into hundreds, if not thousands, of lines of code. With a properly designed set of base code, most of these decisions have already been made, and vital items—such as a coherent error handling strategy—are already implemented. All that remains is for you to plug in the forms and routines that are specific to your individual application.

Any serious application—regardless of size—will need to have some form of infrastructure. By infrastructure, I mean units of code that bind the application's functional units and provide general application support services. A classic example is the error handler whose job it is to maintain application state under erroneous conditions, and provide support services such as logging and tracing. Infrastructure functionality is essential to the application, but often the functionality is not included in any functional or design documentation. This can create problems: now the programmer has to write infrastructure code that has not been factored into the development time estimates. We estimate that using our own application template saves about a month of development time when creating an application from scratch. I'm sure most developers will agree that the majority of projects are developed under stressful time constraints, and an additional month of unplanned activity can mean less sleep! Multiply that by the number of applications your company develops during a year and you can start to see the cost- and time-saving potential of using base code templates.

Timescales are more often than not the major driving force behind an application. However, when the crunch comes, the timescale often succumbs to the more urgent need to iron out bugs and implement overlooked functionality. The problem with not having developed base code up front will manifest itself as a continual series of retrofit changes, each one becoming more difficult as the amount of code to integrate grows. In the reactive rush, standards slip and duplication occurs. How many occurrences of the *bFileExists* function can you find in one of your applications? The problem of duplication will always exist when working under these conditions because programmers on a project rarely have time to share information about functionality that they have added. As a programmer, you will probably assume a function you require does not exist and write it yourself. If that function does happen to exist already, there is a high probability that its code is different, and it might even have a different function name. The contract market is booming, and sometimes a particular programmer has worked with several programming standards from a variety of organizations. In high-pressure situations, the programmer is tempted to treat infrastructure routines as almost incidental. Instead of meticulously sticking to the organization's standards, the programmer might wish to code quickly, using whatever standard comes to mind. Comments will be scarce—if written at all. By this point in the development cycle, all the business can see is slipping deadlines. Code reviews—what are they? Congratulations, you now have most of the ingredients for creating the perfect maintenance nightmare!

By now it should be obvious that using base code has benefits. From a coding perspective, base code allows developers to concentrate on the functionality of the application—that is, the functionality that has been specified and cost-quoted. Most developers would much rather spend their time developing the application functionality because that's where the "clever" algorithms come into play. Writing this code is a real ego boost and many developers take pride in being able to write code that stretches their abilities to the limit. This code is far more likely to contain comments and follow the official coding standards. You can almost hear the programmer crying out for the "work of art" to be reviewed.

Base code encourages code reuse because the average programmer does not want to write *bFileExists*. Knowing that there is a base framework containing this "trainee programmer" type of code, programmers are more likely to actively seek out such a routine rather than write it themselves. However, you should remember that many programmers have limited patience. If you were writing a really cool routine that had to perform different actions based on the operating system, you might scan for a *GetOSPlatform* function in the base code. If such a function did exist, it would be vital that the programmer could find it—in a reasonable amount of time. Intuitively named modules might help here. Another major help is the function's interface. I will cover these topics in more detail later in the chapter.

An application's base code will often need to use specialized API calls, especially for the environmental-type functionality. One example is the Version API functions. In the old days, a badly defined or called API routine would simply cause a General Protection Fault. However, Microsoft got fed up with complaints about such faults—invariably caused by misuse—and built extra layers of validation into the API. Now you can get away with both wrongly declared and wrongly implemented API calls. In most cases the routine just doesn't work but the application is not as likely to crash. Using a good base code template allows complex functionality like this to be abstracted from the application. The developer need not understand how a function works, just that it does. A good base code template can allow developers new to Visual Basic to come to grips with applications more quickly than they otherwise would by concentrating on the business functionality rather than the infrastructure. There are many other reasons you might want to seriously consider using base code templates. Here are some more:

- **Using a base code template means that tried and tested, complex, low-level routines can be added to projects in the knowledge that they already work**. Many of the routines in the TMS Application Template contain complex API calls, which, if the routines were written from scratch, would require extensive debugging and testing. When you are writing an application, the knowledge that some of the messier functions have already been written and debugged can be a great relief.

- **Starting from a set of base code imposes a set of coding and design standards on the developer right from the start.** When an error handling strategy has already been implemented, it is usually much easier to go along with what's already there than to branch out in a different direction. Similarly, when developers become familiar with the naming conventions used throughout the base code, they will be more likely to fall into line with them than to ignore them.

- **Base code allows you to implement a consistent subclassing strategy**. Subclassing is an area that I will be discussing in more detail shortly. For those not familiar with the term, subclassing is basically the concept of taking an existing Visual Basic function or object and replacing it with one of your own so that it is modified functionally.

I hope that by now you have been sold on the idea of base code templates. On all levels, from corporate to project management to development, base code templates are useful. The bottom line, I suppose, is that using some form of template will save you money, time, and effort.

What to Include in a Template

The first step in creating a base template is deciding what to include. The purpose of an application template is to provide the core services that an application is likely to require, but that do not in themselves warrant inclusion in the main application design documentation. The code that makes up the template will in most cases be relevant to many types of application. Some routines will not be needed right from the start, but it is wise to include any routines that might be of use as the project progresses. This section offers a general guide.

Helper Functions

A helper function—such as *bFileExists*—is an obvious start for your template's library, but so too are the less obvious ones such as *ExtractFileName, Extract-PathName,* and *AppendSlash.* At first you might find it hard to think of helper functions to write. You should be able to find a good selection by looking through existing applications. I'm sure you will find many more candidates this way. Looking through existing applications can also help you to identify code that is duplicated between applications and therefore might warrant inclusion. Another way of identifying code for your template is to use a code analyzer on a few of your existing applications. This will help you to identify the routines that are receiving the greatest number of hits, and therefore may prove more useful in template code where you can more easily optimize them.

Common Forms

Common forms can be a real asset to an application. The Common Dialog control is a classic example of a common form. A progress form, About Box, and Message Box are just some of the common forms you can create. Common forms will give your applications a more standard appearance, and again you will not end up with many implementations of the same functionality. A common application MDI form should not be overlooked either. Having such a form will allow you to pre-create the standard menus, such as File, Edit, Window, and Help. Again, this is the type of code that is a bit of a chore to write for each different application.

ActiveX Components

Creating Microsoft ActiveX components can be a powerful way of enforcing business rules. Many applications within an organization will need to access a common set of business rules, creating a uniform look and feel. For example, you could create an ActiveX control that wraps your favorite grid control, and build additional functionality such as allowing the user to cut and paste rows of data. Centralizing these rules into an ActiveX server makes sense. That ActiveX server can then be considered base code.

Subclassing

Subclassing objects and procedures is a powerful technique you can build into your template to change the way that standard Visual Basic elements work. You could, for example, subclass Visual Basic's *Load* method. "Why would I want to do this?" you ask. Well, imagine an application with a complex-state engine that must control what forms can be loaded depending on application state (not an uncommon requirement). By subclassing the *Load* method, you will effectively channel every load request via your function. You can then determine what is being loaded and either prevent the load from occurring, or permit it. In effect, all the state code is in a single place. Programmers need not worry whether it is safe to load a particular object—they just make the call as normal and the subclassed method takes care of the rest. Couple this into your menu control logic and you have the potential to control your application state from a single point! You can subclass many other Visual Basic elements. I will explain how to do this in more detail later in the chapter.

Now you should have a few ideas to start with. Remember that building an application template is a task that should be treated as a project in its own right. Time and budget will need to be allocated for the task; therefore, it makes sense to pin down the requirements beforehand. The success of your template will very much depend on the thought that has gone into its design. In the following sections, I will explain how to perform some of the tasks we have described so far.

SUBCLASSING FUNCTIONS AND SUBROUTINES

To fully understand how subclassing works, you have to understand how Visual Basic resolves which version of a function or subroutine to execute. When Visual Basic encounters a statement such as *Call MySub*, it begins a search for the *MySub* definition. First it looks within the current module, form, or class module for a definition of *MySub*. If it fails to find one, it looks through the rest of the project for a public (or friend) definition of *MySub*. Failing that, it goes to the list of project references (available by choosing References from the Project menu) and resolves each reference in order until it finds the first reference that contains a public definition of *MySub*.

If you check the project references for any project, the first three items in the list you will see are Visual Basic For Applications, Visual Basic Runtime Objects And Procedures, and Visual Basic Objects And Procedures. Because these references contain the definitions for all the intrinsic Visual Basic subroutines, functions, and objects, you will see that, following the rules of the previous paragraph, it is theoretically possible to define local versions of any intrinsic Visual Basic subroutine, function, or object within the program. Unfortunately, this is not the case, as there are some functions that cannot be subclassed for various reasons that I will discuss later in the chapter.

What Are the Benefits of Subclassing?

Subclassing allows you to extend, expand, and even diminish, or degrade, the existing Visual Basic functions and subroutines—perhaps to add extra validation of parameters, perform additional processing to the original function, or even to change the purpose of the function or subroutine altogether. This last choice has obvious pitfalls for users who are not aware that a routine now performs a completely different function than what the manual says, and should be avoided for that reason. For the first two purposes, however, subclassing can add real value to the existing Visual Basic equivalents.

One useful application of subclassing that we have implemented is in replacing the standard Visual Basic *MsgBox* function. The code for our *MsgBox* function is shown here:

```
Public Function MsgBox(ByVal isText As String, _
    Optional ByVal ivButtons As Variant, _
    Optional ByVal ivTitle As Variant, _
    Optional ByVal ivLogText As Variant, _
    Optional ByVal ivBut1Text As Variant, _
    Optional ByVal ivBut2Text As Variant, _
    Optional ByVal ivBut3Text As Variant, _
    Optional ByVal ivBut4Text As Variant) As Integer
'==================================================================
'
'    Module: Message_Box. Function: MsgBox.
'
'    Object: General
'
'    Author - TMS Programmer. TMS Ltd.
'    Template fitted : Date - 01/07/95    Time - 14:27
'
'    Function's Purpose/Description In Brief
'
'    Internal, replacement MsgBox function and statement used in
'    TMS Tools. Allows four buttons, configurable button caption text,
'    and logging of error text to a LOG file. See nInternalMsgBox
'    for more information.
```

>>

```
'
'    This function provides a simple wrapper around frmIMsgBox's
'    nMb2InternalMsgBox method, allowing that method to be called
'    without bothering with the class prefix. As such, its name is
'    not nMb1MsgBox but MsgBox so as to keep its name short and such
'    that it overrides VBA's function/statement of the same name.
'
'    Revision History:
'
'    BY              WHY & WHEN              AFFECTED
'    TMS Programmer. TMS Ltd. - Original Code 01/07/95, 14:27
'
'    INPUTS - See nMb2InternalMsgBox for a description.
'
'
'    OUTPUTS - Possibly nothing, possibly an integer; i.e., as
'              it's a VB function, its return value may be ignored.
'              See nMb2InternalMsgBox for a full description.
'
'==================================================================

     ' Set up general error handler.
     On Error GoTo Error_In_General_MsgBox:

     Const ERROR_ID = "Message_Box - General_MsgBox"

     Call TrTMS2TraceIn(ERROR_ID)
     ' ========== Body Code Starts.==========

     Dim fp      As Form
     Dim sTitle  As String

     ' Create the message box form.
     Set fp = New frmIMsgBox
     Load fp

     If IsMissing(ivTitle) Then
         sTitle = App.MsgBoxTitle & App.Title
     Else
         sTitle = App.MsgBoxTitle & CStr(ivTitle)
     End If

     ' Create and show the message box.
     MsgBox = fp.nMb2InternalMsgBox(isText, ivButtons, sTitle, _
                              ivLogText, ivBut1Text, _
                              ivBut2Text, ivBut3Text, ivBut4Text)
```

```
        ' Destroy the message box form.
        Unload fp
        Set fp = Nothing

        ' ========== Body Code Ends.   ==========
        Call TrTMS2TraceOut(ERROR_ID)

        Exit Function

' Error handler
Error_In_General_MsgBox:

        ' Store error details on stack. Pass procedure name.
        Err.Push ERROR_ID

        ' Add rollback code here...

        Err.Pop

        ' Call TMS error handler.
        Select Case frmErrorHandler.nEhTMSErrorHandler

            Case ERROR_ABORT: Resume Exit_General_MsgBox
            Case ERROR_RETRY: Resume
            Case ERROR_IGNORE: Resume Next
            Case ERROR_END: Call GuDoEndApp
            Case Else: End

        End Select

Exit_General_MsgBox:

End Function
```

This is an example of a routine where we have completely replaced the original Visual Basic functionality. However, it is also possible to use the existing functionality and extend it, as in the following example:

```
Public Property Get EXEName() As String

        EXEName = UCase$(VB.App.EXEName & _
            IIf(App.InDesign = True, ".VBP", ".EXE"))

End Property
```

Here we are simply taking the *EXEName* property of the *App* object and reformatting it to our own standard. Note that to access the original Visual Basic property we must fully qualify the reference. When this is done, Visual Basic ignores the rules above for resolving the location of the routine and instead resolves it directly using the explicit reference.

The potential for subclassing Visual Basic intrinsic functionality should not be underestimated. In the *MsgBox* example alone, the scope you have for customization is enormous. For example, the TMS *MsgBox* function allows you to log any message displayed with the *vbCritical* flag. It contains auto-reply functionality in which you can have the message box automatically choose a reply after a given period of time. You can also configure up to four buttons with custom captions. All this functionality from one Visual Basic method!

Problems with Subclassing

Some Visual Basic functions are not suitable for subclassing. Some functions simply won't subclass because the function names have been made reserved words. *Print* is such an example, as were *CDate* and *CVDate* in Visual Basic 5. Ultimately, there is little that can be done about such functions except create functions with similar—but different—names. This requires that the developers be instructed to use the renamed function instead of the intrinsic function, and thus leaves the door open to inconsistencies within the code.

Functions that have multiple definitions but return a different result type (for example, *Format* and *Format$*) are also not possible to subclass fully. The problem here is that two functions are needed to subclass the function properly, but Visual Basic sees *Public Function Format(...) As Variant* and *Public Function Format$(...) As String* as being the same function and raises a compile-time error of a duplicate function definition. Here, the only option is to subclass the more generic function (in this example, the more generic function is *Format*, as it returns a Variant) and issue instructions to developers not to use *Format$*.

Other functions break Visual Basic's own rules on parameters. An example of this is *InStr*, which takes four arguments, of which the first and fourth arguments are optional. As Visual Basic's rules state that optional arguments must be at the end of a list of arguments, clearly we cannot subclass this function to match exactly the internal definition of it. To get around this, we either have four arguments, with the last two optional, or simply use a *ParamArray* of Variants as a single argument. Both of these solutions require more work within the new version of the function in order to work out which of the four arguments have been supplied.

One "nice to have" feature would be to wrap the subclassed functions in an ActiveX DLL such that the source code was "hidden" from the developers. Unfortunately, this currently isn't possible in Visual Basic. In the beginning of this section, I described the method Visual Basic uses to determine where to find the definition of a function. Remember the three references I listed that always appear at the top of the project references list? Unfortunately, there is no way to prevent those three references from being at the top of the list. This means that the reference to your ActiveX server with the subclassed functions is always below them in the list and, as a result, your subclassed functions are never called. It's a pity that this approach isn't possible, as it would not only hide the details of what extra functionality the subclassed functions contain, but it would also remove the clutter of the extra source code from the application.

Subclassing Objects

Just as it is possible to replace the Visual Basic versions of functions and subroutines, it is also possible to replace the "free" objects that are provided for you during program execution. The *App*, *Err*, and *Debug* objects can all be replaced with objects of your own design, although this does require you to instantiate an instance of each object you are replacing.

Because you are creating new objects of your own, it is essential to include all the properties and methods of the original object and simply pass the calls through to the original object where there is no extra functionality required. An example of this is the *hInstance* property of the *App* object, shown below.

```
Public Property Get hInstance() As Long
    hInstance = VB.App.hInstance
End Property
```

NOTE

Note that *hInstance* is a read-only property of the *VB.App* object so you would not code a *Property Let* for it.

The *App* object

The main uses we have found for subclassing the *App* object are to add new application-level properties and to reformat the output of some of the standard *App* object properties. Typical properties that we find useful to add are *InDesign* (a Boolean value that tells us if we are running within the Visual Basic IDE or as a compiled EXE or ActiveX component), date and numeric formats (from the

Registry), the operating system version details, and various file locations (the application help file and MSINFO.EXE, among others). Other uses for subclassing the *App* object include providing a consistent version number format, and the ability to store Registry settings in different locations depending on the *InDesign* property above (we append either ".EXE" or ".VBP" to *App.ExeName*).

The *Debug* object

This is probably the most difficult and least useful of the system objects to subclass, mainly because an object cannot be created with the name "Debug" and the *Print* method cannot truly be subclassed, as "Print" is a reserved word. For these reasons, it is probably best to leave the *Debug* object alone and, if extra debug-like functions are required, create a completely unrelated object.

The *Err* object

This is probably the most useful object to subclass, as it enables you to apply more consistently your chosen error handling strategy. We add *Push* and *Pop* methods to the error object, and we also make the undocumented *Erl* function a property of the object. In addition, we add an *ErrorStackList* method that allows us to examine the current error stack that we maintain internally within the new *App* object. This allows us to determine, from any point in a program, the routine that raised the current error. For more information on error handling strategies, and an implementation of a replacement "Err," please refer to Chapter 1.

One note of caution with the *Err* object relates to the *Raise* method. Although you should probably add a *Raise* method to your subclassed *Err* object for completeness, you should add code to it to ensure it is never called. The reason for this becomes obvious when you stop to think about it. Your *Err.Raise* method would deal with the error by passing the required details to *VBA.Err.Raise*. This would then generate an error, with the source of the error being your *Err* object every time! When subclassing the *Err* object, you must ensure that *VBA.Err.Raise* statements generate all errors raised in the program.

COMMON FORMS

How many times have you created an "About" form for an application? At the end of the day, all an "About" form does is provide version and copyright information for the application. Copyright information will be standard within an organization, and version information about the program is available via the *App* object. Therefore, "About" is a great example of a generic form that can query the application for the information it needs, and should require no application-specific code in it.

Want a "Tip of the Day" form? Again, this is a generic form that can get its information from a resource file (for the tips) and the Registry (for the last tip displayed and whether to show on startup).

OK, so you've got your error handling sorted out, but you'd like to make it a bit more intelligent than simply showing a message box with the standard Abort/Retry/Ignore buttons. Some errors are prime candidates for the application to retry periodically but still give the user the ability to abort. All you need is to create a form that looks like the message box form, but you should also add a timer. Then all the form needs is a few properties allowing the buttons to be hidden and shown at will, and a property to tell it to automatically retry the error action every *x* seconds. Using the Timer control, the error dialog box can click its own "Retry" button whenever the timer fires. Once you have all this code together, there's no reason why this can't be a generic form. Most people already use *MsgBox* to report errors and that's about as generic as forms come!

Speaking of *MsgBox*, have you ever needed an extra button, or a combination of buttons that's not permitted, or a button with a completely different name than the standard ones? Simply subclass the *MsgBox* function and have your own form that mimics the functionality of *MsgBox*. Now if you need an extra button, you simply need to define a new constant for it and its caption. All the new *MsgBox* code and forms can then become generic, as they are passed all the information they need from the application when the function is called.

Other useful features we have added to our *MsgBox* function include automatic logging of critical messages (where the button includes *vbCritical*) and appending the application title and version details to the beginning of the title text.

HIDE YOUR API CALLS

Unfortunately, Visual Basic still can't do everything. There are times when we need to get information that only the dreaded Windows API can provide. A common requirement is to get version information about a file. Although we can package up the Visual Basic code into a code module and make this part of the base code, we still need to put all of the API declarations and constants at the top of the module. If we're using base code in such a way that we add only the modules we need, things are further complicated by the fact that we then need to declare the APIs as *Private* in each module in which they're used. This way we end up with duplicated definitions, potentially declared differently.

This also allows developers to bypass the rule that API parameters should only be declared *As Any* where this is absolutely necessary. Declaring parameters with a data type of *Any* bypasses the compiler's type checking and allows any data type to be passed to the API. Where this is necessary—such as with *SendMessage*, which can take a long integer or a string as its final parameter—it is best to declare the function twice. This allows you to fully specify the parameter type and the two declarations can then be distinguished by being aliased to different names (such as *SendMessageLng* and *SendMessageStr*).

The best solution to the problem is to remove the API declarations from the Visual Basic code and put them in a type library. A type library performs the same function as the declarations in code, but instead of adding dozens of lines of code, all we need to add to the project is a reference to the type library. Given that one type library can end up being used by many projects, this makes for a much safer and cleaner way of declaring API functions. Constants needed for the API calls and help text (which will appear in the Object Browser) can also be included in a type library.

Type libraries can be a bit tricky to set up and get right but, once created, simplify your project. (Use OLEVIEW.EXE to "de-compile" a type library back to its source—it's an easy way to learn IDL.) The main difficulty in creating type libraries comes from the fact that the API declarations need to be in C format.

I have included a sample type library on the accompanying CD. The TEMPLATE.ODL file is the source file for the type library and can be opened with Notepad or any text editor. The TEMPLATE.TLB file is the compiled type library from the ODL file and is the file that should be selected in the References dialog box. Once that is done, the APIs that have been declared can be browsed via the Object Browser.

To create a type library you need two tools that ship with the Visual Basic CD:

- GUIDGEN.EXE will generate GUIDs for you. (Peet Morris also provides a Visual Basic version of GUIDGEN in Chapter 7.) This is a process that is hidden from you when you create ActiveX components but, put simply, a GUID is the key that is used in the Registry when an ActiveX component is registered. Type libraries require these as well, but whereas Visual Basic generates these and keeps them hidden from you, type libraries require a much more manual process.

- MKTYPLIB.EXE is the type library compiler that will turn your ODL source file into the TLB object file.

REGISTRY TOOLS

GetSetting and *SaveSetting* are valuable tools for getting and saving information to the Registry. However, one of the parameters is the application name, which allows for potential discrepancies between (or even within) applications. To avoid these discrepancies, it is probably best to wrap these functions up in your own functions that hide the application name parameter. This way, you ensure a consistent approach to storing information in the Registry.

Another nice feature that you can implement takes advantage of one of the subclassed properties of the *App* object I mentioned earlier, *App.InDesign*. If your *GetSetting* and *SaveSetting* functions use *App.ExeName* and you have subclassed the *App* object, you can store program information in different locations depending on whether you are running in design mode or as a compiled component.

GetSetting and *SaveSetting* are good for getting and storing program-related information, but sometimes you might need to retrieve information from other areas of the Registry. Functions for doing this require a number of API calls and can be tricky to create. This immediately makes them prime candidates for being written into a common module with more user-friendly parameters than the APIs.

Another example of how subclassing can be used to extend the language would be to add the ability to access any part of the Registry to Visual Basic's Registry functions.

RESOURCE FILES

Resource files are wonderful places for storing strings and graphics that a program might need. Unfortunately, Visual Basic limits us to only one resource file per project, which makes it difficult to use a generic resource file, as we usually require more application-specific data within the resource file.

One way around this limitation is to use a Resource Only Object Server (ROOS). A ROOS is simply an ActiveX component that has the sole purpose of returning data from its own resource file. The ROOS should contain methods to extract data from its internal resource file. You can add all sorts of functionality, such as giving the ROOS the ability to parse tokens and return fully qualified strings. This is similar to how many Microsoft applications work. For example, a ROOS's resource file might contain an entry like this:

```
IDS_ERROR_BADFILEOPEN   "Could not open the file %1, %2"
```

Calling the ROOS method, you could then code:

```
Dim sFileName      As String
Dim vRoosParams    As Variant
Dim oROOS          As MyROOS

On Error Resume Next
sFileName = "C:\MYFILE.TXT"
Open sFileName For Input As #1

If Err.Number <> 0 Then
    Set oROOS = New MyROOS
    ReDim vRoosParams(0 to 1)
    VRoosParams(0) = sFileName
    VRoosParams(1) = Err.Description

    MsgBox oROOS.GetString(IDS_ERROR_BADFILEOPEN, vRoosParams), _
        vbExclamation
End If
```

In this example, an error 53 (File not found) would result in the following message: "Could not open the file C:\MYFILE.TXT, File not found." The ROOS code will in fact be base code that never needs to change. It simply provides an access method to the underlying resource file and gives you parsing functionality. You simply need to create the resource file for the project, attach it to the ROOS, and compile a DLL. You can compile each ROOS with a different class name, like ProjectXROOS or ProjectYROOS for whatever project you are using. This gives you the ability to use multiple resource files within any particular project. Chapter 14 gives a detailed example of how you might build a ROOS.

CUSTOM CONTROLS

Custom controls are a good example of base code that can be reused time and time again. Tired of having to code a *GotFocus* event for every text box to highlight its contents? Why not create a custom TextBox control that handles its own *GotFocus* event but in all other respects acts like a normal text box? The ActiveX Control Interface wizard will generate up to 95 percent of the code you need, leaving you with only a few lines of code to write yourself. A custom control that was generated from this wizard is included with the sample code for this chapter. If you examine the code closely, you will see that the ActiveX Control Interface wizard generated all but four lines!

The sample control simply extends an existing property of another control. However, the wizard makes it equally simple to add custom properties of your own, such as numeric formatting and data validation. For more detailed information on creating custom controls, see Chapter 14. Chapter 6 also provides some information on creating a Year 2000–compliant TextBox control.

DOCUMENTATION

A key area with base code that is often overlooked is that of documentation. It's no good having a library of 20 code modules with hundreds of functions in them if developers have to search through all of them each time they want to see if a common routine already exists to do what they want.

Similarly, if the parameters and return values are not documented, developers might not be able to work out how to call a particular routine or how to interpret the results. When this is the case, the developers will invariably end up writing their own versions of the routine. Consider the following infrastructure routine's interface:

```
GetUserPrivilegeFlags(nUser As Long, _
                nPrivFlags() As Integer, _
                bForcePriv As Boolean, _
                Optional nForcePrivNo As Integer)
```

I know that if I were not intimately familiar with this routine I would be tempted to write my own version. For example, is the array one-dimensional or multidimensional? Do I need to pass the array with values or an uninitialized array?

How on earth are the last two parameters used? You can see the dilemma. The interface is of paramount consideration because it has the potential to scare off any potential users of the routine. Contrast the code above to the same fragment rewritten below:

```
GetUserPrivilegeFlags(ByVal lUserId As Long, _
                      ByRef nPrivFlags() As Integer, _
                      ByVal bGiveSpecificPrivilege As Boolean, _
                      Optional ByVal nSpecificPrivId As PRIVILEGE)
```

By using the *ByVal* and *ByRef* keywords, it is clear what is expected and what is returned. The argument names have been modified to be more meaningful, and the last parameter, *nSpecificPrivId,* has been typed so that a drop-down list of values will be displayed to the user, alleviating any ambiguity for this parameter's value. However, we still have the problem of not knowing the format of the exact requirement for *nPrivFlags*. This problem can be solved by using the Procedure Attributes item in the Tools menu. This allows you to enter a description that appears in the Object Browser when the procedure is selected.

The Object Browser

The Object Browser provides a fairly quick way to scan the contents of a code module. To assist with the scanning process, it is helpful to add a short description to the routines. To do this, select Procedure Attributes from the Tools menu. A description can then be entered that will appear at the bottom of the Object Browser window whenever the routine is selected. The drawback with this is that there is only a limited amount of space available here, and complex functions might require more information to be made available; however, it is possible to use the size bar in the Object Browser window to extend the viewable area. For the lazy ones among you, you can in fact enter procedure attributes directly in the code window. You do this by entering the attribute in the procedure—for example:

```
Attribute GetUserPrivilegeFlags.VB_Description = "My description"
```

The line will be highlighted as a syntax error; however, if you save and reload the file, the *Attribute* line disappears and the description shows up in the Object Browser. Remember that the success of any base code template will be affected by the level of documentation.

Help Files

One approach that we use at TMS is to create a developer help file for the base code. This enables a structured view of the base code to be created. We generally create one help topic per code module, which contains the name and a brief description of each function within the module. Any function that requires more information can be linked to its own help topic, which can provide any detailed information to the developer. This approach has the benefit that keywords can be added to all of the topics, allowing for a search of the information by the developer.

HTML

Using HTML is a similar approach to using a help file, but this approach has the added benefit of being viewable over the company intranet. It also has the benefit of being maintained centrally; when the base code is changed, the developers will immediately have the updated documentation available.

BUILDING YOUR OWN BASE CODE

So far we have discussed why base code is a good idea and some of the techniques that can be used to build it. I hope that by now you're eager to go off and build your own base code. But where do you begin? Who do you get to build it? How do you distribute it to your developers? And most important, how do you put together a convincing business case to justify the project to your boss?

Where Do You Begin?

So where do you start when you want to create your own base code? First remember that the gains to be made from base code are in creating new applications and their subsequent maintenance. To attempt to retrofit base code into existing applications would be difficult at best. Are you sure that the routine you're replacing with a base code routine does *exactly* the same thing?

Second, remember that the beauty of base code is that it is as complete and as thoroughly tested as possible. There's no point in having a set of base code if it's incomplete or full of bugs. It will require a lot of effort to set up initially, but it's worth the effort.

Modules that make up the base code should not have any application-specific code added to them. By its nature, the template must be capable of running as a standalone application in its own right. If you design the template independently of any project, you will be creating a set of base code that will work with any application. It is also important that the base code routines are loosely coupled—that is, each routine should be as self-contained as possible. Never write a base code routine that references elements external to the base code modules. Doing so would in effect prevent you from using the base code in any other project without modification. An ideal strategy would be to have the base code stored in a separate Microsoft Visual SourceSafe project, with the individual projects that use it simply linking to the base project for those modules that they need. Any updates to the base modules would need to be coded only once and the change would then be propagated to each application the next time it was built.

The way you actually construct your base code template will depend very much on where you will be using it. For example, code for an ActiveX control will differ somewhat from code in a full-blown application, which will differ again from an ActiveX DLL. Components without a user interface will probably not require items such as a full-blown message box; however, the base code template for such a component might change the message box functionality to raise some form of remote alert. Template code can be written as objects or as standard modules containing functions, methods, and properties. I advise you to build elements as simply as possible. If you do not need instancing, place your code in a standard module rather than in a class module. The key factor to building your template is to loosely couple everything. Doing this will allow you to extract functionality and reuse it for other templates you want to build.

I have already discussed the importance of your interfaces. You also might want to carefully consider your naming conventions. Because you want the interface to be as intuitive as possible, it is a good idea to use names that break the usual naming standards. For example, you might do this when subclassing existing functionality. To stick rigidly to standards might mean changing the names of procedures or parameters that are well established in the language. This is obviously counterproductive, since the whole idea of subclassing is that the programmer doesn't necessarily know that a change has taken place. Of course, the other problem is that by changing the name of the thing you are subclassing, you are no longer subclassing it!

Who Should Build It?

So you're convinced that base code is a good thing and you've decided to build your own. But which of your developers will you get to do it? Are you going to make it a company-wide development or use a small development team to put it together?

While a large team enables you to put the code together fairly quickly, it makes standards harder to maintain. It also leaves the base code without a clearly defined owner, which makes controlling changes to the code more difficult. A small team ensures high standards of code and a clearly defined ownership. Since part of the object of base code is to abstract complex routines from the application, it also makes sense to use a high-caliber team to create the code.

The code that is created is also going to need to be tested to the highest standards. The developers who are going to use the base code rely on its integrity from day one. If they can't, they are likely to code workarounds for any bugs discovered in the base code, which can then cause problems once the base code is corrected.

Source or Executable?

So do you include the base code in projects as source code or in an ActiveX component? For the reasons discussed above, routines that subclass existing Visual Basic routines must be included as source code in the application. Ideally, as many additional routines as possible should be distributed to the developers in executable form. By placing all the public routines in GlobalMultiUse classes, all the developer has to do is add a reference to the ActiveX component into the project. This also allows the base routines to be subclassed if necessary.

The Business Case

Most companies treat each project in isolation, producing for each a budget and cost-justification. Unfortunately, the project to create a set of base code does not have any immediate impact on the business and is difficult to justify to the business in the short term.

Because the base code must be carefully written and extensively tested before being used in the first project, the business benefits only start to appear about a year after the project starts. Therefore, the project should probably be funded as an internal IT project that can then be recovered from the business in small chunks every time a new application is built on the base code. I cannot stress enough that having no base code will invariably result in either nonstandard code, increased development time, or both. At a time when many organizations are employing the services of third-party contractors, it is important for corporate code to conform to the defined standards of that organization. By having a base to start with, you also increase the likelihood of your standards being adhered to.

Changing Base Code

Just as it is important to create high-quality base code, it is equally important to ensure that base code is changed in a very controlled manner. The base code project within Visual SourceSafe should be regarded as the highest-security project in your organization. As such, only a select core of developers should have anything but read-only access to the project. Remember that any changes to the code will be incorporated in every other application the next time the applications are built.

Controlling changes to the base code is also extremely important. A strict change control process needs to be in place for the base code and every change request must be fully justified. When a change cannot be fully justified, alternative solutions need to be found. See the sidebar on the following page for one possible scenario (along with a solution).

Templates

A nice feature within Visual Basic that was introduced in version 5 is the concept of code and form templates. Now when you add a new form to a project, you no longer get a simple choice between a standard form or an MDI child—you are presented with a whole list of different forms. These are not "common code" in the sense of what we have discussed so far in this chapter, but are close enough to be related.

When you select one of these new types of form, a copy of a prebuilt form is taken and added to your project. In some cases this may simply mean that a few controls have already been placed on the form for you, whereas in other cases there may be significant amounts of code already added. These projects, forms, classes, and modules are all installed in the TEMPLATE folder of your Visual Basic installation.

To create your own templates, simply create the form, module, class, or project that you want to use as a template, and then save the files in the appropriate subfolder of the TEMPLATE folder. Note that when creating a project template, if you do not want the forms, modules, or classes to be individually selectable, you should save them all in the PROJECTS folder.

What to Do When the Base Code Cannot Be Changed

The base code runs as part of an ActiveX DLL with all the functions in a GlobalMultiUse class. Subroutine *Foo* is part of the base code. It currently takes one parameter and is called from six applications that use the base code.

One of the six applications needs an extra parameter to be added to *Foo*. Due to the impact on other applications, this change to the base code is refused. So what can the application do? Simple—subclass *Foo*! This allows us to retain the existing functionality in the base code but to extend it specifically for this application.

It is possible to subclass our own routines in exactly the same way I described earlier the subclassing of the standard Visual Basic routines.

Summary

In this chapter, we've discussed a number of different approaches to using base or template code. You've learned that it isn't necessary to reinvent the wheel every time you sit down in front of the screen. The key to a successful base code strategy is to make sure that it is enforced. There is little point in having a strategy like this if nobody sticks with it. Successful use of base and template code requires a disciplined approach, but can pay huge dividends in the long term.

Mixed Languages with Visual Studio

Peet is a "standards man" and was a member of both the ANSI X3J11 and X3J16 standards groups (C and C++) and was a founding member of the IEEE P1201.1/.2 (API and UI) standards groups. Peet's also a society man: in addition to being a Fellow of the IMIS and the IAP, he is member of the IEEE (and Computer Society) and the ACM.

PETER MORRIS

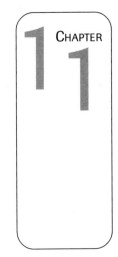

In this relatively short chapter, I want to discuss the concept of mixed language programming (MLP). I'll go into *some* of the pros and cons and considerations of doing MLP with Microsoft Visual Studio. Be warned, though—as the title implies, this chapter cannot be free from other languages; it contains Java, C, and C++ code (and mentions other languages, too, such as FORTRAN and COBOL). None of the other languages is explained in detail, so you might want to skip the code sections of this chapter if you're not up to speed with some of the basics of these particular languages.

WHAT IS MIXED LANGUAGE PROGRAMMING?

From a conceptual point of view, MLP is about connecting code, data, and components that have been constructed using different programming languages. (Did you know that most developers use an average of 2.2 language tools?) However, from a design point of view, MLP is also about choosing the right language up front for the job—the so-called Horses for Courses approach (that is, each language being employed for the purpose for which it is best suited)—and about building reusable code blocks.

One of the most popular approaches to developing components is to apply object-oriented techniques. Object-oriented analysis and design are useful because they enable application designers to approach software development from a higher level of abstraction. Viewing an application as a collection of objects (which have both attributes [state] and behaviors [method]) that interact with each other enables a designer to more effectively model the problem and create an appropriate solution. An object design should be more comprehensible than a series of algorithms. We'll be touching on more object "stuff" throughout this chapter.

In short, MLP lets you take advantage of language-specific features and data structures available in languages outside your main language. Therefore, MLP has the potential to exploit fully the complete range of programming languages within your chosen working set.

Typical MLP Scenarios

The following scenarios in which MLP can be advantageous might help kindle your imagination and help whet your appetite for using MLP.

1. You might be required to write a fast user interface in Microsoft Visual Basic and then call into a remote, platform-independent, Microsoft ActiveX server that was written in Microsoft Visual J++. In turn, that server might want to connect to a couple of DLLs (via COM), one containing collection-oriented Standard Template Library (STL) code written in Microsoft Visual C++ and the other containing code, written in assembly language, for accessing a device such as a hard disk controller. This particular situation is one that every MLP developer dreams about.

NOTE

How portable is Java code really? While I think it's pretty cool in theory, I find that I must agree with Bill Dunlap, Microsoft's Visual J++ Technical Product Manager, when he says that (I'm paraphrasing here) due to the sensitivity of the Java run time to differences in underlying hardware architectures, operating systems, and the virtual machines themselves, the "write once, run anywhere" mantra has all too often been found to translate directly to "write once, debug everywhere."

2. You have the vision to imagine a world in which your mainframe-hosted COBOL code wasn't pejoratively and routinely labeled "legacy code" (for "legacy code" reads "doomed to expire on the mainframe" or perhaps can be relabeled as "heritage code"<g>). The good news is that with MLP, this tried and tested, smoothly-running, expensive, mission critical business logic doesn't need to be ported to be fully exploited by "modern" languages.

3. You have a need to do something that is, by definition, more suited to one language than to another. Name your poison—that's what MLP is all about.

4. For raw speed or flexibility, you've determined that you have only to write a routine or two in Assembler and then link to these routines by calling into a DLL. Easy MLP!

5. You might need pointers in a program you're creating in, say, Visual Basic. Another language *might* be considered more useful simply because that language handles pointers (in the C/C++ sense). We all know that the best programs implement, at each turn, the correct algorithm (putting these before data structures) in the most efficient way possible. More often than not a good algorithm implies some sort of underlying, possibly complex, data structure. Such complex data structures frequently dictate that some pointer manipulation will be required. Ergo, pointers are good for implementing this type of algorithm. An appropriate language for this implementation might be Visual C++ or an assembly language (using the _asm capabilities in Visual C++ or perhaps using Microsoft Macro Assembler [MASM 6.1]). Because they don't support pointers, we probably wouldn't choose either Visual J++ or Visual Basic. No problem—MLP lets us mix 'n match as we please, more or less.

NOTE

Visual Basic cannot (yet) directly use pointers to data or pointers to what's commonly called a "function" (meaning any routine in this context). In this case, the choice between C++, C, or Assembler would most likely come down to some requirement in terms of a clock-cycle count (raw speed) and, perhaps, developer resource.

6. You need to do something that is most suited to a language other than Visual Basic, but the problem doesn't naturally fit into any known language. Normally in such cases you'd resolve this problem by writing your solution in, say, C. (You can pretty much do anything in C correctly!) Alternatively, the proper solution might be to design and write your own language to build certain DLLs. Sound difficult? Don't you believe it—see the section on creating your own "little language," later in this chapter.

What's Required for Using MLP?

To use mixed languages on a development project you need competent developers, the right tools (that's all the tools, with debuggers and profilers included, of course) and you need a very good reason; in other words, what do these other languages offer you that you think you need? For example, if your reason is speed or general performance, consider whether a different language will *really* fix your problems before selecting one. Are you sure that you're using the right algorithm and that it's implemented in the most efficient way possible? Perhaps you should profile your application to make sure that you're focused on the right piece of code, and always do some back-of-the-envelope calculations to ascertain whether you can use your base language in a better way before reaching for some other. After all, it's easier and cheaper to change your existing code using languages you're familiar with than to add to the code using one that's perhaps more alien. However, if you must, and if all else fails, go for it!

I hope you're using Visual Studio, because there are a few languages to choose from—Visual Basic (Visual B++—read the sidebar on page 461), Visual C++, Visual J++, Microsoft Visual InterDev, and last, but by no means least, MASM. What, you mean you didn't know MASM was on your CD? Who among you has already spotted the deliberate mistake? Please forgive me for omitting Microsoft Visual FoxPro—I simply know absolutely nothing about it! Of course, MLP should also allow you to exploit fully your chosen platform and your developer skills.

NOTE

Strictly speaking, a discussion on MLP in Visual Studio should perhaps also mention DHTML, HTML, ASP, SQL, and stored procedures (there, now I've done it!) and whatever else you can think of. Again, because of my personal ignorance, I'm afraid that, just like Visual FoxPro, I've had to omit them. Sorry!

How is MLP Possible in Windows?

As I'm sure I've said elsewhere in this book, one of the truly great and—it must be said—often overlooked features about Windows is the fact that the linkage mechanism (the means by which components connect to one another) is not necessarily defined at the level of the linker. More frequently it's defined at the level of the operating system itself. Throughout the rest of this chapter, linkage defined "early" (by the linker) is referred to as "static linking," while linking defined "late" (by the operating system) is called "dynamic linking." Dynamic linking is at the heart of why MLP is possible in Windows.

You can perform MLP in Windows one of three ways:

- By statically linking object modules that are created using different languages
- By dynamically linking to a "straight" DLL
- By dynamically linking with a COM object

The first two approaches are explained in the following sections. A discussion on dynamic linking with a COM object begins on page 467.

Static linking

Static linking occurs when you use, or consume, a routine that's not defined by your code, but it somehow becomes part of your monolithic executable image on disk.

The original definition of the routine resides in a library of routines elsewhere when you reference it in your code. When you compile your code to object code (meaning the process whereby you convert textual script into real code), the definition of the routine—let's call it *Print*—isn't in your code, it's in a library. However, you don't run object code per se; rather, you run a subtly different form of it: an EXE. You create an executable image from your object code by linking it with other object modules and library files (you also usually link in a bootstrap loader). The linker's job is to bind the object modules and the library routines your object code uses into a single EXE file. During link time the definition of *Print* is literally copied into the resulting executable. Figure 11-1 on the following page shows how this looks diagrammatically.

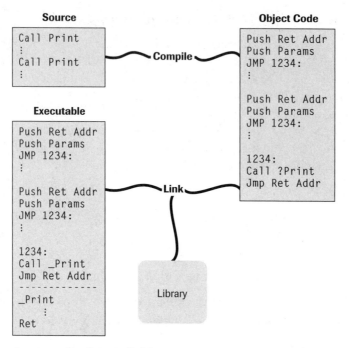

Figure 11-1   *An example of static linking*

Here our source code contains two calls to a routine named *Print*. We haven't defined this routine in our code; it's simply a routine supplied by the language or the library vendor. When we compile our code into an object module you can see that the code has changed; essentially the call to *Print* has been replaced with a *Jump* instruction. A *Jump* instruction transfers program control to a specified location (a bit like a *GoSub* statement). In this example, the specified location is 1234. Notice that before we jump we load a parameter, which is the string to be used as a parameter to the *Print* routine. Don't worry about where this parameter is loaded; just read it as "passes this parameter." The address 1234, which is shown at the bottom of the object code, contains a call to a routine named *?Print*. The question mark here signifies that we still don't have a clue as to where *Print* really is. It's certainly not in this object file! Notice that the two uses of *Print* in the source code have been compressed into one—in other words, we have only one call to the actual *Print* routine. (Or anyway, we will have.)

Next the code is linked. Notice that the linker links not just our single object code file but also includes the library discussed earlier. The linker copies the definition of *Print* from the library and places it into a new file along with the object code. This new file is the EXE file. In addition to providing the definition of *Print,* the linker has also updated the original object code to read *Call _Print*. The definition of *Print* is called *_Print* in the library. No matter.

NOTE

I should say that this static linkage mechanism is still used in most Windows programs today, but it's mixed with dynamic linking, too. I'll explain this in the next section.

This static linking behavior is exhibited in MS-DOS programs. I mean real MS-DOS programs and not "console programs," although these, too, can be statically linked. Static linking behavior also enables an executable to contain all the code it requires. Remember the days when you could give someone an EXE and they could run it simply by entering its name at the command prompt? Of course, those days have long since passed and we're all aware that it's not as simple as that anymore! We've all seen messages saying that we're missing some file or another and that a particular application therefore cannot be run. The missing file is usually a dynamically loaded library that has eluded the program loader; in other words, it can't find some of your code, so how is it supposed to run the application?

WHAT'S IN A NAME?

I find the moniker Visual Basic terribly outdated these days—wouldn't something like "Visual B++" be a much better product label now? After all, isn't C++ purported to be a "better C?" And anyway, when was the last time you saw a language named BASIC that could use and create pointers, forms, classes, DLLs, objects, type libraries, ActiveX controls, documents, and so forth?

While I'm at it, here's another thought: are you a developer who truly deserves to be using *Beginners* All-purpose Symbolic Instruction Code? If you're reading this book, I should think not. Is your company's mission-critical application truly safe in a beginner's hands (by induction, that's both you and the language)? I think it's about time for a name change and I vote for Visual B++— it's better than BASIC. What do you think? Seriously, let me know and I'll forward on the top, say, five suggestions to the Visual Basic team! In fact, I like Visual B++ so much that to try it out, I'm going to use it in the rest of this chapter in preference over Visual Basic!

Dynamic linking

Dynamic linking doesn't differ too much from static linking, as it turns out. The compiler still creates more or less the same old object file and the linker creates almost the same old executable, as shown in Figure 11-2.

Notice that I've changed the name of the library—it's now called an import library. Import libraries contain no code; unlike their static cousins, they contain only information. This information is primarily concerned with where definitions of routines are stored.

Picking up our example at link time, the linker "sees" that the object code needs to use *Print* and therefore must resolve this reference. However, the object code doesn't find the definition of *Print* in the import library, but instead finds a further reference to the routine, something like *X:_Print*. This reference means that the routine is contained within a DLL named X. The linker doesn't find X.DLL, extract the code for *Print*, and then insert it into the EXE it's building; instead, the linker simply places roughly the same reference into the code that it did last time. The EXE *still* doesn't contain the actual code for *Print*; it contains a roadmap that leads the program loader to the definition at load time. In this case, the definition is the *_Print* routine in X.DLL.

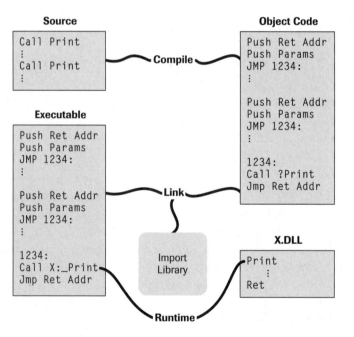

FIGURE 11-2   *An example of dynamic linking*

When the application is loaded, the Windows program loader determines that the code is incomplete. (It's missing the *Print* routine in our case.) The loader sees that the definition of *Print* resides in X.DLL and tries to find it in your file system. Let's assume that the loader finds the definition, loads the DLL into memory, and then searches it for the routine *_Print*. When the loader finds *_Print* it establishes at which address the routine's been loaded (remember, it just did this) and then inserts that actual address into the EXE image that it's still in the process of loading. In other words, as your application is loading, Windows resolves an implicit request for a service or routine in your binary image and replaces it with a call to the actual implementation of the routine.

In truth, the preceding was a somewhat simplified description of what actually goes on. (You really don't want, or probably need, to know all the gory details!) But you should still have a good idea of how clever Windows is!

Mixed static and dynamic linking

Both static and dynamic linking are used in Visual Basic (Visual B++). This is especially true when you're compiling to native code because each module in your project (Class, Module, or Form) is compiled to an object module, which are linked statically by LINK.EXE. However, a Visual B++ application also uses a run-time library, in this case the MSVBVM60.DLL. Because this is a dynamic link library, you can see that a Visual B++ application consists of both statically and dynamically linked code and data.

In fact, Visual B++ applications can also use both forms of dynamic linking (straight DLLs and ActiveX components). Visual B++ applications use ActiveX linking all the time—VBA, the language, lives in such a server component.

The cool things about dynamic linking

A good question to ask at this time is "Why do all this dynamic linking?" The answer is not terribly straightforward because there are many reasons, including some that are historical and that I don't intend to cover here. However, one reason might be that, traditionally, developers have used libraries of routines as a way of accessing the functionality of a component. These libraries implement their routines through an API. Reusing routines like these, packaged as a DLL, is as simple as learning the semantics of the API and linking to the library.

Whatever the reason, however, it's generally a good idea to use and build DLLs because they allow the operating system a greater degree of freedom in how it handles shared resources. The bottom line is that since the linking of components is being done at the operating system level, mixing languages should be much easier to accomplish now than it was in the dark ages of MS-DOS (A-Mess-DOS).

That all said, the traditional approach of using APIs to access the functionality of a software component does have its drawbacks. These drawbacks include evolution of the API, versioning, component communication, and the implementation language. I'll discuss these issues shortly, but first it's time for more history.

Let me tell you a story

Before we had this dynamic linking mechanism, to use MLP we had to find a linker that could link, say, Microsoft C with some other vendor's language. The problem was that such a linker just couldn't exist. Why not? Because each and every language vendor defined their own proprietary object file formats. In other words, the Microsoft linker couldn't understand the object code produced by any other language vendor's compiler, and no other vendor's linker could understand Microsoft C object code. The result was an impasse; and to save everyone's hair from being pulled out, a single-language programming mentality reigned. In fact, to a large degree, it still does.

We've seen that it was very difficult to get languages from different vendors to talk to one another. However, in truth, it was often worse than I've described, because even the languages produced by the same vendor hardly linked up without a fight. I can well remember trying to get code from Microsoft Pascal version 4 to link with Microsoft C code—there were 40 pages devoted to the topic in the Pascal manual and it took me days to figure it out. Man, do I feel old!

Of course, as soon as every vendor's object file format was effectively "neutralized" by Windows, things got a lot easier and I have since been involved with a great many projects where we mixed languages to build an entire system. (Very successfully, too, I might add.)

Mixed Language Approaches

You can actually perform MLP in a variety of ways. The following sections present a few for you to consider.

Using a straight DLL

Probably the easiest way for most languages to communicate is by using a straight DLL, which exports a simple API. In other words, a straight DLL is a traditional DLL. What I mean by "traditional" in this case is a DLL that has an essentially unstructured, arbitrary interface that is in some way referenced via *GetProcAddress*. (If you don't understand, don't worry—you don't need to.). Straight DLLs are cool but they have some warts, too.

Evolution of the API   The evolution of an API is a problem for both the API creator and the software vendors who use the API. Any changes the creator makes to the API after its initial release might break existing applications that consume it. Changes made by the vendors to extend the API can result in inconsistent implementations.

Versioning   Advertising and maintaining different versions of the API can also be problematic. After all, how can an API creator force a developer to check the version of the DLL to ensure it's the version that's compatible with the developer's program? Actually, one way to do this is to create a routine in the API that returns the DLL's version and, at the same time, "arms" the DLL, preparing it for further use. If the developer doesn't call the "version inquiry" routine, any call into the rest of the API will fail. The vendor might want to extend this version logic. They could have each routine mandate that the developer pass to the DLL its own version number (which was returned from the arming API call), or perhaps the version number of the version the developer requires. The DLL version and the required version might be different. If the DLL version is later than the required version, the DLL should run smoothly. If the DLL version is earlier than the required version, it should degrade gracefully—fail predictably, in other words. <g>

Component Communication   Enabling components to communicate with each other is challenging, especially if different developers have created the components. Each developer might use a different technique, such as "pass me a parameter structure," "pass me a pointer," "pass a variadic by value, list of parameters," and so forth. Each developer might also expect parameters to be passed using a subtly different mechanism.

Implementation Language   The programming language you use for creating components greatly impacts how the components will communicate through an API. For example, if you create components in C++ and export classes from a library, it can be a challenge to use C or Visual Basic to create the client of the component. For example, in order to "properly" use a C++ object you need to be able to invoke C++ methods on it. This, in turn, requires you to pass what's known in C++ as a *this* pointer to the method. (The *this* pointer gives the method a pointer to the instance of the object on which it must operate.)

The Fix   An ActiveX DLL has an inherent mechanism, or "rightness," to its exported entry points that brings order to what can sometimes be a truly chaotic environment. The structure of the ActiveX DLL is defined not by a series of exported functions (you can see these by running DUMPBIN /EXPORTS SOMEDLL.DLL) but via a type library (which you can see by using OLEView).

In the case of ActiveX DLLs created in Visual B++, the type library is added by Visual B++ to each ActiveX DLL you build. (More on this later.)

Notice that a call to a straight (non-ActiveX) DLL must be *from* Visual B++ *to* some other language because Visual B++ can create only ActiveX DLLs. For example, say you want to mix C and Visual B++. First you write a DLL in C, and then you call into this DLL from Visual B++—not the other way around. DLLs in Visual B++ are ActiveX DLLs and as such you have no control over defining a non–ActiveX interface to them (unless you're a real hacker).

Of course, this straight DLL stuff is the kind of MLP you're probably already used to handling from the Visual B++ end. You'll be defining external entry points into some DLL via a Visual B++ *Declare* statement:

```
Declare Function GetSystemMetrics Lib "User32" _
(ByVal n As Integer) As Integer
```

This *Declare* statement essentially declares the external *GetSystemMetrics* routine in USER32.DLL to be an external C routine.

The challenge in writing DLLs like this is twofold:

1. Getting parameter data types converted correctly. For example, how is a Date passed? Does Integer mean 16 bits or 32 bits?

2. Passing these parameters to the DLL in the way that it expects them to arrive (not in terms of their definition but their placement in memory). For example, some language compilers support so-called "fast" ways to pass parameters to and from called routines. Normally, of course, parameters are passed on the stack. However, if parameters are instead pushed into registers, a faster call results. (It's quicker to push and pop a value into and out of a register than it is to access the stack.) Pushing to registers is great if, as the called routine, you're expecting to pull parameter values out of registers, of course, but no good whatsoever if you expect to find them on the stack! In the latter case, you'll either be working with garbage or playing with Dr. Watson.

TIP

It's best to compile DLL code using the most basic calling convention available (either *_stdcall* or the Pascal calling conventions) as it's probably the most widely used by clients. By the way, even if you're not calling your C DLLs from Visual B++ today, don't forget that you might want to in the future. Compiling the C DLLs now to use a standard calling convention will protect you later if you decide to call into your back-end DLL from a Visual B++ front end (say).

To resolve both these issues you must *really* know your language compiler. Notice that I don't say "know your language." Most often the language definition will say nothing about how parameters are passed—just that they can be passed! It's up to the language compiler vendors to interpret the language specification as they see fit. If the vendors want to pass parameters using registers, for instance, they're at liberty to do so. You need to check your compiler's documentation and command-line switches to understand how it's working. (See VB5DLL.DOC in the CHAP11 folder on the companion CD for more information.)

Using COM and ActiveX vs. Using a DLL

A DLL is an operating system facility whereas COM is a specification (and some technology) that's been designed from the ground up for building and publishing components and for exporting interfaces. Because COM happens to be implemented largely through the DLL linkage mechanism, you should prefer it to a DLL. However, because language vendors must support it, the DLL linkage mechanism is by far the most common method for connecting objects at run time. Table 11-1 and Table 11-2 on the following page help summarize the pros and cons of using COM/ActiveX and a DLL.

TABLE 11-1   **PROS AND CONS OF USING COM/ACTIVEX**

Pros (subjective)	Cons (subjective)
Well implemented, understood technology.	Registry and installation dependent. (The integrity and "correctness" of the system Registry determines the ultimate integrity of the application that depends on it.)
Designed from the ground up to be portable across architectures; thus inherently cross-platform.	Isolates architectural boundaries.
Part of the operating system.	Based on the Windows operating system.
A Microsoft standard.	A "wholly-owned" Microsoft standard.
Somewhat versioned by the operating system in the form of the GUID and the Registry.	Requires a certain amount of extra savvy on the part of the developer to use with any authority.
Tools such as Visual B++ create COM components by default.	Technology is cutting edge and thus often prone to being misapplied or badly applied by inexperienced developers.
Trendy and fashionable.	The current fad?

TABLE 11-2   **PROS AND CONS OF USING A DLL**

Pros (subjective)	Cons (subjective)
These days, most languages support building DLLs, so the language choice is vast.	Arbitrary interface.
Subject to running afoul of version problems and bad linkage, especially if the DLL doesn't contain a VERSIONINFO resource or if that resource isn't tested by the consuming module.	True DLLs cannot be built by Visual Basic (only ActiveX DLLs can be built that export objects).
Skills required to understand the technology are fundamental.	

COM   COM is a standard (or model) for the interaction of binary objects. An important feature of COM is that objects are precompiled, which means that the implementation language is irrelevant. If you include tokenized code (for example, the p-code in Visual B++ or the bytecode in Java), objects will not necessarily be tied to a specific hardware platform or operating system. COM is also an integration technology. Components can be developed independently and COM provides the standard model for integrating these components. One can think of COM as an enabling technology rather than as a solution in itself.

The major goals of COM are language and vendor independence, location transparency, and reduced version problems.

Language independence   When developing components, you should not need to choose a specific language. In COM, any language can be used as long as it allows functions to be called through function pointers. Even interpreted languages are not excluded if the interpretive environment can provide these pointer services on behalf of the application. You can therefore develop COM component software by using languages such as C++, Java, Visual B++, and Microsoft Visual Basic, Scripting Edition (VBScript).

Location transparency   In addition, you should not have to know in which module and location the file system provides a service. This becomes increasingly important when specific services cannot be provided locally, if services are late bound, or if the process that provides these services changes location. Just as hard-coded paths are problematic in applications, hard-coded dependence on the location of services can also cause errors. COM separates clients from servers, which allows servers to be moved without impacting clients.

Vendor independence   Consider an example of what happens frequently in one of the most current models for software development. A new vendor provides an ODBC driver for your database that is better than the driver provided by your current vendor. It would be a lot of effort if you had to port all existing code to use the new driver. The effort involved might tempt you to keep the existing, less effective driver. But because COM objects export only interfaces, any new object that exposes the same interfaces as an existing object can transparently replace the existing object. Vendor independence extends not just to external vendors, but also internally to objects that can be easily upgraded without recompiling.

Reduced version problems COM requires immutable interfaces. Although this specification requirement does not entirely eliminate version problems, it greatly reduces the extent of the problem.

DLLs in Java

As a language, Java is pretty cool because it gives you the tools you need to do some serious object-oriented development without some of the complications and overhead of the object-oriented assembly language approach in C++. Visual J++ 6 also has a recognizable IDE and, as far as Visual B++ developers are concerned, follows a familiar development metaphor. For Visual B++ developers, Visual J++ 6 is probably the natural choice for creating DLLs as opposed to, say, Visual C++.

If you wanted to get some Java code to work with Visual B++, one easy way to join the two is by utilizing a DLL as a kind of go-between.

Calling out of Java From time to time, Java, like any professional language, needs the native capabilities provided by the operating system. Indeed, the designers of the Java language realized this need long ago, so since Sun Microsystem's Java Development Kit (JDK) 1.0.2 we've been able to call out of Java and into the operating system. We do this through "native methods," also called the Raw Native Interface (RNI). With Java, this need to go outside is especially acute since built-in functionality is incomplete (due primarily to its portability, a common problem with any cross-platform product or technology). Try implementing F1-Help in a Java program for an example of what I mean. As I've stated, Java's creators anticipated this need and had the foresight to define native methods.

In Java, a method that is modified (flagged) as native is implemented in platform-dependent code, which is typically written in another programming language such as C, C++, or assembly language. The declaration of a native method is followed by a semicolon only, whereas an internal Java method declaration would be followed by a block of implementation code.

In Visual J++, Microsoft has extended the native metaphor and named the result J/Direct. For example, they've made it extremely simple to call DLLs, which are declared via Javadoc comment blocks. In fact, J/Direct is so good at allowing you to call out of Java that Microsoft itself uses the technology in the Windows Foundation Classes (WFC) to give Visual J++ great performance when it comes to creating, and even tearing down, your application's user interface.

In summary, J/Direct allows you to call most any DLL directly (a Windows DLL or your own). The Virtual Machine (VM) also takes care of thorny issues such as mapping of data types for you.

Comparing J/Direct to the RNI   J/Direct and native calls are complementary technologies. Using the RNI requires that DLL functions adhere to a strict naming convention, and it requires that the DLL functions work harmoniously with the Java garbage collector. That is, RNI functions must be sure to call *GCEnable* and *GCDisable* around code that is time-consuming, code that could yield, code that could block on another thread, and code that blocks while waiting for user input. RNI functions must be specially designed to operate in the Java environment. In return, RNI functions benefit from fast access to Java object internals and the Java class loader.

J/Direct links Java with existing code such as the Microsoft Win32 API functions, which were not designed to deal with the Java garbage collector and the other subtleties of the Java run-time environment. However, J/Direct automatically calls *GCEnable* on your behalf so that you can call functions that block or perform user interfaces without having a detrimental effect on the garbage collector. In addition, J/Direct automatically translates common data types such as strings and structures to the forms that C functions normally expect, so you don't need to write as much glue code and wrapper DLLs. The trade-off is that DLL functions cannot access fields and methods of arbitrary Java objects. They can only access fields and methods of objects that are declared using the @dll.struct directive. Another limitation of J/Direct is that RNI functions cannot be invoked from DLL functions that have been called using J/Direct. The reason for this restriction is that garbage collection can run concurrently with your DLL functions. Therefore, any object handles returned by RNI functions or manipulated by DLL functions are inherently unstable. Fortunately, you can use either RNI or J/Direct (or both). The compiler and the Microsoft VM for Java allow you to mix and match J/Direct and RNI within the same class as your needs dictate.

Why might you want to call DLL code instead of coding purely in Java? Here are a few reasons:

- A lot of code already exists in C and C++. These languages have been around for a long time, remember, so there's probably a lot of legacy code in existence that could be made available to your Java code via a DLL. If you have such a code base, J/Direct provides an easy way to utilize it that avoids rewriting large bodies of code.

- Java code compiles into what's called bytecode. One strength and, as it happens, one weakness of p-code—oops, I mean bytecode—is that the file format is very well documented (for the VM writers mainly). Hence it is extremely easy to reverse engineer; indeed, a whole raft of third-party utilities ready to download exist that can disassemble bytecode back into easy-to-read source code. Using J/Direct with a native DLL therefore can provide a more secure approach to deploying sensitive applications.

- The Sun Abstract Windowing Toolkit (AWT) is the library from which graphical user interface (GUI) applications are constructed—and it sucks. By using J/Direct you can bypass the AWT to use a more traditional, Windows SDK–type, approach to access the operating system's API.

Here's an example of a Java application (this code is the entire thing) showing how easy it is to call a Windows routine, *MessageBox*, in this case.

```
class ShowMsgBox
{
    public static void main(String args[])
    {
      MessageBox(0, "It worked!",
                "This is a message box from Java", 0);
        }

    /** @dll.import("USER32") */
    private static native int MessageBox(
                                        int hwnd
                                      , String text
                                      , String title
                                      , int style
                                      );

}
```

Simple, eh?

Calling into or out of Java Microsoft's VM for Java has added the ability to treat COM objects as special Java classes. COM integration is best for calling APIs that are wrapped in COM objects, or for ActiveX controls. About the only disadvantage to this wrapping method is that there's a translation layer between Java and COM, so the performance won't be as fast as if you were using C++ (and therefore had one less translation layer).

Creating this type of COM object is really simple if you're a Visual B++ developer, which I assume you already are. Here are the steps. Follow along if you have Visual J++ 6 installed.

1. Select New Project from the File menu. From the New Project dialog box open the Components folder then select COM DLL. Change the Name and Location if you want and click Open.

2. In the Project Explorer double-click the class that's been inserted for you by default (Class1). This will open CLASS1.JAVA in the code editor.

You'll see something like this:

```java
// Class1.java

/**
 * This class is designed to be packaged with a COM DLL output format.
 * The class has no standard entry points, other than the constructor.
 * Public methods will be exposed as methods on the default COM interface.
 * @com.register ( clsid=B6E79300-384E-11D2-B30B-008C7360DC1,
 * typelib=B6E79301-384E-11D2-B30B-0080C7360DC1 )
 */

public class Class1
{
    // TODO: Add additional methods and code here

    /**
     * NOTE: To add auto-registration code, refer to the documentation
     * on the following method
     *    public static void onCOMRegister(boolean unRegister) {}
     */
}
```

Notice that when you generate a COM DLL the opening comments specify a class ID, signifying that this class is a COM class. Visual J++ has an option that lets you specify whether this class should be a COM class. Select Project Properties from the Project menu and then click the COM Classes tab. By default the check box for Class1 is checked, meaning make Class1 a COM class.

3.   Add the following boldface code to make your class look like this:

```java
// Class1.java

import com.ms.wfc.ui.*;

/**
 * This class is designed to be packaged with a COM DLL output format.
 * The class has no standard entry points, other than the constructor.
 * Public methods will be exposed as methods on the default COM interface.
 * @com.register ( clsid=B6E79300-384E-11D2-B30B-008C7360DC1,
 * typelib=B6E79301-384E-11D2-B30B-0080C7360DC1 )
 */

public class Class1
{

    // TODO: Add additional methods and code here
    public int Doit()
    {

        String sText = new String ();
        sText = "Hello from Java";

        return MessageBox.show (
                    sText
                    ,"Java"
                    ,MessageBox.DEFBUTTON1        |
                    MessageBox.ICONEXCLAMATION |
                    MessageBox.YESNOCANCEL
                    );

    }
}
```

4. Build your project by selecting Build from the Build menu. Select Deploy Solution from the Project menu. You're now finished with Java (for the time being).

You can change wfc.ui.* to awt.ui.* in order to use the real, non–J/Direct Abstract Windowing Toolkit (although you'd want to do this only to build cross-platform). You'll find this project in the CHAP11\JAVADLL folder on the the companion CD.

USING A SINGLE ENTRY POINT

One of the most common ways to call into a DLL is to use a single entry point and a service identifier. The service identifier specifies what action to take on a set of parameters. It's like having several routines wrapped into one. Here's some Visual B++ code (better than pseudocode even!) to give you an idea of what this type of call might look like:

```
Const SERVICE_1 As Integer = 1
Const SERVICE_2 As Integer = 2

Private Sub Command1_Click()

    Call Service(SERVICE_1, 1, 2, 3, 4)
    Call Service(SERVICE_2)

End Sub

Public Function Service( _
                    ByVal nService As Integer _
                    , ParamArray Params() As Variant _
                    ) As Boolean

    Dim nRequiredParams As Integer

    Service = True

    Select Case nService

        Case SERVICE_1:
            nRequiredParams = 4
```

```
        GoSub TestParams:

    Case SERVICE_2:
        nRequiredParams = 0
        GoSub TestParams:

    Case Else:
        Service = False

End Select

Exit Function

TestParams:

    If (UBound(Params) + 1) < nRequiredParams Then _
    Err.Raise Number:=5

    Return

End Function
```

You can see that the *Service* routine can handle practically any number of requests. Also, because the routine accepts a variable number and type of parameters (because it's using a parameter array), it's very flexible. Notice too that we're checking that each service is being passed the number of arguments it expects to be working with. You can find this code in the CHAP11\VBSER-VICE folder on the companion CD.

The beauty of coding entry points like this is that to add another virtual entry point, all you have to do is add another service—the interface to the DLL remains the same.

How do you know whether a *Service* routine supports a certain service request before you call it? You probably don't need to know because the routine simply takes no action except to set the *Service* routine's return value to False. Therefore, the only time it can be False is if a service request fails. Of course, many alternative strategies exist for determining whether the *Service* routine is current enough to be useful to you, from checking its version number to having it check a passed GUID with one of its own to verify that you're not going to be disappointed.

USING COM INSTEAD OF NORMAL DLL ENTRY

In Visual B++, you can define a more structured interaction with other languages by using COM for your communications. That is, you can use objects defined via a type library that have been implemented in other programming languages like Visual C++. (Indeed, it's difficult these days to *not* use COM in any Visual C++ development, just as it is in Visual B++.)

However, using COM you can also use objects defined in Visual B++ from, say, Visual C++ or Visual J++. Of course, COM is Microsoft's standard protocol for integrating independently developed software components, so here's a better look at how the connectivity is achieved.

Connectivity Example

Let's say that we use Visual B++ to create an ActiveX DLL that contains a single class called CTest. Let's also say that CTest has a property (defined both as a procedure and as a public data item), a method (sub), and an event. Create the sub with no parameters, name the sub *DoIt*, and within the sub invoke Visual B++'s *MsgBox* routine with *App.EXEName* as an argument. How can this be consumed by a Visual C++ developer?

First compile the Visual B++ project to create the ActiveX DLL. Let's call the project ObjTest, so now we have OBJTEST.DLL. That does it for the Visual B++ piece. Notice that I haven't elaborated on the process here, as I'm assuming that this is not your first foray into building ActiveX components.

Next start Visual C++ and create a new MFC AppWizard workspace (select New from the File menu, then select MFC AppWizard (exe) from the Projects tab). Name the workspace Test. Using the wizard that starts when you click OK, add whatever options you want. If this is your first experience with MFC, C++, or Visual C++ (or all the above), I'd suggest you select Single Document in Step 1 and check the Automation checkbox in Step 3; leave the default choices for all the other options. When you click the wizard's Finish button, the wizard will build an application for you. The resulting application is Windows API, C++, and MFC code. Don't expect to see anything similar to the Visual B++ interface.

Next use the ClassWizard to add the necessary C++ classes to mirror your Visual B++-generated OBJTEST CTest class.

1. Select ClassWizard from the View menu.
2. In the MFC ClassWizard dialog box click the Add Class button and select From A Type Library.

3. Select OBJTEST.DLL from the File Open dialog box. The next dialog box should show _CTest and __CTest highlighted, since it should be your only class. Click OK. The ClassWizard will now add more C++ source code to your project.

Now that all the automatic code has been built, select Find In Files from the Edit menu, enter *AfxOleInit*, and then hit Enter. Double-click the line that appears in the Find In Files 1 tab in your Output window to go to the code that the IDE found. The code will look something like this:

```
// Initialize OLE libraries
if (!AfxOleInit())
{
    AfxMessageBox(IDP_OLE_INIT_FAILED);
    return FALSE;
}
```

This code was inserted because you checked the Automation checkbox in Step 3 of the AppWizard. Before an application can use any of the OLE system services, it must initialize the OLE system DLLs and verify that the DLLs are the correct version. The *AfxOleInit* routine does all we want it to. We need to run this routine, of course, because we're about to talk to—automate—our OBJTEST DLL via OLE and COM.

Navigate through the code to someplace suitable where you can add the necessary code to automate the DLL. I suggest you use Find In Files to locate *void CTestApp::OnAppAbout()*. This is a class function (I can't really explain what this is here, so please just carry on) that's used to create the application's About box. Replace the two lines of code between the C-style braces ({}) with the following:

```
_CTest * pCTest = new _CTest;

if(FALSE == pCTest -> CreateDispatch("ObjTest.CTest"))
{
    AfxMessageBox("Can't create dispatch table.");
}
else
{
    pCTest -> DoIt();

    pCTest -> DetachDispatch();
    pCTest -> ReleaseDispatch();
}
```

You also need to add a statement at the top of the file to include the new header file:

```
#include "ObjTest.h"
```

Next build and run the application. If you followed all my instructions exactly you shouldn't have any trouble building the application. If you do, go over the instructions once more.

So what just happened, from the top?

Using ClassWizard to add the type library caused Visual C++ to add some C++ classes to your project to mirror those in the DLL. Visual C++ will have named these classes the same as your Visual B++ classes prefixed with an underscore. _CTest is our main class.

The code we added to the About box routine creates a new _CTest C++ class instance and stores its address in memory in the variable *pCTest* (a pointer to a _CTest object, if you will). The C++ class inherits some routines (think of *Implements*), one of which we now call: *pCTest -> CreateDispatch()*. This routine connects C++ functions defined in our C++ class _CTest with interfaces in a CTest object—the Visual B++ object, that is. We then call *DoIt*, our routine that does something. You should see the message OBJTEST appear in a message box when this is called (when you select About from the Help menu). Since we're basically through with our Visual B++ class now, we disconnect ourselves from it, which is what *DetachDispatch* and *ReleaseDispatch* do.

NOTE

The class __CTest (two underscores) contains the event we defined.

Can these routines in the C++ classes be called from routines in other languages, perhaps from C? The answer is "Yes," because you can export the routines (make them available as "ordinary exports") by using a class modifier such as *Class _declspec(dllexport) _CTest{};*. However, this exposes the C++ class methods and properties via their decorated names; each will also be expecting to be passed an instance of the class type via a pointer parameter called *this*. All in all, not very easy.

NOTE

The code for the connectivity example can be found on the companion CD in the CHAP11 folder. The project for the CTest class is in the VBCTEST subfolder; the project for the ObjTest DLL is in the OBJTEST subfolder; and the Visual C++ code is in the TEST subfolder.

Calling C++ DLLs from Visual B++

DLLs are separate binary modules that allow developers to share code easily at run time. If you have Visual B++–based client code that needs to use a C++ class (like a dialog box) that lives within a DLL, you basically have three options.

The first option is to write a single C++ function that invokes the dialog box and returns the results to the Visual B++ client. The advantage to this approach is that both the client code and the server code are fairly straightforward. The disadvantage to this approach is that the client code doesn't have a whole lot of control over the dialog box.

The second option is to provide a set of functions in the C++ DLL that manipulate the C++ object. With this approach each function must provide the client code with a handle, and the client code must write a single entry point for each member function it wants to use. The advantage to this approach is that the client has fairly good control over the dialog box. The downside is that the DLL code has to provide wrappers for each class member function (most tedious!), and the client has to keep track of the handle.

The third option is to have the C++ class within the DLL implement a COM interface. The advantage of this method is that the client code becomes greatly simplified. The client gets to use the C++ class in an object-oriented manner. In addition, most of the location and creation details are hidden from the client. This approach means buying into COM. However, that's generally a good thing because just about everything coming out of Redmond these days is based on COM. Using COM from Visual B++ is a good place to start.

Passing a Visual B++ Object to Visual C++

You can pass objects from a function in Visual B++ to most languages that support pointers. This is because Visual B++ actually passes a pointer to a COM interface when you pass an object.

All COM interfaces support the *QueryInterface* function, so you can use any passed interface to get to other interfaces you might require. To return an object to Visual B++, you simply return an interface pointer—in fact, they're one in the same.

Here's an example taken from the MSDN CDs. The following *ClearObject* function will try to execute the *Clear* method for the object being passed, if it has one. The function will then simply return a pointer to the interface passed in. In other words, it passes back the object.

```c
#include <windows.h>

#define CCONV _stdcall

LPUNKNOWN CCONV ClearObject(LPUNKNOWN * lpUnk)
{
    auto LPDISPATCH pdisp;

    if(
      NOERROR ==
      (*lpUnk) -> QueryInterface(IID_IDispatch, (LPVOID *)&pdisp)
     )
    {
        auto DISPID      dispid;
        auto DISPPARAMS  dispparamsNoArgs = {NULL, NULL, 0, 0};
        auto BSTR        name = "clear";

        if(
           S_OK == pdisp -> GetIDsOfNames(IID_NULL, &name, 1, NULL,
                                          &dispid)
        )
        {
            pdisp -> Invoke(
                            dispid
                            ,IID_NULL
                            ,NULL
                            ,DISPATCH_METHOD
                            ,&dispparamsNoArgs
                            ,NULL
                            ,NULL
                            ,NULL
                            );
        }

        pdisp -> Release();
    }

    return *lpUnk;
}
```

The following Visual B++ code calls the *ClearObject* function:

```
Private Declare Function ClearObject Lib "somedll.dll" _
    (ByVal X As Object) As Object

Private Sub Form_Load()

    List1.AddItem "item #1"
    List1.AddItem "item #2"
    List1.AddItem "item #3"
    List1.AddItem "item #4"
    List1.AddItem "item #5"

End Sub

Private Sub ObjectTest()

    Dim X As Object

    ' Assume there is a ListBox with some displayed items
    ' on the form.
    Set X = ClearObject(List1)

    X.AddItem "This should be added to the ListBox"

End Sub
```

Using an ActiveX Control for MLP

What's the difference between an ActiveX in-process server and an ActiveX control? Not much, unless we start talking about n-tier or Microsoft Transaction Server (MTS, also called Component Services).

A control resides on a form, but a server doesn't. As such, the server needs to be set up, meaning that a client needs to add a reference to and then create an instance of some server class using code like this:

```
Dim o As Server.ClassName

Set o = New Server.ClassName
```

Of course, when *o* goes out of scope, your class instance is going to disappear, but we all know this, right?

With a control, there's no need to create an object variable to hold the instance (it's like a global class in this respect). You create an instance of a control up front by setting its name at design time. For example, Command1, the name you assign to the control at design time, is at run time an object variable that is set to point to an instance of a CommandButton class object. The control's lifetime is the same as the lifetime of the form on which it resides.

"Ah," you say, "but I can have multiple instances of my server." By either using a control array, using the new *Add* method on the Controls collection, or by loading multiple control-holding forms you can also have multiple instances of a control. "Ah," you say again, "but I can have many clients use one instance of my server object!" "Ah," *I* say, "so you can with controls; one form serves many consumers." Hands up all of you who have used just one CommonDialog control throughout your application to handle all your common dialogs!

OK, enough with the comparison for now. Because controls reside on a form we tend wrongly to think of them as having to be based on, or represent, something that's manifestly visual (well, at least I do), although we know deep down that this is not necessarily the case. A CommonDialog control isn't visible at run time. Even so, controls do present some type of user interface, right? After all, the CommonDialog control shows dialog boxes. Not necessarily, though— think about the Timer control, which has no user interface at run time. The Timer is a good example of using an object that is not wrapped in an ActiveX server (though you might conversely argue that it should be). It's just a component that presents to the programmer a particular way of being consumed. The Timer control is also pretty cool in that it sits in your Toolbox (which by now might have many panes in it). A Toolbox tab can hold all your server controls; just drag-and-drop them as required.

How about using MLP to create this kind of component? Write the controls in Visual B++, Visual J++, or Visual C++ and then use them from Visual B++. You could write a MatrixInversion or a HashTable server control, or whatever you want. So long as the source language can build controls, you have a natural way of consuming them, in-process!

Here are a few more bits and pieces (minutiae, if you will) about controls and servers:

- Controls normally self-register when they are loaded (in the DLL sense), so they are potentially a little easier to deploy since they don't need preregistering before they're used.

- Control references like Command1 cannot be killed by assigning Nothing to them. Such a control reference is *always* valid, even if the form is unloaded, because if the control is accessed, both the form and the control are recreated (no more Object Variable Not Set messages). Control object references are basically constants (both good and bad, perhaps). If it were legal, we'd have to declare them like this:

```
Const WithEvents Command1 As New CommandButton
```

- All controls are always in scope within a project; in other words, you can't make them private and nonaccessible from outside the form in which they reside. Conversely, a server's object variable can be declared Private. A control object reference is implicitly declared Public.

- Controls (UserControls, that is) can be brought entirely inside an application or compiled to OCXs. (Servers have the potential to be brought inside an application, also).

- Servers are easier to consume out-of-process than controls.

- Controls are easily consumed by other controls. That is, they easily can be used as the basis of another control (a kind of implementation inheritance vs. the strict interface inheritance available to servers).

- A control's initial state can be set at design time via the Properties pane and, as such, controls do not have to have an implicit null state when they're created. This type of initialization is not possible with servers.

- Controls can save their state to a property bag. With some simple abstraction, this could be modified to provide a type of object persistence for controls.

- Controls are supported by user interfaces. The Property Page and Toolbox can be used to interact with them (even before they're created).

- Controls can easily draw or present a user interface—it's their natural "thang," of course. (Imagine seeing how your OLE DB data provider control is linked to other controls at design time!)

- Control instances are automatically inserted into the Controls Collection, which itself is automatically made available.

- Controls have a more standard set of interfaces than servers. For example, controls always have a *Name* property (and a *HelpContextID*, and a *Tag*, and so forth).

- Controls accessed outside their containing form need to be explicity scoped to—they can't be resolved via the References list. Controls can be made more public by setting an already public control-type object reference to point to them, making them accessible to anyone with access to the object reference.

- Control arrays are, well, they're for controls!

- Controls can run in the IDE when they're added to a project at design time, so they are a little easier to set up and debug early on.

- Making a control work asynchronously requires a nasty kludge or two, because controls can never easily be running out of process. To do any form of asynchronous work they need their own thread (or a timer).

- In-process servers present an extra nice ability, through global classes, to act as repositories for compiled, yet shared, code libraries and can be used to create objects (containing modules) that are as useful as VBA itself (such as in the object reference—*VBA.Interaction.MessageBox* and so on). This functionality is also available using controls. At TMS we wrapper the entire C run-time library in this way and make the library available through use of a control typically called CLang. So *CLang.qsort* gets you the Quick Sort routine and so on. Likewise, we also wrapper access to the Registry using a Registry control. So for example you might access the Registry with commands such as *RemoteRegistry.ReadKey* and *LocalRegistry1.WriteValue*.

I give no recommendation here as to which you should use where—there are just too many variables and too many terms to the equation. You decide.

Mixing in Assembly Language

One of the easiest ways to build in Assembler is to build in C, because C allows you to write in Assembler using an _asm directive. This directive tells the compiler that it's about to see Assembler, so it doesn't do anything with your code. The reason for this is that the C compiler's natural output is Assembler;

this is then assembled, during the last pass of the compiler, into machine code. Most C compilers work like this, so it's very easy for any C compiler to support the inclusion of Assembler. The really great thing about doing your Assembler work in C is that you can provide all the boilerplate code using straight C (which saves you from having to fathom and then write all the necessary prologue and epilogue code for the call and parameter resolution stuff). You can then tell the compiler to generate Assembler from C. This process allows you to rough out the bare bones in C and then fine tune the code in the Assembler generated by the compiler. It's also a great way to learn about Assembler programming.

Other Languages

I opened this chapter talking about COBOL, so I guess I'd better briefly describe how you get to it from within Visual B++. The first step is to find a COBOL compiler that can create DLL code—Micro Focus' COBOL Workbench version 4 will do nicely (version 3.4 is the latest 16-bit version). The rest of the steps are pretty obvious. (See Q103226 in the Microsoft Knowledge Base for more information.) You're going to call into the DLL to get at your heritage code. Why rewrite when you can reposition?

Maybe you have a bunch of scientific routines to write and your language of choice for these is FORTRAN (DIGITAL Visual Fortran 5.0 is a good choice here—MLP is especially easy with Visual Fortran 5.0 as it's based on Microsoft Developer Studio).

Building your own little language

I'm getting off the topic a bit so I'll be brief here. Specialized, so-called "little languages" (actually some aren't so little) can be easily created using tools such as lex and yacc. (These tools can be used to build type 2 [context-free] languages as classified by the Chomsky language hierarchy). These tools came from the UNIX world originally but are now widely available for other operating systems, including Windows and MS-DOS. The tool lex builds lexical analyzers and yacc (which stands for Yet Another Compiler Compiler) builds parsers. For example, lex can build a program that breaks down code like $x = a * b * c() / 3$ into identifiable chunks, and yacc can build a program that can check that the chunks make syntactic sense, in the order identified by lex (which is as they're written above). As well as syntax-checking your code, yacc normally generates output code to perform whatever it is that your grammar has just described, in this case math.

Note that yacc can generate any kind of code—it can output C, C++, Assembler, COBOL, or Visual B++. So by using lex and yacc you can create grammars and language compilers to perform specialized tasks. If you want to learn more about these tools see the Mortice Kern Systems Inc. Web site at *www.mks.com*.

Versioning Components

When building applications from components it's vitally important to know what the version number is of the component you're using. After all, you wouldn't want to link with an old buggy version of a control would you?

Using VERSIONINFO

All Visual B++ applications (I'm including ActiveX servers here) have access to a VERSIONINFO resource—Visual B++ inserts one of these into every project for you automatically. If you build an empty project to an EXE and pull out its version information using Microsoft Visual Studio (select Resources from the Open dialog box in Visual C++), it'll look something like this:

```
1 VERSIONINFO
FILEVERSION    1,0,0,0
PRODUCTVERSION 1,0,0,0
FILEFLAGSMASK 0x0L
FILEOS         0x4L      /* Means VOS_WINDOWS32 */
FILETYPE       0x1L      /* Means VFT_APP       */
FILESUBTYPE    0x0L      /* Means VFT2_UNKNOWN  */
BEGIN
    BLOCK "StringFileInfo"
    BEGIN
        BLOCK "040904b0" /* Means English (United States) */
        BEGIN
            VALUE "Comments", "\0"
            VALUE "CompanyName", "TMS\0"
            VALUE "FileDescription", "\0"
            VALUE "FileVersion", "1.00\0"
```

```
            VALUE "InternalName", "Project1\0"
            VALUE "LegalCopyright", "\0"
            VALUE "LegalTrademarks", "\0"
            VALUE "OriginalFilename", "Project1.exe\0"
            VALUE "PrivateBuild", "\0"
            VALUE "ProductName", "Project1\0"
            VALUE "ProductVersion", "1.00\0"
            VALUE "SpecialBuild", "\0"
        END
    END
    BLOCK "VarFileInfo"
    BEGIN
        /* More language stuff. 4b0 is 1200 dec */
        VALUE "Translation", 0x409, 1200
    END
END
```

The bold lines denote the application's version number. Of course, you don't have to have anything to do with this raw resource in Visual B++ because, like most things, this data structure has an IDE interface to it. (See Figure 11-3.)

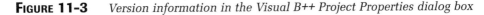

FIGURE 11-3   *Version information in the Visual B++ Project Properties dialog box*

The most important item in a VERSIONINFO is the version number. In terms of code, version numbers are held in App.Major, App.Minor, and App.Revision. I urge everyone to expose these properties through a Project class. If you want to know what version of a DLL or EXE you have, all you have to do is instantiate the component's Project class and ask it!

```
Dim o As Component.Project

Set o =  New Component.Project

MsgBox CInt(o.Major) & "." & CInt(o.Minor) & "." & CInt(o.Revision)
```

Using a GUID

COM assists with versioning. In COM, the version number of the DLL becomes somewhat insignificant. Strictly speaking, the version number is used to indicate which version of the built component you're using. The version number changes whenever the server or component is rebuilt, but it says nothing about what services are available. These services are specified via a GUID. In COM, a GUID is used to version the component's interfaces—facilities it provides, if you prefer. The GUID states what interfaces are available, not which build of the interfaces you're currently using. If the component is significantly different from what you're expecting (meaning that its interface, and thus the services it provides, has changed), its GUID will be different from the GUID of the component you're expecting. There is strictly a two-level version at work here, the actual version number and the GUID. You probably want to check both.

Conclusion

Visual B++, Visual C++, and Visual J++ reflect radically different styles of development. While Visual B++ is a higher level environment especially suitable for implementing user interfaces, Visual C++ is known for providing greater programming control and performance. Java is the man in the middle and is especially relevant for cross-platform (write once, run anywhere) and Web development.

Databases **A**re for **D**orks

Do It Once and Forget It Forever

In fact, there is actually no such person. Lawson is a virtual consultant, an AI application written in Visual Basic 2 with a frequently updated database of Visual Basic knowledge, input by a dedicated team of neophytes. This is why, when TMS requires personal appearances, he must wear a bag over his head (since he could be any one of 30 TMS developers) and why no photograph could be produced.

LAWSON DAVIES

Lawson is a TMS consultant who, on his return from five years working and walking in the Highlands of New Guinea, abandoned the stressful life of itinerant teacher, novelist, and social parasite to enter the more relaxed role of a client/server code warrior. His areas of special interest are design, real ale, system architecture, Islay malts, database connectivity, cricket, distributed systems, and the oeuvres of Brian Eno, Bach, and Gary Glitter (who is now allegedly politically incorrect). From the last book, he found that mentioning what you like to drink in your biography is a fairly certain way of being offered it.

I consider that a man's brain originally is like a little empty attic, and you have to stock it with such furniture as you choose. A fool takes in all the lumber of every sort that he comes across, so that the knowledge which might be useful to him gets crowded out, or at best is jumbled up with a lot of other things so that he has a difficulty in laying his hands upon it. Now the skilful workman is very careful indeed as to what he takes into his brain-attic. He will have nothing but the tools which may help him in doing his work, but of these he has a large assortment, and all in the most perfect order. It is a mistake to think that that little room has elastic walls and can distend to any extent. Depend upon it there comes a time when for every addition of knowledge you forget something that you knew before. It is of the highest importance, therefore, not to have useless facts elbowing out the useful ones.

—Sir Arthur Conan Doyle,

A Study in Scarlet

(Wherein Sherlock Holmes is considering using Memo/Text fields in a Microsoft SQL Server 6.5 database.)

Data is not interesting. Data access is not interesting. Information is interesting, data is not. But data is necessary, like deodorant on a subway train, and therefore has to be addressed. Most Microsoft Visual Basic applications must, regretfully, have dealings with a database somewhere along the line. The current propaganda figure is 95 percent. This data access thing can be a dirty business, so if you have to do it, do it once, do it right, and forget it forever. This means write such a generic and reusable thing that even a gibbering Java programmer will be able to reuse it. How about a middle-tier DLL that you can use over and over again?

DO IT ONCE, DO IT RIGHT, AND FORGET IT FOREVER

In Visual Basic 6, there are many ways to retrieve and manipulate data and quite a few places to stash it once you have it. There are also a wide variety of application architectures possible—ranging from the wildly successful to the frankly disastrous.

Exactly which architecture you choose should (and now *will*—let's be optimistic and pretend that managers don't exist) be dictated by what *you* are most familiar with. This is not what it says in the books—except this one—but it is the truth. In books, the experience of the team and the existing code base are usually ignored. However, in reality we can't choose something we don't know about, and we would be foolish to choose something for a crucial and time-sensitive area of our system that we don't understand quite well. In Visual Basic, one architecture choice can be two-tier systems using Data Access Objects—or even data-bound controls—to access thousands of rows of data at a time and to support hundreds of concurrent users. This is not generally recognized in the Visual Basic community as a passport to success, riches, and fame. However, if it's all you know about, and if the deadline is almost impossible anyway, and if there isn't a design specification—and if, in fact, it is a typical Visual Basic project, regardless of the fact that this is the code equivalent of taking elephants over the Alps—it is probably what you will have to do.

This chapter isn't going to tackle syntax in all of Visual Basic's data access methods. There are books that already cover this. I recommend William Vaughn's *Hitchhiker's Guide to Visual Basic and SQL Server* (sixth edition, Microsoft Press, 1998) for a good, fast start. It looks at some general principles, assesses the options, and attempts to come up with a once-only approach that can be reused (perhaps with tweaks) on many projects.

To pull off this amazing feat, we will have to make certain assumptions, and if your projects don't fit them this approach might not either. However, we will try to make the assumptions nice and general, and also slant them to the more generically difficult areas of data access, where much of The Mandelbrot Set's (TMS) work tends to be. These assumptions will define the kinds of systems we are asked to build—the toughest, and the ones that Visual Basic developers are increasingly being asked to build—big and scalable.

This is mainly because these are the most difficult systems to build, and if we can build these we can build anything. Although some techniques will cover systems that do not have to scale, we are looking here to cover all eventualities, including the lie that there will "never be more than 20 concurrent users; honestly, one of the directors told me."

We shall also assume that you would rather be using objects than not, and that you think tiered systems are a practical proposition and generally the way to try and go for large or scalable systems. Finally, we will assume that even if you don't have to build an Internet-, extranet-, or intranet-accessible system yet, the day is coming when some pointy-headed, simian-browed marketing person or middle-management executive (I always think "executive" derives both from "to execute" and "needing/deserving execution") will say, "Duh, I have a good [sic] idea. We should make the system work on da Web!" When you ask this sort of person for a business justification for this high-risk strategic move, he or she will answer, "Duh, silly, everybody's doing it!"

Our goal is to build a component that wraps your chosen data-access technology into a simple-to-use component with a programming model that is very straightforward for the common things, yet can handle the more complex ones when required. The idea is quite simple, really—get the Database Dork to put all his or her knowledge into a component, and then everybody else can access the data sources they need without having to worry too much about clustered indexes.

Let's Look at Data

"No data yet," he answered. "It is a capital mistake to theorize before you have all the evidence. It biases the judgment."

"You will have your data soon," I remarked, pointing with my finger.

Sir Arthur Conan Doyle,
A Study in Scarlet

We shall begin by looking at data—which we originally called uninteresting. So let's see if we can spice it up a little—nipples.

Data was once central to many people's view of computing—certainly to mine. I was once indoctrinated with Jackson's Structured Design and Programming. His central premise was that computer processing was all about the gap between two different but related data structures. The design process was all about identifying the data structures and the functionality required to transform one into the other. This seemed viable to me when I was working largely in a batch-processing mainframe environment. However, when I moved to working in a client/server model, I encountered a dichotomy. Client/server wants to make data services available to all—usually through memory-loaded working copies—but the prime data, the source of these copies, has to have a high level of data integrity. There is a tension here.

I came to see that the location of data, its scope, and how it is used combine to define the kind of data it is and how we ought to work with it. For me, there are four major types of data.

Master or prime data

This is the data that is almost invariably in a shared database server. It is the most current and most highly trusted data in the system, and it represents the currently committed instance of each data entity. Usually, this sort of data is accessed interactively and concurrently by many data consumers, possibly including batch processes. It is important stuff and has to be secured properly, backed up, and have a restore-from-backup process that actually works. Because it is shared, it is usually placed on a shared server at the same or a higher scope as its usage. Thus, if the system is a departmental one, its prime data will be located on a departmental server, or one that can be accessed by the whole business. It is possible to split this data across a number of servers, but we'll talk a little more about distributed data later on.

Management or business copy data

This kind of data is most often used for reference. It is usually a read-only snapshot of prime data. It is frequently frozen in time or includes some derived summary or aggregation data, so there might be redundancy here. It is usually updated by being re-created through a regular refreshment process, so there might be versions of the same data kept for a period. It is essentially static, unchanging data, so no problems of synchronization arise. This data could be centralized—there's a current vogue for data warehouses—but it could just as easily be distributed, even to the point of being in individual spreadsheets on particular users' machines.

User or operational copy data

In addition to management having copies of the prime data for particular uses, it is quite common for users to have their own copies, usually made with an eye to improving some level of operational efficiency, performance, or service. For instance, a laptop user might carry a copy of his or her own client's records while on the road, to increase response time rather than having to phone the office or wait until returning before checking something. This data is a duplicate. Whether it will need to be synchronized or simply refreshed periodically in the same way as Management Copy Data will depend on its scope and usage. If the responsibility of updating the data is shared, this increases the complexity of synchronization.

However, operational copy data could equally be static data, such as look-up data, which is rarely if ever changed, and if so might be copied to a departmental server from a central source, or even down to individual user PCs to speed the process of consulting it.

Operational copy data can be a subset of volatile prime data copied to a specific location server. Most updates might be made to this local copy, but some might be made to the prime data, in which case a process of synchronizing and reconciling the local copy and the prime data needs to be set up. This is usually done via some transaction logging mechanism, but here the issue of just how real-time the synchronization has to be raises itself.

Work-in-progress data

This is where (usually, we hope) a copy of a subset of prime data is made in order to carry out some specific task. For instance, imagine a software project manager accessing all the timesheets for a given project in order to update the project's progress, write a weekly report, or reconcile progress in time against progress measured by testing. Here a number of changes might be accumulated against a subset of the prime data, and after a particular series of steps for the task are completed, the data with changes is all committed by sending a single transactional unit back to update the prime data. Depending on its size, it can be kept in memory while it is being worked on (an option not without its challenges). However, even if this is the intention, the data can find itself spilling into temporary storage on disk if the machine is under-specified for the task—merely through the ministrations of the operating system. Alternatively, it can be stored on disk anyway, in an attempt to avoid major recovery problems. This is usually the data with the shortest working life.

Tiering and Data

Let's get two-tier out of the way

Having said earlier that we will assume you want to do it tiered (I must get some T-shirts printed: Real Developers Do It In Tiers), I'll start off with two-tiers. I have a good reason for this—to cover choices between DAO, ODBCDirect, Remote Data Objects (RDO), and ActiveX Data Objects (ADO), and also to look at the most successful paradigm for this kind of development. Understanding two-tiers will also give us a basis for noting how familiar Visual Basic practices have to change when you tier.

Where's the data?

This might strike you as a straightforward question—it's in the database, isn't it? Well, the architecture we choose decides where the data is, partly because it will tell us what parts we will have. One way or another, there will be data in all the parts (or, at least, data will be required by all the parts). So let's look at some architectures, find out where the data might be, and examine how to access and manipulate it.

Let's consider a typical client/server usage scenario and see how it suggests itself for database usage. A typical scenario, from the user interface perspective: a customer phones your company and wants to place an order. The order clerk has to first find the customer's details (let's assume this customer is already in the system) by inputting some values. The relevant customer details are displayed. (Perhaps a picklist of possible customers comes back, and the clerk has to do a little narrowing down to get the right customer and customer number to attach the order to.) Once the customer number is available, the customer starts ordering stock items. Each item's availability has to be checked before an order line can be added to the order. Once all the order lines are in place, the clerk is supposed to quote the order number and the total, and if the customer is cool with it all, the clerk places the order.

From the server perspective, a customer picklist has to be created based on some user input. Relevant customer details have to be returned when the customer is positively identified. Stock items and their availability have to be checked for each order line. Finally the order has to be placed. This entire transaction has involved four distinct interactions with the database. The first three are trivial and straightforward in that they are read-only. Let's examine these first.

An ADO Tip

The number of rows that ADO fetches and caches is decided by the *Recordset* object's *CacheSize* property. If you are looking at rows in the cached row range, ADO gets that data from the cache. As soon as you scroll out of the range of cached rows, ADO releases the cache, fetches the next *CacheSize* number of rows back for you, and puts them into the cache. Once you have data flowing back from a production size database and being used, you can watch how your application uses data. What you see can lead you to tune the *CacheSize* property, and this can reduce the number of network trips for data. Reducing network trips is almost always a cool thing to do.

Getting Data Back

This was an unexpected piece of luck. My data were coming more quickly than I could have reasonably hoped.

Sir Arthur Conan Doyle,
The Musgrave Ritual:
The Memoirs of Sherlock Holmes

All we want to display in the user interface is read-only data. So we confront the cursor decision, a danger to all clean-living developers who want to keep their language clean. (See the sidebar on page 499 for more information on cursors.) Some database developers suffer from a kind of Tourette's syndrome, and can only choose cursors. Most know, however, that cursors are an expensive way to fetch data and are rarely used in production-class applications.

Though I had hoped to avoid it, I knew that I wouldn't be able to escape talking about cursors here. So let's look at selecting an appropriate data-access strategy. This is more than just picking between RDO, ADO, DAO, ODBCDirect, ODBC API, and proprietary APIs. It is even more than picking what kinds of cursors (if any) you will use. It is also about deciding when and where we will open connections to the database, how long we will hold them, when and how to use transactions and locking, and how we will get our data to all the pieces of our application in this distributed, component-based architecture we are considering.

First let's deal with the choice of data-access libraries. If you are starting a new project in Visual Basic 6 and you have no particular allegiance (that is, you or your team are not very skilled in another technology and don't have a large investment in an existing code base), the choice is really a strategic no-brainer—choose ADO. However, if there are other factors (for example, you are starting with an MDB back-end and moving to an RDBMS when ODBCDirect suggests itself), weigh the decision up. As a little aide-memoire ("memory aid" for the uninitiated), the companion CD includes a spreadsheet that might help.

The latest version of ADO (ADO 2.0, which ships in Visual Basic 6) is fast. (Check out RDOvsADO in the sample code for this chapter.) It has a low memory and footprint size—although until OLE DB providers for your databases are available, you might have to use an existing ODBC driver along with Kagera [MSDASQL.DLL], the ODBC generic OLE DB provider. Some are shipping with Visual Basic 6 (Jet, Oracle, and SQL Server, for example). However, if you do need to use Kagera, this ups the total footprint size (and incidentally, it doesn't support independently addressed multiple resultsets). ADO 2.0 also now supports events, so you can connect and fetch data asynchronously and react to events when operations have been completed. ADO creates free-threaded objects that are speedy, especially for Web-based applications. If you are familiar with RDO, you'll find navigating the ADO object hierarchy a little different, mainly because you don't have to. Most important ADO objects can be instantiated independently. This seems more convenient, but under the covers many of the other objects in the hierarchy need to be instantiated—albeit not by you directly—and this necessitates more parameters on the instantiation methods you do have to call. ADO allows batch updates, as does RDO. (One of the most interesting things, from a tiering perspective, is the remotable resultset, but we'll come to that later. It has some particularly interesting ways of handling parameter queries).

And now for cursors. At the risk of trying to teach my intellectual betters, I have included a sidebar on cursors on the next page. Experienced database programmers will, or at least should, know about cursors. But a number of Visual Basic programmers are a little vague, and this information is basically a prerequisite for making an informed decision on a data-access strategy. If you are confident in your cursor knowledge, feel free to skip the sidebar—I always have difficulty deciding whether and when to read sidebars myself. If you are going to, now is a good time.

We're back from the valley of the cursors, and if you remember, we've dealt with getting the data we need down and into our user interface. Now, let's deal with changing and updating it.

Beefing Up Two-Tier

The two-tier architecture is pretty widely used today and generally scales to somewhere under the 100-user mark. Standard two-tier suffers from notable limitations:

- Too much data is pulled across the network and dealt with at the client.
- "Functionally rich," fat clients require extra maintenance and limit reuse.
- Databases only scale to a certain number of users.

Using stored procedures in the database is a means of extending the limits of a system. This means you can typically go from a system that in two-tier has a ceiling of 100 users and often as much as double that ceiling.

How do stored procedures do this? To start with, stored procedures can improve database scalability, since they use a database's own optimized code to efficiently process data, and might even use the database's SQL extensions to do specific tasks more efficiently. Stored procedures are also stored in an efficient manner (usually in some precompiled, ready-to-rock state), so they are quick to start as well as rapid to run. Obviously, because they are within the database itself, stored procedures avoid dragging lots of data across a network, since by their nature they must process the data at its source. Stored procedures are frequently used as a way of restricting data access, in that they can be restricted to specific user groups or even individuals. This means that the stored procedure—or its cousin, the database view—is in fact an encapsulation of the data. This can help to avoid the necessity of changing the application if the database structure has to change. There's also an element of reuse with stored procedures because different interfaces and applications can reuse the same stored procedures.

But the land of stored procedures isn't all milk and honey. SQL is not as powerful as more general programming languages such as Visual Basic. Long-running stored procedures can tie up database connections. Stored procedures, again due to their nature, must always run on the same machine as the data, which limits and essentially eradicates hardware scaling of an application.

CURSORS—JUST SAY NO: OR, HOW I LEARNED TO STOP WORRYING ABOUT LOCKING AND LOVE READ-ONLY DATA[1]

The big three in Visual Basic data access libraries—DAO/ODBCDirect, RDO, and ADO—can all implement cursors. The kind of cursor you choose has a vast impact on the performance, concurrency, and thus scalability of your system. Getting it wrong can really hurt. So it helps to know your cursor options carnally.

…in the evening we found a reply waiting for us at our hotel. Holmes tore it open, and then with a bitter curse hurled it into the grate.

—Sir Arthur Conan Doyle,
The Final Problem:
The Memoirs of Sherlock Holmes

1. I must acknowledge one source in particular who over the years has greatly helped my understanding in this area: William Vaughn, author of the highly recommended *Hitchhiker's Guide to Visual Basic and SQL Server* from Microsoft Press. William's book is into its sixth edition, which covers Visual Basic 6 and ADO as well as all the areas he has already covered so well.

>>

Choice of cursor option primarily affects where a resultset will be built, how it will travel to its consumer, how an application can move through the data, and whether and when data in the cursor is updated. For a long time, there have been two ways to look at cursors. The first is the lazy, sloppy, thoughtless way. (At TMS, the shorthand for this is "evil cursors.") Rather than thinking carefully about what cursor functionality is required in each given data access situation and then choosing a cursor that provides a close fit and as minimal and lightweight a set of functionality as can be lived with, many developers choose the fullest functionality and thus the heaviest and most expensive cursor option available. The principle here seems to be, "If it can't be done with the biggest cursor, it can't be done in Visual Basic." In addition, some developers feel that a generic cursor solution is best, rather than taking the trouble to understand the benefits and drawbacks of specific cursor options. In reality though, time spent choosing the most appropriate cursor options is time well spent. If we don't spend it here, much more time will be squandered by our frustrated users as they wait for data to travel across the network or for locks to be released.

The following is a list of options you must decide on when selecting a cursor.

- **Location** This is where the cursor will be physically built—there is also a link with membership, in that the combination of location and membership can control where the data and keys are and how and when they move from client to server. Location has the following options:

    - **Client** The cursor is built on the client. If it is a static cursor, all the data travels across the network at one time, down to the client. This raises questions of capacity—does the client have enough RAM and disk space for this? If the resultset is large, and especially if few of the records in it will become current records, this might be a bad choice. Don't get fooled into thinking that the client is the sink client (where the user interface is) if you open a client-side cursor on a middle-tier machine. When you finally have the resultset on the client, performance can seem fast. As a general rule, client-side cursors scale better, since you are spreading the load across many workstations.

    - **Server** Some databases support building the cursor on the database server machine in a temporary area. SQL Server does this and caches the recordset in the TempDB. Then when the client wants to make a given record the current record, the data for that record travels from the server to the client. Thus, all that is on the client at any given time is the current record's data. This is mainly useful for lightweight clients and large recordsets, especially if you are going to directly access and manipulate only a few of the rows in a large recordset. If you use the server option wisely, it can greatly improve the effect on network traffic. So this option can be the best choice when there isn't much spare bandwidth on a network, or when you have to have a lot of network traffic using client-side cursors. The cursor has to be fully populated before control goes back to the client code, so it can sometimes feel a bit slower, especially if you like to pull the trick of trying to show the first row in the user interface as soon as it is available and then putting the others in while the user is ogling it. Also, try not to have too many of these, especially if they are big and open at the same time—the TempDB is finite too. If you use these, you can't have disconnected recordsets. (See "Returning Changes from a Disconnected Recordset" later in this chapter.) Opening server-side cursors in transactions can have locking implications such as blocking other users. Note also that server-side cursors don't support executing queries that return more than one recordset. Alternatives to server-side cursors are using a client-side cursor, or preferably a disconnected recordset.

- **Membership/Cursortype** This refers to which rows are in the cursor, which aren't, and when the database engine picks them. (Initially, the query processor decides based on the WHERE clause and puts in the resultset.) Also included here is what is in the cursor, in terms of data or just keys (IDs of records). This has an impact on what travels across the network when. This cursor has the following options:

  - **Static** Static cursors usually retrieve a copy of all records in the cursor's membership. Membership freezes when the last row is found (usually when code or the database engine moves the current row pointer to the last row), so data changes made by other users don't join the membership. Often some sort of locks (usually share locks) are kept in place until this is decided. Usually, this means that all the data travels from the database engine across the network to the client and has to be stored there. Static cursors are usually fully scrollable.

- **Keyset** The cursor is built with a key for each record in the membership. Although membership is usually static in that new rows won't be added to the membership, in this case the keys (the IDs) of the records are what initially travels to the client. When a given record becomes the current record, a request goes back to the database for the data for that record, using its key. This means that at any time all the keys plus the data for the current record are likely to be on the client. Because keys, not full records, are being stored, the overhead is less than for static or dynamic cursors. This can help when not all records will be touched (become current record) or where the client has limited data space.

- **Dynamic** Some cursors never close membership—instead they keep asking the cursor driver to requery the database to make sure that rows added, updated, and deleted are taken into account in the membership. This can be very costly to performance, chewing up lots of memory and network resources. Dynamic cursors can change their membership to see changes made by other users. They are fully scrollable and normally updateable—the gold-plated cursor.

- **Scrolling** This is the capability provided by the combination of database engine and cursor driver to let you move from row to row. The following are the scrolling options:

  - **Scrollable** This allows capabilities such as bookmarks so that you can mark a record as you scroll, move the current record and then return to it later, or jump up and down a recordset using Move-Previous and MoveFirst type functionality. This is expensive functionality. Most applications read through a resultset once to put it in the interface, so they don't need this.

  - **Forward-only** This is not really a cursor, but it's usually the first choice, especially when read-only. This provides the capability to go from start to finish sequentially (FIFO—first in first out) through the resultset, making each item in it the current record in turn. This is adequate for most applications bringing back large numbers of rows at a time. (By "large" here, we often mean more than one!) The forward-only cursor is generally the fastest and the lightest on resources.

- **Updateability** This is how your database and cursor driver let you go about changing membership and data values. Updateability has the following options:

>>

- **Updateable** You can maintain data (add, delete, and update new rows) using the cursor's functionality—*AddNew, Delete,* and *Edit/Update* methods on a resultset object are how this normally looks. If you don't use this option (which again is very expensive functionality), you can use action queries. This option is expensive because each row has to be individually addressable, which normally requires a primary key on the table. Use Read-only if you aren't going to update, since it is more efficient.

- **Read-only** This is exactly what it says on the side of the can. This option is cheap on resources and is usually an excellent choice, especially when combined with Forward-only scrolling.

So what do RDO and ADO give you in cursors? Rather than having you wade through another huge table, check out the Visio diagram included on the companion CD. The code for checking this is in the sample RDOvsADO.

So when picking a cursor, you should consider what functionality is needed and then find the cheapest cursor option to implement that will provide it. Once you've made this decision a few times, you'll probably have been through all the normal scenarios—such as these:

Scenario	Cursor Choice	Other Information
Look up data	Read-only, Forward-only, Static	On the server.
Provide a picklist to select from	Read-only, Forward-only, Static	On the client if the number of list options is small, on the server if you have the option and have to provide large numbers. We always try to restrict this kind of query to a maximum size of 50–100 rows (who is going to scroll more?) and show the first 50–100 if more are found, but prompt them to qualify their query more.
Bring back details of one item (chosen from a picklist) into a Detail/Edit screen	Read-only, Forward-only, Static	On the client—we'll do the updates/delete using an action query if we can (not methods on a recordset, but we'll talk more about this later). If you need scrolling, use a client-side keyset cursor.

>>

A useful concept here is that of the current row: essentially, with most resultsets and cursors, only one row of data is "exposed" for dealing with at a time. Scrollable cursors can vary in a number of ways. (Go to the first, go to the last, go the next, go the previous, go to a specific one, or go to one in an absolute or relative position.)

You to your beauteous blessings add a curse,
Being fond on praise, which makes your praises worse.

—William Shakespeare,
Sonnet 84

Cursors are rarely the best way to access your data. But sometimes you need to be able to do the following:

- Scroll forward and backward (browse) through a limited resultset
- Move to a specific row based on a saved value (a bookmark)
- Move to the "nth" row of a resultset in absolute or relative terms
- Update limited resultsets created against base tables using the Remote-Data control

If you don't need a cursor, you will usually find that your application is faster and more efficient. So, how to avoid them? With RDO, if you set the *rdoDefault-CursorDriver* property to *rdUseNone*, all resultsets created by your application will be created *as if* you used the *OpenResultset* method with the *rdOpen-ForwardOnly* and *rdConcurReadOnly* options set, and with the *RowsetSize* property set to 1. *This is often the most efficient way to pass data from the remote server to your application.* ADO doesn't have such an equivalent setting (well, actually, that is a lie—it has an obsolete setting, *adUseNone*, which exists only for backward compatibility)—ADO's default cursor location setting is *adUseServer*.

Although it is also possible to create low-impact resultsets that are also update-able through use of the *Edit/Update* methods, this is usually impractical because the base tables are not directly updateable, so creating an updateable cursor is not possible. This is particularly so in stateless tiered designs.

>>

Whenever you create a resultset with a stored procedure, the resultset is not updateable—at least not using the *Edit/Update* methods. In these cases, you can use the WillUpdateRows event to execute an action query that performs the actual update operation(s).

However you create a cursor, you can usually update the data using one of the following techniques—even if the cursor is not updateable:

- Executing a stored procedure that updates a selected row based on a code-provided key.

- Executing an action query that changes specifically addressed rows. In this case, your code creates a suitable WHERE clause used in the query.

- Using the WillUpdateRows event to trap update operations and substitute appropriate stored procedure calls to perform the actual changes.

Try not to update directly through cursors—it's almost always more efficient to use a stored procedure or an action query. If you are using ADO, use the *adExecuteNoRecords* execution option—this stops ADO from setting any cursor properties.

```
Dim conn As New Connection
Dim sOpen As String, sExecute As String
sOpen = "Provider=SQLOLEDB;Data Source=TMS1;" & _
        "Database=DUDES;User Id=sa;Password=;"
conn.Open sOpen
sExecute = "Insert into DudeMain values(5, 'Chris'," & _
           " 'Star Programmer')"
conn.Execute sExecute, , adExecuteNoRecords
```

It is even harder to justify using a query that creates an unrestrained, off-the-leash kind of cursor against one or more base tables (for example, "SELECT * FROM Table"). Not only is this not a permissible option in protected systems, it can cause serious concurrency problems as you attempt to scale your application to more than a few users. Whenever you create a cursor, be sure to limit the scope to the fewest number of rows possible. In interactive systems (where there is a human operator), fetching more than a few hundred rows is often counterproductive and leads to increasingly complex concurrency problems.

THREE APPROACHES TO CLIENT/SERVER INTERACTIONS

Three approaches suggest themselves for changing and updating data in the typical ordering scenarios, such as the one we have already considered. We'll examine each in turn before making our choice.

Classic Client/Server Computing

Let's get back to the ordering scenario we considered earlier, where we had to find the client, find the thing to order, and then make an order we were having to carry out. Here, our three pieces of server-side work—two reads and an update—would be three separate database transactions/interactions. We pull the data down for the picklist with the first read. We pick a customer ID and use that as a parameter on the next read. We make all changes in the user interface, and when the user is happy, he or she clicks the OK button (or whatever user interface standard we are following). The data goes back—perhaps as parameters on a stored procedure call or an action query—and all the work is done within the database server to make the changes as one database transaction. This is how most early client/server systems were made—it was frequently the model with terminal front-ended applications.

What happens in this approach if something goes wrong? For instance, suppose a business rule, implemented in the stored procedure we called, makes sure that the order we have just input doesn't take the customer's total outstanding orders over their credit limit. Perhaps we even checked for this in the user interface by retrieving the current total order value and credit limit for the customer. In the meantime, however, some other order has also been processed, and that has tipped the balance.

Clearly, the database doesn't get updated. The stored procedure returns something to tell the user interface this and makes sure anything it did to the database is now rolled back (perhaps including assigning order numbers). This model has advantages:

- There are no locks on the database until we do the insert/update work, and then only for the briefest time we can get away with—for example, while the stored procedure is running in the database.

- Our two read routines can be reused in other pieces of functionality within the system. (It is quite likely that the customer picklist read— and the customer details read if it is not too order-processing specific— can be used in a number of places in the system.)

- If we needed to tweak the work process or the user interface, we wouldn't have to rewrite our functionality, we'd just have to reorder it. Thus, if we wanted to take the order details before we checked on the customer, we could do it.

This model aims at making sure that all requests on the server are read-only ones, until the user hits OK. Then all the actions (updates, inserts, deletes) are done in one database transaction. We at TMS like this approach—it isn't a classic for nothing. We have to admit, however, that it won't always work— just because 8 million flies choose it.

Journal/Temporary Entry

Let's look at the stock checking step in our hypothetical application: find the order item with its stock level. We weren't saying, "Lock that stock level until we have finished completing our order." If we don't lock the stock level, we can obviously get situations where, when we first checked, there was enough stock to place the order, but by the time we input our order stock levels have fallen. (We are successful—orders are coming in all the time!) If that is the case, again our poor old stored procedure is going to have to check, raise an error, and offer the customer—via the user interface—the opportunity to accept either a back-order for that item, drop the order line, or drop the whole order.

We could implement this step differently: when we check stock levels, we could say lock, or temporarily allocate, that stock, so that when our order clerk says, "We have that item in stock," it remains true when the order is placed. This can be done as the usual kind of transaction—insert/update records in this allocated stock table. The problem comes if the link between the ordering clerk and this stock allocation table entry goes down before the order is placed and the stock committed.

This problem is usually dealt with by grouping the stock allocation(s) and the order committal into a standard database transaction so that either they both work or neither does. This opens us up to locking problems and also to issues of deciding exactly when the transaction has failed. Has it, for instance, failed if upon committing the order we get a rollback because the customer's credit limit has been exceeded? Does this circumstance mean that all the stock for all the order lines should no longer be allocated? This can mean doing the stock allocations and all the stock checks over again if there is some process for authorizing such orders or upping the customer's credit limit.

Stateful/Transactional/Conversational Servers

Different IT shops have different names for these sorts of servers, but the implications are the same. Essentially, if we go for a solution to the situation above, where we rollback through transactions, our transactions can easily span multiple interactions between the ordering clerk and the database. This is how cursors are often used—when it isn't necessary. It is also how transactions are frequently used. This means that the data might be locked for an extended period—take the extreme case of the ordering clerk dying of a heart attack brought on by the stress of continual uncertainty (due to locking problems) about the length of a task. Suppose also that our system copes with such problems as this, power failures and so on, by writing state data to the local disk for later recovery.

Even if our system users don't die mid-transaction, we are facing a situation of potentially long locks. Add to this a database server that has page-level locking, and make the system one with a high transaction rate and concurrent user numbers, and you have a problem waiting to occur. If we are going to lock, we have to do it in a way that interferes with as few users as possible so that reading data without the intention of updating is still allowed. This is usually done with software locks (the application writes a value when it gets the data and checks the value as it puts it back) or timestamp fields.

Locking and Unlocking

"I shall be happy to give you any information in my power."

Sir Arthur Conan Doyle,
The Naval Treaty:
The Memoirs of Sherlock Holmes

What we are dealing with here is protection against conflicting updates that might break the business rules and corrupt the data. Of course, this is not a new problem and has often been faced in computing. Clearly, even Shakespeare faced this problem and was awakened by nightmares of inappropriate data-locking strategies.

Some data changes are all or nothing replacement changes: I look at a customer record, and I change the surname. Some are not: I look at a balance figure on an account record and change it with a financial transaction. The change this time is incremental; it uses the existing data to help make the change. If the existing data is the wrong data, the resultant change will be wrong. So if another ordering clerk committed an order for that customer faster than I did, my transaction cannot be allowed to complete.

A pessimistic scenario

I or the other user should be stopped from starting a transaction, while the other one is (potentially) already in a transaction. Good—only one working on the data at a time. Bad—only one can work on the data at a time. Imagine a system with three major customer accounts. Each customer has many different people who can phone in orders at the same time, and we have many ordering clerks to allow them to do this. Imagine ten orders for one of our large corporate customers being taken concurrently by ten order clerks. The first one in can lock the data; the other nine must wait. The result? Frustration.

An optimistic scenario

Let's take the same task: ten orders are being taken concurrently. For each order, we read the data and get some sort of indicator of where we are in sequence. All our order clerks go for it—hell-for-leather Online Transaction Processing (OLTP). The first process to complete an order checks to see whether the sequence token it is holding allows it to commit the changes. The token says, "Yes, you are in the correct sequence to change the data," so the transaction commits. The second order process checks its sequence token and finds that the data has changed. The second order process then has to check the data again, to see whether it is going to break the business rules that apply now that the server data has changed. If no rules are broken, the process commits the order. If committing the order would break the rules, the process has to make a decision about which value should be in the database (the value that is there now, the value that was there before the first order was committed, or the value after this second order is committed). Otherwise, the process has to refer the decision back to the second ordering clerk. The choices include: making the change, rolling back the change it was going to make and thus starting all over again (leaving the data as it was after the first transaction), or even forcing the first transaction to rollback too so that the data is as it was before any ordering clerks got to work on it.

Optimistic or pessimistic?

What sort of data is it? Some fields, or even records, might be the sort of data in which no business rules can apply. In that case, the last update must always be the one that defines what data is now in the database. It might be that currently there are no rules, in which case there can be no incorrect sequence. It can be that the data is not volatile or only rarely worked on concurrently. Usually, if you must lock, you must also strive to minimize the time you are locking and avoid locking over user interactions if you can.

The Trouble with Teraflops

Imagine a database with 50,000 account records, perhaps for a public utility. Imagine a user requirement has been allowed to slip through the change control net—perhaps it's even genuinely needed—that allows users to search for customers by the first letter of their surnames. Chances are we will get about 2000 hits when we enter "D".

The prototype convinced the users that they want to see the hits back in a picklist that shows Name and Full Address. Table 12-1 describes the data fields returned for a single hit.

Field	Size (Bytes)
ID	4
Surname	50
ForeName	50
AddressLine1	50
AddressLine2	50
AddressLine3	50
Town/City	50
County	30
Postcode InCode	4
Postcode OutCode	4
TOTAL	342

TABLE 12-1   *The fields in the customer surname query*

So every time we do one of these searches, we can expect 684 KB across the network for each hit. We might consider sending all 2000 hits back in one go. This way, all 2000 have to arrive before the user interface code can load them in the picklist (probably a nice resource hungry grid control). We could send the rows one at a time and try to load the first in the user interface as soon as it arrives.

The issue is one of scalability. System constraints are preventing us from doing what we want to do. The approach we adopt is bound to be a compromise between cosseting bandwidth and providing responsiveness to the user. Since we would actually prefer never to send more than 100 rows back at a time, we can design away the problem.

If the user really must scroll down through hundreds of rows, we can send back the first 100 and then indicate there are more. Then—if we must—we will get the others (although I would prefer to make them narrow their query) in the background while our user is still looking at the first 100. The alternative of bringing the next lot when the user asks for it (usually by scrolling down a grid or list box in the user interface) is very awkward as a user interface, since the chances are high that the user can scroll faster than we can get the data. Even so, there are likely to be strangely jerky and unexpected delays for the user.

We could consider setting up a special index on the server—a covering index for all the fields we need in the picklist, but the index shows only every 50th row. Thus, we bring down the first 100, and if they want more we fetch the index. They choose from the index, and we bring down the 50 that fall between two index entries. Tree views are quite good for this. The new hierarchical cursors in ADO, and the Hierarchical FlexGrid control, are particularly interesting here. If users want more data than we are prepared to send, we could send down the index and let them narrow things down from that. Other user interface solutions are tabs, with each tab representing an index section, such as a phone or address book.

Another question that needs consideration is whether to bring the details of the records back in the picklist, or only the data that is needed for display to do the picking. Suppose that the full size of the record is 700 bytes. This would mean moving 1.4 MB for each picklist. Sounds like a bad idea—imagine the effect on the network.

Once we have the list, how do we work with it? The simplest method is to create objects on an as-needed basis. That is, an object is created and populated with data only after the user has chosen an item from the picklist. It almost never makes sense to create an object and load its data for each entry in a picklist. Our user interface might behave as if that is what we have done, but in reality it will all be a front. There are a number of options for implementation here.

When to Open and Close Connections

One of the most expensive things you can do with a database (at least in terms of time) is opening a connection to it. Try it out with the RDOvsADO sample project in the samples directory for this chapter. This expense in time has led to most database applications, one way or another, opening connections and keeping them open for extended periods, rather than taking the hit of opening the connections more frequently. You'll often see the strategy of a Visual Basic application opening its database connection on application startup, holding it as *Public* property of the application (a *Global* variable in old-time Visual Basic speak), using it everywhere throughout the data access code, and finally closing the connection only when the application shuts down. It once was a good strategy, but the world is changing.

If applications didn't use connections this way, they implemented some kind of connection pooling, wherein a pool of already open connections was used to supply any application. This is because, although database connections are expensive, they are also finite. To begin with, if only for licensing reasons we must usually manage them, but also each connection uses up memory on both client and server machines. Thus, when certain database access technologies require multiple connections per user or application to carry out a task, they can severely impact application performance.

One of the interesting aspects of building middle-tier objects that talk to the database (rather than allowing an application on the client to open its own database connection) is that objects in the middle-tier can open the connections. They might even be on the same machine as the database server, and they can provide connection pooling. When Microsoft Transaction Server (MTS) was introduced as a middleware provider of both Object Request Brokering services and Transaction Process Monitoring, one of its subsidiary roles was to provide pooling of shared resources. Currently, ODBC connection pooling is already provided by MTS. Even without MTS, ODBC 3.5 now provides connection pooling itself. (See Figure 12-1.)

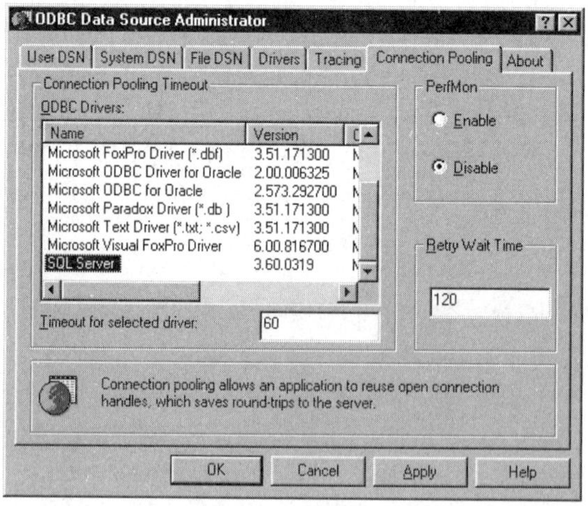

FIGURE 12-1   *Connection pooling with ODBC 3.5*

The effect of connection pooling can best be seen by a project that opens components, which each open and use a connection.

With connection pooling in place, it becomes viable to change the connection opening and holding strategy. It can even be worthwhile to open a connection every time one is required, use it, and then close it, because in reality the connection will not be opened and closed but pooled so as to avoid the cost of repeated connection openings. However, the pool can be limited in size so that the minimum number of active useful connections exist, but idle connections using resources without doing work are all but eradicated.

Deciding Where to Put Transaction Scope

Where should transaction scope lie? Who or what will control it and coordinate commits and rollbacks?

What is transaction scope?

With technologies such as DAO, RDO, and ADO, the transactional scope is limited to some database object or other.

With DAO, that object is the *Workspace* object. Transactions are always global to the *Workspace* object and aren't limited to only one *Connection* or *Database* object. Thus, if you want multiple transactional scopes you need to have more than one *Workspace* object.

In RDO, transactions are always global to the *rdoEnvironment* object and aren't limited to only one database or resultset. So with RDO, to have multiple transaction scopes you need multiple *rdoEnvironment* objects.

If you want to have simultaneous transactions with overlapping, non-nested scopes, you can create additional *rdoEnvironment* objects to contain the concurrent transactions.

With ADO, the transactional scope is on the *Connection* object—if the provider supports transactions. (You can check for a *Transaction DDL* property [DBPROP_SUPPORTEDTXNDDL] in the *Connection*'s *Properties* collection.) In ADO, transactions can also be nested, and the *BeginTrans* method returns a value indicating what level of nesting you've got. In this case, calling one of the standard transaction methods affects only the most recently opened transaction. But if there are no open transactions, you get an error.

ADO can also automatically start new transactions when you call one of the standard close methods for a transaction. For a given connection, you can check the *Attributes* property, looking to see whether the property has a value greater than 0. It can be the sum of *adXactCommitRetaining* (131072)—indicating that a call to *CommitTrans* automatically starts a new transaction, and *adXactAbortRetaining* (262144)—indicating that a call to *RollbackTrans* automatically starts a new transaction.

Cooperating components and transaction scope

Regardless of which object provides transactional scope and methods, the salient point is that there is only one such object for each data access library. Whatever the object, all code that needs to cooperate in the same transaction has to gain access to that same instance of the object. This is a small issue in a two-tier architecture, where all the components are on the same machine (and more often than not where there is only one client executable). There are no process boundaries or machine boundaries being crossed, and the place where the transaction-owning object will be instantiated is a no-brainer.

In a tiered system with a number of cooperating components—perhaps on different machines—some means has to be found of passing object references to the shared transaction-owning object. This is one of the reasons why it typically doesn't make the best sense to build data access code and transaction scope into individual business objects in a tiered system.

Frequently, compromises in design have to be made to allow the passing of this data access object so that a number of business components (which should have no database access specific knowledge or abilities) can cooperate in the same transaction. This is where Microsoft Transaction Server (MTS) solves the problem with a degree of elegance with its *Context* object and the *CreateInstance*, *SetComplete*, and *SetAbort* methods. Taking a lesson from this, a good design pattern is to create a class with the purpose of acting as shared transaction manager for cooperating components, or else to use MTS to do the same thing.

Such strategies allow the grouping of components on different machines in the same transaction and moving the point of transactional control to the place where the sequence of interactions is also controlled. Frequently, this is at some functional location, quite near to the user interface. (See Chapter 2 for more detailed information about business objects.)

Another issue arises here, namely that of stateful and stateless work. MTS prefers statelessness, where everything can be done to complete a unit of work in as few calls as possible between client and server. However, transactional work is by its very nature stateful and built from a series of interactions. This harks back to the three approaches to client/server interaction we considered earlier. This is also discussed in Chapter 2.

Let's Get Tiering

We've already mentioned tiering in terms of cooperating components and transaction scope. So, we're going to make the most of the transactional functionality to fit into Microsoft's Distributed interNet Applications Architecture (DNA). (What, you mean you didn't know they'd trademarked DNA? Does that mean you're not paying the franchising fee either?) The old TLA Lab must have really burnt some midnight oil to make that fit. Please note, this doesn't mean that your application has to be a Web-based application to benefit from the DNA architecture. In fact, as a developer with lots of client/server experience etched in scar tissue on my body, one of the things I was most encouraged about was that (when looked at the right way), Web-based systems and client/server systems are very similar. Thus, I didn't have to unlearn everything I'd sacrificed the last five years to learn. When I discovered this a year or so ago, I was much cheered and sang Welsh songs of triumph involving sheep, beer, and rain.

A Web-based system is of necessity structured in pieces, since it almost never makes sense to put all the work on the client and send everything to it. A Web-based system always has to be aware of the network and scalability. A Web-based system also needs to be as stateless and disconnected as it can get away with. This sounds very client/server–like.

If we are going to consider component-based distributed systems now, we should make a few basic decisions:

Where to put the data access code?

The tiered architecture includes a Data Services tier. Often, this is taken to be the database or data source itself, but TMS would argue that this tier also includes the data access code, which acts as the interface to the system's data sources. Consider the options.

Every business object class implements its own data access code. This can be the same code in many places, which is a maintenance problem. Or, if there are many disparate data sources, there is a lack of consistency.

However, the bulk of data access code, regardless of its data storage format, is likely to provide the same service and thus the same interface. Imagine the advantages of uniformity: all business objects in the same system, regardless of their business rules, using the same data access interface. Thus, there is uniformity for the creation of all generic business services (Create, Read, Update, Delete—the timeless CRUD matrix). This makes it possible to write wizards and add-ins in Visual Basic that generate business objects and all of their common functionality. Since there can be many such business object classes in a system, this can represent a major savings to the project. If a template for the data access class that the business object classes use is created, the internals of supporting different end data sources can be encapsulated behind a standard interface, protecting the business objects from data source changes and protecting the data access code from business rule changes. If data access is provided by a specialized class, this also makes it possible for that class to be bundled as a separate component, which will allow the logical tiers to be physically deployed in any combination. This can have scalability advantages.

The responsibility of the data access service becomes to interface to all supported data sources in as efficient a way as possible and to provide a common interface to any data service consumers. This allows a developer to wrap up RDO or ADO code in a very simple, common interface, but to make the internal implementation as specific, complex, and arcane as performance demands. Such code is also reusable across all projects that use a given type of data source—a handy component to have in the locker if implemented internally in RDO (because it should work with any ODBC-compliant data source) and even more generic if it uses ADO internally. But again, as new unique data sources are required, either new implementations of the component (which have new internal implementations but support the same public interface) can be produced or else extra interfaces or parameter-driven switches can be used to aim at other types of data source.

Essentially, when a request for data or a request to modify data comes in to a business object, (for example, "Move all of Account Manager Dante's Customers to Smolensky") probably via a method call from an action object[2] in a Visual Basic front-end program. The business object's method should find the SQL

---

2. What Jacobson or UML might well call an interface object.

string (or other Data Manipulation Language [DML] syntax) that corresponds to the task required. Once the business object has obtained the SQL string "Update Clients Set Account_Manager_ID = ? where Account_Manager_ID = ?" (or more likely the name of a stored procedure that does this), it passes this and the front-end–supplied parameters 12 and 32 to an instance of a DAO object. The DAO object would choose to link with the data source using ADO/ RDO, and depending on the format of the DML, it might also convert its data type. The DAO object would then update the data in the remote RDBMS and pass back a "successful" notification to the business object (its client).

This gives a preferred application structure, as shown in Figure 12-2:

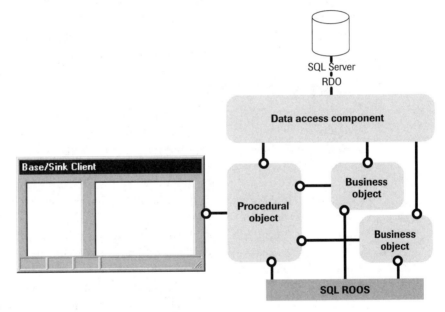

FIGURE 12-2   *Where to put data access code*

The Client creates a reference to a procedural object and calls a method on it. To carry out the work of that method, the procedural object needs to call more than one business object in a transaction. To do this, it creates a reference to a data access component, perhaps in its *Class_Initialize* event procedure. It tells the data access component via a method or property that it wants to start a transaction. Then it creates references to each of the business objects and passes the data access component reference to each of them. The procedural object also maintains its own reference to the data access component. This is so that the business objects will use the same connection and thus be in the same transactional context with the database. The business objects carry out their interactions with the database via the same data access component and thus the same database transaction. Once the business objects have finished with the data access component, they should set it to nothing. To do this, in their *Class-_Terminate* event procedure the business objects must check to see that they have a live reference, and when they find one, they must set it to nothing.

The procedural object can now (perhaps in its *Class_Terminate* event procedure) commit the transaction (if no errors have occurred) and set the data access component's reference to nothing, effectively closing it down. This is the "Do it once, do it right, and forget it forever" principle in action.

What About SQL?

SQL (or another DML in which the data source is very obscure) has to be kept somewhere. Often, it is scattered throughout a system—perhaps bundled into each business object. This is clearly not a good policy. What if the data source changes in type or structure? What if the type of DML changes? The maintenance burden can be high. At a minimum, even if the SQL is easy to find, every business object must be recompiled. The TMS answer is something called a SQL ROOS (Resource Only Object Server). At TMS, we use these as central, easy-to-replace-and-modify repositories for business rule SQL, or anything that is textual (error messages, interface text, and so on). Internally, the mechanism used is a standard Windows one, the resource file (RES) that holds a string table. The ROOS makes calls to this string table, using appropriate off-sets to pull out the correct text and load the methods parameters for return to a calling business server. Many Windows programs use these resource files, either compiled into them or often compiled and linked to as separate DLLs. Visual Basic has a restriction in this regard: we can include only one RES file per project. So to avoid this, and to make string maintenance straightforward without having to recompile a whole application, we do put our RES files into separate DLLs, as illustrated in Figure 12-3. In this way, many DLLs, and therefore many RES files, can be referenced and used in the same project. See the SQLROOS sample on the companion CD for a simple example.

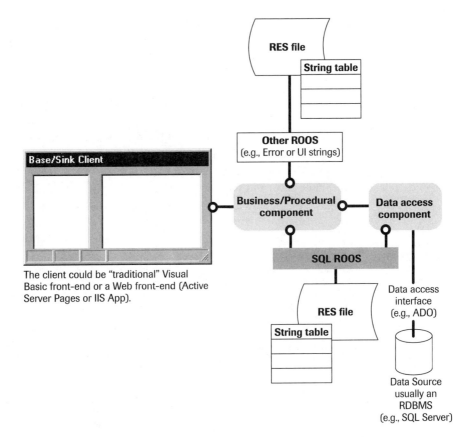

FIGURE 12-3 *Using multiple ROOS's in a system.*

For a given request, the SQL ROOS might return the following information:

1. The SQL statement (including "?" placeholders for parameters)
2. The number of parameters being used in the SQL statement
3. The type (input, output, input/output) of each parameter
4. The kind of query being done (straight select, prepared statement, stored procedure, multiple resultset, insert, update, delete, or other action/batch query)

It makes sense to have a ROOS template project—although some things might change from ROOS to ROOS (mainly the contents of the RES file), the bulk of the code will be exactly the same. Also remember that if you use a ROOS template project, change the base address for each ROOS DLL (and indeed each

DLL) you intend to deploy on the same machine. If you have missed this step, check out the DLL Base Address entry on the Compile tab of the Project Properties dialog box and the associated Help.

So when a business object server has to execute one of its methods that requires retrieval of remote data via a business rule, it uses the SQL ROOS to provide that rule (in the form of SQL, which typically calls a stored procedure). It then adds any data parameters and uses the retrieved SQL and the data parameters as parameter arguments on a method call to the data access server. The data access server in turn submits the SQL and returns a notification of success/failure, any returned parameters, or a resultset (depending on the kind of operation being undertaken) to the business object server. If necessary, the business object server returns any data to its base client. (See Figure 12-4.)

The business or procedural component would obtain a reference to a data access component and pass the SQL (if accessing the SQL ROOS) or else a reference to the SQL into it along with the data parameters.

The data access component would create a connection to the database (perhaps using ADO). Either the business object or the data server then (using the SQL ROOS) finds the SQL and provides it for use (a stored procedure or in-line syntax) along with the parameters. Once the action had been done, it would return to the business/procedural component, unless an error had occurred, in which case it would rollback the transaction and raise an error back to its client (the business/procedural component).

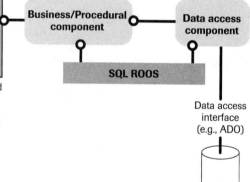

The client could be a Visual Basic front-end or a Web front-end (Active Server Pages or IIS App). It would obtain a reference to a business or procedural component and call methods on it.

Data access interface (e.g., ADO)

SQL Server

FIGURE 12-4   *Using a SQL ROOS*

Static Lookup Data

Static data presents a challenge and an opportunity. (I don't usually go in for management-speak, so I *really* mean this.) The more normalized a data source is, the more joins are likely to be needed in SQL to produce the data for a given instance of a business entity. These kinds of lookup joins can kill performance, and with some data technologies you can reach critical mass when the query becomes too complicated to support. When pulling back an entity, it is also common to have to bring back all the possible lookup values and display them as options to the current setting in a ListBox or ComboBox. Ditto when adding a new instance of a business entity.

Since this data is lookup data it is usually static, so it might be an option (especially for lookups that are frequently used throughout the application) to load or preload the data once, locally, on the client, and use this data to provide the lookup options. This also ends the necessity of making all the joins—you are effectively joining in the user interface.

Thus, it can sometimes be advantageous for performance to have (largely) static data loaded locally on the client PC in a Jet MDB file database, rather than pulling it across a network every time we need to display it. We have to address the problem of when the static data does change, and we need to refresh the static local copy. We could have a central source to check, to compare the state of our data with the central data. This could take the form of a table on an RDBMS, which has a record for each lookup table, held in the data source. When that relatively static data is changed, a date value should be set (indicating the date and time of the change). When the client application starts up, one of its initialization actions should be to check this table and compare each of the lookup table dates with the dates for its own local copies of the lookup tables. If it finds a date difference, it should update its local data.

If it is extremely unlikely that the data will change with great frequency or that working practices will not require frequent data changes during the working day, it is safe to assume that application startup is frequent enough to check for changed lookup data status. However, there is risk here. It might be necessary to design a mechanism that can check the timeliness of our static data every time we would normally have downloaded it. Even then, there is a performance gain: the more static the data, the higher the gain. We would only download the changed tables, and then perhaps only the changes, not all the lookups.

When you have the static data, where do you put it? Such static data can be stored in an MDB and accessed via DAO code, or in flat files, or now in persistable classes. (More on this in a little while.) It can be either loaded by code directly into interface controls or accessed via DAO code, and then the resulting resultset can be attached to a data control, which is in turn bound to interface controls. (In this second option, though, there is a tradeoff of performance, code volume/ease of coding, and resource usage.)

Tiers and Data

Tiered systems built with Visual Basic are essentially systems of class instances provided by a number of physical components. The components can be deployed on a number of machines interacting to produce system behavior. This means the class instances share their data with the system through class interface methods, properties, and events. Figure 12-5 illustrates how data and objects fit together at the simplest level.

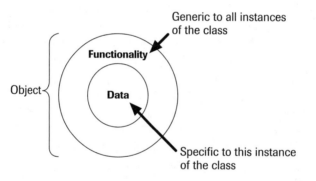

FIGURE 12-5   *Objects and their data*

A class is a template of functionality—it is a generic functional wrapper around data variables. It comes to life when you create an instance of it and give it some specific data to hold in its variables. It is possible to have data-only classes composed only of properties. It is equally possible to have functionality-only classes composed entirely of methods. In both cases, a developer's first reaction to such classes should be to question their design. However, such classes are the exception rather than the rule.

Objects, State, and Data: The Buxom Server

In an object, the data can ultimately come from the two ends of a tiered system: the user (or some other form of) input, or some persistent data storage (usually a database). Some data is transient, ephemeral, short-lived stuff—the data equivalent of a mayfly. Most, however, requires storage and has persistence. It is typically a design goal of scalable COM-based systems that the objects they are made of are as stateless as possible. In other words, specific instances of a class (and thus specific sets of data) stay "live" and in memory for the briefest time. There are many good reasons for this. Principally, this is so that we minimize the impact of idle instantiated objects on server system resources such as CPU and memory. At TMS, for any sizable system we typically would attempt to assess the likely impact of this on a server, as early as possible in the design process. (See the scalability example spreadsheet in the samples directory for this chapter.)

There is always a compromise to be made between the benefits of preinstantiation and the overhead of idle instances. Consider the case of the Buxom server—a publicly instantiable class provided by an ActiveX EXE server, sitting on a machine (The Bar) remote from its clients (thirsty punters like you and I). Its purpose is to stand as the software equivalent of a bartender in a system. Consider the process of ordering a round of drinks from an instance of the Buxom Server.

Preinstantiation: your object hiring policy

When a customer walks up to the bar with tongue hanging out, the management can have taken one of two diametrically opposed attitudes to hiring.

Hire, serve, and fire Management can see the customer and go out and hire a new Buxom server, because there is someone to serve. This will entail advertising, or perhaps going through a staffing agency; interviewing, hiring, perhaps even training. Eventually, there will be a Buxom server to serve the customer. Imagine the customer is typically English (used to queuing and waiting and therefore uncomplaining) so is still there when the Buxom server arrives in a new uniform to take the order. The Buxom server serves the customer, and as soon as the cash is in the register, gets fired by management.

What I've just described is the equivalent of setting the class *Instancing* property of the Buxom server to *SingleUse*. This means that each time a customer wants to get a round of drinks from a Buxom server, we let COM handle the request by starting up a new instance of the ActiveX EXE component, which passes the customer an object reference to a new Buxom server instance. The customer uses the server's properties and methods to get a round of drinks and then sets the object reference to Nothing. The reference to the Buxom server instance drops to 0, COM unloads the class instance and the component that provides it from memory. They are only in memory when a customer uses them. This is good for server resource management but tough on the customer's patience. This was a very Visual Basic 4 implementation, since the alternative of *MultiUse* instancing without multithreading led to blocked requests for service.

Preinstantiation: a staff pool   Management has estimated (the trouble, of course, with estimates is that they have a habit of transforming into promises) that a pool of four permanent bartenders will be enough to handle the volume of customers. They may have to be a little flexible and augment the staff with temporary help at peak periods (happy hour?). So they have already hired some. Now when a customer comes up to the bar—as long as it isn't a terribly busy time—an instance of a Buxom server says, "Hi, what can I get you?" This time, the customer doesn't have to wait for the hiring process to be completed before an order for drinks can be taken.

This is the equivalent of creating a pool manager (did you ever look at that sample?), which holds object references to instances of the Buxom server class and keeps them instantiated when they aren't busy. You can build a separate, generic pool manager, or a multithreaded ActiveX Server that only provides Buxom servers. Typically, pool managers start as standalone ActiveX programs, which have public methods for getting a server and a form to keep the pool-managing component itself alive. Or, they use *Sub Main* in a novel way to provide a message loop, rather than just processing sequentially. Now the Buxom server must have teardown code to clean its properties (its state) after usage so that when it is kept alive it can be used by each customer as if it were newly instantiated. This will avoid the large component instantiation overhead but will place some overhead of idle instances on server resources. However, with good algorithms to manage the pool size dynamically, the overhead can be kept to a minimum and is at least under control.

This is the stateless basis of MTS systems. MTS, however, doesn't exactly do preinstantiation but rather keeps instances that have been used but are now idle alive and waiting for customers for a period of time before allowing them to close and drop out of memory. This is how most Visual Basic systems scale without infinite hardware—by minimizing the number of "live" objects in the system at any given time and thus the amount of resources being used. This is also how—from the database developer's point of view—we can minimize numbers of database locks and connections: by combining object pooling and database connection pooling.

State and the Buxom server

Let's look a little closer at the task of ordering a round of drinks—something I feel well qualified to discuss. We go up to the bar and catch the attention of a Buxom server (we have an object reference to her). This is an art form in itself in some bars. We begin the process of ordering, in answer to her polite, "Hi, what can I get you?" We use her *OrderDrink* method to ask for a pint of Scruttocks Old Dirigible (American translation: a microbrew). She pulls our pint. We wait, since we are synchronously bound. We order a gin and tonic. "Do you want ice and lemon in that?" We don't know—Marmaduke has only just joined the development team. We can probably guess he does, but courtesy and politics dictate that we ask. (He's project manager.) We tell the Buxom server that we'll check and get back to her. Only thing is, he is sitting in the back room with the others, and the bar is very crowded. We fight our way through, check on his ice and lemon preference (he wants both), and fight our way back. All this time, our Buxom server has been idle, consuming system resources but unable to service another order without abandoning her state data.

We carry on with our order: more drinks and some snacks (pork rinds). Then we hand over the money, get our change, and even ask for a tray to carry it all on. We have been interacting with a stateful, conversational server, passing data back and forth. We have been calling methods, or even directly interacting with our Buxom server's properties. (I said we'd try and spice up data access at the outset.) Since the Buxom server was instantiated on one side of the bar and we are on the other, we have also been incurring network overhead with each exchange. For long periods, one or other of us has also been idle, due to the latency of the network and the crowds in the bar. What's the alternative?

Stateless drinking: maximizing your drinking time

So, instead of the unnecessary idling, we implement a single method in the Buxom server named *OrderRound*. The *OrderRound* method carries all the data with it: an indication of the drinks and snacks we want, the Booleans to indicate we want a tray and that there will be no tip (stateless and mean), and even the cash. The returns from *OrderRound* are our round and also some change, we hope. What advantages does this have?

To start, one call and one set of network overhead. Minimal idle time—in fact, we could even make it asynchronous by telling the Buxom server where we're sitting, and she could deliver the drinks (or one of those awful public address systems, firing an event to say our burgers are cooked—there's notable service in most of the places I frequent—far too upscale). As soon as the Buxom server is free, she can dump the state of our order —all taken in as parameters on one method anyway, so no global data is required—and free herself up for the next customer. Such a system will scale better since a single Buxom server ought to be able to turn around more orders in a given period of time.

This is the ultimate statelessness. This is what MTS systems crave (using *SetComplete* to indicate order completion), although it can be an awkward way of thinking for some developers. It is also what most database access techniques would ideally like to achieve. In truth, most of the time we will be somewhere in between highly stateful and stateless, but at least we know what to push toward in our design.

So, the responsibilities of a data access strategy or design don't begin and end at getting data out and into the database; they have to include the dataflow (now there's an IT system term you don't hear so much anymore) around the system. If that system is composed of a number of components spread across a network, an intranet, or even the Internet, this dataflow aspect can take on a great deal of significance, since it is likely to be where performance is won or lost.

Still Not Sure What Data Is Where Objects Are Concerned?

So what is data? (Nothing like getting the fundamentals out of the way early—then there's lots of time for beer.) Funny how, on a software project, if you don't get the basics right the first time, they come back to haunt you (and steal your drinking time) later in the development cycle. In the context of this chapter, Data is sadly not a character from *Star Trek—the Next Generation* (I know, you don't get the time to watch it, you're debugging at the moment) but rather variables holding specific values. Anyone reading this who has already worked on a tiered system will know that, should you ever come to physically distribute your tiers of objects—that is, to have cooperating objects working across more than one machine to constitute the system—you are faced with an object-or-data, reference-or-variable dilemma. Which should you use, raw variables or object references (and through them properties and methods)? To the purist, there is no contest—use the objects. But we are pragmatists. Our jobs are on the line if excellent theory produces appalling performance, so we have to think a little before jumping.

Data—The Currency of an Object System

The flow of data from object to object in a distributed system is the currency of the system. It's the oil that turns the cogs of functionality. Where is an object? An object is instantiated on a given machine, and that is always where it stays (well, almost always—see "Remoting ADO Recordsets" later). One object manipulates another via an object reference, making calls on that object reference to its properties and methods. Those properties and methods—the object's interface—provide access to the object's uniqueness (its data). This paradigm is much easier to grasp and use than an API (application programming interface) is. The object reference is essentially a pointer (4 bytes) to the object. The object doesn't move, therefore referring to an in-process object is fast, an out-of-process object is slower, and a cross-machine object much, much slower. If you want to assess the difference for yourself, the TimeIt[3] application (see the TimeIt subdirectory in the samples directory for this chapter) has some test cases that will allow you to try this[4], or you can add your own. You can even try the Application Performance Explorer that ships with Visual Basic. In the cross-machine scenario, the pain in the butt is that each call to a property or a method is a piece of traffic across the network. (Consider also the effect of *ByVal* and *ByRef* choices for parameters on methods, as illustrated in Table 12-2.) This is going to slow your application down.

---

3. I would like to acknowledge the generosity of Bruce McKinney, who kindly gave permission for this version of TimeIt, which builds on the version he produced for his fine book *Hardcore Visual Basic, 2d ed.* from Microsoft Press, 1997.

4. Please check the Readme file for guidance on how to compile the application and how to add your own tests to it.

Location of Component	Type of Argument	Recommendation
In-process	Large strings (not modified)	Use *ByRef* because it uses a pointer rather than creating a copy and passing it.
Out-of-process	Large strings (not modified)	Use *ByVal* because *ByRef* data is copied into component's address space, this method passes a pointer to the local data, and this doubles the network traffic.
Out-of-process	Object reference	Use *ByVal* because this means you have one-way cross-process marshalling, which is fast.
Out-of-process	Object reference that is going to be replaced	Use *ByRef* so that the original reference can be changed.
Out-of-process	Most things	Use *ByVal*—if you use *ByRef* you can't avoid marshalling by parenthesizing the parameter or using *ByVal* when calling the method.

TABLE 12-2 *Talking with components: ByVal or ByRef?*

Discussions of how to make a system faster also throw an interesting sidelight on the evolution of a programming language. In early versions of a language, your biggest goal is to make it work at all. Often there are only one or two ways to achieve the functionality in the early versions of a language, and to achieve those you have to put in some hours. There are lots of clearly wrong answers and a few clearly right answers. So, if it works, you must have built it right. Then features are added to the language. These sometimes add functionality but more often diversify—more ways to skin the same old cats.

Developers are diverse too, and they react differently to the widening of their choices. Some stay with the same old tried, trusted, and understood ways. Others try every new feature, compare each to the old ways, and make decisions about how and when they will use them. Still others read a bit and wait to be directed by industry opinion. It is hard because Visual Basic has grown exponentially. But enough sidetracks and musings.

How does this affect the data access strategy task we've set for ourselves? Well, unless you are very lucky your data source will be large, shared, on a different machine, and dangerous. You can create your data-retrieving objects locally (on the user's client machine, the sink client) or remotely via a component on the server. The old computer adage, "Do the work near the data," may influence you here, as will whether you have middle-tier objects out on the network. If you have remote objects, you have to consider whether to pass object references or variables, or something else.

Remoting

Efficient passing of data between processes, and particularly across machine boundaries, is critical to the success of scalable, distributed, tiered Visual Basic systems. We've already (I hope) established that passing data in variables that are grouped together on methods—rather than lots of property touching—is the way to go. We also looked at when to use *ByVal* and *ByRef* on parameters. Now we have to look at how we can get the most efficient performance out of remoting. Marshalling data across machines and process boundaries attracts a heavy penalty from COM, so in Visual Basic 4 and 5 a few ways established themselves as favored. They were used particularly for passing large amounts of data, which would otherwise have ended up being collections of objects. Let's remind ourselves of those ways first.

Variant arrays and *GetRows* An efficient way of passing larger amounts of data across process and machine boundaries is as Variant arrays. It is possible to make your own arrays using the *Array* function. But Variant arrays gained in popularity mainly because they were coded directly into the data access interfaces that most Visual Basic developers use. *GetRows* exists on RDO's *rdoResultset* objects and on both DAO's and ADO's *Recordset* objects. The ADO version is more flexible than the DAO and RDO implementations—check out its extra parameters. Using *Getrows* in the data access code looks like this:

```
Public Function GiveMeData() As Variant
    Dim rsfADO  As New ADODB.Recordset  'The Recordset object
    Dim vResult As Variant                'to put data in.

    rsfADO.Open strSQL, strCon            'Open a connection.
    vResult = rsfADO.GetRows            'Park the results in a Variant array.
    GiveMeData = vResult                'Send the Variant array back.
End Function
```

Finally the Variant array reaches the user interface (having perhaps passed through a number of hands, classes, and components) and is used.

```
Public Sub GetData()
    Dim nRowCount As Integer    'A row count holder.
    Dim nColCount As Integer    'A row count holder.
    Dim sCurrentRow As String   'A string to build each row in.
    Dim vData As Variant        'A Variant to hold our data.
    'Call the server and get back a Variant array.
    vData = oDataServer.GiveMeData

    'For each row (rows are dimension 2 of the array).
    For nRowCount = LBound(vData, 2) To UBound(vData, 2)
        sCurrentRow = "" 'Initialize the current row.
        'For each column in the row.
        For nColCount = LBound(vData, 1) To UBound(vData, 1)
            'Add the column data to the current row.
            sCurrentRow = sCurrentRow & Space(2) & _
                CStr(vData(nColCount, nRowCount))
        Next nColCount
        'Add the row to a list box - or use it somehow.
        lstDataRows.AddItem sCurrentRow
    Next nRowCount
End Sub
```

In each case, *GetRows* creates a two-dimensional array, which it puts into a Variant. The first array subscript identifies the column, and the second identifies the row number. The only downside of *GetRows* is that, when you have grown used to manipulating collections of objects and accessing their data through their properties, going back to arrays feels clumsy. It is a specific and increasingly unusual implementation. As a result, at TMS we often use a DLL that turns a two-dimensional Variant array into either a recordset object again (either our own implementation, or less frequently, one of the standalone implementations available in ADO and RDO) on the client-side, purely for ease of coding. (See the Gendata and DataArray projects in the samples directory for this chapter. These projects use *GetRows* with ADO and a custom implementation of the recordset.)

UDTs and LSET   Some people (I was not among them) so mourned the passing of the user-defined type (UDT) into history (since, prior to Visual Basic 6, UDTs couldn't be passed as a parameter) that they came up with work-arounds, to which they became devoted. The UDT has its Visual Basic roots in file access, particularly where files were structured as records.

Imagine a UDT for an Account record:

```
Public Type AccountStruct
    AccountID As Long
    Balance As Currency
    Status As AccountStatus
    AccountTitle As String
    OverdraftAmount As Currency
    AvailableFunds As Currency
End Type
```

Since a UDT couldn't be passed as a parameter, it first had to be converted. Therefore, a corresponding user-defined type that has only one member but is the same size as the original is defined:

```
Type Passer
    Buffer As String * 36
End Type
```

CAUTION

Beware when sizing that in 32-bit Windows, strings are Unicode. Therefore, each character = 2 bytes, so if you need an odd number size (such as 17 bytes because you have a byte member in the original type) you would actually have a spare byte.

We then copy the original user-defined type into this temporary one. We can do this with *LSet*. In the client component, we have:

```
Dim pass As Passer
Dim oUDTer As udtvb5er
Set oUDTer = New udtvb5er
LSet pass = myorig
oUDTer.GetUDT pass.Buffer
```

In the server, we need the same user-defined types defined, along with the following method in our *udtvb5er* class:

```
Public Sub GetUDT(x As String)
    Dim neworig As AccountStruct
    Dim newpass As Passer
    newpass.Buffer = x
    LSet neworig = newpass
    MsgBox neworig.AccountID & Space(2) & Trim(neworig.AccountTitle)_
        & Space(2) & "Current Balance: " & CStr(neworig.Balance)
End Sub
```

To do this, we are copying from one type to the other, passing the data as a string and then reversing the process at the other end. However, as Visual Basic's Help warns, using *LSet* to copy a variable of one user-defined type into a variable of a different user-defined type is not recommended. Copying data of one data type into space reserved for a different data type can have unpredictable results. When you copy a variable from one user-defined type to another, the binary data from one variable is copied into the memory space of the other without regard for the data types specified for the elements.

NOTE

There is an example project in the code samples for this chapter, named UDT-Pass.vbg. This is *not* a recommendation, merely a recap of what was possible!

Visual Basic 6 and remoting

With a few exceptions, this chapter has up until now dealt in long-term truths rather than cool, new Visual Basic 6 features. I haven't done this to hide things from you deliberately. However, passing data from one thing to another is an area where Visual Basic 6 has added quite a few new features, and it's pretty confused in there at the moment. I've attempted to sort them out for you here.

New ways of passing variables (arrays and UDTs)   Visual Basic 6 has made it possible to return arrays from functions. In the spirit of variable passing, rather than property touching, this is likely to be of some help. The new syntax looks like this in the function you are calling:

```
Public Function GetIDs() As Long()
    Dim x() As Long
    Dim curAccount As Account
    Dim iCount As Integer
    ReDim x(1 To mCol.Count)
    iCount = 1
    For Each curAccount In mCol
        x(iCount) = curAccount.AccountID
        iCount = iCount + 1
    Next curAccount
    GetIDs = x
End Function
```

From the client's view, it is like this:

```
Private Sub cmdGetIDs_Click()
    Dim x() As Long
    Dim i As Integer
    x() = oAccounts.GetIDs
    For i = LBound(x()) To UBound(x())
        lstIDs.AddItem CStr(x(i))
    Next i
    lstIDs.Visible = True
End Sub
```

This example has been included in the project group UDTGrp.vbg in the samples directory for this chapter.

Visual Basic 6 has also added the ability to have public UDTs and to pass them between components. Thus, a UDT structure such as we looked at earlier:

```
Public Type AccountStruct
    AccountID As Long
    Balance As Currency
    Status As AccountStatus
    AccountTitle As String
    OverdraftAmount As Currency
    AvailableFunds As Currency
End Type
```

can be passed back and forth to the server thus in the server class's code:

```
Public Function GetallData() As AccountStruct
    Dim tGetallData As AccountStruct

    tGetallData.AccountID = AccountID
    tGetallData.Balance = Balance
    tGetallData.Status = Status
    tGetallData.AccountTitle = AccountTitle
    tGetallData.OverdraftAmount = OverdraftAmount
    tGetallData.AvailableFunds = AvailableFunds

    GetallData = tGetallData
End Function

Public Sub SetAllData(tAccount As AccountStruct)
    AccountID = tAccount.AccountID
    Balance = tAccount.Balance
    Status = tAccount.Status
    AccountTitle = tAccount.AccountTitle
    OverdraftAmount = tAccount.OverdraftAmount
End Sub
```

and called like this from the client:

```
Dim oAccount As Account
Dim tAccount As AccountStruct
For Each oAccount In oAccounts
    tAccount = oAccount.GetallData
    lstAccounts.AddItem tAccount.AccountID & _
        Space(4 - (Len(CStr(tAccount.AccountID)))) & _
        tAccount.Balance & Space(3) & tAccount.OverdraftAmount
Next oAccount
```

Remoting ADO recordsets   The combination of ADO and the Remote Data Service (RDS) client-side library—intended for speedy, lightweight, disconnected data access for Web applications—can be particularly useful for any distributed client/server system, regardless of its user interface type. The client needs a reference to the Microsoft ActiveX Data Objects Recordset 2.0 Library, while the server has a reference to the Microsoft ActiveX Data Objects 2.0 Library. At its simplest, the client code looks like this:

```
Private oDD As DataDonor

Private Sub cmdGetData_Click()
    Dim oRS As ADOR.Recordset
    Set oDD = New DataDonor
    Set oRS = oDD.GiveData
    Set oDD = Nothing
    Set oDataGrid.DataSource = oRS
End Sub
```

While in the server component the DataDonor Class's code looks like this:

```
Public Function GiveData() As ADODB.Recordset
    'A very boring query we can use on any SQL Server.
    Const strSQL As String = "SELECT * FROM authors"
    'We'll use this DSN.
    Const strCon As String = _
        "DSN=pubsit;UID=lawsond;PWD=lawsond;" & _
        "DATABASE=pubs;APP=DudeCli;"

    Dim ors As New ADODB.Recordset

    ors.LockType = adLockBatchOptimistic
    ors.CursorLocation = adUseClient
        ors.CursorType = adOpenStatic
    ors.Open strSQL, strCon
        Set ors.ActiveConnection = Nothing
    Set GiveData = ors
End Function
```

To create a disconnected recordset, you must create a *Recordset* object that uses a client-side cursor that is either a static or keyset cursor (*adOpenStatic* or *adOpenKeyset*) with a lock type of *adLockBatchOptimistic*. (This example is listed in the samples directory for this chapter as RemRset.vbg).

If you return a disconnected recordset from a function, either as the return value or as an output parameter, the recordset copies its data to its caller. If the caller is in a different process or on a different machine, the recordset marshals the data it is holding to the caller's process. In so doing, it compresses the data to avoid occupying substantial network bandwidth, which makes it an ideal way to send large amounts of data to a client machine. Remoting ADO recordsets really has to be done.

The end resultset is a recordset that has been instantiated on the server and then physically passed down to the client. It is no longer connected to the database at all but can be used as a recordset, and if changes are made to it the recordset could be passed back to a server and reassociated with a database connection to allow updates to take effect. This avoids the penalty of continued network overhead because each column and field is referenced for its data and is a strong contender as a replacement for passing Variant arrays.

Returning changes from a disconnected recordset: batch updating   When a recordset is disconnected and has been remoted to a different machine, it is possible to make changes to it using its *Edit*, *Update*, and *Delete* methods. In fact, it is one of the only times when it makes sense to use these methods on a cursor, since we are not using up all the normal resources or actually talking to the database. When you are finished changing things, you pass the recordset back to a component that has a live connection to the database. It uses the *UpdateBatch* method to input all your changes in a single batch.

```
Public Sub ReconUpdate(rs As ADODB.Recordset)
    Dim conn As ADODB.Connection
    Set conn = New ADODB.Connection
    conn.Open "DSN=Universe"
    Set rs.ActiveConnection = conn
    rs.UpdateBatch
```

Fear not the score of other untrustworthy users having updated the same records as you! Just like batch updating in RDO, you have all the tools to sort out collisions, if they occur. However, beware if you are expecting to marshal a recordset from the middle tier to the client machine in order to resolve any conflicts you have. The three versions of the data (original, value, and underlying) are not marshalled, so you need to do some work yourself. (See Q177720 in the Knowledge Base for more on this.)

Creatable ADO recordsets   ADO recordsets can act as a standard interface, even when data is not being accessed from a database using an OLE DB provider, since ADO recordsets can be created independently and filled with data by direct code manipulation. Server code for this in a class is shown on the following page.

```
Private rs As ADODB.Recordset
Private Sub Class_Initialize()
    Dim strPath As String, strName As String
    Dim i As Integer
    ' Create an instance of the Recordset.
    Set rs = New ADODB.Recordset
    ' Set the properties of the Recordset.
    With rs
        .Fields.Append "DirID", adInteger
        .Fields.Append "Directory", adBSTR, 255
        .CursorType = adOpenStatic
        .LockType = adLockOptimistic
        .Open
    End With
    ' Loop through the directories and populate
    ' the Recordset.
    strPath = "D:\"
    strName = Dir(strPath, vbDirectory)
    i = 0
    Do While strName <> ""
        If strName <> "." And strName <> ".." Then
            If (GetAttr(strPath & strName) And _
                vbDirectory) = vbDirectory Then
                i = i + 1
                With rs
                    .AddNew
                    .Fields.Item("DirID") = i
                    .Fields.Item("Directory") = strName
                    .Update
                End With
            End If
        End If
        strName = Dir
    Loop
    ' Return to the first record.
    rs.MoveFirst
End Sub
```

This code is in the DataAware.vbp sample project in the samples directory for this chapter.

Persisting recordsets   ADO *Recordset* objects can be saved to a file by using their *Save* method. This can be valuable if you have a requirement to store data for longer than a run of a program, but without being able to do so in a data source. Imagine a user has made changes to a recordset and then cannot reconnect to a data source such as a remote database. Persisting data can also be useful for a disconnected recordset, since the connection and the application can be closed while the recordset is still available on the client computer. The code for persisting a *Recordset* object looks like this:

```
rsDudes.Save "c:\tms\dudestuff.dat", adPersistADTG
```

and to get the data out from the file again the following code would do it:

```
rsDudes.Open " c:\tms\dudestuff.dat "
```

Files and persistable classes Visual Basic 6 gave classes the capabilities that some other ActiveX instantiables (such as ActiveX Documents and User Controls) have had for a version already—namely, the capability to persist their properties through the *PropertyBag* object. This allows us to store a class's properties between instances. The *Persistable* property in conjunction with the *PropertyBag* object lets a class instance be persisted almost anywhere: a file, the Registry, a database, a word-processor document, or a spreadsheet cell.

Why persist? Most components have properties; one of the great annoyances of Visual Basic's *Class_Initialize* event procedure is that you can't get parameters into it. Typically, *Class_Initialize* is used to set up default values for a class instance. The default values you use are frozen in time when you compile the component, unless you use something like INI settings, Registry entries, files, or command line arguments to vary them. This is where the Visual Basic 6 class's *Persistable* property comes in, allowing you to save a component's values between runs. To be persistable, a class has to be public and createable. When you set a class's *Persistable* property to *Persistable*, three new events are added to the class: ReadProperties, WriteProperties, and InitProperties. Just like in an ActiveX User Control, you can mark a property as persistable by invoking the *PropertyChanged* method in a Property Let or Property Set procedure, as in the following example:

```
Private mBattingAverage As Decimal
Public Property Let BattingAverage (newAverage As Decimal)
    mBattingAverage = newAverage
    PropertyChanged "BattingAverage"
End Property
```

Calling the *PropertyChanged* method marks the property as dirty. The WriteProperties event will fire when the class is terminated if any property in the class has called *PropertyChanged*. Then we use the events and the *PropertyBag* object almost the same way as in a User Control.

There is a twist however: we need a second instance of a *PropertyBag* object so that when the object goes away, and takes its *PropertyBag* object with it, there is a persisted set of properties. The following code shows persisting an object to a text file, but remember that they can be persisted wherever you like, even in a database:

```
Private pb As PropertyBag        ' Declare a PropertyBag object.
Private oBatsman As Batsman      ' Declare a Cricketer.

Private Sub Form_Unload(Cancel As Integer)
    Dim varTemp as Variant

    ' Instantiate the second PropertyBag object.
    Set pb = New PropertyBag
    ' Save the object to the PropertyBag using WriteProperty.
    pb.WriteProperty "FirstManIn", oBatsman
    ' Assign the Contents of the PropertyBag to a Variant.
    varTemp = pb.Contents
    ' Save to a text file.
    Open "C:\tms\FirstBat.txt" For Binary As #1
    Put #1, , varTemp
    Close #1
End Sub
```

The *Contents* property of the *PropertyBag* object contains the *Batsman* object stored as an array of bytes. To save it to a text file, you must first convert it to a data type that a text file understands—here, that data type is a Variant.

Depersisting an object

Once our Batsman is contained inside a text file (or any other type of storage), it is easy to send him wherever we want. We could take the FIRSTBAT.TXT file and send it with perhaps an entire cricket scorecard to our newspaper's office for incorporating into a newspaper report of the day's play. The code to reuse the *Batsman* object would look something like this:

```
Private pb As PropertyBag        ' Declare a PropertyBag object.
Private oBatsman As Batsman      ' Declare a Batsman object.

Private Sub Form_Load()
    Dim varTemp As Variant
    Dim byteArr() as Byte

    ' Instantiate the PropertyBag object.
    Set pb = New PropertyBag
    ' Read the file contents into a Variant.
```

```
      Open " C:\tms\FirstBat.txt " For Binary As #1
      Get #1, , varTemp
      Close #1
      ' Assign the Variant to a Byte array.
      ByteArr = varTemp
      ' Assign to the PropertyBag Contents property.
      pb.Contents = ByteArr
      ' Instantiate the object from the PropertyBag
      Set oBatsman = pb.ReadProperty("FirstManIn")
End If
```

It isn't the same object being created in one place and reused in another; it is an exact copy of the object. This ability to "clone," or copy, an object for reuse offers a lot of potential.

COMPONENTIZING ALL OF THIS

The preceding pages have tried to identify the knowledge that a good data-access component might encapsulate. The next thing to do is design the component's programming model interface. That is a job for another day, and it has been done better than I could have in the excellent article, "The Basics of Programming Model Design," by Dave Stearns of Microsoft.[5]

---

5. "The Basics of Programming Model Design" is due to be an MSDN Article in July 1998. As I write, it hasn't made it onto my MSDN CDs, but I trust by the time you read this it will be available on the CDs and on the MSDN Web site.

Programming on Purpose

A Window on Detailed Design

MARK HURST

Mark is a TMS Associate who is also a writer, painter, pilot, filmmaker, and an enthusiastic—if largely untalented—ragtime guitarist. He risks his life daily by charging through London traffic on a motorbike, and he almost never wears a tie. Since graduating with a computer science degree in 1985, Mark has made a living out of software: he is an accomplished C, C++, and Pascal programmer, and he has also worked as a designer, analyst, system tester, configuration manager, and trainer. Mark has presented at VBITS and the Visual Tools Developers' Academy and has Technical Editor credits on two other recent Visual Basic books, *Using Visual Basic 5* and *Special Edition: Using Visual Basic 6* (both from Que). He has published many articles in industry journals and beyond.

It's a popular myth that Microsoft Visual Basic has changed programming. I disagree. Programming is as hard as it always was—most people who say that Visual Basic projects are easy just aren't doing them right. Perhaps Visual Basic has advanced the state of the art of Microsoft Windows programming a notch or two; but behind the form designers and the wizards lies procedural code, with all the traditional problems developers have come to expect. A dangerous side effect of making a programming tool as easy to use as Visual Basic is the illusion that this somehow dispenses with the need for detailed design—that the code somehow writes itself. The truth, scribbled in the margin of many a project postmortem report, is that programming in Visual Basic is *programming* first and Visual Basic second.

This chapter is about detailed design. To illustrate the kinds of things you need to think about when designing an application, we'll be looking at the design and construction of a window-management scheme, perhaps the most fundamental part of any Windows program. You'll be reading a lot about the graphical user interface

(GUI), but you won't be seeing anything about button sizes, mouse-pointer psychology, or the choice of fonts and colors—the approach in this chapter is from a different angle, addressing the kinds of problems that will sink a GUI no matter how nice the screens look. You'll be seeing the choices Visual Basic offers for designing window-management schemes, some of the obstacles Visual Basic puts in your way, and how you can use some of the more advanced features of Visual Basic to get what you want. In all of this, you'll be focusing on two particular areas: how to use classes to build value-added forms, and how to manage complexity with finite state machines.

MANAGING WINDOWS

The most striking feature of the majority of commercial Visual Basic applications is the set of windows they create and manipulate, including the way the user gets around these windows and the ways in which the windows interact with one another. Often a window-management scheme is something that simply evolves during implementation: the developer might not have a clear idea about how each window will behave with respect to other windows, and the window-management features built into Visual Basic might be the factor that most influences how the design turns out. This isn't so much a poor design strategy as the lack of a strategy, and the resulting problems can be anything from poor usability to insidious bugs.

Visual Basic has a mixed bag of window-management tricks, the simplest of which are *MsgBox* and *InputBox*. These are modal dialog boxes, so you must deal with them before the program will remove them and continue its processing. There isn't much to say about *MsgBox* and *InputBox* except that they are inflexible. In particular, you can't change the button captions, and you don't have complete control over size and position of the dialog boxes. For added flexibility, you can, of course, write your own Visual Basic functions named *MsgBox* and *InputBox* to override the Visual Basic ones. Interestingly, doing this allows you to make nonmodal message boxes, the consequences of which will become clear later.

Visual Basic also has features to support multiple-document interface (MDI) applications, and the decision to build with MDI will have a major influence on the way your application works. MDI has some advantages—chiefly that it is well defined and that Visual Basic will implement some of the features for you (menu management, window arrangements, and so on). On the other hand, adopting MDI for these reasons alone is futile if the application you want to build doesn't fit the rigid MDI model. MDI supports a document model and usually makes sense only if your application is going to work with multiple instances of things that are somehow document-like. Document-like qualities include serialization (binding to permanent storage) and size independence, which gives meaning to the familiar MDI window-arrangement functions *Tile* and *Cascade*.

On the other side of the fence from MDI is single-document interface (SDI). Because Visual Basic has no specific functions to support SDI, however, a more accurate description would be "not MDI." You have much more flexibility when building non-MDI applications, but you lose out on some of the free functionality such as window arrangement, child window menu handling, and Ctrl+Tab to switch between child windows. On the other hand, you have more control over your application's appearance, and you can choose whether to make your child forms modal or modeless.

Finally, you can build hybrid applications that borrow some features from MDI without using built-in functionality. You can, for example, create multiple instances of an ordinary form (forms behave just like classes in many ways), and you can even create MDI parent forms dynamically within a non-MDI application. It's important to consider these issues in advance and to plan a window-management scheme appropriate to the application you want to build.

Modal or Modeless?

Whether you choose MDI, SDI, or your own brand of DIY-DI (do-it-yourself document interface), you'll need to think about modality. Modality is one of the most critical issues in the design of your window-management scheme, since it can significantly affect program complexity. Using modal forms wherever possible helps to control complexity, but it can also get in the way by imposing artificial restrictions on users. Although modality is one of the more contentious issues in user interface design, the evidence in favor of radical modeless design is far from conclusive. Suffice it to say that in this chapter the concern is with the implications of modality on implementation rather than with the psychology of interface design.

When you show a form, Visual Basic lets you specify whether you want to show it modally or nonmodally, using the constants vbModal and vbModeless. This isn't a very flexible way of implementing modes, however; a vbModal form is task-modal, which means it locks out all user input from the rest of the application. This type of modality is really suitable only for pop-up dialog boxes. When you specify vbModal when you show a form, the only way you can show two forms together is if they have a parent-child relationship. This restriction imposes a particular set of design restrictions on your application, and it might prevent you from doing what you want. It's also impossible to display a nonmodal form from a modal form, another potentially intolerable situation.

Consider the example shown in Figure 13-1, which is a non-MDI application with several distinct functions invoked from a main menu. Perhaps it's a database maintenance program, and you would like to be able to refer to display functions while using update functions. In Figure 13-1, I've shown two functions executing at the same time; forms A and C can be considered parent forms for Function 1 and Function 2, respectively. Parent form A is also displaying a child form, form B.

Although the forms shown below are relatively simple, it's likely that you'll want form A to display form B modally, or more specifically, for form A to be inaccessible for as long as form B is on the screen. The conventional way to code this is for form A to call *FormB.Show vbModal*, but this locks all user input from any form except form B—including the main menu. Hence, it wouldn't be possible to reach the situation shown below. The alternative, *FormB.Show vbModeless*, doesn't prevent you from accessing multiple functions at the same time, but it interferes with the design of each function and greatly increases the complexity of the program. Clearly, you need to find something in between.

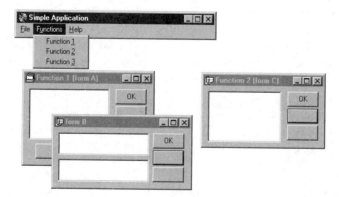

FIGURE 13-1   *An example of function modality: form A is not accessible here*

Visual Basic's built-in support for modal forms is geared toward simple pop-up dialog boxes, but that doesn't stop you from building modes by other means. Forms have an *Enabled* property that, when set to False, effectively mimics what happens to a parent form when it shows a vbModal child. Now that you're in control, however, you're free to enable and disable forms at will, without the restrictions imposed by vbModal.

Returning to the example in Figure 13-1, all you need to do is to create form B as modeless, then disable form A when form B loads and reenable it when form B unloads (or possibly on Show and Hide instead of Load and Unload). This implements a new kind of mode that's more appropriate to your requirements; you might call it "function modality," since you're creating an architecture in which it's permissible to hop back and forth between functions yet each function is effectively a modal cascade of forms. This architecture is only one possibility; a less orthodox architecture is shown in Figure 13-2.

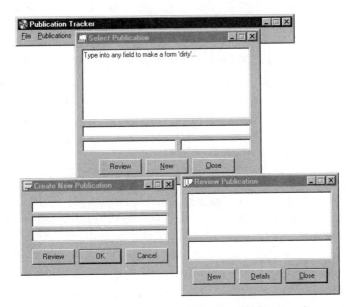

FIGURE 13-2   *The Create New Publication and Review Publication forms swap with each other*

Figure 13-2 shows a database application that's used to keep records of technical publications. Users can choose an existing entry from the list and edit it using the Review Publication form, or they can enter a new publication by calling Create New Publication. Notice that the Create New Publication window has a Review button, and the Review Publication window has a New button. This arrangement could imply multiple instances of each screen, but let's say that the design calls for screens to be *swapped* when these buttons are used. For example, the user could call up the Create New Publication window to enter the details for a new publication and then press the Review button to move immediately to the Review Publication window to enter a review of it. As the Review Publication window loads, it *replaces* the Create New Publication window, which is unloaded. The Select Publication window is disabled when either the Review Publication window or the Create New Publication window is displayed.

There is no elegant way to implement this architecture using Visual Basic's standard modality features. You would somehow have to defer your request for the review form to be displayed until the Create New Publication form was unloaded. You could make it work, but it would be tricky and it would be ugly. You'd be much better off devising a general mechanism to support the kinds of modes you want to enforce.

Toward a General Modality Class

You can both create and manipulate value-added forms by building a CForm-Attributes class (see the "Forms Are Classes Too" sidebar on page 551) and adding the function modality mechanism to it. The central requirement for such a mechanism is to associate a parent with each form you create. You can do this by adding a *Parent* property to the CFormAttributes class:

```
Public Parent As Form
```

Now you have somewhere to store a reference to the parent form, so you need to arrange for this reference to be set when the form is loaded. Since you can't pass parameters to a form's *Show* method (or to the CFormAttributes instance), you need to do this manually from outside the CFormAttributes class. You want to be able to do something like this:

```
Public Sub ShowChild Child:=frmReview, Parent:=Me
```

You could make this a global procedure and give it its own BAS file, but it's better to keep all the code in one place by making *ShowChild* a method of the CFormAttributes class. Obviously, this means you can't invoke *ShowChild* to display the first form in a hierarchy, but the only implication of this is that you need to make sure that the CFormAttributes class recognizes that it has no parent when it is destroyed. You can also dispense with the *Parent* parameter since you already have a *Self* reference in the CFormAttributes class. Here's the method in the CFormAttributes class, which is named *NewChild*:

```
Public Sub NewChild(ByVal frmiChild As Form)
    frmiChild.Show
    Set frmiChild.My.Parent = frmPiSelf
    frmPiSelf.Enabled = False
End Sub
```

The last statement is the significant one because it's the one that disables the parent form and creates a new mode. You need a reciprocal action to reenable the parent when the form unloads, so you need to define another method:

```
Public Sub EnableParent()
    If Not Me.Parent Is Nothing Then Me.Parent.Enabled = True
End Sub
```

Unfortunately, there's no elegant way to bind this to a form unload; you must ensure that you call this method from each *Form_Unload* event:

```
Private Sub Form_Unload()
    My.EnableParent
End Sub
```

In fact, the sample code in CHAP13\atribcls\pubatrib.cls has a generic *UnloadActions* method, which takes the place of *EnableParent*, but this discussion is clearer if I continue to refer to an *EnableParent* method.

That takes care of modal child forms, as long as you invoke them with *My.NewChild* and include the appropriate reciprocal call in the *Form_Unload* event. You can now build on this to extend the mechanism. To cope with the swapping in the sample program, for example, you need to do a couple of extra things: pass on the outgoing form's parent reference to the new form and then prevent the parent from being reenabled when the old form unloads. You can do this by adding a new method and modifying the *EnableParent* method slightly so that the two communicate through a module-level flag:

```
Private bPiKeepParentDisabled As Boolean

Public Sub SwapMe(ByVal frmiNewChild As Form)
    frmiNewChild.Show vbModeless
    If frmiNewChild.Enabled Then
        Set frmiNewChild.My.Parent = Parent
        bPiKeepParentDisabled = True
    End If
```

>>

```
      Unload frmPiSelf
End Sub

Public Sub EnableParent()
    If Not bPiKeepParentDisabled Then
        If Not Parent Is Nothing Then Parent.Enabled = True
    End If
End Sub
```

Notice the check to find out whether the form you're trying to swap to is enabled. If it isn't, it must already have been loaded, in which case you'll just leave the *Parent* property alone. This is an ad hoc test that works in the simple examples shown here, but it might not be general, and so you'll need to extend the mechanism to cope with other situations. For example, the mechanism as it stands won't prevent you from trying to swap to a form that's in the *middle* of a modal cascade—in fact, this would orphan any child forms in the cascade. With a little thought, you should be able to extend the mechanism to allow swapping to remove child forms of the form you're trying to swap to, to prevent swapping between forms belonging to other functions in a function modal situation, or to support any other flavors of modality you care to invent.

Extending the CFormAttributes Class

The beauty of a value-added form class is that it's a simple matter to add new features retrospectively. As an example, let's look at how you can add support for pseudo-MDI minimize and restore behavior. Because all document windows in an MDI application are contained within the client area of the parent window, minimizing that window naturally takes away all of the children, too. This is convenient since it instantly clears the application off the desktop (without closing it, of course).

The MDI window feature in Visual Basic gives you this minimize behavior for free. With an SDI or a DIY-DI application, however, you have no such luxury. Because a Visual Basic form has no Minimize event, you must write code that plugs into the Resize event and decide for yourself when a form is minimized or restored by investigating the *WindowState* property. The behavior we're going to construct will watch for transitions from normal to minimized and from minimized back to normal. (This second operation is usually called "restore.") We'll write the code as a new method of the CFormAttributes class and then simply add a call to it from appropriate Resize event handlers.

Trapping the event, of course, is only half the story—you also need to do something to take away the rest of the forms. One possibility is to set the

WindowState to follow the window containing the trap, but in practice that looks messy because Windows animates zoom boxes all over the place and you end up with lots of task bar buttons (or icons in earlier versions of Microsoft Windows NT). It's quicker and visually more effective to hide all the other forms when you trap a minimize event and to restore them when you trap a restore event. The only tricky part is to remember the prevailing state of each form before hiding it, just in case any were hidden already. Here's the code you'll need:

```
Public PreviouslyVisible As Boolean
Private nPiPrevWindowState As Integer

Public Sub PropagateMinMaxEvents ()
    If frmPiSelf.WindowState = vbMinimized _
            And nPiPrevWindowState = vbNormal Then
        Call HideAllForms
    ElseIf frmPiSelf.WindowState = vbNormal _
            And nPiPrevWindowState = vbMinimized Then
        Call UnhideAllForms
    End If
    nPiPrevWindowState = frmPiSelf.WindowState
End Sub

Private Sub HideAllForms()
    Dim frmForm As Form
    For Each frmForm In Forms
        If Not frmForm Is frmPiSelf Then
            frmForm.My.PreviouslyVisible = frmForm.Visible
            frmForm.Visible = False
        End If
    Next frmForm
End Sub

Private Sub UnhideAllForms()
    ' This is just the opposite of HideAllForms.
End Sub
```

To activate the new behavior, you need to choose which forms will trigger it and call *PropagateMinMaxEvents* from their Resize event handlers. The publication editing program referred to in Figure 13-2 on page 545 has this call coded in the Resize events of all the forms, so minimizing any form hides all the others and shows a single button on the task bar. Restoring from that button restores each form to its previous state. To add minimize behavior to the example application shown in Figure 13-1 on page 544, you would code a single call to *PropagateMinMaxEvents* in the Resize event of the main form (the one carrying the menu bar). This mimics the MDI paradigm more closely because of the definite parent form.

Visual Basic 6 has another trick that you could use here, which is to add custom Minimize and Restore events to your forms through the CFormAttributes class. You can do this very simply by making a small modification to the *PropagateMinMaxEvents* method shown here.

```
Event Minimize()
Event Restore()

Public Sub PropagateMinMaxEvents ()
    If frmPiSelf.WindowState = vbMinimized _
            And nPiPrevWindowState = vbNormal Then
        RaiseEvent Minimize
    ElseIf frmPiSelf.WindowState = vbNormal _
            And nPiPrevWindowState = vbMinimized Then
        RaiseEvent Restore
    End If
    nPiPrevWindowState = frmPiSelf.WindowState
End Sub
```

In case you didn't spot it, calls to *HideAllForms* and *UnhideAllForms* have been replaced with calls to the Visual Basic procedure *RaiseEvent*. This diminutive keyword is very powerful, and you'll see other examples of it later in the chapter. When you define the CFormAttributes instance on a form, a new object, *My*, appears in the code window's Object drop-down list box, and when you choose it, you'll see Minimize and Restore events in the Procedure drop-down list box. These events work in exactly the same way as normal events do, so selecting Minimize inserts an empty procedure named *My_Minimize* into the code. One caveat is that the syntax for defining the CFormAttributes instance is slightly different if you want to see the events:

```
Public WithEvents My As CFormAttributes
```

Unfortunately, the *New* keyword is not allowed in combination with the *WithEvents* keyword, so you'll also need to add a line to the *Form_Load* event:

```
Private Sub Form_Load()
    Set My = New CFormAttributes
    My.LoadActions Me
End Sub
```

Forms Are Classes Too

Forms are really classes in disguise. Once you realize this fact, you can start using it to your advantage. The similarity isn't obvious because you don't have to define instances of forms before you can use them. However, you can use a form's *Name* property to create new instances of the form at run time, just as if it were a class. What's a little confusing is that if you don't create any instances at run time, you always get one for free—and it has the same name as the class. Thus, referring to Form1 at run time means different things in different contexts:

```
Form1.Caption = "My Form"            ' Form1 is an object name.
Dim frmAnotherForm As New Form1      ' Form1 is a class name.
```

The fact that forms are really classes is why defining public variables at the module level in a form appears not to work—trying to assign to these variables causes "Variable not defined" errors. In fact, you're defining *properties* of the form, and these work in exactly the same way as class properties do. To refer to such properties in code, you need to qualify them with the object name, which, you'll recall, is usually the same as the class name. (This is confusing if you do actually create multiple instances.) Even more interesting is that you can also define *Property Let* and *Property Get* procedures, *Public* methods, and even *Friend* functions in forms, just as you can in classes.

Because Visual Basic doesn't support inheritance at the source code level, you can't build value-added form classes; the best you can do is to build value-added form *instances* by adding custom properties and methods to your forms. You can do this by exploiting the classlike nature of forms and writing a form *base class* that contains extra properties and methods you'd like to see on every form. This works very well in practice, although it relies on you adding some standard code to every form you create. To see how this works, let's build some methods to save and restore a form's position when it loads and unloads.

The first thing you need to do is define a class, named CFormAttributes. You'll create a Public instance of this class in every form you create, and this instance will appear as a property of the form. When you store the form positions with *SaveSetting*, it would be nice to use the form name as a key; unfortunately, there isn't any way for an instance of a Visual Basic class to refer to the object that owns it. This means you'll need to define the owner as a property in your CFormAttributes class and arrange to set it when you create the instance. The class is shown on the following page.

>>

```
Private frmPiSelf As Form

Public Sub SavePosition()
    SaveSetting App.Title, "Form Positions", _
                    frmPiSelf.Name & "-top", frmPiSelf.Top
    ⋮
End Sub

Public Sub RestorePosition()
    ⋮
End Sub

Public Sub LoadActions(ByVal frmiMe As Form)
    Set frmPiSelf = frmiMe
    RestorePosition frmPiSelf
End Sub

Public Sub UnloadActions()
    SavePosition frmPiSelf
End Sub
```

Notice that the *LoadActions* and *UnloadActions* methods are also defined. These make the class more general for when you add to it later. To add new properties to a form, you need to adopt certain conventions. First you need to define an instance of the class as a form-level variable:

```
Public My As New CFormAttributes
```

The variable is named *My* because it's pretty close to *Me*, and semantically the two are similar. For example, you can now refer to *My.UnloadActions*. The only other thing you need to do is to make sure the *LoadActions* and *UnloadActions* routines are called:

```
Private Sub Form_Load()
    My.LoadActions Me
End Sub

Private Sub Form_Unload()
    My.UnloadActions
End Sub
```

You do have to pass the owner form reference to *LoadActions* to initialize the class's *Self* property. You can find the complete class on the companion CD in CHAP13\atribcls\pubatrib.cls, and CHAP13\attribs\atr.vbp is an implementation of the program shown in Figure 13-2 on page 545.

DEALING WITH COMPLEXITY

Building a mechanism like the one above is a good way to get a feel for the architectural design of your GUI. However, it's tempting to channel design resources into such details as how many forms you're going to use and what fields you need on each form and to let seemingly peripheral issues such as navigation and modality take a back seat. You can get away with this for smaller projects because it's possible to have an intuitive grasp of the interactions among a small number of forms. In general, however, ignoring questions such as how each form is invoked and which forms can be on the screen at the same time can lead to disaster.

By allowing multiple forms to be active at the same time, you dramatically increase the complexity of the underlying code because manipulating data on one form can affect other forms that are also being displayed. For even a modest-size application, the view ahead is daunting, since you have to examine every possible combination of forms that can be active at the same time and then consider the effects of all possible inputs for each combination. Any modes you've designed will help to limit form interactions, but doing the analysis ad hoc invites unplanned side effects—inevitably, you'll fail to plan for some situations.

Figure 13-3 on the following page shows an application that manages a cascade of forms that lead the user down through successive layers of data. If you use modeless forms, editing the data on form A invalidates the data on forms B and C. You also need to consider what happens if the user closes form A before closing forms B and C. Clearly, you need to decide whether these actions have any useful meaning in the application; if they don't, you can simply prevent them. If they do, you want to know up front because they can affect the implementation. (You don't want the forms to share data, for example.)

You might be feeling skeptical about the complexities of a three-form application. Some simple arithmetic can be illuminating. There are seven possible ways in which combinations of the modeless forms A, B, and C can be active. (Let's call these combinations "states.") Now let's say the user presses the Cancel button on form A. Let's also assume you've decided never to leave forms B and C up when the user closes form A. It's clear that the event handler for form A's Cancel Click can't simply unload the form—it must look around to see what other forms are up and maybe close those forms, too.

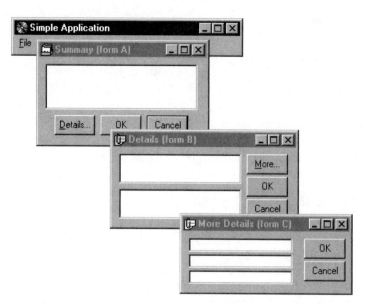

FIGURE 13-3   *A cascade of forms—but modal or modeless?*

If you add another form to the application, the number of states goes up to 15. Even discarding the states that don't contain form A, you are left with 8 different situations to consider in each Cancel Click event handler. In fact, the number of states (combinations of forms) is $2^n - 1$, where n is the number of forms. This number increases *geometrically* as you add forms, which means the number of states gets out of hand very quickly. There is a set of events for which you must consider all of these states, and the handlers for such events need to be aware of the environment and adjust their behavior accordingly.

It should be clear by now that you need a formal way to define the interactions between forms. The model we'll use to track form interactions is the *finite state machine* (FSM). The principles of an FSM, which is essentially an abstract representation of a set of states and events, are described in the following section.

The Art of the State

An FSM is a virtual machine characterized by a set of internal states, a set of external events, and a set of transitions between the states. You might also hear FSMs referred to by the name finite state automata, deterministic finite automata, or simply state machines. FSMs can be used to model an entire application, a small part of it, or both, and they are extremely common in the design of real-time systems, compilers, and communications protocols. FSMs are ideal tools for representing event-driven programs such as GUIs.

States are labels assigned to particular sets of circumstances within the application. Although FSMs are often used to model the GUI part of applications, states are not forms, and events are not necessarily Visual Basic events. You generate a set of predefined events from real-world stimuli and apply them as inputs to the FSM to drive it through transitions into different states. Transitions can have arbitrary lists of actions associated with them, and these actions are executed as you drive the FSM from state to state by repeatedly applying events. An FSM is deterministic because each combination of state and event unambiguously defines the next state to move into.

An FSM can be represented as a state transition diagram or as a pair of tables, one table defining the next state to move into when a particular state/event combination is detected and the other table defining a list of actions to be performed along the way.

Figure 13-4 shows an FSM for a program to strip C comments out of a text stream. (Comments in C are delimited by /* and */.)

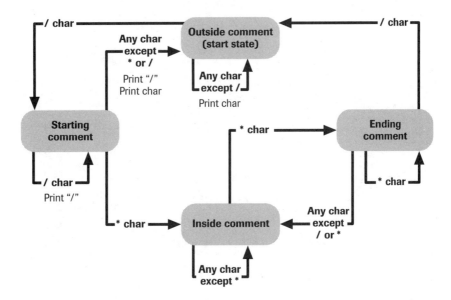

FIGURE 13-4   *Comment stripper FSM*

The bubbles in Figure 13-4 represent states, and the arrows represent transitions between states. Each transition is labeled with the event that stimulates it and the list of associated actions. One state is designated the start state, which is the initial state when the FSM starts to operate. Here is the FSM in tabular form:

STATE TABLE

Event	State			
	Outside	Starting	Inside	Ending
/	Starting	Starting	Inside	Outside
*	Outside	Inside	Ending	Ending
Any other char	Outside	Outside	Inside	Inside

ACTION TABLE

Event	State			
	Outside	Starting	Inside	Ending
/	N/A	Print "/"	N/A	N/A
*	Print char	N/A	N/A	N/A
Any other char	Print char	Print "/"		
Print char	N/A	N/A		

These tables provide the basis for implementing an FSM as a program. An FSM program has the following elements:

- A static variable to track the current state and a set of constants to represent all available states
- A table or equivalent program network to look up a state/event pair and decide which state to move into
- A set of constants to represent FSM events
- A driver loop that captures real-world events and decodes the state/event pair

Modeling a GUI with an FSM

Figure 13-5 shows a GUI fragment modeled on a real application. This application provides a summary and two different detailed views of a database. The forms are modeless, so the user can edit any form on the screen, potentially invalidating data on either of the other forms. Although the maximum possible number of states is seven, the design of this application permits access to only four combinations of forms: A, A + B, A + C, and A + B + C. The only events we'll consider are the button clicks; there are 11 buttons, so 11 is the number of events that must be accounted for in every state.

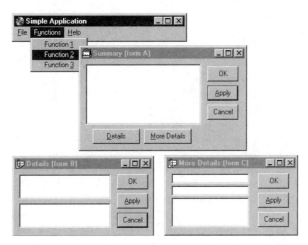

FIGURE 13-5   *A deceptively simple-looking application*

The application has been designed so that only form A's OK or Apply button commits data to the database. Each form has a buffer in which it holds edits to its own subset of the data, and the contents of these buffers are shuffled around as the OK, Apply, and Cancel buttons are manipulated on forms B and C. Figure 13-6 on the following page shows the state transitions for this GUI, and Figure 13-7 on page 559 is a close-up view of two states, showing the actions the application will take on each transition.

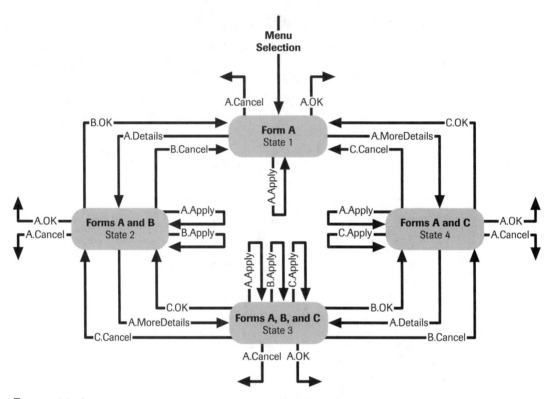

FIGURE 13-6   *FSM for the application shown in Figure 13-5*

Close examination of Figure 13-6 and Figure 13-7 reveals some omissions. There are 11 events, but not all states have 11 arrows leaving them. This is partly because not all events can occur in all states. For example, it isn't possible to click form C's Apply button in state 1. But some events, such as the Details button events in states 2 and 3, are omitted because there just isn't enough space for them. Leaving out events like this undermines a basic reason for using an FSM, which is to verify that you've considered all state/event combinations. This is where the tabular form is a much better representation—it's easier to draw, and it clearly shows all state/event combinations. The two notations complement each other: in practice the state diagram is a useful sketch that conveys the feel of the GUI, while the tables provide a basis for implementation.

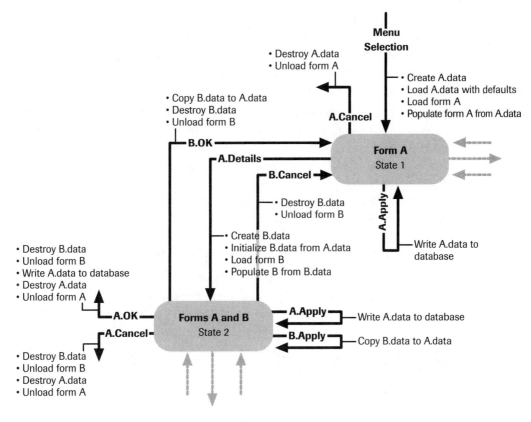

FIGURE 13-7   *Close-up view of a fragment of Figure 13-6*

The End of the Elegance

The finite state machine (FSM) notation is simple and elegant, but you'll run into problems when you try to apply it to real programs. One class of problem, the conditional state transition, is exemplified by the need for validation when you're unloading forms. For example, if you consider form B's OK Click event, you can see that the FSM changes state and does the associated actions *unconditionally*. If you want to do a form-level validation before committing changes, you'll have a problem. In practice, the solution depends on how far you're prepared to go in carrying the FSM through into the implementation of your program. For smaller applications, it's wise to stop at the design stage and just use the state diagram and tables for guidance when writing the program. For more complex programs, you can carry the FSM right through to the implementation, as you'll see below.

For a pure FSM implementation, you can get around the validation issue by introducing extra states into the machine. Figure 13-8 shows a new state between states 2 and 1 for form B's OK event. The only difference is that this state is *transient* because the FSM immediately flips out of it into state 1 or state 2. This happens because you queue an event for the new state before you even get there. Validation states are also required for confirmation, such as when a user tries to abandon an edited form without saving changes.

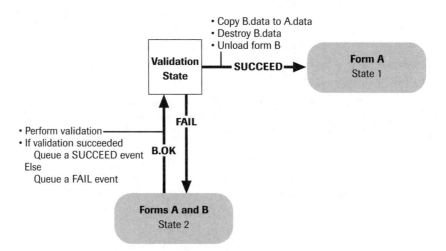

FIGURE 13-8   *Introducing transient states to avoid conditional transitions*

Implementing FSMs

If you want to carry an FSM through to the bitter end, you can implement it directly as program code. This requires a leap of faith because the code can often appear long-winded. In spite of this, if you're taking the trouble to implement the FSM, you'll gain much more by sticking rigorously to the mechanism without being tempted to introduce shortcuts, particularly in trying to avoid repetition of code. Recall that we're using an FSM to *formalize* the design of the GUI, and for a complex GUI the direct translation to code pays dividends by virtually eliminating the need for debugging. By introducing shortcuts, not only do you lose this integrity, but you also make the code harder to read.

Building an FSM with code is a straightforward affair that can be abstracted in a simple conditional statement:

```
If we're HERE and THIS happens Then
    do THAT and GoTo THERE
```

The only thing you have to keep track of is the current state, and most of your effort will be concerned with the mechanics of processing events and invoking the action procedures. You can build an FSM in any language that supports conditional statements, so let's start by looking at an implementation that can be adapted to any version of Visual Basic.

For this example, you will implement the C comment stripper described earlier and build it into a simple application using the form shown in Figure 13-9. The application displays the text as you type, minus any C-style comments. You will drive the FSM in real time—that is, the events will be caused directly by your keypresses, and the states and events will be displayed in the other boxes on the form.

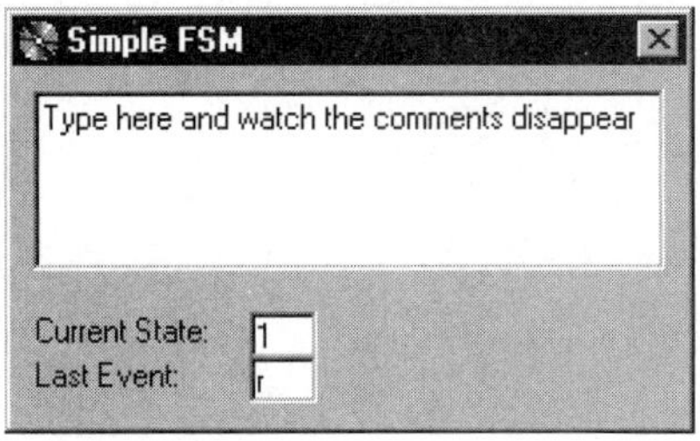

FIGURE 13-9   *The comment stripper FSM program*

The first thing you need is a state, which can be represented as a simple integer. It doesn't matter what data type you choose for the state, since there is no concept of ordering. The only requirement is that the states be unique. In real life, you'll usually want to define constants for the states and events. In this example, however, you're not going to use event constants because it's convenient to represent events with the ASCII codes generated by the keypresses. The states are defined on the following page.

```
Private Const S_OUTSIDE = 1
Private Const S_STARTING = 2
Private Const S_INSIDE = 3
Private Const S_ENDING = 4

Public nPuState As Integer
```

TIP

> If you're defining a group of constants to use as an enumerated type (you're effectively defining a State type here), always start the numbering at 1, not 0. This will help you spot uninitialized variables, since Visual Basic initializes integer variables to 0. Visual Basic 6 allows you to define enumerated types explicitly, but since they are freely interchangeable with longs, the same rule applies. (Unfortunately, none of this applies if you want to use your constants to index control arrays since the designers of Visual Basic chose to base them at 0.)

If you refer to the FSM tables (page 556) for the comment stripper, you'll see that there are 12 different combinations of state and event, so your conditional logic needs to guide you along 12 different paths through the code. To implement this with simple conditional statements, you have the choice of using *If-Then-ElseIf* or *Select Case* statements; for this example, we'll arbitrarily choose the latter. To decode one particular path, the code will contain a fragment such as this:

```
Select Case nState

    Case S_OUTSIDE:
        Select Case nEvent
            Case Asc("/")
                nState = S_STARTING
            Case Asc("*")
                txtOutBox.Text = txtOutBox.Text & Chr$(nEvent)
                nState = S_OUTSIDE
            Case Else
                txtOutBox.Text = txtOutBox.Text & Chr$(nEvent)
                nState = S_OUTSIDE
        End Select

    Case S_STARTING:
        ⋮
End Select
```

You can see that each of the 12 cells in the FSM tables has a piece of code inside a pair of nested *Select Case* statements. The State and Event tables are combined here, so the last statement in each case assigns a new value to *nState* (which we'll assume is a reference parameter). The rest of the code for each decoded state/event pair depends on what you want this particular implementation of the comment stripper to do—in fact, we're just going to add the text to the text box or not, so the actions here are simple. In practice, the code will usually be more manageable if you divide it up so that each state has its own function. Thus, the example above becomes something like this:

```
Select Case nState
    Case S_OUTSIDE DoStateOUTSIDE(nState, nEvent)
    Case S_STARTING DoStateSTARTING(nState, nEvent)
    ⋮
End Select

Sub DoStateOUTSIDE(ByVal niEvent As Integer, _
                   ByRef noState As Integer)
    Select Case niEvent
        Case Asc("/")
            noState = S_STARTING
        Case Asc("*"):
            txtOutBox.Text = txtOutBox.Text & Chr$(nEvent)
            noState = S_OUTSIDE
        Case Else
            txtOutBox.Text = txtOutBox.Text & Chr$(nEvent)
            noState = S_OUTSIDE
    End Select
End Sub
```

Now you have the state variable and the logic for decoding the state/event pairs, and all you need is a source of events. In this example, you'll trap keypresses by setting the *KeyPreview* property of the form and generating an event for each keypress. All you need to do now is feed the events to the FSM by calling a function that contains the decoding logic (let's call it *DoFSM*). The KeyPress event handler looks something like this:

```
Private Sub Form_KeyPress(KeyAscii As Integer)
    Call DoFSM(nPuState, KeyAscii)
    KeyAscii = 0 ' Throw away the keypress.
End Sub
```

In this example, the event codes and the real-world events that map onto them are one and the same—hence, the "action" code in each *DoState* routine can get the ASCII codes directly from the *nEvent* parameter. Most applications don't have such coupling, and you would need to arrange for any such real-world data to be buffered somewhere if you wanted the action routines to have access to it. Consider, for example, the Unix tool yacc (yet another compiler-compiler), which builds table-driven parsers that process sequences of tokens read from an input stream. A parser generated by yacc gets its tokens by successive calls to a C function named *yylex()*, which is the direct equivalent of the KeyPress event handler. The *yylex()* function returns a numeric token equivalent to the *nEvent* parameter, but it also copies the full text of the actual word it recognized into a global variable named *yytext*. This variable is available to any code in the yacc-generated program.

The only element missing from the FSM program is something to initialize the state variable. Recall that one state of the FSM is always designated the start state, so you need a line of code to assign that to the state variable before you start generating events:

```
nPuState = S_OUTSIDE
```

This can go in the *Form_Load* event of the comment stripper program. You'll find the source code for this program in CHAP13\fsm\simple\sim.vbp.

Recursion: See recursion

The comment stripper FSM works OK, but it has a dangerous flaw. It's a flaw that is inherent in event-driven systems, and one that also crops up in regular Visual Basic programs. The problem is reentrant code, and you might have come across it when working with data controls, *Form_Resize* events, or code that uses *DoEvents*.

Let's have a look at a simple example of reentrancy using a data control. The program shown in Figure 13-10 (which is in CHAP13\recurse\broken\rcb.vbp) is about as simple as it gets, with a single data-bound list wired up through a data control to the Visual Basic sample database BIBLIO.MDB (available on the Visual Studio 6 MSDN CD). Assume that the list contains a set of records you need to process somehow and that it doesn't matter in which order the records are processed. Clicking in the list causes a Reposition event, and the program puts up a message box that lets you simulate the kind of Jet page-locking error you might encounter in a multiuser application. You can think of the Reposition event handler as the equivalent of the *DoFSM* function in the comment stripper program.

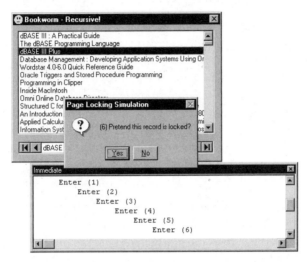

FIGURE 13-10   *Recursion in the data control's Reposition event*

Clicking No when the message box pops up simply continues, and this is where you'd process the new record. Clicking Yes simulates a locking error and simply skips to the next record by calling the *MoveNext* method of the data control's recordset. The idea is that you'll reach the end of the locked page after skipping a few records and so find a record you can process. The problem here is that you're calling *MoveNext* from within the Reposition event handler, which causes *another* Reposition event before the first one has finished—this is recursion. The example program maintains a static variable to count the number of recursions; the count is displayed in the message box, and the program also prints the entry and exit traces for the Reposition event to the Immediate window when you run the program in the IDE. You can also see the effects of the recursion by pressing Ctrl+Break and selecting Call Stack from the View menu.

This example, which comes from a real program, might not have particularly serious consequences because it's a pure recursion that doesn't nest too deeply, and it involves no static data (except for the counter, of course). Generally, however, and particularly when you're devising code such as FSMs to control the loading and unloading of forms, the code will break as soon as you try to invoke it recursively. You might, for example, end up in a situation in which you're trying to load a form from its own *Form_Load* event.

Coming back to the recursive Visual Basic program, it's not immediately obvious how to fix the problem. It turns out that this is quite a common class of problem, and one that conveys the true flavor of event-driven code. What you *want* to do when you find a lock is to exit the event handler and then immediately issue a *MoveNext* on the recordset. Unfortunately, Visual Basic can't do this because as soon as you exit the event handler, control passes back to the run-time system (the <Non-Basic Code> you see when you select View/ Call Stack in break mode). What you need to be able to do is to post some kind of request for a *MoveNext* and have it execute after you've left the Reposition event handler.

Just because Visual Basic won't do this kind of thing for you doesn't mean that you can't implement it yourself. CHAP13\recurse\fixed\rcf.vbp is a modified version of the pathological data control program that uses a simple event queue to achieve what you need. You use an unsorted list box as a convenient event queue and a timer control that continually polls the queue looking for events. There's only one kind of event in the program, so you don't even need to look at its value when you find it on the queue—always consider it a request for a *MoveNext*.

The program works like this: inside the Reposition event, instead of directly calling *MoveNext* when a locked record is encountered, we post an event onto the queue and then exit the event handler. The queue manager (the timer control) then comes along and, finding an event on the queue, kindly calls *MoveNext* for us. Now, however, the *MoveNext* is called from the timer's event handler, and there's no recursion. Notice that it doesn't matter how fast you push event requests into the queue; you never get recursion because the events are processed one by one in sequence.

Adding an event queue to an FSM

To prevent reentrant code, you need to add a queue to the FSM model. Strictly speaking, the comment stripper program doesn't need a queue because it doesn't do anything that will cause recursion. Because it's an example program, however, we'll add the queuing now so that you can build on it when you design real-world FSM programs later.

The queue built in the previous example worked adequately, but it needed a form to carry the list box and the timer control. This awkwardness over essentially nonvisual code has dogged Visual Basic from the start, and it means, for example, that you can't define a queue inside a class or a startup module without creating a dummy form. You could dump the controls onto an existing form, of course, but that's anathema to modular design, and it means you must contrive to load the form before starting the event queue. Getting rid of the list box isn't too hard, but until Visual Basic 5 there was no getting around that timer control without doing something horrific like this:

```
Sub Main()
    Dim nEvent As Integer
    frmMain.Show vbModeless      ' Main program is in here.
    Do
        If bGetEventFromQueue(nEvent) Then
            DoFSM nPuState, nEvent
        End If
        DoEvents
    Loop
End Sub
```

With Visual Basic 5 and 6, however, you can devise acceptable code-only solutions to this kind of problem—in this case, to build an event queue. By using the *AddressOf* operator, you can call the *SetTimer* API function and pass a Visual Basic routine as the timer's callback procedure. This means you can create a timer from pure code, and just like a Visual Basic Timer control, it will invoke the Visual Basic procedure asynchronously at the requested interval. Creating a timer is simple:

```
lTimerId = SetTimer(0&, 0&, 500&, AddressOf MyFunc)
```

The first two parameters are NULL values, which simply signify that the timer isn't associated with any window, and the third is the timer interval, in milliseconds. The last parameter is the interesting one; it passes a pointer to a Visual Basic function that will be invoked by Windows whenever the timer fires. Windows expects this function to have the following interface and to pass the appropriate parameters:

```
Sub MyFunc(ByVal lHwnd As Long, _
           ByVal nMsg As Long, _
           ByVal lEventId As Long, _
           ByVal lTime As Long)
```

NOTE

When working with callback functions, be careful to include the *ByVal* keywords. If you miss a *ByVal*, simply moving your mouse pointer over the parameter name in the Visual Basic debugger is enough to crash Visual Basic. This happens because of Visual Basic 6's instant quick watch feature, which displays a variable's value as a ToolTip. Because Visual Basic thinks you passed a reference parameter (*ByRef* is the default), it tries to dereference an illegal pointer value, which almost always causes an access violation. You can turn off this feature with the Auto Data Tips check box under Tools/Options/Editor.

For now, just ignore the parameters. Make sure to destroy the timer when you're finished with it:

```
Call KillTimer (0&, lTimerId)
```

That takes care of the queue manager, so now all you need to do is provide a queue for it to manage. A simple way to do this is to use a Visual Basic collection:

```
Dim colPuEventQueue As Collection
```

You'll see a more sophisticated use of collections later, but for now you can use one as a simple queue by defining a couple of routines:

```
Sub AddEventToQueue(ByVal niEvent As Integer)
    colPuEventQueue.Add niEvent
End Sub

Function bGetEventFromQueue(ByRef noEvent As Integer) As Boolean
    If colPuEventQueue.Count = 0 Then
        bGetEventFromQueue = False
    Else
        noEvent = colPuEventQueue.Item(1)
        colPuEventQueue.Remove 1
        bGetEventFromQueue = True
    End If
End Function
```

And that's it—a code-only asynchronous queue manager that you can build into a class or a normal module. The program CHAP13\fsm\qman\qman.vbp on the companion CD is the comment stripper FSM program amended to use the new event queue.

BUILDING A BETTER EVENT QUEUE

Remember Message Blaster? Message Blaster is a custom control that lets you intercept Windows messages sent to any Visual Basic control. Windows messages are the raw material of Visual Basic events, but the Visual Basic designers filtered out most of the messages when they decided which events Visual Basic programmers were likely to need. A form's Resize event, for example, occurs *after* the resize has happened, which makes implementing size limits for a resizeable form ugly because you have to snap the size back in the Resize event handler. With Message Blaster, you can intercept the WM_SIZE message and change the form's size with a suitable API call before Windows repaints it.

Now that you know what Message Blaster is, forget it. Visual Basic 6 lets you do all the things that Message Blaster did, directly from Visual Basic code. Message Blaster is an example of a *subclassing* control; subclassing is what Windows programmers do to hook a custom message handler (usually called a window procedure) onto a window, and subclassing controls were an inelegant hack to make this possible in earlier versions of Visual Basic. By allowing Windows callback functions to be coded in Visual Basic, Visual Basic 6's *AddressOf* operator opens up subclassing directly to Visual Basic programmers.

The theory goes like this: You nominate any object that you have (or can get) a window handle for and tell Windows the address of a Visual Basic procedure to call whenever it receives a message for that object. For messages you don't want to handle, you simply call the original message handler. To fix the resizing problem outlined above, you'd write something like this:

```
pcbOldWindowProc = SetWindowLong(Me.hWnd, GWL_WNDPROC, _
                                 AddressOf lMyWindowProc)
⋮

Function lMyWindowProc(ByVal hWnd As Long, _
                 ByVal lMsg As Long, _
                 ByVal wparam As Long, _
                 ByVal lparam As Long) As Long

    If lMsg = WM_SIZE Then
        ' Play with the size here.
    End If

    lMyWindowProc = CallWindowProc(pcbOldWindowProc, hWnd, _
                             lMsg, wParam, lParam)
End Function
```

>>

Any messages that Windows receives for a window are queued so that they arrive in sequence, and you can use this behavior to make a queue for FSMs. The simplest way is to hang a window procedure off an arbitrary control and start sending messages to the queue with *PostMessage*, but this is a bit ugly and can't be done unless you have a form loaded. A better way is to create a window for your own exclusive use behind the scenes. The code is straightforward:

```
lHwnd = CreateWindowEx(WS_EX_TRANSPARENT, "static", _
                "My Window", WS_OVERLAPPED, _
                0&, 0&, 0&, 0&, 0&, 0&, _
                CLng(App.hInstance), 0&)

lEventMsg = RegisterWindowMessage("FSM Event")
```

The choice of *style* and *extended style* parameters is arbitrary and doesn't really matter since you're never going to display the window. Now all you have to do is hook up an event handler to the window and start sending messages. It's a good idea to register a private message as done here, but you could just use any message number greater than WM_USER. It's best to encapsulate the code in Visual Basic functions or a class (CHAP13\fsm\fsmcls\pubfsm.cls shows one possible way), but be aware that the window procedure must be in a standard module. All the constants and Visual Basic declarations for all the functions can be pasted from the API Viewer tool supplied with Visual Basic. This tool is run from the file Apiload.exe, which is located in the Common\Tools\Winapi folder on the Visual Basic 6 CD.

Data-Driven Code

In an ideal implementation of a table-based design such as a finite state machine (FSM), the program is built from the tables themselves. In this kind of program, the tables are embedded in the code and somehow direct the flow of execution. The wisdom of this is clear: the tables are a product of your design process, and using them directly unifies the design—or at least some elements of it—with the code. It's also easier to make design changes because you don't have to translate between logical and physical models.

When it comes to building data-driven programs, working with more traditional Windows programming languages such as C and C++ offers two definite advantages over Visual Basic. First, you can maintain tables of pointers to functions and invoke those functions directly through indexes into the tables. This removes the need for the unwieldy jumble of conditional statements needed in our first stab at an FSM in Visual Basic, reducing the *DoFSM* function to just two statements:

```
void fvDoFSM(int nState, int *nEvent)
{
    (aapvActionTable[nState][*nEvent])();
    nEvent = aanStateTable[nState][*nEvent];
}
```

Second, you can lay out the tables in compile-time initialization statements. This is where the design and implementation intersect since you can lay out the table in a readable fashion and any changes you make to it are *directly* changing the code. Here's what the comment stripper FSM tables might look like in a C program:

```
void (*aapvActionTable[NUM_STATES][NUM_EVENTS])() =
{
//                    E_SLASH     E_STAR     E_OTHER

/* S_OUTSIDE  */ {fvOutSlash, fvOutStar, fvOutOther},
/* S_STARTING */ {fvStaSlash, fvStaStar, fvStaOther},
/* S_INSIDE   */ {fvInsSlash, fvInsStar, fvInsOther},
/* S_ENDING   */ {fvEndSlash, fvEndStar, fvEndOther}
};

int aanStateTable[NUM_STATES][NUM_EVENTS] =
{
//                    E_SLASH     E_STAR     E_OTHER

/* S_OUTSIDE  */ {S_STARTING, S_OUTSIDE, S_OUTSIDE},
/* S_STARTING */ {S_STARTING, S_INSIDE,  S_OUTSIDE},
/* S_INSIDE   */ {S_INSIDE,   S_ENDING,  S_INSIDE},
/* S_ENDING   */ {S_OUTSIDE,  S_ENDING,  S_INSIDE}
};
```

Unfortunately, although Visual Basic has an *AddressOf* operator, the only useful thing you can do with it is pass the address of a function or procedure in a parameter list. (C programmers will be disappointed to find that *AddressOf* isn't really like C's unary & operator.) Although you *can* use *AddressOf* in calls to Visual Basic functions, ultimately you can't do much inside those functions except pass the address on to a Windows API function. This capability is a major leap forward from all versions of Visual Basic previous to version 5, but the fact that you can't invoke a Visual Basic function from an address means that you can't implement an action table like the C one shown above.

Or can you? You can certainly store Visual Basic function addresses in a table by passing them to a suitable procedure. Visual Basic permits you to store function addresses in long variables:

```
Sub AddAddressToTable(ByVal niState As Integer, _
                      ByVal niEvent As Integer, _
                      ByVal pcbVbCodeAddr As Long)
    ActionTable(niState, niEvent) = pcbVbCodeAddr
End Sub
```

Unfortunately, that's as far as you can go with pure Visual Basic. Perhaps a future version of Visual Basic will have a dereferencing operator or maybe a *CallMe* function that accepts an address and calls the function at that address; for now, however, you're on your own.

But don't despair, because you're not sunk yet. Visual Basic doesn't have a *CallMe* function, but there's nothing to stop you from writing your own. You'll need to write it in another language, of course, but if you're one of those Visual Basic programmers who breaks out in a cold sweat at the thought of firing up a C compiler, take heart—this is likely to be the shortest C program you'll ever see. Here's the program in its entirety:

```
#include <windows.h>

BOOL WINAPI DllMain(HANDLE hModule, DWORD dwReason, LPVOID lpReserved)
{
    return TRUE;
}

void CALLBACK CallMe(void (*pfvVbCode)())
{
    pfvVbCode();
}
```

The business end of this code is a single statement; the *DllMain* function is scaffolding to make a DLL. (You also need to use a DEF file to make the linker export the *CallMe* symbol.) Now all you need to do is include a suitable *Declare* statement in your Visual Basic code, and you can call Visual Basic functions from a table!

```
Declare Sub CallMe Lib "callme.dll" (ByVal lAddress As Any)
  ⋮
CallMe ActionTable(nState, nEvent)
```

The source code for the DLL and a Visual Basic program that calls it can be found in CHAP13\callme.

CallMe old-fashioned

The *CallMe* DLL is pretty simple, but it's still a DLL. It turns a programming project into a mixed-language development, it means you have to buy a compiler, and it adds an extra component to the distribution package you're going to have to build when you ship the product. Finding a way to do without a DLL would certainly be an attractive option.

Figuring out the answer simply requires a bit of lateral thinking. You've already seen how API functions that take a callback parameter can invoke Visual Basic functions, so it takes a simple shift of perspective to see such API functions as obliging *CallMe* servers. All you have to do is find an API function that takes a callback function, calls it once, and preferably doesn't do much else.

A quick trawl through the Win32 API documentation reveals *SetTimer* as a possibility since its sole purpose is to invoke an event handler that you register with it. The only problem with this is that *SetTimer* keeps calling the function until you kill the timer, so you must find a way to kill the timer after a single invocation. You could do this by including a call to *KillTimer* in the callback procedure itself, but this is ugly because the mechanism is inextricably bound up with the functions you want to call—if you're building an FSM, for example, all your action functions must look like this:

```
Sub Action1()
    Call KillTimer lTimerId
    ' Real action code goes here.
End Sub
```

The consequence of leaving out a call to *KillTimer* is a ceaseless barrage of calls to the offending function, with who knows what consequences—yuck!

There are other candidates, but one that works nicely is *CallWindowProc*. This function is normally used to attach a custom message handler (a.k.a. a window procedure) to a window; the custom message handler passes on unwanted messages using *CallWindowProc*, which tells Windows to invoke the default window procedure. You're not chaining any message handlers here, and you don't even have a window; but you can still invoke *CallWindowProc* to call a Visual Basic function. The only restriction is that your Visual Basic function must have the following interface:

```
Function Action1(ByVal hWnd As Long, _
                 ByVal lMsg As Long, _
                 ByVal wParam As Long, _
                 ByVal lParam As Long) As Long
```

Windows 95 and Windows 98 let you call a parameterless procedure as long as you trap the "Bad DLL calling convention" error (error 49*), but for reasons of portability—and good programming practice—you shouldn't rely on this.

All you need to do now is to wrap the *CallWindowProc* call up in a Visual Basic function, and you have a *CallMe*, effectively written in Visual Basic:

```
Sub CallMe(ByVal pcbAddress As Long)

    Call CallWindowProc(pcbAddress, 0&, 0&, 0&, 0&)

End Sub
```

Return of the comment stripper

It's time to return to the comment stripper. This time you're going to build a reusable FSM class using everything you've learned up to now—maybe you'll even pick up a few more tricks along the way. To see how the same FSM can be used to drive different external behaviors, you'll also make a slight modification to the program by displaying the text of the comments in a second text box. Figure 13-11 shows the new-look comment stripper. You can find the code in CHAP13\fsm\tabldriv on the companion CD.

---

* The error 49 is generated when Visual Basic detects a stack frame anomaly on return from *CallWindowProc*, although there's nothing wrong with the API call itself. In fact, the error happens earlier, when the *Action1* routine returns to *CallWindowProc*. *CallWindowProc* pushes four parameters onto the stack and expects the action function to remove them before it returns. (This is the Pascal, or *_stdcall*, calling convention.) Our function doesn't oblige since it thinks there were no parameters, but because Windows 95/98 doesn't do stack checking at run time, the error goes undetected. Visual Basic *does* do stack checking, so it detects the error when the API call returns.

Windows NT is less forgiving here—it immediately detects the stack error and raises an exception inside *CallWindowProc*. You can't trap operating system exceptions in Visual Basic, so this kills the program (or kills Visual Basic if you're in the IDE). This, of course, is exactly what should happen, and it's a useful reminder that you shouldn't be taking such liberties! The sample program in CHAP13\fsm\tabldriv on the companion CD uses conditional compilation to demonstrate the use of parameterless action procedures.

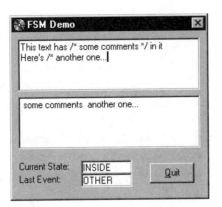

FIGURE 13-11 *Return of the comment stripper*

First the bad news: you won't be able to match C's trick of laying out the FSM table readably in code. Visual Basic fights this on every front: you can't write free-format text, you run out of line continuations, there's no compile-time initialization, and even Visual Basic's comments aren't up to the job. But this is the *only* bad news because using what you've learned about Visual Basic 6, you can do everything else the C program can do.

Let's start by looking at the interface to the FSM class. Since the class is to be general and you don't want to code the details of a particular FSM into it, you need to define methods that can be used to describe the FSM at run time. An FSM description will have four components: a list of states, a list of events, a table that defines state transitions, and a table that associates actions with the state transitions. In principle, the only other interface you need to the FSM class is a method you can call to feed events to the FSM. In practice, the restriction that demands that you put callback functions in a regular BAS file means you also need a method to register the event queue handler function with the FSM.

Here's what the run-time definition of the comment stripper FSM looks like:

```
Set oPiFSM = New CFSMClass

oPiFSM.RegisterStates "OUTSIDE", "STARTING", "INSIDE", "ENDING"
oPiFSM.RegisterEvents "SLASH", "STAR", "OTHER"
oPiFSM.RegisterEventHandler cblEventQueueMessageHandler

oPiFSM.TableEntry viState:="OUTSIDE", viEvent:="STAR", _
                  viNewState:="OUTSIDE", _
                  pcbiFunc:=AddressOf OutsideStar
```

>>

```
oPiFSM.TableEntry viState:="OUTSIDE", viEvent:="STAR", _
                  viNewState:="OUTSIDE", _
                  pcbiFunc:=AddressOf OutsideStar
' ...etc.
```

This code shows how the states and events are defined and also includes a couple of the table-definition statements. *RegisterEventHandler* creates a hidden window to act as the event queue and installs the *cblEventQueueMessageHandler* function as its window procedure. We'll look at the table definitions in a moment, but first let's examine the *RegisterStates* and *RegisterEvents* methods. These work identically, so we'll take *RegisterStates* as an example.

To make the class general, you need to be able to supply this method with a variable number of arguments. There are two ways to do this, but *ParamArray* is the best. The definition of *RegisterStates* looks like this:

```
Public Sub RegisterStates(ParamArray aviStates() As Variant)
    ' Some code here
End Sub
```

ParamArray members are Variants, which is convenient in this situation because the FSM class will allow you to choose any data type to represent states and events. The example program uses strings, mostly because they're self-documenting and can be displayed on the form. In real applications, you might prefer to use enumerated types or integer constants. Without making any changes to the class definition, you could define your states like this:

```
Const S_OUTSIDE = 1
Const S_STARTING = 2
Const S_INSIDE = 3
Const S_ENDING = 4
⋮
oPiFSM.RegisterStates S_OUTSIDE, S_STARTING, S_INSIDE, S_ENDING
```

Or like this:

```
Enum tStates
    Outside = 1
    Starting
    Inside
    Ending
End Enum
⋮
oPiFSM.RegisterStates Outside, Starting, Inside, Ending
```

Enumerated types were introduced in Visual Basic 5. In use they are equivalent to long constants defined with *Const*. Enumerations are better because they associate a type name with a group of constants, so in this example you can define variables of type *tStates* (although there is no run-time range checking). A more important difference is that you can define public enumerated types inside classes, which means you can now associate groups of constants directly with classes. If you were coding a comment stripper FSM class (instead of a *general* class that we'll use to implement the comment stripper), for example, you could define public *tStates* and *tEvents* as enumerated types in the class itself.

The FSM class can cope with any data type for its states and events because internally they are stored as integers and use collections to associate the external values with internal ones.

Here's the code behind *RegisterStates*:

```
Private Type tObjectList
    colInternalNames As New Collection
    colExternalNames As New Collection
End Type

Private tPiList As tObjectList
    ⋮
tPiList.colInternalNames.Add nInternId, key:=CStr(vExternId)
tPiList.colExternalNames.Add vExternId, key:=CStr(nInternId)
```

This code creates two reciprocal collections: one storing integers keyed on external state names and the other storing the names keyed on the integers. You can now convert freely between internal (integer) and external (any type) states. Since you can store any data type in a collection, you are free to choose whichever data type is most convenient.

TIP

Using pairs of collections is a powerful way to associate two sets of values. Usually, one set is how the values are represented in a database and the other set is how you want to display them to the user.

The FSM table itself is created dynamically inside the *RegisterStates* or *RegisterEvents* routine (whichever is called last), using the *Count* properties of the state and event collections for its dimensions. This is shown on the following page.

```
Private Type tTableEntry
    nNextState As Integer
    pcbAction As Long
End Type
    :
ReDim aatPiFSMTable(1 To nStates, 1 To nEvents) As tTableEntry
```

Now you need to fill in the empty FSM table with details of the state transitions and actions. To do this, you make repeated calls to the *TableEntry* method, with one call for each cell in the table. The values you want to insert into the table are successor states, which have one of the values defined earlier in the state list, and subroutine addresses, which you obtain with the *AddressOf* operator. The action routines are all parameterless subroutines, defined together in a single BAS file. Here's what the *TableEntry* method does:

```
aatPiFSMTable(nState, nEvent).nNextState = niNewState
aatPiFSMTable(nState, nEvent).pcbAction = pcbiFunc
```

The *nState* and *nEvent* integers are first obtained by looking up the external names passed as parameters.

Once the table is in place, the FSM is ready to go. In fact, the FSM is running as soon as you define it since *RegisterEventHandler* creates an event queue and registers a callback function to service it. *RegisterStates* puts the FSM into its start state, but it won't actually do anything until you start feeding events to it.

The event queue is implemented as an invisible window created with Windows API functions as described earlier. The only minor problem here is that Visual Basic insists that you define callback functions in normal BAS files, so you can't include the queue event handler in the class definition. You can *almost* do it because you can define the event handler in the class as a *Friend* function; the function you register is a simple shell that calls the *Friend* function, although it still has to be in a normal BAS file. The class must contain the following function.

```
Friend Function cblEvHandler
(
    ByVal hwnd As Long, _
    ByVal lMsg As Long, _
    ByVal wparam As Long, _
    ByVal lparam As Long
) As Long
```

This is a standard window procedure (don't forget the *ByVals*!), and you send events to it using the *PostMessage* API function. A *Friend* function is essentially a public method of the class, but the scope is limited to the current project even if the class is defined as *Public*. A call to *PostMessage* is the essence of the *PostEvent* method, and Windows arranges for the messages to be delivered asynchronously, via calls to the *cblEvHandler* function, in the sequence they were posted.

Calls to *PostEvent* are made in response to external stimuli, and in this case these are all Visual Basic KeyPress events. The calls are made from the KeyPress events, where the translation from ASCII code to an appropriate event value ("STAR", for example) is made. After the FSM is initialized, the KeyPress events are the *only* interface between the FSM and the outside world.

The queue event handler is the focus of the FSM since here is where the table lookup is done and the appropriate action procedure is called:

```
CallMe aatPiFSMTable(nPiCurrentState, wparam).pcbAction
nPiCurrentState = aatPiFSMTable(nPiCurrentState, wparam).nNextState
```

The only other noteworthy feature of the queue event handler is that it contains calls to *RaiseEvent*. The FSM class defines four different events that can be used in the outside world (the comment stripper program in this case) to keep track of what the FSM is doing. These are the events:

```
Event BeforeStateChange(ByVal viOldState As Variant, _
                       ByVal viNewState As Variant)
Event AfterStateChange(ByVal viOldState As Variant, _
                       ByVal viNewState As Variant)
Event BeforeEvent(ByVal viEvent As Variant)
Event AfterEvent(ByVal viEvent As Variant)
```

You saw an example of *RaiseEvent* earlier on page 550; this time, you're defining events with parameters. You define two sets of events so that you can choose whether to trap state changes and events before or after the fact. For the comment stripper, use the *AfterEvent* and *AfterStateChange* events to update the state and event fields on the form.

Doing it for real

The comment stripper is a simple example, and the FSM it demonstrates doesn't deal with window management. As a slightly more realistic example, let's look at an implementation of the GUI from Figure 13-5 (shown on page 557). You'll find the source for this program in CHAP13\fsm\realwrld\rlw.vbp.

The FSM controls the hypothetical Function 1, and the FSM starts when that function is chosen from the Function menu. Other functions would be implemented with their own FSMs, which is a straightforward process because the FSM was built as a class. You're not really implementing the whole program here, just the window-management parts; all the event routines are there, so adding the code to do the database actions would be painless.

The second thing you'll notice, right after you notice those bizarre event names, is that the nice, friendly action routine names have gone, replaced by the anonymous subroutines *a01* through *a44*. With 44 subroutines to code, the only sensible names are systematic ones—using the state and event names as before is just too unwieldy. In fact, the action names are irrelevant because their corresponding state/event combinations are much more useful identifiers. Here's a portion of the FSM table definition:

```
oPuFSM.TableEntry A__, A_Ok_____, EXI, AddressOf a01
oPuFSM.TableEntry A__, A_Cancel_, EXI, AddressOf a02
oPuFSM.TableEntry A__, A_Apply__, A__, AddressOf a03
oPuFSM.TableEntry A__, A_Details, AB_, AddressOf a04
oPuFSM.TableEntry A__, A_More___, AC_, AddressOf a05
oPuFSM.TableEntry A__, B_Ok_____, ERO
oPuFSM.TableEntry A__, B_Cancel_, ERO
```

The key description of this code is "systematic," which is also why we've adopted such a strange convention for the state and event names. We're fighting Visual Basic's unreasonable layout restrictions by making the names the same length so that the list of *TableEntry* calls is readable. You can't quite make a table layout as in the C code example earlier, but the result is an acceptable facsimile that is reasonably self-documenting.

Notice that two pseudostates have been introduced for this example: EXI, which represents termination of the FSM, and ERO, which denotes an error condition. Neither of these conditions should be encountered by the FSM: EXI successor states are never reached because the action routines associated with their transitions halt the FSM, and ERO successor states can be derived only from illegal inputs. The FSM driver function (*oPuFSM.EvHandler*) traps these pseudostates and raises an *FSM_Error* event. This is the FSM equivalent of a *Debug.Assert* statement.

The use of ERO states also permits you to omit coding for state transitions that will never happen. As well as modifying the driver to raise an error on illegal transitions, we've also modified the *TableEntry* method to make the action function optional. In this case, it saves 12 action functions and nicely distinguishes error conditions in the matrix. It's tempting to omit these lines from the list, but you should avoid the temptation vigorously, because if you do so you can no longer tell whether you've covered all possible situations by simply counting the table entries.

Another temptation is to factor code by reusing action routines—for example, *a01* and *a02* appear to be the same, as do *a12* and *a13*. However, discarding *a02* and wiring up *a01* in its place can be disastrous because it introduces a dependency that will cause problems if you later want to change the actions for either transition independently of the other. You could, of course, define a helper subroutine that's called by both action routines. (*ConfirmDiscardEdits* is such a function.) Remember that a *system* is useful because it takes some of the intellectual load off managing complexity, and it goes without saying that circumventing the system—for whatever reason—stops it from being systematic.

One final comment about this example is that it doesn't include validation or confirmation states. Such states would amplify the complexity by adding a new state for each OK and Cancel event, along with 11 corresponding table entries (in this case). In real life, validation and confirmation are best handled by building a conditional mechanism into the FSM. This does *not* mean you should do such processing ad hoc, and control over the successor state should remain with the FSM driver function (*FSM.EvHandler*). This means you can't use Visual Basic's *Form_QueryUnload* or *Form_Unload* event to trigger validation or confirmation since a form unload must always succeed. (Canceling an unload from QueryUnload will cause havoc because the FSM thinks the form has been unloaded and now its state information is incorrect.)

An acceptable way to implement both types of condition is to add an abort transition method to the FSM class:

```
Public Sub AbortTransition()
    bPuTransitionAborted = True
End Sub
```

Now you can modify the FSM driver to check the *bPuTransitionAborted* flag before setting the successor state:

```
Public Sub EvHandler
    :
    CallMe aatPiFSMTable(M_nCurrentState, wparam).pcbAction
    If Not bPuTransitionAborted Then
        nPiCurrentState = aatPiFSMTable(nPiCurrentState, _
                                        wparam).nNextState
    End If
    :
End Sub
```

This might be simple, but it adds considerable complexity to the action routines because you must be very careful about which forms you unload. More specifically, if you cancel a transition, you need to be sure that you don't change anything that characterizes the current state. In this case, the states are defined entirely in terms of forms, so you need to ensure that the action routine has the same forms loaded when you leave that were loaded when you entered. For example, assuming you're in state AB_ (forms A and B loaded), you need either to unload both forms or to leave them both loaded. The following code correctly describes the validation logic for an A_Ok event in this state:

```
Public Sub a12()

    Dim bUnload As Boolean

    bUnload = True

    If frmDetails.My.Dirty Or frmSummary.My.Dirty Then
        If Not bConfirmDiscardEdits Then
            bUnload = False
        End If
    End If

    If bUnload Then
        Unload frmDetails
        Unload frmSummary
    Else
        oPuFSM.CancelTransition
    End If

End Sub
```

AFTER THE DUST HAS SETTLED

Visual Basic was an innovation. A few years ago, the Windows programming club was an exclusive one, and coding for Windows was intensely technical: virtuosity in C was the entrance requirement, and becoming productive relied on mastery of the arcane Windows API. Visual Basic changed all that, opening up Windows programming to all comers and pioneering whole new development cycles by making rapid GUI prototyping a reality.

But there is a darker side. By eliminating the obscure programmatic hoops we must jump through even to display anything on the screen, Visual Basic has taken the technical edge off Windows development, and from the wrong perspective this can have dangerous consequences. Behind the GUI facade, developers face the same problems of design, verification, construction, redesign, testing, and change management that they always have, and without conscientious technical management, these fundamentals can take a back seat while the product is "prototyped" to market.

To ensure success in a Visual Basic project, you need to concentrate on development fundamentals as much as on the database design and graphical veneer, and you must quash unreasonable productivity expectations. Visual Basic is a tinkerer's delight, but the delusion of Visual Basic programming as child's play is short-lived and a recipe for disaster. A Visual Basic project can seem like a whirlwind of fantastic productivity—for the first few months. Only after the dust has settled is the truth apparent: excellent applications happen by design, not by accident.

Didn't I Write That Function Last Week?

Effective Code Reuse

CHRIS DE BELLOT

You first met Chris in Chapter 5. Known internally as "The Dark Dude," Chris is one of TMS's longest-serving employees. During his time at TMS, Chris has given various presentations, including at the Visual Basic Developer Academy. Whenever possible he contributes articles to PC magazines and writes technical white papers for the TMS Web site. Chris mentioned that he is keen on user interface design; however, with his interest in flight simulators and the release of the SDK for Microsoft Flight Simulator 98, user interface design could take on a new twist.

STEVE OVERALL

Those of you who are bound by convention and read books from front to back already met Steve in Chapter 8. To continue, he is a Microsoft Certified Professional who specializes in Visual Basic's Year 2000 issues. In addition to developing solutions for a number of TMS's clients, he trains Advanced Visual Basic programming topics. When Steve has time away from the PC, he enjoys watching cricket and football (the American kind). When lubricated with sufficient quantities of dark and cloudy ale, he can be encouraged to bemoan the current state of English cricket—be warned.

Reusability, as its name suggests, is the ability of something designed for one purpose to be used for other purposes. A good example of reuse can be found in the motor vehicle industry. Low-specification vehicles are usually fitted with blanking plates where more expensive options (such as air conditioning) would normally be located.

Vehicle manufacturers do this for a purpose: to save money. If manufacturers use a generic dashboard and plug the holes in vehicles in which certain items are not selected, they save money because they don't have to create a separate dashboard for every option package. Obviously, it's cheaper to manufacture blanking plates than dashboards! Another advantage is that the manufacturer doesn't have to rebuild the vehicle whenever a customer wants an item installed as an optional extra. The electronics industry also makes use of reusability. If you've ever taken apart your computer, you've probably noticed that the expansion cards plug into the motherboard. The advantage here is that if a complex component fails, you just need to replace a card, not the entire system.

ISSUES AFFECTING CODE REUSABILITY

So if reuse is such a good thing, why not apply it to computer programs? Well, the good news is that you can. Reuse has been around for years. The bad news is that not many companies take advantage of it. Tight schedules, the changing nature of technology, and the difficulty of putting together a top-notch development team all account for the lack of reuse.

Deadline Pressures

Many projects come under pressure when schedules start to slip. When the pressure reaches a certain point, good design, coding practices, and coding standards are often forgotten in a mad panic to deliver. Designing and writing reusable modules and applications takes discipline and the enforcement of consistent standards; unfortunately, these practices are usually the first casualties when a project threatens to overshoot deadlines. (See Chapter 15 for more about how to manage projects successfully in today's competitive and hectic development environment.)

Knowledge of Current Technologies

To develop good reusable code, you must know first what you're trying to achieve through reuse and second how to achieve your goal with the tools you're using. Computer programming languages have come a long way since the early days and most now support the creation of reusable components to some degree. Technology—especially object technologies such as ActiveX and COM—has also improved. Keeping up with the ever-increasing number of languages and technologies can be hard work, and many organizations are tempted to stick with what they know. Although this conservative approach doesn't prevent the development of reusable solutions, it does mean that opportunities to develop more effectively are missed.

Quality of Development Teams

The quality of the development team plays a big part in the process of developing for reuse. The project manager must understand the technology and the business in order to set priorities and justify the effort required to build high-level and reusable business components. Many companies employ project managers who are not technical. This practice is based on the business theory that a manager should be able to apply the same management techniques to any type of project to achieve the same results. The Mandelbrot Set (International)

Limited (TMS) has a policy of assigning project managers who are also good coders. The benefit of a technical project manager is that he or she is acutely aware of problems that can occur and is able to counter them. The project manager can also carry out design and code reviews to ensure that the design is realistic and the code follows the design. This ability is extremely important if external contractors whose work standards are unknown are hired to work on the project.

Analysts and designers also need to be aware of the technology to ensure that the application's design is realistic and achievable in the scheduled time. Often the application design is incomplete when development starts. An incomplete design will almost certainly result in costly redevelopment of certain components. In the worst case, redesign might not be possible because of time or other constraints. If a reusable component is not correctly designed and built, any future development dependent on that component will suffer because of the effort required to rectify the original flaws. A future development team will probably just write its own version of the component.

The programmers have the important job of building the application to specification. Their task will be harder if the specifications and design are not complete or correct. Programmers should also ensure that the infrastructure code is reusable. It is here, in the program's infrastructure, that reusability can have a major impact, not through the reuse of business components but through the reuse of common code—that is, code that can be used by other programmers on the same application or in other development projects. Good communication is needed among programmers so that they all are aware of what code is available. The programmers also need to be sure that any code designed for reuse is well documented so that other team members know exactly how to use a particular unit of code. How many times have you written a particular function, only to discover that it already existed? Or tried to use an existing function but ended up writing your own version because you couldn't figure out the correct parameters for the existing function?

THE BUSINESS CASE FOR REUSE

If you're managing a development project, you should seriously consider reuse—in fact, you should think of reuse as a requirement, not just an option. Whether or not you realize it, reuse is one of the most efficient ways of reducing development time and effort. Unfortunately, many companies develop each application in isolation, viewing each one as a single entity encapsulated within a particular budget. If you intend to implement multiple applications, you'll gain reuse benefits in the form of business components—that is, units of functionality that dictate specific areas of corporate policy. An example of such a policy is "Account managers may authorize discounts of up to 20 percent for regular customers." If you create a single business object to implement this policy for all customer accounts, you'll be able to enforce the integrity of this rule. You'll also have the advantage of being able to change the rule in a single place, which is an important capability given that business rules will change as company policies change.

Business components are not the only area in which you can benefit from reuse. Think of a company that starts each development from scratch, and imagine the number of times a particular unit of code (for example, an error handler or a *FileExist* function) is written. At TMS, we have a reuse strategy. We have an application template that contains core functionality such as error handling, custom messaging, and general utility functions. When we start developing a system for a customer, we give our client the option of purchasing the application template. This creates extra revenue for TMS but, more important, also cuts off about a month of development time because we start building code from this template, which has already been fully debugged and tested. Some companies have unassigned staff between projects with nothing to do. Using such downtime to develop generic "auxiliary" code—the type of code that gets written in almost every project—would be an ideal way to start gearing everyone toward the goal of writing reusable code.

Just because a component is designed for reuse does not necessarily mean that the component must be reused. One benefit of having encapsulated and loosely coupled components is that maintenance becomes much simpler. (Encapsulation and coupling are key elements of reuse and are explained in more detail in the next section.) Imagine a maintenance programmer fixing a bug in a component. If the component is totally self-contained, the programmer doesn't need to know anything about the application outside that component. This makes it easier to control changes in the maintenance phases and allows greater flexibility when allocating people to do the work. Another important advantage of encapsulation and loose coupling is that it's easier to identify components that need to change if maintenance work becomes necessary.

For those of you still not convinced that reusability has real benefits, think of the interface changes made to Microsoft Windows 95. If you're familiar with both Windows 95 and Windows 3.x, one of the prominent interface changes you'll have noticed in Windows 95 is the new look of the controls. Think for a moment of the humble command button. Command buttons previously had a 2-pixel border and bold captions. In Windows 95, the command button changed: the button border is now only 1 pixel wide, and the caption font is no longer bold. You'll also notice that these characteristics change automatically between the versions of Windows. This automatic change in appearance was possible only because the command button, as well as many other controls, does not draw its own borders and captions—a Windows function does it. Imagine the amount of additional development time that would have been required to change the drawing functions if each control had contained its own!

THE KEYS TO REUSE

To achieve effective reuse, you must first understand what makes good reuse. Two attributes are required in any component that will be reused: encapsulation and generic functionality.

As the name suggests, *encapsulation* means that a unit of functionality is enclosed to such a degree that you are able to extract and use that functionality in a physically different environment. The unit of functionality contains everything it requires, and provided that the correct inputs can be applied, it will function in exactly the same way in any environment. The degree of encapsulation can also be expressed in terms of how the unit couples. A unit of functionality that is dependent on many external conditions is said to be tightly coupled. The converse is true of a loosely coupled unit. As a programmer, you'll no doubt have tried at least once to extract and reuse a block of code that had so many dependencies that it was easier to rewrite the code to fit your needs than to reuse it. This difficulty is a direct consequence of a tightly coupled unit and serves to highlight the importance of coupling when designing or coding a unit. The fact that an experienced programmer will understand the issues involved with coupling is one reason why experienced and disciplined programmers are valuable assets to a company.

The second key attribute of reuse has to do with how *generic* a piece of *functionality* is. If you want to use some functionality elsewhere, it stands to reason that the functionality should be able to apply to a number of different situations. Imagine a function written to take a date input and to check that the date is valid and in the range 3/2/1998 through 5/10/1998. The code on page 590 should help you visualize this.

```
Function IsDateOK(DateIn As Date) As Boolean

    If DateIn >= "3/2/1998" And DateIn <= "5/10/1998" Then
        IsDateOK = True
    Else
        IsDateOK = False
    End If

End Function
```

This function is clearly reusable because it has no external dependencies; that is, it doesn't call any other procedures within the application. In terms of actual reuse, however, it's pretty useless unless you specifically want to compare against the same date range in every instance in which you use this function. The function would be far more useful if you were to add inputs for a minimum and a maximum date, because the function could then check whether a date is valid and falls between ranges specified by the routine calling the function. Here is an amended version of the same function; this time, it's more useful because it's generic enough to be applied in a number of situations:

```
Function IsDateOK(DateIn As Date, MinDate As Date, _
                            MaxDate As Date) As Boolean

    If DateIn >= MinDate And DateIn <= MaxDate Then
        IsDateOK = True
    Else
        IsDateOK = False
    End If

End Function
```

For a piece of functionality to be reusable, it doesn't have to be totally decoupled from other routines in the application; in fact, doing so would make reuse impractical. What you must keep in mind, however, is that a unit of functionality is truly reusable only if all of its dependencies are present. To achieve good reusability, you need to set the boundaries or scope of a unit's functionality. For example, a reusable unit might be a single procedure, a collection of procedures, or an entire application. As long as the unit is not coupled to anything outside its bounds, it will be reusable. In programming terms, this means reducing the number of global (for Visual Basic 3) or public variables. In the days of Visual Basic 3, one of the recommended practices was to place global variables in a standard (BAS) module. Programmers should have dropped this practice with Visual Basic 4 because of the ability to encapsulate variables within class or form module properties. However, even in Visual Basic 4, constants still had to be made public because class and form objects couldn't expose constants as part of their interface. One way around this was to write type libraries. But type libraries, being external components, are contrary to encapsulation and can be difficult to maintain across multiple projects or components. To avoid public constants, Visual Basic 5 introduced a feature named enumerated constants, which allows constants to be exposed as part of the interface of the component to which they belong. This addition enables you to completely encapsulate a component. (We'll explain enumerated constants in more detail later in this chapter.)

One of the most widely used bad programming practices is to link areas of functionality with variables of global scope. Imagine an application with a modest 30 public variables. Any unit that couples to those variables is guaranteed to be difficult to reuse in another application because you'll have to recreate these variables and their values. Even in the same application, the state of global variables will change and might depend on certain event sequences, sometimes complex, being executed. Chapter 2 indicates some circumstances in which you can get components to share the same global data, with unfortunate results. And Chapter 4 includes even more on why you shouldn't use global variables.

MEETING REUSE REQUIREMENTS EFFECTIVELY

Visual Basic offers a rich selection of methods to achieve effective reusability. As with many things that involve a choice, you can choose either correctly or incorrectly. In a large computer application, an incorrect choice can mean weeks or months of extra effort. Mistakes will also inevitably occur because of the wide range of options available. For example, you can be sure that many Visual Basic programmers will be eager to create custom controls simply because they now can, thanks to Visual Basic 5 and 6. A particular problem to watch for is the "gold-plating" syndrome, which occurs when a programmer spends too much time adding unnecessary features. Although such features work, they serve only as superfluous gloss on the application—and worse yet, the time spent fiddling with them can jeopardize your schedule.

The following sections provide an overview of the different methods you can use to achieve effective reuse.

Code Reuse Using Objects

Creating and distributing objects is one of the most powerful means of achieving reusability. An object is a discrete unit of functionality. Object components within Visual Basic can be either internal or external to an application, and they can be shared between applications, as shown in Figure 14-1. External object components have an advantage in that they can be physically deployed anywhere on a network. By strategically deploying object components to maximize resources, you can save possibly thousands of dollars when you consider that a typical development's cost comprises both development and deployment overheads.

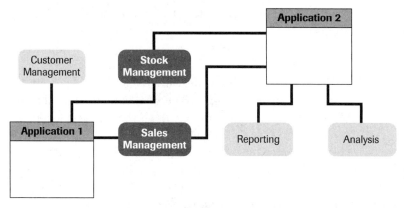

FIGURE 14-1   *Applications sharing object components*

Inherently, object components are loosely coupled and generic. Each object component in Figure 14-1 is totally self-contained and can be used by any number of applications or components. An object component should have no "knowledge" of the outside world. For example, if you have an object component that contains a method to retrieve a list of customers for a given criterion, that method should accept the criterion as input and return the list of customers. It is up to the caller, or client, using the object's, or server's, method to display or process the results. You could code the object's method to fill a list of customers on the form, but that object would be tied to the particular interface component on the form. If you wanted to reuse the object's method in another application, you would need to have an interface component of the same type and name on that application's form. The object would therefore be tightly coupled because it "knew about" the interface.

From a business perspective, object components provide a way of controlling and managing business logic. Business logic consists of rules that can change to meet the needs of the business. By placing such logic in object components and locating these on a server, you can make changes instantly available with low installation overhead, especially since polymorphic (multiple) interfaces in Visual Basic 6 allow you different interfaces within the same component. For example, if a bank were offering an additional 2 percent interest to any customers with over $10,000 in their savings accounts, the functionality could be specified in an account calculations object, as shown in the following pseudocode:

```
Procedure Calculate Monthly Interest For Customer Cust_No
    High_Interest_Threshold = 10000
    Get Customer_Balance for Customer Cust_No
    Get Interest_Rate_Percent

    If Customer_Balance < High_Interest_Threshold Then
        Add Interest_Rate_Percent to Customer_Balance
    Else
        Add Interest_Rate_Percent + 2% to Customer_Balance
    End If

End Procedure
```

In this example, the special offer might have been an incentive that was not anticipated when the application was originally designed. Thus, implementing the functionality in a non-object-component environment would probably involve quite a few additional steps:

- Adding a high interest threshold field to the database
- Adding to the maintenance functionality to amend the high interest threshold
- Amending the monthly balance calculation formula to include an additional calculation
- Shutting down the database to make changes
- Rebuilding the application EXE file
- Testing and debugging
- Reinstalling the application on the client PCs

As you can see, a relatively simple change request can involve a lot of time and money. Using an object component design, you can drastically reduce the amount of effort required to implement such a change. To make the same change in an object component system requires slightly less effort. The differences are explained here:

- The account calculations object calculates interest payments, so locating the code module to change will be fairly simple.

- Because only the account calculations object requires a change, only this component needs to be rebuilt. With this type of design, the object components are most likely to be installed on a server so that only one copy of the object needs to be reinstalled. The object can also be made to work in the new way for some applications and in the old way for other applications without any of the applications changing at all.

- Testing will be limited to the object that has changed because its functionality is completely encapsulated.

This very simple example shows how objects—in this case, distributed objects—offer a major advantage in terms of maintenance. A good example of how shrewd object distribution can save money is one that Peet Morris often uses in his seminars.

If you imagine an application that utilizes a word processor to print output, by installing the print object and a copy of the word processor on the server, each user can access the single installation for printing. Whether you have 5 or 500 users, you still need only one copy of the word processor.

Another advantage of distributed objects is that you can install object components on the most suitable hardware. Imagine that you have several object components, some that perform critical batch processing and some that perform noncritical processes. You can put the critical tasks on a dedicated fault-tolerant server with restricted access and locate the noncritical processes on a general-purpose server. The idea here is that you don't necessarily need all your hardware to be high specification: you can mix and match. The capability to move object components away from the desktop PC means that the client or user interface code can be much smaller and won't require high-end PCs to run. With distributed objects, it's a simple enough task to relocate object components so that you can experiment almost on the fly to determine the best resource utilization.

Cost benefits of object reuse

So far, we've discussed how object components can be reused by many applications and how maintaining applications using this design can be simplified. The reuse advantage should not be underestimated, especially by business managers. Examine Table 14-1, which shows the budget estimate for a warehouse stock inventory and ordering system. The development is estimated to be completed within 12 months from start to finish, including the time required for the project manager and the technical lead to prepare the functional and technical specifications.

TABLE 14-1

BUDGET ESTIMATE FOR A WAREHOUSE STOCK INVENTORY AND ORDERING APPLICATION

Resource	Cost per Day ($)	Duration (Months)	Cost ($)*
1 Project manager	750	12	180,000
1 Technical lead	600	12	144,000
3 Programmer	450 × 3 = 1,350	10	270,000
1 Tester	300	5	30,000
TOTAL	3000		624,000

* Based on working 20 days a month.

Some simple arithmetic shows that if all goes as planned, based on a five-day week, the total cost of the project will be $624,000. The company has decided that this will be the first of three development projects. The second will be a system to allow the purchasing department to do sales-trend analysis and sales predictions. The budget estimate for the second project is shown in Table 14-2.

TABLE 14-2

BUDGET ESTIMATE FOR A SALES-TREND ANALYSIS APPLICATION

Resource	Cost per Day ($)	Duration (Months)	Cost ($)*
1 Project manager	750	10	150,000
1 Technical lead	600	10	120,000
2 Programmer	450 × 2 = 900	8	144,000
1 Tester	300	3	18,000
TOTAL	2550		432,000

* Based on working 20 days a month.

The third project will be a Web application that allows customers to query availability and price information 24 hours a day. The budget estimate for this project is shown in Table 14-3.

TABLE 14-3 **BUDGET ESTIMATE FOR AN INTERNET BROWSER**

Resource	Cost per Day ($)	Duration (Months)	Cost ($)*
1 Project manager	750	9	135,000
1 Technical lead	600	9	108,000
1 Programmer	450	8	72,000
1 Tester	300	4	24,000
TOTAL	2100		339,000

* Based on working 20 days a month.

If we examine all three applications as a single system and then build the applications in sequence, it becomes apparent that the second and third applications will require far less development time than the first because they build on existing functionality. One advantage here is that building the second and third systems need not affect the first system. This situation is ideal for phased implementations. The success of this strategy depends largely on how well the design and analysis stages were completed. Figure 14-2 shows the design of all three applications. The three applications are treated as a single development for the purpose of planning. Reusable functionality is clearly visible, and although the developments will be written in phases, the reusable components can be designed to accommodate all the applications.

In the development of a multiple application system, design is of the utmost importance. It is the responsibility of the "business" to clearly define system requirements, which must also include future requirements. Defining future requirements as well as current ones helps designers to design applications that will be able to expand and change easily as the business grows. All successful businesses plan ahead. Microsoft plans its development and strategies over a 10-year period. Without knowledge of future plans, your business cannot make the most of object component reusability.

Looking back at the application design in Figure 14-2, you can see that all three systems have been included in the design. You can clearly see which components can be reused and where alterations will be required. Because the design uses object components, which as you'll recall are loosely coupled inherently, it would be possible to build this system in stages—base system 1, then 2, then 3.

Let's consider the estimates we did earlier. The main application was scheduled to be completed in 12 months and will have 12 major components. So ignoring code complexity, we can do a rough estimate, shown in Figure 14-3, of how

Didn't I Write That Function Last Week?   Chapter

14

much effort will be required to implement the other two applications. Take the figures with a grain of salt; they're just intended to provide a consistent comparison. In reality, any computer application development is influenced by all kinds of problems. It's especially important to keep in mind that new technologies will always slow down a development by an immeasurable factor.[1]

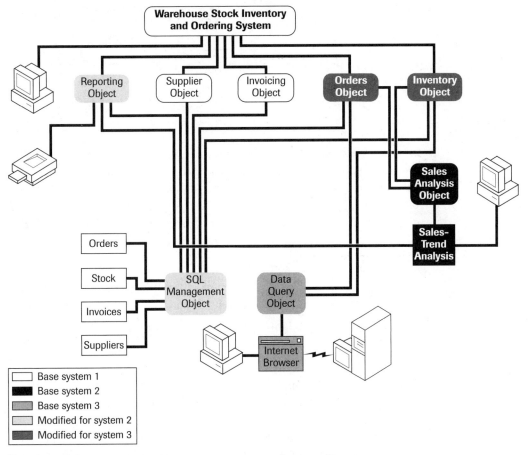

Figure 14-2   *Single development comprising three application systems*

---

1   For those of you interested in estimating and development time issues, we recommend the book *Rapid Development*, by Steve McConnell (Microsoft Press, 1996). He does for project managers what he did for developers with *Code Complete* (Microsoft Press, 1995). See how many of the 36 Classic Mistakes of Software Development you've encountered!

Assumptions (*Time*)

Person-months to code one new unit	1.5
Person-months to modify one new unit for reuse	0.75
Person-months to test one new unit	0.5
Person-months to code one modified unit	0.25

Development Estimate (*Coding and Testing Only*)

Application	Number of Code Units Required for Application		Development Time in Months (Based on Assumptions Above)				Total Time (Months)
			Coding		Testing		
	New	Reused	New	Reused	New	Reused	
Stock Inventory	12	0	18	0	6	0	24
Sales-Trend Analysis	2	4	3	3	1	1	8
Internet Browser	2	2	3	1.5	1	0.5	6

FIGURE 14-3   *Rough time estimate for coding and testing three applications*

The estimates for the three applications when viewed as standalone develop-ments could well be feasible. When viewed as a whole, they give a clear pic-ture of which components can be shared and therefore need to be written only once. The reusable components can be designed from the start to meet the needs of the second and third applications. Although this might add effort to the first project, the subsequent projects will in theory be shortened. Here are the three major benefits:

1. The design anticipates and allows for future expansion.

2. The overall development effort is reduced.

3. Functionality can be allocated to the most appropriate resource. For example, a print specialist can code the print engine without affecting the interface coder.

As you can see, object components provide a number of advantages. Object components are vital to high-level code reuse because of their encapsulation, which allows functionality to be allocated to the most suitable resource. As Fred Brooks points out in *The Mythical Man-Month: Essays on Software Engineering* (Addison-Wesley, 1995), "Only through high-level reuse can ever more complex systems be built."

Object component practicalities

Object components are built using a special Visual Basic module type called a class module. The class module can contain properties, methods, and events and can consume properties, methods, and events from other classes (described

later). Our example diagrams so far have been high level; that is, only the overall functionality of the object has been shown. In reality, an object component
will usually consist of contained classes—each with properties, methods, and
events. Figure 14-4 shows a more detailed example of how applications might
interact with object components.

For the programmer, using object components couldn't be simpler. An object
component is written in ordinary Visual Basic code. To use an object, the programmer simply has to declare the object, instantiate it, and then call its methods
and properties. Two additional and powerful features that greatly increase the
power of object components were added to Visual Basic 5: the *Implements*
statement and the Events capability.

The *Implements* statement allows you to build objects (class objects) and
implement features from another class (base class). You can then handle a
particular procedure in the new derived class or let the base class handle the
procedure. Figure 14-5 on the following page shows an imaginary example of
how *Implements* works. The exact coding methods are not shown here because
they are covered fully in the online documentation that comes with Visual
Basic 6. The example in Figure 14-5 is of an airplane autopilot system.

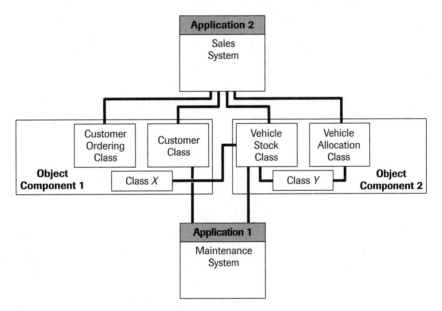

FIGURE 14-4   *Classes within object components*

Figure 14-5 shows a base Autopilot class that has *TakeOff* and *BankLeft* methods. Because different airplanes require different procedures to take off, the base Autopilot class cannot cater to individual take-off procedures, so instead it contains only a procedure declaration for this function. The *BankLeft* actions, however, are pretty much the same for all airplanes, so the Autopilot base class can perform the required procedures.

There are two types or classes of airplane in this example: a B737 and a Cessna. Both classes implement the autopilot functionality and therefore must also include procedures for the functions that are provided in the Autopilot base class. In the *TakeOff* procedure, both the Cessna and B737 classes have their own specific implementations. The *BankLeft* procedures, however, simply pass straight through to the *BankLeft* procedure in the Autopilot base class. Now let's say that the *BankLeft* procedure on the B737 changes so that B737 planes are limited to a bank angle of 25 degrees; in this case, you would simply replace the code in the B737 class *BankLeft* procedure so that it performs the required action.

Visual Basic 4 users might have noticed something interesting here: the Cessna and B737 classes have not instantiated the Autopilot class. This is because the instancing options for classes changed with Visual Basic 5. It is now possible to create a class that is global within the application without having to declare or instantiate it. Here are the new instancing settings:

- **PublicNotCreatable** Other applications cannot create this class unless the application in which the class is contained has already created an instance.

- **GlobalSingleUse** Any application using the class will get its own instance of the class. You don't need to *Dim* or *Set* a variable of the class to use it.

- **GlobalMultiUse** An application using the class will have to "queue" to use the class because it has only a single instance, which is shared with any other applications using the class. You don't need to *Dim* or *Set* a variable of the class to use it.

Only classes in ActiveX EXE projects have every *Instancing* option available to them. ActiveX DLL projects don't allow any of the *SingleUse* options, and ActiveX Control projects allow only *Private* or *PublicNotCreatable*.

The Events capability in Visual Basic 5 and 6 is the second useful and powerful new feature that is available to object classes. Essentially, it allows your object class to trigger an event that can be detected by clients of the object class. The "Introducing the progress form" section on page 607 gives an example of how events are used.

Cessna Control Module
```
Sub FlyPlane

    Dim clsCessna As Cessna
    Dim BankAngle As Integer

    Set clsCessna = New Cessna

    clsCessna.TakeOff
    BankAngle = GetBankAngle(Me)
    clsCessna.BankLeft(BankAngle)
```

B737 Control Module
```
Sub FlyPlane

    Dim clsB737 As B737
    Dim BankAngle As Integer

    Set clsB737 = New B737

    clsB737.TakeOff
    BankAngle = GetBankAngle(Me)
    clsB737.BankLeft(BankAngle)
```

Cessna Class
```
Declarations
Implements Autopilot

Sub TakeOff

    ' This is a nongeneric action, so it contains
    ' no code; in effect, it is a virtual procedure.

    ... code for take-off actions ...

End Sub

Sub BankLeft(ByRef CurrentBankAngle As Integer)

    ' Because this is the same for all planes, we
    ' can use the base method in the Autopilot class.

    clsAutopilot.BankLeft

End Sub
```

B737 Class
```
Declarations
Implements Autopilot

Sub TakeOff

    ' This is a nongeneric action, so it contains
    ' no code; in effect, it is a virtual procedure.

    ... code for take-off actions ...

End Sub

Sub BankLeft(ByRef CurrentBankAngle As Integer)

    ' Because this is the same for all planes, we
    ' can use the base method in the Autopilot class.

    clsAutopilot.BankLeft

End Sub
```

Autopilot Class
```
Sub TakeOff

    ' This is a nongeneric action, so it contains
    ' no code; in effect, it is a virtual procedure.

End Sub

Sub BankLeft(ByRef CurrentBankAngle As Integer)

    ' Generic action, so we can put code here.

    Do Until CurrentBankAngle = 30

        CurrentBankAngle = CurrentBankAngle - 1

    Loop

End Sub
```

FIGURE 14-5   *Example using the* Implements *statement*

Reuse and Modules

With all the wonderful new techniques available it is easy to forget the humble standard module. Standard modules are ideal in cases in which you have an internal unit of functionality that does not need to have an instance and might need to be available throughout the application. One feature of standard modules that is often forgotten, or not known, is that modules can contain properties and methods (but not events). A problem with some applications is that the infrastructure code required to hold the application together is often written in to one or more standard modules each containing a multitude of public variables. Although achieving the desired effect, it can make for extremely difficult debugging and reuse. I'm sure you can all think of an instance when you were not sure if a particular public variable existed that would meet your requirements, and accordingly you created another—just to be sure!

The practice of using public variables drastically cuts down the potential for reuse because the coupling of components becomes unclear. For example, if a particular function depended on the variable *nPuUserPrivilege,* how would you know what area of functionality owned this variable? Sure, you could press Shift+F2 to go to the definition, but the chances are there would be many more such instances. A better way might be to make the variable a public property variable. By doing so you have the added advantage of being able to build event code, giving you the opportunity to perform certain actions whenever the property is accessed. Another benefit is that you can add a description that appears in the Object Browser with the property or method. This can be done by choosing Procedure Attributes from the Tools menu. One technique that is good practice is to give your modules meaningful names and specify the scope when accessing one of its properties. For example, you could have two public properties called *IsTaskRunning* in separate modules and access them individually, like this:

```
If modFileProcessing.IsTaskRunning = True Then ...
If modReportProcessing.IsTaskRunning = True Then ...
```

Standard modules have an advantage in that they cannot have multiple instances and they do not need to be created—they are there right when your application starts. This makes them ideal for general-control flow logic and high-level application control. The sample code below shows part of a standard module whose task is to control the user interface state. Notice in particular that rather than having to set many flags, the whole interface state can be configured by setting just one property.

Form code

```
Sub Form_Load()
    Set basUIControl.MainForm = Me
End Sub

Sub SomeProcess()
    basUIControl.State = UIC_MyProcessStarted

    basUIControl.UpdateProgressBar 0
    For nCount = 1 To 70
        ... do process ...
        basUIControl.UpdateProgressBar (nCount \ 70) * 100
    Next nCount

    basUIControl.State = UIC_ProcessComplete
End Sub
```

Standard module basUIControl

```
Public Enum UIC_StateConstants
    UIC_MyProcessStarted
    UIC_ProcessComplete
    ⋮
End Enum
Private Enum UIC_MenuType
    DisableWhileProcessing
    DisableOnUserType
    ⋮
End Enum
Private m_MainForm As Form

Public Property Set MainForm(frmForm As Form)
    Set m_MainForm = frmForm
End Property

Public Property Let State(nState As UIC_StateConstants)
    Dim mnuMenu As Menu

    Select Case nState
        ' If a process is starting then disable menus that are not allowed
        ' while processing.
        Case UIC_MyProcessStarted
            For Each mnuMenu In m_MainForm
                If mnuMenu.Tag = UIC_MenuType.DisableWhileProcessing Then
                    mnuMenu.Enabled = False
                End If
            Next mnuMenu
        Case ...
End Property
```

The code shown above is totally legal and shows how—with careful planning and design—you can make even "environmental" type code reusable and loosely coupled. Note that the *basUIControl* module stores a pointer to the application's main form. This means that we can manipulate the form without actually knowing anything about it. In this example each menu item is assumed to have a *Tag* value specifying what type of menu item it is. In our logic, when the state is set to process running we use the tag to selectively turn off certain menu items.

In terms of reuse we have several benefits:

- If another UI related function is required, it is obvious where it should go.

- If a programmer needs to use a procedure from this module, it is clear from the Object Browser exactly what each property and method is for —assuming, of course, that you remember to fill in a description.

- It is far easier to see from the Object Browser if a particular property already exists, especially if similar logic is grouped.

The conversion of public variables to properties also gives us an added benefit in the area of application design. Because all our module's attributes now conform to a class specification, there is no reason why we cannot include the module in an object diagram. Normally we view public variables as elements whose scope is global, but in so doing they in effect have no scope—that is, they are not really part of any particular functional area of an application. By converting these variables to properties, we have (as a side effect) scoped these attributes to a specific functional element even though they are global. This can have enormous benefits in terms of application design because we can account for every last member. We are no longer in the position of having tightly coupled control elements. Figure 14-6 on the next page shows a simple program that has been reverse engineered using the Visual Modeler application that comes with Microsoft Visual Studio 98. Note that this sample is intended to illustrate that modules and their associated properties and methods are represented in the same way as class objects. This allows us to account for all elements in an application if we use public properties rather than public variables.

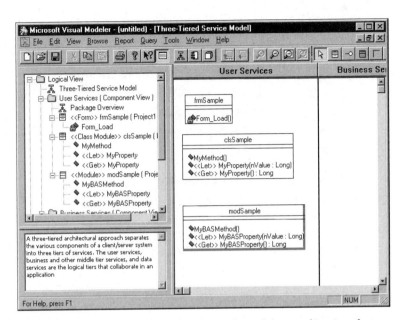

FIGURE 14-6   *An object diagram created by the Visual Modeler application that comes with Microsoft Visual Studio 6*

Forms as Reusable Components

Many developers overlook the fact that forms can make very good reusable components. In addition to the traditional code reuse benefit of reduced development time through the use of previously debugged and tested code, a second, possibly less tangible benefit is user interface consistency across applications. With the exploding office suite market, this need for a consistent user interface has become far more apparent over the last two to three years. A major selling point of all the competing suites is consistency of user interface across the separate suite applications. Consistency reduces wasted time: the user doesn't have to pore over many different manuals learning how things work. Once the user has mastered something in one application, he or she can apply the same skill to the other members of the suite. Reusing forms can be a real win-win tactic. In the long run, you save development time, and the user requires less training.

The types of forms you should be looking to make reusable are what can be considered auxiliary forms. Those that display an application's About information, give spell check functionality, or are logon forms are all likely candidates. More specialized forms that are central to an application's primary function are likely to be too specific to that particular development to make designing them for reuse worthwhile. Alternatively, these specialized forms might still be considered worth making public for use by applications outside those in which they reside.

Writing forms to be reusable

As programmers, we should all be familiar with the idea of reusing forms by now. Windows has had the common File, Print, and Font dialog boxes since its early versions, and these have been available to Visual Basic users through the CommonDialog control right from the first version of Visual Basic. Visual Basic 5 introduced the ability to reuse custom-developed forms in a truly safe way. Visual Basic 4 gave us the ability to declare methods and properties as Public to other forms. Prior to this, only code modules could have access to a form's methods and data. This limitation made form-to-form interaction a little convoluted, with the forms having to interface via a module, and generally made creating a reusable form as a completely encapsulated object impractical.

Visual Basic 5 provided another new capability for forms. Like classes and controls, forms can now raise events, extending our ability to make forms discrete objects. Previously, if we wanted forms to have any two-way interaction, the code within each form had to be aware of the interface of the other. Now we have the ability to create a form that "serves" another form or any other type of module, without any knowledge of its interface, simply by raising events that the client code can deal with as needed. The ability to work in this way is really a prerequisite of reusable components. Without it, a form is always in some way bound, or coupled, to any other code that it works with by its need to have knowledge of that code's interface.

In the following progress report example, you'll find out how to design a generic form that can be reused within many applications. You'll also see how to publicly expose this form to other applications by using a class, allowing its use outside the original application. This topic covers two areas of reuse: reuse of the source code, by which the form is compiled into an application; and reuse of an already compiled form from another application as a distributed object.

Didn't I Write That Function Last Week?   Chapter

14

Introducing the progress form

The form we'll write here, shown in Figure 14-7, is a generic progress form of the type you often see when installing software or performing some other lengthy process. This type of form serves two basic roles. First, by its presence, the form confirms that the requested process is under way, while giving the user the opportunity to abandon the process if necessary. Second, by constantly displaying the progress of a process, the form makes the process appear faster. With Visual Basic often wrongly accused of being slow, this subjective speed is an important consideration.

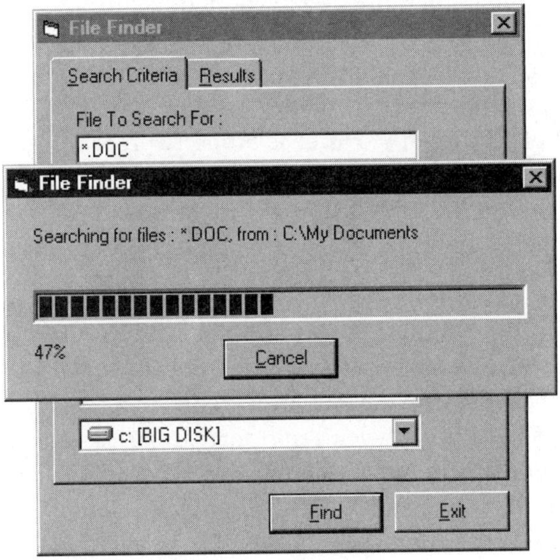

Figure 14-7   *A generic progress form in action*

This example gives us a chance to explore all the different ways you can interact with a form as a component. The form will have properties and methods to enable you to modify its appearance. Additionally, it will raise two events, showing that this ability is not limited to classes.

When designing a form's interface, you must make full use of property procedures to wrap your form's properties. Although you can declare a form's data as Public, by doing so you are exposing it to the harsh world outside your component—a world in which you have no control over the values that might be assigned to that component. A much safer approach is to wrap this data within *Property Get* and *Property Let* procedures, giving you a chance both to validate changes prior to processing them and to perform any processing you deem necessary when the property value is changed. If you don't use property procedures, you miss the opportunity to do either of these tasks, and any performance gains you hope for will never appear because Visual Basic creates property procedures for all public data when it compiles your form anyway.

It's also a good policy to wrap the properties of any components or controls that you want to expose in property procedures. This wrapping gives you the same advantages as mentioned previously, plus the ability to change the internal implementation of these properties without affecting your interface. This ability can allow you to change the type of control used. For example, within the example progress form, we use the Windows common ProgressBar control. By exposing properties of the form as property procedures, we would be able to use another control within the form or even draw the progress bar ourselves while maintaining the same external interface through our property procedures. All this prevents any changes to client code, a prerequisite of reusable components.

The generic progress form uses this technique of wrapping properties in property procedures to expose properties of the controls contained within it. Among the properties exposed are the form caption, the progress bar caption, the maximum progress bar value, the current progress bar value, and the visibility of the Cancel command button. Although all of these properties can be reached directly, by exposing them through property procedures, we're able to both validate new settings and perform other processing if necessary. This is illustrated by the *AllowCancel* and *ProgressBarValue* properties. The *AllowCancel* property controls not only the Visible state of the Cancel command button but also the height of the form, as shown in this code segment:

```
Public Property Let AllowCancel (ByVal ibNewValue As Boolean)

    If ibNewValue = True Then
            cmdCancel.Visible = True
            Me.Height = 2460
        Else
            cmdCancel.Visible = False
            Me.Height = 1905
    End If

    Me.Refresh

End Property
```

The *ProgressBarValue* property validates a new value, avoiding an unwanted error that might occur if the value is set greater than the current maximum:

```
Public Property Let ProgressBarValue(ByVal ilNewValue As Long)

    ' Ensure that the new progress bar value is not
    ' greater than the maximum value.
    If Abs(ilNewValue) > Abs(gauProgress.Max) Then
        ilNewValue = gauProgress.Max
    End If

    gauProgress.Value = ilNewValue
    Me.Refresh

End Property
```

The progress form events

The progress form can raise two events. Events are most commonly associated with controls, but can be put to equally good use within other components. To have our form generate events, we must declare each event within the general declarations for the form as shown here:

```
Public Event PerformProcess(ByRef ProcessData As Variant)
Public Event QueryAbandon(ByRef Ignore As Boolean)
```

Progress forms are usually displayed modally. Essentially, they give the user something to look at while the application is too busy to respond. Because of this we have to have some way for our progress form appear modal, while still allowing the application's code to execute. We do this by raising the PerformProcess event once the form has finished loading. This event will be executed within the client code, where we want our process to be carried out.

```
Private Sub Form_Activate()
    Static stbActivated As Boolean

    '   (Re)Paint this form.
    Me.Refresh

    If Not stbActivated Then
        stbActivated = True

        '   Now this form is visible, call back into the calling
        '   code so that it may perform whatever action it wants.
        RaiseEvent PerformProcess(m_vProcessData)
```

>>

```
          '   Now that the action is complete, unload me.
          Unload Me
      End If
End Sub
```

Components used in this way are said to perform a callback. In this case we show the form, having previously prepared code in the PerformProcess event handler for it to callback and execute once it has finished loading. This allows us to neatly sidestep the fact that when we display a form modally, the form now has the focus and no further code outside it is executed until it unloads.

The final piece of sample code that we need to look at within our progress form is the code that generates the QueryAbandon event. This event allows the client code to obtain user confirmation before abandoning what it's doing. This event is then triggered when the Cancel command button is clicked. By passing the *Ignore* Boolean value by reference, we give the event handling routine in the client the opportunity to change this value in order to work in the same way as the *Cancel* value within a form's QueryUnload event. When we set *Ignore* to True, the event handling code can prevent the process from being abandoned. When we leave *Cancel* as False, the progress form will continue to unload. The QueryAbandon event is raised as follows:

```
Private Sub cmdCancel_Click()
    Dim bCancel As Boolean
    bCancel = False
    RaiseEvent QueryAbandon(bCancel)
    If bCancel = False Then Unload Me
End Sub
```

From this code, you can see how the argument of the QueryAbandon event controls whether or not the form is unloaded, depending on its value after the event has completed.

Using the progress form

The code that follows illustrates how the progress form can be employed. First we have to create an instance of the form. This must be placed in the client module's Declarations section because it will be raising events within this module, much the same way as controls do. Forms and classes that raise events are declared as WithEvents, in the following way:

```
Private WithEvents frmPiProg As frmProgress
```

We must declare the form in this way; otherwise, we wouldn't have access to the form's events. By using this code, the form and its events will appear within the Object and Procedure combo boxes in the Code window, just as for a control.

Now that the form has been declared, we can make use of it during our lengthy process. First we must create a new instance of it, remembering that the form does not exist until it has actually been *Set* with the *New* keyword. When this is done we can set the form's initial properties and display it, as illustrated here:

```
' Instantiate the progress form.
Set frmPiProg = New frmProgress

' Set up the form's initial properties.
frmPiProg.FormCaption = "File Search"
frmPiProg.ProgressBarMax = 100
frmPiProg.ProgressBarValue = 0
frmPiProg.ProgressCaption = _
    "Searching for file. Please wait..."


' Now Display it modally.
frmPiProg.Show vbModal, Me
```

Now that the progress form is displayed, it will raise the PerformAction event in our client code, within which we can carry out our lengthy process. This allows the progress form to be shown modally but still allows execution within the client code.

```
Private Sub frmPiProg_PerformProcess(ProcessData As Variant)
    Dim nPercentComplete As Integer

    mbProcessCancelled = False
    Do

        ' Update the form's progress bar.
        nPercentComplete = nPercentComplete + 1
        frmPiProg.ProgressBarValue = nPercentComplete

        ' Peform your action.

        ' You must include DoEvents in your process or any
        ' clicks on the Cancel button will not be responded to.
        DoEvents

    Loop While mbProcessCancelled <> True _
        And nPercentComplete < frmPiProg.ProgressBarMax
End Sub
```

The final piece of code we need to put into our client is the event handler for the QueryAbandon event that the progress form raises when the user clicks the Cancel button. This event gives us the chance to confirm or cancel the abandonment of the current process, generally after seeking confirmation from the user. An example of how this might be done follows:

```
Private Sub frmPiProg_QueryAbandon(Ignore As Boolean)

    If MsgBox("Are you sure you want to cancel?", _
            vbQuestion Or vbYesNo, Me.Caption) = vbNo Then

        Ignore = True
        mbProcessCancelled = True

    End If
End Sub
```

From this example, you can see that to use the progress form, the parent code simply has to set the form's properties, display it, and deal with any events it raises.

Making a form public

Although forms do not have an *Instancing* property and cannot be made public outside their application, you can achieve this effect by using a class module as an intermediary. By mirroring the events, methods, and properties of your form within a class with an *Instancing* property other than *Private*, making sure that the project type is ActiveX EXE or ActiveX DLL, you can achieve the same results as you can by making a form public.

Using the progress form as an example, we will create a public class named CProgressForm. This class will have all the properties and methods of the progress form created earlier. Where a property of the class is accessed, the class will merely delegate the implementation of that property to the under-lying form, making it public. Figure 14-8 shows this relationship, with the client application having access to the CProgressForm class but not *frmProgress*, but the CProgressForm class having an instance of *frmProgress* privately. To illustrate these relationships, we will show how the *ProgressBarValue* property is made public.

First we need to declare a private instance of the form within the Declarations section of our class:

```
Private WithEvents frmPiProgressForm As frmProgress
```

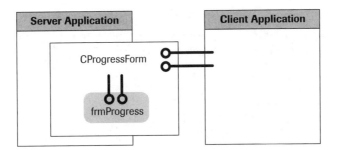

FIGURE 14-8   *Making a form public using a public class as an intermediary*

Here we see how the *ProgressBarValue* property is made public by using the class as an intermediary:

```
Public Property Let ProgressBarValue(ByVal ilNewValue As Long)
    frmPiProgressForm.ProgressBarValue = ilNewValue
End Property

Public Property Get ProgressBarValue() As Long
    ProgressBarValue = frmPiProgressForm.ProgressBarValue
End Property
```

Similarly, we can subclass the PerformProcess and QueryAbandon events, allowing us to make public the full functionality of the progress form. For example, we could subclass the QueryAbandon event by reraising it from the class, in reaction to the initial event raised by the form, and passing by reference the initial *Ignore* argument within the new event. This way the client code can still modify the *Ignore* argument of the original form's event.

```
Private Sub frmPiProgressForm_QueryAbandon(Ignore As Boolean)
    RaiseEvent QueryAbandon(Ignore)
End Sub
```

There is a difficulty with exposing the progress form in this way. The form has a *Show* method that we must add to the class. Because we're using the form within another separate application, this method cannot display the form modally to the client code. One solution is to change the *Show* method of the CProgressForm class so that it always displays the progress form modelessly.

Another possible solution is to use a control instead of a public class to expose the form to the outside world. Those of you who have used the common dialogs before will be familiar with this technique. This enables you to make the form public in the same way as with CProgressClass, but additionally you can add a *Display* method, in which you call the form's *Show* method, showing it modally to the form that the control is hosted on.

```
Public Sub Display(ByVal inCmdShow As Integer)

    '    Display the progress form.
    frmPiProgressForm.Show inCmdShow, UserControl.Parent

End Sub
```

The code for the progress form and the ProgressForm control are on the book's companion CD.

Creating Your Own Controls

A lot of interest in Visual Basic 5 and 6 has been focused on the ability to create custom controls. This ability has greatly extended the capabilities of the product, in a way that some felt should have been possible from the start.

Prior to Visual Basic 4, the custom control was the primary source of reuse. Controls and their capabilities took center stage and appeared to take on lives of their own, becoming software superstars. In some instances, complete projects were designed around a single control and its capabilities! The problem with this was that you couldn't write these wonderful, reusable controls using Visual Basic—you had to resort to a lower-level language such as C++. This situation was hardly ideal, when one of the reasons for using Visual Basic in the first place was to move away from having to get your hands dirty with low-level code.

With Visual Basic 4, the emphasis moved away from controls to classes and objects as a means of reuse. Controls are great as part of the user interface of an application, but they're not really cut out to provide anything else because of their need to be contained in a form. This limitation is significant if you want to write a DLL or a distributed object.

Although the ability to write your own controls is a boon, it isn't the solution for all your problems. Don't overuse this ability just because you can or because you want to. You can do a great deal much more effectively than by resorting to writing a control. Again, beware of the gold-plating syndrome.

Didn't I Write That Function Last Week? CHAPTER

14

Creating the Year 2000 *DateBox* control

The DateBox control is an ActiveX control that provides a means of obtaining and displaying date information in a Year 2000 compliant format. This case study discusses the design goals for the control as well as including a more general discussion of ActiveX control creation in Visual Basic 6.0.

Of utmost importance with the DateBox control is the ability to have a *Date* property whose data type is Date. Chapter 8, which focuses on the Year 2000 problem, discusses the issues around dates being stored in data types other than the Date type, so it is a foregone conclusion that type Date will be used in the control. An interesting problem arises from using the Date type: binding to a data source whose type is Nullable Date is not possible—the control would neither be able to read nor write a Null value from the data source. In real-world applications, it is quite likely that a date value would legitimately need to be Null. For example, date of birth might be optional on an application form if the applicant is over 21. To get around this problem, the DateBox control has a *DateVariant* property that is of type Variant and can be data-bound. Depending on the developer's preference, this property can return a valid date (of type Variant, subtype Date), a Null, or an Empty. The *DateVariant* cannot return an invalid or noncompliant—if the user attempts to read such a date, an error is raised. The *DateVariant* property can be set to an illegal date and this event is treated as if a user had manually typed the value.

The second design goal is to create an interface that allows the user to enter date values in a manner that does not restrict their method of working. A user might choose to enter a date in the format "10/21/1998" or "5 mar 1998." Any valid date syntax is accepted by the control, providing it conforms to either the long or short date format as defined in the Regional Settings of the Control Panel (meaning the Day, Month, and Year must be in correct order). Additionally, when a date is entered, the year must be entered using four digits. The control deems a date to be invalid if a full four-digit year is not entered.

To achieve unobtrusive date input, validation is performed in two stages. The first validation mechanism activates when the control's date value changes, either via user input or programmatically. The foreground and background colors are changed to "error colors" specified by the developer when the control's date is not valid. By default the colors are inverted so that time isn't spent configuring settings if the default will suffice. When a validation error occurs in this first stage the user receives no other prompt. In this way, the user can continue to work unobstructed until such time as he or she feels inclined to rectify the error.

The second stage of validation is triggered when the *DateY2K* or *DateVariant* property is read. When this situation occurs, the error notification is either by message box, Visual Basic error, or a change in the control's text to a predefined message. The error action is selected at design time by the developer.

Because the control is Year 2000 compliant, it follows that the control must display dates in a compliant manner, that is, with a four-digit year. The control's display format can be toggled between the system's Long or Short Date format. However, no matter which format is selected, the control adjusts the format to always use a four-digit year. Note that the system's original format is not modified.

In practice it is not possible to create a property called *Date* because this is a Visual Basic keyword. Therefore the control's date property is actually called *DateY2K*.

The DateBox control is based on the intrinsic TextBox control and contains most of the properties and methods of this base control.

The Properties window does not display picklists for Integer or Long properties as it does with most other ActiveX controls. In order to have a picklist for these properties you need to declare a public enumerated type and set the control's *Get* and *Let* declarations to this type, as shown here:

```
Public Enum DateBox_Error_Actions
    dbx_RaiseError = 0
    dbx_ShowMessage
    dbx_ShowText
    dbx_MessageAndText
End Enum

Public Property Get ErrorAction() As DateBox_Error_Actions
    ⋮
End Property
```

Using the method above will cause the Properties window to display a picklist for the *ErrorAction* property and offer the following choices:

```
0 - dbx_RaiseError
1 - dbx_ShowMessage
2 - dbx_ShowText
3 - dbx_MessageAndText
```

A feature you can make use of here is to have enumerated constant names with spaces. You achieve this by enclosing the constant name in square brackets, as in this example:

```
Public Enum DateBox_Error_Actions
    [Raise Error] = 0
    [Show Message]
    [Show Text]
    [Message And Text]
End Enum
```

The code above will appear in the picklist as

```
0 - Raise Error
1 - Show Message
2 - Show Text
3 - Message And Text
```

In code terms the only disadvantage of using the "pretty" display is that developers wanting to use your control will have to use the bracketed syntax or declare their own constants.

When creating a control that encapsulates an intrinsic control, note that although you can choose to subclass the properties of that control, properties such as *MousePointer* and *DragMode* will appear in the Properties window as non-picklist items. This is because their property *Let* and *Get* procedures are declared as Integer or Long. In this case you can change the property type to Visual Basic's predefined data type, for example, you can use VBRUN.MousePointerConstants as the property type for *MousePointer*. An interesting issue is raised here with regard to coding standards. Take for instance the MSComctlLib.BorderStyle-Constants. They are defined and will appear as shown here:

```
ccFixedSingle
ccNone
```

These are the values you'll see in the Properties window for, say, a ListView control. However, for a TextBox control, you'll see "1 – Fixed Single" and "0 – None." Which style should you use?

One solution to the style problem is to have two sets of public enumerations per property category—one with a pretty display and one that the developer can use. There is an added advantage to this method. Look at this example:

```
Public Enum My_Property_Type
    None = 0
    [Fixed Single]
End Enum
Public Enum My_Property_Type_Internal
    ptMin = -1
    ptNone
    ptFixedSingle
    ptMax
End Enum
```

In this case, if the developer uses the My_Property_Type_Internal constants, validation within the property *Let* becomes much simpler. For instance, to validate input you could code the following:

```
Public Property Let Aproperty(Value As My_Property_Type)
    If Value =< ptMin Or Value >= ptMax Then
        *** Error ****
    Else
        ⋮
    End If
End Property
```

Now if at any time in the future you add or remove an enumerated constant, no change to the validation code is necessary. Alas, you cannot use private enumerated types for your property's values, so you do have to export both enumerations.

One last point on properties: if you declare a property as an enumerated type, hoping that the Property Page Wizard will create a combo selection box for you—it won't! In fact it will not allow you to select that property for inclusion in the property page.

Property pages can be a useful feature to add to your control. A property page is essentially a separate form or collection of forms that you can create to allow the user to set design time properties of your control. You might have seen property pages when you selected Custom from the Properties window, or choose Properties from the popup menu of a control.

There are some problems with property pages. In general I would advise against using them if you have many properties in a particular category or you do not have much development time.

The Property Page Wizard cannot handle lots of controls. That is, it does not error but will place controls off screen if they won't all fit. If you want picklists, you have to create them yourself. Another problem is that not all property page events fire when expected (or at all for that matter), as in the case of LostFocus and GotFocus—there is no way to determine when a particular page has been selected.

Within the property page object, you obtain the control's data using the *SelectedControls* object. The ReadProperties event copies your control's property data into module variables; however, the Initialize event happens before the ReadProperties event. In the Initialize event you cannot access the *SelectedControls* object. What this means in English is that if you want to access your properties during initialization, you can't have it! As the GotFocus event doesn't fire either, this effectively means than you can't easily perform start up logic. If you even want to attempt this feat, it will mean setting lots of flags and writing inefficient code!

Writing a property page is the same as writing a screen form. If the default pages produced by the Property Page Wizard will suffice for your purposes, go ahead and use them. If on the other hand you have special property page requirements, bear in mind that you might have to write most of the code yourself. Also remember that tasks that involve reading control properties at initialization time can prove troublesome.

In addition to the primary design goals, further goals include making the DateBox control adaptable to the end user's needs. In real-world applications it is quite likely that a date input might need to be limited to a specific range. For example, a business rule might dictate that an applicant's date of birth field be in the past or that the applicant's age be within a certain range. The *MinDate* and *MaxDate* properties of the DateBox allow for such rules. Another likely scenario is that the business operates on a five-day week and as a result certain dates—such as delivery dates—cannot be weekend dates. The control allows flexibility here by providing a series of properties:

```
EnableSunday
EnableMonday
⋮
EnableSaturday
```

Setting these properties to a Boolean value allows you to effectively exclude weekdays from the valid date range. Each weekday by default is enabled, and the *DisabledDayText* property lets the developer specify a message to display when a date falls on a disabled day. A point worth mentioning here is that the default error message text that is displayed when a disabled day is entered uses the day name from the locale settings. It is always a good idea to use localized values where possible; for example, display a date using the Long Date or Short Date formats defined in the Regional Settings rather than using a hard-coded format, such as MM/DD/YYYY.

A further feature of the DateBox control is the ability to force the control to keep focus following a validation error. Imagine the scenario in which a user enters an invalid date and then clicks the Save button. It is no good merely displaying an error message—after the warning is acknowledged, the Save button code will continue to execute. By retaining focus, the control effectively blocks any further code execution, saving the developer from having to check for valid values before the save code executes. This feature raises one other issue, though. What if the user hits the Cancel button? First of all you do not want a date validation message to appear, and second you do not want the control to retain focus, which will in effect block the cancel operation. The solution here is to provide a *CancelControl* property. This property can be set at run time to a command button. When the DateBox loses focus to this control no validation occurs, and focus is not retained.

The developer is given the choice of specifying the notification means when a validation error occurs. The control might raise a Visual Basic error, display a message box, display text in the control or a combination of message box and text. For the message box and text methods, developers can override the default messages by specifying their own.

As stipulated previously, it is necessary to allow "blank" dates to be entered. To give greater flexibility, the *DateBlankAction* property can be set to one of the following values:

- Raise an error
- Return Null
- Return Empty

Selecting one of the latter two options only affects the return value of the *DateVariant* property. Because the *DateY2K* property is a Date type it obviously cannot return either of these values—in this case zero is returned by the *DateY2K* property.

In some cases it is sensible to have the control display the current date as a default. This requirement is carried out by the *DefaultDate* property, which can be set to either "Today" or "None."

Didn't I Write That Function Last Week?   Chapter

14

The "business rules" in the DateBox control stipulate that certain dates cannot be valid even though they are legal dates—for example if a two-digit year is entered, or a disabled day's date is entered. The *IsDateLegal* property determines whether a date is syntactically correct regardless of whether or not it's valid. To determine if a date is actually valid the property *IsDateValid* can be checked.

There are two error handling schemes you might need to employ. Property pages should be treated as standalone programs. Neither the control nor its parent will interact with the property page, therefore any error in a property page should employ a standard error transaction scheme in which events are treated as event procedures where the error is discarded.

The control, like the property page, is itself an application. However, the host application can cause events to be triggered within your control. In these instances it is the responsibility of the host application to deal with any errors raised by the control. Within the control itself, use a standard error transaction system. Treat all events as event procedures and discard the error there. Errors that are caused by an invalid action or input by the host application should *not* be discarded at the top level. Just like errors that you specifically want to raise, these should be propagated to the host application.

What can (and can't) Visual Basic controls do?

The following is a rundown of what you can do with Visual Basic 6 controls:

- You can create controls to be used in one of two ways. You can use the well-known ActiveX implementation and create a separate OCX file and, new to Visual Basic 5 and 6, you can create a source code module, with the new CTL extension, and compile it into an application. See the next section for more information on these two methods.

- You'll find built-in support for creating property pages, with the inclusion of the PAG module. Standard Font and Color property pages are also provided (more on these later).

- You can create a control that combines a number of other existing controls.

- You can create ActiveX control projects that contain more than one control in a single OCX file.

- You can create bound controls with very little effort.

- You can use Visual Basic to create controls for use in other languages and within World Wide Web pages.

- With the ability to have multiple projects within a single Visual Basic session, debugging your controls is very easy. Other server projects such as ActiveX DLLs are also simple to debug.

That's the good news. Here are the limitations:

- Controls are not multithreaded within a single instance. They are in-process servers and as such run in the same process as their client. Visual Basic 6 gives you the ability to have only multithreaded objects that have no user interface.

- Because they run in the same process as the client, controls created using Visual Basic 6 cannot be used with 16-bit client applications.

ActiveX or in line? That is the question

When creating controls, you need to be aware of how they are to be distributed or used. Visual Basic 5 was the first version to support controls in code (as opposed to separately compiled objects). This opens the question of whether to compile your controls into traditional ActiveX controls for distribution as separate OCX files or to use them as source code objects and compile them into your application.

As with most things in life, there is no definitive answer, but there are some factors to consider when deciding.

The case for ActiveX controls   Here are some advantages of using ActiveX controls, along with a couple of drawbacks with using in-line controls.

- ActiveX controls can be used in languages and development environments other than Visual Basic, and of course they can be used in Web pages.

- ActiveX controls are beneficial if your control is to be used widely, across many applications.

- With ActiveX controls, bug fixes require only the OCX file to be redistributed. If the control is in line, you might have to recompile all applications that use that control.

- Because they are included in the client as source code, in-line controls are susceptible to hacking. They are more difficult to control (no pun intended) when curious programmers are let loose on them.

Didn't I Write That Function Last Week? Chapter

14

The case for in-line controls Consider the following factors when thinking about using in-line controls:

- You might have to look into licensing implications if you're distributing your ActiveX controls with a commercial application. This is obviously not an issue with in-line controls. (Licensing is covered in more detail shortly.)

- The reduction of the number of files that you have to distribute can make ongoing maintenance and updates easier to support with in-line controls.

Your environment will largely select your deployment policy. If you're writing an application for a system that has very little control over the desktop environment, incorporating controls into your application might well be a way of avoiding support nightmares. If the system supports object-based applications and has strong control over the desktop, the benefits of creating controls as separate OCXs are persuasive.

Licensing implications

Because of their dual nature, controls present unique licensing issues in both design-time and run-time environments. Two main issues are associated with creating and distributing ActiveX DLLs. The first involves licensing your own control. Microsoft has made this deliriously easy. Just display the Properties dialog box for your ActiveX Control project, and check the Require License Key check box at the foot of the General tab. This creates a license key that is placed in the system Registry when your ActiveX control is installed. This key enables the control to be used within the development environment and to be included in a project. When the project is distributed, however, the key is encoded in the executable and not added to the Registry of the target machine. This prevents the control from being used within the design-time environment on that machine. Visual Basic does it all for you!

The second licensing issue surrounds the use of third-party controls embedded within your own control. When you compile your control, the license keys of any constituent third-party controls are not encoded in your control. Additionally, when your control is installed on another machine, the license key for your control will be added to the Registry, but the license keys of any of these contained controls are not. So although your control might have been installed correctly, it won't work unless the controls it contains are separately licensed to work on the target machine.

If you're writing for an in-house development, licensing will be largely irrelevant. For those writing controls for a third-party product or as part of a commercial product, however, licensing is an important issue. You need to be able to protect your copyright, and fortunately you have been given the means to do so.

Storing properties using the *PropertyBag* object

PropertyBag is an object introduced in Visual Basic 5. This object is of use exclusively for creating controls and ActiveX documents.

The *PropertyBag* object is a mechanism by which any of your control's properties set within the Visual Basic Integrated Development Environment (IDE) can be stored. All controls have to store their properties somewhere. If you open a Visual Basic form file in a text editor such as Notepad, you'll see at the start of the form file a whole raft of text that you wouldn't normally see within the Visual Basic IDE. This text describes the form, its settings, and the controls and their settings contained within it. This is where *PropertyBag* stores the property settings of your control, with any binary information being stored in the equivalent FRX file.

This object is passed to your control during the ReadProperties and Write-Properties events. The ReadProperties event occurs immediately after a control's Initialize event, usually when its parent form is loaded within the run-time or the design-time environment. This event is an opportunity for you to retrieve all of your stored property settings and apply them. You can do this by using the *ReadProperty* method of the *PropertyBag* object. This is illustrated in the following ReadProperties event from the DateEdit example control found on the book's companion CD in the CHAP14 folder.

```
Private Sub UserControl_ReadProperties(PropBag As PropertyBag)

    '
    ' Load property values from storage.
    '
    Set m_MouseIcon = PropBag.ReadProperty("MouseIcon", Nothing)

    Set Font = PropBag.ReadProperty("Font", Ambient.Font)

    txtDateEdit.ForeColor = PropBag.ReadProperty("ForeColor", _
        vbWindowText)
```

```
    txtDateEdit.FontName = PropBag.ReadProperty("FontName", _
        "MS Sans Serif")

    txtDateEdit.FontSize = PropBag.ReadProperty("FontSize", 8.25)

    txtDateEdit.FontBold = PropBag.ReadProperty("FontBold", 0)

    txtDateEdit.FontItalic = PropBag.ReadProperty("FontItalic", 0)


    '
    ' Convert any Null dates to empty strings.
    '
    If IsNull(m_MinDate) Then m_MinDate = ""

    If IsNull(m_MaxDate) Then m_MaxDate = ""
```

End Sub

The *ReadProperty* method has two arguments: the first is the name of the property you want to read; and the second, optional, argument is the default value of that property. The *ReadProperty* method will search the *PropertyBag* object for your property. If it finds it, the value stored will be returned; otherwise, the default value you supplied will be returned. If no default value was supplied and no value was retrieved from *PropertyBag*, nothing will be returned and the variable or the object you were assigning the property to will remain unchanged.

Similarly, you can make your properties persistent by using the WriteProperties event. This event occurs less frequently, usually when the client form is unloaded or after a property has been changed within the IDE. Run-time property changes are obviously not stored in this way. You would not want them to be persistent.

The *WriteProperty* method has three arguments: the first is the name of the property you want to store; the second is the data value to be stored; and the third is optional, the default value for the property. This method will store your data value and the associated name you supply unless your data value matches the default value. If you specified a data value that matches the default value, no value is stored, but when you use *ReadProperty* to find this entry in *PropertyBag*, the default value will be returned. If you don't specify a default value in your call to *WriteProperty*, the data value will always be stored.

The following code is from the WriteProperties event of the DateEdit control. It illustrates the use of *PropertyBag*'s *WriteProperty* method.

```
Private Sub UserControl_WriteProperties(PropBag As PropertyBag)

    '
    ' Write property values to storage.
    '
    Call PropBag.WriteProperty("ForeColor", txtDateEdit.ForeColor, _
        vbWindowText)
    Call PropBag.WriteProperty("Enabled", m_Enabled, m_def_Enabled)
    Call PropBag.WriteProperty("FontName", txtDateEdit.FontName, _
        "")
    Call PropBag.WriteProperty("FontSize", txtDateEdit.FontSize, 0)
    Call PropBag.WriteProperty("FontBold", txtDateEdit.FontBold, 0)
    Call PropBag.WriteProperty("FontItalic", _
        txtDateEdit.FontItalic, 0)
    ⋮

End Sub
```

Property pages

Visual Basic 5 introduced property pages, which are of exclusive use to controls. These are dialog boxes you can call up from within the Visual Basic IDE that display a control's properties in a friendly tabbed dialog box format. Each property page is used as a tab within the tabbed dialog box. Visual Basic controls the tabs and the OK, Cancel, and Apply buttons for you. Additionally, you are provided with ready-made Font, Picture, and Color pages to use if necessary, which you should use whenever possible for a little more code and user interface reuse. Figure 14-9 shows the Property Pages dialog box for the DateEdit control.

Visual Basic 6 allows you to create property pages for your control. It is important that you do this. If you have gone to the trouble of writing the control in the first place, you owe it to yourself and others to make the control as easy to use as possible. Designing a property page is no different from designing a form: you can drop controls directly onto it and then write your code behind the events as usual.

When any changes are made to a property using your property page, you need to set the property page's *Changed* property to True. This tells Visual Basic to enable the Apply command button and also tells it to raise a new event, ApplyChanges, in response to the user clicking the OK or the Apply command button. Apply the new property values when the user clicks OK or Apply; don't apply any changes as the user makes them because by doing so, you would

Didn't I Write That Function Last Week?   Chapter

14

prevent the user from canceling any changes: the ApplyChanges event is not raised when the Cancel command button is clicked.

Since more than one control can be selected within the IDE, property pages use a collection, *SelectedControls*, to work with them. You'll have to consider how each of the properties displayed will be updated if multiple controls are selected. You wouldn't want to try to set all of the indexes in an array of controls to the same value. You can use another new event, SelectionChanged, which is raised when the property pages are first loaded and if the selection of controls is changed while the property pages are displayed. You should use this event to check the number of members of the *SelectedControls* collection. If this number is greater than 1, you need to prevent the user from amending those properties that would not benefit from having all controls set to the same value, by disabling their related controls on the property pages.

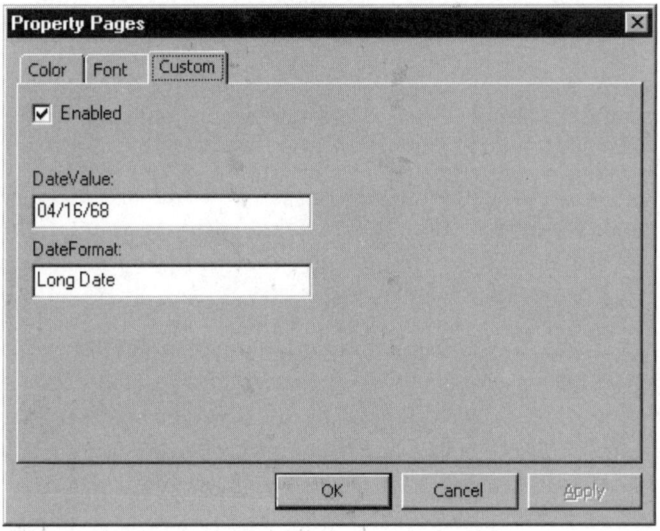

Figure 14-9   *Property pages in use within the Visual Basic IDE*

Binding a control

As mentioned previously, Microsoft has also given us the ability to bind our controls (through a Data control or a RemoteData control) to a data source. This is remarkably easy to do as long as you know where to look for the option. You have to select Procedure Attributes from the Tools menu. This will display the Procedure Attributes dialog box shown in Figure 14-10 on page 629.

This dialog box is useful when you're designing controls. It allows you to select the Default property and the category in which to show each property within the Categorized tab of the Properties window. It also allows you to specify a property as data-bound, which is what we're interested in here. By checking the option Property Is Data Bound in the Data Binding section, you're able to select the other options that will define your control's bound behavior.

Option	Meaning
This Property Binds To DataField	This option is fairly obvious. It allows you to have the current field bound to a Data control. Visual Basic will add and look after the DataSource and DataField properties of your control.
Show In DataBindings Collection At Design Time	The DataBindings collection is used when a control can be bound to more than one field. An obvious example would be a Grid control, which could possibly bind to every field available from a Data control.
Property Will Call CanPropertyChange Before Changing	If you always call *CanPropertyChange* (see below), you should check this box to let Visual Basic know.

By using the first option, you're able to create a standard bound control that you'll be able to attach immediately to a Data control and use. The remaining options are less obvious.

The *DataBindings* collection is a mechanism for binding a control to more than one field. This obviously has a use where you create a control as a group of existing controls, for example, to display names stored in separate fields. By selecting *Title, Forename,* and *Surname* properties to appear in the *DataBindings* collection, you're able to bind each of these to the matching field made available by the Data control.

You should call the *CanPropertyChange* function whenever you attempt to change the value of a bound property. This function is designed to check that you are able to update the field that the property is bound to, returning True if this is the case. Visual Basic Help states that currently this function always returns True and if you try to update a field that is read-only no error is raised. You'd certainly be wise to call this function anyway so that it's ready when Microsoft decides to switch it on.

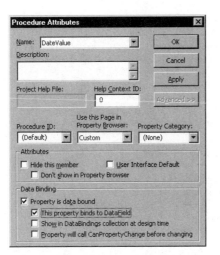

FIGURE 14-10   *The Procedure Attributes dialog box showing Advanced options*

The wizards

Microsoft supplies two useful wizards with Visual Basic 5 and 6 that can make creating controls much easier. The ActiveX Control Interface Wizard, shown in Figure 14-11, helps in the creation of a control's interface and can also insert code for common properties such as *Font* and *BackColor*. The Property Page Wizard does a similar job for the creation of property pages to accompany your control. Once again, standard properties such as *Font* and *Color* can be selected from the ready-made property pages. Using these wizards can prove invaluable in creating the controls and their property pages and also in learning the finer points in their design.

You should use both wizards: between them, they promote a consistency of design to both the properties of your controls and the user interface used to modify these properties. The example DateEdit control used throughout this section was created using both of these wizards. Any chapter about code reuse would be churlish if it failed to promote these wizards. Of course, no wizards yet created can control what you do with the user interface of the controls themselves!

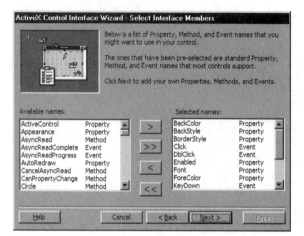

FIGURE 14-11   *The ActiveX Control Interface Wizard*

Controls: a conclusion

The ability to create controls is an important addition to Visual Basic's abilities. Microsoft has put a lot of work into this feature. As a means to code reuse, the abilities of controls are obviously limited to projects that contain forms, but the strength of controls has always been in the user interface.

A lot more could be written about controls—far more than we have space for in this chapter. Do take the time to read the Visual Basic manuals, which go into more depth, and experiment with the samples. After all, writing controls in Visual Basic is certainly much easier than writing them in C++!

Using a ROOS

Another aid to reusability, first mentioned in Chapter 1, is the ROOS (Resource Only Object Server), pronounced "ruse." We've referred to object servers as object components for most of this chapter, but these are two different names for the same object. (To be politically correct, they should really be called ActiveX components, but ROAC is not as easy to pronounce!) A ROOS essentially stores string, bitmap, and other resources that are liable to be changed at some time. Another use for a ROOS is to store multilanguage strings. If you wrote an application to be sold in the United States and in France, using the normal Visual Basic method of setting display text in code would mean that you would have to create two versions of the application: one with English display text and captions and one with French. Obviously, this would create a significant maintenance overhead, because if you have to apply a bug fix to one of the versions, you also need to apply the change to the other. The ROOS is exactly the same in principle as a resource-only DLL as used by many C and C++ programmers. The difference between a ROOS and its DLL counterpart is that the ROOS is an object component and as such can be deployed anywhere on a network and used by any client components.

You can store many types of resources in a ROOS:

Accelerator table	Group cursor
Bitmap resource	Group icon
Cursor resource	Icon resource
Dialog box	Menu resource
Font directory resource	String resource
Font resource	User-defined resource

A ROOS has two components. The first is the resource module, a special file created with an application such as Microsoft Visual C++. The resource module contains all the resources you want to store and retrieve. The second element of the ROOS is a method to retrieve a resource from the resource module. At TMS, we prefer to expand the functionality of the ROOS methods so that string values can be parsed with input parameters. The following example illustrates this.

Resource entries

```
String ID:    400
String value: "The operation completed with % errors"
```

Client code

```
StringID = 400
MyText = GetStringFromROOS(StringID, "no")
```

ROOS code

```
Public Function GetStringFromROOS(StringID As String, _
    Param) As String
    Dim sText  As String

    sText = GetString(StringID)
    sText = MergeString(sText, Param)
    GetStringFromROOS = sText

End Function
```

Result

```
MyText: "The operation completed with no errors"
```

Many projects store custom error messages or other display text in a database file. In an error handler, the custom error text is better in a ROOS because the execution speed is much faster, and many organizations restrict access to make database changes to the database administrator—no good if you're a programmer and have to wait two days to change the caption on a button! Another excellent use of a ROOS is to store icons and bitmaps. Imagine you're lucky enough to have an artist to create all your graphics. You can create a ROOS with dummy resources, and then the artist can add the real graphics to the ROOS as they become available without having to access any source code. (No more multiple access problems!)

Creating a resource module is easy if you have the right tools. You simply enter the resources you want. Each resource has an ID value, which is a long integer. To retrieve the resource from the resource module, you simply use the *LoadRes-Data*, *LoadResPicture*, or *LoadResString* command specifying the resource's ID. Figure 14-12 shows a typical resource file in Microsoft Visual C++ 6. Once the resource module is created (it's actually an RC file), you simply compile it with the RC.EXE program (supplied on the Visual Basic CD-ROM) to create a RES file that you can add to your ROOS project. You can have only one RES file in a single Visual Basic project, but one is plenty! (If you don't have access to Visual C++ or any other tool for creating resource files, you can use an editor such as Notepad. Before attempting this, however, you should study an RC file and a RESOURCE.H file to become familiar with the format.)

Obviously, any client requesting data from the ROOS will need to know the ID value for each resource. In Visual Basic 4, you would need to include your ID constants in each client application, either as hard-coded constants or in a shared type library. With Visual Basic 5 and 6, you can declare all your IDs within the ROOS as enumerated constants, which makes them automatically available to client applications.

Listing 14-1 shows a slightly more advanced ROOS that retrieves string and bitmap resources. The ROOS allows you to merge an unlimited number of tokens into a string resource. To create a string resource with tokens, simply insert a % symbol in the string where the supplied parameter(s) will be substituted.

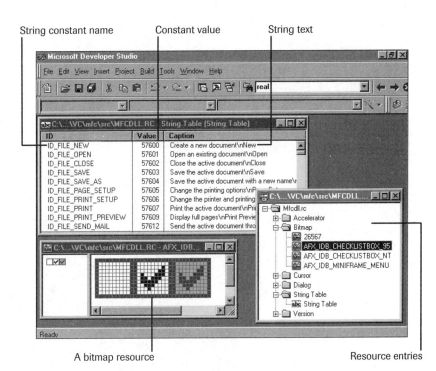

String constant name   Constant value   String text

A bitmap resource   Resource entries

FIGURE 14-12 *A resource file created in Microsoft Visual C++ 6*

```
' The following Enums declare the resource ID of the bitmaps
' in our RES file. The include file "resource.h" generated
' by the resource editor defines the constants to match each
' bitmap. Checking this file shows the first bitmap resource
' ID to be 101; therefore, these Enums are declared to match
' this.
Public Enum BITMAPS


' ***
' *** NOTE: Any new bitmaps added must be inserted between
' *** IDB_TOPVALUE and IDB_LASTVALUE because these constants are
' *** used to validate input parameters.
' ***
```

>>

LISTING 14-1 *ROOS for retrieving string and bitmap resources*

LISTING 14-1
>>

```
        idb_topvalue = 100
        IDB_SELECTSOURCE
        IDB_SELECTDESTIN
        IDB_NUMBERSOURCE
        IDB_COMPLETED
        idb_lastvalue
End Enum


Public Enum STRINGS

    ' VBP project file key ID words
    IDS_VBP_KEY_FORM = 500
    IDS_VBP_KEY_CLASS
    IDS_VBP_KEY_MODULE
    IDS_VBP_SEP_FORM
    IDS_VBP_SEP_CLASS
    IDS_VBP_SEP_MODULE
    IDS_VBP_SEP_RESFILE
    IDS_VBP_KEY_RESOURCE16
    IDS_VBP_KEY_RESOURCE32

    ' Procedure keywords
    IDS_PROCKEY_SUB1 = 600
    IDS_PROCKEY_SUB2
    IDS_PROCKEY_SUB3
    IDS_PROCKEY_FUNC1
    IDS_PROCKEY_FUNC2
    IDS_PROCKEY_FUNC3
    IDS_PROCKEY_PROP1
    IDS_PROCKEY_PROP2
    IDS_PROCKEY_PROP3
    IDS_PROCKEY_END1
    IDS_PROCKEY_END2
    IDS_PROCKEY_END3
    IDS_PROCKEY_SELECT
    IDS_PROCKEY_CASE
    IDS_PROCKEY_COMMENT

    ' File filter strings
    IDS_FILTER_FRX = 700
    IDS_FILTER_PROJECT
    IDS_FILTER_CLASS
    IDS_FILTER_FORM
    IDS_FILTER_MODULE
```

```
        IDS_FILTER_CONFIG
        IDS_FILE_TEMP

        ' Displayed caption strings
        IDS_CAP_STEP1 = 800
        IDS_CAP_STEP2
        IDS_CAP_STEP3
        IDS_CAP_STEP4
        IDS_CAP_NUMBER

IDS_CAP_UNNUMBER
        IDS_CAP_CANCEL
        IDS_CAP_FINISH
        IDS_CAP_CANCEL_ALLOWED

        ' Message strings
        IDS_MSG_NOT_TEMPLATE = 900
        IDS_MSG_COMPLETE_STATUS
        IDS_MSG_TEMPL_CORRUPT
        IDS_MSG_INVALID_CONFIG
        IDS_MSG_CREATE_TMPL_ERR
        IDS_MSG_NO_SOURCE
        IDS_MSG_INVALID_DESTIN
        IDS_MSG_SAME_SRC_DESTIN
        IDS_MSG_QUERY_EXIT
        IDS_MSG_ABORTED

        ' Err.Description strings
        IDS_ERR_GDI = 1000
        IDS_ERR_PROCESS_ERROR
End Enum

' Resource ROOS error constants
Public Enum RR_Errors
        RR_INVALID_BITMAP_ID = 2000 ' Invalid bitmap resource ID
        RR_INVALID_STRING_ID        ' Invalid string resource ID
End Enum

Public Sub PuGetBmp(ByVal ilBitmapID As Long, _
        ByVal ictl As Control)

        ' Check that the ID value passed is valid. This is an
        ' Assert type of message, but the class cannot be part
        ' of the design environment, so raise an error instead.
```

LISTING 14-1

```
      If ilBitmapID <= idb_topvalue Or _
          ilBitmapID >= idb_lastvalue Then

          Err.Description = "An invalid bitmap ID value '" & _
              ilBitmapID & "' was passed."
          Err.Number = RR_INVALID_BITMAP_ID
          Err.Raise Err.Number
          Exit Sub
      End If

      ' Load the bitmap into the picture of the control passed.
      ictl.Picture = LoadResPicture(ilBitmapID, vbResBitmap)
  End Sub

  Public Function sPuGetStr(ByVal ilStringID As Long, _
      Optional ByVal ivArgs As Variant) As String

      Dim nIndex          As Integer
      Dim nPointer        As Integer
      Dim nTokenCount     As Integer
      Dim sResString      As String
      Dim vTempArg        As Variant

      Const ARG_TOKEN     As String = "%"

      sResString = LoadResString(ilStringID)

      If IsMissing(ivArgs) Then GoTo END_GETRESOURCESTRING

      If (VarType(ivArgs) And vbArray) <> vbArray Then

          ' Single argument passed. Store the value so that we can
          ' convert ivArgs to an array with this single
          ' value.
          vTempArg = ivArgs
          ivArgs = Empty
          ReDim ivArgs(0)

          ivArgs(0) = vTempArg
      End If

      nTokenCount = 0

      Do While nTokenCount < UBound(ivArgs) _
          = LBound(ivArgs) + 1
```

```
        nPointer = InStr(sResString, ARG_TOKEN)
        If nPointer = 0 Then

            ' There are more arguments than tokens in the RES
            ' string, so exit the loop.

            Exit Do
        End If



        Call sPiReplaceToken(sResString, ARG_TOKEN, _
            ivArgs(LBound(ivArgs) + nTokenCount))
        nTokenCount = nTokenCount + 1
    Loop

END_GETRESOURCESTRING:
    sPuGetStr = sResString
End Function

Private Function sPiReplaceToken(ByRef iosTokenStr As String, _
    ByVal isToken As String, ByVal ivArgs As Variant)

    Dim nPointer As Integer

    nPointer = InStr(iosTokenStr, isToken)
    If nPointer <> 0 Then
        iosTokenStr = Left$(iosTokenStr, nPointer - 1) & _
            ivArgs & Mid$(iosTokenStr, nPointer + 1)
    End If
End Function
```

REUSE ISSUES FOR THE PROGRAMMER

Good computer programming relies on a structured methodology that consists of a number of individual disciplines. For example, commenting your code as you write it is a discipline that you must practice until it becomes second nature. It is a well-known fact that many programmers either do not comment their code at all or comment it only after it's been written. One of the reasons you should comment code as you write it is that at that time you know your exact thought processes and the reasons behind the decisions you're making. If you were to comment the code two weeks after writing it, you might still understand how it works, but you will probably have forgotten subtle details about why you coded something a certain way or what effects a line of code might have on other parts of the application. If you ever see lots of totally meaningless comments, you can be sure they were inserted after the code was written!

The discipline of coding for reusability is very important and comes only with practice. You will know when you've mastered this habit because you'll start writing less code. You should view any piece of code you write as a potentially reusable component. The experience gained from adopting this practice will help you not only to identify reusable units but also to anticipate the situations in which those units might be used. It will also enable you to make better decisions about how loosely or tightly the code can be coupled—it's not possible or efficient in all cases to decouple a code section completely from the other parts of the application. You should also remember that in a multiple-programmer project, other programmers will look to reuse code that other team members have written. Imagine you want a function and that function already exists: will you write it again or use the existing one? Obviously, you will reuse the existing function unless one or all of these conditions are true:

- You think the code is of poor quality.
- The code doesn't meet your requirements.
- You don't know the code exists.
- The code is poorly documented or commented.

Experience will also help you make the right choices about the way that a unit couples to other units. A good practice to adopt is to write all your code modularly, encapsulating it as much as possible. A typical program consists of a series of calls to functions and subroutines. At the top level—for example, in a text box KeyPress event—a series of calls can be made. The functions that you call from within this event should, wherever possible, be coded as if they were contained in object components; that is, they should have no knowledge of the environment. It is the linking code, or the code in the KeyPress event, that needs to know about the environment. By coding functions and subroutines in a modular way, you can reuse them in a number of situations. You should also avoid embedding application-specific functionality in these top-level events because this prevents the code from being reused effectively. Look at the following sample code, which capitalizes the first letter of each word in the text box Text1:

```
Sub Text1_KeyPress(KeyAscii As Integer)

    If Text1.SelStart = 0 Then
        ' This is the first character, so change to uppercase.
        KeyAscii = Asc(UCase$(Chr$(KeyAscii)))
    Else
        ' If the previous character is a space, capitalize
        ' the current character.
        If Mid$(Text1, Text1.SelStart, 1) = Space$(1) Then
            KeyAscii = Asc(UCase$(Chr$(KeyAscii)))
        End If
    End If
End Sub
```

The functionality in the KeyPress event is tied explicitly to Text1. To reuse this code, you would have to cut and paste it and then change every reference made to Text1 to the new control. The code would be truly reusable if written like this:

```
Sub Text1_KeyPress(KeyAscii As Integer)
    KeyAscii = nConvertToCaps(Text1, KeyAscii)
End Sub

Function nConvertToCaps(ByVal ctl As Control, _
    ByRef nChar As Integer) As Integer

    If ctl.SelStart = 0 Then
        ' This is the first character, so change to uppercase.
        nChar = Asc(UCase$(Chr$(nChar)))
    Else
        ' If the previous character is a space, capitalize
        ' the current character.
        If Mid$(ctl, ctl.SelStart, 1) = Space$(1) Then
            nChar = Asc(UCase$(Chr$(nChar)))
        End If
    End If

    nConvertToCaps = nChar
End Function
```

The *nConvertToCaps* function has no knowledge of the control it is acting on and therefore can be used by any code that has appropriate input parameters. You will often write procedures that you might not foresee anyone else using. By assuming the opposite, that *all* your code will be reused, you will reduce the time you or others require to modify functionality later for reuse.

The effects of not writing for reuse can be seen in many development projects but might not be obvious at first. At a high level, it is easy to break down an application into distinct components and code those components as discrete modular units using any of the methods described above. However, there is nearly always a large expanse of code that doesn't fit neatly into a distinct modular pattern. This is usually the application's binding code—that is, the logic that controls program flow and links various system components. Processes that are not major components in themselves but simply provide auxiliary functionality are normally assumed rather than specified formally, which is yet another reason why estimating can go wrong when this functionality is not considered. The result of bad design of these elements will usually lead to spaghetti code. The following sections discuss some habits that you should practice until they become automatic.

Make Few Assumptions

In an application, you'll often need to use variables that contain indeterminate formats. For example, an application might have several variables or properties storing directory names. When using these variables, you have to add a filename to get a full file specification. How do you know whether the path stored in the variable contains a backslash? Most applications have an *AppendSlash* routine that adds a backslash to a path if it doesn't have one, so you might be tempted to assume the format just because you've run it once in debug mode to check. You need to keep in mind, especially in large projects, that values of variables are often changed by other programmers, so a path that has the trailing backslash in one instance might not in another. Depending on the application, you might discover these errors immediately or not until some later time. In the case of the backslash, rather than rely on it being there, assume it could be missing and use your *AppendSlash* routine to check for it everywhere. You should apply this thinking whenever a particular format cannot be guaranteed.

Develop a Coupling Strategy

Nonspecified code can often suffer problems caused by tight coupling. Because nonspecified code doesn't form part of a major unit, programmers often pay less attention to its interaction with other parts of the application. Where possible, you should pass parameters into procedures rather than use module-level variables. Input parameters that won't need to be changed should always be declared by value (*ByVal*) rather than the default, by reference (*ByRef*). Many programmers choose the by reference method simply because it saves typing.

Another common excuse for using *ByRef* is the argument of speed: passing by reference is a few milliseconds faster than passing by value because Visual Basic has to create a copy of the variable when it's passed by value. But the consequence of misusing *ByRef* can be severe in terms of debugging time. Imagine a seldom-used application configuration variable that gets inadvertently changed by another procedure. You might not detect the error until someone uses the configuration function several times—maybe even long after you've written the code. Now imagine trying to trace the cause of the problem! As a rule, always pass parameters by value unless you explicitly want changes to be passed back to the caller.

The purposes of passing parameters to a procedure rather than using module-level variables are to make it obvious to anyone not familiar with the code exactly what external dependencies are being used, and to allow the procedure to be rewritten or reused more easily. A good practice is to document procedure parameters in a header box. A header box is simply a series of comments at the beginning of a procedure that explains the purpose of the procedure. Any external dependencies should also be documented here. Often programmers do not reuse functionality simply because the parameters or dependencies are unclear or not easy to understand. Imagine a procedure that accepts an array containing 20 data items. If the procedure is dependent on all 20 data items being present, other programmers might find it difficult to use unless it is well documented.

Passing parameters to procedures allows you to create code that is loosely coupled and therefore potentially reusable. The following code fragment shows a would-be reusable procedure that is too tightly coupled to the form it's in to be reused anywhere else in that application, let alone in another application:

```
Sub SearchForFile(ByVal isFile As String)

    ' Disable all buttons.
    cmdClose.Enabled = False
    cmdView.Enabled = False

    ' Process
    ⋮
    labStatus = "File " & isFile
    ⋮
```

The procedure is rewritten here in a more reusable way:

```
Sub cmdProcess_Click()

    Dim ctlDisableArray(0 To 1) As Control
    Dim sFile                   As String

    sFile = filename
    ctlDisableArray(0) = cmdClose
    ctlDisableArray(1) = cmdView

    Call SearchForFile(sFile, ctlDisableArray(), labStatus)
    ⋮
End Sub

Sub SearchForFile(ByVal isFile As String, _
    Optional ctlDisable() As Control, _
    Optional labUpdate As Label)

    Dim nIndex   As Integer

    ' Disable all buttons if any are specified.
    If Not IsMissing(ctlDisable) Then
        For nIndex = LBound(ctlDisable) To UBound(ctlDisable)
            ctlDisable(nIndex).Enabled = False
        Next nIndex
    End If

    ' Process
    ⋮
    If Not IsMissing(labUpdate) Then
        labUpdate = "File " & isFile
    End If
    ⋮
```

Now the procedure is totally decoupled and can be called from anywhere in the application.

Another good practice to adopt is using more flexible parameter types for inputs to a procedure. In Chapter 4, Jon Burn says, "Use Variants for everything." If you take Jon's advice, you should be careful to validate the parameters and display helpful errors. In a simple application, you can easily locate the cause of an error; but if the error occurs in a compiled ActiveX control, it might be a different story. The sample code here is the procedure declaration for a subroutine that fills a list box from an array:

```
Public Sub FillList(ByVal lst As ListBox, anArray() As Integer)
```

Didn't I Write That Function Last Week? CHAPTER

14

The function might work fine, but it's restrictive. Imagine you have another type of list box control that has some added functionality. You won't be able to pass it into this function. It's also possible that someone might want to use this routine with a combo box. The code will be similar, so this is a feasible request. However, you won't be able to use the procedure above with a combo box. If the routine is part of the application, you can rewrite it; more than likely, however, you'll write another routine instead. If the routine is in a DLL file, rewriting it might not be so easy. In the following code, the procedure header is changed to make it more generic and the rest of the code is added as well:

```
Public Sub FillList(ByVal ctl As Control, anArray() As Integer)
    Dim nIndex  As Integer

    For nIndex = LBound(anArray) To UBound(anArray)
        ctl.AddItem anArray(nIndex)
    Next nIndex

End Sub
```

Notice the potential problem now in this routine, however. If any control that doesn't have an *AddItem* method is passed to the routine, it will fail. It might be some time later, when another programmer calls the routine, that the error is detected; and if the routine is in a DLL, it might take some time to debug. What we need is some defensive programming. Always try to code as if the procedure is part of an external DLL in which other programmers cannot access the source code. In this example, you can use defensive coding in two ways: by using *Debug.Assert* or by raising an error.

The *Debug.Assert* method, introduced in Visual Basic 5, evaluates an expression that you supply and, if the expression is false, executes a break. C programmers use these assertions in their code all the time. This method is intended to trap development-type errors that you don't expect to occur once the system is complete. You should never use assertions in a built executable; therefore, the method has been added to the *Debug* object. In a built executable, *Debug.Assert* is ignored, just as with the *Debug.Print* method. You could use an assertion here like this:

```
Public Sub FillList(ByVal ctl As Control, anArray() As Integer)

    Dim nIndex  As Integer

    ' Assert - This subroutine handles only ListBox and ComboBox.
    Debug.Assert TypeOf ctl Is ListBox Or _
```

```
      TypeOf ctl Is ComboBox

  For nIndex = LBound(anArray) To UBound(anArray)
    ⋮
```

This will now trap the error if the routine is running in design mode. Because the debugger will break on the assert line, it's always best to put a comment around the assert so that another programmer triggering the assert can easily identify the problem.

With our example, the assert is not a good method to use for defensive programming because we might put this routine into a DLL, in which case the assert would be ignored and the user would get an error. A better way would be to raise an error. When you raise an error, the code that calls this function will have to deal with the problem. Think of the *Open* procedure in Visual Basic. If you try to open a file that doesn't exist, the *Open* procedure raises the error, "File not found." We can do the same with our routine:

```
Public Sub FillList(ByVal ctl As Control, anArray() As Integer)

    Dim nIndex  As Integer

    Const ERR_INVALID_CONTROL = 3000

    If Not(TypeOf ctl Is ListBox) And _
        Not(TypeOf ctl Is ComboBox) Then

        Err.Number = ERR_INVALID_CONTROL
        Err.Description = "An invalid control " & ctl.Name & _
            " was passed to sub 'FillList' - "
        Err.Raise Err.Number

    End If

    For nIndex = LBound(anArray) To UBound(anArray)
      ⋮
```

This method will work in any situation, but it has two problems. The first problem is not really a problem in this instance because the caller won't be expecting an error. If the caller were anticipating an error, however, we might want to check the error number and perform a specific action. Visual Basic 4 allowed type libraries in which you could declare constants and declarations to include in a project. The main problem with these was that you couldn't create a type library within Visual Basic. It also meant that any client project would need to include the type library, thus increasing dependencies.

Didn't I Write That Function Last Week?   Chapter

14

Enumerated constants is a feature introduced in Visual Basic 5. Let's see how the code looks before we explain what's happening:

```
' General declarations

Public Enum CustomErrors
    ERR_INVALID_CONTROL = 3000
    ERR_ANOTHER_ERROR
    ⋮
End Enum

Public Sub FillList(ByVal ctl As Control, anArray() As Integer)

    Dim nIndex  As Integer

    If Not(TypeOf ctl Is ListBox) And _
        Not(TypeOf ctl Is ComboBox) Then

        Err.Number = CustomErrors.ERR_INVALID_CONTROL
        Err.Description = "An invalid control " & ctl.Name & _
            " was passed to sub 'FillList' - " &
        ⋮
```

The constants are declared between the *Enum...End Enum*, just as in a user-defined type. The *Enum* name can be used to explicitly scope to the correct constant if you have duplicates. Notice that the second constant in the example doesn't have a value assigned. With enumerated constants, if you specify a value, it will be used. If you don't specify a value, one is assigned, starting from 0 or the previous constant plus 1. Enumerated constants can contain only long integers. The big advantage in using enumerated constants is that they can be public. For example, if you create a class, any client of that class can access the constants. Now you don't have to have constants with global scope, and you don't need to create type libraries. In effect, the module becomes more encapsulated.

The second potential problem with the function on the previous page is that the array might be empty—but not the kind of empty that you can check with the *IsEmpty* function. If our sample code were to be passed an array that didn't contain any elements (for example, it might have been cleared using *Erase*), you would get a "Subscript out of range" error as soon as you used *LBound* on it. A much better way of passing arrays is to use a Variant array. A Variant array is simply a variable declared as type Variant that you *ReDim*. If the array has no elements, *IsEmpty* will return True. You can also check that an array as opposed to, say, a string has been passed. The code looks like what you see on the next page.

```
Public Sub FillList(ctl As Control, vArray As Variant)

    Dim nIndex  As Integer

    ' Exit if array is empty.
    If IsEmpty(vArray) Then Exit Sub

    ' Exit if not an Integer array.
    If VarType(vArray) <> vbArray Or _
        VarType(vArray) <> vbInteger Then
        ' Error
```

The techniques described all help you to achieve the following benefits:

- Create reusable and generic code by creating loosely coupled routines and components
- Help others to reuse your code
- Protect your code from errors caused by client code

Group Functionality

You might be surprised at how many applications contain functions that fall into a particular category but are fragmented across the application. Such fragmentation often occurs when many programmers are working on the same application and the module names don't clearly identify the type of functionality the modules contain. The ownership aspect also comes into play: some programmers don't like to amend another programmer's code. Access conflict might also be an issue. It is good practice to familiarize yourself with other modules in the application so that you can group functionality and also identify functionality that you can use. Grouping reusable functionality has the added benefit that it can be extracted in separate DLLs at a later stage.

Document Your Code

Visual Basic now has an excellent Object Browser. You can include detailed documentation about your functions that will prevent others from constantly having to ask questions about routines you have written. Unfortunately, for many programmers, writing documentation is like going to the dentist. It is also a task that never gets included in project plans, so it almost never gets done. It is vital that you increase your estimates to allow time for these tasks.

Refine Your Habits

We've made only a few suggestions here—there are lots more. If you decide on a set of good habits and constantly practice and refine them, your organization will benefit because of the development time you'll save, and you will benefit because you'll need to do much less debugging. Each time you complete a project, review it and identify areas that you could have improved.

Reusability has to be supported by the business, designed by the designers, and coded by the programmers. Unless all sides commit to the goal of reusability, you will be doomed to continually rewrite most of your code.

How to Juggle 30 Balls Blindfolded

Making Enterprise Development a Success

MARK SEWELL

Mark is a director and a cofounder of TMS, and is TMS's expert on software development processes, project management, and team structures. Mark is a Microsoft Visual Basic Certified Professional; cowrote a Visual Basic programmer's product, "TMS Tools"; teaches Visual Basic; and project managed the development of MicroHelp's Code Complete. Mark has presented at VBITS and other conferences and writes many articles. He previously worked for Price Waterhouse, Logica, Sema Group, and IBM. He likes to spend most of his spare time with his wife and children, avoiding anything to do with computers. Mark would like to acknowledge the contribution that Alan Inglis made to the original version of this chapter in the previous edition of this book.

"Once we truly know that life is difficult—once we truly understand and accept it—then life is no longer difficult. Because once it is accepted, it no longer matters."

M. Scott Peck

Software development has been going on for more than thirty years, so you'd think that by now successful development projects would be the norm. Yet consider these statistics: More than 80 percent of all software projects fail. The average large project is a year late. The average small project time estimate is off by more than 100 percent. A project manager's life is a stressful one. The problems are well known and widely published, but in project after project, in company after company, the same mistakes are made over and over again. Plan, estimate, schedule, manage—and when the going gets tough, throw it all away and code. Postmortem reviews reveal the only universal strategy: start at the beginning, keep going until you reach the end, and then stop.

Visual Basic has become much more complex with each new version. Unless projects— particularly large enterprise ones—are properly managed, embarrassing statistics such as those mentioned above will only worsen. This chapter outlines some of the fundamental issues involved in developing large-scale distributed systems using Visual Basic 6. It is aimed at all Visual Basic 6 developers, but project managers who need to understand how the technical environment affects their planning and management should find it particularly useful. System designers and quality assurance (QA) staff who need to understand how important their roles are in delivering a successful project will also find this chapter helpful.

As software development consultants, we at The Mandelbrot Set (International) Limited (TMS) are often asked to comment on why things aren't going quite right with a client's current development project. To find the problem, we normally carry out a project health check and a technical review. We consistently find that in the haste to deliver, Visual Basic developers have abandoned software engineering disciplines that, though not perfect, have evolved over thirty years and are certainly a lot better than the plain code hacking that replaces them. This slack behavior is exhibited by the full range of developers, from junior programmers through project managers. As a result, we keep seeing low-quality, unmaintainable Visual Basic code being written by developers at a high proportion of our client companies, big and small. Why is this happening?

A VISUAL BASIC QUALITY CRISIS?

Men have become the tools of their tools.

Henry David Thoreau

Visual Basic is great! It's an easy, economical, and fast application-development tool, it's a good prototyping tool, and developers love using it. It's fun too! Certainly these comments were true about versions 1, 2, and 3. But with versions 4, 5, and 6 (particularly the Enterprise Editions), things have become infinitely more complex. It is essential that the Visual Basic development mind-set changes—developers need to become much more professional in their approach to programming projects.

Like any high-level programming language, Visual Basic lets the programmer write really awful programs, and with Visual Basic, you can screw up more easily and faster than ever! As with programs in any language, a bad program in Visual Basic can be very hard to maintain. It can be hard to adapt to meet changing business requirements. But with Visual Basic programs, there is a greater danger than with other languages that developers will focus too much on a pretty front end without designing a solid structure on which to hang it.

Important business logic can be attached to GUI widgets rather than placed in reusable objects, making it hard to share and reuse code. And of course, Visual Basic is the perfect tool for maverick code warriors to pump out reams and reams of undocumented and incomprehensible programs. All these factors can lead to severe maintenance and quality problems.

Managers often forget that the Visual Basic coding phase typically takes about 20 to 30 percent of the overall development life cycle. Their expectations of the massive productivity gains to be had from using Visual Basic are totally unrealistic. They have been suckered by the rapid application development (RAD) hype. We feel sorry for Visual Basic—unrealistic plans for it are often drawn up and agreed to, and later the true picture becomes apparent. Then we often hear such laments as, "We can't cut functionality—the business won't tolerate it," or "We can't slip the deadline—it's set in stone," or "We can't throw any more bodies at it without blowing the budget!" When the going gets tough, one or more of the following tends to happen:

- Functionality is cut.
- Deadlines are slipped.
- Bodies are added.
- Quality is reduced.

So what gives? Invariably, it's the quality that suffers the most. And Visual Basic itself gets the blame.

The goals of the organization often conflict with the goals of the Visual Basic team. The organization realizes that building reusable components increases its ability to build better solutions more quickly, whereas individual project teams are typically focused on solving specific problems under tight schedules. The Visual Basic team is pushed so hard that it's next to impossible to consider reuse, despite the fact that the team members would love to generalize their code and make it available to other teams. Unfortunately, they don't have the time to consider problems outside their project.

So is Visual Basic a poor tool for serious enterprise development? We don't think so—quite the contrary. Does Visual Basic 6 solve the problems of the past? It certainly helps. But it can't help solve many of the problems highlighted above because most of those problems relate to people—their attitudes toward Visual Basic software development and the processes they use.

How can Visual Basic software quality be maintained in an enterprise environment? Advanced programmers need the answer. In this chapter, we've listed the simple measures that we consider lead to the production of high-quality Visual Basic 6 applications. We don't aim to present detailed and reasoned arguments. Our views have been honed from years of experience—going all the way back to version 1—observing both good and bad practices in many large organizations developing Visual Basic systems: self-evident truths.

RISK MANAGEMENT

I don't want the cheese, I just want to get out of the trap.

Spanish proverb

Risk is multidimensional, involving business, technical, and people risks that must be managed within the context of the development project's architecture, analysis, design, and implementation phases. (See Figure 15-1.) These risks affect the whole project life cycle. In this section, we'll focus on the technical risks that the introduction of Visual Basic 6 brings.

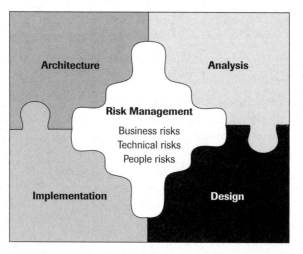

FIGURE 15-1   *Risk management is central to successful system development*

Traditionally, project managers have three major objectives: deliver on time, stick to budget, and create a system that fits its intended purpose. To manage the risks inherent in Visual Basic 6 distributed development, project managers must be aware of business needs, be technically competent and customer focused, and be great team leaders. This kind of development—with its integration of differing, fast-changing components and technologies—has such a high level of risk that some might say only the foolhardy would attempt it. Given such risks, a risk-management strategy is fundamental to successful delivery.

A key factor in heading off problems is moving the technical risks to the beginning of a large project and handling them there. Often, major risks are not addressed until the system test or live running—settings in which the costs of rework or failure are substantially higher. Dealing with the risks early provides a forum for discussing how the project will work and allows broader issues to be addressed. Think of this early technical review as a form of insurance.

Some crucial issues need to be addressed in managing risk: the technical infrastructure, the business environment, and change management.

Technical Infrastructure

Historically, in the mainframe world, we have seen relatively slow evolution of the technical infrastructure and long project-delivery times. This slower pace allows developers to implement a technical strategy that uses a proven technical infrastructure for major system components. The same sort of infrastructure must be established to develop robust systems in Visual Basic 6. Visual Basic 6 Enterprise Edition provides the opportunity for a powerful and flexible development environment, but only if this flexibility is designed into the project. It will be a hefty investment to get it right, and an expensive mistake to get it wrong.

The technical infrastructure includes the hardware, the network, the operating systems, and the tools. All the elements of the infrastructure interact and are constantly changing. This interaction and change is one of the biggest risks. You must work out a method for developing successful systems in this environment.

Visual Basic has recently gone through three releases (4, 5, and 6), all with order-of-magnitude changes in complexity that require very different approaches to development. We've seen Microsoft Windows 95/98, Microsoft Windows NT, and the Internet change the operating environment. Distributed objects and open host operating systems are a reality. Hardware continues to become faster and less expensive. Utility packages such as word processors and spreadsheets have become development tools. The legacy environment, together with these and other tools, forms an ever-changing development infrastructure.

You must be sure of the robustness and performance of the infrastructure under the stresses of live running. If the infrastructure is not proven, then prove it! And keep on proving it!

Business Environment

The business world that our systems support is generally becoming more volatile and is demanding the development of new systems of greater complexity in shorter time frames. We need to develop systems in the context of a corporate business system's architecture that allows rapidly developed systems to integrate and form a basis for future change and development. Systems such as this will help us manage the problems that occur when rapid development approaches are applied to large projects.

Change Management

The more innocuous the modification appears to be, the further its influence will extend and the more plans will have to be redrawn.

Second Law of Revision

You need to anticipate technical and business changes. Databases grow and need restructuring, and underlying system software changes. You should build applications with an architecture that can accommodate change.

Small, simple applications that deliver benefits quickly are preferable to monolithic applications, but the combination of small and very large applications should also provide the same benefit. You need to anticipate the growth of applications—organic growth is natural in successful applications, and you should allow for it.

CRITICAL FACTORS IN SUCCESSFUL ENTERPRISE DEVELOPMENT

Unfortunately, we can offer no formula you can follow that will guarantee the success of your enterprise development. You can greatly improve your odds of succeeding, however, if you adhere to some guidelines as you proceed through the development process. We've discovered, often the hard way, that certain factors are critical to successful enterprise developments.

Insist on Great Project Management

**Misfortunes always come in by a door that has been
left open for them.**

Anonymous

Effective project management is critical to the success of Visual Basic development projects. Strong project management can lead to success even in difficult circumstances. Weak project management can result in failure when success is there for the taking. In the Visual Basic world, many good project managers seem to have mentally wandered off, neglecting their professional responsibilities. The most basic disciplines such as planning, phasing, tracking, managing change, and setting milestones all seem to have been forgotten. Project managers seem to be sucked into a way of working that in their heart-of-hearts they know is wrong—but they do it anyway. The best project managers are prepared to put their jobs on the line to do what's right. They realize that their jobs are at risk anyway. Even the best project managers will be seen to be at fault by someone no matter what the outcome of the project, so why not do the job the right way from the start? *It is essential that proper, disciplined project management occur within every Visual Basic 6 team.*

Visual Basic project managers are typically not technical enough. Project managers cannot lead effectively unless they have credibility within the team and are able to discuss critical design issues. Many of the project managers we speak to don't know, for example, what system resources are, or what the MDI is—even though their team is being forced to code a complex finite state machine as a result of the interface style being chosen.

When we ask a project manager why a substandard Visual Basic application has been released, we normally hear something along the lines of, "The business demanded it quickly," "Our competitors have one, so we had to have one," "We'll use it now and fix it later," "The users expect it now," or "The users are already using it, so we can't withdraw it." The poor management of user expectations and requirements is to blame for much of Visual Basic's bad press. All too often, a manager will allow a program to go live because he or she has failed to adequately manage the expectations of the users (or perhaps of the senior managers).

Visual Basic 6 offers the opportunity to produce component-based solutions. Managing a project of clients and servers in which you do parallel development by using a defined interface (building stubs and then filling them with real functionality) works up to a point; the difficulty comes on the human side.

Parallel development requires a high degree of flexibility and interaction from all members of the team. Developers—especially inexperienced ones—or people who haven't been on a team before find the personal-contract nature of this type of development difficult and would prefer to be told what to do in what order and by what date rather than to make personal, flexible "contracts" with team members. The only way to pull off a parallel development project is by using the following ingredients:

- A great deal of project management effort (micromanaging)
- A highly cooperative, established team
- Long lags and leads

The difficulties compound because of the tendency to fiddle (and to think you can) with declared object interfaces after they are defined.

On the technical front, beware of technical customers—they'll continually want to revisit the design without ever recognizing the impact of this dabbling on the project. Also, even with small teams, on a highly technical project in which people take responsibility for certain areas, the project manager will have trouble keeping on top of the day-to-day technical details. The best way for the project manager to keep track of the details is to delegate responsibility and require written notification (e-mail works well) of how things are progressing.

Know Why You're Taking the Risk

To do great work a man must be very idle as well as very industrious.

Samuel Butler

New, inexpensive technology provides greater access to and more uses for information. With Visual Basic 6, there is a major challenge to technical departments to deliver the technology benefits quickly. Effective development means delivering swiftly and economically so that the business can gain competitive advantage or make strategic shifts.

New technology provides businesses with new opportunities to one-up their competitors. This advantage will be short-lived because the competition will rapidly equal or better the development. This competitiveness produces even more pressure to achieve results in record time.

The same new technology provides IT departments with the challenge of learning about and using it. The pace of change, the visibility of new technology, and the need to exploit it quickly mean that system development has become highly risky. You can lower this risk by ensuring that you understand the technology.

In this context, it's vital to understand how to balance risk and benefit. Only the business managers can judge whether the benefits are worth the risks, so project managers must be able to communicate with the business managers about these issues.

Visual Basic 6 provides even more productivity tools, and tools to build productivity tools, than previous versions. You can reduce the risks if you invest in learning and developing wizards, add-ins, templates, and other reusable components.

Understand Where You Came From

Have the courage to act rather than react.

Earlene Larson Jenke

A traditional corporate environment (such as the one depicted in Figure 15-2) in a large, well-established organization has typically grown up over a period of thirty years or more. During this time, procedures and practices have been implemented to control and manage the development, operation, support, and maintenance of the IT function. The environment is mature.

This type of mature technical environment was relatively slow to change, so methods and people were able to adapt easily to the changes. The environment was relatively simple and stable. This slower change and general stability meant that a small number of well-trained staff could investigate change, develop a coherent technical strategy, and adapt the system management practice to take account of this change. The skills required of the majority of development and support staff were relatively low level.

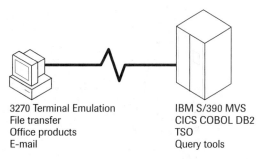

3270 Terminal Emulation   IBM S/390 MVS
File transfer   CICS COBOL DB2
Office products   TSO
E-mail   Query tools

FIGURE 15-2   *A traditional corporate environment*

Understand Where You Are

Make it work first before you make it work fast.

Bruce Whiteside

Today large-scale Visual Basic 6 distributed systems, such as the one depicted in Figure 15-3, are normally attempting to achieve high levels of integration within a business. This implies integration among systems that might require links to e-mail, workflow, document image databases, multiple conventional data sources, and the Internet.

To achieve the necessary integration and performance, you might need to use multiple APIs and protocols. The technical skills required to architect, design, implement, and support such systems are at a significantly higher level than those called for in traditional mature environments.

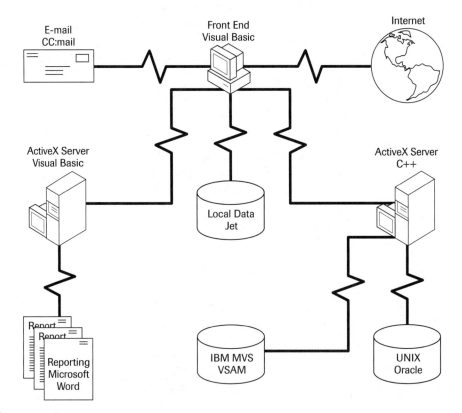

FIGURE 15-3 *A modern corporate environment*

With so many technologies and products involved, the development environment and tools are very fluid. The tools are increasingly complex in order to cope with the complexity of the environment. With the move from Visual Basic 3 to Visual Basic 6, we have seen Visual Basic move through three major leaps in functionality and capability. Practice and skills in this environment are immature.

Build Commitment and Understand Users

Pick battles big enough to matter, small enough to win.

Jonathan Kozol

Project managers and users often have problems with defining project scope and keeping it in line with schedules and budgets. Continual commitment to dialogue is essential to ensure that business domains and technological solutions actually produce benefits in spite of the fact that normally not everyone involved completely understands these domains and solutions. The effect of normal business risks on a project can be greatly magnified to job-threatening and sometimes business-threatening proportions.

Your approach to development must make it possible for you to cope with large projects. Many attempts at rapid development have been based on scaling up small-project development practices. This model of development provides some useful lessons, but it must be placed in a framework designed for large-scale developments.

The development process must allow for managing changes in requirements without excessive bureaucratic burden and large amounts of rework. Often a way to achieve this goal is through prototyping. Visual Basic has always been an excellent prototyping tool that can be used to improve the understanding of requirements. Keep in mind, though, that the techniques for building rapid prototypes are very different from the effective use of Visual Basic 6 for building robust distributed systems. Users must not be misled to think that prototypes are anything other than prototypes. This misconception is a classic way of losing your users' confidence and commitment. (For more information about prototyping, see the "Why Are You Prototyping?" section later in this chapter.)

User commitment and involvement are critical factors to all application development. These factors have traditionally involved a contractual, even adversarial, relationship. On this basis, user commitment and involvement have been relatively easy to manage but not necessarily successful. If you are to speed up development, you must make users part of the development team and involve them continually.

The commitment from the business manager must be to assign to the development team a user who understands the business in sufficient depth to answer developers' questions, has the authority to make decisions on behalf of the business, and can live with the result of his or her decisions. To find such a user and release him or her to an IT project takes commitment. Major projects typically cross functional boundaries. Giving someone authority to make decisions across those boundaries means commitment from the top.

Understand the Technology

Any sufficiently advanced technology is indistinguishable from magic.

Clarke's Third Law

To manage risk on Visual Basic 6 distributed development projects, managers must get closer to the technology. Managers need to be clear about why and how design decisions are made. If you're hanging your career on a technology, you'd better understand that technology. Managers need to know where tools are weak and understand how different architectures perform.

Often when there is a decision to be made about what tools to use, what method to take, and so on, there is no clear-cut choice, so the project management approach must take this uncertainty into account so that correct decisions can be made at the appropriate time. It might be necessary to test different approaches prior to making a decision. Time must be figured into the development schedules for research and benchmarking.

With any major new technology, you should set up a Pathfinder project to investigate the technology. A *Pathfinder project* is a miniature, timeboxed project that identifies the risks within a larger project. Typically, such investigations are not emphasized enough. Users often don't want to pay for something that they see as producing nothing at the end. Instead, you might hear a manager say, "We recognize the need to learn more about the technology, and if our developers need more knowledge, we'll send them to a class." However, with the rapid growth of technology and the complex way in which it applies to existing businesses, there is often not an applicable class, so the Pathfinder approach is a better way of investigating new technology. See the "Creating a Foundation with a Pathfinder Project" section on page 682 for more detailed information about such projects.

One of the objectives of the Pathfinder approach is to provide an initial knowledge base. Providing a knowledge base must be handled carefully, however. Many companies have older, established development environments on which they have spent a great deal of time, effort, and money. They might be reluctant to compromise the status quo by chasing after some new, unproven technology. New skills and methods need to be incorporated alongside existing strengths so that the current knowledge base can be improved rather than undermined or replaced.

At TMS, the approach we have used successfully in setting up Pathfinder projects is to create a small, highly skilled team to develop and prove the infrastructure and the tools. In subsequent project phases (after this Pathfinder project), this team carries out the technical supervision of other teams involved in the project to maintain the technical integrity of the application architecture. This core team, or "SWAT" team, has a role in developing skills in the other teams. It also helps other teams by providing resources to assist in clearing tasks on the critical path.

Some technical decisions have to be made early. For example, the choice of hardware platform or the database management system to be used is often fixed, or at least assumed, before the formal development project is kicked off. Inappropriate decisions at this stage can be very expensive. For example, we know of several cases in which relational approaches were used to address problems that are better suited to Online Analytical Processing (OLAP) solutions. Consequently, effort was expended writing complex SQL and application code to produce functionality that already existed in the OLAP extensions to the relational database. Hasty decisions such as these can lead to a 30 to 50 percent increase in development costs. The ongoing cost of maintenance is also much higher than necessary. Such costs normally don't come to light because of the general ignorance of the appropriate use of technology or through inertia. However, there are kudos to be gained by stepping out, taking a risk, and delivering a better solution ahead of schedule.

It is vital that you understand Visual Basic 6 if you want to use the technology to its full advantage and to avoid pitfalls. Using a sophisticated technology such as Visual Basic 6 without adequate knowledge could cost you your job.

Create a Sensible Management Structure

It was a relief to know that it was just bad management and not technical problems.

Development manager after
firing the head of IS

The rapid development of new tools and operating environments has meant that many information systems development management staff have little understanding of the technical issues and risks involved in these new technologies. As we have said, a key role of a project manager is to manage risk. Rapidly changing technology increases risks dramatically. Technical managers must understand the technology sufficiently to assess risk and act appropriately. The management structure might need to change to ensure that managers are close enough to the technical issues to manage risk. This generally means flattening the structure and devolving responsibility. The implications of this type of change extend to all facets of the information systems development organization, including organizational structures, salary and reward structures, skills planning, and training.

If a project involves prototyping, it might be necessary to give more responsibility at lower levels for managing user relationships and expectations. Prototyping provides an opportunity for developers to work more closely with users and to become more involved with business issues.

Get a Process

Standards were ignored, no method was applied, the system was not designed, staff were not adequately trained, management did not have sufficient technical knowledge to run the project, poor internal support mechanisms, no quality assurance, no test plans, no resources for testing, poor development environment, no risk analysis, 100 percent staff turnover, little documentation, no application architecture.

Project review

Project managers must plan the project and use an appropriate process to deliver the application. The approach they adopt should be based on the business and technical architectures and the project risks. The approach can be pure waterfall, spiral, incremental, or evolutionary. The life-cycle model used should not be dictated by a method but should instead be based on the characteristics of the project. Standards are no substitute for a project manager's experience and judgment.

Given the technical complexity of Visual Basic 6 distributed development, any approach must allow sufficient time for architecture and physical design. Doing these tasks up front can provide significant productivity gains by reducing rework and allowing more tasks to be carried out in parallel.

If Visual Basic 6 distributed development is used for high-profile and high-risk projects, a number of issues need to be addressed. A formal approach to the management, specification, design, and development of applications will be needed. A risk-driven design method that focuses on creating an appropriate application architecture will have to be created.

Visual Basic 6 distributed development lends itself to object-oriented analysis and design and to rapid development. Object techniques can be used to enhance communication between users and development professionals. Version 6 has further extended the object-oriented character of Visual Basic. To make best use of Visual Basic, the development process must reflect this character and take advantage of it. This endeavor will bring challenges in developing the skills of staff and managers.

Visual Basic 6 offers a range of productivity features that must be integrated into the development process. The public ActiveX interface of Visual Basic and the extensibility and configurable integrated development environment (IDE) provide the opportunity to integrate Visual Basic and other tools that automate and control the development process. To exploit fully the power of Visual Basic 6, you need to take its features into account in the development process.

Please refer to Appendix C for details of the TMS Developer's Framework, which combines Visual Basic 6 standards and base code to boost quality and productivity.

Choose a Method

Never confuse motion with action.

Ernest Hemingway

Off-the-shelf development methods are often static prescriptions for "how-to" development; more fluid guidelines and a toolkit of techniques might be more appropriate. However, switching to new methodology entails high costs of adjustment. A better approach is to combine the best of existing practices and standards with the newer techniques to evolve an adaptable in-house Visual Basic 6 distributed development method. The key to a successful method is to manage risk while allowing development to proceed rapidly.

A desire for quality and technical purity encourages a rigorous approach to development. Methods such as SSADM (Structured Systems Analysis and Design Method) promote rigor and tend to be used with a waterfall life cycle. This approach works in traditional environments with skilled project managers. In unskilled hands, the level of rigor tends to be too high. When unplanned backtracking also occurs, costs soar and schedules slip. To counter this excessive rigor, iterative rapid application development (RAD) approaches are used, such as the Dynamic Systems Development Method (DSDM) or the Microsoft Solutions Framework (MSF). These often produce solutions with short lifetimes because they lack the framework more rigorous approaches provide.

Successful users of prototyping and rigorous methods have concluded that no one approach has all the answers. Controlling the development and project management processes is critical to the successful delivery of a system. Design requires high-quality management and good technicians. Controlled RAD applies rigor where necessary, and prototyping for specific goals can accelerate the development process. It allows you to balance the needs of the business, the limitations of a technical infrastructure, and the desire to deliver quickly.

As illustrated in Figure 15-4, a solid component-based architecture and reusable design patterns allow development activities to be carried out in parallel without compromising design quality. Development phases can be decoupled and development speeded up.

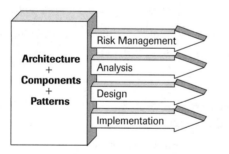

FIGURE 15-4   *Decoupling the development process*

Rapid development is often thought unsuitable for applications in which the design is not visible at the user interface. Using business objects allows design to be taken out of the RAD life cycle. In simple terms, the RAD life cycle then consists of prototyping and gluing together business objects. Business objects, design patterns, and architecture are the key components that capture the design and enable RAD to take place.

ActiveX is Microsoft's component strategy and the core of Visual Basic 6. The features in Visual Basic for enabling reuse provide a basis for developing a pattern- and component-based architecture.

A critical prerequisite for carrying out controlled RAD is that the main risks are understood and minimized. In taking on Visual Basic 6, a new set of risks have been created. Your first Visual Basic 6 project will not be a RAD project, whatever your intention—it will be a learning experience.

Case Study

To succeed, Visual Basic teams must work within an appropriate organizational structure, one in which the process of developing Visual Basic code is agreed on, well understood by all, and adhered to. Although the suggestions in the case study that follows are geared toward a particular real-world organization, some of the generalized suggestions are relevant for any Visual Basic 6 enterprise environment.

We were asked to "recommend an optimum Visual Basic development structure and process, irrespective of current process and structure." This request came from a new client who intended to migrate from mainframe systems. We were asked to consider the following questions:

- How will Visual Basic software quality be maintained?
- How will people multitask across new Visual Basic application development and mainframe application maintenance and support?
- How will Visual Basic applications be installed, implemented, and deployed?
- How will individual projects fit in with an overall distributed architecture?
- How will the optimum culture and attitude be attained?
- How will we make the team dynamic and responsive?
- How will projects be properly planned, tracked, and managed, and who will be responsible for ensuring that this happens?
- How will code reuse be achieved?
- How should the company use prototyping?
- How will external components (for example, ActiveX Servers, DLLs, VBXs, OCXs, and Visual Basic classes) be assessed, procured, and controlled?

The process described below was the result of a series of workshops with in-house staff. A summary of the process is illustrated in Figure 15-5.

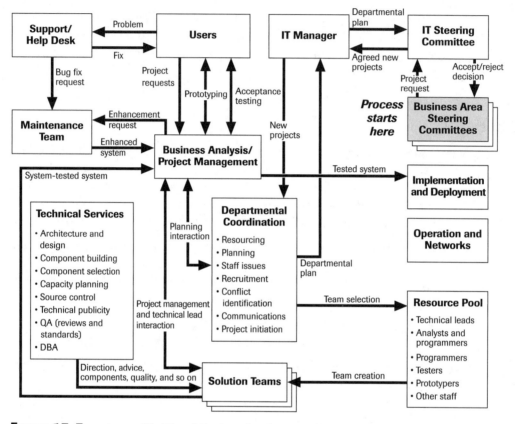

FIGURE 15-5   *A possible Visual Basic 6 development process*

The Process and the Players

The diagram in Figure 15-5 shows *process,* not necessarily *structure,* so the boxes should not be construed as "departments." The approach is very *project-based.* The boxes are essentially people or teams of people, and the arrows are the "things" that pass between them. The following subsections summarize what each person or team does.

Business area steering committees

There is one business area steering committee for each business area. Each committee meets periodically to discuss projects and priorities and to refine its "plan." Business area steering committees look ahead about 12 to 18 months. Any request for a new project they generate has to be submitted to the IT steering committee, where the request is either accepted or rejected.

IT steering committee

When elephants fight, it is the grass that suffers.

African Proverb.

The IT steering committee meets quarterly and takes an overall view across the business areas. The IT manager is the IT department's representative on this committee. Considering both business priorities and the department's commitments and constraints, this committee accepts or rejects and prioritizes project requests from the business area steering committees. Like the business area steering committees, the IT steering committee looks ahead about 12 to 18 months.

IT manager

The IT manager needs to have an accurate picture of the activities of the entire department in order to commit (or not) to taking on a new project at the IT steering committee meeting. The departmental coordination team (see the following section) provides the *departmental plan* for this purpose. The IT manager informs the departmental coordination team of any new projects that have been committed to.

Departmental coordination

**Next week there can't be any crisis. My schedule is
already full.**

Henry Kissinger

This "team" is the key to the process. It receives new project requests, maintains a departmental plan, manages resource levels, identifies project/resource conflicts, recruits staff, manages people issues (such as appraisals), promotes good departmental communications, and so on. When a new project starts, this team identifies a business analyst/project manager (see the next section) and a prototyper from the resource pool (see page 668) for that manager. Also, it creates a team from the resource pool to form a *solution team.* This team always has a *technical lead,* who is the day-to-day project team leader and is the liaison with the business analyst/project manager. The project plan that the business analyst/project manager draws up must be incorporated into the overall high-level departmental plan, and any amendments during the tracking of the project must also be incorporated. Incorporating these changes is an automated process.

Business analysis/Project management

The business analysis/project management team consists of people who are specialists in particular areas of the business. A business analyst/project manager is responsible for a project from start to finish, including both technical and user-related tasks (such as user training). These teams have a lot of user interaction and might receive project and enhancement requests from the users. They manage the requirements specification and prototyping. After the solution team (described below) has built the system, the business analysis/project management team is responsible for performing acceptance testing along with the users before passing the system on for implementation.

Resource pool

The resource pool is a virtual pool of people; that is, it doesn't exist as a team or department and hence requires no management. It's just a pool of people that the coordination team draws from to create solution teams. Its "members" possess a wide range of experience and skills. A person in the resource pool could at any one time be multitasking across projects and wearing different hats on different projects.

Solution teams

Solution teams are formed to actually produce the systems. Solution team members are responsible for the design, code, unit test, and system test of a system. They work closely with the technical services team (see the next section) and have the following responsibilities:

- Ensure that the project design fits with the overall architecture
- Reuse any generally available components
- Have deliverables reviewed and sent through a quality assurance test

Technical services

The technical services team provides a wide range of technical services—mainly to the solution teams—including those listed here:

- Promote reuse by taking generally useful code from solution teams and turning it into robust components that other solution teams can benefit from
- Dictate the overall architecture that solution teams must fit their systems into
- Provide a QA function to ensure that solution teams are producing high-quality deliverables

Users

To get maximum benefit in the Visual Basic/RAD world, users need to become much more heavily involved with projects than they have traditionally—in fact, to the extent of becoming team members. Their role is particularly important during the early stages (such as helping to develop prototypes) of the process and toward the end, at acceptance test time.

Support/Help desk

The support/help desk serves a reactive function, typically receiving problem reports as its stimulus. These reports are either dealt with within the team or passed on to a maintenance team, which fixes problems.

Maintenance team

The maintenance team is a group of people staffed from the resource pool. Typically, a team member stays in the maintenance team for a period of about six months. The primary roles of the team are to deal with any bug fixing in live systems and to add small features requested by users. During slack periods, this team does housekeeping tasks, performs reviews for the solution teams, and the like. A dedicated maintenance team is required so that solution teams are not constantly interrupted by tactical firefighting and therefore have a better chance of sticking to project plans.

Implementation and deployment

This team implements systems in both the test and production environments.

Operations and networks

This team is responsible for the day-to-day operation of the environment, systems, and networks.

The need for consistency, coordination, and design *across* all projects is vital. In this case study, this framework is provided mainly by the coordination team and to a lesser extent by the IT manager and the technical services team.

Getting Started

> After all is said and done, more is said than done.
>
> **Unknown.**

It's all very well to live in an esoteric consulting world of process and structure, but how does one get started on a real-life project? At TMS, we feel that the best way to begin is to define a target process and structure for the organization and to evolve toward this off the back of a pilot, or, as mentioned above, a Pathfinder project. On balance, the Pathfinder approach is better than attempting to set up the new process and structure prior to the first project. And of course, it's essential to have the right people with the right skills.

Skill Requirements

Table 15-1 shows the skills that key personnel require to make a first Visual Basic 6 distributed project a success. This information should form the basis of individual training plans.

TABLE 15-1

SKILLS REQUIRED FOR A SUCCESSFUL PROJECT

Skill or Knowledge	Business Analysis	Development	Technical Services
Business knowledge and business analysis	High	Medium	Low
Project management	High	Low	Low
Database modeling	High	High	Medium
Help files, user documentation, and the like	High	Medium	Low
Awareness of component availability	Medium	High	High
Systems analysis	Low	High	Low
GUI design skills	Medium	High	Low
Visual Basic prototyping	Medium	High	Low
Distributed design	Medium	High	High
GUI testing	Medium	High	Medium
Visual Basic/VBA programming	Low	High	High
Diagnostics, logging, trace, error handling	Low	High	High
Windows operating system and the PC architecture, memory, and so on	Low	Medium	High
Connectivity, performance	Low	Medium	High
Networking	Low	Medium	High
Server operating system and database, DBA	Low	Medium	High
Security, back-out, recovery	Medium	Medium	High
Implementation, installation	Medium	Medium	High

Infrastructure Requirements

As well as finding people who possess the necessary skills to work on your project, you need to put an appropriate infrastructure in place. These infrastructure requirements should be implemented in parallel with the development of the pilot project. Be sure to allow adequate time in the schedules for these extra tasks.

This is the minimalist list of infrastructure requirements that we recommend:

- Corporate Visual Basic 6 distributed architecture and strategy
- General application design standards
- Data design standards
- Distributed guidelines (such as connectivity method, use of stored procedures)
- GUI style guide
- Coding standards
- Distribution, installation, implementation, and upgrade guidelines
- Development environments (such as development, test, and production servers)
- Source control software and associated procedures
- Powerful, standardized developers' PCs fully configured with Visual Basic, Microsoft Access, relevant (and tested) custom controls, and a range of supporting utilities and tools
- Fully configured and tested server database with associated tools to add test data, stored procedures, and the like
- Fully implemented and tested workstation-to-server connectivity (should include network software, drivers, and so on)
- Education and training of those providing any of the above or filling technical roles

THE EARLY STAGES

It is essential that a project get off to the right start. In this section, we detail some of the methods and approaches we use at TMS to make sure this happens.

Vertical Partitioning Means 80 Percent Complete Is 80 Percent Delivered

Who begins too much accomplishes little.

German proverb

Analysis should support the design, implementation, and management processes. If you're using an incremental approach, you should be able to partition the analysis vertically to investigate part of the problem in detail and to defer looking at other areas until later. You should also be able to design and implement each partition without analyzing the other areas in detail. The business architecture will provide the context for any partition. This approach will help you judge the suitability of an application for incremental development and the potential stability of a specific partition.

Partitioning allows you to consider different parts of the problem in isolation. Vertical partitioning allows you to proceed with designing and building the application incrementally with the confidence that rework will be minimal. It also allows the business needs to drive design, build, and roll out. Once the technical foundation is in place, an incremental implementation that meets business priorities can happen. Using an object-oriented approach from analysis to coding allows this incremental implementation to occur.

The careful specification and use of business-oriented ActiveX servers will provide a vertically partitioned design. Late binding and generally decoupling increments will reduce the need for recompilation and rework. From this point of view, out-of-process servers are better than in-process ones. Maintainability should normally rank above performance, a priority you need to make clear early on. (One of the biggest criticisms about a system is often its performance because it's an aspect that is all too visible, whereas maintainability can easily be overlooked since it won't become an issue until after the initial delivery of the system is complete.) Vertical partitioning allows parallel streams of design and build to take place. This partitioning provides rapid development at low risk without increasing costs.

Cut the Politics and Get Serious

The culture acts against quality—"pass the buck" or "shoot the messenger" managers are playing politics, for example, holding back the bad news, hoping other projects will fail first....

Project review

The early stages of a project often bring into focus internal and external politics that can cause project failure. You need to cut through the politics to get the job done right. Challenge inertia and self-interest. If you want to maintain your integrity, this is better than playing politics. But it's just as unsafe. Cutting through politics requires a project manager with guts—preferably one who is financially secure!

Most projects will have some requirements that are relatively simple and don't require great user involvement to achieve. These are ideal deliverables for the early stages of a project. The team is able to demonstrate what it can achieve. The challenge is then to get the right level of user commitment to ensure the same productivity when a high level of user involvement is needed.

To achieve technical objectives, you might have to bypass IT procedures and common practice. You can often circumvent the system like this when you do it on a limited scale. To deliver major projects, however, such practices and procedures might need to be changed.

Dare to Choose Staff Who Have the Right Stuff

**Everyone has talent. What is rare is the courage to
follow the talent to the dark place where it leads.**

Erica Jong

Those who really care about quality and want to do a good job are often considered mavericks by the organization they work for. They don't fit in, they don't play the political game, and they don't strive to move into the management hierarchy.

Staff members who argue their points, don't accept decisions at face value, and insist on doing things the right way can be difficult to manage. They can be thorns in a manager's side. They might insist on being paid more than their manager. They do build better systems, though; they build systems that are maintainable, meet business needs, and are less costly. They probably *are* worth more than their manager.

See the Big Picture, Plan for Change

You can observe a lot just by watching.

Berra's law

Most experienced developers have at some point felt frustrated because the applications they are maintaining or having to extract data from have not been designed for change. They have probably also experienced this frustration from the other side—frustration that they are not provided with the time or resources to develop a system that provides a flexible but sound foundation for future work.

Data from one application is often reused in multiple applications. The second and subsequent uses are often unanticipated, resulting in a range of problems. For example, data quality might be poor or new databases with gross data transformations between the new and the old databases might be required. (See Figure 15-6 for examples of bad and good data management planning.) The problems arise because the original application was not designed in the context of a corporate long-term view. Without a forward-looking view, some data is not captured and overoptimized structures are used. A business architecture provides a logical view of function and data and attempts to anticipate future needs. To design an application successfully (where success is viewed over the lifetime of the application), you must take the bigger picture into account. A well-planned application can grow organically as new requirements emerge. To plan and design solely for the current application creates problems for the future. For example, databases might not be structured flexibly to support future queries; designs might be highly optimized for a particular application but prove to be inadequate for a subsequent application or after maintenance. Producing reusable business rules and generic code tends to take a low priority if the focus is only on the current project. Designing logically, based on a high-level view of core business operations, tends to produce a reusable design that will support multiple applications at the database and code levels.

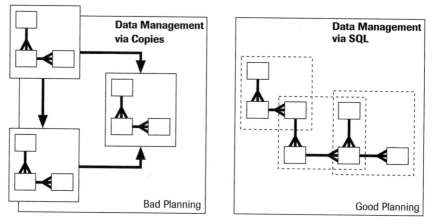

FIGURE 15-6   *Design for the future*

Ways of Ensuring Quality

There are very few people who don't become more interesting when they stop talking.

Mary Lowry

We started this chapter wondering about a Visual Basic quality crisis. As you've seen, many good practices seem to have been ignored. People who should have known better have gotten caught up in the productivity trap made so obvious by this special development tool. So how can you avoid the same trap? The old adage about an ounce of prevention being better than a pound of cure applies to Visual Basic systems development—there's no better way of eradicating problems in a system than by not putting them into the code in the first place.

The best way to improve the quality of Visual Basic team developments is to introduce a formal review process. Reviews are also known as walkthroughs or inspections—nothing new, but rarely found in the Visual Basic world. We believe that defining standards is not enough: the standards also need to be policed, preferably by an independent QA team. Some excellent tools on the market automate this procedure.

The objectives of a review process must include these:

- To ensure standards are adhered to
- To improve the quality of software
- To improve communication between developers
- To improve code reuse

From experience, we've found that a review process is worthwhile only if it has total management backing; that is, implementation should be blocked until all reviews have passed in all circumstances, regardless of the business pressures to go ahead. Essential documents for the review process (both for those being reviewed and the reviewer) are a style guide (or user interface guide) and a set of standards, both of which should be second nature to all developers.

At TMS, we use a three-stage review process:

1. **Requirements.** This review gives the designer and developer an opportunity to ensure that the quality of the requirements specification document produced by the analyst is high enough and that it accurately and unambiguously describes the system.

2. **Design.** This review is further segmented into two reviews:

    - A first design review is carried out about 20 percent of the way through the design phase. This review is informal and normally involves the designer explaining the outline of the design on a whiteboard. This review verifies that the proposed design approach is sound. (It's better to catch any design flaws early on, rather than waiting until a detailed design specification has been produced.) At this point, the team can agree on which reviews should follow; a modified review process can be appropriate depending on the project circumstances.

    - A second design review is carried out at the end of the design phase. This review is much more formal than the initial design review and involves careful scrutiny of the design and the design documents produced.

3. **Code.** This review is also further segmented into two reviews:

    - A first review is carried out 20 percent of the way through the coding phase. This review verifies that the proposed coding approach is sound and that standards are being followed.

    - A second review is carried out at the end of the coding phase. This review is more formal than the initial code review.

While it probably seems that this review process will cause a lot of extra effort, we have found that it actually saves a tremendous amount of time and cost in the long run.

There are, of course, many more ways to improve quality. For example, testing properly, maintaining metrics so that Visual Basic projects can be measured, and doing postimplementation reviews are just a few additional ways of monitoring quality.

Demand More Rigor, Not Less

*It's a funny thing about life; if you refuse to accept
anything but the best, you very often get it.*

Somerset Maugham

A desire for quality and technical purity encourages a rigorous approach to development. Formal methods such as VDM (Vienna Development Method), Z, and B are rarely used in commercial development. But methods that promote rigor (such as SSADM) continue to have a high level of use. Do they work? They can work well in the hands of skilled project managers who know what to use and what to leave out for a specific project. In unskilled hands, the level of rigor applied tends to be higher than necessary, project costs soar, and schedules slip.

In some organizations, the consequence of the failure of rigor is that business managers decide to do their own development. In others, hacking takes over. Visual Basic 3 was one of the main tools of the hackers. To continue to use this approach with Visual Basic 6 is at best a waste and at worst a disaster. The development process for a project should be decided by the project manager with the guidance of the analysts and designers. Prescribing a method from outside the project does not work. A Pathfinder approach provides a mechanism for understanding major projects before you commit large numbers of staff to them.

Teach the Fundamentals

As far as the code is concerned, there appear to have been several passes through it. The later passes introduced several bugs. The person or people involved do not appear to understand the Visual Basic event model.

Code review

Tools and methods are only as good as the people who use them. They are no substitute for training. Staff must know *why* as well as *how*. The *why* comes first.

The basics of computing—how chips work, how memory is used, what operating systems and algorithms do—are all essentials for IT professionals. The lack of this fundamental knowledge means that developers effectively cannot use powerful tools such as Visual Basic 6. They need to understand exactly what the tool is doing and how it works. This knowledge is even more important as the tools become more powerful because they hide so much. To use distributed objects effectively, for example, one has to understand how the technical mechanisms that create the objects work, not just how to make them work. How is a local call turned into a remote call? What is the effect on the network? How does it perform with high transaction rates? What is the impact of other network traffic?

The fundamentals of software engineering must be taught to staff. The principles of data management, security, configuration management, project control, and so on apply to all development approaches. The divisions and disciplines of separate development, test, and production environments are critical to successful implementation. The ability to produce code quickly in Visual Basic 6 doesn't relieve developers and managers of the duty to produce the right code and to use the technical infrastructure correctly and efficiently.

Commit to Staff

Good people are good because they've come to wisdom through failure.

William Saroyan

Good software developers are infinitely better than average ones. The only people worth having on the team are those who are very good and those who are very eager to learn. You can tell people who are good at their jobs a mile off. A team of people who are proud of their work is a thousand times better than a team of average people. High-quality teams lead to real team spirit. At TMS, our hiring process includes a strictly monitored 2½-hour written Visual Basic examination. We never rely on just résumés, references, and interviews. We firmly believe in small, highly skilled teams.

In Visual Basic teams, there is a danger of everyone "doing it all." The Visual Basic 6 box is deceptively small, but there's an awful lot in there (like Dr. Who's TARDIS). Most Visual Basic programmers become jacks-of-all-trades but, of course, masters of none. We therefore believe in specialists across the teams.

Because of Visual Basic's high productivity, it's possible to reach a productivity saturation point long before achieving competency. "Productive incompetent" programmers are the result. Visual Basic programmers need much better education and training. Most employers seem to think that sticking their main-frame programmers in a five-day introductory course is enough. Wrong, wrong, wrong. So many times, we've seen people with inadequate training—for example, with no understanding of the workings of the Microsoft Windows oper-ating system—building mission-critical Visual Basic applications. They assume that they are working in a protected environment with "limitless" resources, just as in the mainframe world. Visual Basic programmers should have a thorough understanding of Windows as well as Visual Basic functionality and syntax. They should also spend at least six months working alongside an experienced Windows/Visual Basic mentor before being let anywhere near an important development project.

Go for the best

One machine can do the work of fifty ordinary men.
No machine can do the work of one extraordinary man.

Elbert Hubbard

Visual Basic 6 distributed development requires that developers have a broad range of technical skills and understanding that covers front-end, middleware, and back-end technologies. Products such as Visual Basic are getting bigger and more sophisticated. Rapid development means shorter analysis, design, and coding stages. Effective staff utilization dictates that the same staff are used across all stages. The implication is that higher-caliber, better-trained, and better-paid staff are needed. Visual Basic 6 distributed development requires stronger analysis because of the more competitive business environment. Design, testing, deployment, and support skills need to be stronger because of the more complex technical environment.

Project managers must be technically competent and have strong business and interpersonal skills. Their management of the users and their own teams has grown more difficult. With the breadth of skills required and the pace of technical change, it is unlikely that team members will have a full set of the required skills. Working together to solve problems, to experiment, to learn, and to cover skill gaps is essential to Visual Basic 6 distributed development. Project managers must build learning time into the schedules. If overall development costs are not to rise, greater productivity must be achieved. The quality of project management is the key issue in building teams and commitment. A project manager must be a good team builder and team leader.

Some of us have had the rare experience of working in highly cohesive, effective, productive, supportive, and fun teams. From a management perspective, productivity and effectiveness are the only important factors. But these two factors don't come without the others; in fact, they are a result of having developed a supportive, cohesive, and fun environment. Unfortunately, such teams often break down after a short period. Few managers have the skills or support to build and maintain such teams. The best organizations have human resources departments that provide management training and facilitate team development. Some managers treat team building with cynicism. They are fools who are making their own jobs much harder.

Many organizations build teams successfully and then destroy them. Staff must be motivated by training, advancement, recognition, involvement, and money. They must not be demotivated by lack of respect, unreasonable pressure, long hours, or lack of consultation on matters that affect them.

In the case study, we recommended a resource pool—but beware. You can have a resource pool of laptop computers, cars, overhead projectors, or any inanimate objects. You can manipulate them with little thought. People deserve better. They are not things to be moved about on a whim. The resource-pool concept needs to be handled carefully. A good team is more important, more productive, and more effective than the best methods, the best tools, or the best organizational structure. The priority must be on building and maintaining a good team. This investment provides the greatest payoff.

If you commit to staff, they are more likely to commit to you. And successful Visual Basic 6 distributed development requires high levels of commitment from staff. They need to spend their own time researching their tools, and they need to be encouraged to do so. Their commitment must be reciprocated in terms of salary, holidays, working hours, personal development, training, respect, and fun. Good staff can command high contract rates and are mobile. Reward them or lose them. The value of providing appropriate rewards outweighs the costs of poor productivity and poor quality. Refer to Chapter 17 for more thorough discussion on staff hiring and retention.

Project teams using Visual Basic for distributed development projects are often weak in their server-side skills. This is particularly serious where this extends to the project management and designers. Project managers might not schedule the time or resources to carry out physical design or be aware of the risks inherent in their project. It is essential for successful completion of any project that a realistic view of the skills required and those possessed be taken.

There are no experts
The true leader is always led.

> Carl Jung

The rate of change in hardware, system software, and development tools means that there are no experts. Visual Basic 3, 4, or 5 gurus are not Visual Basic 6 gurus. With lack of expertise and rapidly changing environments, it's difficult to build a stable and effective technical infrastructure. It's even harder to get good advice on how to use that infrastructure.

A development project is unlikely to have teams with all the skills required in sufficient depth to deliver the project. A realistic assessment of the skills required and those possessed should take place. Any deficiency should be filled for the project and a longer-term solution developed. A good approach is to employ external consultants who have skills transfer as part of their experience.

It makes no sense to incur extra expense by continually running to outside resources for core skills.

Three roles are essential in designing Visual Basic 6 distributed systems:

- The system architect creates the overall conceptual design.
- The system designer carries out the detailed specification of the executable code and the implementation.
- The DBA is the database technical expert.

Other experts, such as language or network gurus, might be required to solve particular problems. In addition to these roles, the complexity of the systems demands external review.

You can learn a lot from those who have more experience, so form a partnership to learn more. The problems are complex, and so are the solutions. You might never know whether you have the best solution because the technology is moving on before it is proved. We repeat, there are no experts!

WHY ARE YOU PROTOTYPING?

Spend sufficient time confirming the need and the need will disappear.

Specification Dynamics

Beware of the prototyping trap. If you ask two programmers on the same Visual Basic team what a prototype is, you're likely to get two different answers. Often the team is unclear whether or not the prototype is a throwaway. Ensure that the term "prototype" is well defined and that everyone (including the users) is familiar with this definition. You might even choose to define different types of prototypes. The big trap is to leave the "prototype" ill-defined. We have seen this lead to much grief on many Visual Basic projects. Prototyping in general has been given a bad name because of frequent misuse.

Delivering quickly is often the justification for a prototyping approach to development. But without control, the "what" that is delivered usually fails to meet the business needs for robustness and maintainability.

To be successful, prototyping must have specific goals, such as these:

- Goals to demonstrate feasibility
- Analysis goals to discover or confirm requirements

- Design goals to prove the technology or an approach to implementation
- Implementation goals to evolve a working system with user involvement within a predefined technical architecture

Uncontrolled prototyping, without goals and a development strategy to produce an application architecture, is doomed. It is hacking with respectability.

Prototyping can be used at various stages during development. The key principle that will ensure that prototyping is used correctly is to precisely define the objectives of the prototype and then ensure that appropriate disciplines are used to deliver these objectives. Rules such as "Prototypes must be thrown away" are unnecessarily restrictive.

CREATING A FOUNDATION WITH A PATHFINDER PROJECT

If you have built castles in the air, your work need not be lost; that is where they should be. Now put the foundations under them.

Henry David Thoreau

You might not have the luxury of being able to start with a small noncritical project to learn about Visual Basic 6 distributed development. If this is the case, start with a Pathfinder project. The concept of the Pathfinder project was developed to handle the risks in large-scale Visual Basic 6 distributed development. It is aimed primarily at the technical risks, but it does provide an opportunity to address business and people risks. It provides a good foundation from which you can build a successful application. (See Figure 15-7.) Such a project is a significant undertaking, usually requiring the full-time attention of three to five of the best development staff for three to six months. This time frame is dictated by the volume of work to be performed and the high caliber of staff needed to perform it. But it is time and effort well spent.

You need to ensure that the application will fit with other applications and will reuse components and ideas. You need to gain appropriate user involvement and commitment. You need to determine team structures and skill requirements and work out the project management approach and the development process. The objectives of the Pathfinder development must be considered nearly impossible to achieve in order to ensure that only commitment from the top and the elimination of politics will achieve them. The Pathfinder project will tackle the difficult things first. It will prove the infrastructure and the techniques for exploiting it. A Pathfinder project kick-starts the process of ongoing research. This process should stop only when the technology stops changing.

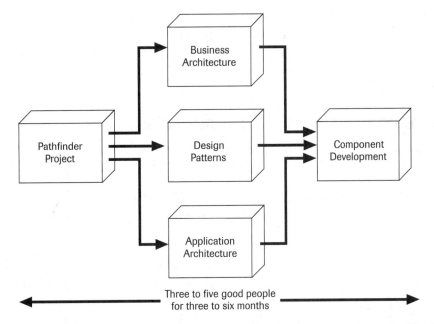

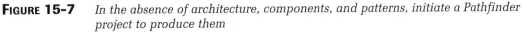

Three to five good people
for three to six months

FIGURE 15-7 *In the absence of architecture, components, and patterns, initiate a Pathfinder project to produce them*

Usually some of the work will have been done as part of other projects. This will reduce the workload, but it will still be necessary to bring the various strands of work together to meet the Pathfinder objectives.

A Pathfinder project will include the following objectives:

- Developing a logical business architecture (This architecture is best expressed as a high-level logical business object model.)
- Developing a technical system architecture that will adequately support all the technical requirements, such as database updates, maintainability, and performance
- Developing design patterns and frameworks to address anticipated design problems, such as bulk data movements, locking strategies, and error handling
- Demonstrating that the technical architecture can deliver at least one significant business requirement to a production environment
- Providing an initial knowledge base
- Developing a core team of technical experts who can provide technical supervision and mentoring to other staff
- Identifying the skills required to complete the project

With a new development tool, it is essential that these areas be revisited and fully understood. The people carrying out the investigation need to be among the best developers. They need to be in touch with day-to-day development issues. They need to know what is important.

PROVING THE TECHNICAL ARCHITECTURE

The doctor can bury his mistakes, but an architect can only advise his client to plant vines.

Frank Lloyd Wright

Can you describe simply how an application is partitioned into a number of discrete components, each of which has a specific purpose? Can you describe how these components interact? Can you describe how and why each component uses the technical infrastructure? Can you describe how a change to a component or to the technical infrastructure will affect the performance of the application? If you have difficulty answering these questions, and the system architecture seems to look like that in Figure 15-8, the application probably doesn't have a coherent and efficient underlying structure to it. Maintenance is likely to be a major problem. An application requires a sound technical foundation that has been proved.

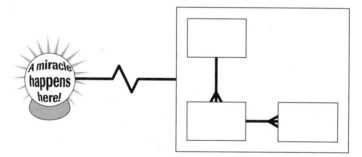

FIGURE 15-8   *A technical architecture?*

Typically, a layered architecture will be adopted to improve maintainability by isolating different implementation technologies from one another and from the core business logic of the application. It is vital that the technology for building components and for communicating among components be thoroughly tested and benchmarked. The robustness and performance characteristics must be understood so that sound designs can be created and technical risks managed.

Layering insulates an application from change. If used appropriately with an object-based approach, layering can reduce dependencies in project scheduling by insulating one part of an application from another.

The layering model can be as simple or as complex as required for the technical environment. For example, at TMS, we have used a 10-layer model to describe and categorize the elements of a complex Visual Basic distributed system. The model shown in Figure 15-9 is for a much simpler system.

Where the application will be physically partitioned, the deployment mechanisms should be understood. In particular, you should assess the process and the impact of repeated deployment. Operations staff who deploy systems should be aware of possible version conflicts and any special installation requirements. In particular, they should understand how the registration database is used by all the applications that they install.

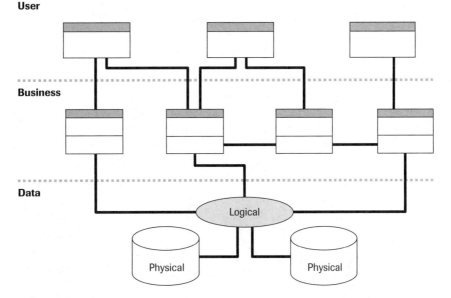

Figure 15-9 *A layered architecture*

Proof of Concept

As mentioned earlier, a key objective of the Pathfinder project is to prove to the business managers and to the IT teams that a business function can be delivered using the application architecture. Using the Pathfinder substantially reduces the perceived risk.

The proof of concept must include thorough testing of the application architecture. Such testing will cover, for example, stress testing the architecture. The architecture should be proven to be a viable basis on which to develop the entire application. Proof of concept includes delivery of the business function into a simulation of a live environment by those who would normally deliver the application. It should be delivered to the user for testing. Difficulties in managing rapid development in the IT department and in the business will be highlighted. Prove that you can deliver. Prove it to the business management, to the technicians, and to the skeptics!

Focusing on Design

Imagination is more important than knowledge.

Albert Einstein

When challenged, most Visual Basic developers would claim they design their applications. Unfortunately, we see little evidence of this. Technical specifications are becoming historical curiosities. It seems that most Visual Basic programmers cannot resist the temptation to start coding on Day 1 and then code, code, and code some more. What's wrong with using pencil and paper and applying a little thought up front to get a handle on a problem? As a contrasting example, tackling a large C++-based development is not easy at the best of times, and developers quickly learn that unless they invest some time in designing carefully, they will waste a lot of time and their development will almost certainly fail. How does this attitude compare with that of Visual Basic developers? We feel that Visual Basic is often abused. It's so easy to build an application that, rather than choose to design, developers build instead; that is, they take the "try it and see" approach to software development. In the Visual Basic 6 enterprise environment, this kind of approach spells disaster.

We recommend that not only must you create a design, you must make sure it fits in with an overall corporate architecture. The application design should be objectized, by building common objects and designing them for reuse. Error handling and debugging aids must be designed in from the start. When it comes to external components and objects, be careful not to include them in your design without properly assessing their quality and their potential impact on your application and on Windows. For example, at TMS, we run all candidate ActiveX controls under the Windows debugging kernel—it's often very revealing! Measure the effect on Windows resources of using a particular control, especially if your design means the control has to be multiply instantiated. More broadly, we recommend that external components and objects be assessed, procured, and controlled centrally—and with much care and thought.

What Is Design?

Design is the process of taking a business requirement and applying the constraints of technology, finance, and time. It is a compromise between the needs of a business and the limitations of the computer. It is a mixture of art and science; it is engineering. Design requires its participants to be masters of business and technology in order to draw the appropriate compromise. Designers need to be communicators and influencers. They need to be leaders.

Designers must possess current business and technical knowledge. The introduction of Visual Basic 6 demands that designers work to understand the new technical environment. A design is a specification for building an application. It applies architectural principle to a specific system. The strategy for implementation must be determined as part of the design. The system must function within the technical infrastructure of a business.

A logical model specifies what is required. For the model to be implemented, it must be tempered with reality. The design model has to be accurate to be implemented. The design model might be very different from the logical model. Rarely can the logical model be implemented directly; unfortunately, many try to do just that. For example, it is well known that a third normal form database design often performs poorly, but it's often tried because a logical database design doesn't take performance into account. A design model has to include all the data, not just the data that was thought of. It has to include all the processing, including the housekeeping and the audit trails. It has to account for peculiarities in database query optimization. It should consider the skills of the team, the build strategy, configuration management, and a host of other things that the analyst who creates the logical model can safely ignore.

Logical modeling should occur at the start of the design—and a long way from the end. Design requires detailed technical knowledge of the implementation environment. That environment includes not just technology but people too. The conversion of a logical data model to a robust and efficient physical design is a complex process that must be performed by the system designer in conjunction with the technical specialists. Only together can they make the appropriate compromises between business needs and technical constraints. The system designer from the application development team is unlikely to have the technical knowledge to make best use of the technology. The technical specialist is unlikely to understand where the business can compromise and where it cannot (or will not).

The process of design starts during the feasibility stage and continues throughout the life of a Visual Basic 6 distributed development project. Design does not follow analysis; it is more likely to precede it. Design is then a process of gradual refinement from high-level strategies to detailed specification that is continually influenced by and influences analysis. Requirements are generally unstable. They might be specified differently by different people. The software crisis is not in requirements gathering and specification, but in design. Designs must be able to cope with change and uncertainty. A successful system will change, but only a well-architected system will cope effectively with this change and at low cost. The focus of a project must be on design.

What Is *Not* Design?

Never play leapfrog with a unicorn.

Confucius on gamesmanship

Certain common techniques can create the illusion of design. Each technique has its proper place in development but does not constitute design in its own right. The importance of design must be considered and acknowledged in project planning. There are no alternatives to design if robust and maintainable systems are to be delivered. In some situations, you can use valid shortcuts, but they must be considered carefully and planned. Design is a compromise between business needs and technological capabilities. This means that design decisions are management decisions and that designers need to be aware of business requirements.

A thin GUI produced from evolutionary prototyping might be placed in front of a set of cooperating business objects derived from a business-object model. But prototyping alone is unlikely to produce a coherent design for business objects. These must be designed separately. Prototyping is not design.

A logical model is not design. It is abstract. A design needs to take into account the implementation environment. In Visual Basic 6 distributed development, the environment and potential impacts on other systems are complex. You need to adopt a benchmarking strategy to test and refine a design.

Data modeling is not design. Data modeling approaches to development assume that processing consists of simple inquiries and updates. GUI interfaces enable highly complex transactions to be built (for example, hierarchies and networks built as a single unit of work). The physical design to achieve performance and data integrity can be complex and can require separate modeling.

CASE tools do not guarantee good design. A mass of diagrams and dictionary prints can give the impression of detailed consideration. CASE tools improve productivity regardless of quality and talent, but they should be given only to those capable of doing the job without the tools. Few CASE tools provide adequate support for physical design. To do so, they would have to incorporate a model of the physical infrastructure and its performance characteristics.

Developing Design Patterns

It might not be possible to capture a generic solution in code effectively, but it might be possible to describe an approach or some techniques that will address the problem. Patterns document design experience. They distill design knowledge and allow it to be reused. Visual Basic 6 distributed systems require that considerable thought be given to software and data architecture. You can understand the nature of some of the problems by using simulation and benchmarking, which can help you evaluate potential solutions. Design guidance can be documented. Solution frameworks can be built to encapsulate partial solutions.

Patterns for the solution and demonstration of layering, partitioning, deployment, locking, database access, error handling, application structure, and so on should be developed using Visual Basic 6. Such patterns will then form the foundation for successful future development. If a preexisting design fits the architecture of the solution, the move from requirement to implementation can happen very quickly, making it seem as if there is no design phase.

When software developers come up with seemingly unrealistic estimates for delivering systems and subsequently achieve them, they are often using preexisting designs. They judge carefully whether their client's requirement fits the architecture of their solution. They work with a limited range of applications. They move from requirement to implementation quickly, beginning with a rapid design assessment to ensure that preexisting designs fit the requirements. Design patterns and application frameworks provide architectures for building applications. Much of the thinking has been done. Provided the new application is a close fit to the pattern or framework, rapid conversion of the requirements to code can be achieved with relatively little effort spent on design.

The application must be judged to fit the design. Careful thought must go into those parts of the application that fall outside the scope of the pattern or framework. But with a close fit, the design process can be shortened.

Examples of design patterns

Consider these four uses of design patterns:

- Front end to back end bulk data movements
- Error handling schemes
- Name and address deduplication
- Executive information systems

These are examples in which design patterns have been derived and used to reduce development costs and project schedules. The first two examples are generic technical problems, and the second two are business problems. In each, a completely coded generic solution cannot be produced, but a large amount of the design work can be reused in a subsequent application. Much of this design work can be captured in templates or libraries of classes.

Visual Basic 6 provides facilities for capturing patterns through two mechanisms: a form of inheritance through the use of the *Implements* keyword; and templates, which provide a starting point for custom code. This starting point can capture the key design ideas without the rigidity of finished and working code.

Benchmark-Driven Design

When choosing between two evils, I always like to try the one I've never tried before.

Mae West

Benchmarking is critical to successful physical design. You should carry it out early using representative models of the system to determine what strategies you should employ for different classes of problems (for example, moving large amounts of data from the front end to the back end or locking). Testing with models should include stress testing in such areas as high transaction rates, multiuser testing, and impacts on other systems. Designing the system incorrectly for these types of problems is expensive once the system has been written. With representative benchmarking carried out early, you should be able to upgrade servers and networks if required. Benchmarking will also give you an early indication of whether the application should be distributed over multiple servers or whether the design can remain simple. Where benchmarks show potential problems, you should evaluate alternative solutions. A set of solutions with varying performance characteristics, costs, and complexities will emerge. This process will enable the designer to select the most appropriate solution from a menu of solutions. These solutions are design patterns.

Benchmark-driven design is essential in Visual Basic 6 distributed applications in which there is a mix of technologies and a large potential for bottlenecks. The aim is to ensure that the technical infrastructure and the approach to using the infrastructure in the application will meet business needs for performance and reliability. To do this, you'll need to develop a model of the system. The performance characteristics and options for Visual Basic 6 (and Visual Basic 5) are very different from Visual Basic 3 or Visual Basic 4. On the whole, versions 5 and 6 have great improvements—improvements that provide opportunities.

Understanding Objects

When the plane you are on is late, the plane you want to transfer to is on time.

The Airplane Law

Visual Basic has gradually become more and more object oriented, and Visual Basic 6 has continued this trend. Whether Visual Basic 6 is fully object-oriented according to some academic's definition is irrelevant. However, it is vital to recognize that the only way to build successful systems using Visual Basic 6 is to develop them from an object-oriented design. An object-oriented design can be developed successfully only from an object-oriented analysis. Object-oriented analysis revolves around the identification of business objects. Identifying business objects responsible for data and function eliminates duplication of data and function.

Using business objects allows you to design incrementally. It also forms a basis for reuse. Using business objects in analysis and design provides traceability and allows the specification to evolve seamlessly by the addition of implementation detail rather than by going through translations from one form of model to another.

Business objects encapsulate data and function and form a natural basis for identifying business-oriented components. Analysis approaches that separate function and data make it more difficult to build a comprehensive component architecture. You will want to package the classes that are developed into larger components—ActiveX servers. These can be considered large objects. The message is that if you are to adopt Visual Basic 6 successfully, you must adopt object orientation.

Business objects are inherently traceable to business concepts and require-ments. Implementing business objects through Visual Basic 6 class modules carries through this traceability into applications. Using a business-object–based application architecture allows the design and coding of objects to be carried out independently of the design and coding of the application. This allows a large amount of flexibility in developing project plans and is the basis of high levels of reuse.

INVESTING IN REUSE

After things have gone from bad to worse, the cycle will repeat itself.

Farnsdick's corollary

As you saw in Chapter 14, reuse is an obvious source of medium- and long-term benefits to an organization. Visual Basic 6 provides a series of features to help in this area. These features require investment of time and, as a result, money for a business to benefit from them. This is where we hit the tired old argument about "Who will pay for reuse?" It should be recognized that reusability is a function of good design. This is true regardless of whether or not reuse is a design objective. A good design supports change, it supports the unknown future, and it is flexible. These characteristics give reusability.

The required investment in many major organizations is in design and design-ers. This is often an unpalatable truth to be faced. You need to actively look for things that can be reused from other applications. Each project should have a task attached to it for "trawling" or "scavenging" for reuse. If the organization has an organized reuse catalog of components and patterns, this is an obvious starting point. However, few organizations appear to have done such cataloging well, if at all.

An effective approach is to schedule a series of short meetings with the design leaders in other projects. At these meetings, discuss the existing application and the new application both technically and from the business point of view and identify similarities. These areas of similarity should point to reuse. Then take a guided tour of the similar parts of each application. Reuse any applicable code, ideas, or good practices. Generally speaking, one workweek should be sufficient for trawling.

Contribute to the reuse catalog, or start one. Reuse comes for free with good design. Duplication is a product of politics.

Finding the Right Tools

Many a time we've been down to our last piece of fatback. And I'd say, "Should we eat it or render it down for soap?" Your Uncle Jed would say, "Render it down. God will provide food for us poor folks, but we gotta do our washin'."

Granny, The Beverly Hillbillies

Basic data modeling tools are adequate for small-scale development. If application development is extended to large-scale Visual Basic 6 distributed development, a sophisticated CASE tool is required that supports object modeling and partitioning the application into components that can be distributed among processors. Such a tool will require a higher level of expertise to use. A source code control system will be required to manage the software and documentation when applications become of significant size or complexity.

An essential part of managing the risk in Visual Basic 6 distributed development is testing performance under realistic stresses. Load-testing tools are available to assist in this process. Other classes of test tools test the user interface and the code structure.

To use such tools effectively, you must first understand them and then use a method to guide their use during development. Most tools and methods are not mature; some might not exist. Test the methods with the tools. Old methods might not be appropriate or might need adapting.

Configuration Management: Just Do It!

The greatest pleasure in life is doing what people say you cannot do.

Walter Bagehot

Configuration management is one of those tedious details that are often not implemented or are poorly observed. The problems caused by the lack of good configuration management become apparent only when it's too late to do the job properly. A project manager must ensure that code versions are managed across all implementation environments. Yes, that does include the mainframe JCL, the SQL, and the documentation. The structure of the database, the versions of any DLLs, ActiveX servers, operating system and network components, and procedures should also be under configuration management. Does your source code control software make it easy to manage the configuration of the entire system? Has anyone figured out how to do it? Probably not, so you'll have some work ahead of you to work it out and get it right. Do it now!

A Visual Basic 6 distributed application can have many interacting pieces of software. Changes in the configuration of each piece can cause ripple effects into other components. Code effects can be managed by maintaining consistent interfaces. Changes in loads and performance characteristics might require changes in other components. New versions should always be extensively tested before implementation. The potential for changes being required or imposed in interfaces grows with the number of interacting components.

Dependencies among components might be disguised. (For example, the query "Select * from X" includes an implied column ordering.) Rolling out an application or a new version can be a nightmare. Configuration management controls need to be handed over at the end of development to those carrying out support. It makes sense to involve support staff early so that their requirements are included in the configuration management plan.

One of the biggest challenges in configuration management is to make the controls supportive to the developer. If they are not, creative talents will be turned toward breaking the system.

DOCUMENTATION

When all else fails, read the instructions.

Cahn's axiom

Documentation might be boring, but it's vital. The following (minimal) documentation set works well for Visual Basic applications:

Functional/Requirements Specification

The requirements should be written down, and this specification should reference a Visual Basic prototype rather than embed screen shots in the document.
As a result, the document and the prototype together constitute the signed-off
requirements. This combination provides a much more realistic representation
of the requirements and leads to a solution that is much closer to what the users
really want.

Design Specification

A concise design specification should be produced (and maintained). It should
describe the key design points.

Excellently Commented Code

This form of documentation is key. In our experience, other forms of documentation invariably become out-of-date. How many times have you been asked
to make a change to someone else's code? Do you trust the documentation, or
do you review the comments and the code itself to find "the truth"? High-
quality module and subroutine headers, excellent block and in-line comments,
and good naming conventions are the best types of documentation possible.
At TMS, we have tools that build "documentation" from the source files—it's
a good test of the standard of commenting.

Test Plan

Testing within Visual Basic teams is generally too informal and ad hoc. Writing
a test plan forces some advance thought and planning.

TESTING

**Any nontrivial program contains at least one bug.
There are no trivial programs.**

**Seventh Law of
Computer Programming**

Historically, testing complex team-based applications has been broken down
into two main areas: unit testing and system testing. In unit testing, the modules

of the system are tested as individual units. Each unit has definite input and output parameters and (often) a definite single function. In system testing, the system is tested as a whole; that is, intercommunication among the individual units and functions of the complete system is tested.

Many of the problems experienced with testing Visual Basic applications occur because testers are trying to apply these conventional methods to systems for which they aren't appropriate. There are fundamental differences in the ways that Visual Basic applications work compared with old-style applications. In Visual Basic applications, you can do things that have no equivalent in a non-GUI application—use a mouse and Visual Basic constructs such as check boxes, option buttons and command buttons, and menus, to name just a few. There are many ways of doing the same thing in a GUI application that would have only one equivalent way in a non-GUI application. An example of this can be found in Microsoft Word, in which you can save a document in at least four ways. To properly test this new type of application, you need to break the old testing methods into four test streams: destruction, window design, navigational, and functional.

Destruction Testing

In this type of testing, the application is tested until it does something it's not supposed to—often in a totally unstructured fashion. You need to come up with a happy medium of what is appropriate. For example, you had 20 days allocated for this testing, and you could let 1 person do this for 20 days or you could let 40 people do this for half a day each. Ideally, about 5 or 6 people for 3 or 4 days each is the best proportion to get the maximum benefit.

Window Design Testing

This kind of test proves that each individual window (such as primary, secondary, pop-up, dialog box, message box) that the system consists of has been designed and built according to the project standards. The best method of ensuring this is in the form of a checklist—that is, points to be checked and signed off by the test reviewer. An example of such a checklist is shown in Table 15-2, but each project should come up with its own checklist for its own project standards and circumstances.

Table 15-2   **Example Window Design Checklist**

Checkpoints	Checked
The form positioning is correct relative to other forms on the screen.	
The form has the correct border style.	
The form has the Max, Min, and Control box set on or off as required.	
The control tabbing order is set and is logical to the user (upper left to lower right).	
Correct colors (foreground, background, fill, and so on) are applied to all controls per project standards.	
The first character of each word of text labels and menu choices is in uppercase text.	
Controls are aligned correctly.	
The text and captions of all controls are in the correct font and size.	
All menus, command buttons, check boxes, and option buttons have mnemonics set.	
All mnemonics are unique.	
Ellipses (…) are included for all routing menu choices.	
Shortcut keys for menu options are set if relevant.	
Command button and menu bar choices are unique.	
A Help menu option or Help command button exists if relevant.	
Command buttons are positioned appropriately on the form.	
A command button is set to be the Cancel default.	
A command button is set to be the Enter default if appropriate.	
Option buttons have a frame or group box.	
A default option button is set for each group.	
Combo box and list box entries are ordered appropriately.	
Enabled and/or Visible control properties are set where relevant.	
Date fields are formatted correctly.	
Image control is used rather than picture control where appropriate.	
3D and non-3D controls of the same type are not used on the same form.	

Navigational Testing

This test determines whether each window can be navigated to by initiation (via all the multiple ways of initiating) of all the different functions from any other appropriate window in the system, without necessarily performing any of the detailed processing that might be required when it gets there. Again, the best format for this test is a checklist, as shown in Table 15-3. Each list is unique to the particular window that is being tested. The list of navigational actions and results can be easily retested and verified by the test reviewer.

TABLE 15-3   **EXAMPLE NAVIGATION DESIGN CHECKLIST**

Navigation	Action Result	Navigation Checked
File : New	Entry fields reinitialized for new input	
File : Open	Windows Open dialog box displayed	
File : Delete	Customer details deleted after confirmation	
File : Print	Windows Print dialog box displayed	
File : Exit	Application terminated	
View : Customer Orders	Customer Orders screen displayed	
Options : Toolbar	Toolbar display toggled	
Help : Contents	Application Help file contents displayed	
Help : Search	Application Help file search displayed	
Help : Using Help	Windows Help file displayed	
Help : About	Application About box displayed	

Functional Testing

Having now tested that an individual window (or group of windows) is designed correctly, contains all the functions it should, contains the required methods for initiating those functions, and can navigate via those functions to all the places it has to go, you can now proceed to the "real" testing of the system. Functional testing ensures that the nuts and bolts functions of the system are actually tested. For example, when you initiate the Save function for a document (regardless of how you do it: via the mouse, the keyboard mnemonic keys, or a keyboard accelerator key), does the document get saved to disk correctly? The list of such tests will be a smaller list once the window design and navigational aspects of initiating a function are separated out. This part of the testing is probably the one that equates most closely (although perhaps not definitively) with the old concept of unit testing.

You would have one of each of these checklists per window in the application. Remember also that automated testing tools can be very useful for testing Visual Basic applications.

You should investigate many other forms of testing, among them these:

- Regression test at check-in
- Automated testing
- Usability testing
- Lots of pure pounding

Also, remember that bug tracking and the collection of metrics are both very important. A properly thought-out test strategy is vital for any Visual Basic 6 enterprise development. Shorten this phase at your peril!

BUILD PLANNING

Visual Basic 6 distributed development would appear to restrict the options for build and integration planning because of the dependencies among different elements of the development. However, by developing components and using layering, you can manage dependencies.

Your build should take advantage of the layered architecture (as shown in Figure 15-10 on the following page) so that builds can start earlier. Because the layers obviously interact, moving ahead in one area might require you to make assumptions that could prove to be false and result in rework. Part of the project manager's job is to understand the risk and balance it with the benefit of producing quicker results.

A thin user interface layer can be built as soon as requirements settle down and can emerge from prototyping. The business logic can be attached behind this layer when that logic is written. The design and build of the data services are likely to be the longest-running tasks. But provided a logical data provider is built to insulate the application from changes in database design, the data provider can be written to interface to a dummy database to provide a test harness for the application. The application will usually be written within a framework that handles generic interface services, error handling, persistence, and so on.

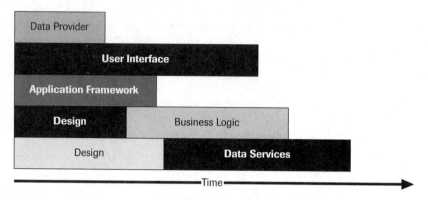

FIGURE 15-10 *Build planning*

YEAR 2000

Year 2000 will cost in the region of $600 billion world-wide to correct.

Gartner Group, 1996

Year 2000 is a well-defined maintenance project—the specification is about as simple as you can get. It is the first project in IT history with an immovable deadline. The consequence of slippage is not just a missed deadline, but the total and catastrophic failure of the organization. The alternative to addressing the problem is to go out of business.

Visual Basic developers are in denial: 90 percent of all applications are affected, not just mainframe code. One bank we know of has developed many Visual Basic systems through the use of freelance contractors. Its own IT department has no support for the language. Today 8 million lines of Visual Basic code are under maintenance by managers. About 5 percent of this code will have to change, and 100 percent will have to be thoroughly tested (incidentally, testing is about 60 percent of the effort). It's really scary.

For a thorough discussion of this topic, refer to Chapter 9. Please refer to Appendix D for details of TMS's Year 2000 Visual Basic services and products, for example Visual DateScope 2000 and VBA2000.

CONCLUDING THOUGHTS

If builders built buildings the way programmers wrote
programs, the first woodpecker to come along would
destroy civilization.

Weinberg's Second Law

This chapter has drawn together a series of ideas that you should take into account when developing a large-scale Visual Basic 6 distributed system. The introduction of Visual Basic 6 means that Visual Basic developers have to change their attitude toward developing higher-quality and more easily maintainable applications. The pursuit of quality must become the prime objective of every member of the team, from the most junior programmer to top management.

You can, of course, improve quality in many different ways, as described early in this chapter. In our discussion, we have touched only on the very basics:

- **Commitment.** Every person involved in a project must be totally committed to the success of the project.

- **Technical excellence.** Insist on the best, and provide support in the form of proper training and the allocation of sufficient hardware and software resources.

- **Communication.** Ensure that the right hand knows what the left is doing. The "mushroom syndrome" must be abandoned forever.

Several basic commonsense steps will help to ensure that quality is maintained in any Visual Basic development:

- **Manage it:** Manage risk carefully.

- **Plan it:** A formal project plan is essential.

- **Design it:** A poorly designed interface to a poorly designed technical infrastructure will invariably result in a very poor system.

- **Test it:** And then test it again. Then get someone else to test it.

- **Review it:** Careful monitoring throughout the development cycle will help to prevent eleventh-hour disasters.

- **Document it:** There is simply no such thing as not having enough time to comment the code properly as you are writing it.

Visual Basic 6 is one of the most powerful tools available to the Windows developer today. And like any powerful tool, in the wrong hands the results can be disastrous. Used correctly, however, Visual Basic 6 can provide unprecedented levels of productivity and sophistication.

Accessibility in Visual Basic

Making Your Applications Work for Everyone

Jean is a Senior Technical Editor at Microsoft Press. After a number of years developing internal applications for a large corporation, she left the world of development to combine her interest in technology with her love of books. Jean has edited books on a variety of topics, ranging from Visual C++ to the Windows Registry, and has edited the first edition of *Advanced Microsoft Visual Basic*. When not working or commuting, Jean enjoys hiking, photography, taking care of her dog Bailey, and just relaxing with a good, nontechnical book.

This chapter focuses on an aspect of programming that is too often overlooked—creating applications that are accessible to people with disabilities. There are few jobs today that don't require the use of a computer. Creating an application that can't be used by someone with a disability essentially denies that otherwise qualified person a job. This type of exclusion is damaging; it can even be illegal for a company to require the use of such software to perform a particular job. This chapter will help you ensure that your applications are accessible to as many people as possible.

WHAT IS A DISABILITY?

For the purposes of this discussion, a disability is simply a physical or mental limitation that makes performing a given task difficult, if not impossible. When used in reference to the software industry, disabilities are normally categorized as shown in the list on the following page.

- Vision: includes such impairments as blindness, low vision, and color blindness

- Hearing: includes deafness and reduced hearing

- Mobility: includes paralysis, weakness, and a wide variety of injuries and diseases

- Cognitive/Language: includes problems with thinking, memory, learning, and general perception

- Seizure: includes epileptic seizures of varying degrees

In the next section, as I go through some of the main features of accessible software, I'll highlight some of the reasons these features are necessary and who will benefit most from them.

THE FUNDAMENTALS OF ACCESSIBILITY DEVELOPMENT

You've probably heard about screen readers for people who are blind and voice activation for people with mobility limitations. Even if you're not designing software specifically to work with these types of hardware, the information in this chapter still applies to you as a developer. Any application you develop with Microsoft Visual Basic should have certain features that make it accessible. The following sections describe some of the more basic features to consider when developing accessible applications and how to implement those features.

Using the Keyboard

One of the most important considerations in the design of an application is how user input will be captured. In graphical user interfaces (GUIs), application developers often tend to focus on capturing input from the mouse. A user typically employs the mouse to perform actions such as clicking buttons, dragging and dropping files and information, and highlighting data. The mouse is a very useful tool and the most convenient method of accessing features of a GUI application.

As a developer, you painstakingly design a user interface that has a lot of buttons, menu options, drop-down lists, and other such features to make sure all the information your application is presenting is a simple mouse-click away. You might spend months working on such an application getting it to look and function just right.

Now it's time for the end user to run your application. As an example, run the NoKeyboard sample application included on the companion CD. (See Figure 16-1.) You'll find that it's functional and simple to use. Now try using it without the mouse. You've just found yourself in a predicament many people find themselves in every day. A number of disabilities can make it difficult or impossible to use a mouse. Quite often, experienced computer users and skilled typists simply prefer to use the keyboard—it can be quicker and more convenient than using the mouse. Whatever the reason, because your application relies so heavily on the mouse, it's totally useless or extremely inconvenient for a very large number of people.

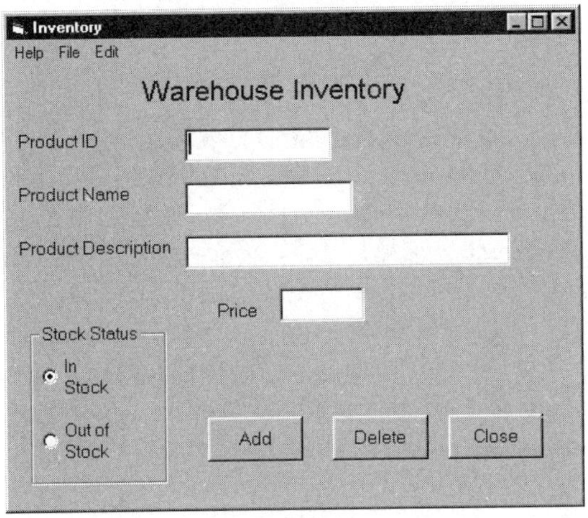

FIGURE 16-1   *Sample application with limited keyboard interface*

What can you do to remedy this situation? You must design keyboard access into all your applications and interfaces. Try running the Keyboard sample. You'll notice it looks very similar to the NoKeyboard sample, but there is one big difference: every action you can perform with the mouse you can also perform using the keyboard. Let's go over some of the changes that were made to the NoKeyboard sample to produce the Keyboard sample.

NOTE

The samples for this chapter that you'll find on the companion CD are to demonstrate user interface features only. You won't find a lot of functionality behind the samples that doesn't relate to displaying and using the interface.

Menu layout

One difference between the Keyboard sample and the NoKeyboard sample is the menu layout—the menu items are in a different order. If you've ever worked in product support, you know you spend a lot of time explaining things that can be found in the online Help. So why not call the user's attention to the Help option by putting it first on the menu? Because that's not where the user is used to finding it. Windows applications have been designed according to standards that allow users to move seamlessly from one application to the next. You might not agree with all the standards, but for your users' sake, don't try to change them. Menu order is especially important for people with visual impairments who expect to find certain interface elements in certain places, and searching around an interface can be a time-consuming and frustrating chore.

Key combinations

Shortcuts are an important part of interface design. All menu options should have an access key. An access key appears as an underlined character in the option name, indicating pressing that key activates that option. Pay careful attention to the keys you are assigning—every key must be unique within each menu or submenu. If your menu includes options that you expect to be used frequently, providing hotkeys (such as Ctrl+S for File Save), also known as accelerator keys, can save the user a lot of time. The user can perform the action without continually activating the menu. Look at the difference between the menus in Figure 16-2.

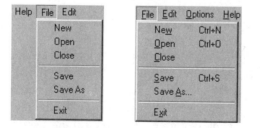

FIGURE 16-2   *Menus from the NoKeyboard sample (left) and the Keyboard sample (right)*

If you're providing functions that are common to most applications, use the most common naming standards and key combinations, such as File Open and Ctrl+O for opening a file. I once had to work with software that had menus you would expect to see, but the keyboard interface drove me crazy. Instead of exiting an application by selecting Alt+F (for the File menu) and then X (for Exit), the interface was designed to select Alt+F and then E. You'd be surprised to know just how many times I hit Alt+F and then X and the computer just beeped at me. Your users will spend a lot less time learning and remembering how to use your application if you give them something they're familiar with.

Navigation

Navigation is the means by which the user moves from one part of a window or dialog box to another, such as from one text box to another. Keyboard navigation is usually accomplished through use of the Tab key and the arrow keys. Setting a logical navigation order makes an application much easier to use than if pressing the Tab key or an arrow key takes the user to unpredictable places. When you create a form in Visual Basic, the tab order of controls on the form is set automatically according to the order in which you place the controls on the form. This can easily make for a strange tab order if you've rearranged the controls or deleted and then added controls. For example, the tab order shown in Figure 16-3 will confuse or simply annoy users. The tab order in Figure 16-4 on the following page is much more intuitive. When your user interface is final, you should determine a logical tab order and then set the *TabIndex* property of each control according to that order (starting with 0).

NOTE

The MSDN Library includes a sample application named TabOrder. You can use this add-in in your Visual Basic environment to set the tab order of your form without setting each individual *TabIndex* property yourself.

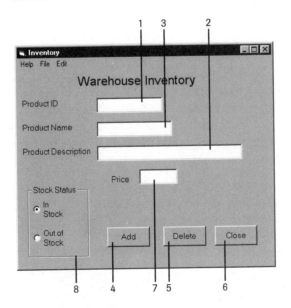

FIGURE 16-3   *Confusing tab order*

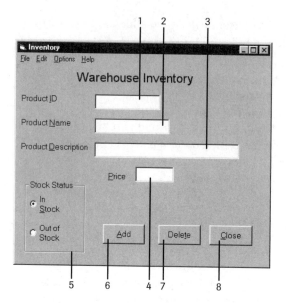

FIGURE 16-4   *Logical tab order*

Navigation order is a common convenience for all users but is especially important for users who don't or can't use the mouse. For example, someone who uses a screen reader will tab through the controls on a form to find out what each control does. Logical navigation makes the interface much easier to use and understand.

Colors

Have you ever walked through an office building and glanced at the computer monitors people are using? If you have, you've probably noticed the great variance in color schemes people set to display on their monitors. Many times I've looked at someone's monitor and wondered how anyone could look at that horrible color combination all day. But I'm just talking about personal preference, right? What does that have to do with accessibility programming?

Color schemes are an integral part of programming. In Visual Basic, you can assign colors to your interface elements easily enough by using control properties. You can set controls to different colors depending on the options the user selects. You can use colors to convey information to the user and to make your application exciting and interesting.

Now remember those awful color combinations. You can't be sure everyone will enjoy the colors you've chosen for your application. What's more, some of the color schemes you see weren't set because people wanted to look at something pleasing to the eye, they were set so that the user could clearly see everything on the screen. An example of such a color combination would be the High Contrast color combination. This setting is available from the Display Properties and from Accessibility Options, both available from the Control Panel. See the section "High Contrast" later in this chapter for further information on this setting.

Color blindness and other visual impairments affect a lot of people in many different ways. You can't accurately guess what color combination every computer user is going to be able to see on the screen. But you can design your application to allow each user to set his or her own colors, avoiding the problem altogether. You can do this by setting the colors in your application based on the system settings the user defined on the Display Properties property sheet. Visual Basic includes a set of constants that represent system colors, such as *vbWindowBackground* and *vbTitleBarText*. We'll be using some of these constants in our color sample applications.

Background patterns

Sometimes it's nice to have an image or a pattern in the background of an application: an image of your company logo, for instance. While this can look nice and seem unobtrusive, a background image can cause a lot of problems for your users. It makes the screen busy, so people with cognitive disabilities can have difficulties focusing on the actual information provided on the screen. Background images can also cause difficulties for users who are color blind, and even those with low vision, because text and labels often end up on top of a busy background. As an example, let's look at the FullColor sample, shown in Figure 16-5 on the following page.

The background image in this case is a picture of Half Dome at Yosemite National Park. It's very pretty and is relevant to the topic of hiking addressed by the application. However, if you're not in high color mode the first thing you'll notice is that this picture is quite ugly. If you are in high color mode and can see all the colors of the picture, you'll notice that the screen is busy, probably too busy for some users. The best solution to this problem is to provide the user with a means of turning off the background image. The ColorOpt sample gives the user an Options menu with a Background menu item that allows the user to turn the background image on and off. This is done with a call such as that on the following page.

FIGURE 16-5   *FullColor sample showing a detailed background image*

```
Const IDB_BACKGROUND As Long = 101
  ⋮
Private Sub ChangeBackground(ByVal bRemove As Boolean)
    If Not bRemove Then              ' Turn the background off
        Set frmHiking.Picture = LoadPicture()
        frmHiking.BackColor = vbWindowBackground
    Else                             ' Turn the background on
        Set frmHiking.Picture = LoadResPicture(IDB_BACKGROUND, vbResBitmap)
    End If
End Sub
```

Notice the *BackColor* setting. The *vbWindowBackground* constant designates the Windows system setting for a window background. By using this constant, the application displays the window background color set by the user's Display options. You can find all the color constants in Visual Basic's online Help under Reference/Language Reference/Constants/Core Language Constants/ Color Constants.

Color coding

The FullColor sample has been designed to give the user a choice between day hiking and overnight hiking and to suggest equipment that should be carried on the selected hike. A simple way to do this is to color code the options. To make the options visible on the picture background, I chose a green color

(&HFF00&) from my system palette at design time as the Required color and a yellow color (&HFFFF&) as the Optional color.

NOTE

Colors are identified by hexadecimal values that represent the intensity of the component colors red, green, and blue. The component values range in intensity from 00 (lowest) to FF (highest). For example, the hexadecimal value for pure green is FF00, or 00FF00—00 for red, FF for green, and 00 for blue. Likewise, pure red would be defined as FF0000.

When you set your colors at design time, you can use the Properties window to set the foreground and background colors for controls and forms using the drop-down palette shown here.

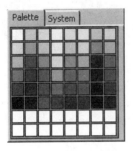

If you select a color from the palette, you'll be selecting from your current system palette, as I did. If you're running in high color, you could be choosing colors that someone running in 256-color or 16-color mode doesn't have. Windows will do its best to substitute, but often the results aren't what you'd like. For now, though, we have a nice application with a pretty background that conveys the information we need. Unless, of course, the user can't read it. The green and yellow I've chosen might be invisible or indistinguishable to someone who is colorblind. These colors might also not be visible to users who have turned the background picture off, depending on what their default window background color is.

The first solution to using the green and yellow colors is to use system colors, as we did with the window background. For the ColorOpt sample, I've set the Required color to *vbHighlight* and the Optional color to *vbWindowText*. However, even these colors aren't enough to distinguish the different options. You should never rely on color alone to convey information. Our final solution is in the ColorOpt2 sample, shown on the following page.

In this sample, we're still using the colors to differentiate the options, but we've changed from labels to check boxes. Now the Required options have check marks next to them as another way to convey the information to the user. Another solution, which you'll see only if you have a screen reader device connected to your machine, is the changing of the check box captions depending on the option selected. If the user has a screen reader connected to his or her machine, you want to turn off the background image and give a nongraphical indication of the options. So in addition to the check boxes, if the ColorOpt2 sample detects a screen reader device it will add text to each caption indicating whether the option is required. See the section "Screen Readers" later in this chapter for information on determining whether a screen reader device is present.

Sound

Computers make noise. I sometimes give my PC a good thunk to reduce the noise. But most of the noise comes from the speakers, and most of the time it occurs for a good reason.

Why applications make noise

The primary uses of sound in applications can be placed into three categories:

- Decoration
- Alert to information on the screen
- Alert to information not on the screen

ACCESSIBILITY IN VISUAL BASIC

CHAPTER
16

An example of sound as decoration would be background music that plays while an application is open. This use of sound doesn't affect accessibility, as long as it doesn't interfere with the alert sounds or screen readers.

An alert to information on the screen would be sounding a beep to draw the user's attention to a visual error message. An example of an alert to information not on the screen would be the beep that sounds when the user clicks an inactive area of the application.

When is sound a factor?

Sound can be a great benefit for people who are blind or have low vision. Sounds provide an indication that something has happened on the screen that requires attention. On the other hand, sound is of no benefit at all to someone who is deaf or hard of hearing. Even for users who don't have disabilities, there are times when they can't hear or don't want to hear sounds. If you're working in a factory, you probably won't hear much coming from the computer. If you're in a library, you don't want your computer beeping and talking. All these situations point out the need for visual cues to work in conjunction with sounds to inform the user of anything important going on in an application.

Audio and visual cues together

The number one rule in using sound in your application is to never use it as the only means of communicating important information. You don't have to give visual indications of every sound all the time, but it should at least be an option. You could put a menu option in your applications that turns sounds within the application on or off, or an option to set whether visual cues will be displayed in conjunction with sounds.

When you supply a visual indication of a sound, make sure it's noticeable. One option is to use the *FlashWindow* function, explained later in this chapter. While *FlashWindow* is designed to provide a quick visual cue that something has happened, you might also want to consider using a visual indicator that remains on the screen for a certain amount of time or until users dismiss it so that you're more likely to get their attention.

Closed captioning

I'm not going to go into the details of adding multimedia elements to your application. But if you do display audio/visual clips in your application, you should provide closed captioning. Closed captioning is the displaying of

713

dialogue and sound effects in an audio clip as text on the screen, similar to subtitles. Microsoft has just developed a new technology called Synchronized Accessible Media Interchange (SAMI) format, designed specifically to provide closed captioning to multimedia software and Web applications. SAMI will be included as part of the Microsoft NetShow 3.0 (which replaces NetShow, Microsoft DirectShow, and Microsoft ActiveMovie) media player. You can also use the ShowSounds Accessibility option, described later, to determine whether you should turn on closed captioning.

Size

The size of a form, as well as the sizes of the objects and controls on that form, impacts users with low vision and mobility impairments. I find often that it's in the nature of a programmer to try to put as much information in one place as possible, but in terms of accessibility and general usability, that's not always the best way to go. Here are a few sizing guidelines to follow when designing your user interface:

- Make sure the interface fits on a 640x480 pixel screen resolution. Users with low vision, and sometimes those just trying to avoid eye strain, keep their resolution at this highest point. Creating an interface larger than 640x480 pixels will cause part of your interface to be hidden and inaccessible to many users.

- Use the system settings to display standard elements. This is pretty simple in Visual Basic. When a user changes the system display settings (from the Control Panel Display properties) and applies those settings, your Visual Basic application will automatically pick up those changes. Try running one of the sample applications that contains a menu. With the sample still running, go to your Display properties and change the font size of the menu. When you click Apply, you'll see that the menu in your Visual Basic application has changed to the new settings. However, the size of the menu doesn't change the size of the form, so the menu might wrap on the form if you don't change the form size to accommodate the menu. You might also need to resize your controls at run time based on the changes to the system settings in order to make sure they're all still visible. See the following discussion on using the Size sample.

- Allow customized sizes. You can allow the user to customize certain properties at run time. For instance, you can allow the user to size a form, at which time you'd adjust the size and spacing of the controls in the *Form_Resize* event procedure. You can also include common dialog controls that allow the user to set the font sizes and styles specifically for your application. Again, you'll need to resize the form controls accordingly. (See the Size sample.)

- Make borders visible. Borders separating screen elements can make a user interface more intuitive, but only if the borders are visible to everyone. To determine an appropriate border size, you should call the *GetSystemMetrics* function, discussed later in this chapter, with the constant values that determine border width and height.

Size example

I've created an example to demonstrate how to dynamically size controls and allow the user to customize the look of an application. This sample application allows the user to size the form and set the font size for all the controls on the form. The form and the controls adjust to fit the changed settings. First let's take a look at the form in design mode.

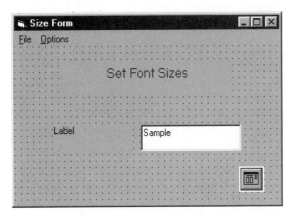

I've kept this example simple by including only three controls—two labels and a text box—as well as a common dialog control. I've also added two menus: File and Options. The Options menu contains one menu item, Font. This item uses the common dialog control to display the Font dialog box, shown on the following page.

By selecting the Font menu item, the user can set the font style and size for all the controls on the form. Let's take a look at the code that does this:

```
Private Sub mnuOptionsFont_Click()
    Dim ctlControl As Control

    ' Initialize the settings and display the Font dialog box.
    With dlgCDialog1
        .Flags = cdlCFBoth ' Display the screen and printer fonts.
        .FontName = labLabel2.FontName
        .FontSize = labLabel2.FontSize
        .ShowFont
    End With

    On Error Resume Next
    ' Run through all the controls, setting the font size and style
    ' according to the user selections in the Font dialog box.
    For Each ctlControl In frmSize.Controls
        With ctlControl.Font
            .Name = dlgCDialog1.FontName
            .Size = dlgCDialog1.FontSize
            .Bold = dlgCDialog1.FontBold
            .Italic = dlgCDialog1.FontItalic
            ' Set the heading size to be larger than the rest
            ' of the controls.
            If ctlControl.Name = labLabel1.Name Then
                .Size = .Size + 4
```

```
        End If
    End With

    ' Resize the controls to fit the new font.
    ctlControl.AutoSize = False
    ctlControl.AutoSize = True

  Next ctlControl

End Sub
```

The first thing we do is initialize the settings for the common dialog control. We set the *Flags* property to *cdlCFBoth* to indicate that we want the dialog box to display fonts that are available for both the screen and the printer. Next we initialize the font name and size to the current settings for the controls. We then call *ShowFont* to display the Font dialog box.

At this point, execution of the Visual Basic routine pauses while the Font dialog box is displayed and the user selects his or her settings. When the user closes the dialog box, the application loops through the controls on the form and assigns the new settings to each one. The label that acts as the heading for the form should stand out from the rest of the controls, so I've increased the font size for that control.

NOTE

Some of the controls on a form might not support the *Font* property. To guard against any errors that might arise, I've included the error statement *On Error Resume Next* to bypass these controls. Chapter 1 of this book warns against problems that can occur from using this statement. I've used it here for the sake of simplicity, but in your own programs you'll probably want to check the control type to make sure the control supports the given property, and use the error checking recommendations described in Chapter 1.

Looping through the controls and changing the settings isn't the final step. The font might now be too big for the controls that were created at design time. Maybe when you designed the controls you were sure to set the *AutoSize* property to True, thinking that would size the controls as needed. Unfortunately, the *AutoSize* property doesn't work like that. Each time the settings are changed, you need to set the *AutoSize* property to False to uninitialize it and then set it to True again so that the control will be resized.

We now have all the code in place so that the user can size the fonts in the application. But what happens if the controls aren't fully visible on the form anymore? Or if the user just wants to see more or less of the form? To accommodate these possibilities, we've made the form resizeable. The user can make the form as big or as small as he or she wants (allowing for screen size). If we leave the controls as we placed them at design time, sizing the form smaller would cut off some controls, while sizing it bigger would leave the controls where they are and just show a lot of blank space on the form. We want the controls to move in proportion to the sizing of the form. For this to happen, the placement of the controls must be changed in the *Form_Resize* event procedure.

```vb
Private Sub Form_Resize()
    Dim ctlControl     As Control
    Dim nHalfWidth     As Integer
    Dim nHalfWBuffered As Integer
    Dim nHalfHeight    As Integer
    Const BUFFER_AREA  As Integer = 100

    nHalfWidth = ScaleWidth / 2
    nHalfWBuffered = nHalfWidth - BUFFER_AREA
    nHalfHeight = ScaleHeight / 2

    On Error Resume Next
    For Each ctlControl In frmSize.Controls
        With ctlControl
            Select Case .Name
                Case "labLabel1"
                    .Alignment = vbCenter
                    .Width = ScaleWidth
                    .Left = 0
                    .Top = 0
                Case "labLabel2"
                    .Width = nHalfWBuffered
                    .Left = 0
                    .Alignment = vbRightJustify
                    .Top = nHalfHeight
                Case "txtText1"
                    .Width = nHalfWBuffered
                    .Left = nHalfWidth
                    .Alignment = vbLeftJustify
                    .Top = nHalfHeight
            End Select
        End With
    Next ctlControl

End Sub
```

The *Form_Resize* event procedure is called every time the user sizes the form, as well as when the form is first displayed. For each of the controls on the form, we set the *Width*, *Left*, *Alignment*, and *Top* properties to determine where on the form the control will be placed. For example, we always want the form heading, *labLabel1*, to be centered on the form no matter what the size of the form is, so we've set the *Alignment* property to *vbCenter*. Because there are no other controls at the same vertical position as *labLabel1*, we can set the *Width* property to *ScaleWidth*, which is the width of the form. That also allows us to place the left edge of *labLabel1* all the way to the left edge of the form, at position 0. The heading will always be at the top of the form, so the *Top* property is also set to 0.

The other controls are sized in a similar manner. Because they are located side by side, they must share the width of the form (*ScaleWidth* / 2) and allow for some white space in between (–100). Run the Size sample, and try setting the fonts to different sizes and resizing the form to see the results.

CREATING A RESOURCE FILE

In the code sample shown above, you see calls to *LoadPicture* and *LoadResPicture*. The call to *LoadPicture* with an empty parameter list removes any picture that has been loaded. To put the picture back on the form, you could call *LoadPicture* with the filename of a picture (BMP, JPEG, and so on) as the parameter. However, it's more efficient to store your picture in a resource file and use *LoadResPicture* to load the picture from the resource file.

To create a resource file in Visual Basic, you first must add the Resource Editor add-in to your Visual Basic project. Select Add-In Manager from the Add-Ins menu to bring up the Add-In Manager dialog box. From the Available Add-Ins list, select VB 6 Resource Editor. Check the Loaded/Unloaded check box in the Load Behavior group, and click OK. You'll now see the VB Resource Editor button, shown here, on the Standard toolbar.

Now that you've included the Resource Editor in your project, you can create a resource file and add the bitmap you're going to use as your background image. (You can also add text strings, icons, cursors, and custom resources to the resource file.) Click the VB Resource Editor button to open the Resource Editor window. Click the Add Bitmap button on the Resource Editor toolbar to open the Open A Bitmap File dialog box. Select the bitmap you want to include in your resource file, and click Open. The bitmap is added to your resource file and assigned a resource ID that you will use as the first parameter in your call to *LoadResPicture*. Save the resource file.

ADVANCED ACCESSIBILITY FEATURES

The Windows operating system provides a number of accessibility features. In Microsoft Windows 9x and Microsoft Windows NT 4 and later, users can set Accessibility Options from the Control Panel. These next sections will describe how to access those system settings and use them in your program design.

Windows Versions

Before we get into system settings and Accessibility Options, I need to emphasize that not all accessibility options are available to all versions of Windows. In this section, you can assume that unless otherwise noted, the settings are valid for Windows 95, Windows 98, Windows NT 4, and Windows NT 5. Where exceptions occur, in the sample programs I've added the Microsoft SysInfo Control 6.0 component to the project and added the control to the form. This allows me to check and make sure we're running on a system that supports the given Accessibility setting, as follows:

```
Dim nOS  As Integer
Dim nVer As Integer
Const WINDOWS_95 As Integer = 1
Const WINDOWS_NT As Integer = 2
Const VER_95_NT4 As Integer = 4

With SysInfo1
    nOS = .OSPlatform
    nVer = .OSVersion
End With

' If Windows 95, Windows 98, or Windows NT 5.0
If (nOS = WINDOWS_95 And nVer >= VER_95_NT4) Or _
    (nOS = WINDOWS_NT And nVer > VER_95_NT4) Then
    ' Check accessibility setting
End If
```

SystemParametersInfo

The *SystemParametersInfo* function provides access to many of the Windows system settings. I'll go over a few of the settings that are most relevant to accessibility development. But first let's take a look at the Visual Basic declaration of this function:

```
Declare Function SystemParametersInfo Lib "user32" _
    Alias "SystemParametersInfoA" (ByVal iAction As Long, _
```

```
ByVal iParam As Long, pvParam As Any, _
ByVal fWinIni As Long) As Long
```

If you don't understand what's happening in this *Declare* statement, don't worry about it. I'll explain enough to allow you to use it effectively in your programs. Just remember that all public *Declare* statements must be placed in a standard module (BAS file) in your Visual Basic project.

NOTE

Declaring an argument As Any as we did in our *Declare* statement goes against the standards established by The Mandelbrot Set (International) Limited (TMS) and as outlined in Appendix A. The parameter is declared As Any here because the return type of that parameter is dependent on the input. However, the preferred method, when practical, would be to create a different *Declare* statement for each possible return value. For example, if you were going to call *SystemParametersInfo* to retrieve information that would be returned as a Long, your *Declare* statement would look something like this:

```
Declare Function WinLongSystemParametersInfo Lib "user32" _
    Alias "SystemParametersInfoA" (ByVal iAction As Long, _
    ByVal iParam As Long, pvParam As Long, _
    ByVal fWinIni As Long) As Long
```

Notice also the prefix *Win* on the function declaration. This is a TMS standard in addition. However, in the samples in this chapter I've left the prefix off the declarations for clarity: you can see the exact name of the DLL functions, as well as the parameter names, and can look them up on Microsoft's Web site or in Visual Studio's online Help if you want more information.

VISUAL BASIC DECLARE STATEMENTS FOR SYSTEM DLLS

Visual Basic ships with a utility called the API Viewer. This utility, located in the Common\Tools\Winapi folder on the Visual Basic CD, reads in a text file filled with Visual Basic *Declare* statements, Type definitions, and Constant declarations for the Win32 API. You can search for the statement you want and then copy and paste it into your application. If you want to really understand how to declare functions from C language DLLs, I suggest you take a look at the chapters in this book by Phil Ridley (Chapter 10) and Peet Morris (Chapter 11).

The settings for the function parameters for *SystemParametersInfo* depend on what system setting you're querying for. The first parameter in the *System-ParametersInfo* function requires a numeric constant.

Keyboard preference

The first constant setting we'll use is *SPI_GETKEYBOARDPREF*, which is defined as follows:

```
Const SPI_GETKEYBOARDPREF As Long = 68
```

Specifying *SPI_GETKEYBOARDPREF* as the first parameter in the *System-ParametersInfo* function indicates that we're querying the system as to whether the user prefers the keyboard to the mouse. The user specifies this setting by selecting Accessibility Options from the Control Panel and then selecting the Show Extra Keyboard Help In Programs option on the Keyboard property page.

NOTE

This option is not available in Windows NT 4.

The second and fourth parameters of *SystemParametersInfo*, *iParam* and *fWinIni*, should be set to 0. The third parameter, *pvParam*, returns True if the user has selected keyboard preference, False otherwise. So your call would look something like this:

```
Dim bUseKeyboard As Boolean

If SystemParametersInfo(SPI_GETKEYBOARDPREF, 0, _
                        bUseKeyboard, 0) Then
    ' Enable and display keyboard shortcuts.
End If
```

You can see an example of this function in the Keyboard sample.

High contrast

The High Contrast option is useful when checking color settings. The user sets this display option by selecting Accessibility Options from the Control Panel, clicking the Display tab, and selecting the Use High Contrast check box. The user sets this option to display a system-defined set of colors that provide a high amount of contrast. This option is especially useful to users who are colorblind. If this option is set, it is an indication to your application that it should be using system colors and hiding all background images.

To find this setting, you need to declare the following user-defined type (UDT) in a module in your project.

```
Type tHIGHCONTRAST
    cbSize             As Long
    dwflags            As Long
    lpszDefaultScheme  As String
End Type
```

You next define the system constants:

```
Public Const SPI_GETHIGHCONTRAST As Long = 66
Public Const HCF_HIGHCONTRASTON As Long = &H1&
```

After declaring the *SystemParametersInfo* function, you can make your call as follows:

```
Dim thc     As tHIGHCONTRAST
Dim lReturn As Long

thc.cbSize = Len(thc)
lReturn = SystemParametersInfo(SPI_GETHIGHCONTRAST, Len(thc), _
                               thc, 0)

If thc.dwflags And HCF_HIGHCONTRASTON Then
    ' High contrast option is on.
Else
    ' High contrast option is off.
End If
```

You can see this function in the ColorOpt2 sample. In that sample, if the high contrast option is on when the application starts, the background picture is turned off by default.

Screen readers

Windows 9x and Windows NT 5 have the ability to determine whether a screen reader device is connected to the computer. You can capture this information by calling *SystemParametersInfo* with the *SPI_GETSCREENREADER* option, as shown on the following page.

```
Public Const SPI_GETSCREENREADER As Long = 70

Dim bScreenReader As Boolean

lReturn = SystemParametersInfo(SPI_GETSCREENREADER, 0, _
                               bScreenReader, 0)

If bScreenReader Then
    ' Screen reader detected; turn off the background and
    ' ensure that all graphic indicators have text explanations.
Else
    ' No screen reader detected.
End If
```

Show sounds

The *SystemParametersInfo* function can be used to determine the ShowSounds setting, but the *GetSystemMetrics* function is the preferred method, so we'll save this discussion for the *GetSystemMetrics* section below.

GetSystemMetrics

The *GetSystemMetrics* function is used to determine system metrics and configuration settings. The Visual Basic *Declare* statement looks like this:

```
Declare Function GetSystemMetrics Lib "user32" _
    (ByVal nIndex As Long) As Long
```

The *nIndex* parameter takes a constant that specifies which system metric to get. The return value depends on the *nIndex* parameter.

The ShowSounds metric

In Windows, the user can set the ShowSounds option on the Accessibility Options property sheet, available from the Control Panel. Setting this option indicates that the user wants to see a visual indication of sounds that occur as part of applications and the operating system. You'll want to check this option in your application and provide visual indications if the ShowSounds option is True.

```
Const SM_SHOWSOUNDS As Long = 70

If GetSystemMetrics(SM_SHOWSOUNDS) Then
    ' Enable visual indicators.
End If
```

One method of providing visual indications of the information the sound is conveying is to use the *FlashWindow* function, discussed below.

Line borders

To set the proper border width and height around a control or image (as discussed in the "Size" section earlier), you would call *GetSystemMetrics* with the following constants:

```
Const SM_CXBORDER As Long = 5
Const SM_CYBORDER As Long = 6
```

GetSystemMetrics will return the width and height measurements in pixels.

FlashWindow

The *FlashWindow* function does just what it says: it flashes the title bar of a window. If a window is active it flashes inactive, if a window is inactive it flashes active. *FlashWindow* also flashes the window's taskbar icon. This function is a visual means of attracting attention to a particular window on the screen. The *Declare* statement for *FlashWindow* is as follows:

```
Declare Function FlashWindow Lib "user32" _
    (ByVal hwnd As Long, ByVal dwflags As Long) As Long
```

You also need to declare whatever constants you'll want to use for the *dwflags* parameter.

```
Public Const FLASHW_STOP      As Long = 0
Public Const FLASHW_CAPTION   As Long = &H1&
Public Const FLASHW_TRAY      As Long = &H2&
Public Const FLASHW_ALL       As Long = FLASHW_CAPTION Or FLASHW_TRAY
Public Const FLASHW_TIMER     As Long = &H4&
Public Const FLASHW_TIMERNOFG As Long = &HC&
```

The FLASHW constants have the following meanings:

- *FLASHW_STOP*: stops the window from flashing and restores it to its original state
- *FLASHW_CAPTION*: flashes the title bar on the window
- *FLASHW_TRAY*: flashes the button for the given window on the taskbar
- *FLASHW_ALL*: flashes the title bar and the taskbar button

- *FLASHW_TIMER*: flashes continuously until the *FLASHW_STOP* flag is set

- *FLASHW_TIMERNOFG*: flashes continuously as long as the window is in the background

NOTE

These flags are actually valid only in Windows 98 and Windows NT 5. In earlier versions of Windows, the second parameter of the *FlashWindow* call is a Boolean value that determines whether the window should flash (True) or return to its original state (False). However, you don't have to check for the Windows version to use the above flags. Any flag you set other than FLASHW_STOP will be interpreted as True and the window will flash.

THE *FLASHWINDOWEX* FUNCTION

The Microsoft Platform SDK includes a function named *FlashWindowEx*. This function is similar to *FlashWindow*, but it offers much more functionality. *FlashWindowEx* is part of the Microsoft Platform SDK, which you can download from the Microsoft Web site. *FlashWindowEx* is available only for Windows 98 and Windows NT 5.

The *Declare* statement for *FlashWindowEx* looks like this:

```
Declare Function FlashWindowEx Lib "user32" Alias "FlashWindowEx" _
    (ByVal pfwi As tFLASHWINFO) As Long
```

You specify the function parameters in a UDT, declared as follows:

```
Type tFLASHWINFO
    cbSize    As Long
    hwnd      As Long
    dwFlags   As Long
    uCount    As Long
    dwTimeout As Long
End Type
```

The first variable in the UDT, *cbSize*, contains the size of the UDT, *Len(cbSize)*. The next variable contains the window handle for the window you want to flash. The next variable, *dwFlags*, contains one of the *FLASHW* flags defined above. The variable *uCount* specifies the number of times you want the window to flash. The variable *dwTimeout* contains the rate, in milliseconds, at which you want the window to flash. If you set *dwTimeout* to 0, the default cursor blink rate will be used.

I've put an example of using this function in the Sound sample. I placed the call within a timer loop so that the window will flash more than once depending on the speed of the system. You can use different types of timing and looping mechanisms if you want the window to flash more than once, but be very careful if you do this. Certain rates of flashing can cause seizures in users suffering from epilepsy. I'm actually not terribly comfortable with the loop I put into the Sounds sample because I haven't placed any restrictions on the actual speed. A flash rate below two hertz is recommended.

Microsoft Active Accessibility

Active Accessibility is an architecture developed by Microsoft designed to make software more accessible. So far, all the methods we've discussed have dealt only with Windows system settings and functions. Active Accessibility provides a whole new set of function calls and interfaces to enable you to create applications that developers of accessibility aids, such as screen readers, can interface with.

That's the good news. The bad news is that Active Accessibility is still a relatively new architecture. As of this writing, Active Accessibility is still on version 1.1. This version has a number of limitations, the first of which is that it's not available on Windows NT 4. If you're developing with Windows 9x, you can install the SDK and implement the functions and procedures in your development project. However, the Active Accessibility SDK will not install under Windows NT 4.

Now for the next problem: Active Accessibility—the SDK and all the documentation—were designed for C++. The SDK comes with a sample Visual Basic 4 program that does run under Visual Basic 6. The SDK also comes with a type library that you can import into your Visual Basic project. The problem with the type library is that the function calls tend to differ slightly from those in the C++ documentation, and they don't come with any documentation of their own.

So, that said, we're going to make do with what we have and get as much out of this technology as possible in preparation for the improvements the Microsoft Active Accessibility group will make in the future. We'll walk through a sample program, AAccess (shown in Figure 16-6 on the following page), that demonstrates how to use some of the object retrieval calls and shows what kind of accessible object information is available.

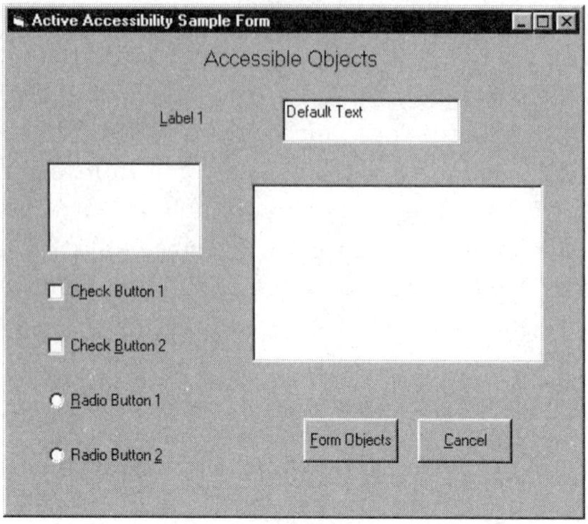

FIGURE 16-6   *Active Accessibility sample program*

Why Should I Use Active Accessibility?

Before starting in on a discussion of how to use Active Accessibility, I need to offer a little more of an explanation as to the purpose of Active Accessibility and how it works.

Active Accessibility uses Component Object Model (COM) technology to expose interfaces that provide a common means of communication among applications. What does that mean? Let's look at an example. Accessible computing often involves more than the guidelines and considerations discussed so far in this chapter. For computers to be accessible to everyone, special devices, known as accessibility aids, sometimes are required. Examples of such aids are screen readers and special input devices. The developers of accessibility aids must create software that communicates with the existing operating system and application software running on the computer. Without Active Accessibility, establishing these communications can be difficult. In order for the accessibility aid software to communicate with the system software, it's required to know or discover a lot of details about the specific types of software. When software applications are created with Active Accessibility, the accessibility aids don't need to know any application-specific details. They can find out what is on the screen and how to use it from the common interfaces exposed by Active Accessibility.

From this, you might have figured out that there are two sides to Active Accessibility: the client and the server. The client is the hardware and software for the accessibility aid that is trying to retrieve information. The server is the software application that is exposing accessible interfaces so that the client can easily retrieve the desired user interface information.

My intent when I started writing this was to demonstrate how to make your Visual Basic application available as a server. Unfortunately, after a lot of work and some discussion with the Microsoft Active Accessibility group, I've discovered that the technology isn't quite ready yet for a Visual Basic server. As I said before, Active Accessibility is still very new, and it wasn't designed for use with Visual Basic. So what I've done instead is demonstrate what can be done from the client side. This will at least give you a chance to see how Active Accessibility works and should help prepare you to use it in the future.

Setting Up Your Project

Before you start building your project, you need to load the Microsoft Active Accessibility SDK (MSAASDK), which you'll find on the companion CD for this book. After you've loaded the SDK, you must create a reference in your project to the Accessibility DLL, OLEACC.DLL. Select References from the Project menu and then click the Browse button to find the OLEACC.DLL file. By default, this file is located in the \Windows\System folder. Once you've created the reference, you can view the Accessibility library through the Object Browser in Visual Basic. When you select Accessibility from the Project/Library drop-down list in the Object Browser, you won't see anything in the Classes or Member Of lists because the Accessibility settings are hidden. You need to right-click in the Members Of pane and select Show Hidden Members to view the Accessibility classes and members.

NOTE

If you're working without a mouse and you want to view the hidden files in the Object Browser, tab to the Members pane and press Shift+F10 to display the shortcut menu. Press H (for Show Hidden Members) on your keyboard and then press Enter.

Another means of accessing the shortcut menu is to enable the Windows MouseKeys option. Select Accessibility Options from the Control Panel, and select the Mouse tab. Check the Use MouseKeys checkbox, and click OK. You can now perform the right-click action in the Object Browser using your numeric keypad by pressing the minus key and then pressing the 5 key.

Retrieving Accessibility Information

Three main functions allow you to retrieve information about objects in an application: *AccessibleObjectFromEvent*, *AccessibleObjectFromWindow*, and *AccessibleObjectFromPoint*. We won't be looking at events here, but we will be retrieving objects directly from a window and from a point on a form.

Retrieving objects from a window

The *frmAccess* form in the AAccess sample contains a number of standard controls, including list boxes, check boxes, and radio buttons. So the first thing we want to do is find out which of these controls are accessible through the Active Accessibility interface. We need to start with a type declaration and a function declaration, which must go in a standard module, in this case *mAccess*.

```
Type tGUID
    lData1             As Long
    nData2             As Integer
    nData3             As Integer
    abytData4(0 To 7) As Byte
End Type


Declare Function AccessibleObjectFromWindow Lib "oleacc" _
    (ByVal hWnd As Long, ByVal dwId As Long, _
    riid As tGUID, ppvObject As Object) As Long
```

The *tGUID* type is a UDT that maps to the C++ *REFIID* structure, often called the class ID. The value we assign to this UDT is the class ID of the interface we want to retrieve. We'll be retrieving the *IAccessible* interface provided by Active Accessibility. *AccessibleObjectFromWindow* will return the *IAccessible* interface for the window object with the given window handle (*hWnd*).

```
Dim oIA     As IAccessible
Dim tg      As tGUID
Dim lReturn As Long

' Define the GUID for the IAccessible interface.
' {618736E0-3C3D-11CF-810C-00AA00389B71}
With tg
    .lData1 = &H618736E0
    .nData2 = &H3C3D
    .nData3 = &H11CF
    .abytData4(0) = &H81
    .abytData4(1) = &HC
    .abytData4(2) = &H0
```

```
        .abytData4(3) = &HAA
        .abytData4(4) = &H0
        .abytData4(5) = &H38
        .abytData4(6) = &H9B
        .abytData4(7) = &H71
    End With


    ' Retrieve the IAccessible interface for the form.
    lReturn = AccessibleObjectFromWindow(frmAccess.hwnd, 0, tg, oIA)
```

We now have an *IAccessible* interface for the form object contained in *oIA*. What we really want is to find out what accessible objects are on the form. For this, we need to make a call to the *AccessibleChildren* function. Declare the function in the *mAccess* module as follows:

```
Declare Function AccessibleChildren Lib "oleacc" _
    (ByVal paccContainer As IAccessible, ByVal iChildStart As Long, _
    ByVal cChildren As Long, rgvarChildren As Variant, _
    pcObtained As Long) As Long
```

The first parameter is the *IAccessible* interface we just retrieved. The second parameter, *iChildStart*, is a zero-based index specifying which child you want to start retrieving. The third parameter, *cChildren*, indicates how many children you want to retrieve. *AccessibleChildren* returns an array of Variants in the *rgvarChildren* parameter. This array can contain either a list of objects or a list of system-defined object identifiers. The final parameter returns the number of objects that were retrieved into the array.

```
    Dim lStart      As Long
    Dim lHowMany    As Long
    Dim avKids()    As Variant
    Dim lGotHowMany As Long

    ' Get the IAccessible interface.

    ' Initialize
    lStart = 0
    ' accChildCount returns the number of children
    ' for the given object.
    lHowMany = oIA.accChildCount
    ReDim avKids(lHowMany - 1) As Variant
    lGotHowMany = 0

    ' Retrieve the form's children.
    lReturn = AccessibleChildren(oIA, lStart, lHowMany, _
                                avKids(0), lGotHowMany)
```

At this point, it appears that we have an *IAccessible* interface for the form and an array of child objects. Unfortunately, a quick look at the *avKids* array in the debugger shows this not to be the case.

Locals			☒
AAccess.frmAccess.cmdOK_Click			...
Expression	**Value**	**Type**	▲
⊟ avKids		Variant(0 to 6)	
— avKids(0)	-1	Variant/Long	
— avKids(1)	-2	Variant/Long	
— avKids(2)	-3	Variant/Long	
— avKids(3)	-4	Variant/Long	
— avKids(4)	-5	Variant/Long	
— avKids(5)	-6	Variant/Long	
└─ avKids(6)	-7	Variant/Long	▼

AccessibleChildren has returned an array of Longs. These Long values represent those system-defined object identifiers I mentioned earlier. Fortunately, one of these identifiers happens to identify the form, so we must search for the form and start again.

```
Dim oNewIA      As IAccessible
Dim avMoreKids() As Variant

' The first call to AccessibleChildren retrieved system information.
' Now we need to find the form object again.
For i = 0 To lGotHowMany - 1
    If oIA.accName(avKids(i)) = frmAccess.Caption Then
        Set oNewIA = oIA.accChild(avKids(i))
        lHowMany = oNewIA.accChildCount
    End If
Next i

' Retrieve the children for the actual form IAccessible interface
' this time.
ReDim avMoreKids(lHowMany - 1) As Variant
lReturn = AccessibleChildren(oNewIA, lStart, lHowMany, _
                             avMoreKids(0), lGotHowMany)
```

If you check the *avKids* array now, you'll see it's full of *IAccessible* objects, as shown on the following page.

In the AAccess sample, I put this functionality in the *cmdOK_Click* event procedure so that we could retrieve the objects and then display them in a list box on the screen. Here are the results.

You might be surprised at the list you see. To start with, if you scroll through the list you'll notice that nine controls were returned. But if you count the controls on the form, you'll find 11 (two labels, one text box, two list boxes, two check boxes, two radio buttons, and two command buttons). The missing controls in the list are the labels. Labels are not included as accessible objects.

The next thing you'll notice is that some of the controls in the list don't have names. We retrieve the name from the *IAccessible.accName* property. For Visual Basic forms and controls, *accName* is the same as the corresponding *Caption* property. The list boxes and the text box don't have *Caption* properties, so their names aren't displayed in the list box.

Retrieving objects from a point

Another means of retrieving information about accessible objects is to query the object at a specific point on the screen. With Active Accessibility, this is done with the *AccessibleObjectFromPoint* function. In our AAccess sample, when the user clicks the mouse we'll find the accessible object at the point of the mouse click and display some of the object's properties in a list box. First let's declare the types and functions we need in our standard module.

```
Type tPOINT
    lx As Long
    ly As Long
End Type

Declare Function GetCursorPos Lib "user32" _
    (lpPoint as tPOINT) As Long

Declare Function AccessibleObjectFromPoint Lib "oleacc" _
    (ByVal lx As Long, ByVal ly As Long, ppacc As IAccessible, _
     pvarChild As Variant) As Long
```

The *tPOINT* UDT maps to the Win32 *POINT* structure, which contains the coordinates for a point on the screen. You pass these *x* and *y* coordinates to *AccessibleObjectFromPoint* to retrieve the *IAccessible* object located at that point. The last parameter, *pvarChild*, returns a Variant. If the value is 0, the *ppacc* parameter contains the *IAccessible* interface of the child object, such as a command button on the form. A nonzero value in *pvarChild* indicates that the *ppacc* parameter contains the *IAccessible* interface of the parent object.

Because we're capturing the mouse location with Click events, the *Accessible-ObjectFromPoint* logic is in a private subroutine that is called by each of the *Click* event procedures.

```
Private Sub GetClickEvent()
    Dim tp      As tPOINT
    Dim oIA     As IAccessible
    Dim vKid    As Variant
    Dim lResult As Long
```

```
' Get the cursor position where the mouse was clicked.
Call GetCursorPos(tp)

' Get the IAccessible interface of the object located under
' the cursor position.
lResult = AccessibleObjectFromPoint(tp.lx, tp.ly, oIA, vKid)

' Add the object's accessibility information to the list box.
On Error Resume Next  ' Not all the acc properties will work
                          ' with all the returned objects.
With lstList2
    .AddItem "Object Name: " & oIA.accName(vKid)
    .AddItem "Default Action: " &  oIA.accDefaultAction(vKid)
    .AddItem "Keyboard Shortcut: " & _
             oIA.accKeyboardShortcut(vKid)
End With

End Sub
```

Now when you run the AAccess sample, you can click the different controls on the form and see what happens. The results will be similar to those shown in this graphic.

You can see that clicking labels doesn't have any effect. This means they're not supported as accessible objects. If you click the Form Objects button, you see the properties for the button in the list box on the right, and the list on the left is populated with the form objects we retrieved with calls to *AccessibleObject-FromWindow* and *AccessibleChildren*. Once the list box on the left is populated, you can click individual list elements and see their properties in the list box on the right. You can also see how the default action changes when you toggle check boxes on and off.

Where Do I Go from Here?

In reviewing the AAccess sample, we've seen how to call the base functions for retrieving accessible objects and how to retrieve some of the properties of those objects. These are the beginnings of using Active Accessibility to expose objects and communicate between applications. The MSAASDK is an evolving architecture, and I recommend that you check the Microsoft Web site for updates to the SDK and to accessibility issues in general. See the section "More Information" on page 739.

MAKING ACCESSIBILITY PART OF YOUR DEVELOPMENT PROCESS

Now that you know some of the technical aspects of making your applications more accessible, you need a means of controlling a development project and ensuring that the accessibility aspects are met. You probably already have a process in place for your development projects. Here we'll go over some suggestions for incorporating accessibility considerations into that process. Keep in mind that a development process is nonlinear; I personally have never known a development life cycle to go cleanly straight through to the end without discovering something new at the next stage that changes what was decided in the previous stage.

The Planning Stage

Every process begins with a plan. This is the stage where you set your goals and decide what it is you want to accomplish with your software application. As you review potential features of your software, determine how these features will be affected by accessibility issues. For example, let's say you decide to put a scrolling banner across the top of your introductory window. Keep a list handy with the disability categories we covered earlier in this chapter. Go through the list and decide whether this feature will impact anyone within those categories in a negative, or a positive, way. Will the scrolling text cause problems for a screen reader used by a blind person? Will someone with cognitive limitations be distracted and confused by the moving text?

It's a good idea at this early stage to include users with disabilities in the discussions. If you don't have anyone on the planning team, find someone to review the plan once you begin to get it outlined. The reviewer should be an expert in disabilities, or you'll need to find several people with different disabilities to be reviewers.

The Design Stage

The design stage is where you decide which options go and which ones stay. Go over the list of features determined in the planning stage, and decide how you're going to implement accessibility into each one. Suppose it was decided at the planning stage that the scrolling banner was a great idea and would add a lot of interest to the application. Now is the time to decide whether you want to provide an option that will stop the banner from scrolling or even remove it altogether. Maybe you want an audio clip that will read the banner the first time it scrolls by. Do you want an option to turn the audio clip off?

The Coding Stage

Developers need to closely follow the guidelines set up in the design stage. Say it's been decided that the introductory window will have a scrolling banner at the top; the banner runs with an audio clip that reads the banner the first time across. But it's also been decided that certain restrictions should apply. If a screen reader is detected, the banner will appear once and not scroll. An option that the user can set will be available to turn off the audio clip. Developers need to find the system and programming tools to implement these design guidelines. There might be cases where the user will find the workaround too difficult to bother with. Since this is an introductory screen, the sound clip begins playing at the same time the user has access to the disabling mechanism. By the time the user can disable the clip, it's already played. So the developers determine this design guideline to be impractical. However, they are free to come up with an alternative. The developers decide to include a button on the introductory screen that will play the audio clip when the button is pressed.

The Testing Stage

Part of the guidelines for testers in any organization should be testing accessibility features. Every test plan should have guidelines outlining testing with the different system accessibility options set. Screen resolutions should be specified, and tests without the mouse should be planned. Most important, find testers with disabilities. If you don't have anyone on staff, organizations exist throughout most of the software-developing world where you can find the testers you need.

Feedback

After you've released a version of your software, always gather feedback from customers to use in your next planning stage. Seek out users with disabilities to find out which features make using the application difficult and which ones are helpful.

LEGAL STUFF

In the introduction to this chapter, I made a brief mention of the legalities of the accessibility issue. I'm not going to pretend to know all the legal issues involved, and as a software developer you're not required to know the intricacies of any legal system. But I do think it's important to point out that a lot of legislation is in place to ensure that people with disabilities are provided the same opportunities in the workplace as everyone else. Companies need to keep these considerations in mind when they create internal software applications, and also when they purchase from outside vendors. If you're a vendor selling software to companies, your product will be much more marketable if it's designed to fulfill the legal requirements of the company or government agency that is purchasing it.

Just a few of the more prominent legislative acts in different parts of the world include:

- The Americans with Disabilities Act (ADA)
- The Rehabilitation Act of 1973, Section 508
- The Telecommunications Act, Section 255

- The Disability Discrimination Act (UK)
- The Australian Disability Discrimination Act

You can find information on these and other acts of legislation on the Internet or from your local government.

MORE INFORMATION

This chapter has highlighted some of the features that should be a part of every development process to ensure that applications are accessible to everyone who needs to use them. While it might be impossible or impractical to include everything mentioned here in every application, you should consider this a strong guideline. For more information on accessibility issues, including detailed guidelines and resources, and on Active Accessibility, check the Microsoft Web site at *http://www.microsoft.com/enable*. Extensive research has also been done on this topic at the Trace Research & Development Center, University of Wisconsin-Madison. You'll find the Web site at *http://tracecenter.org*.

Three Steps to Employment Heaven

How to Find, Recruit, and Retain Great Developers

PETER MORRIS

Peet is a self-confessed Richard P. Feynman nut, a dad, a trained percussionist, a blues guitarist, an avid book reader (OK—book *buyer*, but aren't we all), a "folky," a juggler, and a pilot of light aircraft—but not necessarily in that order! Peet lives in the Regency town of Cheltenham with his wife Fiona and their son Daniel ("Sosij"). E-mail Peet at *peetm.bookteam@TheMandelbrotSet.com*.

As TMS's Human Resources Director, Mark is responsible for all staffing matters, including the recruitment and retention of high-quality staff. Mark believes that dealing with people is the most challenging (and therefore the most rewarding) part of his job. He tries hard to tell someone everyday why he values, appreciates, or admires them. Having just turned forty, Mark spends most of his spare time battling through a mid-life crisis. This has led to him doing some silly things like cutting down on alcohol, banging drums, and playing regular soccer again after a 10 year hiatus.

MARK SEWELL

"The best executive is the one who has sense enough to pick good men to do what he wants done, and self-restraint enough to keep from meddling with them while they do it."

Theodore Roosevelt

Whenever you open a computing newspaper these days, you see more job advertisements than ever before and within them, a higher proportion of Microsoft Visual Basic positions advertised than ever before. This trend will certainly continue with version 6 of Visual Basic. To date, 10 percent more jobs have been advertised in 1998 than there were during the same period in 1997. Big increases in salaries and contracting rates are evident. Three out of every 10 positions remain permanently vacant. So how does an organization differentiate itself so that it can attract and, more importantly, retain great developers?

The first thing to say is that it's very tricky! But an organization can take some practical steps to overcome some of the problems and difficulties of finding good developers. In this chapter, we will outline some of the techniques that we at The Mandelbrot Set (International) Limited (TMS) have used successfully over the years. This is not a classic human resources view, but more a summary of what works for us at the business end of the recruitment process. Perhaps some of our ideas will be useful to you.

WHERE TO START?

First things first, we split our staffing process into these three main steps:

1. Finding
2. Recruiting (including assessing)
3. Retaining

The key to hiring great developers is to recruit the right people in the first place. While all three steps are important, we feel it's worth expending a lot of effort on Step 2, as you'll discover in this chapter.

STEP 1: FINDING GREAT DEVELOPERS

First discuss with others in your organization the main attributes you are looking for—whiteboard the "spec," in other words. Be clear about the type of person you want and the skills required to do the job. For example, we at TMS look to hire developers. Not coders, not programmers. Developers, in our vocabulary, don't just write code or simply program someone else's technical design—coders and programmers do that. Developers are able to develop the designs and architectures they or other programmers need. They never hack code; they think about the code's structure and form first and then write it down. Developers can test and have broad development skills. Now please don't get fired up if you call yourself a coder or a programmer and disagree with the definitions of these terms. They're simply the definitions we use at TMS. That's all, so please don't be offended!

What Sort of Person Should You Look For?

Generally, if we're looking to recruit great developers, we look for people with a good track record in development. It's up to you to decide whether the developer's experience should be in, say, Visual Basic or in Java (that is, whether it's "the brain" and general programming experience you're seeking or whether it's all of the above) combined with experience in the language you're using. When we're recruiting Visual Basic developers we normally expect them to have extensive knowledge of Visual Basic, although if the person were exceptional in every other area, we'd almost certainly take them on and give them the necessary training. The best developers are generally those with logical, methodical minds. They're also usually thoughtful, precise, and, we hope, not impulsive—the best developers think first and act later. We're after the people who think algorithmically (people who understand the necessity of a good algorithm and have the wherewithal to implement it), which is not to say that they should think only in algorithms. A thorough knowledge of algorithms is useful but can always be replaced by someone who "thinks right" and who knows where to look for an existing algorithm.

We are also after people who are in tune with our culture. For TMS, this means they should be first and foremost a team player. If they use too many "I"s instead of "we"s, we have to consider whether they are more comfortable going solo. We have to feel they will fit in with the rest of the family.

Remember that technical people are a bit different from other staff. Typically, they'll want plenty of exposure to the new technologies, such as Visual Basic 6, as well as having some fun while they're at it. Technical people tend to hate bureaucracy, administration, and filling out forms—they can also be harder to manage.

Soft skills (such as interpersonal relations, communication skills, and so forth) are also vital. It's important to be presentable, personable, and coherent.

These are some of the things that we think about. What's important to you? Be clear about what you want.

Qualifications

The qualifications you seek depend on your own personal or company preferences, so, as always, we speak here from our own experiences at TMS. In an ideal world all applicants are vastly experienced and well qualified. Often, obviously, this isn't always the case.

Naturally, we look for experienced and capable developers first. If the candidates are well qualified, it's a bonus, but we don't discount people who fail to meet some sort of qualification threshold. However, we consider a degree a plus, and we're particularly interested in someone with a relevant degree, preferably in computer science or mathematics.

Having a degree versus not having one Someone with an advanced degree normally has a proven ability to solve complex problems and absorb information (although we've seen some interesting exceptions). Somebody with a degree naturally carries more credibility than someone who doesn't have a college degree, and a college graduate is generally easier to present to our clients.

Of course, the best person for the job isn't necessarily the most academically qualified—after all, a degree from the University of Hard Knocks usually means the candidate has pragmatic skills, and we all know that true wisdom is in the actual application of learned knowledge, not just in knowledge per se. That said and human nature being what it is, however, it's often the most academically qualified person who will get the first interview. The bottom line is that having a degree helps, whereas not having one probably hinders, everything else being equal.

MCP certification   Microsoft Certified Professionals (MCPs) have a proven level of competence with Microsoft technologies and tools, so certification is usually viewed as a positive attribute. As a services company, we find an MCP certification is a positive sales feature. However, don't rely on it too much. Conduct your own independent skills assessment.

In summary

Ideally we'd all like to hit what we call "the red zone"—well qualified, lots of experience, and good personal skills. (See Figure 17-1.)

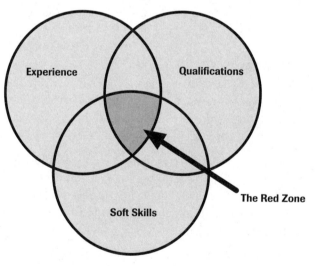

FIGURE 17-1   *Nerdvana: the ideal skill set*

But what's ideal for your organization is for *you* to decide. Which of the three qualifications is most important to you? Brainstorm about what you want and then move on.

Defining the Job Description

Now that you know the sort of person you're looking for, you need to document your requirements. This is vital.

The cornerstone to any employment decision begins with job analysis, which is the systematic assembly of all the facts about a job. The purpose is to study the individual elements and duties. All information related to the salary and benefits, working hours and conditions, typical tasks and responsibilities are required for the job analysis. Competition and equal employment opportunity legislation (the myriad laws, guidelines, and court decisions concerning equal employment opportunity) have made job analysis a mandatory organizational consideration for most businesses.

Job descriptions are written based on job analysis information. A job description describes a job, not an individual doing the job. The job description is derived from a requirement in an organization and is an essential element in the correct selection and evaluation of employees. Job descriptions are also the basis on which a job advertisement is written.

Every job should have a job description, which can be mailed to any interested parties before the interview. The job description might help you easily filter out unsuitable candidates since some will drop out once they've had a chance to see what the job will entail.

Writing style

Job descriptions should be written using brief, clear sentences. The sentence structure should follow the "implied subject-verb-object-explanatory phrase" format. It's generally to your advantage to use action verbs like "programs" and "analyzes," for example.

Sample job description

A job description is a written description of the major duties and responsibilities for any job applicant. On the next page is a sample TMS job description for a developer based on the well-known Hay/MSL format, although we have also included a "person specification" so that everything we want is contained in one document.

JOB DESCRIPTION

JOB TITLE: Developer

REPORTING TO: Project Manager

DATE: As Required

PURPOSE: Work with and mentor the client's own staff on specific projects, and equally for internal company projects. Provide high quality, cost effective technical services within given timeframes and budgetary constraints to ensure optimum customer satisfaction and business-driven solutions.

PRIMARY RESPONSIBILITIES

The key areas of responsibility for the employee are as follows:

1. Ensure that a high quality technical service is provided to both the external client and for internal projects in the specific areas of design, programming, and software testing.

2. Write technical documentation for external clients and whitepapers suitable for publication on the company Web site or in technical magazines as requested by any of the company's managers, in order to maintain the company's profile within the industry and to promote the company's services.

3. Contribute to the development of technical training courses and running briefing sessions on technical issues for the clients' staff as required.

4. Accompany TMS consultants on client visits as required and provide in-depth technical support as necessary in order to maximize all sales opportunities for the company and to ensure the highest quality service for the prospective client.

5. Contribute to company Technical Days by giving formal presentations or leading more general discussions regarding current projects or case studies and ensuring that the overall objective of "knowledge sharing" with colleagues is achieved.

6. Ensure that the company's vision to provide the highest quality software development and client services is achieved and maintained at all times.

ORGANIZATION CHART:

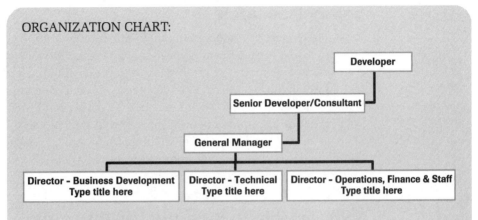

PROFILE OF EMPLOYEE

Essential requirements include:

- Minimum 8 years' experience within the IT industry, preferably within a software services company or consultancy, in a role requiring multiple external client contact and service provision
- Minimum 5 years' hands-on Windows development experience
- Minimum 4 years' hands-on Visual Basic development experience
- Minimum 4 years' hands-on database/SQL programming experience
- Desire and ability to work relatively unsupervised on external client sites
- A self-managing, self-motivated individual who can demonstrate a successful history of remote working
- A quality, focused individual with proven customer interaction skills

Desirable qualifications include

- Graduate-level degree in computer science or other science subject
- Appreciation of software engineering disciplines and methodologies
- Knowledge and experience of traditional or object design, architecture, and implementation
- Working knowledge of any of the following: Microsoft SQL Server, Microsoft Access, and Microsoft Office suite/VBA
- Knowledge and experience of client/server systems development
- Working knowledge of any of the following: Microsoft Windows NT, Java/J++, C/C++, Microsoft ActiveX technology, COM/COM+/DCOM, RDO, ODBC
- Microsoft Certified Professional (version 4, 5, or 6)
- Clean driving record

Salary Research

Research the industry standard remuneration for the position you need to fill, and then add 5 to 15 percent if you want to be competitive. Research salaries regularly and make sure your current workforce benefits from this research as well as any new developer. Also, develop your own company salary policy, stating where you want to be in terms of the salaries and benefits you offer to your staff. For example, do you want to pay at the median level, the upper quartile, or the top decile for the IT industry or for your geographical area? Decide where you want to be, compare where your current salaries fall, and then adjust if necessary.

How to Locate the Right People

The two best ways to locate the right people for your organization are the two that pop immediately into the minds of most people: word-of-mouth recommendations and advertising.

Personal recommendations

Better to hire the devil you know (or at least someone you know) than the one you don't. We're always interested in personal recommendations from existing staff members. More often than not, like attracts like, and usually a good developer will recognize someone from the same stock. It's a kind of "it takes one to know one" philosophy. When someone is recommended to you, ask the person providing the recommendation to qualitatively summarize the skills and qualifications of the potential new recruit. Would the "recommender" be willing to manage or work with the person they're recommending? Also, consider paying a finder's fee to your staff—we do and it works well. Even if we receive a personal recommendation, we still put the candidate through our standard assessment procedure. This step is essential.

Advertising

If you decide to advertise, you'll generally use the job description to compose the advertisement. All the essential qualities must be included in the advertisement so that any potential applicant can decide whether the job is worth applying for.

It's essential to advertise in the right places. Make sure that you advertise, in detail, the role/position you're recruiting for. Don't make the advertisement too general, figuring that if you cast the net wide enough, you might catch other people of potential interest to your company. In other words, don't advertise for Microsoft Windows developers if you're only looking for Visual Basic 6 developers but might also be interested in attracting a C++ developer sometime soon. Advertise for the C++ developer later, when you actually need one, and again, make it clear in that advertisement what you're looking for. By casting the net too wide, you will all too often dilute the information deemed necessary by a potential candidate. You'll also make it appear as if you're trawling for résumés.

People should be interested in the position as described in your advertisement, and you should start the filtering process at this stage. For example, if the position requires long hours, or perhaps working away from home, state this up front in the advertisement—anyone who isn't interested won't apply. Those who do shouldn't mind travelling and working long hours. See? You've already started optimizing the process by generating a shortlist!

Places to advertise   The primary places to advertise to get the best response are as follows:

- **The Web.** We often "e-advertise" on our own Web site (if we have a pressing vacancy) or on other IT employment Web sites. If you have a good profile, and therefore plenty of hits on your own Web site, advertising on your own site makes great sense.

- **The press.** We use the specialist press for advertising key positions. For the more junior positions, we mostly rely on word of mouth and the Web.

- **Agencies.** We rarely use agencies. While they perform a useful role in certain circumstances, we prefer to do our own thing when it comes to recruiting people. No one else knows our business and who we're after as well as we do.

STEP 2: RECRUITING GREAT DEVELOPERS

Once you start receiving résumés, what do you do next? It is essential to have a well defined process so that you are professional, efficient, and responsive with the applications—good people aren't available for long, so you must quickly assess and rank the résumés using an efficient filtering process.

The Initial Filtering Process

We handle only "soft" résumés, meaning that we have them e-mailed to us. We have a strict set of criteria (based on the job specification) that we filter the résumés against. People who are immediately "rejected" are thanked for their interest and informed of our decision right away. We speak to other candidates over the phone to thank them for applying and to assess some of the attributes that are impossible to pick up from a résumé, such as oral communication skills, phone manner, power of description and explanation, and so on. We also ask a small number of (carefully chosen) technical questions. Again, people who are "rejected" at this stage are thanked for applying and informed on the spot. Otherwise, we tell them that we would like to invite them in for an interview.

Interviewing

We tend to interview people in batches, on what we call "recruitment days." Normally we see eight people at hourly intervals. Each candidate gets a general interview and a technical interview and takes a technical test.

The whole procedure takes about half a day. This is quite a lot of time to give up and some people say they can't afford to do so. We do lose a few (what look to be) good people this way, but we regard this as another important part in the filtering process. If a candidate can't give up a reasonable chunk of time for an interview, how keen are they on joining us, really?

At TMS, we have a three-person team, comprising two interviewers and one person to administer tests.

How we interview

We always bear in mind exactly what we're trying to achieve during any interview. Our objectives are as follows:

- To assess a candidate's ability to make informed, intelligent, and objective judgements under pressure (in a limited amount of time and in an interview situation)
- To assess the likelihood that a candidate will share our company's values, goals, and culture
- To assess how well a candidate matches the position being interviewed for

Always keep these points in mind: make them your interview mantra. Also, ensure that you have a structure to your interviews that accomplishes the following:

- Enhances effectiveness by providing a framework promoting the systematic coverage of content

- Is essential for accurate and consistent measurement across a group of interviews
- Is efficient

Interview preparation   This is how we prepare for interviews at TMS:

- Run through the position we're recruiting for in our mind's eye—this is a kind of "mental reminder" of what the job involves and helps us to form a "picture" of the ideal candidate.
- Scan—or better still, study—the applicant's résumé—are there questions we would or should ask about what we see?
- Make sure that we have a pad for taking notes. This is important, because it'll reduce the amount of information that we have to hold in memory.
- Ensure that the interview room is adequately prepared.
- Be sure that we have all the materials that should be given to the applicant.

We always take an instant photo of any prospective employee. We staple this to the notes and résumé so that our recollection is made easier at the end of the day and in the future.

Controlling the interview   Remember that the interviewer controls the interview. Prospective employees should be given an opportunity to ask questions at the end of the interview—inform them of this structure before you start asking them questions. It's important that you separate these two phases, the formal "pull" part of the interview from the more informal "push" part where the candidate usually asks questions.

Sometimes we find it useful to have at least two people attending each interview. For one thing, it gives one of you the chance to "observe" the candidate while the other interviewer is asking a question or listening to a response. Of course, it's also useful to have a second opinion during the debriefing.

Remember that as well as being your chance to assess candidates, the interview is the candidates' chance to assess your company and you as an individual. It's unwise to arrogantly assume that they'll take any job you might offer simply because they turned up for an interview. It's also an opportunity to sell your company. If an offer isn't made, or if the offer is turned down, you still want candidates to have a lasting and positive impression of your company. Keep in mind that they might have an opportunity to do your company a good turn—if they've been impressed with you, that is.

Here are some important things to tell the interviewee about the open position and about your company:

- Tell the interviewee how the company came about and its successes and failures to date.
- Tell the interviewee where the company is going and what its vision and mission statement are. These are what make your company unique.
- Give the candidate details about the position that's being interviewed for, because the advertisement is likely to have been sketchy and perhaps a little vague.
- Tell the candidate what makes your company special: quality, management style, employee care package, company car policy, and so forth. These details combine a reiteration of the company's vision, plus factual information that might otherwise have to be gleaned from an offer letter.
- Perhaps most important, tell the interviewee about the reality of the company, warts and all. Neither one of you wants to be surprised further down the line.

Sample interview questions   Here are some of the interview questions we use:

- Describe in detail what you did the day before yesterday.
- Describe the best boss you've ever had.
- Describe your ideal development environment, everything from the tools you'd use to the philosophy you'd apply.
- Given your personal goals and limitations, what job would be your dream job?
- Having just walked in, what do you think of [company name] so far?
- How did you choose your last job?
- If it were in your power, how would you like to see your current main development tool improved? Have you informed anyone of your views, especially the tool vendor?
- In what ways do you think you can make a contribution to our company?
- What are you reading currently? What have you read recently?
- What are your two favorite technical books? Why?

- What are your own special abilities?
- What do you consider to be your most important contribution or accomplishment in your current position?
- What do you know about [company name] and why are you interested in joining us?
- What does success mean to you?
- What kind of people appeal most and least to you as coworkers?
- What's your definition of a team? Of cooperation?
- Why should [company name] hire you?

Looks for attitude as well as ability. Be careful to spend as much time as possible listening; don't do too much of the talking yourself.

It is important to take notes during the interview and write up a summary as soon as the candidate leaves the room. Do it while your thoughts and impressions are fresh.

Testing

We feel that testing a candidate in a number of different ways is vital. Here are some of the things we do at TMS.

Telephone testing

As we've mentioned, whenever we're interested in recruiting individuals we'll arrange to phone them at home to discuss the position further. At the same time, we'll take the opportunity to probe their technical skills and generally attempt to gauge their personality and how they motivate themselves. As much as possible, we'll effectively conduct an interview with them right then and there. The idea behind this quick phone interview is to optimize the screening process and to save time—both theirs and ours. If you suspect the candidate is less than honest about his or her abilities, you can verify this quickly by asking one or two leading questions about some general development issue or about some appropriate technology. Like any company, we get a few "fakers" applying for jobs; some might be guilty of nothing more than creative writing, whereas others might be trying to deliberately land a job for which they're simply not qualified (figuring that they'll learn the skills on the job and at your expense). Telephone testing is inexpensive and a good way to start the relationship between the prospective employer and prospective employee. We recommend that you *always* take the time to do this prior to conducting the in-person interview.

Technical testing

At TMS, every potential developer we interview is also technically evaluated on a recruitment day. Mostly we use a paper-based written exam, which lasts more than two hours. (The Visual Basic 6 exam currently contains 45 questions.) The test is conducted under examination conditions, which means it's completed in a quiet, supervised room. Those who pass the test and eventually join TMS usually refer to the test as "the test from hell." To pass this test is to feel like you're joining an elite club. Make sure you tell candidates that there will be a test before they come for the interview!

INTRODUCTION AND ABOUT THE TEST

This test paper, once completed, summarizes our understanding of your technical comprehension of Windows' programming using Visual Basic and additionally provides us with a good indication of how you:

- Work under pressure and to strict deadlines
- Go about solving complex problems
- Improvise and form educated guesses
- And most importantly, think

No one is expected to deliver a perfect test paper at the end of two and a half hours (indeed, the design of the question paper and the time limit conspire to prevent this from happening), and candidates with various levels of expertise are of equal interest to us. Given this, and the fact that your completed test paper may be referred to during one of your interviews, it is essential to make an impression during the test. We repeat, however, that it is *not* necessary for you to know the answer to every question, or be a Visual Basic guru, to do well.

Tips on how to answer

It is vitally important to understand and answer the question (and to do it as fully, yet at the same time, since both space and time are limited, as economically as possible). Additionally, it is vital to be verbose and fully suspicious of the questions. Read the wording of each question carefully and try to ascertain what the questioner is after. Always assume that each question is a loaded question, potentially harder than it might at first appear. Once you've written your answer, reread it. Is the answer you gave ambiguous or clear? If you were marking this paper objectively, how would you score the answer on a scale of 1 to 10?

>>

The testing room, and therefore the candidate(s), are "computer-free," so they don't have access to Visual Basic or to any help file text, nor do we provide any manuals. We're not really interested in whether someone can remember the number and order of the parameters to *MsgBox*, for example. That kind of stuff most people look up anyway. No, we're interested in how someone codes and generally solves problems. To give you an idea about what the test aims to find out, see the title page from our test starting on the previous page.

After the test, maintain your own industry average and your own preferred score, the percentage that you would expect someone in your company to attain. Derive this score by having your current employees take the test. (Be sure that they didn't help write the test!) Log their scores and define your passing score.

>>

Exam technique

Although we want you to answer the questions in sequence and not jump about, it is always a good idea to read through the entire question paper before attempting to answer any individual question. (Ten minutes have been allowed for this.) Often, something referred to in a later question helps in the answering of an earlier one—reading the question paper first therefore often has real advantages. This paper contains 44 questions, and you have two and a half hours (plus 10 minutes pre-reading time) to answer as many questions as you can. This gives you on average just over three and a half minutes per question and answer (for all 44).

How we mark the paper

Each question is awarded around 10 points. (Some are higher, some lower.) A total of 440 is the highest possible score. As your paper is being marked, two scores are produced. One score is simply based on how many marks you scored out of 440. (An unanswered question scores 0.) The other score is calculated on the actual questions you answered. That is, it indicates how well you did on the questions that you answered. (Unanswered questions are therefore ignored.)

And finally

Once again, remember that this is not *just* a technical assessment—we're looking to see how you perform here in more general terms. After all, details can be easily found in manuals and in help files! Now, get a fresh cup of coffee, breath deeply, make a real effort to relax, and tell yourself to enjoy the test.

The technical test we have works well for us and we always advise potential employers to evaluate candidates with something similar, whether they're looking to hire contractors or permanent members of the staff. Even an oral test might be sufficient, just so long as it's not too easy. Remember, you're looking to recruit great developers, so, while you might ask someone to explain what Option Explicit is all about, you'll probably want to probe a bit deeper as well. Here are some examples drawn from our current exam to give you a feel for the level of probing and what we think works. The answers are shown in Appendix B in case you want to test your own skills.

THE TMS EXAM

Q1. Given the following code fragment, what will be the output of the *Debug.Print* statement? Explain your reasoning.

```
Dim a As Integer, b As Integer, c As Integer

b = &HFFFF
c = True

a = b = c

Debug.Print a, b, c
```

Q2. Assuming that *lstResults* is a standard Visual Basic list box control, what is the meaning of each of the following code fragments?

```
A.   Debug.Print lstResults.List(3)

B.   For i = 0 to lstResults.ListCount - 1
     ⋮
     Next i

C.   If lstResults.ListIndex = -1 Then
     ⋮
     End If

D.   For i = 0 To lstResults.ListIndex - 1
         lstResults.ItemData(i) = i
     Next i
```

Q3. Write the function *sNumToBin*. This function is passed an integer and returns a string. (Assume 16 bits in the integer.) The string contains the binary equivalent of the passed integral value. For example, if the function were

⟫

passed 42 it would return the string "0000000000101010," and if it were passed –1 it would return "1111111111111111."

Q4. Write the function *itoh*. This function is passed a value and returns a string. The string contains the hexadecimal character equivalent of the passed integral value. For example, if the function were passed 14 it would return the string "E," and if it were passed –1 it would return an out-of-range indicator.

Q5. State how you would position a Visual Basic form (as it is loaded and before it becomes visible) in the center of the Windows desktop. Should the form appear centered irrespective of the screen resolution used?

Q6. State what descriptive, "Hungarian" prefix you would place before the following identifiers (there is no right or wrong answer to this question):

Identifier	Type	Scope	Answer
BM010	Form	Form	
FileOpen	Menu	-	
RecordCount	Integer	Global	
FirstName	String Array	Modular	
VehclNum	Long	Local	
Vehicles	Combo Box	-	
Time	Label	-	

Q7. Part 1: Provide a *full* explanation of the following code fragment. **Part 2:** What, if anything, would change if we simply passed a constant instead of passing *x* both times? **Part 3:** Would changing the line *SomeSub(X)* to *Call SomeSub(X)* affect anything? **Part 4:** Would using *ByVal* cause a change? **Part 5:** State why Visual Basic employs a *pass by reference* parameter passing mechanism instead of a scheme based on pass by value.

```
Private Function SomeFunc(n As Integer) As Integer
    n = n + 1
End Function

Private Sub SomeSub(n As Integer)
    n = n + 1
End Sub

Private Sub cmdTest_Click()
```

```
Dim X      As Integer
Dim Dummy As Integer

X = 1

SomeSub (X)

Debug.Print X

X = 1

Dummy = SomeFunc(X)

Debug.Print X

End Sub
```

Q8. Part 1: Write a small *Form_Load* event handler to multiply instantiate and suitably position a CommandButton control named *cmdDigit* to form a kind of calculator keypad. (Label the controls with digits 0–9.) Assume that at design time a single *cmdDigit* control exists and that its *Index* property is set to 0 and its Caption is "0." **Part 2:** Write a *cmdDigit_Click* event handler to display any selected digit in the caption of a label control named *labDisplay*.

Q9. State as many ways as you can to search a source string for some substring in a case-insensitive way (so that the strings "Tms" and "TMS" match, for example).

Q10. Write the function *NTrim$*. This function is similar to the *?Trim$* functions (where *?* is nothing, *L*, or *R*) already present in Visual Basic, except that it removes any NULL character in a string. A NULL character is a character whose ASCII value is 0.

Q11. Write the function *bFileExists*. This function has a single string parameter and returns either True or False. The function determines whether a file, the fully qualified name of which is given by the string parameter, actually exists or not.

Q12. Part 1: An item of data declared Public in a class can be treated as a property of the class. Additionally, properties can be defined using property procedures. Explain the differences between the two. **Part 2:** Which elements can be "exported" (made visible) from a class?

Q13. What events will the following code fragments cause to be invoked on Form1? In code fragment C, how many instances of Form1 exist once the code is executed?

Code Fragment A

```
Sub main()

    Dim fp As Form

    Set fp = Form1

End Sub
```

Code Fragment B

```
Sub main()

    Dim fp As Form

    Set fp = New Form1

End Sub
```

Code Fragment C

```
Sub main()

    Dim fp As Form

    Set fp = New Form1

    Load fp

End Sub
```

Q14. A project consists of two forms, *Form1* and *Form2*; a module, *Module1*; and a class, *Class1*. *Form1* is the start-up form and *Form2* contains a single button named *Command1*. Each item in this project (except for *Form2*) has the following in its general declarations section:

```
Public n As Integer
```

Additionally, in *Module1*, *o* is declared as *Public o As Class1*.

Form1

```
Private Sub Form_Load()

    Form1.n = 10

    Set o = New Class1

    o.n = 20

    Module1.n = 30

    Form2.Show

End Sub
```

Form2

```
Private Sub Command1_Click()

    Debug.Print n

    Debug.Print Form1.n
    Debug.Print Module1.n
    Debug.Print o.n

End Sub
```

Is the code above legal? Negate any illegalities you see in the code (if any) and state the output to the debug window.

Q15. Write some code to give an example of each of the following:

- Optional arguments
- Parameter arrays
- Collections

Q16. What was VBCP (as shipped with Visual Basic versions 4 and 5), and how was it used?

Q17. What does this code do?

>>

Form

```
Private Sub cmdTest_Click()

    Dim o As Class1

    Set o = New Class1

    Set o.Self = o

    Print TypeName(o.Self)

End Sub
```

Class

```
Private This As Class1

Public Property Get Self() As Class1

    Set Self = This

End Property

Public Property Set Self(o As Class1)

    Set This = o

End Property
```

Q18. Part 1: Given the precedence rules detailed just below (taken from the Visual Basic Help Files), add parentheses to the following code showing clearly how it will be evaluated in Visual Basic. **Part 2:** What does the code print?

```
Dim n As Integer

n = True And &HFF + True And &HFF00 + Not Not True = Not False Or
&HFF + Not True Or &HFF00

Print n
```

>>

>>

When several operations occur in an expression, each part is evaluated and resolved in a predetermined order called operator precedence.

When expressions contain operators from more than one category, arithmetic operators are evaluated first, comparison operators are evaluated next, and logical operators are evaluated last. Comparison operators all have equal precedence; that is, they are evaluated in the left-to-right order in which they appear. Arithmetic and logical operators are evaluated in the following order of precedence:

Arithmetic	Comparison	Logical
Exponentiation (^)	Equality (=)	Not
Negation (–)	Inequality (<>)	And
Multiplication and division (*, /)	Less than (<)	Or
Integer division (\)	Greater than (>)	Xor
Modulus arithmetic (Mod)	Less than or equal to (<=)	Eqv
Addition and subtraction (+, –)	Greater than or equal to (>=)	Imp
String concatenation (&)	Like	
	Is	

When multiplication and division occur together in an expression, each operation is evaluated as it occurs from left to right. When addition and subtraction occur together in an expression, each operation is evaluated in order of appearance from left to right. Parentheses can be used to override the order of precedence and to force some parts of an expression to be evaluated before others. Operations within parentheses are always performed before those outside. Within parentheses, however, operator precedence is maintained.

Q19. Where would you normally use a *GoTo* statement?

As an alternative to the written test (and if you have the resources), you could instead have the candidate write a Visual Basic application in the allotted two and a half hours. Simply set the goal, give the candidate a fully-loaded machine, and then see what he or she comes up with. While this has certain advantages, it also requires more subjective scoring of the applications, and therefore it's harder to compare apples with apples.

Psychometric testing

These days (even with the skills shortage), potential TMS recruits could be forgiven for feeling like they're under the microscope. They're likely to have submitted a detailed résumé, been grilled over the phone and probably attended two interviews, and, of course, taken a technical test! In addition to assessing candidates technically at interview time, we also assess the probability that they will fit in with the company culture. For both their sake and ours, anyone that we feel won't fit in with the way we work simply won't be hired. It makes sense that if a developer is a great technician but perhaps also a total soloist, then, sad as it might be to not have his or her skills in the company, we won't make an offer. To help us ascertain these qualities, we sometimes include some form of psychological profiling, usually a psychometric test.

A psychometric test is a selection tool used by an ever-increasing number of (typically) graduate employers to reduce their shortlist. Tests usually cover areas such as numerical and verbal reasoning; they're not just "psychobabble." In a nutshell, a psychometric test is a standardized sample of behavior that can be described using a numerical or categorical scale. The tests have an advantage over all other forms of assessment in that they are highly standardized. In other words, the test is the same for everyone who takes it. Therefore, all candidates are observed under identical conditions, and their performance is measured objectively against a known and common standard. Also, the methods of interpreting the test results are standard and, once again, objective. There should be no room for error.

The bottom line is that the aim of the test is to match a prospective new employee with both the advertised position and, to a lesser extent, the corporate culture of the prospective employer. For example, if three already successful developers were tested within a team, and a pattern emerged that identified each of them as a highly dominant and extroverted individual, it is unlikely that another developer who is subservient or introverted would fit easily into that same team—or even, for that matter, become a great developer.

Remember to use psychometric tests selectively, and don't become too reliant on them or treat the results as gospel. Mix the tests with the other forms of assessment we've mentioned. Psychometric tests *confirm* your recruitment decision and support your assessment of each candidate to date. The tests should not be used as the decision-making tool. Unfortunately, many inexperienced interviewers fall into this trap.

As part of your overall recruitment process, you should also decide whether you plan to let each candidate have a copy of the results. Some companies do, some don't. It's human nature that most candidates will want to see their results, and many of the psychometric tests around at the moment will allow you to release selected parts of the results.

The Offer

Once all the assessments are complete, the interview team needs to get together immediately to consolidate the information and make decisions. People who haven't made the grade should be informed as soon as possible. We normally do this over the phone and explain the reasoning behind the decision and give plenty of feedback. This is nearly always appreciated, so long as it is done in a positive and constructive way. We also take the opportunity to listen to what the candidate thought of us. We find this approach much better than a brief "thanks, but no thanks" letter.

For people we would like to employ, we always phone and discuss our level of interest and listen to their views. If there is a match, we discuss the remuneration package and reach verbal agreement. (This might take more than one call, obviously.) We follow up in writing as soon as verbal agreement is reached.

You might be left with a strong impression that it is extremely difficult to get a job at TMS. We put candidates through a lot! We are aware that we might be missing out on excellent developers by this very stringent selection process. We realize that many techies are primadonnas and are not prepared to go through all of this when they believe that they can walk into any large corporation and get a job. But for those who persevere, we believe TMS is a good company to work for, and part of the reason for this lies in how we treat our staff once they are with us and the perks we provide: Personal Development Plans (PDPs), regular 1:1s, performance reviews, regular market research on salaries, our family atmosphere, our company culture, our beliefs and values, our commitment to training and development, the opportunities to be exposed to leading edge technology, and so forth. That takes us to Step 3.

STEP 3: RETAINING GREAT DEVELOPERS

Too often, staff can be forgotten once they've been recruited. It's important to have a well-planned induction process and an ongoing career development process. Once you've hired someone, you usually don't want to lose him or her! This employee cost a lot of money to find and train and, after a surprisingly short period of time, accumulates an intrinsic worth that's hard to quantify—Employees' knowledge is of high value. (For example, they know how the company operates and all about its clients.) All in all, you really don't want to lose good people.

One of the ways to address this issue is to realize why people up and leave. People generally do this because:

- They're not being rewarded in a manner commensurate with the effort they're expending.
- They feel they're not valued in some other way.
- They're not being stimulated or challenged in their current role.
- They're not getting the recognition they feel they deserve.
- They can't see how to progress within the organization (or feel that they can't progress, period).

There are other reasons, of course. Typically, remuneration is not the main reason people leave; so long as they're getting a fair rate and they don't have any of the above complaints, they're happy.

Human Resources Management: A Key Role

Natural attrition and turnover of staff is healthy for any organization. A company must ensure that it manages to retain the people it wants to keep and for as long as it wants them. It should be someone's job to make sure that nobody leaves unexpectedly. If anyone leaves like this, that manager has failed in his or her job. Through effective communication and human resources (HR) processes, and in an open, honest, attentive environment, this kind of surprise just shouldn't happen—if it does, something's gone wrong. Did the company not deliver on its promises? Did someone oversell the company's vision and then not deliver on it? Find out why the departing employee is dissatisfied, and then put steps in place to rectify the situation so that no one else leaves unhappy.

In other words, make sure that you have effective and efficient exit interviews, but remember that by the time you get to an exit interview, it's too late to "save" this person. They have already made up their minds to leave and will almost certainly already have another job lined up. Proactive management of your staff while they are employed is absolutely key to staff retention. Be aware of, and deal with, their issues *before* they get so big as to force them to look around for something else. In some circumstances, it will be right for all parties that the individual leaves. But if you know about it early enough, at least you have plenty of time to manage the situation and to recruit and train his or her replacement. In this way, it's a win-win for everyone, and you can mitigate any possible damage.

This HR management needn't be a full-time position, especially in a small company, but make sure someone is responsible for it and gives it a very high priority.

Career Development

We carry out regular human resource reviews via discussions with our staff and questionnaires. Below are some of the issues that we, as a small(ish), distributed, software services company, have identified as being of prime importance.

High-quality communication is vital   Here are some of the ways we ensure that we're giving our employees enough feedback:

- Each manager writes a monthly update for his or her area of responsibility, a monthly report to the staff.
- Only one developer writes a monthly report instead of everyone. This monthly report is comprehensive.
- Quarterly Technical Days are arranged and planned a year in advance. Technical Days are when all the developers get together for a whole day of technical presentations given by the staff to the staff.
- Monthly social get-togethers are arranged, and we schedule a whole year's worth in the calendar in advance.
- We're always available for ad hoc contact and impromptu discussions.

Reducing isolation: site visits and reviews   A schedule of regular site visits and reviews by managers is necessary to evaluate employee performance. Each manager visits each developer a minimum of five times per year for full-day reviews. These visits are a mix of technical visits and more personnel-focused visits. The technical visits are in the minority, but regular technically-focused telephone conferences are also scheduled. The manager takes the opportunity to speak to the client on the visit too, but this should not be the focus. The technical visit includes reviewing the work being carried out by the staff member. Feedback is provided to the staff member in writing. All site visits are written up and published so that all staff members are kept in the loop. The entire program of visits and phone calls is scheduled into manager and staff calendars.

Tools to do the job   It is necessary to provide a comprehensive toolkit for each staff member that enables him or her to do a better job than anyone else around. This toolkit comprises a set of software tools and utilities provided on a number of CDs. Also included on the CDs are TMS's code libraries (see the appendix note on the TDF), coding standards, a copy of our Web site, and other useful documents. Basically, the toolkit contains everything "soft" that might be of immediate use to our developers.

Incentive   We find that giving people a stake in the success of the company, whether through bonuses, shares, share options, profit sharing, and so on is absolutely vital to encouraging their productivity and their commitment to our mission.

Human resources   It is necessary to have a formal process to ensure quality career development. We use two principal mechanisms:

- Personal Development Plans
- Performance reviews

These and other specific processes are discussed in the next section.

Personal development plans

The PDP is a contract between the employee and the company that identifies and agrees on specific developmental needs for the employee over a given period of time, the idea being that performance can be improved through these additional skills and experiences.

To facilitate the PDP, companies need to define a training and development policy. We would suggest something similar to ours, which is: "We will develop the skills of our employees at all levels, to meet the needs of our customers, both internal and external as well as the requirements of our business, taking into account the personal goals of our employees wherever appropriate."

First let's examine how training and development fits in with the PDP.

What is the difference between training and development?　All training is development, but not all development is training. Development is the bigger picture, within which there are formal elements of training. All learning experiences, including the formal elements, are called development. A PDP doesn't just concentrate on formal training courses but includes any experience in which the individual learns something.

How do I define the development needs of my staff?　You should use and refer to a number of different sources. These include:

- The job description
- The performance review (both the Individual Preparation Form and the review form itself). The Individual Preparation Form is a form containing a set of performance and goal-related questions, which are answered by the person being reviewed and then read by the reviewer prior to the meeting. This form forces some pre-thought and pre-planning.
- Individual goals and targets for the year
- Company goals and targets for the year

Call these the "tools" if you like. Your PDP is pulling together all these development needs into one plan of action, linked to which should be an agreed upon set of objectives and outcomes that you and the employee expect to get from the development experience. In this way, you are able to justify the cost of any development against your development budget.

How can we ensure continuity of approach?　Here are a few things we do at TMS to ensure continuity:

1. **Everyone should use the same tools.** All managers with direct responsibility for staff should use the same tools, and all staff should have the same opportunity to prepare their PDP. The PDP is last in line after:

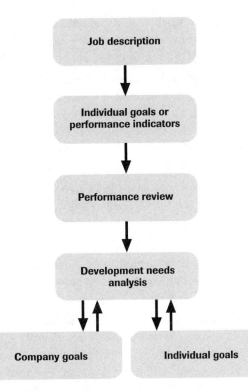

If any of the tools are missing or incomplete, there is little point in attempting a PDP.

2. **Everyone should use the same language.** For companies with large development budgets and/or a large number of staff, it is useful to categorize the development needs as follows:

- Soft skills: time management, stress management, assertiveness skills, presentation skills

- Management development: management of supervisory skills, team building, leadership skills, finance for nonfinancial managers

- Technical: Windows NT, Java, SQL programming, Object Oriented Design, NetWare courses

- Commercial: marketing, finance, human resources

- Quality: courses relating specifically to ISO 9001 procedures and processes

- Professional qualifications: Certified Novell Engineer (CNE), MCSE, advanced degree, MBA, and so on

If you break down your development budget into fields, it becomes easier to track and analyze your development expenses against a particular category of development.

3. **Everyone should categorize the development in the same way.** For example, your categories should include mentoring/coaching, on-the-job training, training temporary replacements to fill in while staff is away, cross-departmental training, internal/external training, professional accreditations, conferences/seminars, industry-specific readings, writing for magazines and books, and orientation for new employees.

10 essential points for managers   We would like to give credit here to *Training and Development: Analysing the Need, Developing the Plan, and Implementing the Strategy* by Sue Mathews. She suggests these 10 key objectives and strategies that managers should be sure to follow:

1. **Keep everyone informed.** When you introduce the idea of a PDP, use a method that delivers the information quickly, accurately, and to everyone in the same way. Sound and effective communication is essential.

2. **Clarify the overall and specific objectives.** Overall objectives refer to the company's development strategy, and objectives and specific objectives refer to the individual's objectives, both job related and personal. Make sure that any development need identified can be linked to the achievement of company objectives, otherwise the development will not be cost effective. The individuals can see what the company is doing and how, and how their own development requirements fit in with the overall strategy and achievement of goals.

3. **Make sure that everyone understands the expected outcomes.** Communicate to staff that every development activity carries outcomes with it; that is, make sure the staff knows what is expected to be different as a result of the development experience, and that their performance will be measured in relation to how well those outcomes have been met.

4. **Realize that all problems cannot be resolved by training or development.** Realize that some problems are not development issues but might be linked to other things, such as inadequate resources or inappropriate systems or structures. Lack of knowledge might contribute to these problems, but training and development will deal with only the symptom—not the cause—in such circumstances.

5. **Set clear and measurable performance criteria.** Make sure that all development activities perform to agreed upon standards and criteria before they are implemented and the cost is incurred.

6. **Recognize that training and development are corporate issues.** Bring training and development off the sidelines and into centerfield. Don't merely pay lip service to it or to PDPs: make sure that a senior manager or a director owns it, and put it on the agenda for management and board meetings and for one-on-one (1:1) meetings.

7. **Development should not just be for the "stars" in the company.** Development opportunities should be genuinely available for everyone; not just a few favored staff members. PDPs and the development budget must ensure that all staff have fair and equal access to development. If they don't, the PDP isn't working.

8. **Don't make training and development an additional organizational "stressor."** If you want staff to get the most out of their development opportunities, make sure that they are supported in managing their workload. If you don't ensure this, staff will not want to attend because of the sheer volume of work waiting for them upon their return—a major development demotivator!

9. **Be prepared to sell your development ideas.** Everyone should be prepared to sell the benefits of their development needs, because not everyone else will share their enthusiasm. Be prepared to think laterally about the best way of learning. (This need not be just through formal training courses.) All development ideas should be justified, because there will always be a cost attached.

10. **Correlate the development activities with the bottom line.** If you can clearly demonstrate how closely the development need or plan is to profit and other corporate issues, the more likely it is to be accepted. Always be prepared to argue the business case.

Other PDP notes

This section contains a step-by-step guide to identifying a development need for a principal accountability in the job description. The aim is to give the employee every opportunity to achieve individual goals and enhance performance in the job.

1. Write and jointly agree upon a job description for each role. Both the manager and the employee should sign to show that both parties agree to the content. The job description defines the job regardless of who fills the position and as such should remain relatively unchanged unless the needs of the business change.

2. Within the job description there will be a number of primary responsibilities. These are the key duties of the job. (Note that these do not
   cover every duty, just the main ones.) Normally you would expect to
   see between five and eight duties depending on the seniority of the
   position.

3. Look at each primary responsibility in turn. Consider what goals or
   objectives should fall out of each primary responsibility. There might
   be only a few goals for some primary responsibilities, but others might
   have numerous goals. The goals are linked specifically to the person
   doing the job and will therefore reflect his or her abilities and length
   of time in the position. Achievement of the goals should be linked to
   the performance review period whenever possible. Employees should
   have 12 months in which to achieve their goals, or as many months as
   possible within the performance review period. Obviously, if this exercise is not carried out until halfway through the review period, the
   goals must reflect the time the employee has to achieve them. Then
   decide how far in advance you are looking at development needs—a
   quarter, six months, or maybe the full year.

4. Transfer the goals to the PDP sheet.

5. For each goal, agree what development need or needs fall out of this.
   You're looking for any additional support or knowledge the employee
   feels he or she must have in order to achieve the goal. In other words,
   you're committing to this development (whatever it may be) so that
   the employee will be confident that he or she can achieve this goal
   within the time indicated. Development does not need to be a formal
   training course. Think laterally and look for the best way of satisfying
   the need.

6. Agree on a date by when this development should take place. Be realistic and link this date to the date by which the goal must be achieved.
   Obviously, the development process needs to take place well before
   the goal is to be achieved.

7. Decide who owns the action for ensuring that the development process is organized and takes place. If it's written down, there will be no
   confusion and the people owning the action will make sure that the
   process takes place because they are accountable for it.

8. Agree with the employee what outcome is expected from the development experience. All development (even mentoring) will have a cost
   to the company, so look at what return on investment can be expected
   from the cost incurred. Clarify the reasons why the development is

necessary and double-check that the development decided upon is actually the most appropriate one to help the jobholder achieve the goal. Both parties now have something concrete to focus on now and at the post-evaluation stage.

9. The PDP should be on the agenda for review at every 1:1 meeting, just to see whether any updates or changes need to be made. If a development process has been completed in between meetings, you need to complete the post-evaluation section and jointly agree how well the original objectives have been met. There will be occasions when the development process has not delivered what was expected, in which case you and the employee must agree on what should be done. Don't hold the post-evaluation meeting too soon after the development process—give employees time to put their newly acquired knowledge into practice.

10. The employee owns the PDP, not the manager. The employees are the ones who should drive the process in conjunction with the manager, not the other way around.

11. When you get to the performance review itself, this form, along with your notes from every 1:1 meeting, will be invaluable. If this form has been completed properly, most of your preparation work for the performance review will be contained here. The ideal scenario is one in which every development process has taken place and every process has had the desired outcome, so every goal has been achieved or even overachieved. If any goal has not been met, this form should give you a record of the reasons why. Whatever the reason, the circumstances should be contained in some way in this form.

12. You might want to modify this form for your customers. Agree with them what the primary responsibilities and the goals relating to the *project* are, and agree on development needs with them, if appropriate. (You might even get them to share the cost.) This form could serve as an excellent record of performance per project, and if the employee completes more than one project in a year, all the forms must be considered at performance review time.

13. This system will be of value only if regular meetings are held to review progress and if the preparation work is carried out in the first place, meaning that current and accurate job descriptions are prepared, primary responsibilities are agreed upon with the employee and reviewed regularly, and the goals are reviewed to ensure that they reflect the business needs as well as the needs of the individual.

Here's an example of a PDP within the seven-month period between January and the end of July 1998 and for goals that were set before January 1998.

SAMPLE PDP

NAME: **LES ARMWELK**

JOB TITLE: HR MANAGER

DEVELOPMENT FOR THE PERIOD: JAN '98 – JULY '98

DATE OF REVIEW: 3/29/98

PRIMARY RESPONSIBILITY: Improve company recruitment process and recruit all new heads per Plan '98.

Goals	Development needed	By when	Owner	Outcome expected
Ensure that all new heads are recruited in time, at the right quality and cost.	Project management training (external).	End Jan '98	LA	Ability to project manage the whole company's recruitment process (100+ heads per year).
	Advanced Interviewing Skills course (external).	End Feb '98	LA	To participate in and make decisions on at least 50 percent of all second interviews by the end of March '98; 70 percent by the end of July '98.
	One-hour sessions with each departmental manager to understand and assess company's Headcount Plan.	End Feb '98	LA	To be able to recommend to the Board the proposed recruitment strategy for each quarter in advance and to make recommendations for change to the Headcount Plan.
Introduce psychometric testing to the company's recruitment process by Aug. '98.	Research an appropriate battery of psychometric tests and present recommendations to the MD.	Research complete by end May '98	LA	To gain MD's approval for tests to be introduced at first presentation.

>>

Goals	Development needed	By when	Owner	Outcome expected
		Presentation to MD by end June '98		To have a working battery of tests in the company that adds value to the recruitment process.
		Presentation to all Dept. Managers by end July '98		

POST EVALUATION

Development need	Actioned	Objectives met? yes/no	If no, next step	Actioned
Project management training (external) by end Jan '98.	YES	Will not be known until end of Plan year, but initial signs are good (Project Plan has been prepared).		
Advanced Interviewing Skills course (external).	YES	YES Les is participating in 50 percent of all second interviews and is on course to exceed the 70 percent target by end July '98.		
One-hour sessions with each department manager to understand and assess company's Headcount Plan.	YES	NO Les requires more detailed financial training in order to understand departmental recruitment budgets.	Two one-hour sessions with the finance director on Profit & Loss and Budgeting & Forecasting.	YES Completed by 15 March '98.
Research an appropriate battery of psychometric tests and present recommendations to the MD.	NO	NO Research is unlikely to be complete by end May '98.	Research to be complete by end June '98. Presentation to MD by mid June '98.	YES YES

Performance reviews

The performance review is intended to summarize the development meeting (which can occur annually or more frequently) between the manager and each of his or her direct reports, during which each jointly reviews training and development activity and work achievements during the past review period and agrees to action plans for training, development, and work-related goals for the coming review period.

The review meeting itself should be seen as a two-way process: as a tool that enables you to assess past performance while also looking ahead at future goals. It helps to guide everyone toward optimizing their abilities so that the end result is that both company and individual goals are met.

The only way company goals can be met is if everyone carries out their own role properly, and so it follows that efficiency and effectiveness must be monitored on a regular basis. The manager and the company should provide every assistance to the employees to enable and allow for optimum performance.

There are many different ways of measuring performance, but the one used most frequently in performance reviews concentrates on measuring achievements against specific goals (or performance indicators). Within the job description are a number of primary responsibilities. From those, the employee and the manager agree to certain performance objectives, or goals, with the intention that shared goals result in a commitment to those goals. The performance of the employee is assessed against these goals over a specific period of time. The overall performance level for the period under review is summarized in one performance rating. Any percentage increase to salaries is directly linked to the performance rating as well as to the company's ability to pay. (This is where the company's revenue and profit come in.)

In general terms, the main purpose of a performance review system is summarized below, although not in any particular order:

- To review past performance
- To set performance objectives for the future
- To help improve current performance
- To set and agree on future goals

- To assess increases or new levels in salaries (Salary levels can go down as well as up, or even stay the same, depending on performance.)
- To assess training and development needs
- To assist in career planning decisions

It is another aspect of communication and an opportunity for you to build a closer relationship with your staff and as such should be seen as a positive step forward.

The review meeting   The following are guidelines for conducting the performance review meeting:

- The review should be a two-way discussion, controlled by the manager.
- The meeting should be conducted with tact, diplomacy, sensitivity, and above all, in a professional manner.
- The manager should never talk "off the record" during the meeting.
- The manager should never make promises during this meeting unless they have been discussed and agreed upon beforehand.
- The manager should not get drawn into discussing salary reviews during the main part of the review; rather, the manager should have an authorized percentage increase to give to employees when they receive their performance rating. (After all, that's really what they're waiting to hear!)
- At the start of the meeting, the manager should briefly outline the format and structure of the meeting and give the employee an idea of the duration. (It's a good idea to schedule at least an hour per review meeting if the review period is six months; otherwise, schedule two hours if the review period is one year.)
- The manager should let staff members know that he or she has reviewed all the 1:1 notes, as well as all client feedback, and their own individual comments in reaching the conclusions contained in the review form itself. Have these forms available during the meeting for reference purposes.
- The manager should work through each section of the review form in turn. The employee should be given the opportunity to comment on what the manager has said and make notes of their comments for the manager to consider before finalizing the wording of the review form.

- The manager should finish the review meeting with details of the overall performance rating and the percentage increase to be assigned to the employee's salary.

- The manager should let employees know that he or she will write up the form and get it to them within two working days of the review meeting for them to sign. Once the manager has the review form back, he or she signs it and makes copies as appropriate.

Follow up   The manager is responsible for these action items after the review meeting with the employee:

- The manager should review his or her own handling of the review meeting as soon as possible, while things are still fresh in his or her mind.

- The manager should review those points where follow-up action has been agreed upon and ensure that the action happens.

- The manager should ensure that any follow-up action that he or she commits to during the review is documented and the individual informed.

The Individual Preparation Form and the review form don't cross-reference each other or follow the same lines in the questions they ask. This might make it more difficult to use any information from the individual preparation form in preparing for the review meeting.

1:1 meetings   The objectives of regular meetings between managers and their direct reports are to provide a regular and focused opportunity for mutual communication, feedback, and exchange of information in the following ways:

- Goal setting, clarification, review, and update
- Performance feedback
- Review of training and development needs
- Communication of information to allow both the manager and the employee to improve their performance
- The upward flow through management of concerns, information, or requests for improvement
- Maintaining and improving the relationship between the manager and the employee

The frequency of the 1:1 meetings depends on the preference of the employee and the manager, but as a guideline, these meetings should be held a minimum of every six weeks, preferably every four weeks. More frequent meetings might be necessary for new employees or for staff undergoing difficulties or tackling steep learning curves. Each meeting should be long enough (usually an hour; no more than two) to cover difficult issues and build enough rapport for open and honest feedback (top down and bottom up). The meeting should be held where there are no interruptions, preferably on neutral territory. The style of the meeting depends on the individual concerned and the areas to be covered in each 1:1. The meeting can be semiformal, very formal, or informal. You might need to use different styles depending on the performance of the employee and the areas that you need to address. Most important is that the style be an effective one.

Try to keep to the same framework (per the template) so that a certain discipline is instilled into the meeting and so that the employee has a chance to prepare beforehand. The actual content of each meeting will vary depending on performance issues. Always agree on any follow-up actions arising from each 1:1. Give the employee a copy of any notes immediately after the meeting for his or her records and as a reference for the next meeting.

The 1:1 process is absolutely key. You should capture any PDP issues within the agenda for any 1:1 meeting. If you hold regular meetings and follow the agenda, your preparation for any performance review will be relatively simple. Similarly, you will give yourself an opportunity to address any problems before they become big issues. Managers who implement regular 1:1 meetings with their direct reports and conduct them properly can ensure an almost 100 percent zero-defect rate in appeals, performance review surprises, grievances, and disciplinary matters.

Project planning

Performance reviews should be viewed as a project, and as such, a project plan should be developed over the whole performance review period, culminating when all performance reviews are to be held. For the purposes of the table on the following page, let's assume that the performance review period is a year that starts in March and ends in February with the review itself. A basic Critical Path Analysis might be as follows.

PREPARATION WORK

Area	Action	Timeframe
Job descriptions and primary responsibilities	Write and agree upon job description with employee focusing on the primary responsibilities.	End of Feb.
Key objectives (or goals)	Isolate agreed-upon goals from each responsibilities and discuss the timeframe for achievement over the 11-month period with the employee.	End of Feb.
	Make sure that you also link the goals to the Individual Preparation Form.	
	Consider asking the clients to give feedback on the employee against the performance areas listed in the Individual Preparation Form; otherwise, you will have no objective feedback on performance in these areas other than the employee's own.	
1:1 meetings	Set up 1:1 meetings in your calendar for every month from March to January.	End of Feb.
Budgets	Board to agree on amounts to be assigned to (a) performance review increases for total company, and (b) percentage increases to be assigned to each performance rating.	Dec.

PREPARATION OVER THE PERFORMANCE REVIEW YEAR

Area	Action	Timeframe
1:1 meetings	Make sure that you hold regular 1:1 meetings with the employee every month to review progress and performance against every one of the goals and objectives.	Every month from March to Jan.
	Obtain regular feedback from the employee's client on his or her performance against predefined goals.	
	Rate the employee's performance against each goal every month using the same criteria as in the performance review form (for example, A, B, C, D).	
	Make sure that the goals and timeframes are reviewed and revised in line with the changing business needs so that they are always current.	
PDPs	Identify any development needs that are agreed upon during these 1:1 meetings with either the employee or the client and transfer these needs onto the	Every month from March to Jan.

Area	Action	Timeframe
	employee's PDP form, ensuring that the development process actually happens (this gives the employee every chance to achieve or surpass their objectives).	
Booking performance review meetings	Book a review meeting in your calendar for every employee who reports to you. You should assume one review in the morning and one in the afternoon (more than this is too many in one day).	First two weeks in Jan.
	Book an appropriate venue.	
	Let each direct report know the date, time, and venue for his or her review throughout February.	

PREPARATION JUST BEFORE THE PERFORMANCE REVIEW MEETING

Area	Action	Timeframe
Individual Preparation Form	Each employee should complete and return his or her preparation form to you at least 10 working days before the performance review meeting.	Mid-Jan.
1:1 meeting notes	If you have held 1:1 meetings every month and assigned a performance rating against each goal as you have gone along, you will have comprehensive records of performance throughout the year. You need only to average these to come up with a rating covering the whole year. It should be a simple process.	Mid-Jan.
Individual Preparation Forms	Read each person's Individual Preparation Form and determine (a) those areas where there is consensus of opinion between you and the employee, and (b) those areas where your opinions on performance differ.	Second two weeks in Jan.
	Where you differ in opinion, determine why and decide which opinion you will discuss at the review meeting.	
Client review forms or notes	Review all the client notes you have for the 11 months and compare these with your 1:1 notes and the Individual Preparation Form notes. As above, determine (a) where there is consensus between the client, you, and the employee, and (b) where the opinions differ.	Second two weeks in Jan.
	Where there is a difference of opinion, decide which opinion you will discuss at the review meeting.	

>>

>>

Area	Action	Timeframe
PDPs	Review the employee's PDP and make a note of any development that had been requested and agreed upon but that had not taken place.	Second two weeks in Jan.
Appraisal form	You can either complete an appraisal form in note form or make comprehensive notes and complete the form after the review meeting. Remember that the employee will still have a contribution to make at the meeting, so don't make it look as though you've already decided what will be included. Wait to hear the employee's side of the story before finalizing the form, although very little in that meeting should be a surprise to either you or the employee if you have held regular 1:1s.	Two working days before the review meeting.

FOLLOW-UP FROM THE REVIEW MEETING

Area	Action	Timeframe
Finishing the performance review	Write up the performance review form and send this to the employee for his or her comments and signature. As soon as you have the signature, you should sign the form as well. When this is done, the performance rating is authorized. Give a photocopy to the employee and keep the original in his or her personnel file.	No more than the three working days after the performance review.
Assigning salary increases	Follow up with a semiformal letter to the employee stating (a) his or her performance rating (b) the percentage increase that has been assigned to this rating, and (c) his or her revised salary with effective date. The original goes to the employee and a copy goes into his or her personnel file. Actual salary increases should be incorporated into your budget.	Immediately.
Setting new goals	Sit down with the employee and mutually agree to new goals and objectives for the coming 11 months, and start the process all over again.	Complete by mid-March so that employees have 10.5 months to achieve new goals.

The Effects of the Year 2000

Some companies are offering "golden handcuffs" (stock options) in response to the Year 2000 situation, meaning they hope the money will keep their employees around. Others are putting off the decision as to whether to offer cash inducements until the situation unfolds and possibly worsens. Many experts, however, feel that golden handcuffs will not have the desired effect. As we've said above, money, typically, will not be enough to keep people. People leave because of unsupportive management, lack of opportunity, or a lack of fit between the company's and the person's values. A fulfilling career, challenge, and fresh skill acquisition are what keep people. We feel that payments based on people staying is really a just form of bribery, and proper career development and training are more important in the long run.

What to Do When Someone Leaves

Of course, if you follow all the advice in this chapter, no one will ever leave. Well, er, maybe they will. Inevitably, employees are going to leave sometime. When this happens, you should treat it as a good opportunity to get some frank feedback about how the company has performed. For example, are they leaving because they've been offered the job of their dreams elsewhere, or are they disillusioned with their current employer? (You!) If they're leaving for the latter reason, others probably are too. This is your chance to find out.

People do come and go—that's life. Don't be disheartened if they go. Just treat it as a valuable opportunity, learn the lessons, and go back to Step 1 again!

MICROSOFT CERTIFICATION AND THE TESTING OF DEVELOPERS

Mark Pearce

Regardless of how much or how little they are paid, bad software developers are always extremely expensive. Hiring developers can all too often be a hit-or-miss affair. You talk to a guy, ask him some questions about his current and past work, and then ask him to answer a few ad-hoc technical questions. He seems personable, maybe even enthusiastic. Perhaps he stumbled over some of the technical questions, but he answered a couple of the others in convincing detail. He certainly seems to be able to "talk the talk," at least superficially. He knows all the latest buzzwords—COM+, MTS, ActiveX servers, polymorphism, etc. But if you don't have, for example, TMS's "Test from Hell," how do you know if the person that you're about to hire has constructed a facade

>>

>>

of technical knowledge specifically to cover up his lack of real-world experience? And how do you measure him technically against the developer that you interviewed yesterday? Given the extremely large sums of money that can be commanded by developers nowadays, what would you give for some form of objective and comparable measurement of a candidate's job skills?

One approach is professional certification. Microsoft offers several different types of technical certification in its products, each designed to show a high level of competence in performing tasks related to the skill being tested. From our point of view, the most important qualifications are Microsoft Certified Professional (MCP) and Microsoft Certified Solution Developer (MCSD). The other popular qualification is Microsoft Certified Systems Engineer (MCSE).

An MCP has passed a mandatory product exam, for our purposes either Visual Basic 4 or preferably Visual Basic 5 (exams #70-065 and #70-165, respectively). Note that these are due to be replaced in the latter half of 1998 with the new Visual Basic 6 exam. The MCSD certification is more advanced and aimed at developers who have to design and develop custom business solutions with Microsoft development tools and technologies. It consists of two mandatory core exams, Microsoft Windows Architecture I and II (exams #70-160 and #70-161) and two elective exams from a list that includes Microsoft Visual Basic 5 (#70-165), Microsoft Access for Windows 95 (#70-069), and Implementing a Database Design on Microsoft SQL Server 6.5 or 7.0 (#70-027 or #70-029). Finally, the MCSE qualification is aimed mainly at people who implement and support networked information systems with Microsoft NT and Microsoft BackOffice. It consists of four mandatory core operating system exams and two elective language/product exams.

Most of these exams cost $100 each to take, are closed-book and computer-administered, between 60 and 90 minutes in length, and consist of a series of multiple-choice questions. They are designed to test the specific skills needed for the job functions being tested. Obviously every job function requires different levels of skills, from memorizing facts to analyzing scenarios, designing solutions, and evaluating options. The exams aim to measure a candidate's performance in these job functions rather than just knowledge of a product or terminology. In my experience, the questions are, on the whole, well researched and well written and do indeed perform a reasonable job of measuring a

>>

candidate's specific job skills. Microsoft insists that none of the exams contain "trick" questions. So let's just say that occasionally a candidate has to read a question very carefully and probably several times—a few questions are more about reading comprehension than about knowledge of the product or skill.

While the exams do have some professional standing in the IT industry and are considered to be fairly demanding, they also have a couple of inherent drawbacks. The first is that each exam is designed to measure general competence in a particular area. Often more useful is the measurement of a specific competence, such as the use of DCOM or an understanding of how to implement ActiveX servers efficiently. As Visual Basic becomes larger and more complex, there is a need for developers who specialize in specific parts of the product. If you're building small teams, with each team specializing in one area, construct your own tests (verbal, written, or computer-administered) to measure thorough competence in that area. By all means follow the Microsoft test format if you want, but engineer your questions to concentrate on the specific areas you need. Refine the questions over time based on candidates' results and feedback. Eventually you will have a test suite tailored to your own requirements.

The second drawback is that the Microsoft exams all use a multiple-choice format. This enables computer grading of tests, without the need for human involvement. However, it is sometimes useful to present open-ended questions, such as asking a candidate to write Visual Basic code to solve a particular problem. Although these types of questions are more subjective and require expert human input to judge the answers, they can also give you more insights into a developer's thought processes and way of working than those questions that use the multiple-choice format. You can also ask more unusual questions. One of my favorites is to ask a candidate what question he or she would add to the test, and how would he or she answer their own question.

My advice is to use the Microsoft exams as a useful tool, and then supplement them with a test of your own design to refine your knowledge of a candidate's technical competence. Be prepared to spend some time constructing your test to ask the right questions in a nonambiguous manner. You are likely to be paying any new hire tens of thousands of dollars, or even hundreds of thousands. It makes no sense to hire just on gut feelings or on inadequate testing.

Coding
Conventions

PETER J MORRIS   MARK DEAKIN

This section is based largely upon our original coding conventions appendix in our first edition, written by Mark Hurst and Peet Morris. It describes the coding conventions we used in preparing most of the source code for this book. These conventions are based on extracts from our in-house TMS Visual Basic programmer's manual, *VB Vogue* (also included as part of the TMS Developer's Framework). You can use this appendix purely to look up type or scope prefixes you don't understand, but you might also want to use our conventions in your own code. Or you might decide to adapt them to suit your own preferences. The important thing is that you have coding conventions and that you apply them uniformly across your code. (If your company is interested in purchasing *VB Vogue*, please send e-mail to the *info@TheMandelbrotSet.com* alias requesting details and availability.)

THE NEED FOR CODING CONVENTIONS

Consistently applied coding standards can improve the following in a software project:

- **Productivity.** Productivity, as applied here to the actual writing of code, means saving "code time" without suffering some inherent quality penalty.

- **Quality.** The quality of code is chiefly measured by its relative conformance to some technical specification and the ease with which it can be maintained.

- **Maintainability.** Maintainable code is both repairable and extensible. Additionally, and in all cases, maintainable code is easy to comprehend, which facilitates achieving speedy, accurate modification.

- **Comprehensibility.** Comprehensible code is both conformant (with some recognized standard) and consistent.

NAMING CONVENTIONS

We use a simplified form of Hungarian notation, a naming convention that takes its name from the nationality of its creator, Charles Simonyi. Certain elements of Hungarian notation are used in Microsoft's Visual Basic manuals. Microsoft also uses Hungarian notation internally as part of its coding conventions, as do many developers around the world. Our simplified form of this notation is used to attach both type and scope information to various object names. Hungarian notation uses character prefixes to denote type, aggregation, and scope, and the full system gets rather complicated. The subset we've chosen for our purposes is defined in the following sections and in the tables that appear at the end of this appendix.

Type Information

Hungarian type prefixes have two parts: a *base type* to represent the base data type and a *modifier* to denote an aggregate type. An example of a base-type prefix is *n*, which denotes an integer, while adding the *a* modifier to the base type denotes an array of integers. An example should make this clearer:

```
Dim nCounter            As Integer
Dim anCounters(1 To 10) As Integer
```

Notice that the variable name itself starts with an uppercase letter, which shows us where the prefix stops and the variable name starts. Sometimes we need to use more than one modifier, such as a multidimensional array:

```
Dim aanStateTable(1 To 10, 1 To 10) As Integer
```

The base types and modifiers we use are listed at the end of this appendix. In fact, we use only one aggregate modifier since arrays are the only single-type aggregates that Visual Basic supports.

Where calls are made to Windows API functions, you might see type prefixes such as *LPSTR* and *sz* that don't appear in our tables: these prefixes are used in the Microsoft Windows documentation. We've found that changing these to match our Visual Basic data types can often conceal errors in the declarations. You might also see *p* used as a modifier to denote a pointer and *pcb* to denote the address of a callback function.

For variables defined with user-defined types (UDTs) and classes, the special base-type prefixes *t* and *C* are used. Although *C* breaks the lowercase rule, we've adopted it because it's used throughout the industry.

Menus are named with the type prefix *mnu*, but the names are aggregated to show the menu structure. For example, the Open item on the File menu is called *mnuFileOpen*. Here are some more standard menu names:

```
mnuHelpAbout
mnuFileExit
```

Scope Information

We also use prefixes to denote an object's scope. Our scope prefixes come between the type prefix and the object name, so we need to make sure they start with an uppercase letter and end with a lowercase letter. This way, the scope prefixes stand out from both the type prefix and the object's name. For example, a private integer variable (scope prefix *Pi*) defined at the module level would be named like this:

```
Private nPiCounter As Integer
```

Variables

Variables are named like this:

```
<type><scope><name>
```

The *name* part is simply the variable name written in mixed case, and the *type* part is a Hungarian type as defined earlier. We don't use type and scope prefixes when naming properties and methods of classes and forms.

The base types and modifiers are given in a table at the end of this appendix. The *scope* part is defined in the following sections.

Local variables

Local variables do not have a scope prefix. Here are some examples of local variable definitions:

```
Dim nCounter  As Integer
Dim sMessage  As String
Dim tThisCell As tTableEntry  ' A user-defined type
ReDim anLookupTable (1 To 10) As Integer
```

Private variables

Private variables defined at the module level have *Pi* as a scope prefix. Some examples follow:

```
Private nPiCounter  As Integer
Private sPiMessage  As String
Private tPiThisCell As tTableEntry  ' A user-defined type
Private anPiLookupTable () As Integer
```

Global variables

Global variables defined at the module level of a standard module (that is, a BAS file) have the module identifier as a scope prefix. The module identifier is a unique two-character prefix that suggests the module name. For example, we might choose *Er* for an error handling module or *Db* for a database module. We also use an additional scope prefix, *Pu*, to identify the variable as public. Here are some examples.

```
Public nPuErCounter As Integer        ' Er for "error handling"
Public sPuErMessage As String
Public anPuTbLookupTable () As Integer ' Tb for "table functions"
Public tPuTbThisCell As tTableEntry    ' A user-defined type
```

Form and class properties (unprotected)

Public variables defined at the module level of classes and forms are properties and do not have scope or type prefixes.

Functions and Subroutines

Public functions and subroutines have scope prefixes in the same way that variables do. Public and private functions also have a type prefix that reflects the type of value returned. The rules for choosing the type prefix are the same as those for variables.

Private subroutines

Private subroutines and functions do not require scope prefixes. Here are some examples of private subroutines:

```
Private Sub OpenLogFile()
Private Sub ClearGrid()
```

And here are some private functions:

```
Private Function nGetNextItem() As Integer
Private Function sGetFullPath(ByVal sFileName As String) _
    As String
Private Function CGetNextCell() As CTableEntry
```

Public subroutines

The rules for choosing scope prefixes for public subroutines are exactly the same as those for variables, as shown here:

```
Public ErReportError()
Public TbInsertTableEntry()
Public DbDeleteItem()
```

Form and class methods

Public functions and subroutines defined in classes and forms are properties and do not have type or scope prefixes.

Form and class properties (protected)

Property Let, *Property Set*, and *Property Get* routines do not have type or scope prefixes.

DLL procedures

When declaring Windows API functions, we use the *Alias* keyword to add the prefix *Win*. For example, *CallWindowProc* becomes *WinCallWindowProc*. When declaring functions in other DLLs, we use the prefix *Dll*.

Parameter lists

Formal parameters are named as local variables but with *i* or *o* added in place of a scope prefix to denote whether the parameter is an input or an output:

```
Sub CrackURL(ByVal siURL As String, ByRef soProtcol, _
    ByRef soPath, ByRef soPath, ByRef noPort)
```

For parameters that are both inputs *and* outputs, we use *io*.

Controls and Forms

We also use type prefixes when naming Visual Basic controls. The prefixes are given at the end of this appendix. Forms are named as if they were controls, even though a form name can also act as a class name. For example, we would name a form *frmPublication* instead of *CPublication*, even though we could create new instances of the form:

```
Dim frmNewPub As New frmPublication
```

Constants

Constants are named in uppercase letters, with no type or scope prefixes. Arbitrary prefixes can be used to group sets of related constants:

```
Const TABLE_SIZE            As Integer = 100
Const DEFAULT_LOG_FILE      As String = "log.txt"

Const ERR_GENERIC           As Integer = 32767
Const ERR_LOGON_FAIL        As Integer = 32766
Const ERR_COMPONENT_MISSING As Integer = 32765
```

Type and Class Definitions

Type names are prefixed with *t*, and class names are prefixed with *C*. These prefixes are also used as the base-type prefixes when naming instances. The rest of the name is written in mixed case:

```
Type tTableEntry
    nNewState As Integer
    lAction   As Long
End Type
```

And in use:

```
Dim tCell         As tTableEntry
Dim CSymbolTable  As New CTable
```

Source Files

Source filenames are restricted to the traditional 8.3 format. The first three characters are reserved for a project identifier, and the default file extensions are retained. The remaining five characters are used to distinguish files in whatever way seems appropriate.

Other Naming Conventions

This is an example of a local string:

```
Dim sCustomerName As String
```

This is an example of a module-level integer:

```
Dim nmCustomerId As Integer
```

Here is a global-level Double defined in the module Mi:

```
Public dPuMiCustomerNumber As Double
```

Here is a global-level Double; the module identifier is not defined or else resident in the project-wide globals module:

```
Public dPuCustomerNumber As Double
```

This is a global array of Longs; the module identifier is not defined or else resident in the project-wide globals module:

```
Public alPuAmounts(1 to 25) As Long
```

This is a global database; the module identifier is Dt:

```
Public dbPuDtCustomers As Database
```

This shows a call to an external DLL function; the result is assigned to a global variable resident in the project-wide global's module:

```
bPuRetCode = bDllIsShareLoaded ()
```

CODING CONVENTIONS

This section outlines a number of conventions we have found useful when writing code. It isn't comprehensive—our in-house manual, *VB Vogue,* contains much more detail than we have space for here. We suggest you use this section as a basis for designing your own coding standards.

Principles

Always code for clarity, not efficiency. Choose variable and function names carefully. Be verbose rather than terse, and parenthesize expressions to make them clearer. Write your code for the reader.

Limit the scope of constants, variables, functions, and subroutines as much as possible. If you have the choice, always use a local object in preference to a global one.

Use explicit type conversions (*CInt*, *CStr*, and so on) when assigning between different variable types.

Some Specifics

Follow these guidelines when you write code:

- Define all variables explicitly. Checking the Require Variable Declaration option under Tools/Options/Editor enforces this. Define variable-length arrays explicitly. (Visual Basic will not enforce this.)
- Always specify the upper and lower bounds in an array definition.
- Define constants, and use them in place of numbers in the code.
- Always use the *ByVal* and *ByRef* keywords in parameter lists. Use *ByVal* where you have a choice.
- Always use the *Private* keyword on functions and subroutines that are not exported from a module.
- Define the types of all variables and function and subroutine parameters explicitly. For example, use *Dim nBufSize As Integer* instead of *Dim nBufSize*, and use *Function nGetChars(nBufSize As Integer) As Integer* instead of *Function nGetChars(nBufSize)*.
- Do not use implicit type suffixes (such as ! and &) in variable definitions.
- In *For* loops, use *Next <Index>* instead of just *Next*.

Follow the general principle of restricting the scope of variables and functions to the barest minimum possible. However, be sure to use common sense. For example, a procedure that logically serves only one form should be "contained" within that form. Likewise, a procedure that could logically serve many forms should be placed in a module, even though it might currently be called only from one form.

Miscellaneous Conventions

This section describes some other conventions worth noting.

Dimensioning variables

Variables should each be dimensioned individually, meaning there should be only one *Dim*, *Public*, *Private*, or *Static* per variable. Multiple dimensions on a line can lead to ambiguity about the scope and type of a variable.

Defining arrays

Both the upper and lower bounds in array definitions must be specified. Do not rely on the Option Base setting (Option Base should not be used).

```
Public anDigits(10) As Integer
```

This dimensions 11 entries in the array if the Option Base is equal to 0, which is its default.

```
Public anDigits(1 to 10) As Integer
```

This dimensions 10 entries in the array, regardless of the Option Base setting, and is the way to dimension arrays.

Using control arrays

Control arrays must be used whenever possible and whenever appropriate in Visual Basic. These make smaller executables, which therefore lead to better performance.

Using operators

Use the addition operator (+) only in numerical expressions. Do not use it to facilitate some string concatenation. This is especially true if using variables of type Variant.

Comparing strings

StrComp is by far the fastest way to compare strings. Use it instead of a language operator (such as =) whenever possible. Binary Comparison is faster than Text Comparison (especially if you're using the *Like* operator), and should be used whenever it is appropriate. Generally, using fixed strings is slower, with the exception of passing strings to API or DLL procedures.

Using parentheses

While a parenthesized expression might be slower to evaluate than a non-parenthesized expression, parentheses should be applied where appropriate to ensure the readability of code.

Initializing variables

Initialize variables through assignment. Initialization or preassignment (in the case of Visual Basic) of variables is a good programming habit to get into.

Initialize variables as close as possible to where they are used. This avoids having to hunt for the initialization:

```
Dim nCount As Integer : nCount = 1 ' for counting iterations
```

or

```
Dim nCount As Integer   ' for counting iterations
nCount = 1              ' initialized
```

Calling subroutines

The *Call* keyword should prefix any call to a subroutine, since it makes explicit what is happening in the code. Using *Call* also avoids the problem of an apparent parameter being merely evaluated.

Setting control properties at design time vs. run time

As a general rule, it is a good idea to do as much in the code as possible. For example, the *Mask* property of a masked-edit control is best set "in code" at run time rather than at design time, because setting it in code generally makes clearer what is going on. This method also makes code more portable (because operational logic is not tied to any form property, such as in the previous example, the code is more portable and generic).

Using *For...Next* statements

In *For* loops, use *Next <counter>* instead of just *Next*. In *For Each* loops (VBA), use *Next <element>* instead of just *Next*. These recommendations are faster.

For...Next loops are more than twice as fast as any equivalent *Do...Loop* and *While....Wend* loops. Not surprisingly, Integer counters are the fastest of all the variable types to use as a counter.

Using the *Me* statement

The *Me* statement should be used whenever possible in the code. Where code in an object module (class or form) refers to objects in the same module, use *Me* rather than the object's name to make the reference implicit, and be assured the code will work with multiple instances of the object.

NOTE

It is not possible to use *Me* when setting an instance of a class or form object to Nothing.

Optional parameters

Visual Basic's typed optional parameters are faster than untyped (Variant) optional parameters. However, note that *IsMissing* does not work with typed optional parameters, only with optional Variant parameters.

IN-LINE DOCUMENTATION

One of the best sources of documentation is the code itself. When you follow a specific coding format and thoroughly comment your code, you're making your program more readable and providing valuable information to yourself and to other programmers who might have to make modifications to the code later.

Formatting

Follow these rules when formatting your code:

- Punctuate your code with blank lines.

- Keep your procedures to a manageable size—preferably not much more than a single screen.

- Keep indentation under control. If you're having difficulty remaining within the right margin, you're probably nesting too deeply.

- Use parentheses to enhance the readability of your code. No one reading your code should have to wonder what you meant when you wrote it.

- Preserve screen real estate wherever possible. For example, when creating a long string, it might be better to build up the string with multiple assignments, such as those shown on the following page.

```
Dim sMsg As String

sMsg = "This is a paragraph that is to appear "
sMsg = sMsg & "in a message box. The text is "
sMsg = sMsg & "broken into several lines of code "
sMsg = sMsg & "in the source code, making it easier "
sMsg = sMsg & "for the programmer to read and debug. "

MsgBox sMsg, vbOkOnly, "Text"

Dim sQRY As String

sQRY = "SELECT Customer.CustomerName, Orders.OrderValue "
sQRY = sQRY & "FROM Customer, Orders "
sQRY = sQRY & "WHERE Customer.CustomerId = Orders.CustomerId"

ReportQry1.SQL = sQRY
```

Code Commenting

The comments in and around the code and, to a lesser though highly important extent, the names and identifiers used within the code, constitute the readable English in a program. Both individually and as a collective, comments animate the code to the reader and help explain what is happening.

Comments typically center upon some sequence point, around which some current "code-wise" activity focuses. In other words, comments explain what has happened or is about to happen in the code. Comments must always therefore provide a narrative or biography of the code—past and present. Additionally, comments are not contained within the "built" Visual Basic code and as such have no overhead attached to them. Don't be afraid to comment code in the belief that it will cause code bloat and the like.

The important rules for commenting are as follows:

- Keep comments up-to-date and directed toward being excessively verbose, if anything.

- A good comment is a high-quality comment. Quality, not quantity, is all important.

- Use capital letters to issue warnings and signal important announcements.

- Comments must be clear and concise—always attempt to add value and never simply restate the obvious.

- Use short comments to say *what* is happening and longer comments to say *how* and *why* the state transition is occurring.

- To reduce the number of comments you use, try to write code that does not require commenting.

- By using clear sentences and parallel structure in comments, you avoid ambiguities and any resulting confusion as to your intent.

End-of-line comments

End-of-line comments should be used to annotate variable or constant definitions:

```
Const MAX_ROWS As Long = 2147483647 ' (2^31)-1 (Max value for
                                    ' long integer)

Const ICONIZED As Integer = 7    ' To startup applications
                                 ' with Shell().
```

In-line comments

End-of-line comments are rarely suitable for annotating code. Where a function or subroutine contains a number of logical blocks, introduce each block with a separate comment indented to the same level as the code. Use as many lines as necessary, and don't use surrounding ***** lines to delimit comments unless something really important is about to happen. Keep comment lines short so that the entire comment can be viewed on a VGA display without scrolling left and right.

Use comments to explain the code, not to echo it; if your comments become very involved, consider restructuring the code. Complicated explanations can also be moved into the function header. The following code shows some examples of appropriate in-line comments:

```
MaxCol = nColumn - 1
XL_NewRow stDataBlock
XL_NewRow stDummyRow

' The dummy row now holds the long form of the column headings.
' Appending this to the main data block gives us both long and
' short headings, one below the other.

XL_AppendBlock stDataBlock, stDummyRow
```

>>

```
' We now need to step through the data array and extract the
' records for each row in turn. Records corresponding to a
' single row all have the same code and description and are
' contiguous in the array (which is sorted on description).
' The row description array returned by GetNextRow is sorted
' on column number.

nDataIdx = 0
Do While nDataIdx < nNumRecs
```

File Headers

Every module should have a header that sits as a comment in the module's definitions area. The header identifies the module and summarizes the external interfaces to it. Here is an example module header:

```
' *************************************************************
' Module          Startup
'
' Filename        tabstart.bas
' Module Prefix   St
'
' Author          A. Developer
'                 The Mandelbrot Set (Int'l) Ltd.
'
' Description
'
' Startup module for the table-driven FSM sample application
'
' Revisions
' 11-12-97, A.Developer
' Added instance checking.
'
' 08-12-97, A.Developer
' Moved global FSM object out of here.
'
' *************************************************************
```

The module prefix is a two-letter code used as a scope prefix that uniquely identifies this module in the project. Module prefixes are significant only for standard (BAS) modules.

Function and Subroutine Headers

A function header is a comment that describes what the function does and summarizes its interface. The description should focus on what the function does, although for complicated or longer functions it might be appropriate to summarize the *how* as well. All nontrivial functions should have function headers, and headers are also recommended for nontrivial event handlers.

Here is an example function header:

```
' ***************************************************************
'
' Synopsis       Create the event queue, and attach
'                an event handler to it.
'
' Parameters
'
'   pcbiNewWinProc           (I) Address of the event
'                                queue callback function
'
' Nonlocal Data
'
'   hwndPiEventQueue         (O) Event queue handle
'   pcblPiEvQueueOldWinProc (O) Event queue default
'                                window procedure
'   lPiFSMEventMsg           (O) Event message number
'
' Description
'
' This is where we create the event queue and attach a
' callback function to it to handle our FSM events.
'
' The event queue is built around a private window that
' we create here. We subclass the window to hook
' pcbiNewWinProc onto it and then register a custom
' message number that we will use to send messages to it.
' The pcbiNewWinProc parameter is a pointer to a VB
' function obtained with the AddressOf operator.
'
' ***************************************************************
```

TYPE PREFIXES

In this section, you'll find tables that include prefixes for various data types and control types.

TABLE A-1   **VARIABLES PREFIXES**

Prefix	Data Type
byt	Byte
b	Boolean
cur	Currency
d	Double
dte	Date
f	Single
hf	File handle (Long)
hwnd	Window handle (Long)
h(... lowercase)	Handle to something (Long)
l	Long
n	Integer
o	Object
s	String
v	Variant

TABLE A-2   **MODIFIERS AND SPECIAL TYPES PREFIXES**

Prefix	Data Type
a	Array <of another type>
C	Class or class instance
t	User-defined type or instance
e	Enumerated type or instance
p	Pointer (used with API calls)
pcb	Pointer to a callback function (used with *AddressOf*)

TABLE A-3

DATA OBJECTS: DAO PREFIXES

Prefix	Visual Basic Data Type
bk	SelBookmarks
ct	Container
db	Database
dc	Document
ds	Dynaset
er	Errors
fd	Field
gp	Group
ix	Index
pa	Parameter
pr	Property
qd	QueryDef
rs	Recordset
rl	Relation
ss	Snapshot
tb	Table
td	TableDef
us	User
wk	Workspace

TABLE A-4

DATA OBJECTS: RDO PREFIXES

Prefix	Visual Basic Data Type
rdoEng	rdoEngine
rdoEnv	rdoEnvironment
rdoConn	rdoConnection
rdoTbl	rdoTable
rdoCol	rdoColumn
rdoPrepS	rdoPreparedStatement
rdoParam	rdoParameter
rdoRS	rdoResultset
rdoErr	rdoError

TABLE A-5 | **CONTROLS PREFIXES**

Prefix	Control Type Description
ani	Animation button
bed	Pen BEdit
cbo	Combobox/Dropdown Listbox
chk	Checkbox
clp	Picture Clip
cmd	Command Button
com	Communications
dat	Data Control
dir	Directory Listbox
dlg	Common dialog
drv	Drive Listbox
fil	File Listbox
fra	Frame
frm	Form
gau	Gauge
gpb	Group Pushbutton
gra	Graph
grd	Grid
hed	Pen HEdit
hsb	Horizontal scroll bar
img	Image
ink	Pen Ink
key	Keyboard key status
lab	Label
lin	Line
lst	Listbox
mci	MCI
mnu	Menu
mpm	MAPI Message
mps	MAPI Session
ole	OLE Client
opt	Option Button

Prefix	Control Type Description
out	Outline Control
pic	Picture
pnl	3D Panel
rdc	Remote Data Control
shp	Shape
spn	Spin Control
tab	SS Tab Control
tmr	Timer
txt	Textbox
vsb	Vertical scroll bar
iml	ImageList
lvw	ListView
pbr	ProgressBar
rtf	RichTextBox
sld	Slider
sbr	StatusBar
tab	Tabstrip
tbr	Toolbar
tvw	TreeView

TABLE A-6

DATA-BOUND CONTROLS PREFIXES

Prefix	Control Type Description
dbcbo	Databound Combobox/Dropdown Listbox
dblst	Databound Listbox
dbgrd	Databound Grid

OTHER CONVENTIONS

Other conventions not listed above can be found in other chapters of this book. For instance, Chapter 1 explains the error handling strategy we use at TMS. Chapter 8 provides a full discussion on how we mandate that dates should be handled in Visual Basic.

Sample Answers to the Technical Test in Chapter 17

PETER J.
MORRIS

MARK
SEWELL

Refer to page 756 for the questions to this exam given by TMS to developer candidates.

A1.

`-1 -1 -1`

The = operator in Microsoft Visual Basic is used for both assignment (such as "*a* is assigned…") and comparison (such as testing the assertion that *b* has the same value as *c*—note the disuse of "equivalent"). The value &HFFFF is synonymous with the value of True and –1, so testing to see if –1 is the same value as &HFFFF yields True, or –1. As an aside, try changing Integer to Long throughout the code; you might be surprised to see –1 –1 –1 output here, too. For yet another result, try changing &HFFFF to 65535 (and use Longs). Finally, try using 65535 with Integer. You'll see it causes an overflow error. A modification to the question, then, is to pose it again using one of these alternative forms and to ask why the results differ. (The answers are exercises for the reader.)

A2.

Code fragment A: Print the contents of the fourth item in the list box *lstResults* in the Debug window.

Code fragment B: Iterate through every item within the list box *lstResults*.

Code fragment C: If a selection has not been made in the list box *lstResults*, then...

Code fragment D: For each item up to the selected item, copy the index of each item within the list box *lstResults* into its *ItemData* property.

A3.

```
Public Function sNumToBin(ByVal nDecimal As Integer) As String

    Dim sBin  As String
    Dim nloop As Integer

    For nloop = 0 To 15

        sBin = IIf(nDecimal And 2 ^ nloop, "1", "0") & sBin

    Next

    sNumToBin = sBin

End Function
```

A4.

```
Public Function itoh(ByVal nByte As Byte) As String

    Const c As String = "0123456789ABCDEF"

    itoh = IIf(nByte <= 15, Mid$(c, nByte + 1, 1), "?")

    ' OR perhaps...

    itoh = IIf(nByte <= 15, Hex$(nByte), "?")
```

```
' OR perhaps...

If nByte <= 15 Then
    itoh = Mid$(c, nByte + 1, 1)
Else
    itoh = "?"
End If

End Function
```

Many answers are possible—some might even include the use of the *Choose* and *Switch* functions.

A5.

Option 1: Insert the following code into the *Form_Load* procedure.

```
Me.Move (Screen.Width - Me.Width) \ 2, _
        (Screen.Height - Me.Height) \ 2
```

Option 2: Set the form's *StartUpPosition* property to CenterScreen at design time.

Screen resolution should not matter. Notice the use of the Integer division operator above; this might show you that someone is conscious of the language (knows about this operator) and is aware that clock cycles are more efficient.

A6.

Identifier	Type	Scope	Answer
BM010	Form	Form	frm
FileOpen	Menu	-	mnu
RecordCount	Integer	Global	gn
FirstName	String Array	Modular	mas
VehclNum	Long	Local	l
Vehicles	Combo Box	-	cbo
Time	Label	-	lbl

Any "sane" prefix is fine, of course.

A7.

1. The code fragment has a function *SomeFunc* and a sub *SomeSub*, both the sub and the function have *ByRef* arguments, and neither return a value. The code *cmdTest_Click* calls both routines. When *SomeSub* is called, a copy of the argument is passed overriding the effect of the implicit *ByRef* in the sub declaration. When *SomeFunc* is called, the argument is passed *ByRef* as declared. The output to the debug window will be *1* and *2*.

2. Both arguments get passed *ByVal* (to a copy of the actual argument), *no errors occur*, and the output to the debug window will be *1* and *1*.

3. The actual argument now gets passed *ByRef*; the output to the debug window will be *2* and *2*.

4. Yes, as in Part 2, the output to the debug window will be *1* and *1* because only a copy is passed.

5. Pass by reference is faster.

As an aside, if *SomeSub* passes *ByRef* (as shown in the question), *SomeSub (x)* succeeds, forcing the "evaluation of *x*" to be passed rather than *x* itself—in other words, forces a *ByVal* result. (The "evaluation of *x*," called an anonymous object, is a value [the result] stored in a memory location other than that occupied by *x*.) However, calling *SomeSub* as *SomeSub ByVal x* doesn't work. It might be worth posing this variant of the question and asking what the difference is. (The answer is an exercise for the reader.)

A8.

```
Private Sub Form_Load()

    Dim nLoop  As Integer

    Const COLS As Integer = 3
    Const ROWS As Integer = 4

    Me.Caption = "Calculator"
    labDisplay.Caption = ""

    With cmdDigit(nLoop)
```

```
                    ' Size form, label, and initial cmdDigit to look right.
                    Me.Height = ROWS * .Height + labDisplay.Height + _
                        Me.Height - Me.ScaleHeight
                    Me.Width = COLS * .Width + Me.Width - Me.ScaleWidth

                    labDisplay.Move 0, 0, Me.Width - _
                        (Me.Width - Me.ScaleWidth), labDisplay.Height

                    .Move 0, Me.ScaleHeight - .Height

                End With

            For nLoop = 1 To ROWS * COLS - 3

                Load cmdDigit(nLoop)

                With cmdDigit(nLoop)

                    .Move cmdDigit(nLoop - 1).Left + .Width, _
                        cmdDigit(nLoop - 1).Top

                    If 0 = nLoop Mod COLS Then
                        .Top = .Top - .Height
                        .Left = cmdDigit(0).Left
                    End If

                    ' Only want 10 numeric buttons so make 'extra'
                    ' buttons nonfunctional.
                    .Caption = IIf(nLoop <= 9, CStr(nLoop), "")

                    .Visible = True

                End With

            Next

        End Sub
        Private Sub cmdDigit_Click(Index As Integer)

            labDisplay.Caption = labDisplay.Caption & cmdDigit(Index).Caption

        End Sub
```

A9.

This list isn't complete. Also, some assume that we're using the *Option Compare Text* statement.

```
InStr(1, "TMS", sSource, 1)

InStr(Ucase$("TMS"), Ucase$(sSource))

sSource = "TMS"

StrComp(sSource, "TMS")
```

A10.

```
Function NTrim$(ByVal sString As String)

    Dim nPos As Integer

    nPos = InStr(1, sString, vbNullChar)

    Do While nPos <> 0
        sString = Left$(sString, nPos - 1) & _
                  Mid$(sString, nPos + 1)
        nPos = InStr(1, sString, vbNullChar)
    Loop

    NTrim$ = sString

End Function
```

Or:

```
Function NTrim$(ByVal sString As String)

    Dim nPos As Integer

    nPos = InStrRev(sString, vbNullChar)

    Do While nPos <> 0
        sString = Left$(sString, nPos - 1) & _
                  Mid$(sString, nPos + 1)
        nPos = InStrRev(sString, vbNullChar)
    Loop

    NTrim$ = sString

End Function
```

A11.

```
Function bFileExists(ByVal sFile As String) As Boolean

    On Error Resume Next

    Call GetAttr(sFile)

    bFileExists = True = (0 = Err.Number)

End Function
```

This is another question for which there are many possible answers. Whichever answer is given, ensure that hidden files, system files, and folder files (directories) are detected—you're looking for the "been there, done that" answer. For example, the normal *bFileExists = "" <> Dir$(sFile)* (used as shown) won't work for such files; a developer who doesn't realize this might cause crucial code to fail, such as the following:

```
Sub MakeFolder(ByVal s As String)

    If Not bFileExists(s) Then MkDir (s)

End Sub
```

A12.

1. Property procedures actually protect the property by only allowing (or disallowing) access to it through these procedures (*Get/Let* and *Set*); they are therefore safer. Property procedures can be used to filter invalid property assignments and give the programmer the option to validate assignment values before actually applying them. A *Public* variable (an item of data declared *Public* in a class) can be arbitrarily accessed and changed. (Many programmers, usually the less experienced ones, don't actually know how to use *Property Set*. This question might enlighten you as to who does and who doesn't.)

2. A class can make only data or functional properties (either explicitly or through property procedures) and methods visible outside of itself.

A13.

Code fragment A: Form Initialize only. No form instance is created. The application terminates immediately.

Code fragment B: Form Initialize only. No form instance is created. The application terminates immediately.

Code fragment C: Form Initialize and Load. There will be one (invisible) instance of Form1 once this code has executed. The application doesn't terminate.

A14.

The code is legal. The output to the Debug window is as follows:

```
30
10
30
20
```

A15.

Optional Arguments: Look out for the use of Variant as parameter type and the use of the *IsMissing* function to test for the presence of the optional parameter.

```
Call MsgBox( _
            sRequired _
          , vbOKOnly _
          , IIf( _
                IsMissing(sDiscretionary) _
              , App.EXEName _
              , sDiscretionary _
              ) _
          )
```

Parameter Arrays: Look for the final parameter to be declared as *ParamArray*.

```
Private Sub ParamTest(ByVal sMsg As String, ParamArray nArray())

    Dim nLoop As Integer

    For nLoop = Lbound(nArray) To Ubound(nArray)

        Debug.Print sMsg & CStr(nArray(nLoop))

    Next nLoop

End Sub
```

Collections: Look for the creation of a collection object as a "New Collection," then look for classes to be added to the collection object using the *Add* method. Then look for the *For Each* operation to iterate through the members of the collection. (An answer in which dictionaries are mentioned demonstrates knowledge in Visual Basic 6.)

```
Dim cColl As New Collection

cColl.Add item:=Class1, key:=12

For Each Class1 In cColl
    ⋮
Next cColl
```

A16.

VBCP was the Visual Basic Code Profiler add-in. It was used to ascertain the execution time of code and to find performance bottlenecks.

A17.

This code outputs Class1 onto the form.

A18.

```
n = ((((True And (&HFF + True)) And _
    ((&HFF00 + (Not Not True)) = Not False)) Or _
    (&HFF + (Not True))) Or &HFF00)
```

-1

You're looking for any mention that an expression like (assuming n is 32) $n = Not\ n = 32$ (where n is now 0, or False if used in a Boolean expression) is very different from $n = Not\ n$ (where n is now -33, or True if used in a Boolean expression).

A19.

Wherever code needs to branch, unconditionally, to a new location within a procedure. An answer along the lines of "I'd never use it because it's bad practice" (does this imply the candidate doesn't use error handlers?) probably ought to be discussed. For example, ask the candidate to explain why he or she wouldn't use it—perhaps you can also have the candidate compare *GoTo* with other unconditional jumps, such as *CallProcedure, Exit, Exit Loop, Exit For, Exit Do, Exit Sub*, and so on. Make a point of asking the candidate to explain the difference between *If SomeCondition Then GoTo* and *If SomeCondition Exit Loop*.

TMS Developer's Framework

PETER J MORRIS

Since 1995, all TMS applications have been built using three interlocking, key building blocks. Collectively these building blocks are known as the "TMS Developer's Framework" (TDF):

- VB Vogue
- Application Template
- Vogue Tools

Each building block can be purchased separately or as a set of complementary components that constitute the "Framework." Each element of the TDF is briefly explained below.

VB Vogue

VB Vogue is TMS's Visual Basic "Developer's Discipline" and Coding Standards reference document. It currently numbers around 70 pages.

VB Vogue is much more than a set of traditional coding standards. As well as defining naming conventions and coding style guidelines, it also includes sections on Year 2000 "readiness," component versioning, guidance on data access methods and structured exception handling techniques—to name but a few. Throughout, it is VB Vogue's aim to give clear explanations and justifications for any advice or rules that it mandates. During VB Vogue's development, TMS made a conscious decision that it be much more than an informational reference book. Our key objective was to ensure it was also instructional and educational. The result: a valuable asset for any development team.

Application Template

TMS's Application Template, or App Template, contains around 18,500 lines of tried and tested infrastructure and support code, and is used on some of the world's biggest Visual Basic development projects. The App Template is actually made up of forms, classes, and modules that collaborate in assisting developers to support the advice or rules given in VB Vogue, allowing the developers to be productive and professional in how they code. For example, the App Template contains the routines necessary to log exceptions using a variety of methods (file, NT event log, database, and so on). Structured exception handling, as we know from development "best practice" (endorsed by VB Vogue), is a mandated facet of any professional development project. By allowing the developer to easily support such professional features, the overhead and burden on the developer is removed from any individual. The result is that any overhead incurred in adding (in this case) structured exception handling is effectively removed. Through logging the precise nature and location of errors, the Debug, Build, and Test cycle is far more efficient and controlled, and in turn offers substantial cost savings. In addition, once the product is shipped, the subsequent pressure on the support or help desk is significantly reduced.

Here is a small taste of what the App Template contains: platform and version checking; standard forms; enhanced replacement Visual Basic intrinsic objects such as Err, App, and Debug; installation support; "real" assertions; storage support (for accessing the Registry, etc.); string handling; and of course, structured exception and error logging.

Ever since its inception, the App Template has been revised for each new release of Visual Basic or whenever a TMS developer can justify a reasonable modification or both. For example, in between Visual Basic 4 and Visual Basic 5, one revision was increased support to assist developers with the Year 2000 problem. This included providing standalone routines to check the validity of any entered date and a new control. The template contains ancillary—although very valuable—components such as the DateBox control. This is an OCX (built using Visual Basic 5 and 6) designed to replace any TextBox control that is used to hold or manipulate dates. A DateBox, unlike a TextBox, mandates that any input sent to it should be "Y2K Safe" and at the same time "map" to whatever the user has set as a preferred Short Date setting. The DateBox control is sophisticated and includes many advanced features such as the ability to define any day of the week as invalid (so that the user cannot, for example, enter a date that is in actuality a Sunday where the date of a "working day" is expected). The control can be set, through design time properties, to generate a variety of behaviors that describe how it should respond to invalid dates. For example, should it generate a Visual Basic exception; should it prompt the user with a customizable error message; should it force the user to reattempt the data entry? And if the answer to the latter is yes, how many times should it force the user to retry before generating an exception?

At the time this book was being written, App Template was being re-architectured into a set of controls, wizards, add-ins, modules, classes, and server-side objects.

In summary, the App Template contains everything that most serious applications should have but isn't part of their specialist function.

Vogue Tools

From the descriptions of VB Vogue and App Template, the user will see that the application of either involves taking actions that will directly manipulate code or form definitions. For example, to fully use the DateBox control, a developer must replace all TextBox controls used to capture dates with DateBox controls. Obviously, this will result in a drawn-out, laborious, and mostly manual alteration of the project's code. Also, as we saw, VB Vogue mandates that exception handlers be added to every routine in a project—again, a tedious manual process would result. Such necessary tedium typically dictates that these critical alterations and additions to the code base are simply not carried out, or that they are applied piecemeal throughout the project. Obviously, both situations are unacceptable and need rectifying.

Vogue Tools are designed to ease any pain involved in applying such rigorous development practices as outlined in VB Vogue and in the updating of existing code, to use, say, the DateBox control. For example, to assist a developer in using the DateBox control, Vogue Tools contains a "lex"-built tool that can be used to replace date-containing TextBox controls with DateBox controls. Typical processing time for an entire project (depending on size) is around 10 seconds. As a further example, to add the necessary exception handling template code to a routine, Vogue Tools contains an IDE Add-In that can do just that with one button click. The current Vogue Tools are listed here:

- Line Number Wizard
- Error Handler Inserter
- Lex DateBox Parser
- Egrep32

Structured Exception Handling Scenario

As mentioned at the beginning of this appendix, all three components—VB Vogue, the App Template, and Vogue Tools—are designed to work together. Let's take a look at how this works with an example of Structured Exception Handling.

VB Vogue mandates that every routine in a Visual Basic application must contain an exception handler. What that handler contains and how it should deal with errors is explained in VB Vogue. (For example, VB Vogue describes how exceptions should not only be caught, but how they should be logged.) However, VB Vogue does not include any of the necessary support and infrastructural code to actually do the next step. That part is delivered through the second component of the TMS Developer's Framework—App Template. Finally, Vogue Tools provides the Error Handler Inserter to insert the appropriate App Template code into the project.

How Are They Provided?

VB Vogue is currently provided as a Microsoft Word 6.0/95 or Word 97 file. In the future, it will be provided as a series of HTML files so that navigation can be achieved using a Web browser.

The App Template is provided as a single Visual Basic project in source code form: in other words, it is runnable. It also includes a .HLP file that contains product documentation. In the future, this will be provided as a series of HTML files so that navigation can be achieved using a Web browser.

Vogue Tools are provided as built executables. Where appropriate to the running of the tool, source code is provided.

If you are interested in purchasing any or all of the TMS Developer's Framework Toolkit, please contact *Sales@TheMandelbrotSet.com.*

Visual DateScope 2000 and VBA2000

KAREN FIELD

TREESJE VERLINDEN

The Mandelbrot Set (International) Limited (TMS) is the sole UK distributor and non-exclusive worldwide distributor of Visual DateScope 2000 (VDS2000) on behalf of Class Solutions Limited. VDS2000 is a developer's toolset designed to aid in the Year 2000 conversion of systems developed specifically in Microsoft Visual Basic.

Originally released in 1996, VDS2000 was the first product of its kind available worldwide, offering support for Microsoft Visual Basic Impact Analysis, Remediation, and Coverage Testing.

Unlike other so-called "generic" or "language-independent" products, VDS2000 has a built-in Visual Basic language parsing engine that understands the language entirely and doesn't just perform simple text searches and other basic tasks. As such, VDS2000 is much better equipped to locate and deal with Year 2000 date-challenged code.

Version 3 of VDS2000 builds on the success of previous versions by providing enhanced functionality and additional features (including eight new impact analysis reports), designed to minimize the time spent performing Year 2000 operations. Version 3 covers Visual Basic versions 3, 4, and 5. In addition, version 3 now supports an optional add-in called VBA2000 (developed in-house by TMS), which works directly with VBA source code imbedded within Microsoft Access databases and Microsoft Excel spreadsheets (in both Office 95 and Office 97).

VISUAL DATESCOPE 2000 FACT FILE

VDS2000 automates the tasks that would otherwise require manual intervention. Adopting an automated approach accelerates the conversion process, provides a framework for control, and reduces the risk of human error. The VDS2000 toolset consists of two primary components, the Scanning Application Component and the Date Function Library Component. These components assist in date identification/impact analysis, renovation, testing, and debugging.

Date Identification Process

The Scanning Application Component consists of an executable application that performs an initial prescan through the Visual Basic or Excel/Access VBA source code extracting the declarations (or definitions) of all the main elements (tokens) that make up a Visual Basic project. You can add numerous Visual Basic projects to the catalog, allowing a repository and date scan of entire systems or of subsystems.

These tokens include the declaration of any controls, DLLs, constants, global variables, modular level and local variables, user-defined type (UDT) names and element names, and any function or procedure parameters. The Scanning Application Component also scans for the many intrinsic Visual Basic date functions and procedures, such as *Now*, *DateDiff*, and *CVDate*.

The Scanning Application Component provides database support by examining the internal structure of any ODBC or Microsoft Jet database, searching for date-related columns or fields and adding these to the repository.

Most date scanning applications will simply search program files for a predetermined set of date-related keywords. The Scanning Application Component recognizes the need for business domain knowledge by allowing the repository to be extended to include user-defined tokens. A scanning application that cross-references a fixed set of date-related keywords would run the risk of entirely missing a business domain date-related variable such as *sEffectiveFrom*.

A hierarchical repository display ensures that the user can work through the components of each project in a logical format and visualize the completion of each logical unit. Compare this with the chore of manually trudging through thousands of lines of code unaided and with no physical indication of work completed—chaos!

The Scanning Application Component provides a Results repository (sorted by module and procedure) of all date-related occurrences identified within each of the specified projects. You can print the repository or use it directly for renovation. (See the next section, "Renovation Process," for more details.) Using the repository of date occurrences, you can return to the Visual Basic project knowing each identified line of code in need of possible modification.

The Scanning Application Component provides an automatic update of the source code with annotations marking each of the identified date occurrences. By automating the majority of the Date Identification process, it is possible to increase accuracy because the risk of human error is reduced. The completion time for the whole process is a fraction of the time it takes to run a manual scan. Consider an average Visual Basic project consisting of 15,000 lines of code. Taking an average of four seconds per line, this could take up to two days to complete for the identification of just one application!

Renovation Process

Visual DateScope 2000 provides a structured and consistent approach to problem solving.

Having identified all date-type occurrences within a system, the process now turns to the renovation of those date occurrences. Using Visual DateScope 2000, you can modify the code directly from within the scanning application.

Renovations can take place without ever having to load Visual Basic, which provides a self-contained conversion environment. There is no context switching.

Year 2000 Library

Once the identification of dates is complete and a method is in place to modify those dates, the question arises as to what to do with the date occurrences. The Date Function Library Component in the Visual DateScope 2000 toolset consists of a library of Year 2000–related date functions designed to erase the threat of the Year 2000 problem in your Visual Basic code. The library has the following features:

- Fully-tested functions appropriate for countless Year 2000 scenarios.
- Consistent approach to fixing date code.
- Completely generic, supporting international dates.
- Handles incorrect input values that are not dates. The reason for this is simple: many companies will hire contract or part-time staff to help in their Year 2000 conversion projects. It is possible that these programmers have little experience in either your business domain or in the Visual Basic language itself. The Year 2000 library therefore tolerates incorrectly applied "fixes."

Testing

Although VDS2000 does *not* test changes, it will certainly increase testing productivity and accuracy. For example, when changing a line of code from within the Scanning Application Component, VDS2000 will automatically add a line of debug code into your source code immediately before your change, if required. Comparative analysis ensures the complete execution of all changed lines of code. An additional debug testing file can be created that shows the "Before" and "After" values of converted dates.

All the debug calls inserted into your code can then be easily removed from within VDS2000 (for production environments).

Information Packs

Contact *y2kservices@themandelbrotset.com* for your information pack, which contains evaluation copies of both Visual DateScope 2000 and VBA2000.

Keeping Current with TMS

PETER J. MORRIS

The Mandelbrot Set (International) Limited (TMS) has arranged to distribute any code updates, book news, further Visual Basic 6 news, tips, errata, or any other book extras via a TMS mail-server newsgroup. Just in case you don't know, a mail-server newsgroup is essentially a machine (server) used to automatically send relevant e-mail to parties who have registered for a certain newsgroup subject.

If you would like to be kept up-to-date, please send e-mail* to *TMS-List-Server@TheMandelbrotSet.com*. Leave the subject line blank and insert this line anywhere in the body of your message:

Subscribe TMSBookList

This subscribes you to the TMSBookList newsgroup on the TMS mail server. Whenever we issue updates, news, and so on, we will distribute them via simultaneous e-mail to everyone who has subscribed to the TMSBookList newsgroup.

---

* TMS promises, at all times, to keep your e-mail address in the strictest of confidence.

Should you wish to unsubscribe from the group at any time, send e-mail to the address given above, but this time insert this line anywhere in the body of your message:

Unsubscribe TMSBookList

You will receive confirmation e-mail back from the server when your communication has been successful. What could be easier?

OTHER NEWSGROUPS

If you would like to subscribe to any other TMS newsgroup, send e-mail to the address given above and insert this line anywhere in the body of your message:

Lists

The TMS mail server will then e-mail back to you a full list of the names of the public newsgroups to which you can subscribe (complete with a description of each newsgroup). Once you know the names of all the different newsgroups, you will be able to subscribe and unsubscribe to them as described in this appendix.

INDEX

Italicized page references indicate figures, tables, or code listings.

push and pop method of error handling, 32

Push method, 31, 442

PVB file extension for compiled Windows CE applications, 211

Q

QA team, policing standards, 675

QED, Windows CE support for processors from, 175

qman.vbp on the companion CD, 568

qualifications for developers, 743–44

quality, ensuring, 675, 701

Quality Tracking templates on the companion CD, 402

QueryAbandon event, generating in the progress form, 610

QueryInterface function, 479

queue event handler in the FSM, 579

queue manager
asynchronous, 568
locating events, 566

R

RAD (rapid application development)
controlled, 664
hype, 651
life cycle, 664

radio buttons on the Component tab of the Project Properties dialog box, 259, 260–61

ragged arrays, 76, 154, 157

RaiseEvent procedure, 550, 579

Raise method
adding to the *Err* object, 442
raising errors in *bDriveExists*, 9

raising an error, 644, *644*

RAM, having software in, 173

rapid application development. *See* RAD (rapid application development)

Raw Native Interface. *See* RNI

raw variables vs. object references, 527

RC.EXE program, compiling the resource module, 632

RDO
avoiding cursors, 504
cursors implemented in, 499
prefixes for, *803*

rdoEnvironment objects, multiple in RDO, 513

RDS client-side library, combining with ADO, 534–35

reading, required for developers, 273

read-only cursor, 503

read-only data, 497

ReadProperties event for a control, 624, *624–25*, 625

real-time capabilities of Windows CE, 181–82

real-time operating system, 181

real-time threads, Windows CE priorities for, *179*

real type, 307

real type extensions, 307

RecentComments Web item, 119

reciprocal collections, 577

recordset, 76–77. *See also cRecordset*
getting at, 95–96
locking, 79–80
persisting, 536–37
retrieving, 78
retrieving with parameters, 81–82
returning from the DAL, 76
serializing, 79
synchronizing, 80–83
updating, 80

Recordset objects, persisting, 537

Recordset property for the *cFactory* interface, *87*, 95–96

recursion, 564–66, *565*

ReDim statement, totally new array for a mistyped array name, 261

U

W

Wait For Components To Be Created startup option in IIS, 113

Watches window in the source-level debugger, 242

waterfall life cycle, 664

wcNoState setting, 129

wcRetainInstance setting of *StateManagement* property, 129

weakly typed language, Visual Basic as a, 365–66

Web, advertising for job candidates, 749

Web application model, 110

Web applications, 110–11
developing, 110
errors occurring outside the Visual Basic code, 125

WEBAPP.MDB database, handling the registration of users, 122

Web-based systems, structure of, 515

Web browser. *See* browser

Web class
adding HTML templates, 116–17
HTML template triggering events within, 117
setting *StateManagement* property, 129

WEBCLASS1.ASP, 114–15

Web class designer
connecting attributes to events, 117
developing *WebClass* objects, 113
warning message issued by, 120

WebClassManager object, *ProcessRetainInstanceWebClass* method of, 130

WebClass objects, 113

Web-enabled devices, Internet Explorer for, 170

Web page, viewing for an IIS application, 114

Web servers, choices for development, 112

Weekday function, 348

WeekdayName function, 353

Weinberg, Gerald, 217

Welcome page, altering in an IIS application, 121

Welcome template, 122–24

whack 'em approach, 94

whitepaper distribution application, 120–30

WillUpdateRows event, 505

Win, prefixing Windows API calls, 325

Win32 API
logging events directly from applications, 19
Windows CE based on, 168, 175–76

Win32 *POINT* structure, 734

WinBringWindowToTop method, 327

window design testing, 696, *697*

WindowedDates project on the companion CD, 372

window handle, 309–10

window procedure, 569

windows
creating for your own exclusive use, 570
managing, 542–43
returning objects from, 730

Windows 98 Date tab in the Regional Settings dialog box, 357

Windows API
getting information from, 443
prefixing calls with *Win*, 325

Windows CE, 166–67
API set for, 175
based on the Win32 API, 168
building devices, 171–74
capabilities of, 173–74
categories of product, 170, 171
components of, 168–70
configurations available, *172*
Control Manager screen, *209*
core components of, 174–84
default error message box displayed by, 207
design considerations for applications, 190–205

The Mandelbrot Set
(International) Limited

The Mandelbrot Set (International) Limited (TMS) is a British "Windows only" software services company that specializes in the design and development of commercial software packages and business solutions using the Microsoft Visual toolset—that is, Visual Basic, Visual J++, and Visual C++. TMS is also a Microsoft Solution Provider.

TMS was the company behind the successful TMS Tools developer's toolkit for Visual Basic 3, and MicroHelp's Code Complete Visual Basic 4 developer's toolkit, which was widely acclaimed as one of *the* developer tools of the year in 1996. The Code Complete technology has since been incorporated into Sax Software's set of Visual Basic Team Productivity tools. For more information, contact *info@saxsoft.com*.

TMS has an excellent reputation for creating innovative solutions and technologies and is recognized as one of the most technically proficient companies in the industry today. The company provides a wide range of development and consulting services to a mainly blue-chip client list. For full details, take a look at the TMS website at:

http://www.TheMandelbrotSet.com

You can also contact TMS directly at:

Mandel House, West End
Northleach, Gloucestershire
GL54 3HG England

Telephone: 44 (0)1451 861212
Fax: 44 (0)1451 861122
E-mail: *info@TheMandelbrotSet.com*

The manuscript for this book was prepared and submitted to Microsoft Press in electronic form. Text files were prepared using Microsoft Word 97. Pages were composed by Microsoft Press using Adobe PageMaker 6.52 for Windows, with text in Melior and display type in Imago Extra Bold. Composed pages were delivered to the printer as electronic prepress files.

COVER GRAPHIC DESIGNER
Tim Girvin Design

COVER ILLUSTRATOR
Glenn Mitsui, Studio M D

INTERIOR GRAPHIC ARTIST
Michael Victor

PRINCIPAL COMPOSITOR
Barbara Norfleet

PRINCIPAL PROOFREADER/COPY EDITOR
Pamela Buitrago

INDEXER
Richard Shrout

MICROSOFT LICENSE AGREEMENT

(Book Companion CD)

IMPORTANT—READ CAREFULLY: This Microsoft End-User License Agreement ("EULA") is a legal agreement between you (either an individual or an entity) and Microsoft Corporation for the Microsoft product identified above, which includes computer software and may include associated media, printed materials, and "on-line" or electronic documentation ("SOFTWARE PRODUCT"). Any component included within the SOFTWARE PRODUCT that is accompanied by a separate End-User License Agreement shall be governed by such agreement and not the terms set forth below. By installing, copying, or otherwise using the SOFTWARE PRODUCT, you agree to be bound by the terms of this EULA. If you do not agree to the terms of this EULA, you are not authorized to install, copy, or otherwise use the SOFTWARE PRODUCT; you may, however, return the SOFTWARE PRODUCT, along with all printed materials and other items that form a part of the Microsoft product that includes the SOFTWARE PRODUCT, to the place you obtained them for a full refund.

SOFTWARE PRODUCT LICENSE

The SOFTWARE PRODUCT is protected by United States copyright laws and international copyright treaties, as well as other intellectual property laws and treaties. The SOFTWARE PRODUCT is licensed, not sold.

1. **GRANT OF LICENSE.** This EULA grants you the following rights:

    a. **Software Product.** You may install and use one copy of the SOFTWARE PRODUCT on a single computer. The primary user of the computer on which the SOFTWARE PRODUCT is installed may make a second copy for his or her exclusive use on a portable computer.

    b. **Storage/Network Use.** You may also store or install a copy of the SOFTWARE PRODUCT on a storage device, such as a network server, used only to install or run the SOFTWARE PRODUCT on your other computers over an internal network; however, you must acquire and dedicate a license for each separate computer on which the SOFTWARE PRODUCT is installed or run from the storage device. A license for the SOFTWARE PRODUCT may not be shared or used concurrently on different computers.

    c. **License Pak.** If you have acquired this EULA in a Microsoft License Pak, you may make the number of additional copies of the computer software portion of the SOFTWARE PRODUCT authorized on the printed copy of this EULA, and you may use each copy in the manner specified above. You are also entitled to make a corresponding number of secondary copies for portable computer use as specified above.

    d. **Sample Code.** Solely with respect to portions, if any, of the SOFTWARE PRODUCT that are identified within the SOFTWARE PRODUCT as sample code (the "SAMPLE CODE"):

    i. **Use and Modification.** Microsoft grants you the right to use and modify the source code version of the SAMPLE CODE, *provided* you comply with subsection (d)(iii) below. You may not distribute the SAMPLE CODE, or any modified version of the SAMPLE CODE, in source code form.

    ii. **Redistributable Files.** Provided you comply with subsection (d)(iii) below, Microsoft grants you a nonexclusive, royalty-free right to reproduce and distribute the object code version of the SAMPLE CODE and of any modified SAMPLE CODE, other than SAMPLE CODE (or any modified version thereof) designated as not redistributable in the Readme file that forms a part of the SOFTWARE PRODUCT (the "Non-Redistributable Sample Code"). All SAMPLE CODE other than the Non-Redistributable Sample Code is collectively referred to as the "REDISTRIBUTABLES."

    iii. **Redistribution Requirements.** If you redistribute the REDISTRIBUTABLES, you agree to: (i) distribute the REDISTRIBUTABLES in object code form only in conjunction with and as a part of your software application product; (ii) not use Microsoft's name, logo, or trademarks to market your software application product; (iii) include a valid copyright notice on your software application product; (iv) indemnify, hold harmless, and defend Microsoft from and against any claims or lawsuits, including attorney's fees, that arise or result from the use or distribution of your software application product; and (v) not permit further distribution of the REDISTRIBUTABLES by your end user. Contact Microsoft for the applicable royalties due and other licensing terms for all other uses and/or distribution of the REDISTRIBUTABLES.

2. **DESCRIPTION OF OTHER RIGHTS AND LIMITATIONS.**

    - **Limitations on Reverse Engineering, Decompilation, and Disassembly.** You may not reverse engineer, decompile, or disassemble the SOFTWARE PRODUCT, except and only to the extent that such activity is expressly permitted by applicable law notwithstanding this limitation.

    - **Separation of Components.** The SOFTWARE PRODUCT is licensed as a single product. Its component parts may not be separated for use on more than one computer.

    - **Rental.** You may not rent, lease, or lend the SOFTWARE PRODUCT.

    - **Support Services.** Microsoft may, but is not obligated to, provide you with support services related to the SOFTWARE PRODUCT ("Support Services"). Use of Support Services is governed by the Microsoft policies and programs described in the user manual, in "on-line" documentation, and/or in other Microsoft-provided materials. Any supplemental software code provided to you as part of the Support Services shall be considered part of the SOFTWARE PRODUCT and subject to the terms and conditions of this EULA. With respect to technical information you provide to Microsoft as part of the Support Services, Microsoft may use such information for its business purposes, including for product support and development. Microsoft will not utilize such technical information in a form that personally identifies you.

- **Software Transfer.** You may permanently transfer all of your rights under this EULA, provided you retain no copies, you transfer all of the SOFTWARE PRODUCT (including all component parts, the media and printed materials, any upgrades, this EULA, and, if applicable, the Certificate of Authenticity), **and** the recipient agrees to the terms of this EULA.

- **Termination.** Without prejudice to any other rights, Microsoft may terminate this EULA if you fail to comply with the terms and conditions of this EULA. In such event, you must destroy all copies of the SOFTWARE PRODUCT and all of its component parts.

3. **COPYRIGHT.** All title and copyrights in and to the SOFTWARE PRODUCT (including but not limited to any images, photographs, animations, video, audio, music, text, SAMPLE CODE, REDISTRIBUTABLES, and "applets" incorporated into the SOFTWARE PRODUCT) and any copies of the SOFTWARE PRODUCT are owned by Microsoft or its suppliers. The SOFTWARE PRODUCT is protected by copyright laws and international treaty provisions. Therefore, you must treat the SOFTWARE PRODUCT like any other copyrighted material **except** that you may install the SOFTWARE PRODUCT on a single computer provided you keep the original solely for backup or archival purposes. You may not copy the printed materials accompanying the SOFTWARE PRODUCT.

4. **U.S. GOVERNMENT RESTRICTED RIGHTS.** The SOFTWARE PRODUCT and documentation are provided with RESTRICTED RIGHTS. Use, duplication, or disclosure by the Government is subject to restrictions as set forth in subparagraph (c)(1)(ii) of the Rights in Technical Data and Computer Software clause at DFARS 252.227-7013 or subparagraphs (c)(1) and (2) of the Commercial Computer Software—Restricted Rights at 48 CFR 52.227-19, as applicable. Manufacturer is Microsoft Corporation/One Microsoft Way/Redmond, WA 98052-6399.

5. **EXPORT RESTRICTIONS.** You agree that you will not export or re-export the SOFTWARE PRODUCT, any part thereof, or any process or service that is the direct product of the SOFTWARE PRODUCT (the foregoing collectively referred to as the "Restricted Components"), to any country, person, entity, or end user subject to U.S. export restrictions. You specifically agree not to export or re-export any of the Restricted Components (i) to any country to which the U.S. has embargoed or restricted the export of goods or services, which currently include, but are not necessarily limited to, Cuba, Iran, Iraq, Libya, North Korea, Sudan, and Syria, or to any national of any such country, wherever located, who intends to transmit or transport the Restricted Components back to such country; (ii) to any end user who you know or have reason to know will utilize the Restricted Components in the design, development, or production of nuclear, chemical, or biological weapons; or (iii) to any end user who has been prohibited from participating in U.S. export transactions by any federal agency of the U.S. government. You warrant and represent that neither the BXA nor any other U.S. federal agency has suspended, revoked, or denied your export privileges.

DISCLAIMER OF WARRANTY

NO WARRANTIES OR CONDITIONS. MICROSOFT EXPRESSLY DISCLAIMS ANY WARRANTY OR CONDITION FOR THE SOFTWARE PRODUCT. THE SOFTWARE PRODUCT AND ANY RELATED DOCUMENTATION IS PROVIDED "AS IS" WITHOUT WARRANTY OR CONDITION OF ANY KIND, EITHER EXPRESS OR IMPLIED, INCLUDING, WITHOUT LIMITATION, THE IMPLIED WARRANTIES OF MERCHANTABILITY, FITNESS FOR A PARTICULAR PURPOSE, OR NONINFRINGEMENT. THE ENTIRE RISK ARISING OUT OF USE OR PERFORMANCE OF THE SOFTWARE PRODUCT REMAINS WITH YOU.

LIMITATION OF LIABILITY. TO THE MAXIMUM EXTENT PERMITTED BY APPLICABLE LAW, IN NO EVENT SHALL MICROSOFT OR ITS SUPPLIERS BE LIABLE FOR ANY SPECIAL, INCIDENTAL, INDIRECT, OR CONSEQUENTIAL DAMAGES WHATSOEVER (INCLUDING, WITHOUT LIMITATION, DAMAGES FOR LOSS OF BUSINESS PROFITS, BUSINESS INTERRUPTION, LOSS OF BUSINESS INFORMATION, OR ANY OTHER PECUNIARY LOSS) ARISING OUT OF THE USE OF OR INABILITY TO USE THE SOFTWARE PRODUCT OR THE PROVISION OF OR FAILURE TO PROVIDE SUPPORT SERVICES, EVEN IF MICROSOFT HAS BEEN ADVISED OF THE POSSIBILITY OF SUCH DAMAGES. IN ANY CASE, MICROSOFT'S ENTIRE LIABILITY UNDER ANY PROVISION OF THIS EULA SHALL BE LIMITED TO THE GREATER OF THE AMOUNT ACTUALLY PAID BY YOU FOR THE SOFTWARE PRODUCT OR US$5.00; PROVIDED, HOWEVER, IF YOU HAVE ENTERED INTO A MICROSOFT SUPPORT SERVICES AGREEMENT, MICROSOFT'S ENTIRE LIABILITY REGARDING SUPPORT SERVICES SHALL BE GOVERNED BY THE TERMS OF THAT AGREEMENT. BECAUSE SOME STATES AND JURISDICTIONS DO NOT ALLOW THE EXCLUSION OR LIMITATION OF LIABILITY, THE ABOVE LIMITATION MAY NOT APPLY TO YOU.

MISCELLANEOUS

This EULA is governed by the laws of the State of Washington USA, except and only to the extent that applicable law mandates governing law of a different jurisdiction.

Should you have any questions concerning this EULA, or if you desire to contact Microsoft for any reason, please contact the Microsoft subsidiary serving your country, or write: Microsoft Sales Information Center/One Microsoft Way/Redmond, WA 98052-6399.